PARLIAMENTARY LAW

HENRY M. ROBERT

Parliamentary Law

WITH A PREFATORY NOTE BY HENRY M. ROBERT III

IRVINGTON PUBLISHERS, INC.
NEW YORK

The Publisher is pleased to dedicate this edition of *Parliamentary
Law* to The National Association of Parliamentarians, who
have encouraged its publication.

—Irvington Publishers, Inc.

Copyright © 1991 by Irvington Publishers, Inc.
Copyright © 1975 by Irvington Publishers, Inc.
Copyright, 1923, by The Century Co.
Copyright renewed, 1951, by Mrs. Isabel H. Robert.

Irvington Publishers, Inc.,
Executive offices: 522 E. 82nd Street, Suite 1, New York, NY 10028
Customer service and warehouse in care of: Integrated Distribution Services,
195 McGregor St, Manchester, NH 03102, (603) 669-5933

Printed in Mexico.

Distributed by Halsted Press,
a Division of John Wiley & Sons, Inc., New York.

Library of Congress Cataloging in Publication Data

Robert, Henry Martyn, 1837–1923.
  Parliamentary law.

  Includes index.
  1. Parliamentary practice—United States.
2. By-laws—United States. I. Title.
JF515.R6448 1975   060.4'2   75–9940
ISBN 0–470–72592–3

INTRODUCTION

Recognizing the need for future generations to be aware of the principles of parliamentary law, and of the unique style Henry Martyn Robert had in recording and demonstrating these principles, the National Association of Parliamentarians is pleased to bring you this edition of Robert's *Parliamentary Law* in honor of our more than sixty years of service to our nation.

Carl Ann Strickeler, PRP
President, National Association of Parliamentarians

PREFATORY NOTE

THIS WORK, now reprinted, comprises the definitive explanatory treatment of parliamentary procedure by the original author of *Robert's Rules of Order*. It contains much valuable information available in no other volume, particularly in the "Question-and-Answer" section, Part VII beginning on page 399.

This book is a "must" for the library of every professional parliamentarian and every serious student of parliamentary procedure.

The work remains in full accord with *Robert's Rules of Order Newly Revised* (1970), the current edition of the standard manual which organizations should now adopt as their parliamentary authority.

This reprinting of *Parliamentary Law* preserves the pagination of the orignal edition, so that existing references to the work will remain correct. Page references to "R.O.R." within this book are to the 1915 edition of *Robert's Rules of Order Revised*.

The small introductory work, *Parliamentary Practice*, mentioned in the original author's preface on page vi, is being reissued jointly with this volume.

—*Henry M. Robert III*
July 1975

PREFACE

WHILE engaged in writing the "Rules of Order Revised," the author was strongly impressed with the impracticability of making a book which would fill the needs of societies and deliberative assemblies for rules of order, and which at the same time would be readable and adapted to the needs of those unfamiliar with parliamentary law. This is especially true of the motions. In "Rules of Order" the first paragraph on each motion shows under what circumstances the motion can be made, what motions can be made while it is pending, to what motions it can be applied, what motions can be applied to it, and whether it can be debated, amended, or reconsidered. These points are needed for quick reference in a meeting, but are very dull reading, especially to one unfamiliar with parliamentary law. The fact that it was necessary to compress the rules of order into a pocket manual required all the brevity consistent with accuracy of statement, and thus prevented illustrations that would have made the matter much more easily understood.

Instead of compromising and combining the two objects in one book, the author decided to make the "Rules of Order Revised" as perfectly adapted to the needs of societies, conventions, boards, city councils, etc., as he was capable of doing in so small a manual, and then to write another book to meet the wants of those desirous of becoming thoroughly familiar with parliamentary law. The two books are in complete harmony: one is adapted to the needs of societies as their rules of order, and therefore is condensed and easy of reference; the other is not suited for such a purpose, but, since it abounds in illustrations, can be read without difficulty by one ignorant of parliamentary law.

The author has not hesitated to repeat statements in different articles when such a course would make the article more easily understood. Examples are given where required. Motions have been grouped where it has seemed important to compare them and to show under what circumstances each should be used. Thus, the half dozen motions used for bringing a question before the assembly a second time are grouped and compared, showing the circumstances under which each should be used, and afterward each one is taken up separately and fully explained. [See p. 79.]

So much trouble has resulted from ignorance of the manner of conducting elections, which is scarcely touched in "Rules of Order Revised," that it has seemed best to devote to it much space. The subject of Discipline is fully explained, and Model By-Laws are given for the guidance of societies when organizing or when revising their by-laws. Out of many years' Parliamentary Law correspondence of the author, there have been selected several hundred Questions and Answers that will be helpful to others besides those who have made the inquiries. They are classified and separately indexed in order to make it easier to find decisions. They form a unique part of the book.

When this large work was nearly completed, it seemed advisable to take out the elementary part and to publish it separately. Accordingly a set of twenty elementary lessons, including seven drills, was prepared with a view to meeting the needs of the novice. To this some useful reference matter was added, and the book has been published under the name of "Parliamentary Practice: An Introduction to Parliamentary Law."

It gives the author pleasure to acknowledge his indebtedness to Mrs. William Anderson for her suggestions, criticisms, and general assistance in the preparation of this work, which have added materially to its value. Her large experience with women's organizations has enabled her to know the needs in many directions. She selected from the author's correspondence a large number of the Questions and Answers used in Part VII, and prepared the Special Index for this part of the work.

That this book may be helpful to those who wish to learn how to carry on the business of societies with the greatest efficiency is the earnest wish of the author.

HENRY M. ROBERT.

GENERAL PLAN

Part I

MOTIONS

Part II

DEBATE; VOTING; NOMINATIONS AND ELECTIONS

Part III

BOARDS AND COMMITTEES

Part IV

OFFICERS

Part V

MEMBERS; HONORARY OFFICERS AND MEMBERS; RESIGNA-
TIONS; DISCIPLINE; QUORUM; SESSIONS AND MEETINGS

Part VI

BY-LAWS AND OTHER RULES

Part VII

QUESTIONS AND ANSWERS FROM THE AUTHOR'S PARLIAMEN-
TARY LAW CORRESPONDENCE

Part VIII

CHARTS AND VARIOUS LISTS OF MOTIONS ARRANGED FOR EAS'
REFERENCE; FORMS; DEFINITIONS

Index

CONTENTS

PART I. MOTIONS

PART I

MOTIONS

(SEE CONTENTS, p. IX, FOR THE CONTENTS OF THESE
FIFTEEN CHAPTERS ON MOTIONS)

PARLIAMENTARY LAW

CHAPTER I

INTRODUCTION

PARLIAMENTARY LAW comprises the rules and customs governing deliberative assemblies. Its objects are to enable an assembly, with the least possible friction, to deliberate upon questions in which it is interested, and to ascertain and express its deliberate sense or will on these questions.

To accomplish these objects, experience has taught that it is necessary to have a presiding officer, a recording officer, and some established rules or customs. The presiding officer is usually known as the Chairman or the President, although in the lower house of legislative bodies he is called the Speaker, and in fraternal and secret societies he has some special title. The duties of the chairman are, in general, to preside over the meetings and see that the rules are enforced. The recording officer is usually called the Secretary or Clerk, though in secret societies various other names are used. The duties of the secretary are, in general, to keep a record, called the Minutes, of the business transacted at the meetings, and to attend to such correspondence as does not naturally devolve upon other officers, or upon committees or boards. If the assembly is an organized society, other officers are usually needed, but a chairman and secretary are all the officers that are strictly necessary for a deliberative assembly.

The rules and customs most commonly adopted by societies in this country are stated in "Rules of Order Revised," and are more fully explained and illustrated in the following pages. The method of organizing and of conducting business in mass meetings, societies, and conventions of delegates is explained in "Rules of Order Revised," pages 275–298. In "Robert's Parliamentary Practice," which is an introduction to this work, are given several drills illustrating in detail the method of conducting business meetings.

It is assumed that the reader has read "Parliamentary Practice," or the forty-five pages covered by the first two lessons which are outlined on page 308 of "Rules of Order Revised," and therefore this elementary instruction is not repeated here. Many readers will think some of the subjects, notably Reconsider, are treated too elaborately. They must bear in mind that there are others who wish to be prepared to meet just such difficulties. Illustrations are freely given in such cases, so as to enable the average reader to understand the subject. If a statement is not understood, it is best to read on, and it will generally be found that further reading makes the meaning clear. It is well to use the Index freely. The Special Index to Questions and Answers, page 401, enables the reader to utilize the author's answers to many questions that may arise in his own mind. If a parliamentary term is not understood, its meaning will generally be found under Definitions, page 568.

No one is ever strong and forceful when he gets near the limits of his knowledge. A teacher should know far more of a subject than he ever expects to teach. A leader in any deliberative assembly should be prepared for every emergency, so that there is no danger of his being tripped up by some expert parliamentarian. While this knowledge greatly increases one's efficiency, it is not wise to make a display of it, or to use it in a way to interfere with carrying out the wishes of the majority of the society. Where there is radical difference of opinion in an organization, one side must yield. The great lesson for democracies to learn is for the majority to give to the minority a full, free opportunity to present their side of the case, and then for the minority, having failed to win a majority to their views, gracefully to submit and to recognize the action as that of the entire organization, and cheerfully to assist in carrying it out, until they can secure its repeal.

CHAPTER II

MOTIONS AND THEIR CLASSIFICATION

Motions. A motion is a proposition that something be done, or that something is the sense, opinion, or wish of the assembly. Business is brought before a deliberative assembly by motions or by communications. In case of a communication, a resignation for instance, before any action can be taken on it, a motion must be made, or the chair must assume one, and the question on the adoption of the motion must be stated by the chair. In order to make a motion, a member rises and addresses the chair by his title, and when he has obtained the floor, he says, "I move," followed by his proposition, as, "I move that we donate $50 to the library"; or, "I move to adopt [or, the adoption of] the following resolution: '*Resolved*, That' etc."; or, "I move to adjourn." In the case of resolutions and amendments, "I offer," or "I propose," is sometimes used instead of "I move to adopt," or "I move the adoption of," as, for example, "I offer [or propose] the following resolution [or amendment]," etc.; or, "I propose that the resolution be amended by striking out '50' and inserting '75.'"

Motions are divided into Main Motions, or those that introduce a subject to the assembly, and Secondary Motions, or those that can be made while a main motion is pending, and that, for the time being, supersede it. Secondary motions are subdivided into Subsidiary, Privileged, and Incidental Motions. This classification of motions is only for convenience. The privileged motions might be called main motions, since they each bring before the assembly a new question that has no relation to the pending question. But their high privilege makes them very distinct from other main motions as to precedence, debate, etc., and it is better to call them privileged motions. Main motions can have all the subsidiary motions applied to them, while no subsidiary, except to amend, can be applied to a privileged motion. All main motions can be debated, while no debate is allowed on any privileged motion, nor on any incidental motion except an appeal under

5

certain circumstances. Privileged and subsidiary motions have a distinct rank among themselves, while incidental motions have not.

Main Motions. A main motion is one that introduces a subject to the assembly for its consideration and action. Since only one subject can be considered at a time, no main motion can be made while another motion is before the assembly. All main motions are debatable and amendable. They are fully explained in the next chapter.

Subsidiary Motions. Sometimes another motion is necessary or desirable in order to dispose properly of a main motion. Motions that help to dispose of a main motion are called Subsidiary Motions. They may be made when the main motion is pending, and when stated by the chair they supersede the main motion and become the immediately pending question. Subsidiary motions are used when the assembly wishes to change the wording of a main question by means of an amendment, to refer a main question to a committee for consideration and recommendation, to postpone action on it to another time, to limit or close the debate, to extend the limits of debate, or to lay the main question aside temporarily when something of greater urgency may require the attention of the assembly.

A subsidiary motion may itself be superseded by another subsidiary motion of higher rank, or by a privileged or incidental motion, which for the time being becomes the immediately pending question. Subsidiary motions cannot be applied to one another, except that most of them can be amended, and debate can be limited or closed upon the debatable ones. For instance, no subsidiary motion can be laid on the table by itself; if it is laid on the table, all pending questions go to the table with it. On page 548 will be found a chart containing a list of all the subsidiary motions, arranged in the order of their precedence or rank, and showing which of them may be amended, and which debated, and which require a two-thirds vote. Each of the subsidiary motions is taken up separately and fully explained in Chapters IV–VII.

Privileged Motions. While a main motion and one or more subsidiaries are pending there must be some method of closing the meeting, taking a recess, and appointing the time for an adjourned meeting. Sometimes, too, a question arises as to the rights and privileges of the assembly, or of an individual member, that requires immediate attention, though other questions are pending. And, again, the society may have adopted a program or order of business which is being departed from, and members may wish the order enforced. The motions to accomplish these various objects are called Privileged Motions, because they are of the highest privilege, being in order while any other motions are pending. The five privileged motions are undebatable because debate is incompatible with high privilege. After the orders of the day are actually taken up, or a motion is made and stated covering a question of privilege,[1] the motion that has had the special privilege of consideration at this time is before the assembly for debate and the application of subsidiary motions, the same as any main motion. The motions fixing the time for an adjourned meeting and to take a recess may be amended, but the other privileged motions cannot be amended. A list of the privileged motions, arranged in the order of their rank, will be found in Chart I, page 548.

Incidental Motions. During a meeting it is sometimes necessary to allow a temporary interruption of the immediate business in order to attend to something relating to the business of the assembly. Examples of such interruptions are: a question of order or an appeal from the decision of the chair; an objection to the introduction of a question that is deemed improper for consideration by the assembly, at least at that session; a motion to suspend the rules in order that something may be done out of its proper order, or in violation of the rules relating to the transaction of business; a motion to divide a question into two or more questions, to consider the question by paragraphs, to create a blank in a pending motion; a motion relating to nominations, voting, or a quorum; an inquiry on a point of parliamentary law involved in the pending business; a request for information in matters relating to pending business or to other business so urgent as to justify interrupting the pending business; a request for leave to withdraw or modify a motion, to read papers, or to be excused from a duty, as, for instance, service on a committee. These various questions are incidental to questions pending, or that have just been pending, or to those it is desired to introduce, or they relate to other business of the assembly, and are therefore called Incidental Questions.

[1] See page 126 for the difference between Questions of Privilege and Privileged Questions.

Incidental questions, unlike subsidiary and privileged ones, have no rank (order of precedence) among themselves. They take precedence of any motion, however privileged, to which they are incidental. Thus, while the motion to adjourn is pending it is in order to make a motion describing the method of voting; or, after it has been voted viva voce to adjourn and before the assembly has been declared adjourned, it is in order to compel the taking of a rising vote by calling out, "Division," or, "I doubt the vote." On the other hand, if an incidental motion is made when a main or subsidiary motion is the immediately pending question, any privileged motion is in order while the incidental motion is pending. No debate is allowed on incidental questions, except on an appeal under certain circumstances, as stated on page 152. If debate were allowed on them it would greatly interfere with business. The prohibition of debate does not, however, preclude a few words of explanation. It is the duty of the presiding officer to see that these remarks do not run into debate. A list of the common incidental motions will be found in Chart II, page 549.

In addition to the four classes of motions, main, subsidiary, privileged, and incidental, there are two motions, to Take from the Table, and to Reconsider, that cannot be placed satisfactorily in any of these classes. These motions are used to bring again before the assembly either a question that has been laid aside temporarily to attend to some more urgent business, or else a question upon which action has been taken the same day or the day preceding. These motions are explained, Take from the Table on page 106, and Reconsider on page 87.

CHAPTER III

MAIN MOTIONS: POSTPONE INDEFINITELY

[For detailed contents of this chapter, see "Main Motions" in Index, page 577.]

MAIN MOTIONS

A MAIN MOTION brings a subject before the assembly for its consideration and action. Since only one subject can be considered at a time, no main motion can be made when any other motion is pending. For convenience they are divided into Original Main Motions and Incidental Main Motions. The only reason for this division of main motions is that it is in order to object to the consideration of an original main motion, while it is not in order to object to the consideration of an incidental main motion.

An *Original Main Motion* brings before the assembly some new subject for its consideration and action. It should be in writing unless very brief, and should usually be in the form of a resolution.

An *Incidental Main Motion* is a main motion that is incidental to or relates to the business of the assembly, or to its past or future action. It is usually made orally, and frequently not in the form of a resolution. The following are examples of incidental main motions: To amend or rescind a resolution or rule already adopted; to accept, or adopt, a report which an officer or committee has been directed to make; to discharge a committee; to appoint a time and place for the next meeting, if the motion is made when no business is pending.

Characteristics of Main Motions. A main motion, or any amendment thereto, must not be in violation of national or state laws, or in conflict with the constitution, the by-laws, or the standing rules or resolutions of the assembly. If it so conflicts and is adopted, it is null and void. A main motion cannot conflict with or be substantially the same as a resolution or main motion previously adopted or rejected by the assembly during the same session, thus bringing up a second time the same question. It cannot cover the same ground as a motion that has been made and has not been finally disposed of, but is in the hands of a committee, or has been postponed, or laid on the table, or will come up as unfinished business, or may be brought before the assembly again by calling up the motion to reconsider which has been made previously. A main motion is not in order that will in any way interfere with freedom of action in the case of one previously introduced and not yet finally disposed of and is thus "in possession of the assembly."

A main motion may have applied to it any subsidiary motion, that is, it may be amended, committed, postponed, etc. When a main motion is postponed or laid on the table, all pending subsidiary motions go with it. When a main motion is committed, only pending amendments go with it. It takes precedence of nothing, that is, it cannot be made while any other question is pending. It yields to subsidiary, privileged, and incidental motions, that is, any of them may be made while a main motion is pending. It is debatable and requires for its adoption only a majority vote, that is, more than half of the votes cast, a quorum being present, except in the cases mentioned hereafter where the effect of adopting the main motion is to change something the assembly has previously done, or to suspend some rule or some right of the members.

As a general rule, when possible, a main motion should be in the affirmative rather than in the negative form. The objection to the negative form is the liability to confusion in the minds of the voters as to the effect of a negative vote on a negative proposition. In many cases, however, the negative form cannot be avoided, because rejecting the affirmative proposition is not always equivalent to adopting the negative proposition. For instance, voting down the resolution, "*Resolved*, That this club is in sympathy with the movement to unite the athletic clubs of the city," is not necessarily the equivalent of adopting the resolution, "*Resolved*, That this club is not in sympathy with the movement to unite the athletic clubs of the city." Many members may vote against the first resolution because they are opposed to committing the club on the question. On the same ground they would vote against the second proposition, so that perhaps neither could be adopted. If it were desired to put the club on record as not in sympathy with the proposed union, it would be difficult to avoid the negative form of the resolution.

When a negative form of motion is offered, the chairman should suggest the proper change if it is capable of being changed into the affirmative form without weakening it. Thus a motion "that we do not approve ——" can usually be changed into a motion "that we disapprove ——," since they are usually equivalent. If the motion cannot be changed from the negative form, or if the mover is unwilling to make the change, the chair, in putting the question to vote, should be very careful to make it clear to the voters what they are voting for. In case of the motion "that we do not approve ——," if the mover declines to modify his motion, the chair in taking the vote could put the question thus: "The question is on the motion 'that we do not approve ——.' As many as are in favor of the motion, that is, as many as do not approve — , say 'Aye.' Those who are opposed to the motion, that is, those who are opposed to expressing disapproval of ——, say 'No.' The ayes have it and the motion is adopted."

EXAMPLES OF MAIN MOTIONS

Resolutions, Motions, Orders. A member wishing to have the assembly consider and act on a certain subject should put in writing what he wishes the assembly to do, or to agree to, and then move its adoption. This is a main or principal motion. It should usually be in the form of a resolution, but the word *"Resolved"* may be dropped and it may be offered in a simple motion, provided it is very short. The Form of the motion is, "I move to adopt [or I move the adoption of, or I offer] the following resolution: '*Resolved,* That the club give a banquet next month,' " or simply, "I move that the club give a banquet next month." In either form it is a main motion. If the motion is of the nature of an order it is better to make the motion thus: "I move the adoption of the following order: '*Ordered,* That during the winter months the reading-room be kept open from 7 to 9 P. M.' "; or, "I move the adoption of the following order: '*Ordered,* That the janitor hereafter be paid $30 a month.' "

Action on Committees' Reports and Recommendations. When a committee reports resolutions or recommendations, a motion should be made by its chairman to adopt or agree to the resolutions or recommendations. If the committee reports facts or opinions no motion is necessary, but if it is desired specially to endorse the report the proper motion to make is to accept the report. All these motions are main motions. If a resolution is referred to a committee and the committee reports it back, recommending its adoption or rejection, no motion is made. The chair states the question on the motion which had been made previously and referred to the committee, thus: "The question is on the adoption of the resolution, etc."; or, "The question is on the adoption of the resolution, the recommendation of the committee to the contrary notwithstanding." [See page 267 for fuller information.]

Action on Communications, Resignations. If the communication is a resignation the proper motion is to accept the resignation. Other communications should in most cases be referred to a committee for consideration and recommendation of suitable action to be taken. In either case the motion providing for suitable action is a main motion.

Approving Minutes. When the minutes are read, without waiting for a motion the chair asks, "Are there any corrections to the minutes?" If there are none he instantly adds, "There being none, the minutes stand approved." The motion to approve (or adopt) is a main motion and is usually adopted, as in this case, by "general consent." If objection is made the chair puts the question to vote without a motion, or some one may make a motion to approve or adopt the minutes.

Ratify, Approve, Confirm. Sometimes action is taken by a national or state society subject to ratification or approval by its constituent organizations. In such cases it is moved in the national or state society to adopt the resolution, or by-law, or amendment, while in the constituent organizations the motion is to ratify the action of the other society. On the other hand, exactly the reverse of this may occur, where a subordinate society, local or state, adopts by-laws or elects officers subject to ratification or confirmation by the parent body.

Sometimes, when there is no quorum present, business of an urgent nature is transacted that certainly will be approved by the society. In such a case, at the next meeting a member states the facts, and, permission being granted, the minutes of that meeting are read, and he then moves, "That the action taken at the informal meeting held on —— day of —— be ratified, and that the minutes be approved as read and be entered on the records." Or, a member may simply report the action taken and move (or some one else may move) that it be ratified. As an illustration of the use of the motion to ratify take the following: A meeting at which the delegates to the state convention are to be elected occurs on such a stormy night that no quorum is present. Since the next meeting will be too late for the election, the delegates are chosen at this meeting, and at the next meeting the fact is reported and the society legalizes the election by ratifying it. Sometimes officers or a committee find it expedient, or even necessary, to exceed their authority, trusting to the society to ratify, and thus legalize, their act. The motion to ratify, or its equivalent, to approve, or to confirm, is a main motion.

Rescind, Repeal, Annul. If the assembly wishes to revoke some action that it has previously taken, it may rescind that action. The motion to rescind is a main motion, and may be adopted by a majority vote if previous notice has been given. But, unlike ordinary main motions, it requires for its adoption a two-thirds vote or a vote of a majority of the entire membership, when previous notice has not been given, because it changes something which the assembly has previously adopted, as explained under Rescind, page 110. On account of the restrictions upon this motion, it is usually better, when practicable, to move to reconsider a vote rather than to rescind it, since a reconsideration requires only a majority vote. The motion to rescind is really one form of the motion to amend something previously adopted, and is subject to all the restrictions adopted for amendments. Thus, nothing can be rescinded in constitutions, by-laws, etc., unless all the rules applying to their amending are complied with. Sometimes repeal or annul is used as the equivalent of rescind.

Discharge a Committee. Similar to the motion to rescind, and under nearly the same rules, is the motion to discharge a committee when made before the committee has reported. After it has reported in full, it is automatically discharged from the consideration of the question without any motion or vote. This motion is explained on page 108.

The motions to postpone indefinitely, to amend, to commit or refer, to postpone definitely, and to limit debate are generally used to assist in disposing of a main motion that is pending, and are therefore subsidiary motions. But sometimes motions in the form of these subsidiary motions are used when there is no main motion pending, and in such cases they are main motions, because they are the original motions that bring the questions formally before the assembly. When these motions are referred to, the subsidiary motions are meant unless it is expressly stated to the contrary.

Postpone Indefinitely. Suppose it is voted to have an excursion on May 2, and at the next meeting it is moved to postpone the excursion indefinitely. This latter is a main motion, but as it practically rescinds action taken by the society, it requires for its adoption the same vote as just described for rescind.

Amend. A motion to amend the constitution, by-laws, rules of order, standing rules, or resolutions, that have been previously adopted and are therefore not pending, is a main motion that may have amendments of the first and the second degree applied to it, or it may be committed, or postponed, etc., the same as any other main motion. Whatever is done to it, unless it is adopted, does not affect the by-laws, standing rules or resolutions, because they are not pending. Standing rules, or resolutions, previously adopted, may be amended by the same vote as required for rescinding action previously taken, as before stated, page 13.

Commit. If the motion to refer a certain subject to a committee or to appoint a committee for a certain purpose is made when no main motion is pending, then the motion to commit or appoint the committee is a main motion. Thus the following, made when nothing is pending, is a main motion: "I move that the subject of the advisability of erecting a suitable building for our society be referred to a committee of seven to be appointed by the chair, with instructions to report as soon as practicable."

Postpone. Suppose the society has voted to have a banquet on July 4, and at a subsequent meeting members wish to postpone the banquet to July 15. Since it is too late to reconsider the vote, it is moved "to postpone the banquet to July 15." This is a main motion, differing materially from the ordinary subsidiary motion to postpone, which means always to postpone the consideration of the main question. There is no main motion pending when this motion to postpone is made, and therefore the motion cannot be a subsidiary one. It is a main motion, which has the effect, if adopted, of changing something the assembly has ordered to be done, like the motion to rescind previously described, and requires the same vote as that motion, namely, a two-thirds vote or a vote of the majority of the membership, unless previous notice of the motion has been given, in which case it may be adopted by a majority vote.

Limit Debate. While no question is pending it may be desired to limit the members during the remainder of the meeting to one speech of three or five minutes on each question. Such a motion is a main motion and therefore is open to debate. It requires a two-thirds vote for its adoption, however, because it deprives the members of a right given them by the rules.

The three motions relating to a Recess, to Adjournment, and to Fixing the Time for an Adjourned Meeting are not always privileged, but are sometimes main motions. The motions to take a recess, and to fix the time to which to adjourn, are main motions if made when no other motion is pending, that is, if made when a main motion is in order. The motion to adjourn is a main motion in a meeting of an assembly that has made no provision for holding another meeting. In such a case, if the motion to adjourn is adopted the assembly would be dissolved. In an organized society, provision is always made for future meetings, so the motion to adjourn in such a society is always a privileged motion. If it is qualified in any way, as, "to adjourn at 12 m.," or, "to adjourn to meet at 2 p. m. to-morrow," it is a main motion.

The motion "to fix the time *at* which to adjourn" is always a main motion, and should not be confounded with the motion "to fix the time *to* which to adjourn," which is always privileged if made when another motion is pending.

Questions of Privilege are privileged to the extent of having the right to interrupt other business, but when under consideration they are main motions and are treated as such in every respect.

Orders of the Day also, whether special orders or general orders, when under consideration are main motions, their only privilege being the right to consideration at that particular time.

POSTPONE INDEFINITELY

This is a motion to reject the main motion, and it cannot be moved if anything is pending except a main motion. It is useful only when the opponents of a measure are in doubt as to whether they control a majority vote. If they are in doubt, by using this motion they can ascertain their strength without risking the adoption of the main motion. If they find themselves in the minority and the motion to postpone indefinitely is lost, the main motion is still pending, and they are free to continue the struggle against it. If they had tested their strength directly on the main motion and had lost, the main motion would have been adopted.

If the opponents of a main motion are confident of a majority, they have nothing to gain by using the motion to postpone indefinitely. On the contrary, they lose time because of the extra debate allowed. If they control a two-thirds vote they can stop the debate by ordering the previous question, but they can do that just as effectually without using the motion to postpone indefinitely. In ordinary societies this motion is rarely of any use.

Sometimes, however, it is used to kill a measure, with the idea that it is not so harsh as voting directly against the main motion. For instance, a large majority may be opposed to a motion to make A an honorary member of the club, and are willing to vote to postpone the motion indefinitely, and yet would hesitate to vote directly against the main motion.

This motion is not only debatable, but opens to debate the entire merits of the main question, because they are necessarily involved in a discussion as to whether the main motion should be postponed indefinitely, that is, killed. Since the question on the indefinite postponement is technically different from that on adopting the main motion, members who have previously exhausted their right of debate, now have another opportunity to debate the main motion.

This motion cannot be amended or have any other subsidiary motion applied to it alone, except the previous question and the motions to limit or to extend the limits of debate, which are applicable to all debatable motions. While the motion to postpone indefinitely is immediately pending, however, it is in order to amend the main motion or to make any of the other subsidiary motions. The various privileged and incidental motions are also in order while this motion is immediately pending. It is the lowest in rank of all motions except a main motion. If a resolution is referred to a committee while a motion to postpone indefinitely is pending, this latter motion is ignored and does not go to the committee.

If the motion to postpone indefinitely is adopted, the vote

may be reconsidered. If it is lost the vote cannot be reconsidered or renewed, because there will be another opportunity to kill the resolution when the vote is taken on its adoption. If a motion to postpone to a certain time is made, and the time is placed so that the effect is to defeat the object of the main motion the same as if an indefinite postponement were moved, it should be treated as if it were the motion to postpone indefinitely. If anything except the main motion is pending, this motion to postpone is out of order. If nothing but the main motion is pending, the motion to postpone is stated and treated as the motion to postpone indefinitely. As an example, suppose there is pending a main motion to accept an invitation to take part in a parade to-morrow. While an amendment to this motion is pending, it is moved to postpone the question to the next regular meeting a week hence. The chair should rule this motion out of order, because it is practically the motion to postpone indefinitely, which is lower in rank than the amendment that is pending. If, however, the motion to postpone to the next meeting is not made until after the amendment is disposed of, the chair should state the question thus, "The question is on the motion to postpone the pending question indefinitely."

The name of this motion, like that of the previous question, is misleading. It is not a motion to postpone, but to reject or kill the main motion. When the word postpone is used without qualification, it never refers to this motion, but to the motion to postpone to a certain time.

CHAPTER IV

AMENDMENTS

[For detailed contents of this chapter see Amendments in Index.]

WHEN a subject is brought by a main motion before an assembly for its consideration, it may be desired to change the wording of the main motion before taking final action upon it. The changes desired may simply make the language clearer, or they may slightly affect the meaning, or they may so completely change the meaning as to defeat the object of the original motion, but, as hereafter explained, they must be germane to the original matter. These changes are called amendments, and may be made by inserting or adding words, or by striking out words, or by striking out some words and inserting others. This last form is a combination of the two other forms of amendments. Any alteration of the wording of a motion is an amendment of that motion.

Instead of altering a few words in a main motion, it may be desired to add or insert one or more entire paragraphs, or to strike out one or more paragraphs, or to strike out one or more paragraphs and insert one or more other paragraphs in their place. The paragraph may consist of a single sentence or it may be the entire resolution. These motions are all amendments, the last one usually being called a substitute. A substitute may replace the entire resolution by a new one on the same subject.

Primary and Secondary Amendments, or Amendments of the First Degree and of the Second Degree. If, while an amendment of any motion except an amendment is pending, a member wishes to have it modified before the vote is taken on its adoption, the proper course is to move to amend the amendment. The original amendment is called a primary amendment, or an amendment of the first degree; the amendment of the amendment is called a secondary amendment, or an amendment of the second degree. An amendment of the first degree can be amended, but one of the second degree cannot. No two amendments of the same question of

18

the same degree can be pending at the same time. But after a primary amendment has been disposed of another primary amendment may be moved, and after its disposal a third may be moved, and so on without limitation. The same is true with respect to secondary amendments.

An amendment of the third degree is not allowed. It is necessary to stop somewhere, and this point has been found to be the best. When a member wishes to move an amendment of a pending amendment of the second degree, his proper course is to speak against the immediately pending amendment and announce the one he will offer if the pending one is rejected. If it is rejected the chair should immediately recognize him for the purpose of moving his amendment.

Amendments must be germane to the subject matter to be amended, that is, they must relate to the same subject. No new subject can be introduced in the guise of an amendment. So, a secondary amendment must be germane to the primary amendment which it is proposed to amend. As a general rule, an amendment is germane to a resolution when the two are so closely related that the adoption, or rejection, or temporary disposal [1] of the resolution would prevent the introduction, at the same session, of the essential idea of the amendment in the form of an independent resolution. But an amendment may be germane to a resolution when they are not so intimately related.

The following illustrations will be of assistance in deciding when an amendment is germane to the main motion:

(a) A motion is pending to confer a certain honor on Mr. Brown, and it is then moved to amend by inserting "and Mr. Jones" after "Brown." This amendment is out of order if the main motion is strictly a personal one intended to compliment Mr. Brown for some act in which Mr. Jones had no share. If no one else shared in the act no amendment is germane that does not bear on the question of honoring Mr. Brown. So, while an amendment would be germane that increased or diminished, or in any way changed, the honor conferred on Mr. Brown, an amendment to insert "and Mr. Jones," or one to strike out "Brown" and insert "Jones," would not be germane and therefore would be out of order.

(b) If, however, in the above-mentioned case, Brown and Jones

[1] See Temporary Disposal, page 80.

conjointly had done the worthy act for which this honor was to be conferred on Mr. Brown, then the amendment inserting "and Mr. Jones" would be germane; but another amendment inserting "and Mr. Smith," who had not participated in the act thus honored, would not be germane.

(c) Suppose a resolution of thanks to the railroads for their courtesy, etc., is offered, and a substitute is moved which condemns the railroads for their discourtesy. The substitute is germane to the resolution, and therefore is in order, because the fundamental idea in the resolution is the attitude of the assembly toward the railroads for their conduct, and a feeling of resentment is germane to a feeling of appreciation. If the resolution relates to a single railroad, it is not in order to amend so as to include other railroads, unless the acts upon which the judgment of the assembly is being passed are practically identical in all the cases. If, however, the original resolution includes two railroads where the acts are not the same, the fundamental idea of the resolution is one of approving or condemning the railroads, and they can all be grouped and considered together just as well as separately, and therefore an amendment inserting other railroads is germane and in order.

(d) Suppose a motion is pending to give $500 to an orphan asylum, and it is proposed to amend so as to have a foundling asylum share in the gift. Whether this amendment is germane or not depends upon the circumstances of the case. If the society is in the habit of making gifts annually to different charitable organizations, and at this time has only $500 available for all its gifts, the amendment is certainly germane, because in this case the underlying fact in the resolution is the appropriation of all the benevolent funds of the society; if it is adopted it cuts off all other appropriations of the kind, and therefore an amendment diverting a part or all of the appropriation to other objects is germane to the resolution. But if the resolution appropriates only a small portion of the funds to the orphan asylum, so that it does not prevent aiding other societies also, then this resolution does not necessarily involve the other societies, and the two appropriations can be considered as well separately, and the above-mentioned amendment would not be germane, and therefore it would be out of order. An amendment changing the amount of the appropriation is, of course, germane.

In the examples given above it is not difficult to decide whether the amendments are germane or not, but cases occur in which the most experienced presiding officers would differ in their decisions. Suppose the following resolution is pending: *"Resolved,* That the immigration of Hindus should be prohibited," and it is proposed to amend by inserting in the resolution the name of another race: Would such an amendment be germane? One presiding officer might hold the view that the underlying idea of the resolution is the preventing of the country's being flooded with foreigners, and that naming one of the largest nations in the world did not necessarily limit the scope of the resolution to that nation if the assembly preferred to act upon others in connection with it: he would therefore rule the amendment in order, leaving it to the assembly to decide whether it would, or would not, insert the name of the other race. Another presiding officer would decide that the resolution was aimed at a particular race, and that an amendment to include another race was not germane, and was therefore out of order.

Suppose, again, that in the case of a resolution conferring a certain honor on Mr. Brown it is moved to amend by inserting "and Mr. Jones" after "Brown," and that, while Mr. Jones has not participated in the act for which it is proposed to honor Mr. Brown, he has performed other worthy acts which entitle him to be honored equally with Mr. Brown. The votes of many members on conferring the honor on Mr. Brown might depend upon whether Mr. Jones was equally honored. There is room for an honest difference of opinion as to whether it is to the interest of the assembly to treat the two cases together or separately, and presiding officers would differ in their decisions.

When such questions arise the presiding officer usually has little time for thinking. He must decide promptly according to his best judgment, and not be sensitive if his decision is overruled by the assembly. He must recognize the right of others to have their opinions, just as he demands the right to his own. The wise presiding officer, however, will never rule an amendment out of order as not germane unless he is absolutely sure that he is right. If there is doubt in his mind, he will either admit the amendment, or, in very important cases, throw upon the assembly the responsibility of deciding whether the amendment is germane or not. In such cases without any motion he submits the question to the assembly thus: "The chair being in doubt will ask the assembly to decide the question, 'Is the amendment germane?' Are you ready for the question?" If no one rises to debate it, or when the debate is finished, he puts the question thus: "As many as are of opinion that the amendment is germane to the resolution [or amendment] say 'Aye.' As many as are of the contrary opinion say 'No.' The ayes have it, the amendment is declared germane, and the question is on the amendment, etc." Or if there are more votes in the negative than in the affirmative he says, "The noes have it, the amendment is declared not germane, and therefore is out of order. The question is on the resolution, etc."

An amendment must not have the effect of making the affirmative of the amended resolution equivalent to the negative of the original resolution. Allowing such amendments would merely waste the time of the assembly. Thus, suppose this resolution pending: *"Resolved,* that our delegates be instructed not to oppose the proposed amendment to our State Constitution." An amendment to strike out "not" is in order, because voting down the resolution of instructions "not to oppose" is not equivalent to instructing the delegates to oppose the amendment. An amendment to insert "not" after "be" would be out of order, because if the amended resolution should be adopted its effect would be practically the same as if the original motion were voted down, in either case each delegate being left free to vote as he pleases. Again, suppose the resolution reads, *"Resolved,* That our delegates be instructed to oppose the proposed amendment to our State Constitution"; an amendment to insert "not" before the word "instructed" would be out of order, while one to insert "not" after "instructed" would be in order. In the former case the effect of the affirmative of the amended resolution is the same as the negative of the original resolution, namely, to leave each delegate free to vote as he thinks best. In the latter case, however, the effect of the two votes is quite different, as instructing the delegates not to oppose the amendment is very different from refusing to instruct them to oppose the amendment, which latter leaves them free to vote as they please. So the word "not," or its equivalent, can sometimes be inserted or struck out, and in other cases it cannot. It depends entirely upon the effect of the amendment, as just shown. Rejecting a resolution is not always equivalent to adopting the opposite, as many may vote against the resolution because they are opposed to the society's committing itself on the subject, and not because they hold views the opposite to those expressed in the resolution.

A motion cannot be amended so as to change it into another parliamentary motion. Thus, a motion to postpone a question to the next meeting cannot be amended by striking out "to the next meeting" and inserting "indefinitely," or inserting any date when there is no meeting, which would be practically the same as inserting "indefinitely." It is not allowable to substitute the motion to postpone indefinitely for to commit, or to substitute a motion to adopt one resolution for a motion to adopt another one that is not germane, though one resolution may be moved as a substitute for another on the same subject, provided it conforms to the conditions heretofore prescribed for an amendment. One form of an amendment cannot be amended so as to change it into another form of amendment. For example, a motion to "strike out" cannot be amended by adding "and insert," etc. As a general rule, one motion cannot be amended so as to include another form of motion, but either of the motions relating to limiting or extending the limits of debate may be amended so as to include the others. For example, a motion to limit each speaker to one speech on the pending question may be amended so as to limit the length of each speech to one minute, and the entire debate to thirty minutes, and that may be further amended so as to allow the leaders on each side to speak for five minutes, with the privilege of reserving a portion of their time for a closing speech. Any main motion may be amended by adding to it instructions for its being printed, or a proviso as to when it is to take effect, provided the motion is not frivolous or improper.

Other Amendments that Are Not Allowed. An amendment must not conflict with a motion already adopted at the same session, nor is an amendment in order that will interfere with the adoption of a motion previously made and still in the possession of the assembly.[1] In such a case the subject will come before the assembly in the course of business, if the assembly so desires, and freedom of action at that time cannot be interfered with by an amendment to another motion, any more than it can by a new motion. [See page 79.]

No amendment is allowed that is frivolous, or that would leave

[1] See In Possession of the Assembly, page 10.

no rational proposition before the assembly, or that is expressed in language which would be out of order if used in debate. It is not permissible to waste the time of the assembly on trifling amendments, nor may a motion be changed by amendments into one that would have been out of order if originally offered in that form. Thus, it is not allowed to strike out the word *"Resolved,"* from a resolution, and thus leave no rational proposition. If the object is to try to kill the resolution without risking a direct vote on it, the proper course is to move to postpone the question indefinitely. Neither can a motion to postpone a resolution be amended so as to postpone it to an unreasonable time.

The Rank, or Order of Precedence, of an amendment is just above, and its Debatability is the same as that of the motion it is proposed to amend, except that an amendment always outranks the motion to postpone indefinitely. Thus, an amendment to the privileged motion to fix the time to which to adjourn outranks all subsidiary and privileged motions, and is undebatable because the motion it is proposed to amend has this high rank and is undebatable; while an amendment to a main motion is outranked by, that is, yields to, all other motions except a main motion and the motion to postpone indefinitely, and is debatable because a main motion has this low rank and is debatable.

When an amendment is debatable the debate must be confined to the merits of the amendment. Thus, if a motion is pending to refer the subject to a committee of five, and an amendment is moved "to strike out five and insert seven," it is out of order to speak against referring the question to a committee, since that is not the immediately pending question. The immediately pending question is on changing the committee from five to seven, and the propriety of this change is the only question that can be discussed. Sometimes the amendment is of such a nature that its discussion necessarily involves the merits of the question to be amended, in which case such discussion, of course, is allowed.

No subsidiary motion except to amend can be applied to an amendment except where it is debatable, and then the previous question and the other motions relating to closing or limiting debate may be ordered, in which case they apply only to it, the immediately pending amendment, unless they are so qualified as to include other pending motions. Thus, an amendment cannot by itself be referred to a committee, or postponed, or laid on the table.

If any one of these motions is adopted while an amendment is pending, the amendment goes to the committee, or the table, or is postponed, together with the main motion. On this account these motions are said not to apply to the motion to amend, while the previous question does apply, because when it is ordered while an amendment is the immediately pending question, the previous question affects only the immediately pending amendment, unless specified to the contrary.

The subsidiary motion to amend requires only a majority vote for its adoption, regardless of the vote required for the adoption of the motion to be amended. Amending only changes the form of the question to be submitted to the assembly for its adoption, and if either side must yield its preference in this matter it certainly should be the minority. When the amended question is put to the assembly for its decision it may require a two-thirds vote for its adoption, as in case of the motion to limit debate. The motion to amend anything already adopted, as by-laws or stand-ing rules, etc., is not a subsidiary motion. It is a main motion, and the vote required for its adoption depends upon what is to be amended, as shown on page 38.

Every main motion and the following secondary motions may be amended: the subsidiary motions, amend, commit, postpone to a certain time, and limit or extend limits of debate; the privi-leged motions, take a recess, and fix the time to which to adjourn; and the incidental motions, division of the question, and motions relating to consideration by paragraph, etc., and to methods of making nominations, and to methods of voting. The amendment of these secondary motions is limited and is extremely simple, as shown hereafter, page 36.

Amendments to main motions may be moved so as to affect (*a*) merely certain words of a paragraph; or (*b*) an entire paragraph or the entire resolution; or (*c*) the motion itself. In the first case the motion may be said to be an amendment of a paragraph, and it should be made in a form similar to this: "I move to amend the first paragraph of Section 2, Article V, by striking out 'three and inserting 'five.'" In the second case it is more properly an amendment of the resolution, or of the by-laws, or of an article or section of the by-laws, as the case may be, and it is made in this form: "I move to amend Article VI by inserting after the second paragraph [or section] the following paragraph [or section] etc."; or, "I move to amend the resolution by striking out the second paragraph"; or simply, "I move to strike out the second paragraph." In the third case the amendment may more properly be said to be an amendment of the motion to adopt, and it should be made in a form similar to that given in the following illustration: Suppose the pending question to be on the adoption of a revision of the by-laws submitted by a committee, which revision reduces the length of the term of the officers, and it is desired not to affect the officers now in service. The proper course is to move "to amend the pending motion, by adding, 'provided the term of office of those now in service shall not be affected thereby.'" So the motion to adopt the amended by-laws could be amended by adding, "provided that Article V shall not go into effect until after the close of this annual meeting." It is the duty of the committee that reports the revision to incorporate in the motion to adopt the revised by-laws all such provisions as these which they deem necessary. Members have a right to move amendments to this motion to adopt, adding other provisions like the above.

Forms of the Motion to Amend

When a resolution, or other main motion, is not satisfactorily expressed and it is desired to modify it, the amendment should be moved in one of these three forms:

To Insert or Add. When it is desired to insert words in a resolution, the following forms are used: "I move to insert 'three' before 'lectures'"; or, "I move to amend the resolution by inserting the word 'three' before the word 'lectures.'" When it is desired to insert a paragraph, the motion is made thus: "I move to insert after the second paragraph the following paragraph." Then follows the new paragraph to be inserted. The exact location of the words to be inserted must be designated by stating the word before or after which they are to be placed. If the insertion is to be in printed matter, the line and paragraph should be specified. The most important word before or after should generally be used, and sometimes both should be used, thus: "I move to insert the words 'of the stockholders' between the words 'meeting' and 'will' in the first paragraph." This is usually necessary where the important word is repeated. In every case the place where the words or paragraph are to be inserted must be accurately described. If the additional words or paragraph are to be at the end, then instead of "insert" the word "add" is used. As it is understood that "added" words are placed at the end, it is not necessary or proper further to describe their location. The form of the motion is this: "I move to add the words, 'and that the committee be instructed to have 500 copies of the ticket printed'"; or, "I move to add to the second paragraph the following words, etc."

The words to be inserted must be inserted at one place. If the insertion of the words necessitates a further change in the wording of the resolution, then this is not the proper form of amendment to use. The form in such case is the motion "to strike out and insert," as shown in the following example: Suppose the following resolution pending: "*Resolved*, That the secretary be directed to prepare a list of members delinquent in the payment of dues, and that he submit a report at the next meeting." Now it is desired to add the treasurer to the committee. But if the words "and treasurer" are inserted after "secretary" the word "he" in the last clause should be changed to "they." In this case "to insert" is the wrong motion. The proper motion is "to strike out the words between 'secretary' and 'submit' and insert the words 'and treasurer be directed to prepare a list of members delinquent in payment of dues, and that they.'" Or, the new resolution could be written out properly and moved as a substitute for the pending one. Sometimes in amending resolutions a grammatical error is inadvertently created. When noticed, the chair should call attention to the error and say that unless objection is made the secretary will correct it, stating at the same time what correction will be made. By this course much valuable time may be saved. If objection is made, which is improbable, the chair, without waiting for a motion, should put to the assembly the question on a proper amendment to rectify the error. In the case illustrated earlier in this paragraph, if the words "and treasurer" had been inserted, the necessary mechanical correction of changing "he" to "they" could have been made by general consent, as just described.

When words or a paragraph are to be inserted or added, their friends should see to it that they are made as nearly perfect as possible by suitable amendments before the vote is taken on inserting them, because after they are inserted it is too late to change them, the assembly having decided to insert the words or paragraph in exactly that shape. Additions may be made to the paragraph, but not such as modify what the assembly has inserted. Before modifying what has been inserted it is necessary to reconsider the vote by which the words or paragraph were inserted, and then to amend them suitably before again voting on inserting them.

While words that have been inserted cannot be amended by inserting or striking out words, it is allowable to amend the resolution by striking out all or a part of the words that have been inserted together with other words, provided the new question is an entirely different one from the question decided by the assembly when it inserted the words. The same principle applies to a paragraph that has been inserted or added. It cannot be amended in any way except by adding to it words that do not conflict with the paragraph as inserted. It cannot be struck out unless other paragraphs are struck out with all or a part of it so as to present to the assembly an entirely different question from the one it has already decided. Suppose a pending resolution contains among other things a paragraph authorizing a committee to rent a hall. This is amended by adding "and to furnish the same." Those added words cannot be amended, but a motion would be in order to strike out the entire paragraph, as that would be an entirely different question. If the hall was to be rented the majority wished it furnished. But it does not follow that a majority wished to authorize the committee to rent the hall, and therefore a motion to strike out the entire sentence or paragraph is in order.

If the motion to insert is voted down, it does not follow that the assembly is unwilling to have the words or paragraph or a part of them inserted elsewhere, provided the new location or the modification of the words makes the question practically a new one. The adverse vote merely shows that the assembly is unwilling to insert these particular words at this particular place. Therefore it is allowable to move to insert the words or paragraph at some other place where the connection will be such as to raise a new question. It may be moved to insert at the same place the same words or paragraph so modified as to make an essentially new question, but it is not allowed merely to change the wording without in any way changing the sense, so as practically to bring the same question before the assembly a second time. To illustrate this, suppose a set of by-laws is being considered and a motion is made to insert a section after the second section of Article II. The motion to insert being voted down, it would not be in order to move to insert the same section at another place in the same article, unless the objections to inserting it in the place first proposed do not apply to inserting it at the new place. The objection may be only to inserting it in this particular article, in which case it would be allowable afterward to move to insert it in a more appropriate article. Common sense must be exercised by the presiding officer so as to give members as great liberty as possible and at the same time to protect the assembly from being imposed upon by useless motions that bring before the assembly questions that it has practically decided already.

Amending the Motion to Insert or Add. The motion to insert (or add) may be amended in any of the three ways main motions may be amended, that is, by inserting (or adding), by striking out, and by striking out and inserting. As previously stated, it is very important that the friends of a proposed amendment make it as nearly perfect as possible by amendments before the vote on the insertion is taken, because they thereby improve the chances of its adoption, and also because, if adopted, it cannot be further changed by amendments.

To Strike Out. When it is desired to strike out words or a paragraph in a resolution, the motion is made thus: "I move to strike out the word 'excessive' "; or, "I move to strike out the word 'the' before the word 'desks' in the third paragraph"; or, "I move to strike out the second paragraph of the first section of Article III." Whenever there is liability to uncertainty as to the word to be struck out, the word before or after it, or possibly both, should be designated, as in the second example given above. The words to be struck out must be consecutive in the motion to be amended.

Amending the Motion to Strike Out. The motion to strike out words can be amended only by striking out words from the primary amendment to strike out. The effect of striking out words from the primary amendment to strike out is to leave the words in the resolution, regardless of whether the primary amendment is carried or lost. When it is proposed to strike out several words, it is allowable to strike out from the primary amendment an intermediate word, and thus to separate the words in the primary amendment, as in this example: A resolution is pending to authorize a committee, "to visit the cities of New York, Cleveland, Chicago, Philadelphia, and Boston." While this is pending it is moved to strike out "Cleveland, Chicago, Philadelphia" from the resolution, and a secondary amendment is moved "to strike out 'Chicago' in the primary amendment." If this secondary amendment is carried, the word "Chicago" remains in the resolution, and the primary amendment is now "to strike out the words 'Cleveland,' Philadelphia,'" which words, it will be noticed, are separated in the resolution. The primary amendment is now in such a shape that if originally offered thus it would have been ruled out of order. If the primary amendment is now adopted, the question is on the resolution as amended, namely, "to authorize the committee to visit the cities of New York, Chicago, and Boston."

The motion to strike out a paragraph is treated differently from a motion to strike out words, as far as amending is concerned. In the latter case, as has been stated, the only secondary amendment allowed is to strike out. In the case of striking out a paragraph, however, it is the duty of its friends to improve the paragraph as much as possible before the vote is taken on striking it out, in the hope of defeating that motion. For this purpose it is allowed to amend the paragraph in any or every way that a main motion may be amended. The motion to strike out a paragraph is a primary amendment and only one amendment of it can be pending at a time, this latter being a secondary amendment. When the paragraph is perfected the question is put on striking it out. If the motion to strike out the paragraph is lost, it may be still further amended.

It will be noticed that the effect of striking out a word from a primary amendment to strike out is entirely different in the two cases of striking out words and striking out a paragraph. If a primary amendment to strike out certain words in a resolution is pending and a word is struck out of the primary amendment, that word remains in the resolution, whether the primary amendment to strike out is adopted or lost. If a primary amendment to strike out a paragraph in a resolution is pending and a word is struck out of the paragraph, that word remains out of the paragraph and therefore out of the resolution, whether the paragraph is struck out or not.

If the motion to strike out is lost, it only shows that the assembly is not willing to strike out those particular words or that paragraph alone. It does not show that it is not willing to strike out a part of them, or all of them provided additional matter is struck out with them. It is only necessary that the new motion shall differ essentially from the one the assembly has already decided.

If the motion to strike out is adopted, the same words or paragraph cannot be put back in the resolution unless they have been so changed by additions or omissions as to present an entirely new question. If in considering a subject by paragraph it is decided to transfer a paragraph or words to another place, it can be done by announcing, at the time the motion to strike out the words or paragraph is made, that a motion will be made later to insert the same words or paragraph in another designated place. This method is necessary when considering a question by paragraph. As the paragraph or words were struck out with the understanding that they were to be inserted elsewhere, this is no violation of the rule that the exact words that have been struck out cannot afterward be inserted without a material modification.

To Strike Out and Insert or to **Substitute,** as the motion is called when it is applied to an entire paragraph or resolution. The two preceding motions, to strike out and to insert, provide for all cases where it is desired to strike out or to insert anything, from a few words to several paragraphs in the pending motion. But frequently it is desired to replace words or a paragraph by other words or another paragraph. If a motion were made only to strike out the words or paragraph, members might hesitate to vote for it because they do not wish it struck out unless certain words or a certain paragraph is inserted, and they cannot be sure that enough votes can be secured to make the desired insertion after the motion to strike out has been adopted. To meet this difficulty it is allowed to combine the two preceding motions in one motion called "to strike out and insert," or "to substitute," as it is called in case of an entire resolution or paragraph that is replaced.

This motion cannot be divided, because its very object would be defeated if any one could require the vote to be taken separately on striking out and on inserting. But for purposes of amendment it would be inconvenient to allow amendments indiscriminately to what is to be struck out and to what is to be inserted, and therefore no amendment of the words to be inserted is in order until the assembly has perfected by amendments the words or paragraph to be struck out. Consequently, when the motion to strike out and insert is made, the chair states the question thus:

"It has been moved and seconded to strike out the words ——
and insert the words ——. Are there any amendments proposed to
the words to be struck out?" When no further amendments are
proposed, the chair says, "Are there any further amendments proposed to the words to be struck out? There being none, the words
to be inserted, which are ——, are open to amendment."

It will be seen that the two parts of the combined motion are
amended the same as if they were two separate independent motions, each being under the rules laid down for that motion. The
debate, of course, may go into the merits of both parts of the motion, since the real question to be decided is the comparative merits of the words to be struck out and those to be inserted.

When the assembly has finished debating and amending the
question, the chair puts the question thus: "The question is on
amending the resolution [or motion, or paragraph] by striking
out the words ——, and inserting the words ——. As many as
are in favor of the amendment say 'Aye.' Those opposed say 'No.'
The ayes have it and the amendment is adopted. The question is
now on the resolution [or motion, or paragraph] as amended.
Are you ready for the question?"

If the amendment is to substitute a new paragraph for one in
the original motion, as in case of amending a set of by-laws which
is under consideration by a society at the time of its organization
and has not yet been adopted, the business proceeds in a manner
similar to this: The chair states the question thus after the new
paragraph has been read: "It has been moved and seconded to
substitute the paragraph just read for the second paragraph of the
first section of Article III of the pending by-laws. Are there any
amendments proposed to the paragraph to be struck out?" When
no further amendments are proposed, the chair says: "There
being no amendments [or, no further amendments] proposed to the
paragraph to be struck out, the paragraph to be inserted is open
to amendment." The comparative merits of the two paragraphs
are open to debate, and, before the vote is taken on making the
substitution, the two paragraphs should be perfected by amendments as heretofore described under the separate motions, to insert, and to strike out. When no further debate or amendment
is desired, the chair reads first the paragraph to be struck out, and
then the paragraph to be inserted, reading them both as they
finally stand after being perfected by amendments. He then puts

the question thus: "The question is on amending the pending by-laws by substituting the paragraph last read for the paragraph in the pending by-laws [or, in the by-laws reported by the committee]. As many as are in favor of the motion to substitute [or, of the amendment] say 'Aye.' Those opposed say 'No.' The ayes have it and the motion to be substituted [or, the amendment] is adopted." The chair proceeds at once to have the next paragraph read and asks, "Are there any amendments proposed to this paragraph?" and thus continues until an opportunity has been given for amending each paragraph or section of the by-laws. When the by-laws have been perfected by amendments, the question is put upon adopting or agreeing to the by-laws as amended.

If it is desired to replace an entire resolution by another one on the same subject, the proper course to pursue is for a member to obtain the floor when nothing is pending but the main motion, the resolution, and say, "I move to substitute for the pending resolution the following: *"Resolved,* That, etc.,*"* reading the proposed substitute. The chairman states the question thus: "It is moved and seconded to substitute for the pending resolution the following: *'Resolved,* That, etc.' [reading the resolution]. Are there any amendments proposed to the pending resolution?" The pending resolution should then be perfected by amendments, if it has not been done already, as has been explained in case of striking out a paragraph. When no further amendments are offered, the chair says, "There being no further amendments proposed to the pending resolution, the substitute is open to amendment. It reads as follows: *'Resolved,* That, etc.' " The substitute is then perfected by amendment, as in the case of inserting a paragraph. When its amendment is apparently completed, the chair asks, "Are you ready for the question?" No one claiming the floor, he reads, or causes to be read, first the pending resolution and then the proposed substitute, after which he says, "The question is, 'Shall the resolution last read be substituted for the pending resolution?' As many as are in favor of the substitution say 'Aye.' Those opposed say 'No.' The ayes have it and the motion to substitute is adopted. The question is now on the resolution as amended. Are you ready for the question?" In stating the question to be voted on, instead of using the words above mentioned the chair may say, "The question is on substituting the resolution last read for the pending resolution."

The adoption of the motion to substitute has no effect except to put the substitute in the place of the resolution or paragraph which it replaces. Therefore, if a resolution or paragraph has not been adopted, but is pending and must be voted on, then a resolution or paragraph substituted for it becomes the pending question and must be voted on. A paragraph or section or article of by-laws or standing rules, etc., that has been previously adopted, is not pending to be voted on, and therefore when another paragraph, section, or article is substituted for it, the substituted paragraph, section, etc., becomes a part of the adopted by-laws, standing rules, etc., and no further vote is taken. Thus, only one vote is taken in case of substituting a paragraph, etc., for a paragraph of an adopted set of by-laws, etc., while two votes are necessary in case of by-laws not adopted, first on making the substitution and next on adopting the by-laws as amended. In the case of adopted by-laws the question is on substituting something for something already adopted, and if agreed to there is no further question in the case, because the substituted matter has taken the place of something already adopted. But in the other case the substituted matter takes the place of something that has not been adopted, and therefore it is subject to being voted on, the same as was the matter it has replaced. Members may vote for a substitute for a motion that is pending, not because they are in favor of its final adoption, but because they are opposed to the pending measure and wish to load it down with such extreme provisions that it can never be adopted. Voting for the substitute only puts it in the place of the pending main question against which they intend to vote.

If the motion to strike out and insert, or to substitute, is adopted, all the rules relating to matter struck out apply to what has been struck out; and all the rules relating to the matter inserted apply to the matter that has been inserted or substituted, exactly as if the two motions had been made separately. If the motion to strike out and insert, or to substitute, is lost, the only question the assembly has decided is that that particular change shall not be made. It does not show that the assembly is opposed to striking out the words or paragraph, nor that it is unwilling to make the desired insertion somewhere else, but that it is unwilling to replace the words or paragraph in the manner specified. Any motion may be made in reference to the group of words or paragraph that was to be struck out, or was to be inserted, except one that is practically identical with the one voted down.

If the vote on striking out and inserting, or substituting, is reconsidered, the chair asks if there are any amendments to the words or paragraph it is proposed to strike out, and if there are none, or when there are no more proposed, he calls for amendments to the words or paragraph to be inserted, just as was done originally. When both those to be struck out and those to be inserted are amended as much as the assembly desires, the chair puts the question on striking out and inserting, or substituting.

This motion to strike out and insert is the proper motion to use when it is desired to strike out words that are not consecutive. The motion should be made to strike out the entire sentence, or enough to include all the words it is desired to remove, and to insert such a sentence or words as is desired. If the changes extend over much of a paragraph or resolution, it is better to write a new paragraph or resolution and offer it as a substitute.

It is not in order, except by general consent, to strike out words at one place and to insert different words at another place. This is a combination of two motions that is not permitted. A sentence or paragraph, however, may be transferred to a different place by striking out and inserting.

Amending a Preamble. When a resolution has a preamble, the preamble is not open to amendment until the assembly no longer wishes to amend the resolution. The chairman then asks if there are any amendments proposed to the preamble. This is done because the amendments made to the resolution may necessitate a change in the preamble.

Amending a Resolution with Several Paragraphs. When the main motion consists of a number of paragraphs, or sections, etc., as in adopting a set of by-laws, the paragraphs are taken up separately in their order, the chair asking in each case, after it is read, whether any amendments are proposed to that paragraph. After the paragraph is discussed and amended, without taking any vote on it the chair reads, or directs to be read, the next paragraph and proceeds as before, until the entire resolution or by-laws, etc., has been considered. The chair then states that the entire by-laws are open to amendment. It is then in order to move further to amend any of the paragraphs, or to insert a new paragraph. Finally the question is put on adopting the entire resolution, or by-laws, etc. For an illustration of this, see Amending By-Laws page 368. When paragraphs, sections, articles, or resolutions are numbered, and one of them is struck out or inserted, it is not necessary or usual to amend the numbers, since the necessary correction of the numbers is made by the secretary.

AMENDMENT OF THE VARIOUS MOTIONS

The motion to Adopt (Accept or Agree to) a main motion may be amended by adding instructions or a proviso in addition to changing the words of the resolution it is proposed to adopt, as in the following examples: Suppose a motion to adopt a set of by-laws is the immediately pending question: it is in order to move to amend the motion by adding, ''provided they shall not take effect until after the close of this annual meeting''; or the motion to adopt could be amended by adding, ''and the secretary is instructed to have 500 copies printed and to mail one copy to each member.'' Amendments of this nature are strictly amendments of the motion to adopt, while an amendment affecting an entire paragraph is an amendment of the resolution or other thing which it is proposed to adopt, and an amendment affecting certain words in a paragraph is an amendment of the paragraph, as well as an amendment of the resolution.

The motion to Ratify may be amended as described above in the case of the motion to adopt.

The motion to Rescind (or Repeal) is subject to amendments increasing or diminishing the portion to be rescinded, but if the part to be repealed is increased, the notice previously given does not apply, and the vote required is the same as if no notice had been given. Where previous notice is required, as in case of adopted by-laws, no amendment is in order that increases the amount to be rescinded.

The motion to Commit (Refer to a Committee) may be amended by specifying the committee, if there are any standing committees, and also by giving it instructions. If the reference is to a special committee, then it may be amended by specifying the number to constitute the committee, and how it shall be appointed, and when it shall report, and by giving it any other instructions.

The motion to Postpone to a Certain Time may be amended as to the time, and also by making the question a special order for a specified time. The time to which it is postponed must fall

within the session at which the motion was made, or the next succeeding business session. A motion to amend the time so that it
would not fall within the time of the present or the next session
would be out of order, but after a motion has been adopted fixing
the time to which to adjourn, that is, fixing a time for holding an
adjourned meeting, then an amendment postponing the question to
that time would be in order. If the motion to postpone is amended
so as to make the postponed question a special order, the amended
motion, namely, to postpone and make a special order, requires a
two-thirds vote, while the amendment required only a majority
vote. [For a full discussion of the subject see Postpone to a
Certain Time, page 57.]

A motion to Close Debate at a Future Time, to Limit the Number
and Length of Speeches, or to Extend the Limits of Debate, may
be amended by changing the limits prescribed by the motion; or it
may be amended by including any other limitations as to length
and number of speeches and length of debate. Thus, a motion to
limit each member to one speech may be amended by adding, ''no
speech to exceed three minutes in length and the debate to be closed
and the question to be put at 2 P. M.'' The amendment requires
only a majority vote, while the amended motion requires a two-
thirds vote for its adoption.

The motion to Fix the Time to Which to Adjourn, that is, to
fix the time for holding an adjourned meeting, may be amended
by changing the time, and by adding or changing the place for
the meeting.

The motion to Adjourn cannot be amended, unless it is qualified
in some way, or unless it is made in an assembly before any provision has been made for a future meeting, so that its effect, if
adopted, would be to dissolve the assembly, and in these excepted
cases the motion to adjourn is a main motion and may be amended.

The motion to Take a Recess may be amended as to the time.

Questions of Privilege, when raised by a member, are not subject to amendment until a motion on the subject has been made
and stated by the chair. Then that motion may be amended as any
other main motion.

A Call for the Orders of the Day cannot be amended, but when
an order of the day is under consideration it may be amended like
any other main motion.

A motion for the Division of the Question may be amended so

as to make a different division, but each separate question must be a proper one to be adopted if all the rest fail.

A motion to Consider a Question by Paragraph, or Seriatim, may be amended so as to consider it by articles, or sections, or in some other way.

A motion prescribing the Method of Taking a Vote may be amended as to the method. A motion to Appoint Tellers, like every other motion that involves numbers, may be amended as to the numbers.

A motion to Close the Polls may be amended as to the time when they are to be closed, and to Reopen the Polls may be amended as to the length of time they shall remain open.

A motion relating to the Method of Making Nominations may be amended as to the method; and one relating to Closing Nominations may be amended as to the time for closing. A list of Motions that Cannot be Amended will be found on page 553.

Amend as a Main Motion

In all the rules that have been given for amendments it is assumed that to amend is a subsidiary motion, that is, that it is moved while a main or secondary motion is the immediately pending motion. Whenever the motion to amend is referred to, the subsidiary motion is meant, unless it is specifically stated to the contrary. The subsidiary motion to amend is designed to modify the pending question, and the only effect of its adoption is to make a change in the question upon which the assembly is afterward to take a vote to decide whether it will agree to the motion as modified. Since amending a motion does not necessarily imply its adoption after it is amended, the subsidiary motion to amend requires only a majority vote, regardless of the vote required for the amended motion. Thus, the motion to Limit Debate requires a two-thirds vote, but an amendment to it requires only a majority vote.

But the motion to amend is sometimes applied to constitutions, by-laws, standing rules, or resolutions that have been previously adopted and therefore are not pending. In such cases the motion to amend is a main motion, and is necessarily treated differently from the subsidiary motion to amend. Like other main motions, it cannot be made while any other motion is pending, and is subject to amendments of the first and second degree. When the main motion to amend has the effect of striking out an entire resolution, rule, by-law, or set of by-laws, or constitution already adopted, it is usually called "to Rescind" or "to Repeal," which is simply one form of the main motion to amend. To amend a resolution or standing rule already adopted requires a two-thirds vote, or a vote of the majority of the membership, unless previous notice has been given, in which case it requires only a majority vote. [See page 110 for Rescind, and page 368 for Amending By Laws, etc.]

Filling Blanks

It is often convenient in making a motion that involves numbers, or dates, or names, to leave a blank to be filled by the assembly with such numbers, or dates, or names as it may prefer. If they are in the motion when made, they may be changed by the ordinary method of amending. If there will probably be several amendments, it is sometimes better to create a blank by striking out the number, or date, or name, and then to treat the motion as if it had been made with a blank.

The principal advantage of having a blank instead of using the ordinary method of amending, is that, in amending, the first proposition made is the one last voted on, and the last one made is the first one voted on, regardless of their relative importance; whereas in filling blanks the different propositions are voted on in a much better order, as shown hereafter, the order in filling in names being different from that. used in filling in numbers or dates.

To Create a Blank. The motion to create a blank by striking out a number, etc., is an incidental motion, like the motions relating to methods of voting or of dividing the question, and is therefore undebatable. It cannot be amended. Since it relates to the method of amending the resolution, it is in order when the immediately pending question is on the resolution, or on an amendment of the first or of the second degree which amendment would be struck out if the blank is created. It may be made in this form: "I move to create a blank in the resolution by striking out the words 'July 4th.'" After the vote creating the blank is announced, the business proceeds the same as if the resolution had originally contained the blank, except that the chair announces in their order the number, or date, or name that was in the resolution, next the one in the proposed primary amendment, and then the one in the proposed secondary amendment, if any have been proposed. He then asks if there are any more propositions for filling the blank.

Filling a Blank. A blank is not filled by the ordinary method of amending, nor is the method of filling it with names the same as of filling it with a number or a date. According to the circumstances of the case, the chairman inquires, "Of how many shall the committee consist?" or, "What date shall be inserted for the concert?" or, "Of whom shall the committee consist?" Members then suggest numbers, or dates, or names. No member, except by unanimous consent, can propose more than one. The chair repeats each number, date, or name as it is suggested, and when all who wish have made their suggestions, which require no seconds, a vote is taken on the different names, numbers, or dates as described below.

Filling a Blank with Names, or Nominations. In filling a blank with names, if the number of the names is stated and no more than this number are proposed, the chair usually accepts this as an expression of the wish of the assembly that the blank should be thus filled. If the motion is to appoint a committee, he puts the question upon appointing the committee consisting of these members. If the motion does not specify the number, the chair takes a vote on each name, beginning with the first one proposed, and all that receive a majority vote are inserted in the blank. If more names are suggested, or more nominations, as they are called, are made than are provided for in the motion, the chair takes a vote on each name in the order of nomination, beginning with the first and stopping as soon as a sufficient number have received a majority vote. Usually the persons first suggested for an office are more likely to be the choice of the assembly than those suggested later, and it is fairer to vote on them first, instead of last, as is the case where the ordinary method of amending is adopted. The advantages of using the method of filling blanks, or the nomination method, as it is also called when the blanks are to be filled with names, is illustrated under Viva Voce Nominations and Elections, page 205.

Filling Blanks with a Number or a Date. In filling blanks with numbers or dates, the usual practice in this country is to take the vote first on the largest number, or the longest time, or the most distant date, except where it is evident that a different order is necessary to enable the assembly to vote first on the proposition that will probably receive the smallest vote. Suppose a motion pending donating a blank sum to a hospital, and the blank is now to be filled. Various sums are proposed, $300, $400, $500, and $600. The vote is taken first on the largest amount, and if it is preferred by a majority it is inserted in the blank. If it is not the choice of the majority, the next largest sum, $500, is voted on, and this will command the vote of all its friends and also of all those who preferred $600. If these combined votes do not constitute a majority, the vote is taken on the next amount, and so on until a majority vote is obtained. Suppose that the vote was taken on $500 first, as might be the case if the ordinary method of amending was used, and that a large majority preferred $600. They might be afraid to vote down the $500 proposition for fear that one of the lower amounts might be adopted. By voting first on the largest sum the real preference of the assembly is more certain of being ascertained. If, however, the resolution authorized the sale of property at not less than a blank price, the vote should be taken first on the smallest amount, since that would usually command the smallest vote. The vote would increase as the price rises, until it reaches a majority at the lowest price at which they are willing to sell.

In case the blank is one of time, the longest time is voted on first. If the blank is to be filled with a date, the most distant one is voted on first. If, however, it is evident in any case that the reverse order will more surely enable the assembly to express its will, the chair should put the questions in that reverse order. The guiding principle is to begin at that end of the series which is least likely to be adopted, and this is most commonly found in the largest sum and the longest time.

The number of propositions for filling a blank is not limited. They do not require to be seconded, nor can they be amended or have any other subsidiary motion applied to them. They may be debated.

Blanks in a resolution or other motion should usually be filled while it is pending. But where a large majority feel confident that the motion will not be adopted and that it is a waste of time to fill the blanks, they may order the previous question and thus force an immediate vote on the resolution before the blanks are filled. Since a two-thirds vote is required to order the previous question, and since probably only those that are opposed to the resolution would vote for the previous question while the resolution is incomplete, there is but little danger of the resolution's being adopted with its blanks unfilled. If by any accident a resolution or other motion should be adopted with unfilled blanks, it would be necessary to fill the blanks before taking up other business. When a motion is adopted that is incomplete, the motions to carry it to completion have the right of way before any new business can be transacted. The most common case of incomplete motions is in the appointment of committees, and under that head it is fully treated and some further information is given in regard to filling blanks as they occur in such motions. [See pages 48, 49.]

CHAPTER V

COMMIT, OR REFER

In nearly all clubs and other societies there is much work that cannot be done directly by the society itself or its officers, either on account of the nature of the work or because of lack of time. Resolutions and other main motions frequently are brought before the assembly in such a crude form that they cannot be properly amended without consuming too much time. Two or three carefully selected persons can prepare proper amendments in much less time than can be done by the entire assembly, while the assembly in the meantime can attend to other business. These selected persons are called a committee, and the motion to refer the resolution to them is called to Commit, or to Refer. There may be any number of committees at the same time to which different subjects have been referred. Any member of the assembly is free to make suggestions to a committee, and, if he requests it, a reasonable opportunity must be given him to appear before the committee and to present his views. When the committee reports its recommendations to the assembly, they may be discussed and adopted or rejected, either as reported or after modification. Thus, referring a question to a committee does not interfere with the right of members to discuss it before taking final action upon the question. The judicious use of committees enables an assembly to do vastly more work and to diminish the chances of hasty, ill-advised action.

Sometimes there is introduced in a meeting a resolution that cannot be acted upon intelligently until an investigation of the facts in the case has been made. Such a resolution should be referred to a committee to investigate and report the facts with their opinion or recommendation.

Again, there may be a question before the assembly of such a delicate nature that it is best not to have the details brought before the assembly. By referring it to a large committee so representative that it has the confidence of the entire society, the assembly will usually be satisfied with a report giving only the recommendations of the committee without the details upon which the recommendations are based. In such cases, however, it is very important that the committee is not partisan.

Sometimes there is before an assembly a very important matter upon which there is difference of opinion among the leaders, and which should be discussed until, if possible, an agreement is reached; but the majority of the assembly have wearied of the debate, and yet do not wish to act on the measure until it has had thorough consideration. In such a case the proper course to pursue is to refer it to a large committee of which the leaders on both sides and others who wish to discuss the question are members. If the committee is not large, it is sometimes good policy to invite to the committee meeting all who are likely to oppose the resolution and request them to take part in the discussion. By this method the opposition have had an opportunity to express their views, and the debate will be mainly confined to the committee instead of occupying the time of the assembly, many of whose members would be bored by the lengthy discussion.

In conventions of delegates meeting once a year there is so much business to be transacted in a limited time that it is almost necessary to require all resolutions to be carefully considered by a committee previous to coming before the assembly for action. In such a case it is usual to appoint a large committee on resolutions, which continues in existence as long as the convention does, and to which are referred all resolutions as soon as introduced. Sometimes this committee is required by the by-laws or standing rules. This committee also prepares and submits resolutions demanded by courtesy or custom, such as a resolution of thanks for hospitality, etc., as explained under Committee on Resolutions, page 273.

All the committees that have been mentioned are called special or select committees because they are selected to consider and report on a special subject, and when this is done the committee automatically ceases to exist. Committees that are permanent are called Standing Committees. [For a full account of the different kinds of committees see Chapter XXII, page 243.]

When the Motion to Commit or to Refer May Be Made. The only motions that can be referred to a committee are main motions with their pending amendments, and debatable appeals. When a resolution, or other main motion, is referred to a committee, the pending amendments go to the committee also, while a pending motion to postpone indefinitely is ignored. The motion to commit is out of order if any motion is immediately pending except the main motion which it is proposed to commit, or an amendment to it of the first or second degree, or the motion to divide or to postpone indefinitely the main motion, or a debatable appeal.

While as a general rule it is in order to refer to a committee any main motion, yet this rule, like most others, is subject to the rule of reason, of common sense. Motions that are manifestly absurd or unreasonable are out of order, even though they conform to the literal interpretation of the rules. [See Dilatory and Improper Motions, page 177.] Thus, a motion cannot be referred to a committee when such reference necessarily defeats the object of the motion. The chair should rule out of order a motion to refer a resolution to a committee to report at the next meeting when the resolution requires action to be taken before that meeting. So, too, it is out of order to move to refer to a committee a motion to adopt a committee's report, or a motion to proceed to an election, though both of these are main motions. To refer such motions to a committee is simply absurd. [The chart, page 548, shows what motions may be made when commit is immediately pending.]

Form of the Motion. The motion to Commit, or to Refer, is made in a form similar to the following: (1) "I move to refer the resolution [or, that the resolution be referred] to the committee on finance"; or, (2) "I move to refer the resolution to a committee consisting of Mr. A, Mr. B, and Mr. C"; or, (3) "I move to refer the resolution to a committee of five to be appointed by the chair [or, nominated from the floor], with instructions to report at the next meeting"; or, (4) simply, "I move to refer the resolution to a committee"; or, (5) any of the above-mentioned forms with the words added, "with full power." These five different forms are used as follows:

(1) The first form is used when it is desired to refer the resolution to a standing committee or to a special committee that has already been appointed. After stating the question, since it is debatable, the chair asks, "Are you ready for the question?" It is in order now to discuss the propriety of the commitment, or the question as to whether another committee would be more suitable, or to move to amend by changing the committee or by adding instructions. The debate must not go into the merits of the question to be referred to the committee. When the debate has ceased and the amendments have been disposed of, the question on committing the resolution is put to vote and, if carried, the chair announces the result thus, "The ayes have it, the motion is carried [or adopted], and the resolution is referred to the committee on finance with instructions to ——"

(2) The second form is used when the mover wishes to designate the members of the special committee to which he proposes that the resolution be referred. Any member may debate the propriety of the commitment, or may move to amend by inserting an additional name or names, or by striking out a name, or by striking out a name and inserting another in its place, or by adding instructions. If the motion is carried, the chair announces the vote thus: "The ayes have it, the motion is adopted, and the resolution is referred to a committee consisting of——" repeating the names of the committee and the instructions if there are any.

(3) The third, or complete, form of the motion to refer is used when it is desired to refer the resolution to a special committee, specifying the size of the committee, and its method of appointment, and giving it instructions. Any one or more of these points may be omitted, but it is usually better to include them all in the motion to refer to a special committee. Any of them may be changed by amendments, and if any have been omitted they may be inserted. After the motion to commit has been adopted, even if all the points mentioned have been covered, it is still necessary to appoint the committee before other business can be transacted, unless the committee is to be appointed by the chair. [See page 256 for the different methods of appointing committees.] If any of the points have been omitted in the adopted motion, they are treated as shown below under the fourth form of the motion.

(4) The fourth form is used when the object of the mover is simply to have the motion referred to a committee, leaving to

others the privilege of suggesting the kind of committee and other details. When this form is used the procedure is as follows: As soon as the motion is made and seconded, the chair states the question thus: "It has been moved and seconded to refer the resolution to a committee. Are you ready for the question?" The motion is then open to debate and amendment. If a member wishes it referred to the standing committee on resolutions to be reported at once, he moves, "to amend by striking out 'a committee' and inserting 'the committee on resolutions with instructions to report as soon as possible.'" If a member wishes it referred to a special committee, he moves to amend by adding the necessary words, as, "of three to be nominated by the chair." When the assembly has finished amending the motion to commit, the chair puts the question on the completed motion, announces the result, and proceeds, in accordance with the motion as adopted, to appoint or nominate the committee, or to have it elected. [The Appointment of Committees, including their nomination and election, is fully treated on pages 256–264.]

Sometimes when the chair states the question on the motion simply to refer, there is no response to the question, "Are you ready for the question?" In such cases it is generally better for the chair, without waiting for motions, to put the various questions on completing the motion to refer, so as to get it into one of the preceding forms. These questions are usually settled by general consent, in the order given below, until one of the other three forms of the completed motion is obtained, and then a vote is taken on the completed motion. The first question asked by the chair, if there are appropriate standing committees, is, "To what committee shall the resolution be referred?" When this question receives only one answer, and that specifies a standing committee, the chair accepts this as the will of the assembly, and states the question on the completed motion, puts it to vote, and, if it is carried, announces that the resolution is referred to the designated committee. If several committees are suggested in answering this question, the chair takes a vote on each until one receives a majority vote. They are voted on in the following order: (1) Standing committees in the order in which they are suggested; (2) special committees in the order of their size, the largest being voted on first.

If the only answer to the chair's first question is, "A special

committee," he immediately asks, "Of how many shall the committee consist?" This is the first question asked by the chair, if
there are no appropriate standing committees, as in such case it
is useless to ask, "To what committee shall the resolution be
referred?" When various numbers are suggested, the chair immediately puts the question on the different numbers, beginning with
the largest, until one of them receives a majority vote, and then
announces that the committee will consist of that number, and
asks, "How shall the committee be appointed?" If only one
number is suggested, the chair accepts that as the will of the
assembly and proceeds to the next question as just stated. He
proceeds in the same way if the answer to the first question, instead
of being "A special committee," is "A committee of ———,"
specifying the size of the committee.

The next question is, "How shall the committee be appointed?"
The answer to this question may be (1) "By ballot"; (2) "By
nominations from the floor"; (3) "Nominations by the chair"; or
(4) "Appointment by the chair." If only one method is suggested, the chair assumes that to be the will of the assembly and
proceeds as though a vote had been taken. If more than one
method is suggested, the vote is taken on each of them, in the
order given above, until one is chosen. The most common methods
are "Nominations from the floor" and "Appointment by the
chair." This is usually the last question asked by the chair, as
he never asks what instructions are to be given the committee
unless he thinks instructions necessary. If a member wishes the
committee to be instructed, he can move to amend by adding the
instructions, or he can wait until the committee has been appointed
and then move that the committee be instructed so and so.

When the method of nomination is settled, the chair states
the question on the motion to refer, and puts it to vote thus: "The
question is on referring [or, on the motion to refer] the resolution
to a committee of five to be nominated from the floor. Are you
ready for the question?" If no one rises to speak or make a
motion, he continues: "As many as are in favor of the motion
say 'Aye.' Those opposed say 'No.' The ayes have it, the motion
is adopted, and the resolution is referred to a committee of five
to be nominated from the floor. Members will please nominate
[or, Nominations are now in order]." Nominations are then made
and acted upon as described on page 258.

If, when the chair states the question on the motion simply to refer, no one rises to speak or to make a motion in response to his inquiry, "Are you ready for the question?" and he thinks a majority wish to consider the resolution at that time and are opposed to referring it to a committee, time may be saved by the chair's putting the question at once on the motion to refer. If the motion is voted down, the assembly is saved the trouble of settling the details about the size and appointment of the committee, which are of no consequence since the resolution is not to be referred to a committee. Should the chairman be mistaken and the motion to refer be adopted, then it is necessary to settle all the details afterward in the same order as has just been given for their settlement.

If the assembly evidently wishes to consider and act on the question immediately, and yet a small minority is using much time in debate and in efforts to amend the motion, the proper course is to order the previous question on the motion to refer and its amendments, if any are pending. This requires a two-thirds vote and if carried stops debate and further motions to amend, bringing the assembly immediately to a vote on the motion to refer and its amendments. If the motion to refer is voted down, time is saved that might have been spent in uselessly completing the motion to refer. If the motion to refer is adopted (which is not probable when two thirds voted to order the previous question on it while it was incomplete) it is necessary only to determine the details as to the committee in the same order as when settled in advance.

In completing the details after the simple motion to refer has been adopted, each detail is announced as soon as decided, and no vote is taken on the completed motion, because it has already been voted to commit the resolution. When the details are settled in advance, these are really amendments to the pending motion to refer, and it is necessary to take a vote on the completed motion.

(5) The fifth form of the motion to refer differs from the others only by adding to one of them the words "with full power." It is used when it is desired to refer a resolution to a committee with full power to take final action in the case, this power, of course, being limited to what the society can do itself. The committee, if thus authorized, is clothed with all the power of the

society, as far as the matter referred to it is concerned, and when its work is completed it reports for the information of the society what it has done.

Recommit. When a resolution that has been reported by a committee is again committed, it is said to be "recommitted." When it has been moved to recommit a resolution and various committees are suggested, they are voted on in the same order as in case of a first commitment, except that the former committee, if it has been suggested, is voted on before other committees of the same class. Thus, if previously it was referred to a standing committee and that committee is suggested, it must be voted on before voting on any other standing committee. And so the previous special committee takes precedence of other special committees. In every other respect the rules applicable to the motion to commit apply equally to the motion to recommit. If the matter is recommitted without specifying the committee, then the resolution goes back to the committee that reported it. In such case the motion may be made either "to recommit the resolution" or "to refer the resolution back to the committee." If it is referred to another committee, the regular form of the motion to commit is used. When a resolution or any matter is recommitted, all action previously taken by the committee is ignored, regard being paid only to what the assembly refers to the committee.

Committee of the Whole and Its Substitutes. Sometimes, instead of referring a question to a small committee, it is desired to discuss it in the assembly with all the freedom of a committee, which may be done by referring it to the "committee of the whole," or by considering the question "as if in committee of the whole," or by "considering it informally." The first method is used in the U. S. House of Representatives, the second in the U. S. Senate, and the third in ordinary assemblies only. These three motions may be considered as forms of the motion to commit, and when the chair inquires what kind of committee is desired, these forms may be proposed, as well as standing and special committees. If all five are proposed they are put to vote in the following order: committee of the whole, as if in committee of the whole, consider informally, refer to a standing committee, and finally refer to a special committee. It is only when it is desired to take up the question immediately and consider it with all the freedom of a committee that an ordinary assembly uses one of the first three methods. The motion for this purpose is made as follows: "I move that we go into committee of the whole, to take under consideration———"; or, "I move that the assembly [or club] do now resolve itself [or go] into the committee of the whole, to take under consideration———"; or, "I move that the resolution be considered as if in committee of the whole"; or, "I move that the resolution be considered informally." These different methods of considering a question by the entire assembly with all the freedom of a committee are explained hereafter on pages 290–293.

Debate on the Motion to Commit. If the motion to commit is adopted, the main motion and its amendments go to the committee and come back to the assembly with the committee's report, at which time they are open to discussion. If the motion to commit is lost, the main question and its amendments, if any, are before the assembly for debate and such action as the assembly desires to take. Therefore, there is no need of discussing the merits of the main question while the motion to commit is pending, and, because of this, the debate is limited to the reasons for and against referring the main question to the designated committee, and for and against its size, the method of appointment, and instructions. When an amendment is offered, the debate is limited to that amendment. Thus, if it is moved to amend by striking out "three" and inserting "five," no debate is allowed except on the relative merits of three and five.

From the above it will be seen that the debate on the motion to commit is very limited, just as it is with the motion to postpone. In both cases the main question will come before the assembly again, at which time the discussion may take place.

Motions that Are in Order when to Commit is Immediately Pending. While the motion to commit is immediately pending, it is in order to amend that motion, as already shown, by specifying or changing the committee; by specifying or modifying the method of its appointment; or by giving it instructions or power, or by modifying its instructions or power. Like all other debatable motions, the previous question may be ordered on it, or the debate may be limited. If while the motion to commit is the immediately pending question one of these motions to close or to limit debate is adopted without specifying the motions upon which it is ordered, it applies only to the motion to commit, without in any way affecting the main motion. The motion to commit cannot be committed or postponed indefinitely. It cannot by itself be laid on the table, or postponed to a certain time. These latter motions are designed for the purpose of having the question brought before the assembly again at a more convenient time, and it would be an absurdity if, in the meantime, the main motion could have been disposed of so there would be nothing left to refer to a committee when the motion to commit was taken up for consideration. If either of these motions, to lay on the table or to postpone, is adopted when the motion to commit is pending, it applies to all the pending questions, taking to the table, or postponing the main motion and all pending subsidiaries including the motion to commit. When the questions come up again for consideration, the motion to commit is again pending in the same condition as when the motion to lay on the table, or to postpone, was made.

While the motion to commit is the immediately pending question, it is in order to make any privileged or incidental motion that the occasion may demand. The new motion supersedes for the time being the motion to commit, but the consideration of the latter is immediately resumed when the new motion is disposed of, unless this is prevented by the action taken on the new motion.

The motion to commit, even though it contains instructions, cannot be divided, because if divided and the first part, referring the resolution to the committee, is lost, the remaining question, which would be on the instructions, is absurd, as there would be no committee to instruct. A separate vote, however, may be obtained on instructions by moving to strike them out. Instructions, or additional instructions, may be given a committee by the assembly at any time up to the time of its making its report.

The vote on the motion to refer, whether the motion is adopted or lost, may be reconsidered, provided the motion to reconsider is made before the committee has taken up the subject. After the committee has begun its work it is too late to reconsider the vote on committing the resolution, or appointing the committee, but the committee may be discharged at any time, as explained [page 108].

To Commit as a Main Motion. To appoint a committee to report or to act on a matter not before the assembly, or to refer to a committee a matter not before the assembly, is a main motion, not a subsidiary one. The subsidiary motion to refer, or commit, is applied to resolutions that are pending at the time. But it is often desirable to appoint a committee on a subject not before the assembly, as in the following case: A member rises, and after being recognized by the chair, states that the heating and ventilation of the hall is a subject of much complaint, and he moves that a committee of three be appointed by the chair to investigate the subject and report with their recommendation as to what remedial measures should be adopted. Now, this motion is evidently a main motion, as it brings before the assembly for its action a new question. It is a main motion, whether in form it appoints a committee to do a certain thing, or refers to a committee something that is not pending at the time. It is not in order if any other motion is pending, and is subject to all the rules applicable to other main motions. The forms of the motion are similar to those given for the subsidiary motion to commit, but they must be adapted to each particular case, as shown on pages 254–255.

To Discharge a Committee. It is seldom necessary to make a motion to discharge a committee, because a committee is discharged from the consideration of a subject by the mere act of making its report to the assembly, and cannot thereafter resume its consideration unless the assembly recommits the matter. When it is thought advisable to take a matter out of the hands of a committee, the committee should be "discharged" if it is a special committee; it should be "discharged from the further consideration of the subject" if it is a standing committee. [See pages 108–109.]

General Remarks on the Motion to Commit. In actual practice a great deal of time can be saved by a tactful chairman in settling the details connected with motions to commit. He can often see when there is no opposition to a suggestion, and instead of taking a vote he can accept it at once. Of course, if any one objects, thus showing that there is opposition, he must put it to vote. But general consent enables all these details to be quickly agreed upon in most cases.

The proper size of a committee is dependent upon its duties. A committee for action should always be small and in sympathy with the action to be taken. If a member who is not in favor of the proposed action is appointed on a committee, he should at once ask to be excused and some one else should be appointed in his place. Likewise, if a resolution is referred to a special committee for amendment, and a member is nominated or appointed on it who is opposed to the essential idea of the resolution, he should ask to be excused and some one else should be nominated or appointed in his place. One who does not wish to improve the resolution so that it may be adopted cannot honorably serve on a committee appointed for that very purpose. But if the committee is for investigation, or for considering and reporting upon a subject upon which there may be great difference of opinion, it is important that the committee should be large and be comprised of representative members of the different parties in the assembly. If this is done, the discussion of troublesome and delicate questions may be mostly confined to the committee meetings, and both parties will feel confidence in the report, or reports if there is a minority report, because each party has confidence in its representatives on the committee. [The chapters on Committees and Boards, and their reports and action thereon, Part III, should be read in connection with this chapter.]

CHAPTER VI

MOTIONS TO DEFER ACTION

To Postpone to a Certain Time and to Lay on the Table Compared

When it is desired to defer action upon a question that is pending before the assembly, it may be done by either postponing the question to a certain time or laying it on the table. Which of these motions should be used depends upon whether it is wished to set a definite time in the future for the consideration of the question, or whether it is desired to lay the question aside in such a way that the assembly by a majority vote may at any time resume its consideration.

In the first case the question is postponed to some definite time, and it cannot be taken up before that time except by suspending the rules by a two-thirds vote, which makes it the safer motion for deferring action for any length of time. In the second case the question is "laid on the table," to be "taken from the table" at a more suitable time, or when a majority chooses to consider it. Its proper parliamentary use is to lay aside a question temporarily in order to attend to something more urgent. As soon as the interrupting matter is attended to, the question should be taken from the table, as described on page 106, and properly disposed of. Since a question may be taken from the table at any moment and finally disposed of by either its friends or its foes who happen at the time to be in the majority, it is not always safe to leave a question on the table for any length of time.

Since laying a question on the table does not interfere with resuming its consideration whenever the assembly wishes to do so, there is no need of debate on the motion to lay on the table.

It could not be amended without destroying its essential feature and thus converting it into the motion to postpone to a certain time. Therefore the motion to lay on the table cannot be debated or amended. On the other hand, postponing a question to a fixed time takes the question out of the control of the majority until the specified time arrives. There may be a difference of opinion as to the best time to which to postpone the question, or even as to the expediency of postponing it at all. The motion, therefore, should be, and is, debatable and amendable.

In an ordinary meeting of a society, if a motion that has been postponed to a certain time is not reached when the assembly adjourns, it becomes unfinished business at the next meeting, and is announced by the chair at the proper time. But if a motion is laid on the table it never comes before the assembly until it is voted to take it from the table. The motion to take from the table may be made during the session at which the question was laid on the table, or during the next session in societies with regular meetings as often as quarterly. If the motion is not taken from the table during either of these sessions the situation is the same as if the motion had never been made. It has not been adopted or rejected.

When the motion to postpone or to lay on the table is adopted, all pending questions are postponed or go to the table together, and when taken up for consideration they are all in exactly the same condition that they were just previous to being postponed or laid on the table. If on account of lapse of time any pending motion has become absurd, it is ignored. Thus, suppose that when the question is laid on the table the motion to postpone to 2 P. M. is pending, and that the question is not taken from the table until 3 P. M. In this case the motion to postpone is ignored. Orders for the previous question and to limit debate expire with the session, and therefore these motions, if pending, are ignored if not taken up for consideration until the next session. Postponing or laying on the table a motion to amend or rescind anything already adopted, as by-laws, does not carry with it the matter to be amended or rescinded, because such matter has already been adopted and is not pending before the assembly.

With this general statement as to the differences between the two motions, they will now be described in detail.

POSTPONE TO A CERTAIN TIME, OR DEFINITELY

When it is desired to defer action on a pending question to some definite day, or meeting, or hour, or until after a certain event, the proper motion to make is to postpone the question to that day, or meeting, or hour, or until after that event. This motion is referred to as the motion to postpone, the term never being applied to the motion to postpone indefinitely, which is the motion to kill, not to postpone.

The debate on this motion is limited to the propriety of the postponement and the suitability of the time. The merits of the question are not open to discussion while the motion to postpone is pending, unless they are essentially involved in the question of the propriety of the postponement. If the motion to postpone is lost the debate is resumed, and if it is voted to postpone the question there will be an opportunity for debate when the question is taken up at the designated time.

The motion to postpone may be amended by changing the time, or by making the question a special order for a certain time. While a majority vote may adopt any of these amendments, it requires a two-thirds vote to adopt the motion to postpone when it includes making the question a special order.

It would not do to allow a subsidiary motion to be separated from its main motion, and then have one of them postponed to another time, and the other left before the assembly for consideration and final action. Therefore, when a question is postponed, all adhering or attached questions go with it. When the specified time arrives and the consideration of the question is resumed, the business is in exactly the same condition it was in immediately before the motion to postpone was made, except that if the question does not come up until the next session it is divested of motions limiting or closing debate.

Chart I, page 548, shows that to postpone outranks the motion to postpone indefinitely, to amend, and to commit the main motion; that is, when any of them is the immediately pending motion it is in order to move to postpone the pending questions. If the division of the question or the method of consideration of the question is immediately pending, though they are incidental questions, it is in order to move to postpone the main question, and if adopted these motions are postponed also, just as in case of subsidiaries. An appeal from the decision of the chair may be postponed, but if the appeal adheres to the main question in such a way that action on one may affect the other, then they are both postponed to be considered at the designated time. Thus, if an appeal from the decision of the chair as to an amendment's being germane is postponed, it would be manifestly improper to proceed with the consideration of the amendment or the main question and take final action upon it, and then afterward to take up the appeal and perhaps reverse the decision of the chair. In such a case the only proper thing to do is to postpone all the questions together and then to decide the appeal first, and afterward to take up the other questions and act in accordance with the decision of the assembly. Therefore, if the appeal is postponed the main question is postponed with it. But the appeal may be from a decision that does not affect the main question, in which case the appeal may be postponed by itself and then the consideration of the main question is resumed.

As previously stated, subsidiary motions cannot be postponed alone. If the motion to postpone is adopted when a subsidiary motion is immediately pending, then all the pending questions are postponed to the designated time. No privileged or incidental motion can be postponed except an appeal, but a question of privilege or an order of the day when actually before the assembly for consideration is treated as a main motion and can be postponed or have any other subsidiary motion applied to it. The incidental motion to divide a question or to consider a question by paragraph, or otherwise, adheres to the main motion just as a subsidiary does and is postponed with the main motion.

While the motion to postpone is immediately pending, it is in order to make any privileged or incidental motion that the occasion may demand, and to make the subsidiary motions to lay on the table, the previous question, to limit debate, and to amend the motion to postpone, and also to make the motion to reconsider. As soon as the vote is taken on the interrupting question, the consideration of the motion to postpone is resumed, unless it is prevented by the action taken on the interrupting question.

In specifying the time to which it is proposed to postpone a question, whether it is in the original motion to postpone, or in the amendment to it, it is necessary that the time should fall within the present or the next business session. In societies having frequent meetings of a religious, literary, scientific, or social nature, at which business may be transacted, and also having regular business meetings monthly or quarterly, a question may be postponed to the next regular monthly or quarterly business meeting, provided the question is not of such a nature as to require earlier attention. In organizations of the kind just referred to, no important business that can be delayed without injury should be transacted at any meeting except at the regular monthly or quarterly business meeting. Where societies have regular business meetings, even though as frequently as weekly, it is not allowed to postpone a question beyond the next business meeting, and thereby to put it out of the power of a majority to consider the question at that meeting. If it were permitted to postpone a question beyond the next regular business meeting, say for a year, a minority, while temporarily in power, might introduce measures favored by their opponents and postpone them for a year, and thus prevent their being considered as long as there were less than two thirds in favor of them. No resolution is in order while one covering practically the same ground is under the control of the assembly and not finally disposed of, that is, is in the hands of a committee, or has been postponed, or laid on the table.

If it is desired to consider the question at a time that does not fall within any of the regular sessions provided for, it is necessary first to vote that, when the assembly adjourns, it adjourn to meet at the desired time. As this motion, to fix the time for holding an adjourned meeting, is one of the highest privilege, it may be made when any other motion is pending. After its adoption, the adjourned meeting being provided for, it is in order to move to postpone the question to this meeting. The fact that a question cannot be postponed beyond the next regular business meeting does not prevent an agreement or understanding among the leaders that it will not be considered until a certain time in the future, and then it may be postponed from meeting to meeting until the time agreed upon arrives. While such agreements are morally binding on the parties who make them, they cannot be enforced by the chair, and they do not prevent the assembly at any session from acting upon the postponed question if a majority chooses to do so.

The time to which a question is postponed must not be such

as to make the motion unreasonable or absurd. Thus, a resolution requiring something to be done at a certain time cannot be postponed to a time later than that specified. The effect of such a motion if adopted is to kill the resolution, not to postpone it until a more suitable time. An amendment that has a similar effect is also out of order.

No question can be postponed to another time so that it will interfere with one previously postponed, unless by a two-thirds vote it is made a special order. Thus, after a question has been postponed to 3. P. M., a motion to postpone another question to a time that would obviously interfere with that order is out of order, while one to postpone it to 2 P. M. or even to 3 P. M. would be in order, because they would not interfere with the question previously postponed to 3 P. M. Any number of questions may be postponed to the same hour, in which case they are taken up in the order in which they were postponed, as explained on page 133.

If it is desired to consider a question before the time prescribed by the program or order of business, it cannot be done by postponing or by laying on the table all of the previous business by a single vote. Each item of business may be postponed, or laid on the table, or otherwise disposed of, by a majority vote after it has been stated by the chair. But a subsidiary motion cannot be made until the main motion to which it is subsidiary is actually pending. If two thirds of the assembly wish to take up a question out of its proper order they can do so by suspending the rules. Thus, if a motion is made to postpone the hearing of the reports of committees, the chair must rule the motion out of order, but at the same time he should state that the proper motion is "to suspend the rules and take up such and such a question." [See page 145.] This latter motion should be used whenever it is desired to take up a question out of its proper order, whether this order is due to an order of business, or a program or ritual, or to the fact that the question had been postponed to a certain time. It requires a two-thirds vote for its adoption because, having decided upon a time for the consideration of the question, interested members have a right to make their plans accordingly so as to be present and prepared at that time. This could scarcely be done with safety if the question could be taken up previously by a majority vote. Yet, as experience has shown, it is advisable to allow the assembly by a two-thirds vote to suspend the rules for certain purposes, so it has been found best to allow a question by a two-thirds vote to be taken up before the time appointed for its consideration. On the day the vote to postpone is taken, or on the next succeeding day, it is in order to reconsider the vote on the postponement, as shown under Reconsider, page 88.

The subsidiary motion to postpone means "to postpone the consideration of the pending questions." Suppose there is pending a motion to have an excursion on September 3, and it is moved "to postpone the excursion to September 15." Such a motion is out of order, as it does not propose to postpone the consideration of the question but to modify it. It is an amendment and not the subsidiary motion to postpone, and should have been made thus: "I move to amend by striking out '3' and inserting '15.' "

The form of this motion is, "I move to postpone the question," or, "I move that the question be postponed," to, or until, the desired time, day, or meeting, or until after a specified time. When a question is postponed it becomes a general order for the specified time. The motion to postpone may have added to it the words, "and be made a special order," or it may be made in this form: "I move that the question be postponed and made a special order for" the desired time. If this is adopted by a two-thirds vote the question becomes a special order for the time specified. [See Special Orders, pages 134–136.]

When the hour arrives to which a question that has not been made a special order has been postponed, it cannot interrupt the question then under consideration, but as soon as that question has been disposed of, it has the right of way over everything that was not assigned before it to the same or an earlier hour, or has not been made a special order. Even if a member has obtained the floor and has made a motion, provided it has not been stated by the chair, any member may call for the orders of the day, and the chair must announce the question that was postponed to that time. Or, if he doubts the wish of the assembly to take up the orders, he may state that the orders of the day are called for, and then put the question, "Will the assembly proceed to the orders of the day?" If the vote is in the affirmative, the orders of the day are taken up in their proper order, as described in the chapter on that subject, page 133, which should be read in connection with this one.

Postpone as a Main Motion. Sometimes it is desired to postpone something that is not pending before the assembly. In such a case the motion to postpone is a main motion, not a subsidiary one. A subsidiary motion can be used only when there is a motion pending to which it is subsidiary. The main motion to postpone cannot be made if any other motion is pending. The following are illustrations of the use of the main motion to postpone: (1) When a committee notifies the assembly that it is prepared to report, and the assembly wishes to postpone hearing the report until another time, since there is no question pending, the motion appointing the time for hearing the report is a main motion. The motion could be "to postpone the reception of [or receiving or hearing] the report until 4 p.m.''; or "that the report be received [or heard] at 4 p. m.'' If either of these motions is adopted the committee's report becomes the order for 4 p. m., and at that hour is announced by the chair unless a question is then pending, in which case it is announced as soon as pending business is disposed of. The reception of the committee's report could be postponed by using any of the other forms of the motion to postpone. (2) If a society has decided to have an excursion on September 4 and at a later meeting wishes to postpone it to September 15, it can be done by adopting a main motion "to postpone the excursion to September 15,'' or by rescinding the vote on having the excursion and then adopting a new motion on the subject. Since this changes action previously taken by the society, it requires for its adoption a two-thirds vote or a vote of a majority of the membership, unless previous notice has been given.

Lay on the Table.

When it is desired to suspend the consideration of a question to attend to something more urgent, and yet to retain the right to resume its consideration whenever the assembly pleases, the proper motion to make is "to lay the question on the table.'' On account of the importance of this motion, and because when legitimately used it does not finally dispose of the question or even injure it, but only immediately stops debate and amendment and lays the question aside temporarily, it is allowed to have the highest rank of all subsidiary motions, and is undebatable and unamendable and requires only a majority vote for its adoption.

It is a principle of parliamentary law that a deliberative assembly cannot be compelled to take final action on a proposition without full debate, except by a two-thirds vote. On this principle, a two-thirds vote is required for ordering the previous question, that is, closing debate now; and on closing debate at a future time, or in any other way limiting the right of debate. When the motion to lay on the table is used to suppress a question, it is equivalent to a combination of the motions to postpone indefinitely and the previous question with the high rank of the latter, and therefore it should require the same vote as the previous question, namely two thirds, for its adoption. In all ordinary societies the previous question alone, or it and postpone indefinitely, should be used for immediately suppressing a question, and the motion to lay on the table should be reserved for its important and legitimate use. In any society where members persist in using this motion to kill the question, a rule should be adopted requiring a two-thirds vote to lay a question on the table. Even after an assembly has ordered the previous question, or that the debate close and the vote be taken at a certain hour, it is in order for a mere majority to lay on the table the questions that have not been disposed of, and thus be able to attend to urgent business. It does not seem reasonable to insist upon a two-thirds vote to stop or to limit the debate and yet allow a bare majority to kill the measure without any debate.

So important is it for the assembly to have the power by a mere majority vote to lay aside a question temporarily, that if this motion is lost it may be made again and again the same day, provided there has been material progress in debate, or a change in the condition of the pending business since it was last moved, or there is some urgent business requiring immediate attention. The change in the business or the progress in debate must be sufficient to make it practically a new question whether the assembly will now lay the pending proposition on the table. A motion to adjourn made and lost is not sufficient business to justify the renewal of the motion to lay on the table, but taking a vote on adopting an amendment is sufficient, because many may have been opposed to laying the question on the table before, who would favor it now after the amendment has been disposed of. The chair must be careful that this high privilege is not taken advantage of to obstruct business. As shown under Dilatory Motions, page 177, whenever it is apparent that the motion is being used for obstructive purposes, the chair should decline to recognize it. For instance, if the assembly by an overwhelming vote has twice declined to lay a question on the table, the chair should not again recognize the motion while that question is pending, unless something very important has occurred in the meantime that makes it doubtful whether the assembly is not now ready to lay the question aside.

A debatable appeal is the only incidental motion that may be laid on the table, and if it is of such a nature that its decision does not affect the main question it does not adhere to that question, and laying it on the table does not carry with it the main question. To illustrate: While a resolution is before the assembly a member interrupts, claiming that a certain matter is a question of privilege; the chair decides against him, and from this decision he appeals, and the appeal is laid on the table. The appeal may afterward be taken from the table and the chair's ruling sustained or reversed, but in neither case would the decision affect the main question that was pending at the time the ruling and appeal were made. In such a case, when the appeal is laid on the table the consideration of the interrupted question is resumed. But if an amendment is ruled out of order and an appeal is taken and that is laid on the table, the main question would go there too, because if the appeal is afterward taken from the table and the chair's decision reversed, it might very materially affect the result. The motion to lay on the table, since it cuts off all debate on the appeal, prevents a discussion that might change the opinions of many as to the correctness of the ruling. All main motions may be laid on the table, and when one is laid on the table it takes with it all adhering motions.

Nothing would be gained by allowing the privileged motions [Chart I, page 548] to be laid on the table. After a question of privilege or an order of the day, however, has been actually taken up for consideration, it can be laid on the table, and if this is done the chair immediately announces whatever business was pending, or was then in order, when the question of privilege was raised or the orders of the day were called for.

Neither the motion to lay on the table nor to take from the table can be reconsidered, because if the motion to lay on the table fails it may be repeated whenever there is any probability of its being adopted, and if it succeeds the question can be taken from the table as soon as the interrupting subject is disposed of.

Even after the ordering of the previous question up to the moment of taking the last vote under the order, the questions not yet disposed of may be laid on the table. When taken from the table at the same session they would still be under the order for the previous question and could therefore be neither debated nor amended. If not taken from the table until the next session, the previous question is exhausted and the debate may be resumed.

It is not in order to lay on the table a class of questions, such as reports of committees. Only a single report or main question and what adheres to it can be laid on the table by one vote. If it is desired to reach a question out of its order and the friends of the measure command a two-thirds vote, they should move to suspend the rules and take up the desired question. If they cannot command a two-thirds vote their only recourse is to lay on the table the intervening questions one by one as they come up. But usually this can be, and is, arranged by unanimous consent. If desired, and no one objects, any class of business or any particular question may be taken up at any time out of its order, and as soon as it is disposed of the regular order of business is resumed. Or sometimes, as a question or class of business is reached, it is suggested that it be "passed over," and if no one objects the chair announces the next question or class of business, and as soon as it is disposed of, the assembly returns to the one that by general consent has been passed over.

When a question has been laid on the table it remains there, unless taken up, until the end of the session; and, in the case of organizations with regular meetings as frequent as quarterly, it remains on the table until the close of the next regular business session. As long as it is on the table no motion or resolution is in order, the adoption of which would interfere with its adoption should it be taken from the table. The proper course is to take the question from the table and then move to amend it by substituting the new resolution for the old one.

Perhaps no motion, except to adjourn, is more frequently made in such a way that it should not be recognized by the chair. It is often made while rising by calling out, "Mr. Chairman, I move to lay it on the table," without waiting for recognition by the chair. Any one after that can claim the floor and debate the question, as the maker of the motion did not have the floor and was therefore out of order in making his motion. Again, it is frequently made before the mover of the main motion has had an opportunity to claim the floor to debate his motion, although until he has had a reasonable opportunity to claim the floor no one else has a right to it. The very high privilege given this motion, and the temptation to take an improper advantage of this privilege, makes it incumbent on the chair to protect the minority as far as possible in their legitimate right to debate questions before they are finally disposed of, and he should therefore be very particular to allow this motion to be made only by one who is entitled to the floor and has obtained it.

The form of this motion is, ''To lay the question [or resolution, or pending questions] on the table''; or, ''That the question [or resolution, or pending questions] be laid [or lie] on the table.'' The motion must not be qualified in any way, but the member when making it may state at what time he proposes to move that it be taken from the table. This does not prevent any one else from making the motion to take the question from the table at an earlier time. Its high privilege is given the motion to lay on the table only in consideration of the fact that it places the question on the table at the pleasure of the assembly. If the motion is made with a qualification, instead of ruling it out of order, the chair should state it properly. Thus, if the motion is made to lay the question on the table until 4 p.m., the chair should state the question as being on the motion to postpone the question to 4 p. m.

CHAPTER VII

MOTIONS AFFECTING THE LIMITS OF DEBATE

CLOSING OR LIMITING DEBATE.

THE right of debate is inherent in the conception of a deliberative assembly. The very name *deliberative* carries with it the idea that the assembly is for the purpose of deliberating on, that is, debating, questions before taking final action upon them. So important was this right of debate considered that the old common parliamentary law made all motions debatable, and placed no curb on the length of the debate, except that each member was permitted to speak in debate only once on every question, that he could not read any part of his speech without permission of the assembly, and that he must confine his speech to the pending question, and must not waste time with repetitions or frivolous remarks.

It has been found that advantage will be taken of such privileges by small minorities to block all business and prevent adoption of measures favored by the great majority of the assembly. Consequently the common parliamentary law of the present day makes all questions of high privilege undebatable, and allows the right of debate on any motion to be suspended by a two-thirds vote, the vote required for suspending the rules. If two thirds of the assembly have made up their minds on a question, so that they wish to limit the debate in any way, or to stop it altogether and immediately put the question to vote, it is only fair to allow them to do so, as under such circumstances there is little hope that fuller debate will change enough votes to enable the minority to become the majority. It would not, however, be for the best interests of the assembly to allow a bare majority to limit or close

67

debate, as this power could be used to prevent the minority from discussing any question the majority wishes adopted, or suppressed, without debate, even though the majority has but one more vote than the minority. This would destroy the deliberative character of the assembly. Therefore debate should not be closed or limited by a majority vote, but it should be allowed to be done by a two-thirds vote, and this is the common parliamentary law in this country to-day.

There are assemblies, like the U. S. House of Representatives, that have such an enormous amount of business that debate must be relegated to committees, and a majority must have the power to limit or close debate in the House. With as many as four hundred members having the right to speak one hour each on every debatable question, it would be impracticable to transact business, when the opposing parties are nearly equal, unless the majority could limit or close the debate. So incompatible is this, however, with the idea of a deliberative assembly that, although Congress allows a majority to suppress a question without debate by the use of the motion to lay on the table, it does not allow a majority to adopt a measure without opportunity for forty minutes' debate, twenty minutes on each side. It accomplishes these objects by adopting a rule requiring a two-thirds vote to take a question from the table, and then using the motion to lay on the table for the purpose of suppressing the question; and by adopting other rules allowing a majority to order the previous question, and, after it has been ordered, allowing forty minutes' debate, twenty minutes in favor of and twenty minutes in opposition to the proposition, unless the proposition has been previously debated. By means of these rules a proposition or main question may be suppressed instantly by a majority vote without debate, or adopted with only twenty minutes' debate on each side. These rules, or at least rules with a similar effect, seem necessary to enable Congress to transact its business, but they are simply rules of the House and are not adapted to ordinary assemblies. Organizations with more business than they can transact under the ordinary rules should adopt some such special rules that will enable them to attend to their important business during the limited time at their disposal. [See page 366.]

When debate has been closed or limited on any motion, until the vote is taken on that motion, the debate is equally closed or limited on any debatable motion that may for the time being supersede it. Thus, if a resolution and its amendment are pending, and debate on the amendment is ordered to be closed or limited, the order to close or limit debate would apply to a debatable appeal from a decision of the chair made before the vote was taken on the amendment. The same would be true in regard to the motion to reconsider, and the question reconsidered, made under similar circumstances. Privileged motions are undebatable, but when the question of privilege (which is one of the privileged motions [see Chart I, page 548]) or an order of the day is actually before the assembly, it is treated as a main motion and is debatable. The prohibition of debate, in the case of these two privileged motions, applies only to the question as to whether the privileged motion shall be allowed to interrupt the pending business. When such a privileged question interrupts and supersedes a question upon which debate has been closed or limited, the order closing or limiting debate does not apply to the interrupting question. The latter, the interrupting question, is privileged to interrupt unprivileged questions, without in any way being affected by them.

The motions to close or limit debate outrank all the subsidiary motions except to lay on the table, to which they yield, as shown by Chart I. They cannot be laid on the table alone, but they go to the table with the main motion when it is laid on the table.

An order closing or limiting debate is in force only for the session during which it was adopted. If the question upon which it was ordered is brought before the assembly at a future session, it is divested of the order closing or limiting debate, and is open to debate the same as if the order had never been adopted. The same is true if the question is referred to a committee, even though the committee reports at the same session. The reasons for wishing the debate closed or limited do not usually apply to the next session, nor to the question after the committee has made its report. Besides, the members present at the next session should not have their privilege of debate limited without their consent.

In addition to these rules that apply equally to all motions closing or limiting debate, there are given below additional rules that apply only to a motion closing debate now, called the Previous Question, and those that apply only to a motion limiting or extending the limits of debate.

THE PREVIOUS QUESTION

WHEN an assembly is wearied with a debate it often gives expression to its feeling by calls of "Question." If no one has the floor or rises to speak, the chair usually accepts this as indicating that the debate has closed and asks, "Are you ready for the question?" And then, if no one claims the floor, he proceeds to put the question. If a member has the floor or rises to speak, such calls are discourteous and out of order, and should be instantly suppressed by the chair the same as any other disorderly conduct. If a debatable question is immediately pending and a large majority of the assembly is desirous of closing the debate and at once proceeding to vote, the proper course to pursue is to move the Previous Question.

The Previous Question is the name given to the motion "To close debate now, stop further motion to amend, and proceed to voting on the immediately pending question and such others as are specified." It may be moved on any debatable motion that is immediately pending, and it may be moved even after the assembly has ordered debate to be closed at a future time. It is undebatable and cannot be amended, although, as shown below, an effect similar to amendment, by changing the motions on which it is proposed to be ordered, can be produced in another way.

The forms of the motion to close debate now are as follows: "I move [or demand, or call for] the previous question," in which case it applies only to the immediately pending question; or, "I move the previous question on the pending amendment [or amendments]," in which case it applies only to the pending amendment or amendments as specified; or, "I move the previous question on the motion to commit and its amendments"; or, "I move the previous question on all pending questions," in which case it applies to all the pending motions. While this motion cannot be amended, yet when made in one of these forms any one can move the previous question in one of the other forms, and the vote is taken first on the one covering the largest number of questions, and, if that is lost on account of failure to receive a two-thirds vote, then the vote is taken on the motion covering the next smaller number of questions.

After the previous question has been moved and seconded, no subsidiary motion, except to lay on the table, is in order until it is rejected or its effect exhausted as shown hereafter. During this time the questions not yet voted on may be laid on the table, or a privileged or incidental motion may be made.

Putting the Question. Since no subsidiary motion, except to lay on the table, is in order after the previous question has been moved, and since it is undebatable, the chair should immediately state and put the question thus: "The previous question is moved and seconded [or demanded, or called for] on the pending amendment [or such other motion or motions as were specified]. As many as are in favor of ordering the previous question on [specify the motions] will rise." If the number rising is such that the chair is sure of the result, he directs those standing to be seated. If he is not sure as to the result of the vote, he counts, or causes to be counted, those standing and then directs them to be seated, after which he continues, saying, "Those opposed will rise." He treats the negative vote in the same way, and then if the vote has been counted he announces it thus: "There are 80 votes in the affirmative and 40 in the negative [or, 80 in favor of and 40 opposed to the motion]. There being two thirds in the affirmative [or, in favor of the motion], the affirmative has it and the previous question is ordered on the amendment [describe it]. As many as are in favor of the amendment say 'Aye.' Those opposed say 'No.' The ayes have it and the amendment is adopted. The question is now on the resolution as amended, which is, '*Resolved, That, etc.*' [read the amended resolution]. Are you ready for the question?" The resolution is now open to further debate and amendment, since in the supposed case the previous question was ordered only on the amendment. If the affirmative vote is 79 instead of 80 the vote is announced thus: "There are 79 in the affirmative [or, in favor of the motion] and 40 in the negative [or opposed]. There being less than two thirds in the affirmative [or, in favor of the motion], the negative has it and the motion is lost. The question is now on the amendment [state it]. Are you ready for the question?" In case the assembly is not familiar with the previous question, it is well for the chair before taking the vote on ordering it to state that it requires a two-thirds vote for its adoption, and he should also say exactly what its effect will be if adopted.

Suppose the previous question is ordered on all pending questions when there is pending a series of motions consisting of a resolution with an amendment, the motion to commit with an amendment, and the motion to postpone to a certain time. In this case the vote is instantly taken on the postponement; and, if that is lost, next on the amendment to the motion to commit, and then on commit; and, if that is lost, the vote is taken on the amendment and finally on the resolution. If the motion to postpone is adopted, all the remaining questions of the series are postponed to the designated time. If that time is during the same session and the questions are again taken up, there can be no debate upon them because the order closing the debate is still in force. But if the postponement is to another session, then when taken up the questions are debatable and amendable, as the effect of the previous question is exhausted at the close of the session at which it was ordered. If the motion to postpone is lost and the motion to commit is adopted, the resolution and its amendment go to the committee and the previous question is exhausted. When the committee reports back the resolution and its amendment, even if it is at the same meeting, they are free from the previous question and are open to debate and amendment, as the reasons for closing debate previously do not apply to the questions when they come from a committee.

Since the preamble cannot be considered until after the debate and amendment of the resolution have ended, it follows that if the previous question is ordered on a resolution before its preamble has been considered, the previous question does not apply to the preamble, and the chair immediately asks if there are any amendments to the preamble. When the debate and amendment of the preamble are finished, the chair puts the question upon the resolution, including the preamble.

Reconsideration of the Previous Question and Votes Taken Under It. The vote on the previous question may be reconsidered, provided that no vote has been taken on a pending question since the previous question was ordered. As the previous question can be neither debated nor amended, no one would vote for reconsidering a vote on it except for the purpose of voting to reverse the vote. Hence, instead of voting first on the reconsideration and then on the previous question, it is usual to vote only on the reconsideration, and if that is carried it is considered as also reversing the vote on the previous question, and the chair announces the result accordingly. Thus, if an affirmative vote on the previous question is to be reconsidered, the chair puts the question thus: "It has been moved and seconded to reconsider the vote ordering the previous question. As many as are in favor of reconsidering the vote say 'Aye'; those opposed say 'No'; the ayes have it and the vote ordering the previous question is reconsidered. The question is now on the resolution [state the pending question]. Are you ready for the question?" If the noes are in the majority the chair announces the vote thus: "The noes have it and the motion to reconsider is lost. The question is on the resolution. As many as are in favor, etc." As the previous question had been ordered on the resolution, the chair does not ask if the assembly is ready for the question, but immediately puts it.

After debate has been closed and votes taken on one or more of the pending questions, it is in order to reconsider these votes, but not the previous question. Under the same circumstances it is also in order to reconsider votes on amendments, and other motions subsidiary to the main motion that were voted on before the previous question was ordered. If the reconsideration is moved before the previous question is exhausted, as explained below, it is undebatable and the questions reconsidered are undebatable, because the previous question is still in force. But if all the questions on which the previous question was ordered have been voted upon before the reconsideration is moved, then, the previous question being exhausted, the reconsideration and the motions reconsidered are relieved from the previous question and are debatable and amendable the same as if the previous question had never been ordered.

Exhaustion of the Previous Question. The previous question is said to be exhausted when every question upon which it was ordered has been voted on, or those not voted on have been referred to a committee, or postponed indefinitely, or else the session at which the previous question was ordered has ended. If any of the questions on which the previous question was ordered are laid on the table or postponed definitely, the previous question is not exhausted until the close of the session. If they are taken up again during the same session they are still undebatable and unamendable. Thus, if the previous question is ordered on an amendment, as soon as the vote is taken on the amendment the previous question is exhausted, and then everything is treated exactly as if the previous question had never been ordered. If, later, it is moved to reconsider the vote on that amendment, the motion to reconsider and the amendment are both debatable, and the amendment is open to amendment. If, however, the previous question is ordered on both the amendment and the resolution, the previous question is not exhausted until the resolution itself is voted on. Therefore, if, previous to voting on the resolution, it is moved to reconsider the vote on the amendment, the reconsideration and the amendment are both undebatable, and the amendment is not open to amendment, because the previous question is still in force, being only partially executed. When the previous question is exhausted the condition of the business is the same as if it had never been ordered. Any motions that are made afterward are treated the same as they would be if the debate had never been closed.

If the previous question is lost, it may be renewed after sufficient progress in debate or business to make it practically a new question.

In organizations having a rule allowing a smaller number than one third to order a vote to be taken by yeas and nays (by roll-call), the previous question may sometimes be used to advantage in stopping the making of motions to amend an undebatable motion. A great deal of time is consumed in voting by roll-call, and a minority might waste much time if there were no way to stop their offering amendments and then demanding a vote by roll-call. On this account the previous question can be ordered on any amendable motion, even if it is undebatable. In ordinary societies a majority vote is required to order a vote taken by roll-call, and this could not be obtained if two thirds, the number necessary to order the previous question, were opposed to the roll-call. Therefore there is no use for the previous question in an ordinary assembly except when the immediately pending question is debatable.

To Limit or Extend Limits of Debate [1]

According to the old common parliamentary law, when a member obtained the floor he was entitled to it as long as he was able to speak on the pending debatable question. But this rule is so unreasonable that it has generally been abandoned, and in mass meetings, and in ordinary societies with no rules to the contrary, it is now generally accepted that no member can speak more than

[1] This should be read in connection with pages 183-184.

twice on the same question, nor longer than ten minutes at a time. But, while this may be best as a general rule until the assembly adopts a rule of its own on the subject, still there are times when it is desirable to cut down the speeches in number or length, or to specify the length of debate or when the debate shall close, or to allow longer speeches or more of them than are allowed by the rules. The motions to produce these results are of the nature of a motion to suspend the rules relating to the number and length of speeches allowed in debate, and therefore, like the motion to suspend the rules, they are undebatable and require a two-thirds vote for their adoption. They are in order whenever the immediately pending question is debatable, and they apply to it and such other pending motions as are specified in the motion to limit or extend the limits of debate. Therefore these motions, like the previous question, should always designate the motions upon which the debate is to be limited or extended.

The limitation of debate applies also to all debatable subsidiary motions, to a debatable appeal, and to the motion to reconsider, which are made while the limitation is in force, whereas an extension of debate applies only to the motion or speech specified in the order. This is the only difference in the rules applicable to motions limiting debate and those extending the limits of debate. The reason for this difference is that the object of limiting debate on a question is to enable the assembly to dispose of that question quickly, and therefore the restrictions on the debate should apply with equal force to interrupting questions; but an extension of the limits of debate is made usually for the purpose of giving a single speaker more time, or of enabling a particular question to be more thoroughly discussed, and it does not follow that more liberty should be given to the discussion or interrupting questions.

Motions affecting the limits of debate may be made in any of the following or similar forms: "That debate be closed, and all pending questions be put at 9 P. M."; or, "That debate on the pending resolution or any subsidiary motions that may be proposed, be limited to one hour, at the close of which the questions shall be put on all motions then pending"; or, "That debate on the pending resolution and its amendments be limited to one speech of three minutes from each member who has not already spoken on the question"; or, "That Mr. A's time be extended five minutes"; or, "That the time for debate of the resolution be extended, and that the question be put at 4 P. M."; or, "That, in the debate on the pending resolution, Mr. A and Mr. B be allowed fifteen minutes each, to be divided at their pleasure between their two speeches, and that all other members be limited to one speech of five minutes, and that on any amendment proposed no member shall speak more than once nor longer than one minute"; or, "That general debate on the pending resolution be limited to forty minutes, no member speaking more than once or longer than five minutes, after which each member shall be allowed to offer one amendment, the debate upon which shall be limited to one speech of three minutes in favor of, and the same in opposition to, the amendment." These examples are sufficient to show how an assembly may limit the debate to suit the circumstances of the case.

A motion limiting or extending the limits of debate may be amended by changing the limitations, and any of the forms of the motion may be amended by adding any of the others. While this motion is pending, the main question may be laid on the table, taking with it the motion limiting or extending the debate; or, the previous question may be ordered, these two subsidiaries being of higher rank, as shown by Chart I, page 458. While a motion limiting debate is pending, any privileged or incidental motion that the occasion demands is in order.

While an order limiting or extending the limits of debate is in force, any motion may be made that could be made if this order had not been adopted, except that when a definite length of time for the debate has been adopted, or an hour has been appointed when it shall close and the question be put, neither the motion to refer to a committee nor one to postpone definitely can be made before the vote on the order has been reconsidered and reversed. The reason for this. is that appointing a time for closing debate implies that at that time the question will be voted on, and therefore, after adopting such an order, postponing the question or referring it to a committee conflicts with action previously taken by the society at the same session. If a motion has been adopted closing debate at 3 P. M., it is in order any time previous to 3 P. M. to move to extend the time for closing debate to 4 P. M.; or, to close debate at 2 P. M.; or, to limit the number and length of speeches. So, while an order is in force limiting the number and length of speeches it is allowable to make a motion limiting the number and length of speeches differently.

or to move that debate be closed at a certain hour. Since these motions are in the nature of a suspension of the rules and require a two-thirds vote, they can be made without reconsidering an order already adopted even when they conflict with that order.

If debate has been ordered to close at a certain time, and before that time arrives the pending question is laid on the table, and is taken up at the same session but not until after the hour for closing the debate has passed, all debate is cut off just as if the previous question had been ordered. If it is desired to prevent this, some one who has voted in favor of closing debate should move to reconsider the vote ordering the debate to be closed, or move to extend the time for closing debate.

As stated previously, an order limiting or extending the limits of debate is in force only during the session at which it was adopted. The members attending one session of a society cannot dictate to those attending the next session in regard to a particular debate. If some of the questions on which debate was limited or extended are not finally acted upon until another session, they are then under the regular rules of debate, the same as if the order had never been adopted. The same is true of the questions if they have been referred to a committee and are reported back during the same session. But if the questions are laid on the table or postponed to a time within the session and are again taken up during the session, then the order limiting or extending the limits of debate is in force. When the final votes have been taken on all the questions upon which debate was ordered to be limited or extended, then the order is exhausted, and if any one of these votes is reconsidered it is free from the order and is open to regular debate.

The order limiting or extending the limits of debate may be reconsidered any time before its exhaustion, that is, while it is still in force, even though the order has been partially executed. In this it differs from the previous question, which, as previously stated, cannot be reconsidered after the order closing debate has been partially executed. Since the motion to limit or extend the limits of debate is undebatable, the motion to reconsider the vote on it is also undebatable. After all the questions upon which the debate has been limited or extended are voted on, the motion limiting or extending debate is exhausted, so that, if these votes are reconsidered, they are open to debate the same as if the previous debate had not been restricted or extended. If the motion to reconsider is made while the restriction of the debate is still in force, then the restriction applies also to the debate on the reconsideration and the motion to be reconsidered.

The Main Motion to Limit Debate. The motion to limit debate is a subsidiary motion of high rank, as a main motion is pending when it is made. But sometimes, especially in conventions, it is desired to limit debate for the entire session. Such a motion is a main motion and can be introduced only when no motion is pending. As a main motion it can be debated, amended, etc., the same as any other main motion. But since it interferes with the freedom of discussion as much as the subsidiary motion to limit debate, it requires the same vote for its adoption, namely, two thirds.

CHAPTER VIII

MOTIONS TO BRING A QUESTION AGAIN BEFORE THE ASSEMBLY

PRINCIPLES INVOLVED.

AN assembly, having expressed its will upon a question, should not be annoyed by having what is practically the same question brought before it again before anything has occurred to change the opinion of its members. At another session other members may be present and they may hold different views on the subject, but it would be intolerable to permit the defeated members to renew their motion, or to introduce a similar one, during the same session. It is therefore one of the principles of parliamentary law that when an assembly has decided a question, it is not permissible during the same session, unless a voter on the winning side has changed his mind, to introduce the same question, or one so similar that the action in the two cases would naturally be the same. It is also an established rule that no question can be introduced that is so similar to one already introduced in the assembly and only temporarily disposed of (by being laid on the table, or postponed, or committed) that the adoption of the new motion would interfere with the freedom of the assembly in dealing with the previous motion when it comes before the assembly again. Another principle of parliamentary law is that an assembly has a right by a two-thirds vote to suspend any rule of parliamentary procedure that does not protect absentees or a minority smaller than one third. These principles taken together give to members the greatest freedom for introducing and discussing questions that is compatible with the best interests of the entire assembly.

In again bringing up questions that have been decided by the assembly, a distinction must be made between those that have been temporarily, and those that have been permanently, disposed of.

QUESTIONS TEMPORARILY DISPOSED OF

Questions are temporarily disposed of by being Laid on the Table, or Postponed to a Certain Time, or Referred to a Committee. Questions so disposed of are again brought before the assembly by Taking them from the Table, or Taking them up Out of their Proper Order or before the proper time, or by Discharging the Committee from their further consideration. When a question is temporarily disposed of, it is still under the control of the assembly, and no question is in order that is identical with it, or that might interfere with it, as explained above. For example, if a resolution providing for an excursion on June 7 has been laid on the table, or postponed, or referred to a committee, it would be out of order to move to have a picnic June 7, or to have an excursion June 5. The adoption of either of these motions might interfere seriously with the motion previously introduced, when it comes before the assembly again. To attain either of these objects the original resolution must be brought back and amended.

Take a Question from the Table. A question laid on the table is absolutely at the disposal of the majority of the assembly after the business for which it was laid on the table is transacted. If afterward the motion to take the question from the table is made when business of the same class, or unfinished or new business, is in order, it must be recognized in preference to another main motion that has been made but has not yet been stated by the chair. It may be made by any member regardless of how he voted on the motion to lay the question on the table. If a majority wish to take a question from the table while another question is pending, they can do so after laying the pending question on the table. Like the motion to lay on the table, it is undebatable and unamendable, and requires only a majority vote for its adoption. When a question is taken from the table it is in the exact condition it was when laid on the table. The motion to lay on the table, if lost, can be renewed as soon as there has been progress in debate or business, and if carried, the question can be taken from the table by a majority vote at any reasonable time, as just explained. Therefore there is no use in allowing a reconsideration of the motion to take from the table, and consequently a question laid on the table cannot be brought before the assembly again by a motion to reconsider the vote laying it on the table.

Take Up a Question Out of Its Proper Order, or Before Its Proper Time. A question postponed definitely is not under the ~~needs 2/3~~ control of a bare majority of the assembly until the time arrives to which it was postponed. Being the order of the day for that time, it comes then before the assembly for its action, as described on page 133. But sometimes, after assigning a time for the consideration of a question, the assembly wishes to take it up before the designated time arrives. If a majority were allowed to do this, the minority, while in a temporary majority, might take up and act on a question in the absence of the majority, who were relying on its not being taken up until the appointed time. In fact, there would be no use for the motion to postpone if a majority could take up a question before the appointed time, since it would then be practically identical with the motion to lay on the table. In order to make the designation of a future time of real service, it has been found necessary to require a two-thirds vote to take up a question before its appointed time, whether this time is due to the adoption of a program, or order of business, or to the question's having been postponed to that time. Taking up a question before its proper time is really a suspension of the rules, and differs in this respect from the motion to take from the table. It is understood that a motion laid on the table can be taken up at any reasonable time, during that session or the next in assemblies with meetings as often as quarterly.

This motion, to take up a question out of its proper order, or before its appointed time, like the motion to take from the table, cannot be made when any other motion is pending, and cannot be debated or amended. The vote postponing a question may be reconsidered if the motion is made on the day or the day after the vote was taken, as explained later under Reconsider. For fuller information in regard to taking up a question out of its proper order, see page 145.

Discharge a Committee. A question that has been referred to a committee is in the hands of the committee until its report is made. A committee may take advantage of this power, however, and neglect to make its report promptly, or for other reasons the assembly may wish to get the question out of the committee's hands so as to take action on it. This can be done by discharging the committee. As this annuls action previously taken by the assembly, it, like the motion to rescind, requires a two-thirds vote or a vote of the majority of the membership for its adoption, unless previous notice has been given, in which case it may be adopted by a majority vote. This motion to discharge a committee cannot be made when any other question is pending, except when a committee has made a partial report and there is a motion made to accept the report, or to accept the report and continue the committee. To discharge the committee may then be moved as an amendment and be adopted by a majority vote. A motion to discharge a committee should never be made when its full report has been made, since there is no committee then to be discharged.

Before, but not after, the committee has taken up the question referred to it, the question may again be brought before the assembly by a vote to reconsider the vote referring it to the committee. But the motion to reconsider must be made on the day, or the day after, the question was committed. For further information on discharging a committee, see page 108.

For further information on discharging a committee, see page 108.

QUESTIONS FINALLY DISPOSED OF

Questions are finally disposed of by Adopting, Rejecting, or Postponing Indefinitely the motions or propositions. When a question is thus disposed of, it may be brought before the assembly again by a motion to Reconsider the vote disposing of it, or to Rescind the action taken, or to Amend the adopted proposition, as in case of by-laws, resolutions, etc.; or it may be done by Renewing (repeating) the motion if it was lost. Which of these four methods should be adopted depends upon the circumstances of the case.

Reconsider. To provide against the results of hasty action without mature deliberation, American parliamentary law has introduced the motion to reconsider the vote on a question. The defeated party would always wish the vote reconsidered, while the interests of the assembly demand that there shall be no reconsideration unless some one of the winning side has changed his opinion. Accordingly, the rule has been established that the motion to reconsider can be made only by one who voted with the prevailing side. It may be seconded by any one. In order to make it effective it has the peculiar privilege of being in order when another has the floor and a motion of the highest rank is pending, and, while it cannot be considered then, the mere making of the motion suspends for a limited time all action under the vote it is proposed to reconsider. To prevent its too great interference with the work of the assembly, the time for making the motion is limited to the day and the next calendar day after the motion that it is proposed to reconsider was made. It is too late to reconsider a vote after action that cannot be undone has been taken as a result of the vote. For instance, it is too late after the treasurer has paid a bill to reconsider the vote authorizing the payment. No motion can be reconsidered if it can be brought again before the assembly equally well by a majority vote on some other motion. Thus, the vote on laying on the table or taking from the table cannot be reconsidered because the same result can be accomplished by the proper use of these same motions.

The debatability of this motion is the same as that of the motion to be reconsidered: if the latter is debatable the motion to reconsider is debatable; if it is undebatable the reconsideration is undebatable. While the motion to reconsider is immediately pending, if it is debatable the whole merits of the question to be reconsidered are open to debate. The reason for this is that the merits of the question it is proposed to reconsider are necessarily involved in the question as to the expediency of reconsidering the vote. The motion to reconsider cannot be amended or reconsidered, nor can it be repeated after it has been adopted or rejected, unless the question in the interval has been materially amended. A majority vote is all that is required to adopt the motion to reconsider.

One form of this motion is used to protect the assembly from the action of a temporary majority in a meeting that does not fairly represent the society. Its effect is to suspend action until another day, thus giving notice to the society of the proposed action. It outranks the other form of the motion to reconsider and can be applied only to votes adopting, or rejecting, or postponing indefinitely a main motion. Its form is, "To reconsider the vote on —— and have it entered on the minutes." Its peculiarities are explained on page 104. The motion to reconsider is fully treated hereafter, page 87.

Rescind. In case an assembly wishes to annul some action previously taken, any member may move to rescind the resolution or order. This is a main motion with no privilege, except that notice that the motion to rescind the vote will be made at the next meeting may be given when another question is pending, just as in the case of the notice of the motion to reconsider. When proper notice is given, only a majority vote is required to rescind a resolution or order, or any other main motion, except a by-law or similar rule that provides for its amendment by a two-thirds vote. Without notice, it requires a two-thirds vote, that is, two thirds of those voting, or else a majority vote of the entire membership, to rescind any action previously taken. The reason for this is that, while as a general rule the minority of a society should yield to the majority, yet, on account of the small quorum usually required, the attendance at a meeting may be very small and unrepresentative, so that a majority vote may represent the views of only a small minority of the society. So important is it sometimes to be able to rescind certain action without notice, that a two-thirds vote without notice is allowed to rescind resolutions and other main motions, provided that nothing that the assembly cannot undo has been done as the result of the resolution, or other main motion.

The motion to rescind is a main motion and is subject to all the rules applicable to main motions as given on pages 9–11. The debate on the motion to rescind necessarily enters into the merits of the question to be rescinded, and it yields to all secondary motions, that is, any of them that the occasion demands may be made while the motion to rescind is immediately pending. This motion is fully explained on page 110.

Reconsider and Rescind Compared. When it is possible to use the motion to reconsider, it is usually preferable to the motion to rescind or to discharge a committee, which latter motion is practically the same as to rescind. If it is desired to act on a question immediately, reconsider has the advantage over rescind in that the reconsideration has the precedence of all new ques-tions while rescind has not; and reconsider requires only a majority vote while rescind requires a two-thirds vote, or a vote of a majority of the membership, at the meeting where the original motion was adopted, and even at later meetings it requires the same large vote unless previous notice has been given. On the other hand, suppose a resolution is adopted at a convention by a temporary majority when many of the members who are opposed to it are absent from the hall, and no one who voted with the winning side is willing to move a reconsideration. In such a case the only remedy is to rescind the resolution, and this may be done at the same meeting, or at any time later, without notice if two thirds are opposed to the resolution; or it may be done by a vote of a majority of the accredited delegates, which can be obtained in a convention more easily than a two-thirds vote. If neither of these can be obtained, notice may be given that the motion to rescind will be made at the next meeting, and then only a majority vote is required to rescind the resolution, even though the two meetings are held on the same day. In an ordinary society the motion to reconsider cannot be made except at the meeting during which the resolution to be reconsidered was adopted, because there is no meeting the next day: whereas the motion to rescind may be made at any meeting regardless of the time that has elapsed.

A motion rescinding or repealing a by-law is the same as the motion to amend by striking it out, and it is under the rules for amending the by-laws.

Amend a Resolution or Rule Previously Adopted. An adopted resolution or standing rule may be amended without notice by a two-thirds vote, or by a vote of a majority of the membership; or if notice is given at the previous meeting, or in the call for this meeting, it may be amended by a majority vote. It will be noticed that the vote required is the same as is required for rescinding a resolution or standing rule. In fact, rescind is merely one form of the main motion to amend. When it is desired to modify some previous action taken by the assembly, before anything has occurred that the assembly cannot undo, it may be done in the following ways: (a) Reconsider the vote, and reject the motion or amend it and adopt the amended motion. This is the proper and the best way if it is practicable, because all action under the motion is stopped as soon as the reconsideration is moved, and only a majority vote is required for whatever action is desired.

(b) Rescind the action taken, which requires notice or a large vote as described, and then if any further action is desired, adopt a proper resolution. (c) Amend the adopted resolution as just described. Which of these is best in any particular case depends upon circumstances. Reconsider is generally the best when it is practicable. If the object is merely to annul the previous action and it is not practicable to reconsider the vote, the proper motion is to rescind. If it is not desired to rescind the previous action but to modify it, amend is generally the proper motion to use, although sometimes it may be desirable to rescind the unexecuted part of an order or motion. [See also Amend as a Main Motion, page 38, and Amending By-Laws, etc., pages 368-374.]

Renewing a Motion. As has been previously stated, when an assembly has expressed its will as to a certain question, it is unreasonable to allow the same question to be introduced as often as the defeated party may desire. When a main question has been decided either affirmatively or negatively, it is not allowed at the same session to introduce the same question again, nor one so similar to it that the decision of one necessarily implies the decision of the other. The assembly at one session, however, cannot bind the assembly at another session, except by adopting something in the nature of a by-law, etc., that requires previous notice. Hence a main question that has been decided at one session of an assembly may be introduced again at the next and future sessions.

Secondary motions, that is, those that may be made while a main motion is pending, may be renewed whenever the progress in debate or business is such that the previous decision does not necessarily imply that the decision will be the same this time. While the form of the question is the same both times, the real question must be different. Thus, the question on adjourning before an amendment is voted on is different from the question on adjourning after the vote is taken on the amendment. This renewal of motions is explained more fully on page 113.

CHAPTER IX

RECONSIDER, AND RECONSIDER AND ENTER ON THE MINUTES

RECONSIDER

As has been stated heretofore, it would be impossible to transact much business in a deliberative assembly if there were no limit to the number of times the assembly could be called upon to consider and act on the same question. Yet hasty, unconsidered action is so common that it has been found an advantage to allow most votes to be reconsidered once, provided the motion is made within a limited time by one who voted with the winning side. In ordinary societies with frequent meetings, often weekly, and with quorums consisting perhaps of less than ten per cent. of the membership, it is also important to provide some method of preventing a very small minority of a society, that may be temporarily in the majority, from committing the organization to a course disapproved by the large majority of the society.

These two objects are accomplished by the American motion to Reconsider. When it is desired to reconsider hasty action, the motion is made in the simple form of "to reconsider" the vote: when it is desired to prevent final action on a main motion until another meeting of the organization on another day, the motion is made in the form of, "To reconsider the vote and have it entered on the minutes," the practical effect of which is to enable any two members to prevent final action on any main motion without at least one day's notice. The fact that this form of the motion is qualified by "and have it entered on the minutes" does not mean that the simple motion to reconsider is not recorded like other motions. This form of the motion scarcely expresses its exact meaning, which is, "To reconsider the vote on ——, and to have the motion to reconsider entered on the minutes to be called up at the next meeting on another day." The unqualified form of the motion to reconsider is used in all cases except when it is desired to prevent final action on a main motion until another day. The points in which the second form differs from the simple motion to reconsider are explained further on page 104.

The motion to reconsider may be made only on the day on which the vote to be reconsidered was taken, or on the next succeeding calendar day, a legal holiday or a recess not being counted as a day. Ample time is thus given in a convention having sessions lasting several days to think the matter over and to attempt to persuade voters on the winning side to change their votes. If no one on the winning side is prepared to change his vote on the next day, it is for the best interests of the society that the matter be considered as settled, so far as reconsideration with its high privilege is concerned. In ordinary societies a session lasts only an hour or two, and it is at least a week before there is another meeting. Unless an adjourned meeting is held the next day, the motion to reconsider in such societies can be made only at the meeting where the motion to be reconsidered is made. If no one makes the motion at that meeting, the vote cannot be reconsidered, but at any time the society may rescind the action taken, or again introduce and adopt a resolution that was lost.

The motion to reconsider must be made by one who voted with the prevailing side, for it is not to the interest of the assembly to permit this motion to be made unless some one who voted with the winning side has changed his opinion, or at least is sufficiently in favor of giving the minority another opportunity of presenting their case, to be willing, himself, to make the motion to reconsider. If a motion is lost for lack of a two-thirds vote, the negative, even though it is a minority, is the prevailing side. Any member may second the motion, since the change of a single voter from the winning side to the losing side may change the result. Of course a member may vote with the winning side merely for the purpose of moving a reconsideration. There is no way to prevent this, but it would rarely be done except when the mover is quite sure that he represents the real majority of the society and that he will be sustained eventually. If a member uses this or any other motion for improper purposes, the evil must be met as described under Dilatory Motions, page 177.

In order to make the motion to reconsider effective without interfering too much with pending business, it is necessary to allow this motion the following high privileges: (a) It may be made when any other motion whatever is pending, even when another member has the floor, though it cannot interrupt a member while speaking or making a motion, nor can it interrupt the voting. It may be made after it has been voted to adjourn, provided the mover rises and addresses the chair before the assembly has been declared adjourned. The principle involved is that nothing can be allowed to prevent the making of the motion to reconsider as early as possible, because it cannot be made after anything irrevocable has been done as the result of the vote it is proposed to reconsider. It is therefore necessary to allow a member to make this motion even if he cannot obtain the floor. (b) The mere making of the motion to reconsider has the effect of stopping all action under the vote to be reconsidered, unless finally disposed of sooner. [This question is fully explained on pages 91, 92.] This privilege renders it unnecessary to interrupt pending business any longer than is necessary to make the motion. The motion having been made, the reconsideration may be attended to at the convenience of the assembly.

As has been previously stated, the motion to reconsider may be made after it has been voted to adjourn, provided the mover rises and addresses the chair before the assembly is declared adjourned. If the making of the motion to reconsider would not affect the vote on adjourning, the chair, immediately after announcing the motion, declares the assembly adjourned, in accordance with the previous vote. If, however, making the motion to reconsider requires some action of the assembly to prevent its serious interference with something the assembly has decided upon, the chair must again put the question on the motion to adjourn, because moving the reconsideration has so changed conditions that there is uncertainty as to whether the assembly now wishes to adjourn.

To illustrate: Suppose, after the assembly has voted to adjourn, but before the chair has declared the adjournment, a member rises and moves to reconsider the vote on an amendment to a resolution that was laid on the table or was postponed to the next meeting. The making of this motion could not possibly affect the vote on the motion to adjourn, and therefore the chair, after announcing the motion to reconsider, declares the meeting adjourned. But suppose the vote to be reconsidered is one authorizing the engagement of a lecturer who can be secured only if prompt action is taken, and the object of the resolution will be defeated if the matter goes over to the next regular meeting. The chair should announce the fact that the reconsideration has been moved, and that unless it is acted upon before adjournment the lecturer cannot be engaged. He should then put the question again on the adjournment, and when this motion is voted down the motion to reconsider should be taken up and disposed of. [See also Illustration (8), page 99.]

Taking Up the Reconsideration. The reconsideration itself has the rank of the motion to be reconsidered, and therefore is taken up at such time as the motion would have been in order had it not already been made. The reconsideration of a main motion, if moved when nothing is pending, is announced immediately by the chair. If business is pending at the time, the chair states the question on the reconsideration as soon as a motion of that class, or unfinished or new business, is in order. If the chair neglects to announce the reconsideration at the first opportunity, any member may ''call up'' the reconsideration. If called up, it is taken up in preference to any main motion competing with it for consideration. But to entitle it to this preference the mover must rise and address the chair before another question is stated. If he cannot attract the chair's attention until another member has been recognized, he should say that he rises to call up the motion to reconsider, and the chair should say, ''The motion to reconsider the resolution on —— is called up. The question is, 'Will the assembly reconsider the vote on the resolution?' Mr. A has the floor,'' recognizing the mover of the reconsideration. Any one may call up the reconsideration of a vote adopting, rejecting, or postponing indefinitely a main motion, but as a matter of courtesy, if there is no reason for prompt action, it is usually left to the one who moved the reconsideration, if it is evident that he is acting in good faith.

If it is a subsidiary motion that is to be reconsidered, the chair announces the motion when made, and states the question on the reconsideration the moment it is in order to make that subsidiary motion if it had not been made previously. Illustration: Suppose, after an amendment is adopted, a motion is made to postpone the question to the next meeting, and while this motion is pending it is moved to reconsider the vote on the amendment. The chair immediately announces the motion to reconsider, but does not state the question on it until after the pending question on the postponement is disposed of. If the postponement is lost, the chair immediately says, "The question is on reconsidering the vote on the amendment," etc., repeating the amendment. If the postponement is adopted, when the time to which the question was postponed arrives, the chair states the question in a form similar to this: "The next business in order is the consideration of the resolution, '*Resolved*, That, etc. [repeating the resolution] and its adhering motion to reconsider the vote on the amendment [repeating the amendment].'" The chair then assigns the floor to the member who moved the reconsideration.

For another illustration, suppose that after amendment No. 1 has been rejected, amendment No. 2 is moved, and then that the question is laid on the table: now it is moved to reconsider the vote on No. 1. The chair announces the reconsideration when it is moved, but no action is taken upon it until the question is taken from the table and amendment No. 2 is disposed of, at which time the chair immediately states the question on reconsidering the vote on amendment No. 1.

In an ordinary society with regular meetings as often as quarterly, the effect of making the motion to reconsider continues until the close of the next regular business session, if not called up sooner. When the effect of the motion to reconsider has expired without its being called up, the vote that it was proposed to reconsider is in full force, the same as if the motion to reconsider had not been made. If in such a society it is called up and not finally acted upon, but is laid on the table or postponed to another day, the motion to reconsider carries with it the question to be reconsidered, and its effect continues just the same and expires just the same as if it, the motion to reconsider, had not been laid on the table or postponed.

In an organization meeting less often than quarterly, as a

convention meeting annually, the effect of moving a reconsideration does not extend beyond the session; the adjournment of the session terminates its effect if the motion to reconsider has not been called up, or if it has been called up and has been laid on the table or postponed. In such an organization a motion to reconsider cannot be postponed to another session, and a motion to reconsider that is on the table when the session adjourns is dead, and the vote to which it is proposed to reconsider is in full force.

When the motion to reconsider is called up, the difference between the two forms of the motion, to reconsider, and to reconsider and enter on the minutes, ceases, and the chair states the question in exactly the same way in the two cases. In either case he would state the question in a manner similar to this: "The motion to reconsider the vote on the resolution, '*Resolved*,' etc. [repeating the resolution] is called up. The question is on reconsidering the vote adopting the resolution." If the motion to be reconsidered is debatable then the reconsideration is debatable, and in this debate the merits of the question to be reconsidered may be entered into as fully as if it were the immediately pending question. The motion to reconsider an undebatable question is undebatable. The motion to reconsider is undebatable if the reconsideration comes up while the previous question is in force, whether the vote to be reconsidered was taken up under the order for the previous question or not. An order limiting debate applies in a similar way to the motion to reconsider. For example, suppose the previous question is ordered on a resolution and its pending amendments, and that before they are all voted on, it is moved to reconsider the vote on an amendment that was voted on before the previous question was ordered. As soon as pending amendments are disposed of, the chair puts the question on the reconsideration, and if that is carried he at once takes the vote on the amendment. No debate on the reconsideration or the amendment is allowed, because the previous question is not exhausted until the vote is taken on the main question.

The motion to reconsider cannot be amended, or postponed indefinitely, or referred to a committee, but the motion to reconsider a main motion may be postponed to a certain time, or laid on the table, in either case carrying with it the question to be reconsidered and the motions adhering to it. It would be absurd to refer to a committee the question as to whether the assembly should reconsider a question, but the assembly might prefer to take up the question of reconsideration at another time, and of course this would require that the question to be reconsidered should be postponed also. The previous question and other motions relating to closing or limiting debate may be applied to the motion to reconsider a debatable question.

When the motion to reconsider is before the assembly for debate, members who have previously exhausted their right of debate can now speak again on the question to be reconsidered. Technically the question is different from what it was before, but practically it is the same, because a discussion of the reconsideration necessarily involves the merits of the question to be reconsidered. If the reconsideration is carried, the question is before the assembly in precisely the same condition it was just before the taking of the vote that has been reconsidered. Consequently if a member has exhausted his right of debate on that question for the day he cannot now speak upon it. He should have spoken when the reconsideration was pending. Any motion that was in order just before the taking of the vote just reconsidered is now in order.

A majority vote is all that is required to reconsider any vote that can be reconsidered regardless of the vote required on the motion to be reconsidered. If the motion to reconsider is lost it cannot be renewed, except by unanimous consent. If it is adopted the question cannot be reconsidered again, unless when previously reconsidered it was so materially amended as to make the second reconsideration an entirely new question.

Reconsideration of a Main Motion. If a resolution or other main motion has been adopted, rejected, or postponed indefinitely, and afterward, on the same or the next day, a member who voted with the winning side has changed his opinion and wishes the question to be further discussed, he should take advantage of the first occasion when there is no pending question and obtain the floor and move "to reconsider the vote on the resolution on —— " Any one may second the motion. When the chair states the question on the reconsideration he assigns the floor to the member who moved the reconsideration, and this is the time to discuss the question and show why the assembly should take different action. The main question is just as debatable now as if it were the immediately pending question. When the debate is finished the chair puts the question on the reconsideration and announces the result. If the reconsideration is lost the vote on the main question stands, and it cannot be reconsidered again except by unanimous consent. If the reconsideration is carried the chair announces the fact thus: "The ayes have it, and the vote on the resolution on —— is reconsidered. The question is now on the resolution, which is as follows: [Reads the resolution.] Are you ready for the question?" The question is now open to debate and amendment, it being in the exact condition it was just before it was previously voted on. If the member who moved the reconsideration had said he intended to offer an amendment, the chair should have assigned him the floor even though another had already risen to claim it. After his amendment has been offered, he is entitled to the floor in preference to others. After this, however, he has no preference, and other amendments may be offered by any one, the procedure being the same as if the main motion had never been voted on.

In the above case the motion to reconsider could have been made while another question was pending, but ordinarily nothing would be gained thereby, as it could not be taken up until all pending questions were disposed of.

Reconsideration of an Amendment While the Main Motion Is Pending. In this case, as soon as the member who wishes the amendment reconsidered obtains the floor he moves "to reconsider the vote on the amendment —— " [stating the amendment]. If nothing is pending but the main motion or it and the motion to postpone indefinitely, the chair states the question at once on the reconsideration, and assigns the floor to its mover, who should then give the reasons for the reconsideration. If a secondary motion other than postpone indefinitely is pending when the reconsideration of the amendment is moved, the chair announces the reconsideration, but does not state the question on it until all pending secondary motions except postpone indefinitely are disposed of. If after debate the reconsideration is carried, the chair states the question on the amendment and recognizes the mover of the reconsideration if he claims the floor. The amendment is now open to debate and amendment just as it was before it was voted on.

The same principle applies in reconsidering any other secondary motion, that is, the chair states the question on the reconsideration as soon as the motion to be reconsidered would be in order if it had not been made already.

Reconsideration of an Amendment or Other Secondary Motion after Final Action Has Been Taken on the Main Motion. After a main question has been acted upon it is too late to reconsider the vote on a motion subsidiary to it, unless the vote on the main question is also reconsidered. Thus it is absurd to reconsider a vote on postponing or amending a question that has already been disposed of and is not in the possession of the assembly. In such a case it is necessary to reconsider the main motion and then the subsidiary one, taking first the question last voted on; or, still better, to make one motion and one vote cover all the questions to be reconsidered. When one motion is made to cover all the questions to be reconsidered and the chair states the question on the reconsideration, the only one of the questions open to debate is the one most distant from the main question, and this is the proper time to state the objections to it in its present form, and what is to be proposed in its place if the vote is reconsidered. Unless sufficient reasons are given for reconsidering, it is not to be expected that the motion will be adopted. If the motion to reconsider is carried, the chair states that the votes are reconsidered and that the question is on the amendment, or whatever the reconsidered question is, that is farthest removed from the main question. The question is now in the exact condition that it was before that question was voted on, so that each of the reconsidered questions is open to debate and amendment, and must be put to vote again in the same order as before, as if it had never been put to vote. This is illustrated below.

Instead of the above described method of reconsidering a main motion and its subsidiaries by one motion and one vote, it may be done by separate motions and votes. In this case the mover should announce his purpose at the beginning when he moves to reconsider the vote on the main motion. When the chair states the question on the reconsideration, he should assign the floor to the mover, who should give his reasons for wishing the reconsideration, and then move to reconsider the amendment or other subsidiary. If this is carried and there is another subsidiary to reconsider, the chair assigns the mover the floor again to move the other reconsideration, since the maker of one motion of a series is entitled to the floor to complete the series. While this method is commonly used, the other one is preferable.

The steps to be taken in reconsidering the vote on a rejected amendment of the second degree after the resolution has been adopted illustrate the procedure in other cases of reconsideration, and are as follows:

(1) Move to reconsider the votes on the resolution and amendments of the first and second degree.

(2) Debate on reconsidering the amendment of the second degree.

(3) Take a vote on reconsidering all the three votes. [Carried.]

(4) Debate and vote on the amendment of the second degree.

(5) Debate and amend (if desired) and vote on amendment of first degree.

(6) Debate and amend (if desired) and vote on resolution.

After each vote is announced, as well as after every motion is made, the chair should distinctly announce the pending question. While this is always the duty of the chair, it needs special emphasis in case of a reconsideration as just described. It will be noticed that if separate motions to reconsider are made, the one motion and one vote required in the first three steps given above will be replaced by three motions and three votes, even though the chair refuses, as he should, to allow amendments until all the motions of the series of reconsideration have been made.

Illustrations. The following illustrations will make more clear the procedure where it is desired to reconsider a vote. In actual practice it is seldom necessary to reconsider any votes except those adopting or rejecting a main motion or a primary amendment. Verbal corrections can usually be made by general consent, thus avoiding a reconsideration. For brevity's sake it is assumed in the following examples that the chair knows that Mr. A, who moves the reconsideration, voted on the prevailing side. If the chair is not sure of this he should ask how he voted. It is also assumed that the motion is seconded. It does not matter how the seconder voted, or even whether he was present when the vote was taken which it is proposed to reconsider.

(1) *To reconsider a resolution after it has been adopted or rejected.* When nothing is pending Mr. A moves "to reconsider the vote on the resolution on ——," and the chair immediately

states the question thus: "It is moved and seconded to reconsider the vote on the resolution on ——. Mr. A." Mr. A, being thus assigned the floor, gives the reasons for the reconsideration, after which the question is open to debate by others. The debate may go into the merits of the resolution the same as if it were the immediately pending question. If the question is decided affirmatively the chair says: "The ayes have it and the vote on the resolution is reconsidered. The question is on the resolution, which is, '*Resolved*, That,' etc. [reading the resolution and asking], Are you ready for the question?"—unless Mr. A has indicated that when the resolution was reconsidered he wished to offer an amendment, or to make some other subsidiary motion, or to debate it, in which case the chair assigns him the floor without asking the above question. The question is now in exactly the condition it was before the resolution was voted on, and therefore it can be debated and amended and must be disposed of by a vote just as if it had never been voted on. If the motion to reconsider is lost, the chairman announces the fact and proceeds to the next business. Whether adopted or lost, the motion to reconsider cannot be renewed except by unanimous consent.

(2) *To reconsider an amendment of the first degree while the resolution is pending.* Mr. A moves the reconsideration, if he can get the opportunity, while the resolution is the immediately pending question. If there is no other chance, he must make his motion while another subsidiary motion is pending, or even while another member has the floor, but he cannot interrupt any one who is speaking. In the first case, when the resolution is immediately pending, the chair at once states the question on reconsidering the amendment: in the other case he announces that the motion is made, but he waits to state the question on the reconsideration until there is no question pending except the resolution. The chair states the question on reconsidering the amendment as soon as the resolution itself is the immediately pending question. He must not wait for the mover to call up the motion.

(3) *To reconsider an amendment of the first degree after the resolution has been adopted or rejected.* Mr. A moves "to reconsider the votes on the resolution —— and its amendment —— " [describing the resolution and its amendment]. If nothing is pending the chair states the question and assigns the floor to Mr. A, who then explains why the votes should be reconsidered. The

debate would naturally be confined mainly to the amendment, but may go into the main question also if it has any bearing on the reconsideration. If the reconsideration is carried the chair announces it thus: "The ayes have it and the votes on the resolution and the amendment —— are reconsidered. The question is on the amendment" [stating the amendment]. After the amendment is disposed of, the question is stated on the resolution.

(4) *To reconsider a primary amendment which has been amended and then adopted.*[1] Suppose a resolution pending contains the word "pine," and it is moved to strike out "pine" and insert "poplar": it is then moved to amend this primary amendment by striking out "poplar" and inserting "cherry." Both amendments are adopted, so that the word "cherry" is inserted in the resolution.

(a) Afterward, if it is desired to replace the word "cherry" by the word "poplar," it is necessary to reconsider the votes on both amendments as described in the next illustration (5).

(b) If it is desired to replace "cherry" by "pine," it is necessary to reconsider the amendment striking out "pine" and inserting "cherry," and then to reject the amendment and thus leave "pine" in the resolution.

(c) If it is desired to replace "cherry" by "mahogany," it is necessary to take the steps just described in (b), and then move to strike out "pine" and insert "mahogany." It would not be in order to move to strike out "cherry" and insert "mahogany," because "cherry" has been inserted and therefore cannot be struck out.

(5) *To reconsider an amendment of the second degree while the resolution is immediately pending.* Mr. A moves "to reconsider the votes on the amendment —— and its amendment ——" [describing the primary and the secondary amendments]. The chair states the question and assigns the floor to Mr. A as shown in previous illustrations. If the reconsideration is adopted the chair states the question on the amendment of the amendment, and proceeds exactly as if the amendment had never been voted on, except that Mr. A is recognized in preference to others until he has had an opportunity to offer his secondary amendment, or to make the speech for which the reconsideration was moved.

[1] It will be well for the reader to write down the resolution and the amendments as shown in the illustration in "Parliamentary Practice" p. 192.

(6) *To reconsider a negative vote on the motion to commit while an amendment to the resolution and a motion to postpone to a certain time are pending.* When Mr. A makes his motion to reconsider, the chair announces the motion, but he cannot state the question on the reconsideration until the vote is taken on the postponement, which outranks commitment. If the postponement is lost, the chair immediately states the question on the reconsideration of the motion to commit, because to commit outranks the pending motion to amend the resolution. If the postponement is carried, all the pending questions go over to the designated time, at which time the chair states the reconsideration of the motion to commit as the immediately pending question.

(7) *Suppose, just after a vote is taken adopting a resolution but before the result is announced, a motion is made to reconsider a vote rejecting an amendment.* The chair at once states the question on the reconsideration as it must be acted upon before the result of the vote on the main question can be announced. If the reconsideration is voted down, or if the amendment after being reconsidered is again lost, there is no necessity for again taking the vote on the resolution, because there has been no change in the main question, and therefore the chair immediately announces the result of the vote previously taken. If when reconsidered the amendment is adopted, then, the main question being changed, the vote previously taken is ignored and the main question as amended is put to vote.

(8) *Suppose it is voted to adjourn, and before the chair has declared the assembly adjourned, a motion is made to reconsider the vote fixing the time for the next meeting.* It makes no difference whether the adjourned meeting was appointed by adopting the privileged motion fixing the time to which to adjourn, or by adopting a main motion to that effect. It is clear that to be of any use whatever it is necessary to act on the reconsideration before the chair declares the assembly adjourned, so, since the question is undebatable, he immediately states the question on the reconsideration. As soon as the reconsideration and the question reconsidered are disposed of, the chair declares the assembly adjourned without any further vote.

(9) *Suppose that, after an amendment to a resolution is lost, it is moved to refer the resolution to a committee, and before this is voted on the question is laid on the table, after which it is*

moved to reconsider the vote on the amendment. Whenever the question is taken from the table the immediately pending question is on referring the resolution to a committee. If that is carried the resolution goes to the committee and the motion to reconsider is ignored. The committee reports back the resolution with such amendments as it recommends, in this case including, if it wishes, the amendment that it was moved to reconsider, regardless of whether the amendment had been adopted or rejected by the assembly. If the motion to commit is lost, the chair then states the question on the reconsideration of the amendment. In the case explained above, if another amendment was pending when the motion to refer was made, after this motion to refer was lost, that amendment would be the pending question, and after it was disposed of the chair would announce the reconsideration as the pending question.

In all cases of secondary motions like the above, the chair does not wait for the reconsideration to be called up, but states the question on it as soon as it is in order. These illustrations are sufficient to show the correct procedure in any use of reconsideration likely to arise.

Questions that Cannot Be Reconsidered. The motion to reconsider is, as a general rule, not applicable to the following cases:

(*a*) To votes on motions that can be renewed after progress in business or debate.

(*b*) To an affirmative vote in the nature of a contract, when the other party to the contract has been notified of the vote.

(*c*) To a vote on the motion to reconsider.

(*d*) When other motions are provided that will practically accomplish the same object.

(*e*) After something has been done as a result of the vote that the assembly cannot undo.

(*f*) After a vote has been partially executed (except in case of an order limiting debate).

The following are cases of votes that have been partially executed and therefore cannot be reconsidered: (1) A resolution and an amendment are pending. The previous question is ordered on all pending questions and the vote is taken on the amendment. It is now too late to move to reconsider the vote ordering the previous question, as it has been partially executed. (2) In case a committee has taken up a question referred to it, it is too late to reconsider the vote referring the matter to the committee. (3) It has been voted to nominate and elect by ballot the delegates and alternates to a convention. After the election of the delegates it is desired to do away with the nominating ballot for the alternates, and to have them nominated from the floor. It is too late to reconsider the vote ordering the nominating ballot, because the order has been partially executed. The proper course to pursue is to rescind the unexecuted portion of the order. A vote, however, limiting or extending the limits of debate may be reconsidered after it has been partially executed, because it is to the interest of the assembly not to allow any modification of the limits of debate unless a large majority desire it. The debate may raise such questions as to materially modify the views of members in regard to the expediency of limiting the debate, and a majority should have the right to reconsider the vote and do away with the limitations.

The motion to reconsider cannot be renewed, unless it was withdrawn or unless the question to be reconsidered has been materially amended since the reconsideration was previously moved. The list of motions that cannot be reconsidered on page 553 is in accordance with these principles.

To Reconsider and Enter on the Minutes

Necessity for and Proper Use of This Motion. The motion to reconsider, as has been explained, provides sufficiently against hasty action which the majority of the assembly that adopted it wishes to modify. But it does not protect a society with a small quorum and frequent meetings from the deliberate action of a temporary majority that represents only a small minority of the entire membership. Both houses of the English Parliament have small quorums, and a majority of the members are not expected to be present at every meeting, so that in these respects they are very similar to ordinary voluntary societies. They have protected themselves from the danger mentioned above by requiring notice of main motions, so that there is ample time to notify absent members. Such a rule would be exceedingly inconvenient in ordinary societies, and in them it is required for only a few important motions, such as to amend the by-laws. Societies with very small quorums are sufficiently protected from the action of small or packed meetings by the proper use of the motion to Reconsider and Have Entered on the Minutes.

The legitimate use of this motion is to enable two members to prevent for the day final action on important main motions that have been sprung upon the assembly without notice, and that would probably be decided differently if time were afforded for consultation and for notifying absent members. It practically permits two members to require at least one day's notice before final action is taken on a motion permanently disposing of a main motion.

Since no one would make this motion who was really in favor of the vote that prevailed, it follows that a member who is opposed to the prevailing party must vote with it, or else he must change his vote to that side before the vote is announced, so that he can move to reconsider the vote and have it entered on the minutes. This motion is especially useful in cases so flagrant that, before the vote.is taken, members know that the members present do not fairly represent the society in the pending matter, and therefore some of them should vote with the prevailing side, and then move to reconsider the vote and have it entered on the minutes. If none of the defeated party voted with the prevailing side, one of them could change his vote before the vote is announced. Should this be neglected, then some one should give notice that at the next meeting he will move to rescind the resolution or action thereon. This will enable a majority at the next meeting to rescind the action taken, provided nothing has been done as the result of it that the assembly cannot undo. The motion to rescind, or the notice of it, does not suspend action under a resolution, as reconsider does, and therefore it is useless to give the notice if the resolution requires something to be done before the next meeting.

Improper Use of the Motion to Reconsider and Enter on the Minutes. The requirement that the motion to reconsider and enter on the minutes must be made, like the simple form of the motion to reconsider, by one who voted with the prevailing side, protects the assembly to a great extent from being annoyed by members of the minority making this motion uselessly, even at meetings where the attendance is normal. But there is an improper use of this motion, as explained below, that at times may seriously interfere with the assembly unless its danger is fully understood and proper steps taken to meet it.

As has already been stated, merely making this motion suspends until another day action under the vote it is proposed to reconsider. Advantage of this may be taken by any two factious members to defer to the next meeting important business that should be attended to before the next regular meeting. If this is attempted the assembly should immediately vote that when it adjourns it adjourns to meet next day, at which time the reconsideration may be taken up and disposed of at once. If the main motion is of such a nature that deferring action on it to the next day is equivalent to postponing it indefinitely, then the motion to reconsider and enter on the minutes is out of order.

To illustrate the above, suppose the following case: A society with regular weekly meetings, learning that a distinguished person is to be in their town the next week, unanimously vote to invite him to be present at their next meeting and address them. Immediately after they have voted to adjourn, but before the chair has declared the assembly adjourned, a member rises and moves to reconsider the vote of invitation and have it entered on the minutes. The member having voted with the prevailing side for this very purpose, and the motion being seconded, no invitation can be sent until the motion to reconsider is voted down, and this cannot be done until the next meeting, which will be too late. In such a case the proper course is for some one immediately to rise, address the chair, and move that when the assembly adjourns it adjourns to meet at such and such a time, specifying the day and hour. This motion is in order even though the assembly has voted to adjourn, as the assembly is not adjourned until so declared by the chair. If this motion is adopted, an adjourned meeting is provided for, which may be on the next day, at which time the reconsideration would be called up and voted down and then the vote giving the invitation is in force. Under these circumstances, as soon as the motion is made providing for an adjourned meeting, it is probable that the motion to reconsider would be withdrawn, when of course the motion fixing the time for an adjourned meeting should be withdrawn also. Should no one think before the assembly is adjourned to provide for an adjourned meeting, the only course left for the majority is to have a special meeting called as quickly as possible, stating in the call that the meeting is called to take up the reconsideration of such and such an invitation. If the members know how to defeat such sharp practice, it will probably never be resorted to.

Points in Which the Motion to Reconsider and Enter on the Minutes Differs from the Motion to Reconsider.

(1) To reconsider and enter on the minutes outranks the simple form of to reconsider, and when made supersedes the latter, which is treated as if it had never been made. Even if it had been voted to reconsider, provided the vote had not been announced, the motion is in order. After the vote on the reconsideration has been announced, whether it is carried or lost, it is too late to make the other form of the motion. If this motion did not outrank the simple form of the motion to reconsider it would be nearly useless, because it could usually be forestalled by the prompt making of the motion to reconsider by the member in charge of the motion just voted on. The motion to reconsider would be immediately voted down and the other form of the motion could not be made.

(2) To reconsider and enter on the minutes can be applied only to an affirmative or negative vote on adopting, and an affirmative vote on postponing indefinitely, a main motion; and to a negative vote on the consideration of a main motion whose consideration has been objected to. These are the only votes that finally dispose of the main question, and are therefore the only ones to which the motion can be applied. It would generally be a hindrance rather than a help to allow this form of the motion to be applied to the various privileged, incidental, and subsidiary motions.

(3) To reconsider and enter on the minutes can be made only on the day the vote to be reconsidered was taken. The next day the motion simply to reconsider accomplishes the same object as having it entered on the minutes the day before would have done, namely, to bring the main question before the assembly again on another day than the one when the vote was originally taken.

(4) In an assembly, like a convention, whose regular sessions are not as frequent as quarterly, the motion to reconsider and enter on the minutes cannot be made on the last day of the session unless there is to be a business meeting afterward, and at the last business meeting any one may call it up. Since this form of the motion cannot be called up during the meeting at which it is

made, and its effect is exhausted when the session closes, there would be no use for this form of the motion at the last meeting of the session. The simple form of the motion to reconsider should be used.

(5) The motion to reconsider and enter on the minutes cannot be applied to votes on motions the object of which would be defeated by delay to another day. For instance, it would be absurd to allow two members to prevent the assembly's asking a visitor to address them at that time, or accepting an invitation to anything occurring on that day, and yet that would be the effect of allowing the motion to reconsider and have entered on the minutes to be applied in such cases.

(6) The motion to reconsider and enter on the minutes cannot be called up on the day it is made, unless that is the last day of the session of an assembly having regular meetings less frequently than quarterly, and in this case any one can call it up at the last business meeting of the session. If in an ordinary society this motion could be called up at the next meeting on the same day, its object would be defeated by fixing the time for an adjourned meeting, say, in fifteen minutes and then adjourning. The interval between the meetings would be too brief to enable absent members to be notified, and the object of the motion would be defeated. It is necessary to require that it cannot be called up on the day it is made.

After the day on which the motion to reconsider and have entered on the minutes is made, it is treated exactly as if it had been made in the simple form of reconsider. The object of entering it on the minutes has been accomplished when it has delayed final action on the main question until another day from the one on which the original vote was taken. It cannot be withdrawn when it is too late for any one else to move the reconsideration.

CHAPTER X

TAKE FROM THE TABLE; DISCHARGE A COMMITTEE; RESCIND; RENEWAL OF A MOTION

TAKE FROM THE TABLE

[Read in connection with this pages 80, 81.]

As stated heretofore, a pending question may be laid on the table at any moment by a bare majority, without allowing any debate or amendment. This is done on the theory that the question is only temporarily laid aside on account of more urgent business, and that its consideration will be resumed, at which time opportunity will be given for debate and amendment. On this account the motion to take a question from the table takes the precedence of other main motions that have not been actually stated by the chair, provided it is made when business of the same class, or unfinished or new business, is in order. A question laid on the table remains there, if not taken up previously, until the close of the session; and in assemblies having meetings as often as quarterly, unless taken up sooner, it remains on the table until the close of the next regular business session. If not taken up within the time limit, the question is as if it had never been made, and therefore it may be introduced again.

If nothing is pending and there is no order of business, or program, or rule that would prevent the consideration at this time of a motion that has been laid on the table, a member rising to move to take the question from the table should be assigned the floor in preference to any member rising to introduce any main motion except one of a series already begun. A member wishing to have a question taken from the table should obtain the floor immediately after a pending main question is disposed of and

106

move to take the question from the table. If the chair recognizes another member as having obtained the floor, the first member should at once say, "Mr. Chairman, I rise to move to take a question from the table." It is not too late for him to do this even if the other member has made a motion before the first member can attract the chair's attention so as to state for what he has risen. The chair should recognize the motion to take from the table in preference to any main motion, and even if he has stated another question, he must ignore the fact and recognize the member who rose to make the motion to take from the table, provided the member rose and addressed the chair before the other question was stated. This motion cannot, however, interrupt a series of motions, but must wait until the series is disposed of. [See R. O. R., p. 30.]

The form of the motion is, "To take from the table the resolution on ——," or, "To take up the report of the financial committee." It is undebatable, and cannot be amended, committed, postponed, laid on the table, or reconsidered. Privileged and incidental motions may be made while this is pending. Its effect is to bring before the assembly the question laid on the table with all its attached questions in exactly the same condition they were when they were laid on the table, except that if not taken from the table until the next session the previous question and motions limiting, or extending the limits of, debate are exhausted. Members who had exhausted their right of debate cannot again speak to the question if it is taken up on the same day it was laid on the table. The chair should drop any subsidiary motion that has become useless on account of the delay in taking up the question, as for instance, a motion to postpone to a time that has passed.

A vote on the motion to take from the table cannot be reconsidered, as the same object can be accomplished within a reasonable time by renewing the motion if it is lost, and by laying the question on the table again if it is carried. If it fails it may be repeated again and again, but it cannot be repeated until some business has been transacted since it was last voted down. If it is desired to take from the table a question while another question is pending, the proper course is to lay on the table the pending questions and then the other question may be taken from the table. When taken from the table, the question cannot again be laid on the table until there has been material progress in debate or in business.

DISCHARGE A COMMITTEE

[Read in connection with this page 82.]

When a motion is referred to a committee, the subject matter is in a condition, as far as the assembly is concerned, very similar to what it would be if it had been postponed to the time when the committee reports. A motion cannot be offered in the assembly that is identical with the one that has been referred to a committee, or that in any way interferes with the freedom of the assembly to deal as it pleases with the report of the committee. If it is desired to consider the new motion, it is necessary first to bring back the question from the committee, as it would be absurd for the assembly to consider and act upon a question while a committee is considering a similar proposition referred to it. The question may be brought back before the committee has actually begun its consideration, by reconsidering the vote committing the question, which may be done by a majority vote on the day, or the day after, the question is committed. After the committee has begun its work on the question it is too late to reconsider the vote.

If the vote committing the question cannot be reconsidered, the only way to bring the question immediately before the assembly is to discharge the committee. If the committee is a special one with no other duty, the proper form of the motion is, "To discharge the committee to which was referred the resolution on enlarging the library, and that the resolution be now taken up for consideration." If the committee has other duties, the motion is made in this form: "To discharge the committee on resolutions from the further consideration of the resolution." If this motion is adopted by the proper vote, as explained below, the chair announces the result and then states the pending question thus: "The committee is discharged [or, discharged from the further consideration of, etc.], and the question is on the resolution [or amendment]," etc. [reading the resolution or amendment immediately pending when the resolution was committed]. The above-mentioned motions may have added to them, "and that the resolution be now considered," but this is unnecessary, as the chair should state the question on the resolution when the committee is discharged. The motion to discharge may have added to it the words, "and that the resolution be considered at [or, be made the special order for] 4 P.M.," or similar words.

The motion to discharge a committee requires a two-thirds vote, or a vote of a majority of the entire membership, except in the following cases, when it requires only a majority vote: (1) when notice of the motion to discharge the committee was given at a previous meeting, or in the call for this meeting; (2) when the committee makes a partial report; (3) when the time arrives at which the committee was instructed to report and it fails to do so. These exceptions are necessary to prevent the business of the assembly from being delayed by a committee. With these rules the majority of an assembly can prevent a resolution from being smothered in a committee, while at the same time a committee that is acting in good faith and doing its duty cannot have the subject referred to it taken out of its hands after the committee has begun its work by less than a two-thirds vote, unless previous notice of the motion has been given. The previous notice has all the privilege of notices of amendments to the by-laws and of making the motion to reconsider; that is, if necessary it may be given even after it has been voted to adjourn, provided the chair has not declared the assembly adjourned.

When a committee makes its report to the assembly, that report is in the possession of the assembly, and the committee is automatically discharged if the report is a final one. Therefore it is improper to move "to accept the report and discharge the committee," unless the report is only a partial one, or a report of progress, because if the final report has been made by a special committee there is no committee to discharge, and if it was made by a standing committee the committee, having made its report, cannot resume its consideration unless the matter is recommitted.

The motion to discharge a committee is an incidental main motion and cannot be made when any other motion is pending. It should never be used after a committee has begun its work, unless there are urgent reasons for immediate action, or the committee is dilatory in making its report. It is debatable. Privileged and incidental motions may be made while it is pending, and the subsidiary motions may be applied to it.

An assembly at any time may by a majority vote give instructions or additional instructions to a committee. Instead of discharging a committee the assembly may instruct it to report at some reasonable specified time. It would not be in order to move "that the committee be instructed to report in five minutes," or in any other impracticable time, and thus be enabled at the end of the five minutes to discharge the committee by a mere majority vote. Instructing a committee to report at a specified time may be moved as a substitute for the motion to discharge a committee.

RESCIND OR REPEAL

[Read in connection with this page 84.]

A motion to annul words or sentences of the constitution, by-laws, or rules of order, etc., is usually referred to as the motion to strike out, or to amend by striking out. A motion to annul a by-law, or a paragraph or section of the by-laws, etc., is referred to as a motion either to strike out, or to rescind or repeal, the by-law or paragraph, etc. A motion to annul the entire constitution, by-laws, or rules of order, or an entire standing rule or resolution, is referred to as a motion to Rescind or Repeal. There is really no difference between the motions to rescind and to strike out something that has previously been adopted. They are both main motions and cannot be made when any motion is pending. They are debatable, the debate being on the merits of what it is proposed to rescind or strike out. The various subsidiary motions may be applied to them, the same as to other main motions. The rules relating to either motion apply to the other, as there is no difference between them except that the motion is generally called rescind when it applies to an entire rule or resolution, and is called amend or strike out when it applies to only a part. Thus, when the by-laws, as is usual, require notice and a two-thirds vote for their amendment, the same motion and vote is required to rescind them. To rescind, when notice is required, like to strike out a by-law, etc., cannot be amended so as to increase the amount to be rescinded or struck out.

A resolution or standing rule may be rescinded without notice by a vote of a majority of the entire membership, or by a two-thirds vote, that is, two thirds of those voting. If notice is given at the previous meeting, a mere majority vote is all that is necessary to rescind any resolution, order, or standing rule that has been previously adopted. These limitations are necessary in order to have stability in the actions of an assembly. If a bare majority could undo the action of the assembly at any time without any notice, it might prove very troublesome where the meetings are frequent and the quorum small. The majority of a quorum may not exceed five per cent. of the membership, and so small a number should not have the power to rescind action taken by the assembly unless notice has been given of the intention. When notice has been given, a majority of those who choose to attend and to vote should have the power to rescind a resolution or standing rule that required only a majority vote for its adoption, and was adopted without any previous notice.

Since an organization may rescind any resolution it has adopted, by a similar vote it may countermand or modify any action taken by its subordinates that it could countermand or modify if the action had been taken by the body itself, provided the resolution does not relate to a matter placed under the exclusive control of the subordinate body by the by-laws of the higher body. Thus a society may countermand any action taken by its board, and the board may countermand any action taken by the executive committee. Afterward the higher body may take any other action on the case that it deems advisable.

When a temporary majority takes some action that is evidently not approved by the majority of the society, a member in the opposition should vote with the majority and then move to reconsider the vote and have it entered on the minutes. This stops action in the matter until the next meeting on another day, thus giving an opportunity to notify absentees, so that at the next meeting the society may be fairly represented, at which time a majority will decide the question. Should no member who voted with the temporary majority be willing to move to reconsider the vote, then one of the opposition should give notice of a motion to rescind the resolution or action just taken, which motion will be made at the next meeting. This notice may be given while no one is speaking, even though another member is entitled to, or has, the floor. Any member may give this notice of the motion to rescind, regardless of how he voted. This notice does not require a second. At the next meeting, if the member who gave the notice fails to move to rescind the resolution or other action, any member may make the motion to rescind. Notice having been given, only a majority vote is required for its adoption. If no member has given previous notice of the motion to rescind the resolution, any member may make the motion. If this motion is adopted by a two-thirds vote, or by a vote of a majority of the membership, the resolution is rescinded. If the motion fails, but seems sufficiently popular to warrant it, then notice should be given of the motion to rescind as just described, and at the next meeting the resolution may be rescinded by a majority.

The motion to reconsider should be used in preference to rescind whenever possible, since the mere making of the motion to reconsider instantly stops all proceedings under the motion to be reconsidered, and it requires only a majority vote for its adoption. But on account of this the motion to reconsider must be made by one who voted with the prevailing side, and it must be seconded even when it is to be entered on the minutes to be called up at the next meeting; and it can be made only on the day, or the next day after, the vote was taken that it is proposed to reconsider. But, even so, whenever the motion to reconsider can be made it should be given the preference.

In an assembly where most of the members are present at the meetings, as a convention of delegates, for instance, the motion to rescind may be used more conveniently, because in such a meeting there is but little difference between a vote of a majority of the membership and a majority vote, and the motion to rescind anything except the constitution or by-laws or rules of order may be adopted by a vote of the majority of the membership without giving any previous notice. In an ordinary society it is usually impracticable to secure even the attendance of a majority of the membership, much more so to obtain so large a vote in favor of rescinding a proposition.

An assembly cannot rescind a resolution or any vote under which action has been taken that cannot be undone by the assembly. For instance, if a bill has been approved and has been paid, it is too late to rescind the order of approval. If any action of the nature of a contract has been taken and the other party has been informed thereof, it cannot be rescinded. Thus an election to membership, or to office, cannot be rescinded after the elected party knows of the election, although by amending the by-laws the term of office may be changed or the office done away with. So acceptance of resignations or expulsion from membership or office cannot be rescinded, provided the party involved was present or has learned of the action. The unexecuted part of an order or resolution may be rescinded. For example, when an order has been adopted requiring nominations and the election to be by ballot, and the nominating ballot has been taken, and it is desired to make it the electing ballot, it is out of order to make such a motion or to move to reconsider or to rescind the order or resolution. But it is in order to move to rescind the unexecuted portion of the order, and if that is adopted the motion can be made to declare the nominating ballot to be the electing ballot. This would, however, be out of order if the by-laws required the election to be by ballot.

In a few extreme cases it has been voted to rescind a certain resolution and expunge it from the record. This is intended to be a very strong expression of disapproval of the resolution. Such a motion, to deface the records, requires a vote of the majority of the entire membership, and it is doubtful if even that vote is sufficient to authorize such action. If such a motion is carried, the secretary, in the presence of the assembly, encircles the record of the adoption of the resolution and writes in ink across it, "Rescinded and Ordered Expunged ——" [entering the date of its being rescinded and signing the entry officially]. Nothing in the record can be obliterated or cut out, because if done it might be impossible to determine whether something else has been blotted or cut out. As the record remains so it can be read, there would seem to be nothing to justify the action of expunging it. Nothing is accomplished more than would be done by rescinding the resolution and adopting a resolution strongly condemning the action taken.

RENEWAL OF A MOTION
[Read in connection with this page 86.]

As has been explained on page 79, a question that has been decided by the assembly cannot, as a general rule, be introduced again during the same session. In cases where members have changed their opinions, or the assembly has been largely increased by the entrance of members opposed to the action taken, the question may be brought again before the assembly by one of the motions, to reconsider, to amend, or to rescind. With many of the secondary motions a slight progress in the business, or even in the debate, changes the condition of the business so as to justify the renewal of the secondary motion that has just been rejected. The fact that the assembly declined to adjourn before the vote was taken on a certain question does not show that it would not adjourn immediately after that vote was taken. The conditions under which the various motions may be renewed are as follows:

A motion that is withdrawn is treated as if it had never been made, because the assembly has not expressed its opinion upon it, and therefore it can be renewed.

As long as the vote on a motion may be reconsidered, that motion cannot be renewed. And if, in an ordinary society, a main motion is adopted, rejected, or postponed indefinitely, and a motion is made to reconsider the vote, and then the question is laid on the table or postponed to the next session, the main motion cannot again be introduced until after the close of the next session, because it will either come up at that session as a postponed question, or it may be taken from the table. In an organization having meetings only annually or semiannually, like national and state societies, a motion laid on the table stays there during that session only, so that it may be renewed at the next session.

If a main motion has been adopted, rejected, or postponed indefinitely, it cannot be renewed during the same session, but under certain circumstances the question may be brought before the assembly again as explained under Reconsider, page 82, Amend Something Already Adopted, page 85, and Rescind, page 84. At the next session, however, the main motion may be introduced again, if it failed, or it may be rescinded if it was adopted. If a series of resolutions is lost, any one or more of the series may again be offered at the same session, provided enough is omitted to make the new question so different from the former question that some of those who voted against the entire series may favor the new proposition.

The motion to postpone indefinitely cannot be renewed, because if it is lost the assembly will have another opportunity to vote on practically the same question when the vote is taken on the main question, the motion to postpone indefinitely being simply a motion to reject the main question.

The motion to amend cannot be renewed at the same session, but the vote on it may be reconsidered, and thus another opportunity obtained for discussion and action on the amendment, the same as if it had been renewed. After it is too late to reconsider the vote rejecting an amendment to the minutes, the amendment may be again moved, since it is never too late to correct the minutes. The same amendment to the constitution, by-laws, rules of order, or standing rules may again be renewed, but all the preliminary steps of notice, etc., are required as at first.

The motions to commit, to postpone to a certain time, for the previous question, and those limiting or extending the limits of debate, if lost, may be renewed after material progress in business or debate, so that the question put to the assembly is practically different from the one decided negatively before.

The motion to lay on the table may be renewed without any limitation, except that it cannot be made unless there has been such business transacted, or such progress in debate, since it was last made, that it is practically a new question whether the assembly under these circumstances will lay the main question aside temporarily; or unless something has arisen that is urgent and was not known by the assembly when it previously declined to lay the question on the table, as, for example, the arrival of a distinguished visitor whom it was desired to introduce to the assembly and invite to make a brief address.

The motion to take from the table may be renewed again and again, but not until the business that was taken up after it was lost when last made has been disposed of.

The motion to reconsider a question that has not been materially amended since the motion to reconsider was previously made, and an objection to the consideration of a question, cannot be renewed.

The motion to suspend the rules cannot be renewed for the same purpose during the same meeting, but it may be renewed at another meeting held the same day.

The motion to adjourn and to take a recess may be renewed without limitation, provided there has been business transacted or material progress in debate since they were last moved. The motions to adjourn, to take a recess, and to lay on the table made and lost do not constitute business that justifies the renewal of a motion.

The motion to fix the time to which to adjourn, that is, to fix a certain time for an adjourned meeting, cannot be renewed at the same meeting, but it may be reconsidered; or a motion may be made to fix a different time for an adjourned meeting.

A call for the orders of the day, if the assembly refuses to proceed to them, may be renewed, but not until after the disposal of the subject before the assembly at the time of the refusal.

If a question of privilege or a point of order is decided adversely by the chair, it cannot again be raised during the same session, unless upon appeal the decision is reversed.

If a decision of the chair is sustained upon appeal, no appeal involving the same principle can be made afterward during the same session.

CHAPTER XI

MOTIONS RELATING TO ADJOURNED MEETINGS AND TO ADJOURNMENT; FIX THE TIME TO WHICH TO ADJOURN; RECESS; QUESTIONS OF PRIVILEGE

MOTIONS RELATING TO ADJOURNED MEETINGS AND TO ADJOURNMENT

EXPERIENCE has shown that the best interests of the assembly require that the motions relating to appointing an adjourned meeting, to closing a meeting, and to taking a recess shall take the precedence of all other questions whatsoever, because otherwise the assembly might be prevented from appointing an adjourned meeting, or be kept in session indefinitely against its will. By giving these motions precedence over all others, it is impossible to keep an assembly in session many minutes beyond the time when adjournment is desired by the majority. A member having the floor cannot be interrupted for these motions without his consent. Sometimes the member having the floor yields it for one of these motions, with the understanding that when the sitting is resumed he will be entitled to the floor. If no arrangement of this kind can be made, it is necessary to wait until he yields the floor (he cannot hold it longer than ten minutes), and then, if the majority wishes to adjourn, it is more than an even chance that the first member to claim the floor will move to adjourn, or be willing to yield the floor for that motion. These motions cannot be made by members calling them out, either from their seats or when standing, unless they have been recognized by the chair as having the floor. When the motion to adjourn, for instance, has been made in this improper manner, and a member

117

afterward rises to claim the floor for debate or to make a motion, the chair is obliged to recognize him as entitled to the floor, because it is only by general consent that the motion to adjourn, or any other motion, can be recognized when made informally.

There are three motions in use relating to adjourning, which rank in the following order: (1) To Fix the Time to Which to Adjourn, that is, to fix the time for holding an adjourned meeting; (2) To Adjourn, that is, to close the meeting now; (3) To Take a Recess, that is, an intermission. They are undebatable because of the fact that their high rank allows them to interrupt all other questions, which would greatly hinder business if they were debatable. High rank is incompatible with debate, but where the dignity or rights of the assembly or of a member are involved, or the enforcement of an order of business previously adopted by the assembly is concerned, though they are privileged questions ranking only after those relating to adjourning, their undebatability lasts only until it is decided whether they will be permitted to interrupt pending business. After the question of privilege or the order of the day is actually before the assembly, it is debatable.

The motions to fix the time for an adjourned meeting and to take a recess, if made when no business is pending, are main motions without any privilege. So also the motion to adjourn is a main motion if made in an assembly that has made no provision for a future meeting, or that has already appointed a time for adjournment.

Fix the Time to Which to Adjourn

When, in an assembly that has made no provision for an adjourned meeting, it is desired to hold such a meeting, a motion like this should be made: "That, when the assembly adjourns, it adjourns [or, stands adjourned] to 8 p. m. next Thursday"; or, "That, when we adjourn, we adjourn to meet to-morrow night at eight o'clock in this hall." If the assembly has no fixed place for meeting, this motion should include the place as well as the time for the adjourned meeting.

It is preferable to make this motion when no other business is pending, in which case it is simply a main motion that can be debated and amended and have applied to it any of the subsidiary motions. In some cases it is desirable to refer the motion to a committee to recommend a time and place for an adjourned meeting. But it sometimes happens that, after the advisability of holding an adjourned meeting has become apparent, there is no opportunity for introducing a main motion, and then this highest of all privileged motions is the only recourse. A member having the floor cannot be interrupted by this motion. If the one wishing to make it fails to obtain the floor, he can usually secure the consent of the member who is assigned the floor, before he has commenced speaking, to yield the floor to him for a moment to make the motion fixing the time for an adjourned meeting. If there is no other opportunity to make his motion, he can do it even after the assembly has voted to adjourn, provided the chair has not declared it adjourned; but it should not be deferred until the motion to adjourn is made, if this can be avoided. It cannot be made during the voting. There is no way to prevent the motion's being made, and therefore there is no necessity for its unduly interfering with business.

This is the highest of the privileged motions, taking precedence of all others if made while other business is pending in an assembly that has made no provision for another meeting on the same or the next day. Under all other circumstances it is a main motion. When referred to, the privileged motion is always meant, unless the contrary is stated. When privileged, it is undebatable. It may be amended as to time and place, and these amendments are undebatable. No other subsidiary motion can be applied to it when it is a privileged motion, except that the previous question may be ordered to prevent amendments from being moved, though it is seldom that anything would be gained thereby. The motion to fix the same time cannot be renewed at the same meeting, but it may be reconsidered. Sometimes this motion, instead of specifying the time for the adjourned meeting, provides for the assembly's being called together again by the chair or by a committee, thus: "That when we adjourn we adjourn to meet at the call of the chair." The essential thing in this motion is that it shall provide for the next meeting.

Every permanent organization should provide in its by-laws for its regular meetings, and also for a method of calling special meetings. Conventions and other bodies holding sessions lasting several days should adopt a program, or order of business, or order of exercises, as it is variously called. By doing this the use of this motion in such organizations is avoided, except when it becomes desirable to hold an adjourned meeting of one of the regular or special sessions, as in the case of an annual meeting for the election of officers, etc., when the assembly is unable to complete the work assigned by the by-laws to the annual meeting.

The motion "to fix the time *to* which to adjourn" is a very different motion from one "to fix the time *at* which to adjourn." The former motion fixes the time for holding an adjourned meeting, whereas the latter motion fixes the time for closing the present meeting, and is always a main motion. A motion appointing the time and place for holding the next annual convention in a state or national organization is not the same as this motion to fix the time to which to adjourn. The former appoints a time and place for a meeting provided for by the by-laws, which meeting is an independent session and not an adjournment of the present meeting. The absolute necessity for the convention's deciding the question makes the motion fixing the time and place for the next convention a question of privilege [see page 126], which outranks all motions except these three relating to an adjourned meeting, adjournment, and recess.

ADJOURN

[Before reading this, read pages 117, 118.]

When it is desired to close a meeting,[1] the proper motion to make is "to adjourn." This word strictly means "to another day," but it is used now as the equivalent of "to close the meeting now," and has nothing to do with whether the assembly meets again on another day, or on the same day, or never meets again. The question of the time when the assembly shall meet again should be decided before the motion to adjourn is made, though, as has been previously stated, it may be done even after it is voted to adjourn, provided the motion to fix the time to which to adjourn is made before the assembly has been declared adjourned.

Whenever the effect of its adoption is to dissolve the assembly, the motion to adjourn is a main motion that may be debated, amended, or referred to a committee, or have any other subsidiary motion applied to it. This is the case in a mass meeting until some provision is made for an adjourned meeting or for calling

[1] For difference between Meeting and Session, see page 358.

another meeting. The motion to adjourn is also a main motion without privilege in a convention of delegates, before the adoption of any program and provision for holding another meeting; and during the last meeting provided for by the program, since its adoption in either case would dissolve the assembly. Usually in such cases the motion is made to "adjourn sine die,"[1] or "without day," which means to dissolve the assembly. Whatever form the motion has, if it is adopted and its effect is to dissolve the assembly, the chair, after announcing the vote, should declare the assembly "adjourned without day," or "sine die."

If a time has been appointed for the adjournment of the meeting by adopting a motion to that effect, or a program or order of business, or if the by-laws fix the hour for adjournment, the motion to adjourn is not a privileged motion. In such a case high privilege would probably prove more of an annoyance than a benefit. If the motion to adjourn is qualified in any way it loses its privileged character. Thus, "to adjourn to 2 P. M. Tuesday" and "to adjourn without day" are main motions.

Every permanent society with meetings as often as quarterly has by-laws that provide for future meetings, and usually there is no fixed hour for adjournment, so that the motion to adjourn in such societies is always a privileged motion. In boards and committees future meetings are provided for, or they can be called by the chairman, and there is no fixed hour for adjournment, so that to adjourn is always a privileged motion in boards and committees. Unless specified to the contrary, whenever this motion is referred to, the privileged motion to adjourn is meant.

The privileged motion to adjourn takes precedence of every other motion except to fix the time to which to adjourn, to which it yields. It cannot be made when another member has the floor, or during a division, or while verifying a vote. It is undebatable and cannot be amended or have any other subsidiary motion applied to it. While the motion to adjourn is undebatable, it does not mean that there should not be a brief conference after it has been made, when, in the opinion of the chair, the interests of the assembly are conserved thereby. In meetings, such as conventions, holding sessions lasting for days, there are usually notices to be given before the close of each meeting, and the chair should not put the question on adjourning, or taking a recess,

[1] Pronounced sī-nē dī-ē.

until he has given an opportunity for announcing all such notices. There may be important business that should be attended to before adjourning, in which case it should be stated, and a request made that the motion to adjourn be withdrawn. If it is not withdrawn it must be put to vote, and it will probably be voted down, as the importance of not adjourning has been stated. Such remarks and requests are not debate, and the chair has the power and the duty to keep them within proper limits, and to allow only such as the interests of the assembly demand. These remarks apply especially to annual meetings of societies whose by-laws prescribe that certain things must be done at these meetings, and that certain other things cannot be done at any other meetings. In such meetings care must be exercised not to adjourn until all the business has been attended to, or an adjourned meeting has been provided for.

On account of the right of any member to demand a division of the assembly on any vote, that is, that a rising vote shall be taken, the chair must be careful not to declare the assembly adjourned until a reasonable opportunity has been afforded for a division to be called for. All votes are usually taken by voice (viva voce),[1] or by show of hands, without counting. But if a single member, without even rising, calls for a division, it is necessary to take a standing vote, and a majority may require the vote to be counted, in which case the number voting on each side is entered in the minutes. In order to afford time for this, unless there is a decided majority on one side, the chair should announce the vote on an adjournment in this form: "The ayes seem [or appear] to have it; the ayes have it; the motion is carried [or adopted], and we stand [or, the assembly stands] adjourned [or, adjourned to two o'clock to-morrow afternoon]."

When the adjournment closes the session so that the next meeting will be at the time of the next regular session as appointed by the by-laws, the chair simply declares the assembly adjourned, without saying anything about the next meeting. If an adjourned meeting has been provided for, he should always state the time to which the assembly stands adjourned. If the adjournment dissolves the assembly, as in case of the final adjournment of a convention, or a mass meeting with no provision for a future meeting, he should declare the assembly "adjourned without day."

[1] Pronounced vī-va vō-sē.

If, immediately after declaring the assembly adjourned, the chair learns that a member had risen to move a reconsideration and had addressed the chair before the adjournment was declared, it is his duty to ignore the declaration of adjournment and to call the assembly to order at once and state the facts and allow the motion to reconsider to be made. He then announces the motion to reconsider, and proceeds according to the motion it is proposed to reconsider, the same as if the motion to reconsider had been made before he had declared the adjournment. A similar course should be pursued whenever the chair declares an adjournment without recognizing a member who was entitled to give a notice or make a motion that is in order after the assembly has voted to adjourn.

The motion to adjourn cannot be reconsidered, but if lost it may be renewed again and again, provided there has been material progress in debate or business since it was last made. On account of this, like the motion to lay on the table, it may be used for obstructive purposes unless the chair prevents it, as explained under Dilatory Motions, page 177.

Effect of an Adjournment upon Unfinished Business. The effect of an adjournment upon the pending business depends upon whether or not it closes a session of the assembly.

(1) If it does not close the session, business is resumed at the next meeting where it was interrupted, just as if there had been no adjournment. Such business is, however, subject to any rules, program, or order of business that may have been adopted.

(2) If it closes a session of an assembly that does not meet regularly as often as quarterly, all pending business falls with the adjournment, and if taken up at the next session it must be introduced anew. Annual conventions of national and state organizations fall under this rule. The objections to allowing business to go over for six months or a year surpass the advantages. [See Session, page 358.]

(3) If the adjournment closes a session of an assembly having regular meetings as frequently as quarterly, the unfinished business goes over to the next meeting, and it is taken up under its proper heads as prescribed by the adopted order of business. This is the case with ordinary clubs and societies having regular meetings once a month or oftener. The business of Standing Committees and Boards also falls under this rule.

(4) If the body is an elected or appointed one, as a board of managers, and the term of office of a certain portion of the members has expired and new members have been appointed or elected since the adjournment, then the adjournment puts an end to unfinished business, which, if taken up at the next meeting, must be introduced anew.

In committees, except committees of the whole, the motion to adjourn is used just as in the assembly, except that, when a special committee has completed its business and finally adjourns, it is better form to vote to "rise," which is equivalent to the motion to adjourn without day and is therefore a main motion. A committee of the whole cannot adjourn to another time: it can only "rise and report." Where a committee adjourns without having appointed a time for its next meeting, the adjournment in effect is at the call of the chairman of the committee, as he can at any time call a meeting of the committee. The motion "to adjourn at the call of the chair" is therefore never made in committee.

RECESS

[Before reading this, read pages 117, 118.]

An intermission during a day's proceedings of a deliberative assembly is called a recess. Recesses are often taken for meals, and while the ballots are being counted in an annual election. When the session lasts for several consecutive days, as with an annual convention, and an adjournment is taken over to the day after the next, for instance, then the convention is said to take a recess until that day. If, however, a society has regular meetings, say weekly, lasting usually for a day or a part thereof, and a meeting is adjourned to meet in a day or two, the interval between the two meetings is not spoken of as a recess, but the second meeting is referred to as an adjournment of the first meeting, and the two meetings together constitute a single session.

A recess may occur (1) from having adopted a program or order of business providing intermissions for meals, or other purposes; (2) or from having voted that when the assembly adjourns it adjourns to meet at a certain hour the same day, or, in case of a convention, on another day, in which case, when an adjournment is voted, the chair states that the assembly stands adjourned to that time; (3) or from having adopted a motion "to take a recess for —— minutes," or, "that a recess be taken until 2 P. M.," or, "that the assembly take a recess until ——."

In the first case, on the arrival of the time set for the adjournment the chair announces that the assembly stands adjourned, or in recess, until such and such an hour. If a member is speaking at the time, the chair may at his discretion permit the speech to be finished, unless some one calls for the orders of the day. He may take a vote on proceeding to the orders of the day, that is, carrying out the program, or, if no objection is made, he may at once declare the assembly adjourned until the specified hour. Like any other order of the day, when the time arrives the assembly may by a two-thirds vote decline to enforce it immediately. In the second case, since only the time for holding the adjourned meeting has been determined, the chair waits until the assembly votes to adjourn, and then states that the assembly stands adjourned to the specified time. In the third case, as soon as it is voted to take a recess, the chair announces that the assembly stands in recess, or adjourned, to the specified hour. In all cases of recess, whether they arise from the motion to take a recess or not, the chair should announce the time at which the assembly is to reconvene, and when that hour has arrived the chair calls the assembly to order and the business proceeds the same as if there had been no intermission, except in cases where the program or order of business provides otherwise.

The motion to take a recess for a specified time takes effect immediately upon its adoption. If made while other business is pending, it is a privileged motion taking precedence of all others except the motions to fix the time to which to adjourn, and to adjourn, to which it yields. It may be amended as to the time, but no other subsidiary motion can be applied to it, except that the previous question can be applied to it in order to prevent motions to amend, though in ordinary societies this is useless. It is undebatable. It cannot be reconsidered, for if the motion for a recess is carried the assembly is not in session until the recess is over, and if the motion is lost it may be renewed after there has been sufficient progress in debate or business to make it a new question.

Take a Recess as a Main Motion. The motion to take a recess, if made when no question is pending, is a main motion subject to debate, amendment, etc., the same as any other main motion. The motion to take a recess at a future time is always a main motion without any privilege.

QUESTIONS OF PRIVILEGE

As a general rule, when a question is under consideration by the assembly no new question can be introduced until the other one is in some way disposed of. While a subject is pending the motions in order relate either to the disposal of that question, or to adjournment, or to the enforcement of the rules, or are in some way incidental to the pending business. But at times there arise questions that affect the rights and privileges of the assembly or of a member, and that require immediate attention. Experience has resulted in establishing the parliamentary principle that such questions, called Questions of Privilege, shall take precedence of all other questions except those relating to an adjourned meeting, or to adjournment, or to a recess.

Questions of Privilege must not be confused with Privileged Questions, which latter include motions to fix the time for an adjourned meeting, to adjourn, to take a recess, to raise a question of privilege, and to call for the orders of the day. Questions of privilege are divided into questions affecting or relating to the privileges of the assembly, and questions of personal privilege. If the two classes of questions come into competition, a question affecting the privileges of the assembly outranks a question of personal privilege.

Questions of privilege relating to the assembly are like the following: questions relating to the organization or existence of the assembly; or to the comfort of its members, as the heating, lighting, ventilation, of the hall, and freedom from noise and other disturbance; or to the conduct of its officers or employees; or to the punishment of a member for disorderly conduct or other offense; or to the conduct of reporters for the press, or to the accuracy of published reports of proceedings.

Questions of personal privilege are such as relate to the individual as a member of the assembly, as, for instance, charges that have been circulated against his character that if true would disqualify him from membership, or the case of a member's learning, after minutes have been approved, that he is credited with offering a resolution to which he is bitterly opposed. He can rise to a question of personal privilege and insist that the error in the minutes be corrected. He cannot rise to a question of personal privilege in order to correct a speaker's incorrect statement of his views or argument, or to request information, etc. Such incidental matters are attended to by requests for permission to correct the speaker, or by requests for information, or by raising points of order. In ordinary societies it is very seldom that a question of personal privilege can arise.

When a question of privilege arises, the member desiring to bring it before the assembly should preferably choose a time when no other business is before the assembly. If there is no such opportunity, he should wait until a member yields the floor, and then rise and address the chair, and as soon as he attracts the chairman's attention, without waiting for recognition, he should say, "I rise to a question of privilege." The chair, though he has assigned the floor to another member, should at once direct him to state his question, which he does, and the chair decides whether or not it is a question of privilege. From this decision any two members may appeal. The decision and the appeal are undebatable. If the question is decided to be one of privilege, the chair immediately assigns the floor to the member who raised the question, even though he has previously recognized another as having the floor. The latter member should resume his seat. The question that was pending is now laid aside until the question of privilege is disposed of, after which the consideration of the former is resumed, the chair assigning the floor to the member who was entitled to it when the question was interrupted by the question of privilege. The privileged matter may be disposed of without any motion, or it may be necessary to make a suitable motion.

When this privileged motion has been made and the question stated by the chair, it is treated exactly like any other main motion, its privilege extending only to giving it the right to interrupt any question except the privileged motions relating to an adjourned meeting, adjournment, or recess, and it cannot be interrupted by the orders of the day. Therefore it is debatable, and it may be amended and have any other subsidiary motion applied to it, and it yields to the motions relating to an adjourned meeting, or to a recess, and to incidental motions. It is like any main motion in regard to reconsideration and renewal.

If the case is one of exceeding urgency it may interrupt a

member even while speaking, as, for instance, when street doors have been opened, exposing the rear of the hall to so much noise that the members sitting there cannot hear the discussion. When the question is not so urgent the chair should not allow it to interrupt a member while he is speaking. If a member attempts such an interruption, the chair may recognize the question as one of privilege, but not of such urgency as to justify its interrupting a member's speech. In such a case, as soon as the speech is finished the chair recognizes the member who raised the question of privilege. The following is a case of this kind: Suppose a member were to claim as a question of privilege the right to interrupt another member while speaking, in order to introduce a motion requiring that a certain reporter withdraw from the assembly hall and that he be refused admission to the hall until he offers an apology to the assembly and promises to retract in his paper the false statements he has published in regard to the proceedings of the previous day. The chair, in such a case, should recognize it as a question of privilege that would be in order as soon as the member has finished speaking, but not of such urgency as to justify interrupting a member while speaking. As soon as the floor is vacant, the chair should recognize the member to raise his question of privilege.

CHAPTER XII

MOTIONS RELATING TO THE ORDER OF BUSINESS

THE various motions relating to the order of business can be most readily understood by treating them together. The expressions Order of Business and Orders of the Day are frequently synonymous, but the order of business laid down in the by-laws or rules of order should usually be referred to as such, and not as the orders of the day. The order of business for any particular meeting, which is the prescribed order, modified perhaps by having special orders and general orders made for that meeting, is known as the "orders of the day." If it is desired to transact business out of its proper order, it may be done by a two-thirds vote, as described at the close of this chapter.

CALL FOR THE ORDERS OF THE DAY

Whenever the prescribed order of business is deviated from, instead of raising a question of order, a member "calls for the orders of the day," which means that he demands that the orders of the day be complied with, that is, that the next subject in the order of business be taken up. As a single member, while another has the floor and is speaking, has a right, without recognition by the chair and without a second, to raise a question of order or to demand that the rules be enforced, so a single member, while another has the floor, has a right, without recognition and without a second, to call for the orders of the day. As a point of order must be raised at the time the rules are violated, and is undebatable, so the orders of the day must be called for at the time they are deviated from (except in case of a special order) and the call is undebatable. If a new question is permitted to be introduced and the debate has begun, it is too late to call for the orders of the day until that question has been disposed of, unless the hour has arrived for which a special order has been assigned. The objector must rise as soon as the new subject is introduced, regardless of the fact that another has the floor, and say, "Mr. Chairman." As soon as he attracts the chair's attention he adds, "I call for the orders of the day," or, "I demand the regular order." The chair should then immediately say, "The orders of the day are called for [or, The regular order is demanded]. As many as are in favor of proceeding to the orders of the day, say 'Aye.' Those opposed, say 'No.' " If the negative side is less than two thirds the chair says, "There being less than two thirds in the negative, the ayes have it and the orders of the day will be proceeded with." He then announces the next subject in the order of business. If there is a two-thirds vote in the negative the vote is announced thus: "There being two thirds in the negative, the noes have it and the orders of the day will not be taken up. The question is on the resolution," etc. [stating the question that was interrupted by the call for the orders of the day]. A two-thirds vote in the negative is required to prevent the orders of the day from being enforced, because such action is a suspension of the rules. Instead of taking a vote on proceeding to the orders of the day, the chairman may rule the new motion out of order and announce the next business in order. In this case the new motion can be introduced at that time only by suspending the rules, as explained on page 156. [See Illustrations at the close of this chapter.]

ORDER OF BUSINESS

Every deliberative assembly, except a mass meeting for a special purpose, should have some plan, or program, or order of business, so as to insure an opportunity for the consideration of the most important business. If there is no order in which business must be transacted, the member who first obtains the floor has the right to introduce any resolution he pleases, provided it relates to matters with which the society is concerned and comes within the rules of propriety as laid down under Dilatory and Improper Motions, page 177. An ordinary society with meetings weekly, fortnightly, or monthly, lasting only an hour or two, is sufficiently protected by adopting an order of business that merely prescribes the order in which the different classes of subjects shall be considered, without specifying the time allotted to each. The meetings are so frequent and short that it would be a hindrance to allot the same amount of time at each meeting to each class of subjects. At one meeting a committee's report might occupy the entire time, while at the next meeting there might be no report from any committee.

The better way, usually, for such societies is to prescribe only the order in which the business shall be transacted, leaving the amount of time to be devoted to each subject and class of subjects to those who attend the meeting. The order that experience has shown to be the best in organizations with regular meetings as often as quarterly is as follows:

(1) "Reading the minutes of the preceding meeting, and their approval." Occasionally, owing to the absence of the secretary or to some other cause, this is neglected, in which case the minutes of all the meetings that have not been approved should be read at the opening of the next meeting. They should be read and approved separately in the order of the dates of the meetings. When there is more than one meeting in the day, the minutes are read only at the opening of the first meeting of each day.

(2) After the minutes of the preceding meeting or meetings have been read, the first business to be attended to is the "Reports of Officers, Boards, and Standing Committees of the society." If they have any reports to make to the society, such reports should certainly be heard in preference to any proposition coming from one who is only a member of the assembly.

(3) If a matter has been referred to a special committee which is now ready to report, an opportunity should be given the committee at this time. Hence the next class of subjects in the order of business should be "Reports of Special Committees."

(4) Sometimes there is a very important subject that the assembly wishes to consider at the next meeting in preference to everything except the minutes and reports of committees. In such a case it should be postponed to the next meeting and made a special order. Accordingly, after committees' reports are disposed of, the first order of business is "Special Orders." If there is

more than one special order, the one first made is taken up first. If a special order was pending at the adjournment of the previous meeting, it precedes the others.

(5) After the minutes, the reports of officers and committees, and special orders have been disposed of, the business that was undisposed of at the previous meeting should be taken up at the point where the adjournment interrupted it. If any question, except a special order, was actually pending at the time of adjournment, its consideration is resumed. When it is disposed of, the general orders for the previous session that were not reached are taken up in their proper order, and then the questions that were postponed to this meeting. These postponed questions, or general orders, as they are called, are taken up in the order in which they were made. It will be seen, then, that it is necessary to dispose also of "Unfinished Business and General Orders" before any new business can be introduced.

(6) The meeting is now open to "New Business." If some new business is of great importance, or if for some other reason it is desired to consider it earlier in the meeting, it can be done by general consent or by suspending the rules by a two-thirds vote. In the same way, any item of business may be taken up out of its proper order. In other words, the order of business is conformed to unless at least two thirds of those who vote wish to deviate from it. Usually, however, it is not necessary to have a formal vote, since in such cases it is arranged informally by general consent.

The order of business stated above is the most natural one, and is the customary one in societies with regular meetings as frequent as quarterly. It may be summarized thus:

Order of Business.

(1) Reading and Approval of Minutes.
(2) Reports of Officers, Boards, and Standing Committees.
(3) Reports of Special (Select) Committees.
(4) Special Orders.
(5) Unfinished Business and General Orders.
(6) New Business.

In societies with sessions lasting only a few hours the above order of business will suffice until experience has shown how it may be improved for the particular society. If it is desired to modify it, a suitable order of business should be prepared and adopted, just as rules of order are adopted. It may be modified for any meeting by making a question *the* special order for that meeting, or a special order for a certain hour, as explained hereafter, or by suspending the rules and taking up a question out of its proper order. These motions are undebatable, and, since they interfere with the established order, require a two-thirds vote for their adoption.

ORDERS OF THE DAY

The order of business adopted by the society as modified by the making of special orders for the meeting, or postponing questions to the meeting, constitutes the Orders of the Day for that meeting. These orders are divided, according to their importance, into General Orders and Special Orders. The distinction between them is that, as a rule, a general order cannot interrupt pending business, and therefore can be made by a majority vote; while a special order, when the hour appointed for it arrives, can interrupt pending business, and therefore can be made only by a two-thirds vote.

General Orders comprise all the subjects designated in the order of business for which no hour is designated, and also all questions postponed to the meeting, even though they have been postponed to a designated hour, provided they were not made special orders. In an ordinary society, with sessions lasting only one or two hours, nothing is accomplished by designating the hour to which a question is postponed, except to prevent its being taken up before that hour unless the rules are suspended by a two-thirds vote. The postponed question cannot be taken up at the designated hour unless everything in the order of business before general orders has been disposed of. The reason for this is that it requires only a majority vote to postpone a question to a designated time, and a bare majority cannot change the order of business that has previously been adopted. If it is desired to have the question considered at a certain time, regardless of the regular order of business, then it is necessary that the question be made a special order for that time, which requires a two-thirds vote, as explained farther on.

Even if general orders have been announced and the designated hour has arrived, the question postponed to that hour cannot be taken up until all questions that were previously postponed have been disposed of, because general orders rank in the order in which they were made, the question first postponed being taken up as soon as general orders are announced. In no case, however, should a general order be taken up before the time for which it was made. The chair should announce the general orders in their proper order, and if he should fail to do so any one can call for the orders of the day, as already explained.

In a convention lasting several days there is usually some time allowed every day for miscellaneous business, during which postponed questions should be taken up before new questions are allowed. The chair should announce these questions in the order in which the votes were taken on postponing them. If the hour is designated for considering a question, another one may afterward be postponed to an earlier hour. Suppose a question is postponed to 4 P. M., and later another question is postponed to 3.45 P. M. Now, if the latter question is taken up before 4 P. M. and is not disposed of at that hour, it cannot be interrupted by the other question. It is not proper to call for the orders of the day when 4 P. M. arrives, because general orders can never interrupt a pending question. It would not be proper to postpone a question to so short a time before the hour to which another question had been previously postponed that it will manifestly interfere with the previous order. But if two thirds of the assembly wish a question to be postponed and to have the precedence over one already postponed, they can accomplish it by making the preferred motion a special order.

In the case mentioned above, if the question postponed to 3.45 P. M. has not been taken up when 4 P. M. arrives, it cannot then be taken up until the one postponed to 4 P. M. has been disposed of, because the latter was postponed first. The principles governing all such cases are these: (1) General orders cannot interrupt a question after it has been stated by the chair. (2) General orders made at the same time rank in the order in which they are arranged in the motion making the order. (3) General orders made at different times rank in the order in which they were made, provided that no order is taken up before the time to which it was postponed.

A Special Order is a resolution, report, or other main motion, or other matter that has been assigned to a certain meeting, or hour of that meeting, with the high privilege of having the right to be considered at the time specified, even though it interrupts another question, or conflicts with some rule of the assembly. It cannot be taken up before the designated time, except by a two-thirds vote.

A special order may be fixed for a certain hour; or after a certain event, as an address; or it may be a special order for a meeting; or it may be *the* special order for a meeting. In the first two cases, when the designated time arrives, the special order can interrupt any question except a special order that was made before it was made, or a question of privilege, or a question relating to adjournment or recess. When a question is made a special order after an event, it follows the event immediately, and is treated precisely as if it had been made for an hour that had arrived. When the question has been made a special order for a meeting that has an order of business that provides for special orders or for orders of the day, it cannot be called up earlier than the order of business provides, unless the rules are suspended. But if there is no provision for special orders or orders of the day in the order of business, then any one may call for the orders of the day at any time after the disposal of the minutes. If several special orders are made for the same time, they take precedence in the order in which they were made, the first having the preference. If the question has been made *the* special order for a meeting, it is announced as the pending business immediately after the disposal of the minutes of the previous meeting.

To Make a Special Order. Making a special order suspends the rules that would interfere with its consideration at the designated time, and therefore requires a two-thirds vote. The motion to make a special order is debatable and may be amended by a majority vote. A special order may be made in any of the three ways following: (1) by adopting a motion postponing the pending question to a certain time and making it a special order; or (2) by introducing a question and moving that it be made a special order for a certain time; or (3) by adopting a program specifying the hour when certain subjects shall be taken up.

(1) In the first case, the motion is a form of the motion to postpone, and may be made thus: "I move to postpone the question and make it a special order for the next meeting [or, for 9 P. M. at the next meeting]"; or, "I move to postpone the question and make it *the* special order for the next meeting." The latter form is used only when it is desired to devote the entire meeting, or as much of it as is required, to the consideration of the special order.

(2) When the question is not pending, the motion to make it a special order is a main motion, and can be made only when nothing is before the assembly. If it is desired to make a resolution a special order, the motion may be made in a form similar to this: "I move that the following resolution be made the special order for 4 P. M. at the next meeting: 'Resolved, ——' " [reading the resolution]. If this motion is adopted by a two-thirds vote, the effect is to postpone the question and make it a special order for the time specified. If it is a committee's report which has not yet been made, the motion could be made thus: "I move that the report of the committee on revision of the by-laws be made the special order for the next meeting." While this is a main motion, it requires a two-thirds vote for its adoption, just as any other motion to make a special order, and for the same reason, namely, that it suspends all rules that may interfere with its consideration at the designated time.

(3) The third method of making special orders is by adopting a program for a meeting, designating the hour when each topic shall be considered. This is very common in conventions lasting several days. The program is prepared usually by a committee, and when submitted is, like other reports, a main question, open to debate and amendment. Although there is no statement to that effect, yet the form of the program implies, as explained under Program in this chapter, that each question will be disposed of before the hour arrives for taking up the next subject. When special orders are made by either of the other methods, there is no implication as to any limit of time for their consideration.

When special orders that were made at different times come into conflict, they take precedence in the order in which they were made, the one first made outranking those made afterward. If they were made at the same time and for the same hour, they take rank in the order in which they are arranged. If they were made at the same time and for different hours, as a program for a convention, each subject has the preference at the hour fixed for its consideration, and can then interrupt the pending question, even though that question is a special order, since such a program implies that the time for each topic is limited to the time before that appointed for the next subject. Suppose, for instance, that special orders have been made for 3.45 and for 4 P. M., and that when four o'clock arrives the special order for 3.45 has not been disposed of: if the special order for 4 P. M. was made after the order for 3.45 was made, it cannot interrupt the pending question, but must wait until the earlier special order is disposed of; if, however, the special order for 4 P. M. was made before, or at the same time as, the 3.45 special order was made, when 4 P. M. arrives the special order for that hour must be announced, thus interrupting the pending business. As soon as the interrupting question is disposed of, the consideration of the interrupted one is resumed, provided the hour has not arrived for the consideration of another special order that was made before or at the same time that the interrupted one was made. The principle is that when a special order is made it cannot interfere with one already made, nor be interfered with by one that is made afterward. If it is desired to do this, it is necessary first to reconsider the vote creating the special order that is to be interfered with.

It does not interfere with a special order made for 5 P. M. to make one for 4 P. M. afterward, for if the latter is still pending at 5 P. M. it is necessary only to call for the orders of the day to bring before the assembly immediately the question as to whether the assembly will proceed to the orders of the day, that is, take up the special orders for 5 P. M. If the question is decided in the negative by a two-thirds vote, the orders of the day cannot again be called for until the pending question is disposed of.

Program, or Order of Business, for a Convention with Designated Hours for Each Subject. In conventions lasting an entire day or several days, an order of business like the one described on page 132 would prove unsatisfactory. It is necessary to designate not only all the subjects, or class of subjects, that must be attended to, and the order in which they are to be considered, but also the day and in most cases the hour when each important question is to be taken up, and the hours for opening and closing each meeting. This program should cover the entire session of the convention. Sometimes speakers are selected for the opening addresses on certain topics which are afterward open to discussion, in which each member is limited to one speech of one or two minutes, as designated in the program. Sometimes distinguished speakers, not members of the convention, are invited to deliver addresses. Usually the program is so crowded that the slightest deviation from it is unfair to the succeeding speaker or subject, and to the members who have come especially to hear the speaker or the discussion assigned to that hour. The assembly has the power by a two-thirds vote to extend the time of a speaker or subject, but it is rarely expedient to do it when it interferes with the subject that follows. If the program is disarranged at one point it is usually very difficult to avoid many other changes.

Program Committee. The success of a convention is largely dependent upon its program being properly prepared and advertised. As this must be done before the opening of the session, it is necessary that a strong program committee be appointed at the previous convention, or by the president or the board or the executive committee at least three or four months before the session begins. When the program has been completed, the committee should have enough copies printed so as to have a sufficient number left for the use of the delegates at the convention after copies have been mailed to every constituent society. The constituent societies should be furnished with copies of the program some weeks previous to the convention, so as to stimulate interest in the meeting. This is especially important when there are to be addresses by distinguished speakers.

On account of the necessity for having the programs printed and distributed in advance, the committee must have the authority to decide upon a program, to engage speakers when that is thought advisable, and to determine the time for the various subjects to come before the convention. This enables members who cannot attend all of the meetings to make their arrangements to be present when the subjects in which they are specially interested are being considered. Generally the power to work out details is supposed to belong to the program committee without any provision being made for it in the by-laws. If this has not been established by custom, the by-laws should be so amended as to provide for it.

The program should be submitted to the convention at its first business meeting, and should be adopted. During the convention changes may be necessary or advisable. Speakers may fail, and there may be reasons that justify other changes in the program. All proposed changes should go to the program committee, which continues in existence until the convention adjourns sine die. It may report at any time, recommending changes upon which the assembly votes. A two-thirds vote or a vote of a majority of all the registered delegates is necessary to make a change in the program.

When a program or order of business is adopted, since it designates the hour for each subject, it is implied that the consideration of any subject is limited to the time previous to that appointed for taking up the next question, or, in other words, that the assembly has ordered debate closed before the arrival of the hour assigned to the next subject on the program. The chairman, therefore, should not wait for a call for the orders of the day, and if they are called for, he should usually not take a vote on proceeding to them, but when the hour arrives for the next subject he should announce the fact, even though it is necessary to interrupt a member while speaking. He immediately puts to vote all pending questions, if there are any. No amendment or debate is allowed, but the motions to commit, to postpone, and to lay on the table should be permitted, though without debate. Of course privileged and incidental motions are in order. If the majority wish more discussion on the question, final action on it may be deferred by the use of the subsidiary motions mentioned above, but the chair should not allow any more time to be consumed by these motions than is strictly necessary to ascertain whether the assembly wishes to defer action on the question. If the chair is satisfied that the vote fairly expresses the will of the assembly, dilatory motions and divisions should not be permitted.

When the chair announces the time for closing the discussion, any one may move that the time for considering the pending question be extended a certain number of minutes. Since this motion, if adopted, changes the order of the assembly, it requires a two-thirds vote. If the chair allows the discussion to extend beyond the allotted time, any one may call for the orders of the day, and the chair proceeds as just described.

When a speaker has been invited or appointed to speak for a certain time and he overruns his time, he should not be called to order, nor should the orders of the day be called for. It would be extremely discourteous to an invited speaker. Still, it is the duty of the presiding officer to enforce the rules, and when the speaker's time has expired the chair should immediately indicate it in as quiet a way as possible, as by tapping on a book with a pencil. A good method is to inform each speaker when he comes to the platform that a certain signal will be given one or two minutes, as agreed upon, before the expiration of his time, and that it will be repeated at the close of his time.

A similar case is likely to occur when several persons have

been invited to address a meeting, where addresses are limited as to the time to be occupied in their delivery. As in the previous case, the presiding officer should inform each speaker as to how he will be warned that his time has nearly expired. The chairman or, in large assemblies, the time-keeper should notice the time that each speaker begins, and give the warning signal at the proper time.

If, in either of these cases, when the time has expired the speaker is evidently closing his speech and will have finished in a moment, the chair should not interrupt him. Otherwise, after giving the signal for stopping, the chairman should rise and advance to the front of the platform, thus indicating to the speaker that the chairman wishes to speak. If this hint is not taken, the chairman must interrupt the speaker and say that the speaker's time has expired. Great tact is needed in such cases to avoid, as far as possible, hurting the feelings of the speaker, and at the same time to protect the other invited speakers from having their time infringed upon. No one should be invited to deliver an address, especially when others have also been invited to speak at the same meeting, without being informed as to the limit of time allowed him. Every invited speaker should consider that he is in honor bound not to interfere with the program of the meeting. Being the guest of the assembly, he should scrupulously refrain from causing embarrassment by interfering with the rights of other guests by unduly prolonging the meeting, or by forcing the presiding officer to intervene in order to protect the rights of others.

Program of a Meeting in an Assembly Not a Deliberative One. The program referred to in this article is the program or order of business of a deliberative assembly that designates the hours for taking up some or all of the business to come before it. The rules given do not apply to the program of a meeting that is social or literary, etc. Many societies devote the first part of the meeting to business and the rest, the greater part, to other exercises, for which latter part they have what is termed a program. The program is usually under charge of a committee, the society not interfering with it in any way. The committee fills vacancies in the program as they occur, without reporting to the society for approval. The society is not acting as a deliberative assembly in this social or literary part of the meeting, so that members cannot make motions, or call for the orders of the day, or raise questions of order, etc. Sometimes, however, during the non-business part of the meeting it seems advisable to transact some business that has been neglected. The chairman, in such cases, states the facts and either awaits a motion or puts the question on his own responsibility. If it is a member who thinks of the neglected matter, he should privately call the attention of the chairman to it and leave it to him to bring the matter before the assembly at the proper time. If the chairman prefers, he may call on the member to state the case or present his motion.[1]

Illustrations. The following illustrations show the method of carrying out in an ordinary society the usual order of business as given on page 132, and also the procedure when the orders of the day are called for under different circumstances:

(1) In an ordinary society with weekly or fortnightly meetings, it is usually unnecessary to have an order of business any more definite than that given on page 132, which is the customary order in societies that have not adopted a special order of business. As this prescribes only the order in which the different classes of business are to be taken up, it is easily conformed to. After the minutes have been read the chairman asks, "Are there any corrections to the minutes?" If there is no response he adds, "There being none, the minutes stand approved [or, are approved]." He then calls for reports from such officers, boards, standing committees, and special committees as are required to report at this meeting. He calls for these reports in the order just mentioned, omitting those that the chair knows have no report to make. If there are standing committees that should report, he asks, "Are any standing committees prepared to report?" or he calls on the different committees by name, calling first on the standing and then on the special committees, preferably in the order of their importance. The report of a committee is made and treated as described on pages 267–289.

When there are no more committees to report, the chair usually says, "New business is now in order"; or, "The meeting is now open to new business"; or, "What is the further pleasure of the meeting [or society, or club]?" While this is the ordinary procedure, it is possible that the previous meeting adjourned while business was pending, or before all the orders of the day had been disposed of; or that some matter was postponed to this meeting; or

[1] See "Parliamentary Practice," page 162.

that some question was made a "special order" for this meeting. In any of these cases the chair does not announce new business until these preferred questions are disposed of, first announcing the special orders, then the unfinished business, and then the postponed questions. Unfinished business includes all the orders of the day of the previous meeting that were not disposed of. If there is more than one postponed question, the different ones are announced in the order in which they were postponed, the one first postponed being taken up first.

Sometimes it is desired to take up a question that was laid on the table at the same or the previous meeting. This can be done while questions of the same class are being considered, or at any time after unfinished business has been announced, or when new business is in order. Thus, a report of a committee that has been laid on the table either at this or the preceding meeting may be taken from the table by a majority vote while committees' reports are in order, or when unfinished business or general orders (postponed questions) or new business is in order.

(2) Suppose a case like the one in the last illustration, but that a special order for three o'clock at this meeting had been made at the previous meeting, and that when that hour arrived the assembly was considering any question except a special order that had been made prior to the making of the special order for three o'clock. In such a case, any time after three o'clock, even though another member has the floor and is making a motion or a speech, a member has a right to call for the orders of the day, and thus demand the enforcement of the regular order.

(3) Suppose an order of business, as in the preceding cases, and that a special order has been made for 3 P. M. When that hour arrives, it is the duty of the chair to interrupt pending business and to announce the special order. But the chair should use judgment in interrupting the proceedings, since in many cases time may eventually be saved by a slight delay. If the report of a committee is being read, and a few minutes is required to finish the reading and to dispose of the report, it would be unwise to interrupt it. If a member has nearly finished a speech, the chair should wait a moment until it is finished, and then announce the special order thus: "The hour having arrived that was appointed for the consideration of the resolution on ——, the question is on the resolution, 'Resolved, ——' " [reading the resolution that is the

special order]. Should the chair neglect to announce the special order at the designated time, any one may call for the orders of the day, and then the chairman must announce the special order, or else put the question to the assembly as to whether it will proceed to the orders of the day. When the special order is disposed of, the business that was interrupted is resumed at the point where it was broken off.

If the resolution was made merely a special order for the meeting without designating the hour, it has no right of consideration in preference to reports of boards and committees, because these reports precede special orders in the orders of business.

(4) Assuming the same order of business as in the previous illustrations, suppose all business preceding and including special orders has been attended to and a member offers a new resolution. The chair should not recognize it if there is any unfinished business from the preceding meeting, or any question postponed from that meeting. If the chair does recognize it and any one calls for the orders of the day, the chair must either announce the proper business, or else put to vote the question as to whether the orders of the day will be taken up. As stated hereafter, it requires an opposition of two thirds to prevent the enforcement of the orders. But if no objection is made to the deviation from the order of business before the chair states the new question, it is then too late to call for the orders of the day until after that question has been disposed of. The reason for this is that special orders have been already disposed of, and general orders cannot interfere with a pending question. But the majority may at any time lay the pending question on the table, and then the chair should at once announce the next order of business.

(5) Suppose an adjourned meeting of a society is being held with an order of business, as in the previous illustrations. This meeting is legally a continuation of the preceding meeting, of which it is an adjournment. Therefore, after the minutes are read, the order of business is resumed exactly where it was interrupted by the adjournment. If reports of boards and committees had been acted upon at the previous meeting and there are none for this adjourned meeting, then special orders are the first order of business after the reading of the minutes. All special orders that have not been disposed of should be taken up in their proper order, as heretofore described. If a special order was pending at

the time of the previous adjournment, its consideration would be resumed first, since it would necessarily be the ranking special order. After the special orders are disposed of, if any question was pending at adjournment, it is taken up, and then the general orders in the order in which they were made.

(6) In a convention having a session lasting several days, where a program or order of business has been adopted covering each day of the convention and designating the hour for each subject, it is the duty of the chair to interrupt the business when the hour arrives that was assigned to a new subject, and to announce that subject. When a convention adopts a program of this kind, it is understood that the time for each subject is limited, in order not to interfere with the next one. If a resolution is pending, the chair should immediately put it to vote, the same as if an order had been adopted closing debate at this hour, except that he should entertain a motion to commit, or to postpone, or to lay on the table. No debate is in order, but amendments should be allowed to the first two of the above-mentioned motions. No amendment to the resolution itself is allowed, except by general consent, after the expiration of the time allowed the subject. The time allotted to the subject may be extended by a two-thirds vote, in which case debate and amendment are allowed until the expiration of the extended time.

Suppose, in a case like the above, a resolution is postponed and made the special order for a certain day and hour. When that time arrives, the postponed question ranks as a special order just after those assigned to this time by the program, which was adopted before the other question was postponed and made a special order. Thus, if the program provides for reports of standing committees at 3 P. M., and reports of special committees at 5 P. M., and a resolution has been postponed and made a special order for 4.30 P. M., when the hour of 4.30 arrives, the orders of the day cannot be called for if reports of standing committees are still being considered, as they are the orders for that time. But if these reports have been disposed of and other business has been taken up, then the orders of the day may be called for at 4.30, or afterward, and the pending business may be interrupted even though a member is speaking at the time.

To Take up a Question Out of Its Proper Order

Experience has shown that as a general rule societies should adopt an order of business or program for its business meetings, instead of leaving the order to chance, depending upon the member who first secures the floor after a main question is disposed of. Yet unforeseen things may occur that render it very important that action be taken upon a matter before the time set for it in the order of business, or upon a matter that has been postponed to another meeting.

If a member desires to interrupt the regular order so as to take up something out of its proper order, or to introduce a new question, he should, when the pending question is disposed of, obtain the floor and say, "I request general consent to take up the [or, to introduce a] resolution on ———." The chair repeats the request, and asks if there is any objection. If there is none, the chair says, "There being no objection, Mr. A has the floor." If the resolution is a new one, Mr. A now offers it. In either case it has now become a part of the orders of the day, just as if it had originally been assigned this place in the order of business. If, while the new question is pending, it is desired to return to what was the regular order of business, it cannot be done by calling for the orders of the day, unless the time appointed for a special order has arrived, because the modified orders of the day are being complied with. The proper course is to lay the pending question on the table.

When the chair asks if there is **objection** to the introduction of the new resolution, if a single member says, "I object," the chairman says, "Objection is made. The next business in the regular order is ———," announcing the next subject in the regular order. But any one may move "to suspend the rules and take up the resolution on ———"; or, if it is desired to introduce a new resolution, he should move "to suspend the rules that interfere with the introduction of a resolution on ———." If either of these motions is adopted by a two-thirds vote, the chair at once assigns the floor to the member who asked for general consent to take up or offer the resolution, and this resolution now becomes a part of the orders of the day, just as in case general consent had been given for its introduction. If the resolution is a new one, it must be formally offered as soon as the rules are suspended.

The motion, to suspend the rule and take up a question out of its proper order, cannot be made when any other question is pending. It is undebatable, and cannot have any subsidiary motion applied to it. While it is pending, any privileged motion except a call for the orders of the day is in order. The reason for this exception is that it is absurd to allow a call for the orders of the day to interfere with the assembly's deciding whether it will suspend those very orders. Incidental motions arising out of this question may interrupt it. A vote on it cannot be reconsidered. If it is lost the motion cannot be renewed at the same meeting, except by unanimous consent, but it can be made again at another meeting, even if held the same day. Thus, if the motion to take up a certain question out of its proper order failed at a morning meeting, it may be made again in the afternoon.

CHAPTER XIII

QUESTIONS OF ORDER; APPEAL; OBJECTION TO CONSIDERATION; SUSPENSION OF THE RULES

QUESTIONS OF ORDER

IT is the duty of the presiding officer to see that the business is carried on in its proper order, that decorum is preserved in debate, that order is preserved in the hall, and in general that the rules of the assembly are observed. While it is the duty of the presiding officer to enforce the rules, members may differ from the chair as to whether the rules are being violated, or the chair may not have noticed a violation of the rules. In either case, the member who thinks there is a breach of the rules has the right to raise the question as to whether they are being violated, and this is called "raising a question of order," or "making a point of order." The point of order must be made at the time the breach of order occurs.

This question of order must be decided by the chair, unless in a doubtful case he prefers to have the assembly decide it. If any two members are dissatisfied with the decision of the chair, they may appeal from the decision, one making the appeal and the other seconding it, as explained farther on under Appeal. If the chair is in doubt, instead of deciding the question himself, he may at once submit the question to the assembly. Suppose a point of order has been made against an amendment that it is not germane to the resolution, and the chair is in doubt as to whether the point is well taken or not. He may at once put the question to the assembly in a form similar to this: "Mr. A makes the point of order that the amendment is not germane to the resolution. The chair is in doubt and submits it to the assembly. As many as are of the opinion that the amendment is germane to the resolution, say 'Aye.' As many as are of a contrary opinion, say 'No.' The ayes have it and the amendment is germane. The question is on the amendment. Mr. B has the floor.'' The question should always be put so that the affirmative vote is on the side of the question's being in order. If the affirmative side wins, the chair at once assigns the floor to the member entitled to it at the time the point of order was made. There can be no appeal from the decision of the assembly, and therefore, when the chair submits the question of order to the assembly, it is debatable whenever an appeal would have been debatable. [See page 151.] Each member is allowed but one speech, as in case of an appeal. The presiding officer, before deciding a question of order, may call upon experienced members for their opinions, which they usually give from their seats to avoid the appearance of debate. Since these suggestions are only for the assistance of the chairman, no one has the right to make them unless requested by the chairman.

In all cases except those relating to transgressions of the rules of speaking or to indecorum in debate, a question of order is raised as follows: When a member observes a violation of the rules that he considers will do harm if allowed to pass, and yet the chair takes no notice of it, he rises, even though a member is speaking, and without waiting for recognition says, "Mr. Chairman, I rise to a point of order." The chair directs him to state his point, after which the chair decides whether the point is well taken, that is, whether what he objects to is out of order. If the chair agrees with the member he says, "The gentleman's point is well taken," and acts accordingly. If the chair disagrees with the member he says, "The chair thinks the gentleman's point not well taken," and he directs the speaker to continue. For instance, suppose an amendment has been moved and has been stated by the chair, and a member thinks it is not germane to the pending resolution: he rises to a point of order as just described, and if the chair sustains the point, the chair at once rules the amendment out of order. If, however, the chair thinks the amendment is not out of order, he says he thinks the point not well taken, and permits the business to go on. In either case any two members may appeal from the decision of the chair.

If the case is one of transgression of the rules of speaking or of indecorum in debate, the question of order is usually raised by the chairman's calling the speaker to order. How this should be done must be left to the judgment of the chair. A nervous, excitable presiding officer is unfit to preside over a turbulent assembly. A presiding officer who is calm, cool, and courteous while every one else is excited, and who is familiar with the duties of the chair and is impartial, can nearly always keep the assembly under control. The moment a speaker attacks the motives of another member, or refers to his opponent by name, or uses an offensive epithet, the chair should rap with the gavel if in a large assembly, or tap with a pencil in a small hall, or in some other way attract the attention of the speaker, and then proceed according to the circumstances of the case.

If the language used has not been seriously offensive and yet is becoming personal, the chair should interrupt the speaker by gently rapping and saying, "The gentleman will please avoid personalities"; or, "will please avoid using names of members: no name can be used when the member can be described otherwise"; or, "The gentleman will please not refer to the motives of members," as the case may be. In such a case he permits the speaker to continue, provided he continues in order. It is better for the chair to caution members as soon as he sees that they are becoming excited, and never permit matters to go so far as to require severe discipline.

If a member uses opprobious epithets or offensive language, or is disrespectful to the presiding officer, the chair should immediately rap, rise, and say, "The gentleman is out of order, and will take his seat." He then directs the secretary to take down the objectionable language, which is read, and then the speaker is asked if those are the words he used. If he denies them, the chair either corrects the words as recorded, or puts the question to the assembly as to whether these words were used by the gentleman. If the assembly decides affirmatively, or if the speaker acknowledges having used the words, and does not withdraw them or apologize, the chair states that the first business before the assembly is as to what punishment shall be imposed upon the member for the offense. If the member withdraws the offensive words or apologizes for his disrespect, the matter is usually dropped, though he has lost his right to the floor. The permission of the assembly is required before he can continue his speech. If he does not withdraw the offensive words or apologize, the procedure is as described under Discipline, page 334.

If the chairman keeps cool and courteous, yet firm, it will rarely if ever be necessary to resort to extreme measures. Members may in the heat of debate use offensive personalities, but if they are quickly stopped, and the language they have used is recorded and quietly read by the clerk, they recognize its impropriety at once, and will usually withdraw it and make an apology, and the whole matter is closed.

While it is the duty of the chair to enforce the rules as to decorum in speaking, yet if any member observes such a breach which the chair does not correct, he has the right to raise a question of order by rising immediately, while the member is speaking, and saying, ''Mr. Chairman, I call the gentleman to order.'' The chair directs the speaker to take his seat and the member to state his point of order, unless it is so evident that this is unnecessary. The chair then rules on the point raised. If he thinks the speaker in order, he so rules, and directs him to continue his speech. If he thinks the speaker is out of order, the chair proceeds in the same way as when the chair calls the speaker to order. In the case of objectionable language, the member who raised the question of order is the one to indicate the words to which he objects.

A question of order can be raised only by the presiding officer or by a member who is entitled to vote, and not by a non-member who has been granted the privileges of the floor and of debate. It must be raised at the time the breach of the rule occurs. After a member has finished his speech, it is too late to call in question the propriety of language used in the earlier part of his speech. After an amendment has been debated it is too late to rule it out of order, even though it is unquestionably not germane. If any motion or action is in violation of the laws of the state, or of the constitution or by-laws of the assembly, or if for any other cause the motion or action is null and void, then it is never too late to raise a point of order against it.

A question of order, like all other questions or inquiries put to the chair, cannot be debated, or amended, or laid on the table, or have any other subsidiary motion applied to it. When the order of business is deviated from, instead of raising a point of order, the proper course is to call for the orders of the day as shown on page 129.

It is a mistake to be constantly raising points of order in regard to little irregularities, especially in assemblies unfamiliar with the technicalities of parliamentary law. The rules of parliamentary law are designed to expedite business and protect the minority, while at the same time they enable the assembly to express its deliberate sense on the questions before it. Parliamentary law should be the servant, not the master, of the assembly. The assembly meets to transact business, not to have members exploit their knowledge of parliamentary law. A business meeting is not a class in parliamentary law. It is a nuisance to have the time of the assembly wasted by a member's raising points of order on technical points when no harm is done by the irregularity. If the chair chooses to put a question without waiting for a second, or to state a question properly according to the intent of the mover when the question as made was out of order, it is foolish to raise a point of order.

APPEAL

While it is the duty of the presiding officer to decide questions of order when raised, it is the privilege of any two members to appeal from this decision, one making the appeal and the other seconding it. As has just been stated, when the presiding officer is in doubt, he may, before deciding the question of order, consult such members as he chooses, or he may put the question to the assembly for its decision. If, when he decides such a question or makes such a ruling, a member objects to it and attempts to discuss it, the chair should suggest that the member appeal from the decision of the chair, since the question is undebatable unless on appeal. Members have no right to criticize the chair's rulings unless they appeal from his decision to that of the assembly. He is entitled to his opinion as much as any other member, and he must rule in accordance with that opinion. If others differ from him, they should not hesitate to appeal and thus obtain the decision of the assembly. There is no more cause for a feeling of delicacy about appealing from the decision of the chair than about differing from a member in debate. Appealing relieves the chair from responsibility in the case, throwing it upon the assembly, and therefore an appeal should be welcomed by the chairman.

When a decision or ruling is made to which a member objects, he may instantly rise, though another has the floor, and say, "Mr. Chairman, I appeal from the decision of the chair." If a member is on the floor at the time, the chair directs him to take his seat, states the exact point at issue, his ruling thereon and his reasons therefor, and then states the question thus: "The question is, Shall the decision of the chair stand as the judgment of the assembly?" While this is the old established parliamentary form and the preferable one, in ordinary societies the question is sometimes put thus: "Shall the decision of the chair be sustained?" This is allowable and may be preferred by many on account of its simplicity. Sometimes the question is stated thus: "Shall the chair be sustained?" The objection to this form is that it is more personal to state the question as one of sustaining the chair, rather than his decision or whether the decision of the chair shall stand as the decision of the assembly.

If the question of order relates to transgression of the rules of speaking, to indecorum in debate, or to the priority of business, or if it is raised during a division of the assembly, or while an undebatable question is pending, the appeal is undebatable, and therefore the chair immediately after he has stated the question puts it to vote thus: "As many as are in favor of the decision of the chair standing as the judgment of the assembly, say 'Aye.' As many as are of a contrary opinion, say 'No.'" Or, "Those in favor of sustaining the decision of the chair, say 'Aye.' Those opposed, say 'No.'" The question must always be put on sustaining the decision of the chair, not on sustaining the appeal. The chair may vote on an appeal. On a tie vote, including the chairman's vote, the decision is sustained, on the theory that the decision of the chair stands until it is reversed by a majority.

In the cases just mentioned no debate is allowed, because there would rarely be anything gained by allowing debate, while in those involving personalities or indecorum there might be danger of making matters worse if debate were permitted on an appeal. When an undebatable question is pending, its decision should not be delayed by interjecting a debatable one. In all cases except those mentioned in the previous paragraph an appeal is debatable, but only one speech is allowed each speaker. In cases of a debatable appeal, if no one rises to claim the floor when the question is stated, the chair asks, "Are you ready for the question?" just as he does in the case of all other debatable questions. Before putting the question, the chair has the right, without taking the floor, to answer arguments made against his ruling and to give additional reasons for the decision.

An appeal may be made from any ruling of the chair except when another appeal is pending. In such a case, to avoid complications, the decision of the chair must be submitted to at once. Afterward, however, when no business is pending, the correctness of the chair's decision can be brought before the assembly by a resolution or motion covering the case. An appeal must be made at the time the decision or ruling is made. If any business or debate has intervened, it is too late to appeal.

While an appeal is pending, privileged and incidental motions are in order. If the appeal does not adhere to the question pending when it was made, that is, if its decision would not in any way affect the pending question, then the appeal may be laid on the table or have any other subsidiary motion applied to it, except to amend, without in any way affecting the main question. As soon as the appeal is thus disposed of, the consideration of the interrupted question is resumed, and the floor is assigned to the member who was entitled to it at the time the question of order was raised. But if the appeal adheres to the question pending at the time it was made, then no subsidiary motion, except those closing or limiting debate, can be applied to it without affecting the main question. For instance, suppose, while a question is pending, some one raises a question of privilege, and the chair rules that it is not a question of privilege. From this ruling an appeal is made, and the appeal is laid on the table. The decision of the main question, which was pending, is in no way affected by the reversal of the decision of the chair when the appeal is taken from the table. Therefore, as soon as the appeal is laid on the table the consideration of the interrupted question is resumed. But if the appeal is from the chair's ruling an amendment out of order as not germane, laying the appeal on the table or postponing it to another time would lay on the table or postpone the main question also, because the appeal adheres to the main question so that it, the main question, may be materially affected if the decision of the chair is reversed. In such a case it would be as absurd to allow an appeal to be laid on the table as to allow an amendment to be laid on the table without carrying with it the main question.

An appeal can be made only from a decision of the chair. It cannot be made from an answer to a parliamentary inquiry, from an answer the chair may give to any other question, from any opinion expressed by the chairman, or from an announcement of the result of a vote. In the last case a division should be called for, and if there is still doubt as to the correctness of the declaration of the vote, a count by tellers may be ordered by a majority vote. For instance, if in answer to a parliamentary inquiry the chair should state that a certain motion was out of order, no appeal could be made from this answer, since it is not a decision of a parliamentary question that has actually risen. To bring the question before the assembly on an appeal, some one should make the motion, even though the chair has stated it was out of order. As soon as the chair has ruled it out of order, an appeal may be made from this decision.

Objection to the Consideration of a Question

It is the right of every member of a deliberative assembly to introduce questions for its consideration and action. Mass meetings are usually called for a special purpose, and societies are organized with some definite object in view, which should be stated in the by-laws. Questions introduced that are outside the objects specified in the by-laws, or outside the objects of the meeting as defined in the call for the meeting, should be ruled out of order by the chair. But many questions that cannot legitimately be ruled out of order may be objectionable to most of the members on the ground that they are useless, contentious, or otherwise objectionable, or that there are more important questions which should be considered and which require the entire time covered by the session. In such a case, when the question is first introduced, before it has been debated, a member should rise and, without waiting for recognition by the chair, say, "Mr. Chairman, I object to the consideration of the question." If a member has the floor at the time, the chair directs him to be seated, and immediately puts the question to the assembly in a manner similar to this: "Mr. A offers the following resolution ——," which he reads, and then he continues: "Mr. B objects to its consideration [or, Its consideration is objected to]. The question is, 'Will the assembly consider it?' [or, Shall the resolution be considered?] As many as are in favor of its consideration will rise. Be seated. Those opposed will rise. Be seated. There being two thirds opposed to the consideration of the resolution, it will not be considered.'' If there is less than a two-thirds vote in the negative, the chair announces the result thus: "There being less than two thirds opposed to its consideration, the resolution is before the assembly." As it requires a two-thirds vote in the negative, that is, two thirds of the votes cast, to prevent the consideration of a question, it is generally better to vote by rising, or by show of hands in a small assembly, instead of by the voice. In a large assembly it is better to vote by rising. Unless the first vote is clearly one-sided, so that there can be no doubt about it, the chair, instead of announcing the vote, should say: "The chair is in doubt. All in favor of the consideration of the resolution will rise and stand until counted." As soon as the count is made by the chair, or the secretary, or by tellers appointed by the chair, according to the size of the assembly, the chair says, "Be seated," and, announcing the number of votes, he continues, "Those opposed will rise." After the negative vote has been counted and announced, he announces the result.

An objection to the consideration of a question needs no second. It can be made only against original main questions when first introduced, but not after debate. Incidental main questions, as the report of a committee on a subject upon which it has been ordered to report, or an amendment to the by-laws, cannot be objected to, but the report or opinions of a minority of a committee may be objected to. The report of a committee which it has not been ordered to make can be objected to, just as any other original main motion. The consideration of petitions and communications from members or subordinate organizations may be objected to, but not communications from a superior organization. An objection to the consideration of a question cannot be debated or have any subsidiary motion applied to it.

When an objection to the consideration of a question has been sustained by a two-thirds vote, the question cannot again be introduced during the same session except by unanimous consent, or by reconsidering the vote refusing its consideration. This motion to reconsider, which is undebatable, can be adopted by a majority vote. An affirmative vote on the consideration cannot be reconsidered.

An objection to the consideration of a question is in several respects similar to a question of order. Either of them can be made when another has the floor, and if not made promptly cannot be made at all. Neither requires a second nor can be debated, and as the chair can call a member to order, so he can, on his own responsibility, put the question on the consideration of a question that for any reason he thinks should not be considered during that session. After the debate has begun, or a subsidiary motion has been stated by the chair, it is too late to object to the consideration of the main question.

A two-thirds vote in the negative is required to prevent the consideration of a question, because it suspends the right of a member to introduce a question to the assembly. Objecting to the introduction of a question is a very different thing from objecting to granting a request, or to permitting something to be done that can be done only with the permission of the assembly. A member has an inherent right to offer a resolution in a deliberative assembly, and nothing less than a two-thirds vote can deprive him of this right. The minority of a committee, however, has no inherent right to submit a report. Its report is usually received as an act of courtesy, but if a single member objects, a majority vote is required to authorize its reception. For similar reasons, if objection is made, it requires a majority vote to receive communications or petitions from those who are not members of the society.

Suspension of the Rules

If it were not for the common parliamentary law, the minority of an assembly that has no rules or by-laws would have no protection from the tyranny of an impassioned majority. Yet, however unreasonable a majority under great excitement may be, in their calm, sober moments they are usually ready to adopt reasonable rules to govern the assembly and to protect those who may happen at any time to be in the minority. Although it is necessary for every society to have its own rules, adapted to its own special needs, yet there are times when some of these rules, instead of being a help, are a great hindrance to the transaction of business, and if they affect none but those present at the meeting they should be capable of being suspended. Experience has shown that some rules should never be suspended even by a unanimous vote, while there are others whose suspension should be allowed, some by a unanimous vote, others by a two-thirds vote, and still others by a majority vote. No rule can be suspended if the negative vote is as large as the minority protected by the rule, as otherwise the rule would be of no value. Thus, if there is a rule requiring a four-fifths vote to admit non-members to the hall, the rule cannot be suspended by less than a four-fifths vote.

Rules that Cannot Be Suspended Even by a Unanimous Vote. The fundamental organic rules of a society as embodied in its constitution or by-laws cannot be suspended by a unanimous vote. These rules were originally adopted by the entire society, and provision was made therein for their modification, and in no other way can they be modified. For instance, the qualifications for membership cannot be suspended by a unanimous vote, nor can a rule requiring the election of members and officers to be by ballot, provided these rules are placed in the by-laws. The by-laws are designed to contain such rules as cannot be suspended, and they cannot be changed except after notice has been given to the members, and then usually at least a two-thirds vote is required to adopt the amendment. Such fundamental principles of parliamentary law as the right to vote being limited to members cannot be suspended, so that the right to vote cannot be given to a non-member even by a unanimous vote.

Rules that Can Be Suspended by a Unanimous Vote. By a unanimous vote, or general consent, any or all rules relating to the transaction of business may be suspended, provided absent members are not affected thereby and there is no interference with the secrecy of the ballot. A rule requiring notice to be given to amend the rules of order cannot be suspended by a unanimous vote, for its object is the protection of absentees and they have not consented to its suspension. A motion directing the secretary to cast the ballot for a certain person is out of order, provided there is a rule requiring the vote to be by ballot. The reason is that the secretary's casting a ballot is not a ballot vote at all, the essential feature of the ballot vote being secrecy, and no one can vote on a motion directing the secretary to cast the ballot without exposing his vote. If the by-laws require a ballot, there is no way to suspend the rule, or have the vote taken in any other way, because no member can object without exposing his vote. If it is required by the rules of order, but not by the by-laws, then the rule may be suspended by a two-thirds vote. If it is required by only a standing rule of the kind described on page 367, it may be suspended by a majority vote. If it has been ordered by a vote during the meeting, the vote can be reconsidered and reversed, or it may be rescinded.

Rules that Can Be Suspended by a Two-Thirds Vote. Rules relating to the priority of business, to business procedure, to admission to the hall, or to participation in debate by non-members, etc., may be suspended by a two-thirds vote. If two thirds of those present and voting wish, for the time being, to suspend one of these rules, they should be permitted to do so. For instance, a large number present who are specially interested in a subject that is on the program for, or was postponed to, 4 P. M., must leave at that hour, and wish to take it up at 3 P. M. They can move to suspend the rules and take up the desired subject immediately, or at 3 P. M., and if this is adopted by a two-thirds vote their object is accomplished. It would not be safe to allow a majority to change the order of business, as this power could be readily used by a temporary majority to take up a question out of its proper order, so as to take advantage of their opponents during their absence from the hall. Experience has shown that the best interests of a deliberative assembly are subserved by allowing a two-thirds vote to suspend such rules as relate to the program or order of business, or to how often and how long a member may speak, or to what persons shall be admitted to the hall, and even the rule that members only may speak. While the rules may be suspended so as to permit a non-member to take part in the debate, they cannot be suspended so as to permit a non-member to vote. The right to vote affects the entire organization, and for the time being would give the non-member the most important privilege of membership, and thus would suspend the by-laws. This, of course, cannot be done.

Any motion that has the effect of suspending some right or privilege of members requires a two-thirds vote, even though it is not made in the form of suspending the rules. The previous question, motions limiting or extending the limits of debate, and an objection to the consideration of a question, are examples. The very name "deliberative assembly" carries with it the idea that members have a right to introduce questions and to have these questions "deliberated" on, or discussed, before they are called upon to take final action. Other members have equal rights in regard to other questions, and since these rights may come into conflict, experience has shown that it is best for the assembly to have the power by a two-thirds vote to suspend these rights in any special case. All the rules above referred to relate to the transaction of business in the meetings, and may be classed under rules of order.

Rules that Can Be Suspended by a Majority Vote. It is a fundamental principle of parliamentary law that one session of a deliberative assembly cannot interfere with future sessions except by adopting by-laws or rules of order, both of which require previous notice and a two-thirds vote, and therefore may be assumed to be an expression of the will of the entire organization. Some slight exceptions to this rule are necessary as far as the next succeeding session is concerned in societies having regular meetings as often as quarterly. It is necessary to allow a question to be postponed to a certain hour, or even to be made a special order, for the next session. So a question may be referred to a committee to be reported on at a future session. All these exceptions should be provided for in the rules of order adopted by the society.

It has been found best in ordinary societies that a resolution or order of a continuing nature adopted at one session should be binding on future sessions, until it is rescinded or suspended. Such resolutions and orders are called standing rules. Such a rule does not interfere with the rights of future sessions, because any session may suspend the rule for that session by a majority vote. A majority vote may amend or even rescind the rule, provided notice of the proposed action was given at the previous meeting. If no notice was given, it may be amended or rescinded by a two-thirds vote, or a vote of a majority of the membership. On the day the rule was adopted, or the next succeeding day, a mere majority may reconsider the vote on the rule and vote it down.

CHAPTER XIV

DIVISION OF A QUESTION; CONSIDERATION BY PARA-GRAPH; MOTIONS RELATING TO NOMINATIONS; MOTIONS RELATING TO VOTING

DIVISION OF A QUESTION

HOWEVER complicated a resolution or motion may be, if it is so written that it cannot be divided, the objectionable parts must be eliminated or modified by amendments. A motion cannot be divided unless each of the propositions into which it is to be divided is suitable for adoption if all the others are rejected. If such a proposition is very complicated, it is often better to refer it to a committee, with instructions to prepare and submit a suitable substitute. If desired, the committee may be instructed to divide the resolution in a specified way and to submit two or more separate resolutions.

If a series of resolutions is offered in which the different resolutions are upon distinct subjects, then upon the demand of a single member, the resolution must be divided so that only the resolutions relating to one subject will be voted upon at a time. If a separate vote on only one subject is desired, the resolution, or resolutions, on that subject may be specified in the call for a division of the question thus: "Mr. Chairman, I call for a division of the question, so that the resolution in regard to the Orphan Asylum shall be considered separately." Upon this demand, the chair says that a division of the question is called for, and the resolution in regard to the Orphan Asylum will be considered separately. He then states the question on the resolution relating to the Orphan Asylum, and after it is disposed of he states the question on the adoption of the other resolutions as a whole. Often a committee on resolutions submits at one time a series of resolutions on entirely unrelated matters, but they must be divided at the request of a single member. This request or demand must always be made by calling for, or demanding, a "division of the question," not simply a "division." Calling for a "Division" is a demand that the vote be taken by rising, as explained under "Division of the Assembly," page 167.

If a motion, or a resolution, or a series of resolutions, is on a single subject, and yet so written that it can be divided into two or more propositions each of which is capable of standing alone as a rational proposition that could have been offered independently of the others, then the question may be divided by a majority vote on a motion to divide the question in the manner specified in the motion. The motion is out of order if it specifies a division such that any one of the propositions would be absurd if adopted when all the others were rejected. For instance, it would be absurd to allow a division of a motion "to refer to a committee with instructions," for if the motion to refer is lost there will be no committee to instruct.

The division must be a simple clerical division requiring the secretary to do nothing but insert the formal word "That," or "*Resolved*, That," or "*Ordered*, That," before the word beginning each new proposition; and to omit conjunctions, and to replace pronouns with the proper nouns, where required. Thus, take the following resolution: "*Resolved*, That a vote of thanks be extended to Mr. B, and that he be refunded his expense in the investigation of the causes of the fire." This may easily be divided into two independent resolutions, thus:

"*Resolved*, That a vote of thanks be extended to Mr. B"; and:

"*Ordered* [or *Resolved*], That Mr. B be refunded his expenses in the investigation of the causes of the fire."

It is not in order to move a division that requires the rewriting of a resolution to a much greater extent than stated above. If more changes are required, a division should not be moved, but the changes should be made by amendments, or by referring to a committee with instructions. In case several names occur in a resolution and a separate vote is desired on each, instead of moving a division, the proper course is to move in succession to strike out each name upon which a separate vote is desired, or to include several names in one motion to strike out. By a motion to strike out an objectionable sentence, or paragraph, or resolution, the assembly is brought to a separate vote on the objectionable part just as effectively as if there had been a division of the question. This is the proper method to pursue when the resolutions or paragraphs are so written that they cannot be divided. Take the following case:

"*Resolved*, That a committee of five be appointed by the chair to examine and report on a site for our club building.

"*Resolved*, That the committee be authorized to obtain an option on the site they recommend, and to pay a reasonable price therefor."

Many would prefer to vote separately on these resolutions, but if they were divided (which they cannot be) and the first one were lost, the pending question would then be on the second resolution, which would be absurd. The proper way to get a separate vote on the second resolution is to move to strike it out, as shown under striking out a paragraph.

A call, or motion, for a division of a question can be applied only to a main question, and in certain cases to amendments, and is in order up to the moment of commencing to take the vote on that question, even though the previous question has been ordered. It takes precedence of the motion to postpone indefinitely, and yields to privileged motions and to such others as may be properly incidental to it, and to all subsidiary motions except to amend and to postpone indefinitely. It is undebatable. It may be amended as to parts into which it is proposed to divide the question, but no other subsidiary motion can be applied to it. Instead of amending this motion in the ordinary way, it is usually more convenient to proceed as in the case of nominations and filling blanks, so that the different methods of dividing the question are voted on in the order in which they are proposed, unless different numbers of questions are proposed. In this case the largest number is voted on first, as in filling blanks, and for the same reasons.

When a question has been divided into a series of questions, all motions adhering to the original question adhere to the separate ones. Thus, if the motion has been made to adopt a resolution, and it is afterward divided into several resolutions, as soon as one is disposed of the chair states the question on adopting the next.

If a series of resolutions is moved as a substitute for another series, the question cannot be divided, but objectionable parts must be disposed of by amendments. It would not always be possible to determine which resolution of the substitute series is to replace a certain one of the original series. But if a motion is made to strike out several paragraphs of such a nature that the paragraphs can be acted upon separately without incurring the risk of having an absurd question placed before the assembly, then the question may be divided by a majority vote. The same is true of an amendment to insert several paragraphs. It is seldom, however, that anything is gained by dividing an amendment. The motion to strike out usually accomplishes the same purpose.

In actual practice questions are commonly divided by consultation and general consent. Much time may be saved usually by adopting this method rather than by formal motions and votes. If any one objects, or there appears to be too much difference of opinion to be quickly adjusted, the chair should require a formal motion to divide the question.

CONSIDERATION BY PARAGRAPH

When a question consists of paragraphs or sections all bearing on the same subject, or else closely related to each other, it is frequently better not to divide the question, even if it is capable of division. The adoption of an amendment to one paragraph may necessitate amending a paragraph already adopted, which would be troublesome. The proper way to consider such questions is by paragraph, or seriatim, as it is sometimes called. By this method, after the question has been stated by the chair on the adoption of the resolution or other paper, he states that "It will be considered by paragraph, each paragraph after being read being open to debate and amendment only, no vote being taken on adopting the paragraph." He then reads, or causes to be read, the first paragraph, and asks, "Are there any amendments proposed to this paragraph?" If there are none, or when no more are offered, he says, "There being none [or, There being no more amendments proposed], the next paragraph will be read." When all the paragraphs have been read, the chair should state that the entire resolution or paper is now open for amendment. This is the time to insert new paragraphs, or to make any amendments to the original paragraphs necessitated by changes in the later ones. Changes required in the numbering of the paragraphs, sections, or articles on account of altering their position, or striking out some or inserting new ones, are made by the secretary and not by formal amendments.

When the body of the paper is satisfactorily amended, the preamble, if there is one, is taken up in the same way and perfected, since the amendments made in the other part of the paper may require an amendment to the preamble. On this account, if the previous question is ordered before the preamble has been considered, it does not apply to the preamble unless it is so specified. When no more amendments are offered, the chair puts the question on the adoption of the resolution or paper as amended.

If, during the consideration of any paragraph, a motion to lay on the table, to postpone, to commit, or to postpone indefinitely is adopted, it applies not only to that paragraph but to all the others, that is, to the entire pending question. The previous question and motions to limit or to extend the limits of debate may be applied to amendments of a single paragraph. If, while an amendment is pending, one of these latter motions is adopted, without specifying to what it applies, it applies only to the pending amendment. When a question is divided, there are two or more questions just as distinct as if they had been moved separately, so that any subsidiary motion adopted after the division applies only to the one proposition immediately pending. But when a question is considered by paragraph, the paragraphs are not separate questions, as when a question is divided. The paragraphs are considered separately only for convenience in amending.

No vote is taken on adopting the separate paragraphs, a single vote being taken on adopting the whole. When the bad method of adopting each paragraph is followed, a vote must not be taken on adopting the whole paper, because when each paragraph has been adopted the entire paper has been adopted. When the paragraphs are adopted separately, each paragraph goes into effect immediately upon its adoption, and it cannot be changed except after reconsideration. If it is a set of by-laws that is being considered, after the paragraph requiring notice for its amendment has been adopted, it is too late to reconsider any votes, and no change can be made, except in accordance with that paragraph.

When a resolution or other matter containing two or more paragraphs is before an assembly, the chair should exercise his judgment as to whether it would be more convenient to consider it as a whole or by paragraph. If the chair thinks it ought to be considered by paragraph, he proceeds as already described; and if any member wishes to save time by acting on it as a whole, he moves that "it be considered as a whole." If it will not cause much discussion or amendment, the chair should simply state the question as a whole, and if any member wishes it considered by paragraph, he at once moves that it "be considered by paragraph." These two motions, to consider by paragraph and to consider as a whole, are undebatable, and cannot have any subsidiary motion except to amend applied to them. They apply only to main motions and amendments, and yield to all privileged motions, to such motions as are incidental to them, and to all subsidiary motions except to amend and to postpone indefinitely.

In practice, the question of considering a resolution or other paper as a whole or by paragraph is usually settled without a formal motion or vote. It is a question upon which there would seldom be difference of opinion, so that the chair's action in the case would usually be acquiesced in.

MAKING NOMINATIONS

After the question of an election has been taken up, if there are no rules to the contrary, any one can make a motion specifying the manner of making nominations. This motion cannot be debated or have any subsidiary motion applied to it except to amend. The nominations may be made from the floor, or by "open nominations," as it is sometimes called; or by a nominating committee; or by a nominating ballot. When made from the floor, any member may rise and address the chair, and, when recognized, say, "I nominate Mr. A." Sometimes in large conventions the member who makes a nomination follows it with a speech advocating the cause of his candidate, and then the nomination is seconded by one or more members, each making a speech. In ordinary assemblies, however, it is not usual to make nominating speeches. In small bodies the nominations of members of committees are usually made by members from their seats without addressing the chair. It is not necessary that a nomination be seconded.

If a nominating committee is appointed and the election is to take place immediately, the committee should at once retire and agree upon a nomination, or a ticket, and report to the assembly.

In some societies it is not necessary to consult the nominees, though it is usually expedient to do so, and it should always be done in organizations meeting only annually, like conventions, because after the report has been made the nominees may decline the nomination. When the committee submits its report, no vote should be taken on adopting or accepting it, but after repeating the nominations the chair should ask if there are any more nominations. Any member may now claim the floor and nominate some one else for the office, as the appointment of a nominating committee does not preclude nominations from the floor. If the candidates are voted for viva voce, or by show of hands, or by rising, the vote is taken on the different names suggested in the order in which they are mentioned, the vote being first taken on the one reported by the committee. The negative should always be put as well as the affirmative, and if there are more affirmative votes than negative for a candidate, he is declared elected, even if he receives only one vote. Since no vote is taken on the other nominations after one is elected, it is necessary for those favoring a candidate to vote against the others.

Another method of nominating is by taking a nominating ballot. This is frequently improperly called an informal ballot, and sometimes leads to adopting a motion to make this "informal" ballot the formal one. By this nominating ballot the preferences of the members of the society are ascertained with greater accuracy than in any other way. The ballot is taken in the same way as an ordinary ballot, and when the result is announced it shows how many favor each candidate. Then the regular or electing ballot is taken. Sometimes, when the nominating ballot shows that one candidate has an overwhelming majority, so that there is no possibility of getting a different result on a formal ballot, it is voted that the ballot taken be declared the electing or formal ballot, and thus time is saved by avoiding a second ballot. But this destroys the usefulness of the nominating ballot and it should never be done. It cannot legally be done if the by-laws require the vote to be taken by ballot, as this is a viva voce vote. Secrecy in voting is one of the objects of balloting, and this is defeated by allowing a motion like the above, or even asking for unanimous consent. [For fuller explanation of Nominating Ballot, see pages 207–209.]

Closing and Reopening Nominations. In ordinary deliberative assemblies there is rarely any use for a motion to close nominations. When the chairman thinks there will be no more, he inquires "Are there any more nominations?" and if there is no response he proceeds to take the vote on the nominees. If law or custom requires the nominations to be formally closed, a motion to that effect should be made and put to vote, but not until a reasonable time has been given for nominations. As this motion, like the previous question, deprives members of their rights, it requires a two-thirds vote for its adoption. It may be amended as to the time when nominations shall be closed, but can have no other subsidiary motion applied to it. It yields to privileged and incidental motions, and is undebatable.

When closed, nominations may be reopened by a majority vote. The motion, like the motion to close nominations, may be amended as to the time, but no other subsidiary motion can be applied to it, nor can it be debated.

DIVISION OF THE ASSEMBLY

It is customary to take a vote first by the voice, viva voce, or else by show of hands, that is, the right hands are held up first by those in the affirmative, and then by those in the negative. Sometimes the viva voce vote is referred to as voting by ayes and noes, because the affirmative answer "Aye" and the negative "No." The objection to using this term is that it is liable to be confused with voting by "yeas and nays," which is the same as voting by roll-call. Usually either of these two methods, viva voce or showing hands, the simplest and quickest methods of voting, will suffice to show which side has the majority. But if the two sides are nearly equal these methods are not sufficiently accurate to satisfy every one, and the chair, instead of announcing what appears to be the vote, should immediately take a rising, or standing, vote. If, when those voting in the affirmative rise, he sees from the number standing that a count will probably be necessary to determine the vote, he may direct them to remain standing until counted. If the assembly is small, he counts those standing, or directs the secretary to do so, and then says "Be seated. Those opposed [or, The negative] will rise and remain standing until counted." He then announces the number of votes on each side, which should be entered on the minutes, and declares the result. In a large assembly he should appoint at least two tellers, one from each side of the question, to count and report to the chair the number of votes on each side. The chair has the right and the duty to take the necessary steps to satisfy himself as to the vote before announcing it.

On the other hand, the assembly has the right to have the vote taken, so that it may be satisfied that the announcement by the chair is correct. If the vote is at all close and the chair neglects to take a rising vote, any member without even rising may call, "Division," or, "I doubt the vote," and the chair is obliged to take the vote again, this time members voting by rising. A call for a division does not require a second, is not debatable, and cannot have any subsidiary motion applied to it. Sometimes a division is called for, not because there is any doubt as to the vote, but because the vote is so small that there is doubt as to its being a correct expression of the views of the assembly.

If members are not satisfied with the standing vote, they may by a majority vote order a count or any other method of ascertaining the vote, as described farther on. A single member cannot require time to be consumed by a count or other method of voting when the majority are satisfied with a standing vote.

Whenever a vote has been taken only by voice or by show of hands, it is in order to call for a division immediately after the vote has been announced. The chair cannot take away this right of a member by hastily announcing the vote and the next business in order. A member forfeits this right, however, unless he claims it immediately after the chair announces the result. When the assembly votes to adjourn, the chair should never declare the assembly adjourned until a reasonable opportunity has been given for any one to demand a division, unless a rising vote has been taken. After the adjournment has been properly declared, it is too late to call for a division.

While members have a right to demand a division, this right is given merely to insure a deliberate vote and that no mistake is made as to what the vote is. It should never be used when the vote is large and there is no question as to which side is in the majority. It can do no possible good in such a case, and therefore can be used only for obstructive purposes, and should be treated as a dilatory motion.

Motions Relating to Methods of Voting

Various questions arise, in connection with voting, which are usually settled by general consent, but may require formal motions and votes. They are incidental to the pending question and therefore are in order while it is pending, sometimes even after a vote has been taken on that question. They cannot be debated or have any subsidiary motion, except to amend, applied to them. They require a majority vote for their adoption. One of the most common of these incidental motions is one prescribing the method by which the vote shall be taken when it is desired to have it taken in some other way than by the voice or by show of hands. In the chapter on Voting all the usual methods are described. If one form is suggested or moved, any one may suggest or move another form. Instead of treating the second as an amendment, it is usual to proceed as in filling blanks, putting the question on the various forms suggested in the order of the time and trouble required for taking the vote, as follows: (1) Ballot; (2) Roll-Call, or Yeas and Nays; (3) Division and Count; (4) Rising. If the assembly is large it may be desired to divide it by having the affirmative go to one side and the negative to the other side of the hall, and be counted; or, one party to pass between tellers and be counted, and then the other; or, each side in succession to rise and be counted.

There is nothing gained by taking the vote by yeas and nays, that is, by roll-call, in an ordinary society where the members are not responsible to a constituency and the vote is not published. It is doubtful if it is ever justifiable to take a vote by yeas and nays unless the proceedings are to be published. It consumes much time, and then the secretary is required to enter in the minutes the names of all voting on each side, and, if they do not constitute a quorum, enough more names, of those who are present and do not vote, to make a quorum.

Closing and Reopening the Polls

When the vote is taken by ballot, as is usual in electing officers of permanent societies, the ballot may be taken during a meeting of the society, and the ballots be collected by the tellers in baskets or other receptacles. In this case, as soon as the tellers collect the ballots, the chair should ask, "Have all voted who wish to do so?'' If any members have been overlooked by the tellers, they should indicate it by rising or holding up the hand, and the tellers should collect their ballots. Should any members enter after the polls are closed, they cannot vote unless upon motion it is voted to reopen the polls. This motion may be simply to "reopen the polls," or to reopen them for a specified time, as three minutes. At the close of the specified time the chair announces the polls closed. If no time is specified, when the chair thinks all have voted, he again inquires if all have voted who wish to do so, and if there is no response he again declares the polls closed.

In the other ways of balloting, in which the members deposit their ballots in a box, the balloting may be done during a meeting of the society, or at another time, as described under Elections, page 215. The polls may be closed by adopting a motion to that effect, made after all have had a reasonable opportunity to vote. If the motion is made after all have voted, the chair should inquire if all have voted who wish to do so, and if there are any wishing to vote he should delay putting the question on closing the polls until they have had an opportunity to vote. It is usually better to leave the closing of the polls to the chairman, who should close them as soon as all have voted who wish to do so, and not until then. When the chair on his own responsibility declares the polls closed, any one may say, "I object," and then the chair should immediately put to vote the question on closing the polls. A two-thirds vote is required to close the polls, just as it is required to close debate. Only a majority vote is required to reopen the polls.

When the balloting is done at some other time than during a meeting of the society, the hours for opening and closing the polls are decided in advance by the by-laws or rules of the society, or by a special vote. In such case the polls cannot be reopened, since the society is not in session at the time.

The motions to close and to reopen the polls are made only in case the vote is by ballot. They are undebatable, and cannot have any subsidiary motion applied to them except to amend. They yield to privileged motions. [For further information concerning voting by ballot see the chapter on Nominations and Elections, pages 204–217.]

CHAPTER XV

INQUIRIES AND REQUESTS; DILATORY AND IMPROPER MOTIONS

REQUESTS GROWING OUT OF THE BUSINESS OF THE ASSEMBLY

SOMETIMES in the midst of business a member needs information on some point to enable him to act intelligently, or he wishes permission to do something, or to be excused from something. If these requests are of such an urgent nature that their object would be defeated by delay, they may interrupt a member even while speaking. They cannot be debated or have any subsidiary motion applied to them, except in rare cases when from their very nature they may be amended. The fact that one of these incidental questions is pending does not prevent the making of any privileged or incidental motion.

Parliamentary Inquiry. When a member is in doubt as to which motion to use in order to accomplish a certain object; as to whether a certain motion he wishes to make is in order; as to the effect of the adoption of the pending motion; or when he is in need of any further information on parliamentary law that is necessary to enable him to act intelligently in regard to pending business, or to business he is about to introduce—the proper course for him to pursue is to "rise to a parliamentary inquiry." He should never interrupt a speaker to make his inquiry unless necessary. If he thinks the speaker is out of order and is not sufficiently sure of it to raise a point of order, he should interrupt the speaker by rising to a parliamentary inquiry. He should clearly state his point and then ask the chair if the speaker is not out of order.

If the floor is occupied when a member wishes to make his inquiry, he rises and says, "Mr. Chairman, I rise to a parliamentary inquiry." The member speaking should stop, and the chairman should direct the interrupting member to state his inquiry. When he has made his inquiry the chair answers it and the inquirer resumes his seat. If the inquiry relates to the speaker's being out of order, the chair acts in accordance with the answer given to the inquirer. There can be no appeal from the answer to the inquiry, which is only the opinion of the chair, because an appeal can be made only from the decision of the chair. If a member acts in opposition to the opinion of the chair and is ruled out of order, then an appeal may be made.

If the inquiry is made when no one else has the floor, the member may proceed as just described, or he may rise and obtain the floor just as if he were going to make a motion, and ask his question as soon as recognized by the chair. In this case, if he wishes to make a motion he may retain the floor while the chair is answering his question, and then immediately make his motion if the answer is favorable. Neither a parliamentary inquiry nor the chair's answer can be debated or have any subsidiary motion applied to it.

A member has no right to ask a question on parliamentary law unless it is necessary in order to guide him in his actions at that time. The chair is supposed to be an expert parliamentarian and able to inform members as to correct parliamentary procedure in ordinary cases. Before answering the inquiry, just as before deciding a question of order, he may consult or ask the opinion of persons of experience. A request for information is not a parliamentary inquiry unless it involves a question of parliamentary law.

Request for Information. When the information that is desired does not relate to parliamentary law, the procedure is similar to that just described for a parliamentary inquiry. The member, however, on rising while another has the floor, says, "Mr. Chairman, I rise to a point of information." If the information is to be furnished by the speaker, the inquirer rises and says, "Mr. Chairman, I should like to ask the gentleman a question." In a large assembly the chairman should ask the speaker if he consents to be questioned. If he declines the request, he continues his speech and the inquirer must resume his seat. If he consents, the chair directs the inquirer to ask his question, which must not be addressed to the speaker in the second person, but must be in the third person and spoken through the chairman, thus: "Mr. Chairman, I should like to ask the gentleman if the third sentence of his resolution could not be struck out without interfering with the object of the resolution. He would then remove the only objection many of us have to it." The answer should be addressed to the chair also, as members are not permitted to address each other in debate. The second person cannot be used except when it applies to the entire assembly or to the chairman. When the speaker consents to the interruption, the time lost comes out of his time. On this account, when his time is short a speaker may decline to be interrupted, even though willing to be questioned if he had sufficient time. In a smaller assembly less formality is often observed. Thus, when the inquirer says he wishes to ask the speaker a question, the chairman simply turns to the speaker, who, without waiting for the chairman to speak, immediately consents or declines to be questioned.

If the floor is not occupied when a member makes the request, he obtains the floor and then asks for the desired information. If any business is pending, the request must have a bearing on that business, or else must be of a sufficiently urgent nature to justify the interruption. Even after it has been voted to adjourn, if a member rises and says, "Mr. Chairman, I rise to a point of information," the chair must tell him to state his point. The question must relate to something necessary to be known before the adjournment is pronounced, as, for instance, regarding a clear understanding as to obtaining tickets for an excursion to be taken before the next meeting.

Request for Leave to Withdraw or Modify a Motion. Before a motion has been stated by the chair its maker has a right to withdraw or modify it, but after it has been stated he can neither withdraw nor modify his motion without the consent of the assembly. If, when a motion is made by Mr. A, Mr. B wishes it withdrawn or modified, and thinks Mr. A will consent, Mr. B should rise before the question is stated by the chair, and, without waiting to be recognized, say something like this: "Mr. Chairman, I should like to ask the gentleman to withdraw his motion

for the present, as there is some very important business relating
to —— that should be attended to immediately"; or, "Mr. Chairman, I should like to ask the gentleman to accept the following
amendment ——," which he then states. If the request is refused,
the chair says so, and proceeds to state the question on the motion
as made by Mr. A. If Mr. A is willing to accede to the request,
he says, "Mr. Chairman, I accept the amendment." In the first
case the chairman says, "The motion is withdrawn." In the
second case he says, "Mr. A accepts the amendment. It is moved
and seconded to ——," stating the question as if the motion had
been originally made in its modified form. If the chairman states
the question after Mr. B rises and addresses the chair, this does
not deprive Mr. A of the right to withdraw or modify his motion.
It is the duty of the chair to notice members who rise and address
him, and should he neglect to do so the member loses none of his
rights thereby. In such a case the chair proceeds exactly as if the
question had not been stated.

After the question has been properly stated by the chair it
belongs to the assembly and cannot be withdrawn or modified
without its consent. Mr. B in this case, even when another has
the floor, provided he has not begun speaking, rises and says,
"Mr. Chairman." As soon as he attracts the chairman's attention,
he adds, "I want to ask the member to withdraw his motion,"
giving the reason. If the request is for the acceptance of an
amendment, the procedure is similar.

If Mr. A. declines to accede to the request, that ends the matter.
If he agrees to the suggestion, then the chair states the request
clearly and asks if there is any objection. If there is none, he
announces the result, that is, that the motion is withdrawn, or that
it is amended, as the case may be. In case of an amendment he
should announce it in a manner similar to this: "There being no
objection, the resolution is amended by striking out —— and inserting ——. The question is on the resolution ——," reading it
as amended. As stated under General Consent, page 190, the fact
that members do not object when objections are called for does not
imply that all the members are in favor of the proposition, but
only that the minority believe that no good will be accomplished
by their objecting. Thus, it is useless to object to the withdrawal
of the motion to adjourn when it is seen that, if objection is made,
the motion to adjourn will be defeated by an overwhelming vote

in order to attend to the other business. Time is saved by giving general consent and thus avoiding formal votes in such cases as withdrawing a motion.

If objection is made to the withdrawal of a motion, any one can move "that permission be granted for the withdrawal of the motion to ——," specifying the motion. This does not require a second, because the maker of the motion has already consented, and thus two persons favor it. This motion cannot be debated, or amended, or have any other subsidiary motion applied to it. If the motion is lost, the matter is dropped. If it is adopted, the chair announces that the motion that was previously pending is withdrawn, since its maker has already agreed to its withdrawal.

If objection is made to the acceptance of a suggested amendment, the proper course is to offer the amendment formally. When an amendment is formally offered, the maker of the original motion may say, "I accept the amendment." The chair then asks if there is any objection, and if any is made he immediately states the question on granting the desired permission. If permission is granted, he says, "The amendment is accepted, and the question is on the motion ——," which he reads as amended. When a motion is modified the seconder may withdraw his second.

When a motion has been withdrawn, the business is treated thereafter just as if it had never been made, and it can be made again by any one. Any motion may be withdrawn, even though it has been amended and the previous question has been ordered on it, except that the motion to reconsider cannot be withdrawn after it is too late to renew the motion, unless unanimous consent is given. If this were allowed, enemies of the reconsideration could make the motion and then withdraw it when it is too late for its friends to renew it. The same rule applies to withdrawing notice of a proposed motion.

Reading Papers. A paper upon which the assembly is to act must be read when the question is stated on it, and, if there is debate or amendment, it must be read again when the question is put on it. A single member has the right to insist on this, however long the paper may be. It is only by general consent that the second reading can be dispensed with.

With these exceptions, no member has a right to have a paper read for his convenience. A member who was not present when the paper was read, even if absent on duty, has no right to demand its reading for his benefit. If a single member could have a paper reread at his pleasure, business could be greatly hindered thereby. But when a member requests the rereading of a paper, and the request is evidently in good faith and the paper is not long, the chair should comply with the request. If any one objects, the chair should put the question to vote, or any one may move that the report be reread. If the paper is a long report it is better for the chair to put the question at once, thus: "Mr. A. requests that the report be reread. As many as are in favor of having the report reread say 'Aye'; those opposed say 'No.' " A majority vote grants the request.

If during debate the speaker wishes to read or have read any printed document, or copy thereof, or even a written speech, and any one objects, he cannot read it unless leave to read it is granted by a majority vote. If it were not for this rule, members might occupy the full time allowed them by the rules in reading printed documents or speeches prepared by others. However, where it is evident that no improper advantage is being taken of the privilege, it is customary to permit members to read their written speeches, and also to read reasonably short extracts from printed documents. But if any one objects, the procedure is exactly as just described in case of a request to have a paper reread.

To Be Excused from a Duty. In most societies there are no duties required of members, except the payment of annual dues. In some societies a certain amount of attendance on meetings is required, and sometimes members are obliged to prepare papers, or in other ways to take part in the literary, artistic or other work of the society. Holding office and serving on committees and boards is also sometimes compulsory. In such cases, the duty being compulsory, the member cannot demand as a right that he be relieved from it. He must request that he be relieved from the duty, which request is made and treated as described .in the next section.

A member may be incapacitated for performing a duty that is required of him, so that the society may be interested in having a successor appointed. In such a case the request to be relieved from the duty has a bearing on the organization of the assembly, and is therefore a question of privilege. Such a case would be the serious illness of the secretary, or an emergency causing the chairman of an important committee in a convention to be called away suddenly. Wherever the duty is not compulsory the member has the right to resign, which is treated under Resignations.

Request for Any Other Privilege. Sometimes a member wishes to make explanations of something he has said or done, or wishes some other privilege. Whatever the nature of the request, the member making it must rise and address the chair by his proper title, and wait until he attracts the attention of the chairman before continuing. After a motion is made he must not rise to make a request until the chair has stated the question on the motion, unless the request is of such a nature that its object will be defeated by waiting until the question is stated. Thus a request for the withdrawal or modification of a motion, if not made before the question is stated, cannot be granted by the maker of the motion without the consent of the assembly. Therefore the member wishing the motion to be withdrawn or modified must not wait for the motion to be stated.

The same principle applies to interrupting a speaker with a request. It may be done if necessary, but it is disorderly to interrupt a speaker if the request could be made just as well after the speaker has finished. When the speaker yields the floor, any one may rise to make a request, even though another has risen first and has been recognized by the chair. As a general rule, a request should be made so as not to interrupt a member after he has begun speaking. When a request is made, the chair should repeat it and ask, "Is there any objection?" If none is made he should say, "There being no objection, the gentleman will proceed," modifying his statement to suit the case. If objection is made, the chair immediately states the question thus: "Mr. A requests ——. As many as are in favor of ——," putting the question so that every one may understand exactly what he is voting for or against. A request cannot be debated, but explanations and short remarks should be allowed when the chair thinks they will assist the assembly in deciding the question more intelligently. If made while another question is pending, no subsidiary motion can be applied to it, unless from its nature it allows of amendment.

DILATORY MOTIONS

It has been seen that it is to the interest of a deliberative assembly to allow nearly all motions to be reconsidered and to allow some highly privileged motions, as to adjourn and to lay on the table, to be renewed again and again. It is also found best to permit a single member to demand a division, which requires a rising vote to be taken, and any member may raise a point of order, and any two may appeal from the decision of the chair. But these high privileges, granted to any one or two members, may be deliberately used by two or three factious members to obstruct business, and in ordinary societies, with business sessions not exceeding two hours in length, they could be used so as to prevent business from being done if the presiding officer were obliged to recognize motions when they are clearly made for dilatory purposes.

To protect the assembly from this improper use of proper parliamentary forms, the chair should not recognize motions that are evidently merely dilatory. If there is any doubt whatever in the case, the benefit of the doubt should be given to the maker of the motion. But if a motion to adjourn is made near the beginning of the meeting, or while there is a large amount of important business not yet attended to, it is evidently not made in good faith. A motion to lay on the table a question of great importance that must be settled that day, when there is no urgent matter requiring attention, cannot be made for any other purpose than to obstruct business.

IMPROPER MOTIONS

Motions that conflict with the constitution or by-laws or other rules of the society, or with national or state laws, or with a motion that has been adopted by the society at the same session which has not been rescinded or reconsidered and rejected are improper, and should be ruled out of order. If they are adopted they are null and void. So a motion is out of order if it conflicts with a main motion, or is of such a nature that its adoption might interfere with the freedom of the assembly in acting on the previous main motion when its consideration is resumed. A main motion is in the possession of the assembly after it has been stated by the chair until it has been finally disposed of by being adopted or rejected or postponed indefinitely; or, if it has been temporarily disposed of, it is in the possession of the assembly until so much time has elapsed that it is too late to bring it again before the assembly except by renewing the motion. If a main motion has been finally disposed of, and the motion to reconsider, in either of its forms, has been made and not called up, the main motion is in the possession of the assembly until it is too late to call up the motion to reconsider. In such a case as above referred to, if the new motion were adopted it might seriously interfere with the other motion that had been laid on the table, postponed to another time, or referred to a committee. The one first offered must be brought back to the assembly and the desired amendments may be offered. The assembly having decided to lay the question aside temporarily, or having referred it to a committee, it is plain that practically the same or a similar subject should not be brought before the assembly until the original question is again taken up.

A motion that is frivolous, trivial, or absurd, or that reflects upon the motives of others, or that uses discourteous language in a way not permitted in debate should be ruled out of order. The only exception is the case of a motion closing with a resolution of censure, or one preferring charges against a member. The language used must always avoid all unnecessary harshness. The principle involved is that a member cannot take advantage of his privilege to offer a resolution, and then place in the preamble or resolution language that he would not be permitted to use in debate.

A motion that introduces a subject not provided for in the objects of the society as stated in the constitution or by-laws is out of order. Under Renewal of Motions, page 113, will be found a list of motions that cannot be renewed during the same session, and also the conditions under which certain secondary motions may be renewed.

Amendments are not permitted that are not germane to the motion to be amended; that have the effect of making the affirmative of the amended motion equivalent to the negative of the un-amended motion; that are identical with a question already adopted or rejected at the same session, or with a question that is on the table, postponed, committed, or is in any other way in the possession of the assembly.

When factious members, whose motions are not recognized, appeal from the ruling of the chair, if the chair is sustained on an appeal, he need not entertain any further appeals from members of the same faction on rulings of the same general nature. The assembly, by sustaining the chair, has decided that they are using dilatory methods, and therefore the chair must treat them as obstructionists. Great care should be exercised in this matter not to infringe upon the rights of the individual as long as he is acting in good faith, and even when he is merely "filibustering" he should not be interfered with more than is necessary to protect the assembly in its right to do business.

Part II

CHAPTER XVI

DEBATE

DECORUM IN DEBATE

IN order to debate a question, a member must rise and address the presiding officer by his title, and be assigned the floor. He must always address his remarks to the chair, never using a member's name where it is possible to describe him otherwise, as for instance, "the gentleman who last spoke." He may deny the correctness of a statement of facts, but he must never ascribe improper motives to a member, or use discourteous language. Thus, if a member states a fact of which he was not an eye-witness, it would not be out of order, though injudicious, for one who was an eye-witness to say in debate, ' The gentleman's statement in regard to —— is false.'' But if both were eye-witnesses such language would be out of order. Instead of it the speaker could say, "I am satisfied that the gentleman was entirely mistaken as to the facts in the case.'' In no case is a member to call another a "liar" or to refer to his statement as a "lie,'' as in either case the member is accused of misrepresenting the facts with the intention of deceiving, whereas in the case mentioned above the speaker is not charged with knowing that his statements are false.

NUMBER AND LENGTH OF SPEECHES

According to the old common parliamentary law, when a member obtained the floor he was entitled to it as long as he was able to speak on the pending debatable question. He was obliged to confine himself to the question under consideration, and he was not allowed to read anything without permission of the assembly. But as long as he could speak on the question without evidently wasting time with absurd or frivolous arguments, or repetitions, or unnecessary slowness of speech, there was no parliamentary way for any one else to obtain the floor without his consent. In order to adjourn it was necessary to obtain his consent, which he might not give except upon condition that when the assembly meets again he is entitled to the floor. In the U. S. Senate, senators have held the floor until physically exhausted, while in the U. S. House of Representatives, a rule has been adopted limiting each speaker to one speech of one hour on each question. The Senate limits the number of speeches on the same question on any one day to two for each senator, but no senator can speak a second time on the same day on the same question until every one desiring to speak has spoken.

While these rules may be adapted to Congress, they would be intolerable in ordinary societies that meet not oftener than weekly, and whose sessions rarely last beyond two hours. If they were considered as establishing the common parliamentary law that would be in force until rules were adopted, it would be impracticable for a mass meeting containing a few factious members to transact business.

While no rule is adapted to all bodies, it is necessary to have some restrictions on debate that will be in force in assemblies before they have adopted rules of their own. The rule that, unless permission is given by the assembly, no member shall speak longer than ten minutes at a time, nor more than twice on the same question on the same day, nor speak a second time until every one has spoken who desires to speak, has been generally accepted as giving the best results in most cases, and is the present practice in societies in the United States. In societies to which the rule is not well adapted, a suitable rule should be adopted as soon as practicable. Five minutes is a better limit than ten minutes in many societies. At any meeting the limits of debate may be changed by a two-thirds vote, as shown on page 67.

The maker of a debatable motion is always entitled to the floor for the purpose of debate as soon as the chair states the question on his motion. He cannot be deprived of this right, if he claims it promptly, by any one's making a motion or addressing the chair before he does. When a motion is made by order of a committee, the reporting member of the committee should be recognized in preference to others, since the assembly should have the advantage of the committee's study of the case. It is to the interest of the assembly to hear both sides of a case, and therefore as far as practicable a member who is opposed to the last speaker should be recognized. The member who introduces a question is allowed to close the debate, provided he has not already exhausted the twenty minutes, the extreme limit of time, allowed each member for debate.

If a member who has the floor for debate allows another member to make an explanation, the time is charged to the one who has the floor, the same as if he himself continued speaking.

DEBATABILITY OF MOTIONS

Main Motions. The right to debate every main question before taking final action on it belongs to every member of a deliberative assembly, and this right cannot be interfered with except by a two-thirds vote.

Subsidiary Motions. The subsidiary motions, except those relating to the limits of debate, are debatable in proportion to their interference, if adopted, with the freedom of the assembly to consider and act upon the main question at its pleasure. Thus, if the motion to postpone indefinitely is adopted, the main question is killed the same as though it had been rejected, and therefore the whole question is as debatable as if the main question were the immediately pending question. The adoption of an amendment to the main question finally changes the main question, and therefore an amendment is debatable and should be thoroughly debated before being voted on. Since the motion to commit, if adopted, only defers debate and action on the main question until the committee reports, the debate is limited to the propriety of the commitment, to the number and personnel of the committee, and to its instructions. The merits of the main question cannot be debated, since they will be open to debate when the committee reports. The motion to postpone definitely, if adopted, only defers action until the specified time when the main question will be up for debate and action, so the debate is limited to the propriety of the postponement to the designated time. The motion to lay on the table, if adopted, does not interfere with the right of the majority to take the question from the table and debate and act upon it, and therefore it is undebatable. The previous question and motions to limit or extend the limits of debate are undebatable, because their very object is to prevent the consuming of time in debate. They require a two-thirds vote for their adoption, however, because of their interference with the freedom of debate.

The Privileged Motions are all undebatable, because if debate were allowed on motions having such high rank they could be used to hinder business greatly. High privilege is incompatible with the right of debate. Although calling for the orders of the day and raising a question of privilege are undebatable, yet the orders of the day and the questions of privilege after being taken up are debatable. The motions for a recess and for appointing a time for an adjourned meeting, if made when no other question is pending, are treated as other main motions, and are therefore debatable. The motion to adjourn is always undebatable in an organized society. In a mass meeting, however, previous to adopting any provision for holding an adjourned meeting, the motion to adjourn is a main motion with no special privilege, because if adopted the assembly would be dissolved with no provision for convening it again.

The Incidental Questions, with the exception of an appeal and a resignation, allow of no debate. Their high privilege of interrupting any questions to which they are incidental makes it inexpedient to allow them to be debated. But an appeal may involve questions of vital importance which should not be decided without being open to debate. An appeal from a decision of the chair in a case involving indecorum, or violation of the rules of debate, or priority of business, is usually so simple that the best interests of the assembly demand that it be decided without debate, like other incidental questions. No debate is allowed on an appeal made during a division of the assembly, or while an undebatable motion is pending, or while any motion upon which the previous question has been ordered is pending. In all other cases an appeal is debatable, but no member is allowed to speak more than once.

The motions to amend and to reconsider are debatable to just the extent that the motion to be amended or to be reconsidered is debatable. The motion to take from the table is undebatable, as is the motion to lay on the table. The motions to rescind, to ratify, and to amend anything previously adopted are main motions, and are always debatable. The motions to reconsider, to rescind, to ratify, and to postpone indefinitely are not only debatable, but they open to debate the merits of the question to be reconsidered, rescinded, ratified, or postponed indefinitely.

The fact that a motion is undebatable does not prevent the presiding officer from permitting questions to be asked and answered, or explanations to be made, before putting the question to vote. This is not debate. The presiding officer permits the conference only so long as he thinks it will assist the members in deciding how to vote.

CHAPTER XVII

VOTING

VIVA VOCE [1] VOTING

AN assembly expresses its will or opinion on a question by voting upon it. Whenever practicable the question is put in such a way that it may be answered by yes or no. A proposition is submitted to the assembly in the form of a resolution or motion, offered or made by one member and seconded by another. The question on the adoption of the motion is then stated to the assembly by the chair for its consideration. When the assembly is ready to take action upon it, the chair "puts the question" to the assembly as to whether it will adopt the motion, directing those in favor of the motion to say "Aye,"[2] and when they have responded he directs those opposed to say "No." Whichever side is the more numerous he declares "has it," and he then declares the motion adopted or lost, as the case may be. This is termed "voting," or "taking the vote." A majority of the votes cast is all that is necessary for the adoption of any motion excepting those for which common parliamentary law or the rules of the society prescribe a greater vote. In the case of a motion requiring a two-thirds vote for its adoption the chairman does not declare it adopted unless there are two thirds in the affirmative. The exact form of putting the question on the various motions will be found by referring to the Index, under Putting the Question.

The method just described is always adopted unless otherwise

[1] Pronounced vī-vá vō-sē.
[2] Pronounced like *eye* and *I*; it means "yes."

ordered, except in certain assemblies where the voting is usually by "show of hands," that is, by raising the right hand. Where such is the custom, it must be understood that that method of voting is covered by the term "viva voce" as used in this book. The question is put thus: "As many as are in favor of the resolution will hold up their right hands. Down. Those opposed will signify [or manifest] it in the same way. The affirmative has it and the resolution is adopted."

VOTING BY RISING

If the difference between the affirmative and the negative votes is not sufficient to show clearly which side has won, the chair should take the vote again, this time by a "rising vote." In putting the question he says: "Those in favor of the motion will rise. Be seated. Those opposed will rise. The affirmative has it and the motion is adopted [or, The negative has it and the motion is lost]," etc. If, when those in the affirmative rise, the chair sees that there will be difficulty in deciding without a count which side has won, he should count those standing, or direct the secretary to do so. If the assembly is large he should appoint two or more tellers to count the voters on each side. In case of several hundred voters, two tellers should be appointed for each section of the hall so as to expedite the count. As soon as the two tellers for a section agree in their count, they may report to the presiding officer, who, when all have reported, announces the number of votes on each side and declares the motion adopted or lost, as the case may be. Instead of each pair of tellers reporting directly to the chair, they may all report to the chairman of the tellers, the first one named, and he reports the aggregate votes to the presiding officer. The tellers should be nearly equally divided between those in favor of and those opposed to the motion.

Sometimes the chair is satisfied as to the viva voce vote, while some members are not. In such a case any member has a right to compel a rising vote to be taken. This he does by simply calling from his seat, "Division," immediately after the chair announces the viva voce vote. [See Division of the Assembly, page 167.]

While a single member can compel a rising vote to be taken, it requires a majority vote to order a count. If a single member could force each vote to be counted, very little business could be transacted in large assemblies. Since the presiding officer is obliged to declare the vote, he must have the right to order a count when the vote is so close that he cannot decide it otherwise.

GENERAL CONSENT

Much time is wasted in some assemblies by taking formal votes in routine matters where there is evidently no difference of opinion. Sometimes very complicated cases can be settled quickly by means of "general consent." Suppose, after the adoption of a resolution, a serious grammatical error is discovered, due to the adoption of an amendment of the second degree. Instead of going through the long process necessary according to the rules to correct the error, the chair should call attention to it, and read the resolution as it should be, and ask if there is any objection to the correction. It may require some consultation before a suitable correction is agreed upon, but when this is done the corrected resolution is treated the same as if the correction had been made by the necessary formal motions and votes. When the chair asks if there is any objection to a proposed action, and none is made, it is virtually a unanimous vote, and the chair should in the above-mentioned case announce the result by saying: "There being no objection [or, By general consent], the resolution is corrected so as to read as follows: ——." Minutes are usually approved in a similar way, the chair saying as soon as they are read: "Are there any corrections? [Pause.] There being none, the minutes stand approved."

BALLOT VOTING

The methods of voting just described—viva voce, show of hands, rising, and general consent—have the objection of exposing one's vote; but they occupy so little time that they are always used in ordinary assemblies, except when a secret vote is required in order to get an expression of the real opinion of the assembly. In elections, in cases involving the acceptance or the expulsion or other punishment of members, and in all cases of a similar nature, the voting should be by ballot, so as to be absolutely secret. It is usual for the by-laws to require officers and boards to be elected by ballot. Where not required by the rules, it takes a majority to require a vote to be taken by ballot.

This method of voting is explained in connection with receiving members, elections, etc., as will be seen by consulting the Index, under Ballot.

Voting by Roll-Call (Yeas and Nays)

Voting by roll-call is tedious, and is useless except where the voters are responsible to their constituents and the names of those voting on each side are published. It is very useful in legislative assemblies, city councils, boards of education, etc., and often serves to prevent improper action by putting each member's vote on record. To make it of any value, however, a small minority must be able to require a yea and nay vote, and this provision must be in the by-laws. The U. S. Constitution provides that one fifth of the members present in either House of Congress may order a vote to be taken by yeas and nays. Some small bodies require the vote to be taken by yeas and nays on the demand of a single member. If there is nothing in the rules on the subject, it requires a majority vote to order the vote to be taken by roll-call. This majority vote could never be obtained at the only time it is needed. If the majority wish to do something they ought not to do, they certainly would not vote to put their individual votes on record.

Besides the time spent in calling the roll of the entire membership of the society, it is necessary to make a record in the minutes of the names of those voting "Yea," and of those voting "Nay," and of enough others present and not voting to make a quorum, when a quorum does not vote. This record must be read at the next meeting. There is nothing to justify such a waste of time in ordinary societies. Voting by yeas and nays is fully explained in "Robert's Rules of Order Revised," page 197.

Absentee Voting

It is a general principle of parliamentary law that the right to vote is limited to the members of an organization who are actually present at the time the vote is taken. Each member must vote in person, so that a member temporarily leaving the hall cannot authorize another to cast his vote for him in his absence. There are, however, some exceptions to this rule, as voting by mail, which is used in some organizations when it is desired to secure a fuller vote than can be obtained in a meeting of the society, and proxy voting, which is allowed in stock corporations, as explained on page 194.

Voting by Mail. A full vote of the society is very desirable when it is proposed to amend the by-laws, and yet it is impossible in many large societies to obtain the attendance of a majority of the members at a meeting. Under such circumstances a vote by mail secures a fuller and fairer expression of the will of the society than a vote of only those present at a meeting.

There are societies whose membership extends over a state or large district, so that a large proportion of the members do not wish to incur the expense of attending the annual meeting in order to vote for the officers. In such cases it is better to have the nominations and elections by mail, thus enabling every member to vote.

In many state and national organizations, members appointed on boards and committees are so scattered that much of their work must be done by mail. The old rule that nothing can be done by a committee except when it is in actual session was designed for committees of legislative bodies and of local organizations, and not for committees whose members are scattered and where no provision is made for reimbursing the expenses of travel and hotel bills incident to a meeting of the committee. The spirit of the old rule, however, must be carried out. In all cases where it is practicable, and the minority desire it, and the matter is not urgent, action should be delayed until there is a meeting of the committee. If the matter is urgent, discussion and voting by mail or telephone should be permitted. In no case should advantage be taken of the liberty to vote by mail so as to suppress the views of the minority. It must be kept in mind that the committee does not possess this liberty when it is practicable for it to meet, unless every member is consulted and no one objects, or unless the society has authorized the committee to vote by mail. Sometimes local committees or boards take action in a case by means of the telephone, but this can be done only when every member is consulted and no objection to this method of voting is made.

Voting by mail cannot be adopted unless authorized by the by-laws. It involves so much trouble that it is scarcely ever used except in elections and in voting on amendments to the by-laws. Its use in elections is explained on pages 233, 234. In voting by mail on an amendment to the by-laws the procedure is as follows: The proposed amendments should be numbered and printed, and on a separate slip should be printed the ballot, with instructions like the following form, the date being the date on which the ballots are to be counted.

Ballot for Amendment to By-laws.

May 12, 19—.

1st Amendment   Yes, No.

2d Amendment   Yes, No.

N.B. Draw a line through either "Yes" or "No" for each amendment, leaving unmarked the one you wish to vote, and place the ballot within the smaller envelope, which you should seal. Sign where indicated on the smaller envelope and enclose it in the larger addressed envelope. Seal, stamp, and mail immediately.

Besides the proposed amendments to the by-laws and the ballot, there is sent to each voter two envelopes, the smaller one having printed on it "Ballot for Amendments to By-Laws," and also a dotted line with the words "Signature of Voter" underneath. The larger one is addressed to the secretary. The secretary opens the outer envelopes and turns over the sealed inner envelopes to the chairman of the tellers, or committee, previously appointed to count the ballots. The tellers count the ballots as described under Elections, page 223, the tally sheets, however, being in the following form:

1st Amendment.

Yes. 〰〰〰〰〰〰〰〰〰 〰〰〰〰〰〰   75

No. 〰   5

2d Amendment.

Yes. 〰〰〰〰〰〰〰〰〰〰   50

No. 〰〰〰〰〰〰 /   31

Their report is made thus:

1st Amendment

No. of votes cast 80

No. necessary for adoption...................................... 54

No. voting Yes 75

No. voting No 5

2d Amendment

No. of votes cast 81

No. necessary for adoption...................................... 54

No. voting Yes 50

No. voting No 31

If an envelope is not signed, it is treated as a blank and ignored. This is necessary because the only guaranty that the ballot is cast by a member is the signature of the voter. If neither the Yes nor the No is crossed out, that ballot for that particular amendment is treated as a blank and ignored, as there is nothing to show for which side the ballot was intended; but this does not affect the votes for the other amendments on that ballot.

Voting by Proxy. As has just been stated under Absentee Voting, proxy voting is an exception to the general rule that the right to vote is limited to the members who are actually present and vote in person. It is used only in stock corporations where the control is in the majority of the stock, not in the majority of the stockholders. If one person gets control of fifty-one per cent. of the stock he can control the corporation, electing such directors as he pieases in defiance of the hundreds or thousands of holders of the remaining stock.

The laws for stock corporations are nearly always made on the theory that the object of the organization is to make money by carrying on a certain business, using capital supplied by a large number of persons whose control of the business should be in proportion to the capital they have put into the concern. The people who have furnished the majority of the capital should control the organization, and yet they may live in different parts of the country, or be traveling at the time of the annual meeting. By the system of proxy voting they can control the election of directors without attending the meetings.

A "proxy" is a power of attorney by which A authorizes B to act in his place, as his substitute for specified purposes. The word "proxy" is also used to designate the person who holds the proxy. The form of a proxy is shown on page 564. It should always be irrevocable, and therefore should be limited to a specified meeting and its adjournments. If it were not made irrevocable the maker could at any moment revoke it, and if this were done freely endless confusion would result.

Proxy Voting is not permitted in ordinary deliberative assemblies unless the laws of the state in which the society is incorporated require it or the society by-laws provide for it. It is incompatible with the very idea of a deliberative assembly, and should be allowed only in stock corporations where it is the stock that is voted. Even there its use is generally limited to voting at the annual meeting for directors, for the ratification of acts of the directors, for enlargement or diminution of capital, and for other vital changes in the policy of the corporation. These proposed changes are stated in the circulars sent to the stockholders just before the annual election requesting the proxies of all stockholders who do not expect to attend the meeting. The secretary usually sends to each stockholder a printed notice of the annual meeting, which notice states that the stock-transfer book will be closed at a specified date (usually ten or twenty days before the meeting) and that it will be reopened the day after the annual meeting; also a printed proxy blank with the name of the proxy inserted, and a stamped addressed envelope for enclosing the proxy. If revenue stamps are required on the proxy, they are affixed by the one requesting the proxy. The proxy must always be witnessed. Any one may be the witness. If the proxy is given by a corporation, it should be signed for the corporation by its president, or a vice-president, and the corporation's seal should be affixed and attested by its secretary, or assistant secretary, or other proper officer. The proxy should be sent immediately to the person for whom it is intended, or to the secretary.

The stock-transfer book is closed at least ten days before the annual meeting, to enable the secretary to prepare a list of stockholders and the number of shares held by each. Stock is voted as shown by the stock book when posted, so as to show all the transfers received at the office up to the time of closing the transfer book, regardless of who actually owns the stock at the time of the annual meeting. No notice is taken of sales of stock made after the specified date for closing the transfer book, nor of sales made previously if the stock has not been presented by that date for registry.

The proxies sent to the secretary should be listed, with the number of shares covered by each, so as to reduce to a minimum the clerical labor at the annual meeting. Proxies that are presented at the annual meeting should be checked by the secretary for the number of shares each represents. If this is not done before the voting begins, it must be done before the tellers count the votes. The proxies are usually pinned to the ballot for the directors, the ballot being signed by the person casting it, who is the person holding the attached proxies. In other words, the tellers must have evidence that each vote is cast by one who legally represents the number of shares of stock specified, and therefore the vote must be by a signed ballot, which of course cannot be secret.

Usually very few attend a stockholders' meeting, a few persons holding a large number of proxies being the only ones present.

The business of such organizations is transacted by the directors, who usually meet immediately and elect the officers and a small executive committee. Proxy voting is not allowed in the meetings of the directors. [See Election of Directors in Stock Corporations, page 234.]

CHAPTER XVIII

ELECTION OF MEMBERS OF SOCIETIES

THE method of electing members varies greatly in different societies, depending upon the attitude of the societies toward increasing its membership. Some societies, especially benevolent ones, are ready to welcome almost any addition to their numbers, and have no election of members or rules on the subject, but allow any one to join by simply paying the small annual dues. Others require the applicant to be elected by a majority vote, the motion being made by any member, without any previous notice. Many require the application to be made through a committee, the application being endorsed by two or more members, and then, if the committee recommends the election of the candidate, a two-thirds, or three-fourths, or even a larger vote is required for the election. In some cases a single negative vote will defeat the election. Sometimes the number of members is limited, so that applications are put on the waiting list, and when a vacancy occurs the first one on the list is proposed by the membership committee.

The method of voting on the election of members varies. In some societies the voting is viva voce, and in others, by some form of ballot. In the case of viva voce voting, a separate vote may be taken on each candidate, or a single vote may be taken on the entire group. In the latter case a separate vote may be obtained on any objectionable candidate by moving to strike out his name. In societies, however, where there will probably be negative votes cast, the election should always be by ballot. In balloting, each candidate may be voted for separately, or all the candidates may be balloted for on one ballot. Each society must adopt for itself the method best adapted to its own needs. No one method is best for all societies.

A rejected application cannot be renewed during the same session, but it may be renewed at any subsequent session, provided the society has no rule to the contrary. A committee, however, would rarely report again an application shortly after its rejection. The vote rejecting an application can be reconsidered if the motion is made by one who declares that he voted in the negative. A vote admitting a member may be reconsidered, provided the motion to reconsider is made before the member has learned of his reception. Allowing the reconsideration of the vote on the reception of a member, under the limitations mentioned, is for the best interest of the society. Members may learn facts during the meeting, after the vote has been taken, that would have changed their votes had they known them in time, and these changes of votes may affect the result. The two general methods of electing members, by viva voce vote and by ballot vote, will now be explained in more detail.

Viva Voce Election of Members

In societies not exposed to the danger of having undesirable persons proposed for membership, there is no objection to allowing members to propose new members from the floor, and to proceeding immediately to their election by a viva voce vote. When there is no rule to the contrary, this method is allowable, a majority vote being all that is required for election. The member who proposes a new member obtains the floor and makes a motion similar to this: "I move that Mr. A be elected [or, received as] a member of the society." This motion must be seconded and may be debated the same as any other main motion.

The motion to elect a candidate for membership usually cannot be amended, because no amendment can be germane. It is a proposition that a designated person be elected a member of a designated society. His election usually in no way affects the election of any other member, so the name cannot be changed; nor can the word "member" be changed, nor can the word "society" be changed. There is an exception to this rule when a society is limited in its membership. If in such a society there is only one vacancy, then, when a member is proposed, a motion to amend by changing the name would be germane, because the election of the first candidate would prevent the election of the second. This should never occur in viva voce elections, however, as a club with limited membership should always elect by ballot.

Instead of allowing members to propose candidates from the floor, the rules of societies usually require the applications to be made through a standing Membership Committee, even when the elections are viva voce. If this committee is unfavorable to the application it makes no report on the case, because there is but little probability of the candidate's being elected when the committee makes an adverse report. Still, by a majority vote the society can order a report to be made. If the committee decides favorably on the application, at the proper time for it to report, a member of the committee, usually its chairman, rises and says: "Mr. President, the Membership Committee has directed me to report the names of A, B, and C, with the recommendation that they be admitted to membership [or, received as members]. I move that they be received as members." Or, a form similar to this may be used: "By direction of the Membership Committee, I move that A, B, and C be received as members of this society." Since this motion is made by order of a committee, it is endorsed by at least two members and therefore requires no further second. If a separate vote is desired on one or more candidates, the proper course is to move to strike out those names. The voting being public, the making of this motion and voting for it does not increase the publicity of the opposition. This is the only way to prevent the election of undesirable candidates, except by rejecting the entire group, in which case none of them can be proposed again during that session. Where a very small number can prevent an election of a candidate, the election should be by ballot, so as to protect the negative voters. This is not so necessary when the opposition must be large to prevent the election.

ELECTING MEMBERS BY BALLOT

Electing members by ballot has the great advantage of not making known those who vote in the negative. For this reason it should always be adopted when the rules allow a small minority to defeat the election. If the by-laws require members to be elected by ballot, the rule cannot be suspended even by unanimous consent, because, if unanimous consent were asked, the opposition could not object without showing their opposition and thus defeating the very object of the ballot, namely secrecy.

When the election is by ballot, the members are proposed by the Membership Committee, as has just been described. The chairman appoints tellers to distribute, collect, and count the ballots, and to report the vote to the society. The number of tellers required is dependent upon the number of voters and the number of candidates. There should never be less than two tellers. Their duties and the advantage of having an ample number of tellers are explained under Tellers, page 221. The methods adopted for balloting for members are simpler than those used for electing officers, because there is much less liability of attempted fraud.

There are two general methods of voting by ballot on the reception of members—one with small balls, from which is derived the term "Ballot," and the other with slips of paper. The same methods are also used in voting as to whether a member is guilty of charges preferred against him, and on his expulsion, and on other important questions that can be answered by yes or no, and whenever it is desired to preserve secrecy in the vote. The two methods are as follows:

(a) Balls. Many organizations use small white and black balls, or small white balls and black cubes. The white ball is used for the affirmative and the black ball or cube for the negative. From this is derived the expression "black-balled," meaning rejected. An ordinary ballot box is rectangular in shape, with a partition dividing it near the middle. The first compartment, into which all the balls are placed before the voting begins, has an opening in the end sufficiently large for a man to insert his hand, take a ball of the color he desires, and put it into the second compartment through a hole in the partition. Before voting begins, the ballot-box is inspected by the president to see that the second compartment is empty. The box is then passed by the tellers to the members, each member putting one ball from the first compartment into the second compartment, so that no one except himself sees the ball he is voting.

This method of voting places all members on their honor to vote honestly. There is no way to detect the fraud if a member puts in two balls, except by counting the number of voters and the number of balls put into the second compartment. Neither the dishonest voter nor the fraudulent vote can be detected.

Partially to remedy this defect, another style of ballot-box is used, one with two compartments, each having a hole over it for inserting the ball. One is marked "white" and the other "black." The voter takes from another box the ball he wishes to vote, and holds his hand so that the teller may see that he has only one ball, without seeing the color of the ball. Then, holding both hands together, the voter places the ball according to its color in the hand opposite the proper hole, and, holding each hand over a hole so that no one can see into which the ball is dropped, he drops the ball. The president should inspect the box before the voting, and after the tellers have removed the balls, to see that it is empty. This method requires the members to come to the ballot-box, so that the tellers can see that they have but a single ball. It is more troublesome than the other method, but is a better guard against double voting.

(b) **Slips of Paper.** In using this method, the chair, after appointing tellers, announces the name or names of the candidates. If there is only one candidate, he directs the members to write "Yes" or "No" on the paper slips that have been distributed by the tellers, and then directs the tellers to collect the ballots. The ballots are collected and counted and reported as shown hereafter, and the chair announces the result. If there are several candidates to be voted for, the chair should instruct the members to write on the left of their ballots the names of all the candidates whom they intend to vote for or against, and to the right of each name the word "Yes" or "No," according as they vote for or against the candidate. In counting and reporting the ballots, the tellers must treat the votes for each candidate the same as though the candidates were voted for on separate ballots. In other words, each candidate's votes are independent of those cast for the others.

Collecting Paper Ballots. In some organizations members go to the ballot-box and deposit their paper ballots. In others the ballot-box, or basket, or hat, or other receptacle, is passed by the tellers to the members in their seats, and each member deposits his ballot. This is a simple method, and there is no objection to it where there is no danger of fraudulent voting. In such cases there is no objection to the ballot slips being deposited without being folded, and there is the advantage that it facilitates counting. Under ballot voting for officers, page 219, is explained the precautions necessary when there is liability of fraudulent voting.

As soon as the ballots are collected, the chair should ask if all have voted, thus giving an opportunity to any one who has been overlooked by the tellers to make the fact known. When all have voted, the chair says, "The polls are closed," and the tellers proceed to count the ballots. [See page 223.]

While the tellers are counting the ballots, no one else should be allowed at the table where they are at work. As the votes are all affirmative or negative, their duties are very simple. As soon as the count is made, the teller first named reports to the assembly thus: "Mr. President: For Mr. A there are 60 votes in the affirmative and 3 in the negative; for Mr. B there are 58 in the affirmative and 4 in the negative; for Mr. C," etc. The chair repeats the report, and adds, "Messrs. A, B, and C are received as members of the society," or "Messrs. A, B, and C are elected members of the club."

ELECTION OF MEMBERS BY BOARD OF DIRECTORS

In many clubs the members are not elected directly by the club, but indirectly, by means of a board of directors, or managers, or governors, to whom all applications are made. This board, in some organizations, reports at every meeting of the society the names of all who have made application since the last meeting, so that members may have an opportunity to communicate to the board any objections to the reception of any applicant of which they have knowledge. The board does not act on the case until its next meeting after having reported the application to the society. The board also reports at each meeting of the society the names of all members received since the last meeting.

ELECTION OF MEMBERS WHERE THE MEMBERSHIP IS GREATLY SCATTERED

In this case the following method is pursued in some societies that are very careful about receiving new members. The written application for membership, endorsed or recommended by two or sometimes by three members, must be on file at the headquarters of the society about thirty days before the regular meeting at which it is to be acted upon. The president appoints for each application a committee of investigation consisting of two or three members. Two or three weeks before the regular meeting a printed notice of the meeting is mailed by the secretary to every member. This notice states what business is to come before the meeting, and contains a list of all candidates for membership to be voted for.

with their addresses, and in each case the names of the members who recommended the candidate and the names of the investigating committee. Members who know anything that should prevent the reception of a candidate are expected to communicate the facts to the chairman of the investigating committee.

Some plan of this kind is necessary where the membership is scattered all over a state, or perhaps over the entire United States, since the applicants may be unknown to the committee and to the members actually present at the meeting when action is taken.

CHAPTER XIX

NOMINATION AND ELECTION OF OFFICERS, BOARDS, AND STANDING COMMITTEES

NOMINATIONS

WHEN it is desired to choose some one to fill a certain position in a society or any deliberative assembly, instead of making the ordinary motions it has been found more convenient to nominate persons for the position. A nomination is practically a motion that the nominee, the person nominated, be chosen for the position. A nomination is usually made viva voce, like any other motion, by a single member, in which case it is called a "nomination from the floor" or an "open nomination"; or it may be made by a committee appointed for the purpose, known as the "nominating committee." Nominations may also be made by ballot, called a "nominating ballot," or by mail, as explained hereafter, page 233. Whenever nominations are referred to, viva voce nominations are meant unless one of the other methods is specified. A nomination differs from the ordinary motion in that it does not require a second; that there is no limit to the number of nominations; that in case of viva voce voting the voting is in the order of the nominations, beginning with the first one nominated instead of beginning with the last one named, as with amendments; and that the voting ceases as soon as any candidate receives a majority vote. If a motion is made similar to this, "That A act as secretary of this meeting," and no other name is suggested, the chair should put the question to vote, the same as in case of any other motion. But if the motion is also made to amend by striking out A and inserting B, he should treat it as filling a blank, and at once modify the question, saying, "A and B have been nominated for secretary. Are there any more nominations?"

Sometimes the term "nominate" is used in proposing candidates for membership in a society. There is a clear distinction between proposing a person for office and for membership, unless the membership is limited. Electing some one to fill an office prevents the election of any one else to that office, and therefore it is allowed to propose, or "nominate," additional candidates for the office. The case is somewhat similar in nominating members when there are more nominations than vacancies. The case of boards or committees is similar, for, while there is more than one position to fill, the number of positions is limited, so that the election of one member does to a certain extent interfere with the election of others, and therefore they are treated the same as in the case of officers. The election of a member of a society in which the membership is unlimited, on the contrary, does not interfere with the election of any one else as a member, and therefore when he is proposed it is not allowed to propose another candidate to compete with him for election, as in the above-mentioned cases of nominations.

To illustrate the advantages of the nomination method over the ordinary motions, suppose five candidates, A, B, C, D, and E, are proposed in the order mentioned. If the method of the ordinary motion and amendment were followed, A's election would be first moved, and then it would be moved to amend by striking out A and inserting B, and then a motion would be made to amend that amendment by striking out B and inserting C. Having reached the limit of amendments, the friends of D and E can only ask their friends to vote against all other candidates, and say that as soon as there is an opportunity they will move to amend by inserting the names of their respective candidates. If C is the choice, only three votes would be necessary to settle the election, the votes being in the affirmative on the two amendments and then on the amended main motion, so that but little more time would be consumed than by the nomination method. But if C were voted down, then it would be moved to amend the amendment by striking out B and inserting D; and if that were lost it would be moved to strike out B and insert E. If this last amendment is either adopted or lost, it would be necessary to take a vote on the amendment of the first degree, and then on the main motion whether amended or not.

By the nomination method the five candidates would be nominated in succession by a friend of each. The candidates would then be voted for in the order of their nomination, beginning with the first and stopping as soon as one receives a majority vote, that is, more ayes than noes. This is the fairer method, as the first nominees are more probably the choice of the assembly than the later nominees; and yet, the amendment method requires the votes on the first nominees to be taken last. The amendment method also takes more time, as it requires five different votes to be taken to elect either A or B, whereas the nomination method requires only one vote to elect A and two votes to elect B. Nominations cannot be amended. They are seldom debated, though sometimes the member making the nomination makes what is termed a nominating speech. This also is sometimes done by one or more seconders of the nomination.

If any person is nominated who is unable or unwilling to serve, he should immediately decline. If he was previously asked whether he would accept a nomination and did not decline, it is an imposition upon the society for him afterward to decline and to put the society to the trouble of selecting another candidate.

Nominations by Committee. Usually a committee is appointed in advance to submit nominations for the various offices and boards to be elected at an annual meeting of a society. If the committee is well selected its nominees are almost certain of election. It should be reasonably sure that the persons nominated are willing to serve if elected. In case a nominee withdraws before the election, the committee should meet immediately and agree upon another nomination, which should be reported even though the committee has previously made its report. Although a committee is automatically discharged when its report is made, nevertheless a nominating committee, in order to complete the work assigned it, is automatically revived, by the withdrawal of a nominee, provided the withdrawal occurs before the balloting begins. When called upon for its report, the chairman of the committee rises and says: "Mr. President, your [or, the Nominating] Committee makes [or submits] the following nominations: President, Mr. A; Vice-President, Mr. B"; etc. No other motion is made. The committee has virtually moved that this ticket be elected. The president announces the nominations thus: "The Nominating Committee makes [or submits] the following nominations: President, Mr. A," etc. [reading all the nominations]. "Are there any further nominations?" Nominations may now be made from the floor, as described in the next paragraph. Since the usual method of electing officers and boards is by ballot after they have been nominated by a committee, this entire subject is fully treated under Nominations by Committee and Election by Ballot, page 212.

Nominations from the Floor. A nomination from the floor is made by a member's rising and saying, "I nominate Mr. A." This he does not do until the president has called for nominations or has announced that nominations are in order. The president repeats each nomination thus, "Mr. A is nominated," "Mr. B is nominated," etc. No second is required, though sometimes one or more members second the nomination to give it their endorsement. The maker and the seconders of a nomination have the right to advocate the claim of their nominee when making or seconding the nomination. As soon as the chair announces one nomination, another may be made in the same way, and so on, as long as members wish to nominate. No one, except by general consent, can nominate more than one member of a board until all have had an opportunity to nominate. When the chair thinks no more nominations will be made, he inquires, "Are there any further nominations?" If there are none, he proceeds to take the vote on the nominations by whichever method the society has prescribed. In a large assembly it is generally well for the president to announce that "Nominations are closed" before proceeding to the election or other business; but the mere proceeding to the election or other business, if no objection is made at the time, closes nominations by general consent. [See in this connection Closing Nominations, page 166.]

In small assemblies nominations are frequently made by members from their seats without the formality of rising. In very large assemblies, on the other hand, members should address the chair as they rise.

Nominating Ballot. In some organizations it is the custom to nominate by ballot instead of from the floor. It is sometimes called an informal ballot, but the more correct designation is a nominating ballot. Its object is to ascertain the exact preference of the members, which can be expressed with secrecy by this method.

Since each member has the opportunity to nominate on his ballot a candidate for each office, he has not the right to nominate from the floor, unless the assembly by a majority vote authorizes such nominations. The ballot is conducted just the same as the ordinary ballot [see page 210], but the tellers' report does not state the number necessary for nomination, because every one voted for is nominated.

The real value of the nominating ballot is that it shows the preferences of the members without electing any one. This enables members to vote more intelligently on the electing ballot. Suppose 100 nominating ballots were divided among five candidates thus, A 25, B 23, C 20, D 18, and E 14, and that those who vote for the last three candidates prefer either of these candidates to either A or B. The nominating ballot shows that if they combine on one candidate they can elect him, since they control 52 votes of the 100. In societies where the elections are by a plurality vote, the nominating ballot is specially useful, as may be seen by the foregoing illustration, for in such a case A would have been elected on the first ballot even though seventy-five per cent. of the society were opposed to him. [See Plurality Vote, page 234.]

Any nominee who is unable or unwilling to serve should decline the nomination immediately. If one of the nominees receiving the largest number of votes declines, a motion should be made to take another nominating ballot for that particular office. The majority will then decide whether conditions have so changed as to make another nominating ballot desirable. To illustrate the importance of this, suppose the nominating ballot gives for president the preferences thus: A 60, B 30, C 8, and D 2. In such a case the chances are that B is not the second choice of the 60 who voted for A, so that if A declines they would prefer some one else to B. In this case a motion could be made to reopen nominations and allow nominations from the floor, or to have another nominating ballot, or to combine the two methods. In the last case the motion could be made thus: ''I move that nominations for president be reopened, and that nominations be allowed from the floor, after which another nominating ballot be taken.''

In some organizations that use the nominating ballot, the attempt is made to limit the voting at the electing ballot to the two nominees for each office receiving the highest number of votes for that office on the nominating ballot. Such action suspends one of the rights of members, and therefore, like motions limiting the right of debate, requires a two-thirds vote. Unless two thirds favor it, it is likely to do more harm than good. Sometimes this limitation is placed in the by-laws, which is a great mistake. In the case illustrated above, a by-law limiting the voting to A and B would deprive the majority of their right to vote for their choice. Such a by-law has led to worse results, as in a case where the nominating ballot gave 95 votes for A and 5 votes for B, and A declined. This left B the only eligible candidate according to the by-laws, as interpreted by the society, and he was elected, though ninety-five per cent. of those voting were opposed to his election. Sometimes the by-laws state that the two candidates receiving the largest number of votes on the nominating ballot shall be the official nominees. This does not prevent members from voting for other candidates, because voting is not limited to the nominees. Such a rule only prevents printing on the tickets the names of other candidates for the office.

Sometimes a motion is made to declare the nominating ballot the electing ballot. If the by-laws require the election to be by ballot, the motion is out of order, since it does away with the ballot. This is also the case with the motion that "the secretary [or some other member] cast the ballot of the society for Mr. A." ,The essential thing in the ballot is its secrecy, and no one can vote on such motions without exposing his vote.

Viva Voce Elections

In mass meetings and in many societies the elections are viva voce. In a mass meeting the presiding officer is nominated by one who is appointed for the purpose of calling the meeting to order, nominating the chairman, and presiding until the chairman is elected. He does not call for other nominations, but acts as chairman, and immediately puts the question on his nominee. In societies using this method of voting in elections, the officers and boards are nominated by a nominating committee and from the floor, or from the floor alone. If the officers are elected in succession, the second officer is not nominated from the floor until after the first one is elected.

If the nominations are made by a committee, the viva voce election is conducted in the following manner: The time for the election having arrived, the president says: "The next business in order is the election of officers for the ensuing year. The nominating committee will please report." The chairman of the nominating committee rises and says: "Mr. President, your nominating committee submits [or makes] the following nominations: President, Mr. A; Vice-President, Mr. B"; etc. The president reads all the names and then says: "Mr. A is nominated by the committee for president. Are there any more nominations for president?" Now any one may nominate from the floor, as described under Nominations from the Floor, page 207. If the election is to be viva voce, when the nominations have ended, the president repeats the nominations and says: "As many as are in favor of Mr. A for president say 'Aye.' Those opposed say 'No.'" If there are more ayes than noes, he continues: "The ayes have it and Mr. A is elected president." If the noes are in the majority he says, "The noes have it and Mr. A is not elected. Those in favor of Mr. M [the next nominee] say 'Aye.' Those opposed say 'No,'" etc. If Mr. M is not elected, the president puts the question on the next nomination, and so on until one receives a majority vote, that is, more ayes than noes, and then the chair declares that one elected, and says: "The committee nominates Mr. B for vice-president. Are there any other nominations for vice-president?" The other officers are elected in the same way.

It will be noticed that it is necessary for the friends of a candidate to vote against the other candidates, because if one of the others receives only two votes, and yet only one person votes against him, he receives a majority vote and is elected. In such a case of negligence the only remedy is for some one to call out immediately, "Division," whereupon the chair proceeds to take the vote again, this time taking a rising vote. As soon as one receives a majority vote, the office thereby being filled, no votes are taken on the remaining nominees.

BALLOT ELECTIONS IN SMALL SOCIETIES

In small societies a very common method of electing officers and boards at their annual meetings is to have nominations made from the floor, and then to have the vote taken by ballot. Sometimes the officers are elected separately, and sometimes they are all voted for on one ballot. There is a great advantage in not voting for the second officer until it is known who is elected to fill the first office, but it takes so much time that the plan is seldom used in large societies or conventions. In a small society the separate election of officers may be combined with any form of nomination.

When officers are voted on separately, which is done only when there are few offices to fill, or few voters, the election is conducted as follows: The chair announces that "The business before the assembly is the election of officers. The chair appoints X and Y as tellers. The tellers will distribute blank slips [which should be provided in advance by the secretary], one to each member, who will immediately write on the slip his choice for president. Are there any nominations for president?" If a nominating committee has been appointed, the president calls on it to report before calling for nominations from the floor. The committee makes all its nominations at one time, and the president repeats the committee's nominations for each office just before calling for nominations from the floor, as in case of viva voce elections. When the nominations are ended, the chair directs the tellers to collect the ballots, which they do in any convenient receptacle, the only essential points being that none but members vote, that no member puts in more than one ballot, and that the vote is secret. This does not mean that a member cannot show his ballot to another member, but the tellers have no right to look at the ballots when collecting them so as to be able to identify any one's vote. When the tellers have collected the ballots, the chair should inquire if all who wish to do so have voted. Any member who has been passed over by the tellers should hold up his ballot so the tellers can see it, and it should be collected by one of them. The chair should then direct the tellers to count the ballots, which should be done preferably in another room.

Any business may be transacted while the tellers are out, and in some cases there is no objection to proceeding to elect another officer, taking care, however, not to proceed to an election that might be affected by the result of the preceding one, the ballots for which are being counted. New tellers may be appointed for the second election, and these two sets of tellers will enable the election to be expedited. Both sets of tellers should be given an opportunity to vote in elections held while they are counting ballots. When the tellers report, the chair repeats the report and announces who is elected. The tellers should never announce the result.

If all the offices are balloted for at the same time, at least four tellers should be appointed. In this case the chair should direct the members to write the name of the person for whom they vote immediately under (or after) the name of the office he is to fill. The method of counting the ballots in this case is described on page 223, and the form of the tellers' report on page 561.

NOMINATIONS BY COMMITTEE AND ELECTION BY BALLOT

Nominations by Committee. Officers and boards of large societies are usually nominated by a committee and elected by ballot. In conventions this method of nomination and election is always followed. Since the report of the committee usually consists of a printed ticket, the committee must be appointed early enough to allow for the printing. In an annual convention of delegates the by-laws should provide that the committee be appointed in advance by the Executive Board or Board of Directors, or, at the first meeting of the convention, by the convention itself. It may be appointed by any of the methods mentioned on page 254, except that it should never be appointed by the president, because in case of his renomination it would prove embarrassing. Unless the by-laws or a resolution of the society prescribe the method, the nominating committee should be appointed by the assembly. In local societies having frequent regular meetings, it is well for the by-laws to require the nominating committee to be appointed at least a month before the annual meeting. In some organizations the printed ticket is mailed to the members previous to the annual meeting. In others it is posted in their club-room at least a week before the annual meeting.

The nominating committee previous to submitting its report should, if practicable, satisfy itself that the nominees will, if elected, accept the offices and perform the duties thereof. This is especially necessary in large organizations where the voters are numerous, and in conventions of delegates.

In nominating the officers, consideration should be given to the duties to be performed. In some societies the president is merely the presiding officer at its meetings, and in such societies he should be chosen on account of his ability to preside. A poor presiding officer almost always means trouble. In other societies the principal duties of the president are of an administrative nature, and his ability in this line is of more importance to the society than his ability as a presiding officer.

In some societies the only duty of the vice-president is to preside in the absence of the president. In others he assumes all the duties of the president in case of the death or resignation of the latter. In still others the several vice-presidents are the heads of different departments of work. These duties should be considered in nominating these officers.

The secretary, or clerk, or recorder, or scribe, as he is variously called, is in most societies a very important officer, and the nominating committee should be careful to nominate some one who would keep accurate records, and would avoid boring the society with attempts to exhibit his literary talents.

Other officers and boards should be selected in a similar way for their efficiency, and not for social or complimentary reasons. Much trouble has resulted in societies as a result of failure to observe this rule.

Usually the nominating committee reports a ticket with only one nominee for each office, but sometimes the by-laws require them to report two nominees for each office. It is doubtful if any good is accomplished by this. If the committee desires the election of one candidate, it can select for the other a person whom it would be impossible to elect. Those who are opposed to the nominations of the committee have their remedy in nominating their candidates from the floor when the committee reports, and then "scratching" the printed ticket, that is, crossing out the objectionable names and replacing them by the names of their candidates. If it is desired to have the committee report two nominations for each office, both parties should be well represented on the committee, and the first nominee for each office should be chosen by the majority and the second nominee by the minority of the committee.

In some societies the so-called Australian Ballot is used, in which case the duties of the nominating committee are somewhat different, because under that system all the nominations are printed on the ticket and it is necessary to indicate by a mark which nominee is voted for. This should never be confounded with the single ticket system, in which only one name for each office is printed, and therefore there is no occasion for designating by a cross for which of the several nominees the vote is cast. [See Australian Ballot, page 231.]

Report of the Nominating Committee. This report consists simply of a list of the offices to be filled, each office being followed by the name of the nominee. It may be simply in writing if the number of voters and offices to be filled is small, or if the election is not to be held until a future day. If the voters and offices to be filled are numerous, and the election is to be held immediately, it is usually better for the committee to report a printed ticket with a nominee for each office, and a blank space below each name in which the voter may write the name of a candidate that he prefers. These tickets can be used for ballots at the election. If the election is held on another day, the tickets, or ballots, should not be printed until after the committee has reported, and the ballots should include the nominations that have been made from the floor.

Presenting the Committee's Report. When called upon for the committee's report, the chairman rises and says: "Mr. President, your nominating committee makes [or submits] the following nominations: President, Mr. A," etc., reading the ticket and handing it to the president and then resuming his seat. The president reads the ticket again, or has it read by the secretary, or, in very large assemblies, by the reading clerk or official reader. The president then asks if there are any more nominations, after which any member may nominate a candidate for any office to be filled, as described under Nominations from the Floor, page 207. If it is evident that there will be many nominations from the floor, the chairman should call for nominations for each office in succession, taking them in the same order as they are on the ticket reported by the nominating committee.

Preparing the Ballots. If the tickets are printed it is well to have them distributed before the committee reports, so that members who wish to do so may "scratch" their tickets as they hear nominations that they prefer to those submitted by the committee. The change may be made by writing the preferred name under the one reported by the committee. It is better, though not necessary, to cross out the printed name. When there are several to be elected to the same office, as to membership on a board, it is necessary to cross out the name of every candidate for whom it is not intended to vote. If there are more names left than vacancies to fill, all the votes for that office except those written in are ignored. If there are 6 names left and only 5 to be elected, the tellers cannot determine which of the printed names are voted for, and therefore they must reject all but the written ones. This does not affect the other votes on the same ticket. Whenever

a ticket or ballot is printed and more than one are to be elected
to the same office, the number to be elected should be stated above
the names of the nominees for the office. If there are a number of
members ineligible to the office, the fact in some way should be
called to the attention of the voters. In a small society it might
be sufficient for the chair to state the by-law that makes certain
persons ineligible, and then to repeat the names of those ineligible.
Where there are large boards, one third going out of office each
year, members may not remember the names of those holding over.
Some by-laws make all who have held office for, say, three years
consecutively, ineligible for one year thereafter to any office. The
voters should be informed as to all ineligible persons. When the
ballot is printed, it is well to have on it full directions with the
names of the ineligibles, so that there will be no excuse for any
votes being cast for ineligible persons. If a member is in doubt
as to any point, he should rise, address the chair, and make his
inquiry.

When the nominations are all made, the next step is the election
by ballot. A nomination is really a motion that the nominee fill
the specified office, and consequently, if accepted, adopted, or
agreed to by a majority vote of the assembly, the nominee is elected
to the office unless the by-laws specify how the officer shall be
elected. An assembly, therefore, cannot "accept" two nominees to
the same office, any more than it can elect two.

Election by Ballot in an Ordinary Society. The election may
take place immediately after the nominations, or at a future time.
In some societies the nominating committee, previously appointed
or elected, reports a ticket at the opening of the meeting, this
ticket having been posted previously where it could be examined
by the members. Immediately after the report of the nominating
committee an opportunity should be given for nominations from
the floor, and these are posted adjacent to the committee's ticket.
The election should be held early in the meeting, in order that if
the first ballot fails to elect there is time for further balloting.
If the voters and candidates are few, there is no necessity for a
printed ticket. In making out the tickets, the offices should be
arranged in the same order as in the ticket submitted by the nominating committee. It would be well for the secretary to supply
uniform slips upon which the tickets should be written. If the

voters and offices to be filled are numerous, it might be well for these slips to have printed on them the title of the office, with space below for writing the name of the person voted for.

If the election is held immediately after nominations are closed, the voters necessarily will be obliged to write their own tickets, unless the nominating committee submits a printed ticket. In the latter case the voter uses that ticket, changing it to suit his views.

Ballots may be collected in either of the following ways:

(*a*) The tellers pass a basket, or a ballot-box, or any other receptacle among the voters, who themselves deposit their ballots in the receptacle. Sometimes the ballots are required to be folded, which gives the tellers a little more trouble, but makes it more difficult for any one to put in more than one ballot. If two ballots are folded together, both are rejected as illegal. This method of collecting the ballots is probably the most common in ordinary societies, because in them there is but little danger of fraudulent voting. The tellers should never look at the names on the ballots, but they should see that no one votes who is not entitled to do so. It is impossible for them to see that no one puts in two ballots, especially if they are not folded. In using this method of collecting the ballots it is necessary to trust to the honor of the members, since it is impossible to prevent members from putting in more than one ballot. If there are more ballots than voters, another ballot should be taken.

(*b*) Another method of collecting the ballots is to have the ballot-box placed on a table, and the members to pass by it and to deposit their ballots, or, better still, to hand them to a teller who deposits them. This latter method makes it very difficult to have any illegal voting. The tellers must be sure that those who vote are entitled to do so, and that after voting they do not join those who have not voted. This can easily be arranged by the chair's directing all the members to move to the part of the hall nearest the ballot-box, and then those who have voted to occupy the vacant part. If the ballots are handed to a teller to place in the box, it is impossible for any one to put in two ballots unless they are folded together, and in that case they are both rejected. If the ballot is not folded, it should be handed to the teller face down, so that no one can see for whom the vote is cast. It is safer, of course, to require the ballots to be folded, and it requires no more time to count them if an additional number of tellers is employed.

(c) In very large assemblies much time may be saved if it is practicable to have several ballot-boxes and sets of tellers. These may be placed in different parts of the hall, or in outside rooms, and the assembly divided into an equal number of groups, one group to each ballot-box. By a little care the tellers for each group can see that their group votes without confusion. The tellers should not permit any one to vote whom they do not know to be a member, unless he is vouched for by some other member whom the tellers know.

(d) In societies with extensive and scattered membership, where the tellers are unacquainted with the members, some method must be adopted to prevent voting by those not entitled to vote. In case the voting members are required to register, they should at that time be supplied with a badge or something of that kind to designate them. Sometimes before receiving a ballot the member is required to give his name and even have another member identify him. His name is called out and then checked on the alphabetical list of members in attendance, and he is then furnished with a ballot. This is generally sufficient protection against fraudulent voting. If greater protection is desired, some of the methods described in the next chapter, under Elections in Conventions of Delegates, may be used with slight modifications.

The method of counting the ballots and of reporting the result is explained in the next chapter, pages 223–228.

CHAPTER XX

ELECTIONS

(Continued).

ELECTIONS BY BALLOT IN CONVENTIONS OF DELEGATES.

THE method of making nominations described on pages 212–214 is used in conventions the same as in ordinary societies. If the nominating committee is not appointed in advance, it should be elected or appointed on the first day of the convention. It should report as soon as practicable, because in the case of most conventions it is better to use a printed ballot containing the names of all the nominees, those nominated from the floor as well as those reported by the committee. The printed ballots should be ready for the election, which should never be left to the last day of the convention, because it may be necessary to have several ballots before all the offices are filled.

In conventions of delegates the method of voting by ballot is necessarily modified on account of the fact that the right to vote is limited to those who have proper credentials. In such bodies all delegates must present their credentials to the credentials committee, and that committee reports to the convention a list of the delegates with proper credentials. When this report has been accepted, it constitutes the roll of delegates to the convention. Only those whose names are on that roll can vote on its acceptance, and thereafter none can vote except those that were on that roll and those that are afterward added to it from time to time as the credentials committee reports additional delegates. The credentials committee should furnish the delegates with some badge or certificate that will show that they are accredited delegates and are therefore entitled to admission and to a seat in the hall, and that they have the right to vote. The credentials committee should coöperate with the tellers in identifying the voters, as shown on page 220.

To insure that none but delegates vote, different methods are pursued. If none but delegates are admitted to the floor of the hall, or if the convention is small and the members are known to one another, any of the methods already described for voting in an ordinary assembly may be adopted. But in elections in large conventions it is usually better to exercise more care, and to use stationary ballot-boxes into which the ballots are put by one of the tellers, to whom the ballot is handed by the voter. The objection to allowing the voter to put in his own ballot is the difficulty of preventing a person from putting in more than one ballot. Even if the teller detects the fraud, it is generally too late to prevent it, and he has no way of identifying the fraudulent votes. It takes no more time for the voter to hand his ballot to the teller than to put it into a box. If the ballot is not folded it should be handed to the teller face down, and he should insert it in the ballot-box without exposing the face. Preferably, ballots should be folded even when handed to a teller. No voter should ever be allowed to put into the ballot-box an unfolded ballot, as it is easy to put in two ballots without being detected. As heretofore stated, if two ballots are folded together both are rejected as illegal.

Care should be exercised to prevent any one from voting twice. One precaution is to have the voter give his name, and show his certificate or badge, as he hands his ballot to the teller. An additional precaution is to have the teller repeat the name, so that all in the vicinity can hear, before putting the ballot into the ballot-box, while another teller, or a credentials committeeman, checks the name on the alphabetical list of delegates. This publicity prevents any attempt to vote under another's name, while the check prevents repeating. When printed tickets are used, these are often given out only to delegates, and only one to each delegate. If the delegate spoils his ticket, he must return it in order to obtain another. In order to procure his ticket he must show his certificate, or other evidence of his being a delegate, and give his name, which is called out and checked. These precautions are sometimes neces-sary in large conventions in which the delegates are unknown to the tellers.

Where the number of delegates is large, a number of ballot-boxes should be provided and the delegates should be divided into a similar number of groups, so that the voting will not consume too much time. A member of the credentials committee who is familiar with the part of the list of delegates covering this group sits beside the tellers and checks the name of the voter. The teller then, in the presence of the voter, places the ballot within the ballot-box. Under Credentials Committee, on page 283, is shown how the territory covered should be divided into districts for convenience in registering, and the register should be divided into a corresponding number of sections. This same grouping of the delegates should be used in balloting at the election, the tellers being divided into a corresponding number of sub-committees, numbered the same as the credentials sub-committees and as the sections of the register. A member of each credentials sub-committee should coöperate with the corresponding set of tellers, since he is familiar with his section of the register, the duplicate copy of which he takes with him to the polls.

As an illustration, let the case be taken of the election of the officers and directors in a state convention of 600 registered delegates. For registration purposes the state has been divided into 5 districts, the register into 5 sections, and the credentials committee into 5 sub-committees. Each of these sub-committees has had a separate table conspicuously marked with its number and a description of the territory included in the district. These same tables should be used by the corresponding sub-committees of the tellers. All of the directions given on pages 284, 285 for assisting delegates to find their proper places for registering, and to prevent confusion in entering and leaving the room, should be followed at the election. When a member enters the room to vote, since he has his identification card with the number of his district, he proceeds at once to the table with that number. This is the same table at which he registered. The ushers, when necessary, should assist the delegates in finding their tables. At each table are the tellers, a ballot-box, and a credentials sub-committeeman with the section of the register of that district, to whom he gives his name and shows his identification card. As soon as his name is checked he is furnished with a ticket, if the tickets have not been previously distributed. He then goes to a table, marks his ticket to suit his views, returns to the tellers of his district, handing one of them his folded ballot, and leaves the room by a different door from the one by which he entered. The object of this is to prevent the confusion arising from members' entering and leaving by the same door, where there is a crowd. If members have been furnished tickets before the election, so that there has been an opportunity to mark them, they hand them to the teller by the ballot-box immediately after showing their identification cards. As soon as the name of a voter is checked, the teller places the ballot in the ballot-box.

If it is desired to take additional precautions to prevent fraudulent voting, the plan described above may be modified as follows: Each blank ballot, before being delivered to the voter, is initialed by the teller in charge of the blank ballots for that district. At the same time the name of the voter is checked by the credentials committeeman, or the teller, in charge of the register for that district. This prevents the issuing of more than one ballot to the same person. When the voter has marked and folded his ballot, he hands it to the teller in charge of the ballot-box, who, after seeing that it is properly initialed, places it in the ballot-box. This is to insure that no ballots are voted except those obtained from the person in charge of the ballots. As an additional precaution, the teller in charge of the ballot-box may place his initials on each ballot. The initials of the two tellers should be placed so that they can be seen when the ballot is folded. These two tellers should belong to opposite parties, and each one should have associated with him a teller of the other party. These precautions, if the tellers are properly selected, reduce the liability to fraud in voting to a mimimum.

The precautions just described are excessive in most cases. Every convention must decide for itself just how its elections shall be conducted. In some cases it is difficult to find members to accept office, and therefore there is no need of taking precautions against fraudulent voting. In others there is great rivalry for office, and every reasonable means should be taken to prevent illegal voting.

The Tellers. It is so common to appoint tellers who are unfitted for the duties they are to perform that it would seem that there is but little realization of the importance of their duties. Very serious difficulties arise in societies because of mistakes of the tellers, resulting sometimes in placing in office persons not elected. When this is discovered after the new officers have been installed, as has occurred in large societies of intelligent people, it is bound to cause trouble. Tellers should be as careful and accurate as an auditing committee, and therefore it is generally best to have them appointed by the president. Usually the chair appoints the tellers, but if any one objects, it requires a majority vote to authorize him to make the appointments, as it is not his right any more than to appoint other committees. If he is authorized only to nominate the tellers, it is treated as in case of his nominating a committee. If he appoints tellers without express authorization, the assembly by a majority vote can change them. This change should be made if he betrays his trust and shows partizanship in his appointments. In the case of large organizations it is frequently better to have the president authorized before the annual meeting to appoint tellers, so that they may have an opportunity to prepare properly for their work.

The tellers, like a committee of investigation, should never be appointed from one party. They must command the confidence of all. And consequently, when there are two parties in the election, the tellers should be equally divided, or nearly so, between them. In such cases the president should consult the leaders of the two parties, and appoint tellers satisfactory to them. But in no case should incompetent or contentious tellers be appointed. Some very good people are so constituted that they cannot work well with others, and consequently should not be appointed tellers. No teller has a right to insist upon doing everything himself. If he cannot trust any of the other tellers he should ask for some additional tellers whom he can trust, or ask to be excused, because each teller can do but half of the work, as shown hereafter. If there is only one set of tellers, the president should designate the one to act as chairman of tellers. If there is more than one set, he should appoint an additional teller to act as chairman, and sometimes a vice-chairman also, who should belong to the opposite party. When possible the chairman should be one having had experience as a teller, as well as having good judgment. Usually it is better to have four tellers in a set working together, though two can do the work equally well where there is no great rivalry for office and each has confidence in the other. Where the number of voters is large and there are many offices and candidates, it is usually advisable to have several sets of tellers, as shown on page 230.

Tally Sheets. Tally sheets, that is, sheets for the record of the votes for each candidate, should be prepared by the tellers as soon as the nominations are made. If the candidates are numerous, it may be more convenient to have separate sheets of paper for each office. In this case the first sheet should be headed "President," and the surnames of all the nominees for president would be written in a column on the left side of the sheet, arranged alphabetically, each surname being followed by the corresponding Christian name, thus: "Jones, John M." In case of a married woman who may be voted for under two names, the entry may include both names, thus: "Brown, Mrs. Isabel H.," and underneath in parenthesis, "(Mrs. Lawrence W.)." A vertical line should be drawn to the right of the names of the nominees, and a horizontal line just above the name of each nominee. Below the names of the nominees should be left space for adding the names of candidates who may be voted for in addition to those who are nominated. In some societies a single tally sheet will be sufficient for all the officers, while in others several sheets will be required, and in some a single sheet for each office is needed. If tally sheets have not been prepared in advance, as should always be done if possible, it will generally be found better policy to take the time to prepare them, as just described, before commencing the count.

Counting the Ballots. The various methods of collecting the ballots have been explained in the previous chapter. In the case of two tellers, it is assumed that the additional precautions described on page 221 are unnecessary and have not been taken. When the polls have been closed, the tellers take the ballot-box into a room where they can be alone, though if necessary several sets of tellers could occupy tables in different parts of the same room. No one else should be permitted in the room while the ballots are being counted. The ballot-box is opened and the ballots emptied on the table and counted. It is well to place them in piles of any convenient size, as 20, 25, or 30, since this may be of service in the recount that will be necessary if the total number of ballots is greater than the total number of voters checked on the roll. If the ballots are in excess of the checks on the roll, some one has voted who was not checked; if the ballots are fewer than the checks, then some one was checked who did not vote. If the ballots are in excess of the checks on the roll, the fact must be noted and reported to the assembly as a part of the tellers' report, as shown hereafter. If the ballots are fewer than the checks, it is of no consequence and the matter is ignored, since it simply shows that a delegate after being checked failed to hand in his ballot. The ballots may be counted either before or after the votes for each candidate have been counted. Another check that may be applied is to count the printed ballots on hand before the polls are opened after they are closed. The difference should be equal to the number checked on the roll plus the number of spoiled tickets exchanged for new ones. The spoiled tickets should be kept with the unused ones and the checked roll, and turned over to the chairman of tellers. The tellers should examine the ballot-box before the voting begins to see that it is empty, and at the close to see that all the ballots have been removed. As both parties have a representative present when the tickets are issued and also at the ballot-box, they should be satisfied that the election has been fairly conducted.

If there are only two tellers, or only two in each group, one teller opens and reads the ballots, and the other makes the record on the tally sheet. Since there is no check on the inaccuracy of either teller, this plan should never be adopted except in very small bodies where very accurate tellers can be secured.

If there are four tellers, two of them, belonging to opposite parties, look over each ballot together while one of them reads it aloud; or one of them may open and glance at each ballot and pass it to the other, who reads it aloud and then places it where there is no danger of its being mixed with the uncounted ballots. Each of the other two tellers has a tally sheet, on which he makes a vertical line to the right of the name of the candidate as it is called out. The marks are made in groups of five, the fifth line being drawn diagonally across the four vertical ones, as shown in the Form of Tally Sheet, page 562. Grouping thus in five facilitates the counting, while, when there are more than two tellers and two are keeping the count, one calls out "Tally" whenever a diagonal line is drawn, so that if the count does not agree it is detected at once and the count must all be gone over again. If a candidate is voted for who was not nominated, and is therefore not on the tally sheet, his name should be entered when first called. If there is any possibility of a contested election, the tally sheets should be in ink, and should be signed by the tellers and deposited, together with the ballots, with the secretary, who should retain them until satisfied that they will not be required. They are the legal evidence of the votes cast at the election and should not be defaced in any way. When all the ballots have been entered on the tally sheet, the total number of votes cast for each candidate should be entered opposite his name to the extreme right, or immediately under his name. Then the number of votes cast for the candidate for each office should be added together, and if in any case this number exceeds the number of ballots cast, it shows there has been a mistake in counting the votes for this office, and it is necessary to make a recount of the votes for this office alone. If the total votes for any office is less than the number of ballots, no notice is taken of it, since it is probably due to some one's failing to vote for that office.

In crediting votes, common sense must be exercised and an effort made to ascertain and to carry out the intention of the voter. It is folly to attempt to enforce unnecessary rules with strictness, such as requiring a particular kind of cross to be placed in a specified space adjacent to each name voted for, when there is only one name under the title for the office, and therefore there can be no doubt for whom the vote is cast. Such rules are necessary where ballots are used with several names printed under some of the titles, so that it is necessary to have some way of designating which of the candidates is voted for. But when the ticket is printed or written with only one name for each office, such a rule as the above cannot possibly be of any service, and if enforced, results in disfranchising some of the voters. When only one name is printed or written under the title of an office, the vote should be credited to that candidate. If the voter does not wish to vote for any candidate for that office, the printed name, or names, should be crossed out. If it is desired to vote for another candidate, the preferred candidate's name should be written in the blank space below, and the printed name, or names, may be crossed out. If the voter neglects to cross out the printed name, but writes in a new name, it is quite evident that the vote was intended for the candidate whose name is written in, and it should be so credited. No cne would write a name on a ballot under the title of an office without intending to vote for that person.

When a married woman's name is written in several ways, the ballot is not vitiated even if two or all of the names are written on the same ballot under the same office, for it is evidently intended to better describe the candidate, and must not be treated as though it were a vote for more than one person. All the names on the ballot are credited as one vote for the candidate. Ballots with any one of these various names must be credited to the same candidate. No attention is paid to middle names unless they are necessary to distinguish two candidates. Thus, for example, ballots for "Mrs. Brown," "Isabel H. Brown," "Mrs. Isabel Brown," "Mrs. Lawrence Brown," "Mrs. Dr. Brown," "Mrs. Dr. Lawrence W. Browne," if these names are all evidently intended to describe the same person, must be credited to the same person. The misspelling of names and inaccuracies of initials, or even their omission, should be ignored by the tellers, provided there is no doubt as to the person for whom the vote is intended. The essential thing is the intention of the voter as shown by the ballot itself. If the intention of the voter cannot be determined from the ballot alone, it is rejected as an illegal vote. A case of this kind is one with the name illegible, or one where there are more names written in than there are positions to fill, as for a board of managers. The rejection in such a case does not apply to the entire ballot, but simply to the particular vote that is illegal. The ballots that contain illegal votes should be put in one package properly marked, so that they can be examined if the assembly deems it advisable.

Although, as just stated, votes should be credited according to the intention of the voters whenever such intention is clear from the ballots themselves, yet every effort should be made to have the ballots correct. When practicable, the names of nominees for each office should be written in large, plain letters and conveniently displayed in the hall. Where names are peculiar in their spelling and where the names of two nominees have some similarity, the chair should call special attention to the fact.

If a member has accepted a nomination and his name is printed on the ticket reported by the nominating committee, it does not prevent his being nominated from the floor to another office. If votes are cast for a candidate for several different offices on the same ballot, he must be credited with a vote for each office, and if elected to two or more offices he has the right, if present, to choose which one he will accept; if he is absent the assembly should decide by a majority vote which office he shall fill, and then proceed to another election to fill the vacancy.

If, in unfolding a ballot, two are found folded together, both are rejected as fraudulent. They should be so marked and preserved. If a blank paper is found folded in a ballot it does not vitiate the ballot, and no notice is taken of the fact. Blank pieces of paper folded as ballots are ignored, though sometimes a memorandum of them is made for the purpose of accounting for all the ballots cast, or for all the apparent voters. Members who do not wish to vote sometimes adopt this method of avoiding voting and at the same time concealing the fact. The blanks are not votes and must not be counted as such, but every ballot, however defective, must be counted as a ballot if it has a name on it that is not crossed out.

If the tellers are not unanimous as to how they should credit a vote, they must report the facts to the assembly and ask for instructions. When asking instructions, they should be careful not to show how the decision would affect any of the candidates. The chair decides the question raised, but any one can appeal from his decision, as on any question of order. The tellers are not judges of election. The assembly decides all doubtful questions.

When completed, the tally sheets should be signed by the tellers and disposed of as stated on page 230.

Tellers' Report. The tellers proceed to make out their report as soon as the tally sheets are completed. In the case of the annual election of officers and a board of directors, the report could be headed, "Tellers' Report of Ballot for Officers and Directors at the Annual Meeting of the Aëro Club, May 11, 19—." If each of the ballots contains votes for candidates for all the offices, so that the number of ballots cast for each office is the same, then immediately below the heading should be entered the number of ballots cast and the number necessary for an election, which, unless there is a by-law to the contrary, is always a majority of the entire number of ballots cast by legal voters, whether the ballots are rejected as illegal or not. Thus the number of ballots cast for any office is the number of legal voters who voted for somebody for that office, whether the person voted for was eligible or not. Below the number of votes necessary for election should be stated the number of illegal ballots, if any. The number of illegal ballots, added to the number of votes credited to the candidates for each office, should be equal to the entire number of votes cast.

The number of ballots cast should be followed by the title of each office as a sub-heading, arranged in the same order as on the ballots, which should be the same as in the list of officers in the by-laws. Under each title should be written the names of the various candidates for that office, with the number of votes cast for each, the list being arranged in order according to the number of votes received, the one receiving the highest number being first.

Sometimes voters do not vote for candidates for all the offices, so that the number of votes for president, as an example, may be more than those for treasurer. In this case, instead of stating it once at the beginning of the report, it is necessary to state the number of votes cast and the number necessary for election under the title of each office, just before stating the number of votes for each candidate. The number of votes necessary for election to any office is a majority of the votes for that office, which is not necessarily a majority of the ballots voted. In the case of a board where there are several to elect, every ballot is counted that has on it a single name for the board. If a printed ballot is used, it should state the number of members of the board to be elected, and give the names of members of the board that hold over, so that they will not be voted for. The name of every candidate not voted for should be crossed out. If more names are left than places to fill, the ballot cannot be counted for any members of the board, but like other illegal ballots must be counted in stating the number of votes cast and the number necessary for election.

When the report is completed, it should be signed by all the tellers, who should return to the assembly hall and report through their chairman. As soon as he can obtain the floor, he says something like this: "Mr. President, your tellers, having counted the ballots cast for the officers and directors for the ensuing year, report as follows [or, submit the following report]." He then reads the report made as just described, hands it to the president, and takes his seat. The report should never state who is elected, as the tellers have no authority to decide that question. [For a Form of Report of Tellers, see page 561.]

Declaring, or Announcing, the Election. When the president receives the tellers' report, it is again read, either by the president or by some one designated by him. After the number of votes for each candidate for an office is read, the president should announce the election of the candidate receiving a majority of the votes cast for that particular office. If in any case there is not a majority vote, he announces, "There is no election," and proceeds with the reading of the report. In the case of an election of a board of directors or a standing committee, it is possible that more candidates may receive a majority vote than there are places to fill. In such a case, if there are five places to fill and eight receive a majority vote, the chair announces as elected all of the first five that received more votes than the other three. If only three receive more votes each than the sixth one, that is, if the fourth, fifth, and sixth are a tie, then the chair announces the election of only the first three, and a new ballot must be taken for the other two directors. In other words, in order to be elected on a board, a candidate must have a vote as large as a majority of the number of ballots cast for members of the board, even though some of the ballots may contain the name of only one candidate, and must also have more votes than any candidate who is not elected.[1]

If there is a failure to fill any of the offices, the president, after reading the tellers' report, should immediately direct the tellers to distribute blank pieces of paper to the members, and should then give instructions to the latter as to what offices are to be filled, and should direct them to write the title of each office, and under (or after) each title the name of the candidate voted for. If there is a failure to elect many of the officers, it may be easier to use any surplus of printed ballots, it being understood that it is not necessary to cross out the names under offices already filled, as the ballots are counted only for the offices that the president has stated are to be filled.

If the election is one where there is a possibility of its being contested, both the tally sheets and the report should be in ink, and the tally sheets, together with the ballots, should be turned over to the secretary, who should seal them and preserve them until there is no liability of a recount's being ordered, after which time they should be destroyed. If the election is not questioned within a month there is usually no use to preserve them. In most societies there is no possibility of the report of the tellers being questioned, and therefore the tally sheets may be in pencil, and

[1] See Drill on Election of Delegates and Alternates in Parliamentary Practice, page 152.

they and the ballots may be destroyed as soon as the annual meeting adjourns. The tellers are in honor bound not to divulge the vote of any one that they may recognize by the handwriting or otherwise.

If for any reason the election is not completed at the annual meeting, the assembly should adjourn to another day to complete its work. The annual election of officers and boards is assigned to that meeting, and that meeting should not end until that duty is performed, even if necessary to hold several adjourned meetings. The intervals between these adjourned meetings should be as short as possible, and no other business should be attended to until the elections have been completed.

In large conventions of delegates, when there are several sets of tellers, as described on page 220, each having charge of the voting of one section of the delegates, each set of tellers proceeds until the tally sheets are completed and signed, and then they are handed to the chairman of tellers. When all the tally sheets are received, the chairman calls the tellers together, and all doubtful questions should be settled and the tally sheets corrected before attempting to make out the report, which is done the same as if there had been one set of tellers. It may be found that different sets of tellers settled the same question differently. If after discussion the tellers are not unanimous, the facts should be reported to the assembly and instructions requested. [See page 227.]

Where it is desired to guard against every possible fraud, one teller from each party should look over the report of each section of tellers while one of them reads the report aloud. A teller from each party at the same time might, though this is not necessary, look at the tally sheet to see if the figures are the same, and the other tellers should write down the figures as they are called off, and afterward add together the number of votes for each candidate as reported by each set of tellers. From these figures the chairman makes out the tellers' report as already described. [See page 561 for Form of Tellers' Report.]

CHAPTER XXI

ELECTIONS (*Concluded*): MISCELLANEOUS ELECTIONS

AUSTRALIAN BALLOT IN SOCIETIES AND CONVENTIONS.

THE so-called Australian Ballot is admirably adapted to political elections, for which it was designed in order to diminish the chances for bribery and fraud. The attempt to use it in some societies and conventions, for which use it is ill adapted, has caused unnecessary difficulty in conducting fair elections.

Political elections are essentially different from elections in deliberative assemblies, and what is a good method for one may be a very bad one for the other. In the former case there is no assemblage of the voters where open nominations may be made, where tellers may ask for instructions, and where decisions may be made upon all questions relating to the election upon which the tellers are not unanimous. In the ordinary society or convention the voters are in session, and can attend to their business without the machinery necessary in political elections, where there is no assemblage of the voters. In the political elections there are always several distinct parties, sometimes five or six, each of which nominates a distinct ticket, and in some cases each of these tickets contains fifty or more names, making two or three hundred names on the ballot sheet. In an ordinary society or convention, on the contrary, there are no such organized parties which nominate party tickets in advance. It is seldom that there are more than two parties, and usually the contest is limited to a few offices. Under such circumstances the Australian Ballot should never be used. [See page 236 for further comparison of political elections and elections in deliberative assemblies.]

The Australian Ballot is used in political elections as described on page 237. As stated there, it varies in different places, the only essential thing in the ballot being that the names of all the nominees are printed on a single sheet of paper under the direction of the government whose officers are to be elected, instead of being printed on separate party tickets under party management. Special means are taken to prevent repeating, that is, voting more than once, or impersonating another, or using any ballot except the one delivered to the voter by the election officer at the polls.

If a society or convention wishes to use the Australian Ballot, it is necessary first to determine upon some method of making nominations, since they all must be printed on the ballot. Of course it would be impracticable to allow single members to nominate, as is done in open nominations (nominations from the floor). The by-laws should prescribe the number of signatures required to a nomination, and should designate to whom, and how long before the annual meeting, the nomination must be sent. If it is desired to have a nominating committee, the nominations should be sent to the chairman of that committee, and the committee should attend to having the ballots printed. If there is no nominating committee, the nominations should be sent to the secretary, who should attend to having the tickets printed, arranging the nominees for each office alphabetically under the title of that office. In case there is a nominating committee, its nominations for each office could lead the list of nominees for that office, the others being arranged alphabetically. To the right or left of each name there should be a small open square for the purpose of allowing a cross to be placed in the one adjacent to the name of the candidate for whom the vote is cast. Below the list of nominees for each office there should be ample room for writing the name of a person not nominated. Where a name is written in the blank space after the names of the nominees for an office, it is understood to be a vote for the person whose name is written, as there can be no other possible reason for writing it there. But if several names are printed and none written under the title of an office, it is impossible to determine for which nominee for that office the ballot is cast, unless all the other names are crossed out, or else that name is indicated in some way by a cross. Directions similar to these should be printed at the top of the ballot sheet:

When the name of more than one candidate is printed under the title of an office, the one voted for should be indicated by a cross, X, marked in the square beside his name. If it is desired to vote for one whose name is not on the ballot, his name should be written just below the printed names of the nominees for the office.

Since the Australian system was designed for the express pur pose of preventing frauds, all the precautions mentioned on pages 220–222 are taken to prevent illegal voting. The methods in use in political elections are described hereafter [page 236]. As heretofore stated, this method of voting is not adapted to ordinary societies, especially where tickets are printed with the name of only one nominee for an office.

NOMINATIONS AND ELECTION BY MAIL

Where the members of an organization are scattered so that it is difficult to secure the attendance of a fair representation of the society at a meeting held for the purpose of conducting an election, the method of voting by mail is often adopted. The nominations are made thus: The secretary sends by mail to every member a blank nominating, or preferential, ballot, and two envelopes prepared as shown under Voting by Mail, page 193. When the ballot has been filled out it is placed in the smaller envelope, which, when sealed and signed by the voter, is enclosed in the larger envelope, which should then be mailed immediately. If the secretary receives them, he sends the inside envelopes unopened to the chairman of the committee, who preserves them unopened until they are opened by the committee. The committee opens and counts the ballots the same as if they had been deposited in a ballot-box. The chairman of the committee is responsible for the envelopes not being opened except by the committee. The signature of the voter on the envelope is necessary as a guaranty that the vote is cast by a member. The tellers are in honor bound not to divulge any vote that they may notice.

The report of the committee on nominations may be made in various ways, depending upon the nature of the society and the election. Each society must decide these questions for itself. If the election is also to be oy mail, the committee may be authorized to report simply a printed ticket containing the names of all the nominees for each office, arranged in the order of the number of votes received by each, the number being printed in parenthesis after each name. Sometimes the committee is instructed to report only the two or three nominees for each office receiving the highest number of votes. The committee should usually hand the written ticket to the secretary, who should have it printed and mailed with enclosed envelopes and instructions to every voter. The ticket is prepared just as in the case of using a ballot-box. All the names on the ticket must be crossed out except the ones voted for, or, in the case of many nominations for the same office, the one voted for may be checked. Of course, when the voter wishes to vote for one not on the ticket, he should write that name in the ticket, crossing out the printed names of the nominees for that office.

The ballots, enclosed in signed envelopes, are mailed as in the case of the nominating ballot just described. They are counted the same as in ordinary elections, and the result mailed to every member. In case of an election by mail where there are several candidates for an office, it will frequently happen that no one has a majority vote. To avoid this, some societies limit the voting to the two nominees having the largest number of votes. It is a very objectionable practice to limit the right of voting, even to the nominees. If one candidate were very popular and received nearly all the votes, and if he were to decline the nomination, the society would be forced to elect one of the minority candidates, who might have received only two or three votes. Voting is not limited to nominees unless the society has adopted such a rule. The better way is not to limit the right of voting, and, if the election is by mail, to allow a plurality vote to elect. If the one elected declines, the vote should be taken again. If the election is in a meeting, the balloting should be repeated until the offices are filled, but where the election is by mail it is not practicable to repeat it over and over, and therefore it is well to allow a plurality vote to elect. A candidate has a plurality when he has more votes than any other candidate for the same office. If there is a tie vote, it should be decided by lot. [See also Voting by Mail, page 191.]

ELECTION OF DIRECTORS IN A STOCK CORPORATION (PROXY VOTING)

Under Voting by Proxy, page 194, the proxy is explained, and its form is given on page 564. As there stated, it is used only in stock corporations, where it is desired to ascertain, not the will of the majority of the stockholders, but the will of the holders of the majority of the stock.

The secretary has usually procured from stockholders enough proxies, in the name of one or two of the directors, to enable the directors to vote a majority of the stock. As these proxies are obtained mostly before the meeting, they can be examined and the number of shares represented by each marked on it, and lists made out showing how many shares each holder of proxies is entitled to vote. If additional proxies are received at the meeting, they should be entered on the proper lists by the secretary. All the proxies should be attached to the lists, as vouchers for their accuracy. These lists may be used as ballots, space being left at the top of each for the names of the directors voted for and for the signature of the voter.

Since such meetings are usually attended by very few persons, the names of the proposed directors are written at the top of a sheet of paper which is signed by the voter. Below is a list of the shares of stock voted by him, first placing his own name and the number of shares he owns, and then the names, etc., of the stockholders whose proxies he holds. If he does not know the number of shares owned by each, these blanks are filled by the secretary, who always assists the tellers and must have the stock books at the meeting. If the proxies have not previously been given to the secretary, they must be attached to this ballot. If they have been given to the secretary, then the list as made by the secretary can be used as the ballot, the voter signing it after entering the names of the directors for whom he votes.

Two tellers are appointed to count the votes. If there is any opposition, it should be represented by a teller, in order to give confidence in the count. The real work of the tellers is the verification of the number of shares that each voter is entitled to vote. This may be done by examining each ballot separately, first seeing that the attached proxies are correct, and then that the list on the ballot agrees with the proxies. Next it is necessary to see that the number of shares entered in the list agrees with the stock book, or with the secretary's list of stockholders containing the number of shares owned by each on the day the stock-transfer book was closed. If any errors are detected, they must be corrected. If a proxy is not signed, or is not witnessed, or is voted by one not legally entitled to vote it, it must be rejected, and the total number of shares voted on the ballot changed accordingly. If the number of shares placed opposite a name on the ballot is found incorrect, the necessary corrections must be made before the ballots are counted.

When the ballots have been thus verified they may be counted easily, because usually there is only one ticket and rarely more than two. Since the tickets are never scratched, it is necessary only to enter the number of shares voted on each ballot under the proper ticket, and then to add these figures and find the total number of shares voted for each ticket. The tellers then report to the society the total number of shares of stock voted, and the number voted for each ticket, and the president declares the ticket receiving the largest number of votes elected, as the laws generally provide for plurality elections in stock voting.

Where defects are found in a ballot, either in the proxies or in the number of shares credited a stockholder, the tellers should call the attention of the voter to the error and to their correction of it, so that if he wishes he may appeal to the society. A rejected proxy, unless withdrawn by the one attempting to use it, should have written across it "Rejected," or "Defective," with the signatures or initials of the tellers. Proxies and ballots must be preserved for a reasonable time when there is a possibility of any question's being raised as to the legality of the election.

Election by Roll-Call

In certain national conventions the by-laws allow a certain number of votes to each state, or for some other reason make it advisable to vote by roll-call. Where the vote is by states, the delegates from each state elect a chairman of their delegation, who answers to the roll-call, announcing the vote of his state, which may be all for one candidate, or it may be divided. The procedure is practically the same as in taking the vote by yeas and nays, as described in "Robert's Rules of Order Revised," page 197.

Political Elections and Elections in Deliberative Assemblies Compared

Much of the trouble in elections is due to confusing political elections with elections in deliberative assemblies, which have but little in common. In a deliberative assembly the voters meet together; there must be a quorum present; nominations are made usually by a nominating committee and also from the floor; tellers are appointed to count the ballots and report the facts to the assembly; the assembly settles all doubtful points and declares who are elected; a majority vote is necessary for election; and if any of the offices are not filled at the first ballot, the balloting is continued until all the offices are filled.

Not one of these things is true of political elections. In political elections the voters do not assemble; there is no quorum or nominations from the floor; and there are no tellers to count the ballots and report to the voters for them to decide all doubtful points and declare who are elected; a plurality elects, instead of a majority; nominations are not made by a committee appointed by all the voters or by the presiding officer, nor are nominations made from the floor by individual voters, but they are made by party conventions or primary elections, or petitions signed by a specified number of voters, or by a combination of these methods. Formerly, printed party tickets were used universally, each ticket having the name of only one candidate for each position. With such a ticket a voter who preferred another candidate for a particular office crossed out the objectionable name and wrote below or beside it the name of the preferred candidate. This is the established custom, and the natural way where ballots are used that contain no more names than there are positions to fill, as in the case of a ticket reported by a nominating committee.

A new form of ticket has been adopted by many states, generally called the Australian Ballot, but in reality a variation of that ballot. By this system no ballots are allowed but those furnished by the government whose officers are to be elected, and these contain on the one ballot the names of all the nominees for all the offices to be filled at that election. To the right or left of each name is a little square, and the voter must place a cross in the square opposite to the name of the candidate for whom he wishes to vote. This is the simplest possible method of indicating one's vote with such a ballot. It would be difficult to count the votes correctly on a large ballot sheet containing many names unless all these detailed instructions are complied with. The attempt to combine this method with the single printed ticket reported by a committee, and nominations from the floor not printed on the ticket, should never be made. It simply complicates matters without any possible benefit.

General Remarks on Elections

Deliberative assemblies vary so much in their size, in their constituency, and in their object, that a method of conducting the election of officers that is suited to one may not be at all adapted to another organization. It would be folly for a music club of a dozen members to adopt the method of election described on pages 218–230, and it would be equally unwise for a convention of a thousand delegates to adopt any of the simple methods that are suited to small assemblies. Each society or organization should adopt the method best adapted to its own case.

A person may be nominated for more than one office, and if elected to two or more, he may choose, if present, which one he will accept. If he is absent, the assembly should decide by a majority viva voce vote which office he shall fill. In considering the eligibility of an officer to reëlection, one who has served more than half a term is considered as having served that term.

In electing members of boards by ballot, if a majority vote is received by more than there are places to fill, those places are filled by those receiving the highest number of votes. If a tie interferes, the tie is decided by lot, unless the assembly continues the balloting, which latter is much more satisfactory and should be done if time permits. If the term of office of the members of the board elected at one time varies, those receiving the greatest number of votes take the longest term. All ties are decided by lot.

A very common mistake made in regard to elections is to assume that only one ballot will be necessary, and therefore the election is held so near the close of the meeting that if the first ballot fails to elect the officers, there is not sufficient time for other ballots. The constitutions of some large organizations that meet in convention only once a year require the election of officers to be held on the last day of the convention, and the program places the report of the tellers in the afternoon of that day, so that if there is no election on the first ballot it may be impossible to ballot again on account of lack of quorum. This is not an imaginary danger, for it has proved a very serious difficulty. Members should not assume that because they have voted for officers they can leave the convention with safety. Elections should always be held at a time that will allow of the balloting being repeated if necessary. This is especially important in conventions of delegates who come from distant points, so that it is impracticable to hold an adjourned meeting at another time. No convention should hold its election later than the day before the last of the session, and in some cases this is too late unless a plurality vote is allowed to elect. The important work of the convention is the election of officers and boards that carry on the business during the year, and this should be attended to while all the delegates are present, allowing always for a failure to elect on the first ballot.

Since the purpose of a ballot is to ascertain the preference of the voters, no rule should be adopted that may defeat this purpose, unless it is absolutely necessary to protect the society. To require, as some societies do, that a cross should be placed in front of, or after, each name on a printed ticket, with only one name for each office, is unreasonable, and therefore the requirement is very likely to be overlooked, resulting possibly in the ballot's being thrown out as illegal. There certainly can be no doubt for whom a ballot is intended when there is only one name for an office, whether it is written or printed. A cross does not make the voter's wish any more certain. Such unreasonable rules as this cause many of the troubles in societies. More common sense and fewer useless rules are needed.

Rules of this class, unless in the by-laws, should be regarded as directory rather than obligatory. Thus, if the ballot has printed on it directions that when a new name is substituted for a printed one the new name must be written below the erased one, it should be considered as advisory for the convenience of the tellers. If the new name is written on the side of the old one, the ballot should not be rejected. If ballots are rejected for such trivial defects as omitting a cross, or making a wrong kind of a cross, or writing a new name in the wrong place, when it is clear for whom the vote is intended, to be consistent, a candidate should not be credited with a vote if there is an error in the spelling of his name. The courts have held that ballots should be credited to candidates when from the ballot itself it is clear for whom the vote was intended, provided that there is no law on the subject. If the by-laws require certain formalities they must be observed, but printed instructions on the ballot, even though adopted by the assembly, cannot throw out a vote not in conflict with the by-laws, if the ballot shows clearly for whom it was intended.

PART III

BOARDS AND COMMITTEES

CHAPTER XXII

BOARDS, STANDING COMMITTEES AND SPECIAL COMMITTEES COMPARED

VERY little work could be accomplished by a society if nothing were done except at its meetings by the action of the society as a whole. Investigations as to facts, preparation of resolutions expressing the views of the society on certain matters, making arrangements for carrying out some order of the society, such as to secure a hall, or to engage a lecturer, or to plan for a banquet, etc., can be done better by a few persons, known as a committee, acting for the society, than directly by the whole society.

Many societies are formed for social or other purposes of such a nature that most of the members do not wish to be annoyed with its business. They prefer to turn over the management of the business to a few chosen members known by some such name as the Board of Directors or Managers. Then, again, there are organizations whose membership is so scattered that it is impracticable for them to meet frequently, and so their business between the meetings must necessarily be managed by a few selected persons. This is especially true of state and national organizations, made up of numerous constituent or subordinate societies. These societies appoint delegates, who meet in convention once in one, two, or three years for a period of less than a week, to elect officers and a board of directors to carry on the work until their successors are elected.

The groups of members selected for these various purposes are in a general sense committees, because certain duties or powers belonging to the society are committed or intrusted to them. The great mass of the work of most societies is done by them, and therefore it is important fully to understand their duties and powers. They are naturally divided into two great classes, called Boards and Committees, which differ in some very essential points. One must not be misled, however, by names, as the name Executive

Committee or Standing Committee is frequently given to what is essentially a board.

A *Board* is appointed to act for the society in an administrative capacity. The board exists permanently, but its membership is chosen for a definite period, usually one, two, or three years. Between the meetings of the parent body, the society, the board has all the power of the former, except as limited by the by-laws or orders of the society. It cannot, however, delegate this power, or rescind any action of the society, or conflict with such action in any way, whereas the parent body, unless prohibited by the by-laws, may countermand action taken by the board and give it instructions which the board is bound to obey.

In ordinary societies and conventions a *Committee* is appointed, either for some special purpose, automatically expiring as soon as that purpose is accomplished, or for some general purpose which requires the committee to remain in existence permanently, to take care of all business that may arise of the class assigned to it. The first kind of committee is called a Special or Select Committee, because it is selected to attend to some special thing, the committee expiring when that thing has been attended to and its final report has been made. The other kind is called a Standing Committee, because it is always in existence, the old members not going out of office until their successors are appointed.

Standing Committees in legislative bodies, city councils, and similar bodies are usually committees to which are referred matters to be reported back to the body for its action. They are appointed usually for the period of the existence of the parent, or appointing, body, and expire with it. Such legislative bodies never appoint boards. In ordinary societies, however, there are rarely such standing committees. A standing committee appointed by an ordinary society or convention is more like a board than like a committee. It is a permanent body, the members being changed annually, biennially, or triennially, as the society may determine, just as with boards, and the committee has charge of a specific line of work, just as a board has charge of the general work of the society.

Special Committees are so distinct from boards that there is no danger of confusing them. They can be readily distinguished from standing committees by the fact that they are appointed, as just stated, for a specified purpose and expire as soon as that purpose is accomplished and their report is made. A committee on credentials or the order of business, etc., appointed during a convention, is a special committee even though it continues in existence till the close of the convention, because the committee does not have a permanent existence, but expires with the session. If a committee is appointed to submit a revision of the by-laws at the next convention, and therefore continues in existence for a year or more, it is a special committee, because it ceases to exist when its special object has been accomplished and it has made its report to the organization. If such a committee is provided for in the by-laws as a permanent one, so that the members continue in office until their successors are appointed, then it is a standing committee.

Boards and Standing Committees, Appointed by a Convention. A Convention, as the term is used in this work, is an assembly of representatives, or delegates, appointed by its constituent or its subordinate societies for that single session which usually lasts from two to six days. It is known by various names, as convention, congress, convocation, conference, association, assembly, etc. It hears reports from its officers, boards, and committees, and elects officers and the board for the ensuing year or term of years, determines general lines of policy, and adjourns sine die, leaving to the board the real work of the organization until a new convention meets. Immediately after the convention the new board organizes, elects an executive committee, if it is authorized to do so, appoints such other committees as are needed, and attends to such business as is required by the by-laws, or may have been turned over to it by the convention. The board meets quarterly or semiannually, as required by the by-laws or by its rules, and also just before the assembling of the convention to finish its business for the year, at which meeting it adopts a report to be presented to the convention. During the five or six days the convention is in session the board has nothing to do. Its work begins after the convention has adjourned and ends before the convention meets. During this interval it has full power to carry on the work of the organization, provided it never takes any action in conflict with the rules and acts of the convention.

In addition to a board, many conventions appoint a number of standing committees, each of which has charge of a specified department of work, just as the board has charge of the general work of the organization. These standing committees are usually appointed by the incoming administration, either by the board, or by the president, usually the latter, as described by the by-laws. Like boards, they should meet and organize at the close of the convention, and each one at its last meeting previous to the meeting of the convention should adopt a report of the work of the preceding year, to be presented to the convention. The duties of standing committees are so various that, while some may meet only two or three times a year, others may be obliged to have weekly meetings. The rules for the transaction of business are the same as for boards. The standing committees may be subordinate to, or independent of, the board as determined by the by-laws. Which is best depends upon the nature of the duties.

Boards and Standing Committees of an Organized Society Having Weekly or Monthly Meetings. The difference between boards and standing committees appointed by a convention, and those appointed by a local society, is that those appointed by a convention are organized and do all their work after the expiration of the convention, and make their reports to another convention, whereas those appointed by a local society do their work and report to an existing society with more or less frequent meetings. The society is in constant touch with its board and committees, and may, at any of its business meetings during the year, give them instructions, or refer subjects to them, or receive reports from them. The power of the board in such societies varies greatly. In some it is quite limited, while in others the entire administrative authority of the society is given them.

CHAPTER XXIII

BOARDS

Duties and Powers. A Board may be defined to be a group of of persons appointed by an organization to act for it between its meetings, or, in case of a stock corporation, to act for it altogether. In this work the term "board" is used in this sense, regardless of whether it is called the board of managers, or directors, or trustees, or the executive board, or the executive committee, or the standing committee, or by any other name. The term executive committee is used, as described hereafter, for a smaller board appointed by the board to act for it between its meetings. The parent organization may meet only annually, or biennially, or even triennially, at which time it hears the reports of its officers and the board, determines general lines of policy, elects the officers and a new board, and adjourns, leaving to the board and to the officers the real work of the organization. When the organization is a local society with regular business meetings as often as weekly, or monthly, or even quarterly, the board is not usually given so much power, because the society itself can attend to much of its business at its regular meetings. In such cases the board is usually required to report at least as often as quarterly. It always submits an annual report at the annual meeting.

A board cannot adopt rules in conflict with rules of the organization appointing it. It cannot delegate its power to an executive committee, or change its quorum, unless authorized to do so by the body that appointed it. It may adopt rules for the conduct of its business, but these rules must not be in conflict with the rules of the appointing power. Such rules will continue in force until amended, suspended, or rescinded in accordance with the parlia-

247

mentary authority adopted by the organization. This avoids the necessity of adopting rules each year, and prevents any board from putting it out of the power of a majority of a future board to suspend or rescind the rules, or to adopt such rules as they choose, without notice. It has not the right, however, to adopt a rule limiting the power of the majority of the membership of the board.

When the board has duties that frequently require prompt action, or in cases where the members are so scattered that it is inconvenient to attend to the business, the by-laws of the organization should authorize the board to appoint from its membership a small executive committee which can meet frequently and attend to the business in the intervals between the board meetings. As a general rule, the members of the executive committee should be so situated that they can have a special meeting without difficulty. Though called an executive committee, it is not strictly a committee: it is a miniature board, and all the rules applicable to boards apply to it. Like a board, its quorum is a majority of its members, unless the by-laws provide otherwise.

While a board cannot appoint an executive committee, unless so authorized by the by-laws of the society, or turn over its powers to an officer or committee, it may appoint committees to investigate and report, or to carry out an order of the board. The society has intrusted the board with the responsibility of administration, with the understanding that a majority of the members must meet to decide questions. The principle involved is that an agent cannot turn over to another his powers as agent unless so authorized by his principal.

An emergency may occur that requires immediate action when it is impossible to have a meeting of the executive committee. In such a case the responsible officer must act, consulting such members as may be reached by telephone or otherwise, and then report the facts at the first meeting and have his informal acts ratified. A board or an executive committee must keep a record of all its acts, and it can act only when it is in session with a quorum present at a properly called meeting. Unanimous agreement outside of such a meeting is not a legal act of the board.

Boards of directors, or managers, of a stock corporation practically control the entire business of the corporation. There is an annual meeting of the stockholders to hear the report of the board and to elect a new board, but this meeting is attended by very few except the members of the board, the voting being done almost entirely by proxy. Though there may be thousands of shares of stock, probably not more than a dozen stockholders attend the annual meeting, because the voting is by stock and by proxy. The directors being elected, they immediately meet and elect such officers as are required, and an executive committee, which is sometimes as small as two. The board of directors has nearly all the powers of the corporation in its hands, the stockholders usually doing nothing except to elect the directors. In all things, however, the board must comply with the statutes of the state in which it is incorporated.

Appointing of Boards. The by-laws should provide for a board, specifying the number of members, how they shall be elected, etc., just as in the case of the officers. Its powers should also be clearly defined. Sometimes the officers constitute the board, and sometimes all the members of the board are elected. More commonly the board consists of certain officers and a number of elected members. The board, or a certain portion of its members, should be chosen at each annual meeting by ballot in the same way as the officers are elected. It has generally been found best to elect only one half or one third of the members at a time, their term of office being either two or three years, as the case may be. This plan insures the board from having at any time a majority of new members. Since all of the members of the board are voted for on the same ticket, more candidates may receive a majority vote than there are places on the board to be filled, and some ballots may be cast for only one or two members of the board, thus raising a question as to the number of votes necessary to elect. The method of deciding who are elected in such a case is described under Elections, page 229, and in the Drill on Electing Delegates in Parliamentary Practice, pages 152, 153. In societies meeting frequently the society itself can and should fill vacancies in its boards, but vacancies in boards appointed by a convention should be filled by the board itself. The by-laws of the convention should authorize the board of directors to fill, until the next meeting of the convention, all vacancies in its membership and in the offices. This is necessary because the convention ceases to exist when it adjourns sine die, and there must be some way of carrying on the business during the year before the next convention is held.

Organization of a Board. Immediately after the annual meeting the board should meet and organize. If a part of the members hold over, the former chairman, or in his absence the secretary of the board, should preside while a presiding officer is being elected. If neither the chairman nor the secretary is present, the member longest in continuous service on the board should preside until a chairman is elected. If the entire board is newly elected, the meeting should be called by the member whose name heads the list of the members of the board as announced by the chairman. Besides a presiding officer, called either the president or chairman of the board, a secretary should be elected. When a board has frequent meetings and important business, it is often best to elect a vice-president, or vice-chairman if the presiding officer is called chairman.

The procedure just given is the one usually followed when the by-laws do not specify who shall be the officers of the board. In organizations meeting not more frequently than once a year, it is usual for the by-laws to make the president and the secretary of the convention ex-officio president and secretary of the board.

Conduct of Business in a Board Meeting. A board must actually meet, the same as a society or a convention, in order to transact business. A brief record should be kept of the business done, the same as required in an ordinary society. As heretofore stated, the board can act only when it is in session. The meeting must be a regular one, or one properly called, every member being notified thereof, or an adjournment of such a regular or called meeting. Every act of the board must be entered in the minutes of the meeting at which the action was taken, and obviously there can be no minutes of a meeting that never occurred. Therefore unanimous agreement of the members outside of a properly called meeting is not the act of the board. To make it the act of the board it must be properly ratified at a legal meeting of the board. The rules of the parent organization are in force in the board, with the following exceptions: Motions need not be seconded; members may speak as often as they choose; and the chairman, without leaving the chair, may make motions and take part in the discussion as much as any other member, and may vote on all questions. If the board is small, or in any case if it is seated around an ordinary-sized table, members do not rise to make motions or to debate, nor does the chairman rise to put the question.

In fact, subjects are often discussed without any motion having been made, all the freedom of a committee being allowed. This is especially true of an executive committee. How far the formalities of ordinary assemblies may be dispensed with to advantage is a question to be decided by the board or the executive committee itself. But, in the end, the chairman must always put the question to vote and announce the result.

At each board meeting the executive committee should make a report of all that it has done since the last meeting of the board. This is necessary to enable the board to know the present condition of its business. The board may give instructions to the executive committee, or countermand any of its acts, since the executive committee is under the orders of the board, just as the board is under the orders of the parent organization. The report of the executive committee may be oral unless the board requires it to be in writing. Whether made orally or in writing, it must not withhold any information that might be of interest to the board. Since the report purports to be a full one, a failure to make it complete is practically a false report. The report may be a very brief statement of what has been done since the last report was made, or it may consist of the minutes of the various meetings of the committee. It is for the board to decide what kind of report it desires. Usually a simple oral statement of what has been done is all that is necessary. This statement is usually made by the executive secretary, in case there is one, and where there is none it is made by the chairman or secretary of the committee or some other member. No action need be taken on this report, as it is only for information. Sometimes it is voted to accept the report, but this is entirely unnecessary. An executive committee should never attempt to forestall action by the board. Questions that do not demand attention before the board meets should be left to the board. The same principle applies to the board in its relation to the society.

Annual Report. The board makes an annual report to the parent organization and such other reports as that organization requires. These reports are always in writing. Instead of giving a full account of the transactions of the board, they should omit unnecessary details, and should summarize the important work done in such a manner as to be interesting to the society, and should recommend any action they desire the society to take. Since the board is more competent than any committee to prepare such resolutions, the report should close with resolutions to carry out all its recommendations. A failure to do this wastes much time, either in requiring a special committee to consider the recommendations and prepare and report suitable resolutions, or in the assembly's attempting to do the work itself. A board, like a committee, should always regard it as an essential part of its duty to prepare the resolutions necessary to carry into effect its recommendations.

The *report of a board* is usually prepared by the executive committee, if there is one. If there is none it is prepared by the secretary, or the president, according to which one is the more active in the management of the business. This varies in different societies. The board may, however, appoint any of its members to prepare its report. When the report is submitted to the board, it may be amended to any extent. It must be formally adopted by a vote before it becomes the report of the board. It should be properly written out as finally adopted by the board, and signed by the president and the secretary. It is never signed by the members concurring in the report.

When the report of the board is called for by the presiding officer of the assembly, it is presented by the reporting member of the board, and read from the platform by him or by the reading clerk (official reader). If the report contains recommendations and resolutions, or resolutions alone, the reporting member of the board should, as soon as the report is read, say, "Mr. President, by direction of the board, I move that the resolutions be adopted." If the report contains recommendations without resolutions, he should move the adoption of the recommendations. If the report contains neither resolutions nor recommendations, he should make no motion, because no action of the assembly is necessary on a mere statement of facts or opinions. Sometimes it is voted to accept the report, but if such a motion is made it should not come from a member of the board. The assembly cannot change the report in any way, but when the resolution is pending to adopt the resolutions, or recommendations, they may be amended, or divided, or otherwise treated, the same as if they had been offered by a committee or by an individual. In publishing the report of the board, any changes made by the assembly should be distinctly indicated as shown in "Rules of Order Revised," page 209.

The objection to adopting recommendations is the uncertainty as to the effect of their adoption. If the recommendation is that a bill be paid, its adoption probably authorizes the payment of the bill. If the recommendation is that charges be preferred against a member for certain offenses, its adoption does not prefer the charges, but leaves to others the preparation of the charges and all the motions necessary to prefer them and to provide for the trial, work that should have been done by those who made the recommendation. But there are many cases where there is room for difference of opinion as to the effect of adopting the recommendation, and the safest course is to embody in the resolutions all the recommendations in the report and move the adoption of the resolutions.

CHAPTER XXIV

COMMITTEES

Purposes for Which Formed

A Committee consists of one or more persons appointed for one of the following purposes:

(1) To consider and report suitable action upon a resolution or other main motion referred to it. [See page 269.]

(2) To consider and report back, with its recommendation in each case, all resolutions or other main motions, or all of a certain class, that may be offered during a session of a convention. Example, Committee on Resolutions, page 273.

(3) To consider a subject and report a resolution covering the action it recommends the society to take. Example, Committee on Revision of the By-Laws, page 277.

(4) To investigate a certain matter and report the facts, with its opinion thereon if so ordered. Example, Committee to Find a Suitable Site for a Club-House, page 278.

(5) To execute an order of the society. Example, Committee of Arrangements for a Banquet, etc., page 279.

(6) To represent and act for the society in a certain matter. Example, Delegates to a Convention, page 280.

(7) To receive and count the votes, or to receive and act upon

the credentials of delegates to a convention. Example, Tellers and Credentials Committee, page 281.

(8) To take charge of a certain class or department of the work undertaken by an organization, and to report to it the work done. Example, Standing Committees of a Society, page 285.

All of these are special committees, except the last one, which is a standing committee. The difference between special and standing committees is explained on page 244.

In the first case (1), mentioned above, a main motion is pending which it is desired to refer to a committee, and therefore the subsidiary motion to refer, or commit, is used. In the second case (2), the committee is appointed usually by virtue of a by-law or rule previously adopted, which is the better plan in a convention; or it is appointed as the result of the adoption at the meeting of a main motion to appoint a committee. In the last case (8), the standing committees are appointed in accordance with provisions in the by-laws. In all the other cases mentioned above, the motion to appoint the committee is a main motion, except in the few cases when there is a main motion pending at the time, which is referred to the committee and the committee is given the necessary instructions and power. Small committees are usually composed of an odd number of members, three or five, or possibly seven, in ordinary societies. With an even number of persons on a small committee the difficulty of securing a report is greatly increased. Thus, in a committee of four, it is necessary to have three present at every meeting, and if all four are present three must agree to the report to make it the report of the committee, because it requires three to constitute a majority of four. But three is also a majority of five, so that with a committee of five there can be twice as many absentees from the meetings, and twice as large an opposition, if all the members are present when they adopt the report, as with a committee of four, without endangering the report. On the other hand, it is sometimes an advantage to have an even number on a committee where it is given full power to act in a case. A committee of four, for instance, cannot take final action if more than one member objects, all the members being present.

The subject of committees will be treated in the following order: (1) Appointment of Committees, page 256; (2) Organization of Committees, page 264; (3) Conduct of Business in Committees, page 265; (4) Preparing, Submitting, and Adopting the

Reports of the various kinds of committees mentioned above, treated separately, page 267; (5) General Remarks on Adopting Reports of Committees, page 287.

APPOINTMENT OF COMMITTEES

Every organization has the right to decide for itself how its committees and boards shall be appointed. Sometimes the method is prescribed in the by-laws. Where this is not done, the assembly by a majority vote decides the question at the time the committee is appointed.

If the member who makes the motion to commit or to appoint the committee is very familiar with the subject, he is usually put on the committee, but this is not at all necessary. The interests of the assembly should control the selection, and the maker of the motion to refer, or to appoint the committee, may be entirely unsuitable for appointment on the committee. Whoever appoints a committee has the power at the time the committee is appointed to appoint the chairman. When appointed or nominated by the chair, the person first named is chairman. When appointed or nominated by any other method, unless the chairman is named, the first person named acts as chairman unless the committee elects some one else, which it has a perfect right to do. In the case of special committees, since the committee is so short a time in existence, it is very likely to allow the first-named member to continue as chairman, and therefore it is important that he should be a competent person.

Committees may be appointed by any of the eight methods listed at the beginning of this chapter. No one of these methods is best under all circumstances. In a small society with no rivalry of candidates, it would be a waste of time to adopt the plan that is best suited to a very large organization with many candidates for office and intense partizan feeling. When merely the method of nomination is stated, it is understood that the election is viva voce. The ballot method of election is generally adopted for boards and delegates, but scarcely ever for special committees.

(a) **Appointment by the Chair.** In large assemblies it is safer to place upon the president the responsibility of appointing committees. If he is held responsible for their selection, there is a greater chance of obtaining suitable committees than if the choice is left to the entire assembly. If the chair betrays the confidence of the best interests of the society, some of the other methods of placed in him and appoints his friends on a committee, regardless appointing committees should be adopted in the future, unless the method is prescribed by the by-laws. This danger is so slight, however, compared with the danger of a bad selection if left to open nomination and viva voce election in a large assembly, especially in a mass meeting, that it is generally safer in large assemblies to have the committees appointed, or at least nominated, by the presiding officer unless they are elected by ballot.

Sometimes the by-laws authorize the president to appoint all committees. This gives the power to the president of the society, and is not the same as giving the power to the chairman of the meeting, who may be a different person. It may be necessary to have a special committee appointed when the president is not present, and therefore a by-law requiring such a committee to be appointed by the president might prove very inconvenient, unless there is a provision for its suspension. In many organizations the following rule would be a good one:

The president shall appoint all standing committees, unless before their appointment this rule is suspended by a two-thirds vote, or a vote of the majority of the membership. He shall appoint all special committees unless in any case this rule is suspended by a majority vote.

This enables the majority in an assembly to appoint a special committee in any way they think best, while under ordinary circumstances the president appoints all committees, special and standing. Societies differ to so great an extent that each one must adopt a method of appointing committees that is best suited to its own needs.

Unless the power to appoint committees is given the president by the by-laws or by a vote of the assembly, he must not assume it. There being no by-law on the subject, if the assembly wishes to give him that power in any particular case, it should be incorporated in the motion appointing the committee. If the motion to commit does not state how the committee is to be appointed, the words "to be appointed by the chair" can be inserted as an amendment.

When the chair appoints the committee, he announces the names of the members of the committee to the assembly, the same as if they had been elected. No vote is taken, as his announcement ends the matter. If he is not prepared to announce the committee at the time, he must state that the committee will be announced later during the session. Until the committee has been announced to the assembly, it cannot act, unless the chair has been authorized to .appoint the committee after the adjournment.

(b) **Nominations by the Chair and Viva Voce Election.** This method is adopted when the assembly desires the advantage of having the committee selected by the chair, and yet wishes to retain the veto power. In this case the presiding officer says: "The chair nominates Mr. A, Mr. B, and Mr. C. As many as are in favor of these gentlemen's constituting the committee say 'Aye.' Those opposed say 'No.' The ayes have it and the committee consists of Messrs. A, B, and C." Since the chair was authorized only to nominate, not to appoint, the committee, it is not necessary to elect those nominated by the chair. Before the vote is taken, any one can move to strike out one or more names, and, if this motion is carried, the chair must replace those names by others. No motion is in order to strike out one name and insert another, because the chair alone has been authorized to nominate the committee, the society reserving only the right to confirm his nominations.

This method has the advantage of utilizing the knowledge and judgment of the chairman in the selection of the committee, while the society is protected to a great extent by its power to reject any objectionable nominee.

(c) **Nominations from the Floor and Viva Voce Election.** This is a common method of appointing ordinary committees when the committee is not named in the motion creating it. It is also used frequently for electing boards and delegates in small societies when the positions are not specially sought after. It allows every member the opportunity to name one member of the committee, and yet does not consume much time. Its disadvantage is due to the unwillingness of members to vote openly against an objectionable nominee, and yet there is no other way to prevent his election if he is among the first nominated.

No one can nominate from the floor more than one member of a committee, except by general consent, until every member has had an opportunity to nominate. In nominating by ballot, each member is allowed to nominate as many members of the committee as there are places to fill, but if this were allowed when nominations are made from the floor, it might result in such confusion as to destroy the usefulness of this method of nomination. However, the entire committee is sometimes nominated by one member, and if no one else makes a nomination the chair assumes general consent and announces those nominated as the committee. Or, he may ask if there are any other nominations, and if there are none he may put the question as to whether these nominees shall constitute the committee. If, however, any one else makes a nomination, the chair ignores all the nominations made by the first member, except the first one, as the nomination made by the second member shows that general consent was not given to the first member's making all the nominations.

If it is desired to appoint a committee by this method, when the chair asks, "How shall the committee be appointed?" some one should say (except in a very large assembly), "By nominations from the floor." If no other suggestion is made no vote is taken, and the chair immediately says, "Members will please nominate." Any member may then nominate one member of the committee, which he does in a small assembly without rising by merely calling out the name of his nominee thus, "Mr. A." The chair immediately announces the nomination thus, "Mr. A is nominated." Nominations are not seconded, and it is not customary to obtain the floor to nominate members of a committee. If the assembly is large, however, members should rise and say, "Mr. Chairman, I nominate Mr. A," or simply, "I nominate Mr. A." Especially is it necessary to rise in a large assembly when all are not entitled to vote. In this way the assembly is assured that nominations are made only by those who are entitled to vote.

If no more nominations are made than there are places on the committee, the chair says, "Are there any more nominations? There being none, Messrs. A, B, and C constitute the committee." A vote may be taken, but it is useless, as the assembly by declining to make any more nominations has shown that it wishes these nominees to constitute the committee. It may be said they are chosen by general consent.

If there are more nominations than there are places on the committee, the chair, as soon as all the nominations are made, says: "Messrs. A, B, C, D, E, and F are nominated. As many as are in favor of Mr. A say 'Aye.' Those opposed say 'No.' The ayes have it and Mr. A is elected. As many as are in favor of Mr. B say 'Aye.' Those opposed say 'No.' The noes have it and Mr. B is not elected. As many as are in favor of Mr. C say 'Aye' ": and so on until the proper number of members is elected.

No vote is taken on the other nominees, as there are no vacancies left on the committee. The only way that the later nominees can be elected is by the voting of their friends against some of the earlier nominees. If there is only one vote for a nominee and none against him, he is elected. Therefore a negative vote does not necessarily mean opposition to the nominee so much as it means preference for another nominee.

No vote on the method of election is necessary when it is desired to use the viva voce method. All voting is done this way unless ordered otherwise, except in certain assemblies where raising the right hand is used. Where such custom prevails it must be understood that that method of voting is covered by the term "viva voce" as used in this work.

(d) **Nominations by a Committee and Viva Voce Election.** This method of election is frequently used when there are no seekers for positions on the boards and standing committees. It has the advantage of enabling the nominating committee to select carefully the members of the board or committee, and to name only those who are fitted for the work and are willing to serve. The right of members to nominate is not interfered with by this method, because they have the right to nominate from the floor after the nominating committee reports. Since the election is viva voce, but little time of the assembly is consumed. If, however, there is rivalry for the positions, it is better to have a ballot election so members can vote secretly.

Making nominations by a nominating committee is described on page 212, and electing by viva voce vote has just been explained in the preceding section (c).

(e) **Nominations from the Floor and Ballot Elections.** Election by ballot takes so much time that it is rarely used for ordinary committees. It is, however, commonly used in the election of boards, and frequently in the election of delegates. In the case of important committees, it may also be used to advantage. This is especially true where the assembly wishes to choose the members directly, and yet recognizes the danger of a viva voce election on account of the strong disinclination of members openly to vote against an unsuitable nominee who is present. All voting is done viva voce unless the assembly orders otherwise. If it is desired to have a ballot election with nominations from the floor, a member should make a formal motion, thus: "I move that the committee

APPOINTMENT OF COMMITTEES 261

be nominated from the floor and elected by ballot." Or, members may call out, "Nominations from the floor and ballot." If no other method is suggested, the chair should accept this as the will of the assembly. If other methods are suggested, the chair takes a vote on the different methods, beginning with the most difficult one, which would probably have the least number of advocates.

As soon as the method is decided, the chair says, "Members will please nominate." When it appears that no one desires to make another nomination, the chair proceeds thus: "Are there any more nominations? There being none, the chair appoints Mr. A and Mr. B tellers, and they will distribute the blanks for ballots. Each voter will write on his blank the names of the members for whom he wishes to vote. He is not limited to those nominated, but may vote for any member of the society." As soon as it is decided to vote by ballot, the secretary should prepare suitable slips of paper for the ballots, which the tellers should distribute when so directed by the chair. Since committees may be elected at any meeting, when many members are without pencils, ample time should be allowed before the ballots are collected. It is, however, the duty of members to be prompt and not waste the time of the assembly.

When the chair thinks the ballots are ready, he directs the tellers to collect and count them and report as described under Elections, page 223.

(f) **Nominations by a Committee and Ballot Election.** In electing boards and delegates and some important standing committees in large societies and in conventions, it is generally better to combine the method of election just described with nominations made by a committee. The committee, called a nominating committee, consisting usually of from three to five members, may be appointed by any method the society may choose. If it is desired to have the nomination and election of delegates by this method, when the chair inquires, "How shall the delegates be appointed?" some one should obtain the floor and make a motion similar to this: "I move that the delegates and alternates be nominated by a committee of three to be appointed by the chair, and that they be elected by ballot." In small societies this motion is frequently made at the meeting when the delegates are to be elected. In this case the committee immediately retires and agrees upon a list and reports it at the same meeting In larger organizations the nominating committees should always be appointed at a meeting previous to the one at which the election occurs.

When the committee is ready to report, the president calls on its chairman for the report. The chairman rises and says, "Mr. President, your committee submits the following nominations for delegates and alternates." He then reads the written list of nominees and hands it to the president, who again reads it and hands it to the secretary and asks, "Are there any more nominations for delegates?" Now, any one can nominate from the floor as heretofore described, because ordering nominations to be made by a committee does not deprive members of the right to nominate from the floor. When no other nominations of delegates are desired, the president asks, "Are there any other nominations for alternates?" If there are many nominations, it is well to have the names written on a blackboard so all can see them. When the nominations are completed, the election is conducted as described in the previous section (e).

(g) **Nominations by a Nominating Ballot and Ballot Election.** This is a very common method of electing boards as well as the officers of an organization. Its advantage is that it shows the exact preferences of the members, as each one nominates secretly all the members of the board or committee, which is not possible by any of the other methods. When the result of the nominating ballot (or preference ballot, or informal ballot, as it is variously called) is announced, the members know the preferences of the assembly and can thus vote more intelligently in the electing ballot, which follows immediately. If members are going to decline to serve, they should do so when the nominations are announced, and not wait until they are elected. The declining of a nominee for a board or a committee does not call for a reopening of nominations, as it frequently does in the case of a nominee for an office. Since several members of the board or committee have been nominated by each voter, their first, second, third, etc., choices have been given sufficiently to guide the assembly in its voting.

Nominations from the floor are not permitted when a nominating ballot is taken, unless authorized by a majority vote, because every member nominates on his nominating ballot. When a committee nominates, it is necessary to allow nominations from the floor in order to preserve the freedom of the assembly. When nominations are made by the chair, nominations cannot be made from the floor, but the freedom of the assembly is preserved by allowing the rejection of all objectionable nominees.

The form of this motion is, "I move that nominations and the election be by ballot." [See Drill on Nomination and Election of Delegates, etc., "Parliamentary Practice," pages 147–158.]

(*h*) **Nominations and Election by Adopting a Motion Naming the Committee.** This is a very common method with ordinary committees, and is frequently used in appointing delegates when members are not seeking the appointment. It should rarely, if ever, be used in electing boards or standing committees. The motion is made in a form similar to this: "I move to refer the resolution to a committee consisting of Mr. A, Mr. B, and Mr. C"; or, "I move that a committee consisting of Mr. A, Mr. B, Mr. C, Mr. D, and Mr. E be appointed to examine our constitution and by-laws and report as soon as practicable such amendments as they recommend for adoption"; or, "I move that Mr. A, Mr. B, and Mr. C be appointed delegates to the State Convention." The first illustration is the subsidiary motion "to commit," because a main motion is pending when it is made. In the other two cases the motion to appoint the committee is a main motion. They can be amended just as any other motions of the same class. If desired, the names of any members of the proposed committee may be struck out and others inserted, or all the names may be struck out and a blank created by one motion, thus: "I move to strike out 'A, B, and C,' thus creating a blank"; or, "I move that a blank be created by striking out the names of the committee." If this motion is adopted, the blank is filled as described on page 40.

Sometimes a motion is adopted like one of the three illustrations given above, except that the names of the committee are omitted. The motion may be to "refer the resolution to a committee of three," for instance. In such a case, as soon as the motion to refer is adopted the chair asks, "How shall the committee be appointed?" Any member may obtain the floor and move "that the committee consist of Mr. A, Mr. B, and Mr. C." Or, before the question is put on the motion to refer, it may be moved to amend that motion by striking out "of three" and inserting "consisting of Mr. A, Mr. B, and Mr. C."

ORGANIZATION OF COMMITTEES

As soon as practicable after the appointment of a committee, it should be called together by its chairman, if one has been appointed. If no chairman has been appointed, then the first-named member calls the committee together and acts as chairman until a chairman is elected by the committee. A special committee is usually in existence so short a time and its duty is so restricted that it seldom exercises its right to elect a chairman, accepting the first-named member as chairman if none has been appointed. When the committee is nominated from the floor or elected by ballot, the first member named may not be best adapted for chairman, and the committee should not hesitate to elect another chairman if its interests demand it. The chairman may not be in sympathy with the report of the committee, in which case the committee may elect a new chairman unless he was appointed by the power that appointed the committee; or they may appoint another member to make the report. The reporting member, that is, the one who makes the report for the committee, should always be in favor of the report, and usually should be its strongest advocate on the committee, as he has to represent the committee on the floor of the assembly.

A majority of a committee must be present in order to transact business unless the assembly has authorized a smaller quorum, which it should usually do in case of very large committees.

Since a committee is not required to keep a record of its proceedings, there is no necessity for electing a secretary, the chairman keeping such memoranda as he may think necessary. But with most standing committees, and sometimes with special committees where a number of meetings are held, it is often important to know what was done at a previous meeting, and in such cases it is better to have some one act as secretary at the meetings. The committee may elect a secretary, or the chairman may ask a member to act in that capacity. The secretary merely keeps memoranda of what is done, as far as may be necessary to enable the committee to continue its work at the next meeting. These are not treated as minutes, that is, they are not read and approved at the next meeting, nor are they copied in a book and preserved. They are simply temporary memoranda, which are destroyed when no longer needed for reference.

Should the chairman neglect to call the committee together, any two members have the right to do so, notifying every member of the committee. In the same way, a meeting may be called at any time after the first meeting, that is, by the chairman or by any two of the members of the committee, unless the committee has adopted an order requiring a larger number, as a quorum for instance, to sign the call for a meeting. Very large committees should not leave it in the power of any two members to call a meeting of the committee.

If a committee is assigned a duty that must be performed immediately, it should retire from the hall as soon as appointed and attend to that duty. If the committee is to make a report, then when it returns to the hall its chairman should rise as soon as he can obtain the floor and should state that the committee is prepared to report. The report is made either then or at a future time, as may suit the convenience of the assembly.

Committees should not meet while the organization is in session unless their work cannot be performed otherwise. Usually the committee should meet as soon as the society adjourns and either attend to their work or appoint another time for meeting.

CONDUCT OF BUSINESS IN COMMITTEES

It may be laid down as a sound principle of parliamentary law that there should be no restraint of the individual except to the extent that is necessary for the good of the whole assembly. The larger the assembly and the more complicated its business, the greater the necessity for rules restricting the freedom of the individual members. In a small body, like ordinary committees with probably less than a dozen present, the enforcement of the rules of parliamentary law adapted to large assemblies would be not a help but a positive hindrance to business. Obtaining the floor by rising and addressing the chair before making a motion or speaking, and the seconding of motions, while necessary in a large assembly, are absurd in a committee. Members do not rise when they make a motion or speak, nor are motions seconded. The meeting is informal, and the chairman takes an active part in the discussion. He even makes motions without leaving the chair, and puts them to vote. In making a motion, however, he would not use the ordinary formal terms, but merely make it as a suggestion, and then after discussion he should put the question on adopting the proposition. Members, in the same way, may make informal suggestions which are discussed and finally voted on, perhaps after having been materially modified.

Since one of the principal objects of referring a question to a committee is to enable the question to be more thoroughly discussed than is practicable in the assembly, there is no limit in committee to the number of times a member may speak on a question, and the committee cannot close or limit the debate. If advantage is taken of this privilege to obstruct the business of the committee, the fact should be reported to the assembly, which may remove the obstructing member from the committee, or may adopt an order limiting or closing debate in the committee, or take such other action in the case as it may deem advisable. A committee cannot punish a member. In case of disorderly conduct on the part of a member, it should report the facts to the assembly.

A committee must always give to members of the society who request it a reasonable opportunity to express their views on the matter under consideration. In this way much time of the society may be saved, a large part of the discussion taking place in the committee. Only members of the committee, however, have the right to attend the committee meetings. Others may attend only when the committee invites them or gives them permission to attend.

Since the assembly desires the maturest judgment of the committee, it is necessary to allow more freedom in reconsidering votes in committee than is permitted in the assembly. Therefore there is no limit to the number of times questions may be reconsidered or as to the time when the motion to reconsider may be made, and it may be made by any member who did not vote with the losing side. Thus, a member who was absent from a meeting when certain action was taken may move a reconsideration, regardless of the time that has elapsed. To prevent a misuse of this privilege, it is necessary to require a two-thirds vote to reconsider or rescind a vote in committee, unless all the members who voted with the prevailing side are present, or have received ample notice that the reconsideration would be moved at this meeting, in which case only a majority vote is necessary.

All papers referred to a committee must be carefully preserved and returned to the secretary of the society without being defaced. It is not permitted to write amendments on the papers referred to a committee. They must be written on a separate sheet.

CHAPTER XXV

REPORTS OF COMMITTEES

ORAL REPORTS

WHEN a committee to which has been referred a resolution makes an oral report, its chairman stands and says: "The committee to which was referred the resolution on ———— reports it back [or, has directed me to report it back] with the recommendation that ————." The form of the recommendation is given on pages 270, 271 for all cases that may occur. In the case of a committee on resolutions the forms of the oral report are given on pages 274–276.

PREPARING WRITTEN REPORTS

Reports of committees are not usually dated or addressed. The report of a standing committee should be headed thus, "Report of the Committee on ————." The report of a special committee should always at the beginning show clearly what the committee was ordered to do. In the case of standing committees the name of the committee is sufficient. If the recommendations require any action on the part of the society, the report should close with a resolution or resolutions to carry into effect the recommendations. The adoption of a recommendation that a thing be done is a very different thing from doing that thing, or from ordering it to be done. Too much care cannot be taken to close the report with a resolution that completely covers all action that the society should take in the case.

A committee's report should always be written in the third person, even though the entire work has been done by the chairman and though the report is signed only by him. When a report contains a number of facts, opinions, or recommendations, they should usually be summarized near the end of the report just before the resolutions. The report may be signed by all the members agreeing to it, or the committee may authorize the chairman to sign it. In the latter case the chairman adds the word "Chairman" after his name, which he should never do except when he signs the report alone for the committee. This he cannot do unless so authorized by the committee. It is better to have a very important report signed by every member agreeing to it. The signatures may immediately follow the body of the report, or they may be preceded by the words, "Respectfully submitted." What is in the report of the committee must be agreed to by a majority vote at a meeting of the committee, of which every member has been notified, or at a meeting that is an adjournment thereof, a majority of the members being present. It must never be referred to as the report of the majority, but always as the report of the committee. [On page 286 is explained the circumstances under which committees may act without meeting.]

MAKING REPORTS

The chairman of a committee usually makes its report to the assembly. If in any particular case the chairman is not in sympathy with the action of the committee, another member, called the reporting member, should be appointed to make the report on that subject. This is because the reporting member should be prepared to give the reasons for the recommendation and to answer criticisms. If the order of business specifies a time for hearing committees' reports, it is the duty of the presiding officer, when the time arrives, to announce the fact and to call upon each committee in succession for its report. He should never call upon the chairman of a committee for his report, nor should the committee chairman refer to it as his report. Although the chairman may have written every word, the report is not his, but is the committee's. When no time is set for hearing the report, the committee chairman should avail himself of the first opportunity, after it is ready, to obtain the floor and to announce that the committee is prepared to report. The president may direct him to report then, or the assembly may appoint some other time.

Minority Report. If the minority wish to present their views to the society, they may put them in writing, signed by all who approve of them, and, if permission is granted, they should present them immediately after the committee has reported. They have not the right to make a minority report, but the privilege is rarely refused. In a case of this kind the chairman of the committee, after presenting the committee's report, says that the minority desire to present their views. The president says that if there is no objection the views of the minority will be heard. If objection is made, some one may move that the views of the minority be heard, or received, or the president may put the question without waiting for a motion. If permission is granted, the president calls for the views of the minority, which are then presented and read by the member who has been chosen to present them. If the committee's report contains a resolution, the views of the minority are not submitted until after the president has stated the question on adopting the resolution. In this case the member reporting for the minority should move to substitute the resolution recommended by the minority for the one recommended by the committee. If the committee's report does not call for action by the society, no motion is made to adopt either report. The society has been furnished the desired information, and that ends the matter as far as the committee is concerned. This minority report is more properly called the views of the minority. [See pages 557–560 for examples of Reports of Committees.]

REPORTS OF VARIOUS KINDS OF COMMITTEES AND ACTION THEREON

[Reports of the different kinds of committees mentioned on page 254 are treated here in the same order as given there.]

(1) **A Committee to Consider and Report Suitable Action on a Resolution Referred to It.** This is the common case of a resolution's being committed or referred to a special committee. In societies with much business to transact, it is usually better not to spend much time in considering resolutions that are offered in an

unsatisfactory shape. Such resolutions should be referred to a committee whose duty it is to consider carefully the questions and recommend suitable action by the society. When the committee meets, the entire resolution should be read by the chairman, after which the action of the committee depends upon its attitude toward the resolution. The report in all cases is an oral one, though amendments proposed by the committee, unless very simple, should be in writing on a piece of paper separate from the one containing the resolution. If the committee proposes amendments, the committee chairman should move their adoption. In other cases no motion is made because the motions to adopt the resolution and its amendment, if there is any, were pending when they were referred to the committee, and are therefore pending when they are reported back to the assembly.

Since a special committee has only one thing to attend to, its chairman is pretty sure to be in sympathy with the majority of the committee on the question referred to it, and therefore he usually makes the committee's report. As soon as this report is made, the president repeats the recommendation, and then reads what has been referred to the committee, and states the question before the assembly, as illustrated below.

(a) If the committee is in favor of the resolution exactly as it stands when committed, its chairman should be directed "to report the resolution back with the recommendation that it be adopted." In this case the president says: "The committee to which was referred the resolution on —— recommends its adoption. The resolution is, 'Resolved, That —— [reads the resolution]. The question is on the adoption of the resolution [or, on its adoption]."

(b) If the resolution when referred had an amendment pending, and the committee favors the amendment and the resolution when amended, the chairman should be directed "to report it back with the recommendation that the pending amendment be adopted, and that resolution as thus amended be adopted"; or with the recommendation "that the resolution and pending amendment both be adopted." In this case the president, after repeating the recommendation and reading the resolution and the amendment, should state the question on the pending amendment. After it is voted on, the question is stated on the resolution as it then stands.

(c) If the committee is in favor of the resolution but is opposed to the pending amendment, its recommendation should be, "that the pending amendment be rejected [or, not adopted] and that the resolution be adopted." In this case the president, after repeating the recommendation and reading the resolution and the amendment, says: "The question is on the adoption of the amendment, the recommendation of the committee to the contrary notwithstanding." The question must always be put on adopting the motion, never on rejecting it. After the vote is taken on the amendment, the question is on the resolution as it then stands.

(d) If the committee is opposed to the resolution and is unwilling to recommend any modification of it, its recommendation should be, "that it be not adopted." The president, after repeating the recommendation and the resolution, states the question thus: "The question is on the adoption of the resolution, the recommendation of the committee to the contrary notwithstanding."

(e) If the committee favors the adoption of the resolution in a modified form, it should either agree upon suitable amendments, or after discussion appoint a member to rewrite the resolution. In the former case the entire work is done by the committee. If the resolution consists of more than one paragraph, the paragraphs are taken up singly for amendment, just as is done in the assembly, the later paragraphs not being open to amendment until the earlier ones are disposed of, as explained on page 371. After the committee has agreed upon the amendments, which may be a substitute, the chairman should be directed "to report the resolution back with the proposed amendments and the recommendation 'that the amendments be adopted, and that the resolution as thus amended be adopted.'" The amendments should be put in writing on a separate sheet of paper and handed to the presiding officer when the oral report is made. The sheet may be headed thus: "Amendments Proposed to Resolution on Renting a Hall." Under this the amendments should be entered like this: "Amend by striking out 'fifty' and inserting 'sixty.'" Or the report may be in writing, as shown on pages 557-558.

As soon as the report is made, before taking his seat, the committee's chairman says: "By direction of the committee, I move the adoption of the amendments." The president then says: "The committee to which was referred the resolution on —— reports it back, with the recommendation that it be amended as follows: [repeating the amendments], and that the resolution when thus amended be adopted. The question is on the first amendment reported by the committee, which is to insert —— after the word ——. Are you ready for the question?'' Instead of taking a separate vote on each amendment, the question may be stated and put on all the amendments at once, if no objection is made. If objection is made, a brief informal conference among the leaders will often save time by providing for taking a separate vote, perhaps on only a single amendment. A member who wishes a separate vote on an amendment should call for a ''Division of the question'' when the president is about to take a vote on all the pending amendments together.

If, in the last case mentioned, there had been an amendment pending when the resolution was referred to the committee, the recommendations should state whether the committee recommends the adoption or the rejection of the pending amendment, and the chair should state the question on that amendment first, and then on the committee's amendments. If the committee recommends an amendment to the pending amendment, the president states the question first on the secondary amendment proposed by the committee, and, when that is disposed of, the question is on the primary amendment as it then stands. Afterward the amendments to the resolution proposed by the committee are taken up, at which time they are open to debate and amendment. After the committee's amendments have been acted upon, the resolution is open to further amendment from the floor. On page 557 is given a form for a written report in a case like this.

If the amendments are very numerous, it is better to rewrite the resolution and submit the new one as a substitute for the original. In this case a member is appointed to prepare the substitute which is open to amendment by the committee. When it is perfected, a motion is adopted directing the chairman to report back the resolution with the substitute and the recommendation that the substitute be adopted. When the report is made, the reporting member moves the adoption of the substitute, and the president states the question thus: ''The committee to which was referred —— reports it back with a substitute which it recommends for adoption. The resolution is as follows: [reads the resolution]. The substitute recommended is 'Resolved, ——' [reads the substitute]. The question is on substituting [or, on the motion to substitute] the resolution submitted by the committee for the original resolution. Are you ready for the question?'' If no one rises he puts the question thus: ''As many as are in favor of substituting the committee's resolution for the original one say 'Aye'; those opposed say 'No.' The ayes have it and the motion to substitute is adopted. The question is now on the resolution as amended. Are you ready for the question?'' If no one rises to claim the floor, the president puts the question on the pending resolution, that is, the resolution recommended by the committee which has been substituted for the original one. If members wish to move amendments to either the original resolution or the substitute, the procedure is as shown on page 33.

(2) **Committee on Resolutions.** Instead of appointing a separate committee for each resolution when proposed, in conventions it is generally more convenient, as well as more satisfactory, to appoint one large committee, called the Committee on Resolutions, to which is referred all resolutions offered by individual members and all recommendations of officers and committees that are not in the form of resolutions. It is the duty of this committee to prepare and submit to the convention suitable resolutions to carry into effect the recommendations referred to it, and also to recommend the action which, in its opinion, the convention should take in each case referred to it. The committee may make any of the recommendations mentioned on pages 274–276, and the proceedings are the same as there described.

This committee should be provided for by a by-law, or by a rule adopted by a convention, which requires all resolutions and recommendations to be referred to a committee on resolutions, unless the rule in any particular case is suspended by a majority vote. In large conventions with much business, the resolutions should be handed to the secretary, who at convenient times passes them to the president. The order of business should provide a time at each meeting, or at least each day, for offering resolutions. When that time arrives, the president reads or causes to be read from the platform all the resolutions received, announcing that they are referred to the committee on resolutions. If no time is specified on the program for reading the resolutions or for miscellaneous business, the president has the resolutions read at such time as he deems best.

If it is desired to consider any one of these resolutions immediately, some one should move, as soon as it is read, to suspend the rules that interfere with the immediate consideration of the resolution. As this motion, if carried, suspends only a standing rule, it requires merely a majority vote for its adoption. Or, a motion may be adopted ordering the committee to report the specified resolution back at a certain time.

In some conventions, where improper or contentious questions are liable to be introduced, it is well to allow the committee on resolutions by a three-fourths vote, or a vote of two thirds of its members, to decide not to report a resolution. A larger vote should be required in such a committee to suppress a question than is required in the convention. In the convention it requires a two-thirds vote to sustain an objection to the consideration of a question. If it is desired to give the committee this power to suppress a resolution, provision must be made for this in the by-law or resolution authorizing the committee, as otherwise the committee is obliged to report back the resolution even though unanimously opposed to it.

When the committee is called on for its report, the chairman proceeds to the platform and says: "Mr. President, the committee on resolutions, having had under consideration the following resolutions which were referred to it, has directed me to report as follows: Resolution offered [or proposed] by Mr. A and seconded by Mr. B, 'Resolved, That ——' [reading the resolution]. The committee recommends its adoption." The resolution is handed to the president, who says: "The following resolution has been reported by the committee on resolutions with the recommendation that it be adopted: 'Resolved, That, ——' [reading the resolution]. The question is on the adoption of the resolution. Are you ready for the question?" When the first resolution has been disposed of, the committee chairman again rises and says: "Resolution offered by Mr. C and seconded by Mr. D: 'Resolved, That, ——' [reading the resolution]. The committee recommends that it be not adopted." The president proceeds as just stated, except that he says: "The committee recommends that the resolution be not adopted. The question is on the adoption of the resolution, the recommendation of the committee to the contrary notwithstanding." If the committee recommends that the resolution be amended and then adopted, the committee chairman, after reading the resolution, says: "The committee recommends that the resolution be amended by striking out —— and inserting ——, and that as thus amended the resolution be adopted. By direction of the committee I move the adoption of the amendment." The president, after receiving the resolution, says: "The committee on resolutions reports the following resolution and moves an amendment to it, and recommends that the resolution as thus amended be adopted. The resolution is as follows: [reads the resolution]. The committee moves to amend by striking out —— and inserting ——. The question is on adopting the amendment."

The resolutions that originate with the committee are usually reported last, the committee chairman saying: "By direction of the committee on resolutions, I move the adoption of the following resolution [or resolutions]: 'Resolved, That ——' " which he reads and hands to the president. The reporting member moves the adoption of all resolutions and amendments proposed by the committee, but he makes no motion in cases where the committee recommends the adoption or rejection of a motion referred to it. The signatures of the mover and the seconder are affixed to the written motions that are referred. If the committee recommends an amendment, the chairman moves the adoption of the amendment.

When the committee reports a number of resolutions, it is well first to report in one group all of those that the committee recommends to be adopted to which, in the opinion of the committee, no objection will be made. In such case the committee chairman reports thus: "Mr. President, the committee on resolutions having had under consideration the following resolutions referred to it, has directed me to report them back, with the recommendation that they be adopted. Resolution proposed by Mr. A and seconded by Mr. B: 'Resolved, That ——' [reading the resolution from the platform]. Resolution proposed by Mr. C and seconded by Mr. D: 'Resolved, That ——,' " thus reading all the resolutions of the group. The president then says: "If there is no objection, a single vote will be taken on the adoption of these resolutions, which are all reported favorably by the committee on resolutions." If no objection is made he continues: "There being no objection, the question is on the adoption of the following resolutions: [The resolutions are then read from the platform again.] As many as are in favor of the adoption of these resolutions say 'Aye,' etc." If objection is made to taking a single vote on all the resolutions, or a division of the question is called for, the president asks how the member wishes the resolutions divided. It may be that there is only one resolution upon which a separate vote is required, and time can frequently be saved by an informal talk concerning the matter by the leaders. The same is true in regard to a number of amendments reported by the committee, which can often be disposed of in one or two groups.

If two or more of the resolutions referred to the committee relate to the same general subject, the committee may find it advisable to prepare a single resolution, or a series of resolutions, and report it as a substitute for the resolutions on that subject. In such a case the reporting member should read all the resolutions, and then say that the committee recommends the adoption of a substitute for them all, which he should read and then move its adoption.

The committee on resolutions should be authorized to report every day of the convention, some time for this report being designated in the program or order of business. Its reports are oral, except the resolutions and amendments proposed, which are in writing, preferably typewriting. When typewritten they should, for the convenience of the secretary, be in duplicate whenever the proceedings are to be published.

A committee of this kind is not automatically discharged when it makes a report, as is a committee to which a single question is referred. In the case of a convention, as long as the session lasts the committee continues to exist, unless the convention limits the time during which resolutions may be handed in, in which case the committee ceases to exist as soon as it has performed all the duties assigned it, or the time limit for offering resolutions is reached.

Some conventions receiving a large number of reports, with recommendations from its officers and committees, have a Committee on Recommendations of Officers and Committees in addition to the committee on resolutions. It is doubtful as to there being anything gained by thus dividing this work between two committees, referring the recommendations of officers and committees to one, and resolutions offered by individual members to the other. Similar questions may come before both committees which can be handled more satisfactorily if the committees are combined. A large committee on resolutions has all the advantages without the disadvantages of two committees. It can divide itself into two sub-committees, one doing the preliminary work on the recommendations and the other on the resolutions referred to it. These sub-committees report to the committee, which may adopt or modify the resolution and recommendations submitted. Sometimes it may be desirable to have even more than two sub-committees to do the preliminary work.

Since the committee on resolutions does so much of the preliminary work of the convention, and is largely responsible for the ultimate form of most of the resolutions adopted, it should be large and composed of the strongest and fairest-minded of all parties, so that its resolutions 'will carry weight with the convention. Its chairman should be sufficiently familiar with parliamentary law to write resolutions and to make reports in proper form. Hearings on the questions referred to a committee should be given to all who request that privilege. Before making an adverse report on a resolution, or recommending a vital amendment to it, the committee should give the one who proposed it an opportunity to defend the resolution. If a resolution is not in proper form, the committee, if it approves the subject matter, should recommend an appropriate substitute. If this committee is properly constituted and does its duty, the convention will be saved much time that otherwise would be spent in debate and attempts to modify the resolutions reported.

(3) **A Committee to Consider a Subject and Report a Resolution Covering its Recommendation.** Sometimes there is a subject upon which it is desired to take action, but no one is prepared to offer a resolution covering the matter. In such a case a motion should be made to refer the subject to a committee, or to appoint a committee with instructions to report a resolution covering the case. This is not the subsidiary motion to commit or refer, as there is no motion pending to be referred to the committee, and there can be no subsidiary motion unless there is a motion pending to which it is subsidiary. The motion to refer, in this case, is a main motion and may be made in either of the following forms: "I move to refer the date and place of meeting of the next convention to a committee of five to be appointed by the chair, with instructions to report by resolution to-morrow morning"; or, "I move that a committee of five be appointed by the chair to consider the various invitations that have been received for the next convention, with instructions to report as soon as practicable a

resolution providing for holding the next convention at such time and place as it deems best.''

The report of the committee need be nothing but a resolution, which should always be in writing. If the committee makes no report in writing except the resolution, the chairman of the committee should make such explanation of the case as may be necessary to enable the society ·to understand it.

Since no resolution is referred to the committee, it is generally best to discuss freely the subject in committee before any resolution is drafted. After a full discussion, one member should be requested to draft a resolution covering the matter referred to the committee. If the subject is of such a nature as to call for a written report, one member should make a draft of the report, giving the required information and closing with one or more resolutions which the committee recommends to be adopted. [See page 559 for the form of the report.] This draft is discussed and amended and finally adopted. A clear copy of the report should then be made, which is signed by the chairman for the committee, or by all the members of the committee who agree to the report. It may be necessary to have two or more meetings of the committee before the work is finished. Finally the chairman is directed to submit the report, and the committee ''rises,'' that is, adjourns sine die.

When the committee reports, its chairman reads the report, if written, or makes an oral report as heretofore described. In either case, before taking his seat he reads the written resolution, moves its adoption, and hands the report to the president. The president then says: ''The committee recommends the adoption of the following resolution: [reads the resolution]. The question is on the adoption of the resolution.'' No vote is taken on adopting the report, even when it is a written one, as it is merely explanatory of the resolution, which is the only thing for the assembly to adopt. A committee should never submit its recommendations in such a shape that it is necessary for others to prepare and offer resolutions to carry out the recommendations. No one can do this as well as the committee, who have carefully investigated the matter and have made the recommendations. [For the form of the report see page 559.]

(4) **A Committee to Investigate a Certain Matter and Report the Facts with Their Opinions Thereon.** Sometimes there are

matters upon which a society wishes a statement of facts after a thorough examination by a small number of judicious persons. For this purpose a committee is appointed to investigate and report the facts. In most cases the committee can with advantage be instructed to report also its opinions and recommendations, which latter, when practicable, should always close with a resolution.

When the committee meets and confers upon the matter, it may be found advisable to appoint one or more sub-committees, of one or two members each, to investigate certain matters and to report at an adjourned meeting. The committee may find it advisable to invite some persons, not necessarily members, to appear before it. When all the facts in the case have been ascertained, the committee proceeds to prepare its report as described in the last case. If the report contains only a statement of facts and the opinion of the committee, its chairman, on submitting the report, makes no motion, as there is no necessity for the assembly's taking any action on the report. The assembly cannot alter one word of the report, which contains nothing but a statement of facts and the opinion of the committee thereon. The president therefore, when the report has been read, merely announces the next business in order. If, however, the report closes with a resolution, or merely with a recommendation, the committee chairman moves the adoption of the resolution or recommendation. [For the form of the report see page 559.]

(5) **A Committee to Execute an Order of the Society.** If a society wishes to have some definite action taken, it appoints a committee to take charge of the matter. Cases of this kind arise when a society wishes to appoint a committee to attend to having the society incorporated; to make arrangements for a concert or a course of lectures; to obtain subscriptions or to collect funds; or to act as ushers to seat the audience, or a committee on hospitality to provide accommodations for guests. A committee of this kind should have full power to do everything that is necessary for the proper accomplishment of the work assigned it without having to call on the society for additional power. It usually does its work through its individual members, or through small sub-committees, instead of in committee meetings. It should, however, meet as soon as the committee is appointed, and decide how its work is to be done. When its work has been accomplished, it

should usually have another meeting and close up the business. If its work is such as to call for a report, as when finances are involved, the report should be prepared and adopted and submitted to the society as heretofore described. If the committee handles money, great care should be exercised and all funds should be turned over to the treasurer of the society as promptly as possible. When it is desired to limit the expenses that a committee's duties may necessarily involve, it can be done by adding to the motion appointing the committee a provision like this in case of a banquet: "Provided, that the cost per plate shall not exceed $2.50"; or like this in case of a concert: "Provided, that the indebtedness incurred shall not exceed $50 more than the value of the tickets subscribed for in advance."

The motion to appoint a committee of this kind may be made in the following form: "I move that the club give a banquet at the close of the next annual meeting, and that a committee of three, to be appointed by the president, have full charge of all the arrangements, with power to add to their number, and to appoint sub-committees consisting in whole or in part of those who are not members of the committee"; or thus: "I move that the club give a concert next month, and that it be in charge of a committee of three, to be appointed by the president, with full power." Custom has authorized the use of the expression "with full power" as meaning "with all the power that is possessed by the society in regard to the particular thing referred to the committee."

(6) **A Committee to Represent and Act for the Society in a Certain Matter.** In case different societies wish to coöperate, and yet it is impracticable for them to meet together for consultation, they should each appoint a few members to represent the society, and these representatives, or delegates, as they are usually called, should meet and act for their respective societies. These delegates are actually committees, and may be instructed to any extent by the societies appointing them. When a society is either a constituent or subordinate member of a greater organization, the constitution of the latter organization determines the power of the delegates. In other cases, unless authorized by the society, its delegates or committees have no power to bind the society.

Committees of this kind do not usually organize, as they have no business to transact or report to make as a committee, and therefore have no need of a chairman. In some national organizations the delegates from all the societies in a state are required to act together in certain matters, and therefore the delegates from each state organize and elect a chairman, unless a chairman is provided for in the by-laws. If they are required to make a report to the society, it is prepared and made as heretofore described. No motion is made nor is a vote taken in the society on adopting the committee's report, as it is simply a statement of facts for the society's information.

(7) **Tellers and Credentials Committees.** The *Tellers* are a committee appointed to count the vote and report it to the assembly. In case of a ballot vote, they also prepare and collect the ballots. Since their most common use in ordinary societies is in the election of officers and boards, the subject is treated in that connection. [See Tellers, page 221.]

A *Credentials Committee* is appointed to receive and examine the credentials of delegates and their alternates; to furnish those who have proper credentials with a suitable badge or card as evidence of their being duly accredited delegates or alternates; to report to the convention the names of such delegates and alternates, and the names of contestants with the facts in cases where there are disputes as to which credentials should be recognized; and also to furnish the tellers with a copy of the register of delegates and to coöperate with the tellers in identifying delegates.

A Convention is composed mainly of delegates appointed by its constituent or subordinate societies. Its membership also includes ex-officio members, such as its own officers, and usually the chairmen of its standing committees and of such other committees as are instructed to report to the convention. These should be members of the convention, whether delegates or not. Frequently the presiding officers of the constituent societies are ex-officio members of the convention. The number of delegates to which each society is entitled is limited by the by-laws of the organization. Each society, in order to insure its having a full representation, usually appoints some alternates to take the place of any delegates who fail to attend. The delegates and alternates must be furnished with some evidence of their appointment, and this certificate, called the credentials, should be signed by the secretary of the appointing society and preferably by the president also. The convention may adopt a form for the credentials, or the form on page 562 may be used. If the convention has adopted no rule on the subject, one certificate can be given, including the names of all the delegates and alternates. In this case the delegate holding the certificate must identify the other delegates and alternates when they register.

In such conventions it is usually necessary to reserve the main hall for the members, who for the purpose of identification are furnished with badges. In this way the voters are not mixed with the non-voters, rendering it easier to determine the vote when it is viva voce or by rising. Such precautions are necessary when there are several hundred voters. In voting by ballot for the officers, some large organizations require each voter to present a card, furnished by the credentials committee, showing that the holder is entitled to vote.

In order to examine the credentials of delegates and to furnish badges and cards when required, it is necessary to have a Credentials Committee appointed in advance of the meeting of the convention, either by the president or by the board of managers, as provided in the by-laws. By this plan the committee can, and should in the case of a large convention, meet a day before the convention, so as to examine the credentials of members as they arrive. There is no reason why this committee should not be appointed from those not delegates to the convention. Most, or even all, of the members may be members of the local society with which the convention meets. Each delegate whose credentials are substantially correct, after signing the register hereafter described, should be furnished with a card, or badge, or both, showing that he is a delegate. Small technical defects should be overlooked in ordinary conventions. Even if a delegate has lost his credentials, or has not been furnished with them, if there is no reason to doubt his statement that he was appointed a delegate, the committee may report him as a delegate and furnish him with a delegate's card, etc. Where there is no inducement to or suspicion of fraud, it is not well to be too particular about enforcing the rules as to credentials. On the other hand, carelessness in providing one's self with proper credentials and taking care of them should put the delegate to enough inconvenience to prevent the repetition of the neglect. If an error is made and is afterward discovered, it can be rectified.

If there is a contest between two delegates each claiming the office, the committee hears the evidence and reports in favor of the one the committee thinks is entitled to the place. The convention decides which one shall be recognized as delegate. This rarely, if ever, occurs in any convention except a political one. In many cases the difficulty is to find enough members who are willing and can afford to attend the convention. In case of many religious conventions, each of the local churches adopts a resolution authorizing its minister to appoint as many delegates as the church is entitled to, or a resolution appointing as delegates such members as attend the meeting. In either case, the minister should be furnished with a copy of the resolution, which he should hand to the credentials committee together with a list of the delegates.

The credentials committee should make a partial report at the opening of the convention, before any business is transacted, so that it may be known how many delegates are present. In some conventions the names of all delegates who have presented proper credentials are reported. In state and national conventions of delegates of ordinary societies, it is not necessary or customary to read the names, but the number present should be reported. In national conventions it is also of interest to know how many are present from each state. Each convention decides for itself as to what details shall be included in the report of the credentials committee. If the register is kept as shown on page 563 the number of registrants at any moment can be readily found by adding the check marks in each of the two columns on the right of the pages of the register. No action is taken on the report unless the names of the delegates are reported. If the names of the delegates are reported, the report of the committee is adopted either by a formal vote or, if no one objects, by general consent. If a contest is reported, neither party to the contest can vote until the assembly decides which is entitled to the seat. The committee should make additional daily reports, provided more delegates register, as it is necessary to know the number registered in order to determine the quorum, which is a majority of the number registered. The committee continues in existence until the convention adjourns, because members may arrive at the last moment and wish to register.

Register of Delegates and Alternates. In the case of a very large convention where it is desired to be particular in regard to the credentials of delegates, the constituent bodies should be asked or required to send to the chairman of the credentials committee, at least a week previous to the opening of the convention, the names of all delegates and alternates. The list, called the Register of Delegates and Alternates, should be prepared in duplicate by the committee before the opening of the convention. [See page 563 for the form of the register.]

To reduce the time occupied in registering, it is well to divide the state, in case of a state convention, into districts, or groups, of one or more contiguous counties, or of counties arranged alphabetically. No district should have more than 150 or 200 delegates. To each of these districts is devoted a section of the register, these sections being numbered consecutively. Each section consists of 3 or 4 sheets (12 or 16 pages) of foolscap paper upon which are typewritten in alphabetical order the counties in the district; and under each county the names of the societies represented, alphabetically arranged; and finally, under each society, the names first of the delegates, and then of the alternates, each being entered alphabetically. Each section of the register should be bound with a cover of stiff paper, and numbered.

In case of a national convention the method is the same as just described, each district consisting of states instead of counties.

The credentials committee should be divided into as many sub-committees of two as there are sections of the register. In addition, there should be a few members of the committee in reserve for filling temporary vacancies. Each sub-committee should be provided with a section of the register, in duplicate, and with a table, pens, and ink. Each should also have badges and identification cards sufficient for all the delegates and alternates in its district. These tables should be separated as far as practicable, and the number of the district, and the counties it covers, distinctly displayed. At the entrance to the room there should be a bulletin showing the counties or states in each district, and the number of the district. Ushers should be provided to show to the delegates the tables at which they are to register. If practicable, the delegates after registering should leave the room by a different door from the one by which they entered. The chairman and vice-chairman of the credentials committee should see that every possible step is taken to enable the delegates to enter and to leave the room without confusion, and to register rapidly.

A delegate, having reached his proper table, hands his credentials card to the committee (who retain it), and announces at the same time his county, or state, his society, and his name. As soon as his credentials are found to be correct, he signs his name in the register to the right of his typewritten name. He is then furnished by the committee with a badge, and also with an identification card when one is required. This card certifies that Mr. —— is a delegate to the convention. It should be numbered the same as the district to which the delegate belongs, and in some conventions must be shown in order to obtain a ballot or to vote at the election of officers. The number on his card will indicate to him the number of the table at which he will obtain his ballot and vote at the election. The place of voting for each group, or district, should be the same as its place of registering.

The alternates register the same as the delegates, and receive their badges in the same way. It is not as important that they receive cards as is the case with delegates, because they do not vote. Care should be exercised by the sub-committees to see that the delegates and alternates receive their identification cards, because after signing the register and receiving their badges they often neglect to obtain their identification cards. The badges and cards should never be issued until the register has been signed. The chairman of the committee, with the assistance of the vice-chairman, should supervise the sub-committees and ushers, and should see that they are well instructed and are performing their work properly. All doubtful questions should be acted upon by the entire committee. After the first rush, one or two sub-committees can usually attend to all the business. The duplicate copy of the register is for the use of the members of the credentials committee when coöperating with the tellers at the election of officers, etc., as explained on page 220.

(8) **A Standing Committee to Take Charge of a Department of Work.** Many organizations, local, state, and national, carry on work that can best be divided among a number of standing committees. Each of these committees has a definite class of work assigned to it, of which it has complete control, subject to the by-laws and orders of the parent organization. As explained on page 244, such committees are practically boards, differing from the board of managers only in the fact that the field of operations of each is very limited. Sometimes an organization will have a dozen or more of these standing committees in addition to the board of managers. They are not subject to the board unless made

so by the by-laws, which is sometimes done in national societies. Organizations differ so greatly that each must decide for itself whether it is advisable to make its standing committees subject to the orders of the board of managers.

Standing committees of local societies can meet the same as special committees, and are under the same rules. No action can be taken, except at a meeting properly called and at which a quorum is present. The report must be adopted at such a meeting in order to be the report of the committee.

In state and national organizations it is not always practicable to enforce the ordinary parliamentary principles that the names of the members of a committee must be announced to the assembly before the committee can act, and that nothing can be done by the committee except when it is in session and a majority is present. The convention meets not more frequently than once a year, and those present rarely exceed from one to three per cent. of the members of the constituent societies. On this account it is often impracticable, during the session of the convention, to obtain the consent to serve of some members whom it is desired to appoint on standing committees. Sometimes much correspondence is necessary before the president can appoint a single committee, and usually this correspondence cannot begin until after the convention adjourns. The president should always select the chairman first, as his consent to serve may depend somewhat upon what colleagues he has, and therefore he should be consulted in reference to them before they are appointed. Usually the members of each standing committee are selected from different districts of the territory covered by the organization, and thus the members are so scattered that the committee can never meet. Ordinarily each member attends to the work of the committee in his district, and any business that requires the action of the entire committee must be done by correspondence.

Each member should send an account of the work done by him to the chairman in time for the latter to prepare a report of the work done by the committee during the year, which report must be submitted to the convention. [A simple form for such a report is given on page 559.] As long as the report is merely an account of the work done, it is usual for the chairman to prepare and sign it as chairman without submitting it to the committee for approval. But he is not authorized to include any recommendation in the report that has not been adopted by a majority vote at a meeting of the committee, unless the recommendation has been sent to every member and has been approved by a majority of the entire committee. If the chairman wishes to make recommendations that have not been authorized by the committee, they must not be included in the report, but should be offered as recommendations proposed by the chairman on his own responsibility.

The reports of committees of conventions and of any other kind of large meetings should always be read from the platform. If the reporting member cannot read so as to be heard by every one in the hall, the report should be read by the secretary or by some one appointed for the purpose who can be heard. It is an imposition on the assembly for a report to be read so that many cannot hear it. Unless the report contains recommendations, when the reading is finished the president calls for the next committee's report, or whatever is next in order. No action is taken on a report that contains only an account of what the committee has done. The convention cannot change it in any way. If the report closes with resolutions or recommendations, the reporting member should move their adoption.

GENERAL REMARKS ON ADOPTING REPORTS OF COMMITTEES

In the foregoing pages the method of presenting the report of a committee to the assembly has been described, and also the forms of stating and putting the question. It is rarely advisable to adopt, or accept (which means the same thing), the report of a committee. The better form is to adopt the resolutions recommended by the committee. In case the report contains recommendations that are not followed by a resolution to put them into effect, the recommendations should be adopted or rejected. If they are adopted, a committee should usually be appointed to draw up a resolution to carry the recommendations into effect. If, however, the assembly adopts, or accepts, the report of a committee, it thereby adopts the entire report, including statement of facts and the opinions and recommendations and resolutions contained in the report. The assembly can in no respect change a committee's report, and it cannot make the committee say anything it has not said. If it wishes to adopt the report with certain exceptions, the assembly may strike out the objectionable parts and adopt the report as thus amended, or it may amend the report in any other way. The committee's report is thus treated just as any proposition submitted by a member, the assembly modifying it as it pleases before adopting it. This does not change the committee's report, and if the report is entered in the minutes or published, the record must show clearly what the committee reported. If the proceedings are published, the report may be published as submitted, followed by a statement that "The report was adopted after being amended as follows——." Or the report may be prefaced by a note, thus: "The report was adopted after the words printed in italics were inserted and the words enclosed in brackets were struck out"; and then the amendments would be incorporated in the report, showing clearly what the committee reported and what the assembly adopted.

Frequently with some committees of national or state organizations nearly all the work is done by the chairman, and therefore there is a tendency to refer to the report as "the report of the chairman," and sometimes even the president makes the mistake of calling on "the chairman of —— committee for his report," instead of calling for "the committee's report." The chairman sometimes writes the report in the first person, constantly using the pronoun "I." At other times the expression "your chairman" is used. All of these errors should be avoided. The report is not the report of the chairman, but of the committee, and the pronoun "I" can scarcely be used with propriety for a committee. As the report is being made to the convention, the expression "your chairman" can apply to no one except to the chairman of the convention. If it is necessary in the report to refer to the chairman of the committee, the expression "the chairman" or "our chairman" should be used, always avoiding the use of the first person singular. As far as possible, reference to the individual members of the committee by name should be avoided.

The motion "to receive" a report should never be made except when objection is made to allowing the report to be made. When the report has been read it already has been received and is the property of the assembly. The motion "to accept," which is equivalent to "to adopt," a report has the objection of being misunderstood by many persons, who confound it with "to receive." The motion "to adopt the report and discharge the committee" should never be made, except when the report is only a partial one, because the reception of the report by the assembly, if it is a final report, automatically discharges the committee from the consideration of the question. If the report is only a partial one, sometimes called a report of progress, the committee, unless it is discharged, continues its work without any order of the society. Sometimes it is voted "to accept the report and continue the committee," but such action is entirely unnecessary. [Various forms of reports of committees are shown on pages 557–561.]

CHAPTER XXVI

COMMITTEE OF THE WHOLE AND ITS SUBSTITUTES

COMMITTEE OF THE WHOLE

SOMETIMES in large assemblies it is desired to consider a question with all the freedom of a committee. This can be done by the assembly's resolving itself into a Committee of the Whole. The motion is made thus: "I move that the assembly do now resolve itself into a committee of the whole to take into consideration ——"; or, "I move that we go into committee of the whole to consider ——"; specifying the resolution or subject to be considered. This is really a motion to commit, the committee consisting of the whole assembly.

If this motion is adopted, the president appoints a chairman of the committee and takes his seat as a member of the committee. The secretary does not keep minutes of the proceedings in committee of the whole, but he, or an assistant secretary, should keep a temporary memorandum of the business transacted, which may be destroyed after the assembly has acted on the committee's report. Members must obtain the floor before making motions or speaking, and formal votes must be taken, just as in meetings of the assembly. Members may speak on a question as often as they obtain the floor, provided that, when several rise to speak, preference is given to one who has seldom had the floor. The committee cannot close or limit debate, or lay a question on the table, or postpone or commit it. Nor are any of the privileged motions in order. The committee cannot take a recess, or adjourn to meet at another time, or appoint a time for another meeting, nor can a question of privilege be raised, or the orders of the day be called for. When its business has been attended to, a motion is made in this form: "I move that the committee rise and report ——," stating what the committee has agreed upon as the result of its de-

290

liberations. Although the committee ceases to exist if this motion is adopted, yet it is necessary, just as with the privileged motion to adjourn in the assembly, to allow it to be made at any time when the mover can obtain the floor, and also not to allow it to be debated or amended, because otherwise a few members could prevent the committee's ever reporting. Of course it cannot be made when another has the floor or while the committee is engaged in voting.

If the committee wishes to adjourn before completing its work, the motion is adopted "to rise and report that the committee of the whole has had under consideration [state the subject], and has come to no conclusion thereon." If the assembly has fixed an hour for its own adjournment, when that hour arrives, the chairman should say, "The hour for the adjournment of the assembly having arrived, the committee will rise." The president immediately resumes the chair, and the chairman of the committee reports that the committee has come to no conclusion.

The committee cannot punish members for disorderly conduct, but it may order the gallery and hall cleared of all non-members. If members take advantage of the freedom allowed in committee, the committee should rise and report to the assembly for the assembly to take suitable action. The assembly may punish the refractory member, or may limit the debate in committee, or take such other action as the case calls for. The assembly then resolves itself again into committee of the whole to consider the question, the chairman of the committee resuming the chair. If the committee should be so disorderly that its chairman cannot control it with his limited powers, the president should resume the chair and declare the committee dissolved. The assembly is then in session, with all its rules in force.

The quorum of the committee of the whole is the same as the quorum of the assembly, unless the assembly authorizes a different quorum. If the committee finds itself without a quorum, it must rise and report the fact to the assembly, which then adjourns. In case of a convention where it is possible to secure the attendance of absentees from the hall, the convention, instead of adjourning, may take measures to secure a quorum as described under quorum, "Rules of Order Revised," page 259. If a quorum of the committee is obtained, the president directs the committee of the whole to resume its session.

When the committee rises, the president resumes the chair, and the committee chairman, in large conventions standing on the platform, says: "Mr. President, the committee of the whole has had under consideration ——, and has directed me to report the same with the following amendments" [reading the amendments]; or he makes such other report as will suit the case. The forms of reports given on pages 557-558 may be used just as with other committees.

As if in [or Quasi] Committee of the Whole

This is a somewhat simpler form of committee of the whole, and is used instead of it in the U. S. Senate. Instead of appointing a chairman of the committee and leaving the chair when the assembly has voted "to consider the resolution as if in committee of the whole," the president simply announces that the motion is adopted, and that "the resolution is before the assembly as if in committee of the whole," and retains the chair. The question is now considered with all the freedom of a committee, as already described. When no further amendments are offered, the president asks if any further amendments are proposed, and if no one rises to claim the floor, he at once rises and says: "The assembly, acting as if in committee of the whole, has had under consideration the resolution on —— and has made certain amendments," which he reads. No motion is made to adopt the report or the amendments, as the report itself is equivalent to a motion to adopt the amendments. The president then states the question on the amendments, and a single vote is taken on adopting them all, unless objection is made or a division of the question is called for, in which case the question must be divided as explained on page 160.

While acting as if in committee of the whole, any proper motion is in order, the same as if the question was being considered in the assembly in the ordinary way, but the adoption of any motion except an amendment puts an end to the quasi committee. Thus a motion to postpone the consideration of the question to the next meeting is in order, which is not the case in committee of the whole. If the postponement is adopted, the regular order is resumed and the president announces the next business in order in the assembly. To obtain the same result, if the resolution had been referred to the committee of the whole, it would be necessary that the committee adopt a motion to rise and report a recommendation that the resolution be postponed, etc.; that the committee chairman make the report; and that the assembly vote to postpone, etc. So it will be seen that considering a question as if in committee of the whole is simpler than referring the question to the committee of the whole, and is usually preferable in assemblies not very large.

No entry is made in the minutes of what is done while acting as if in committee of the whole, but the secretary keeps a temporary memorandum of the motions and votes, just as in committees. In fact, the motion to consider a subject as if in committee of the whole is a form of the motion to commit.

INFORMAL CONSIDERATION

When a resolution is considered in committee of the whole, or as if in committee of the whole, all the amendments must be voted on twice, first by the committee and then by the assembly. In ordinary societies a simpler method is to consider the question informally, which in effect is equivalent to suspending the rule limiting the number of times a member may speak in debate upon the resolution and any amendments of it. Such informal consideration avoids the complications of referring the question to a committee consisting of the entire assembly, to be considered and reported back for final action by the assembly.

When it is desired to consider a question informally, a member moves "that the resolution [or question, or subject] be considered informally." This is a form of the motion to commit. The debate on it is limited to the propriety of considering the question informally. If carried by a majority vote, the president announces the fact and adds: "The question is now open to informal consideration. There is no limit to the number of times a member may speak to the question." The motion applies only to the resolution and its amendments at this meeting, so that if the motion is temporarily disposed of by being laid on the table, or postponed, when it comes up at another meeting it is under the ordinary rules of debate.

While a question is being considered informally, the debate by a two-thirds vote may be limited in any way or closed; or the regular rules of debate may be put in force by a majority's adopting a motion "that the regular rules of debate be in force," or "that the question be considered formally." As soon as the main question is disposed of, temporarily or permanently, the informal consideration automatically ceases.

CHAPTER XXVII

OFFICERS

A SIMPLE deliberative assembly requires only two officers, one to preside over the assembly, and the other to keep a record of its proceedings. The first is known as the Chairman or President, etc., and the other as the Secretary or Clerk, etc. In addition to these, legislative assemblies have as additional officers a Sergeant-at-Arms, a Doorkeeper, a Postmaster, and a Chaplain. Sometimes large conventions in session for several days require similar officers. The duty of the Sergeant-at-Arms is to maintain order in the assembly, under the direction of the chairman. In Congress he is also the paymaster. The Doorkeeper is intrusted with the enforcement of the rules relating to admission to the hall, and has supervision of the janitor and charge of the rooms, furniture, etc., of the assembly. The Postmaster has charge of the mails, and the Chaplain opens each day's sittings with prayer.

All of these officers are elected by the assembly, and each is empowered to appoint all of the employees or subordinates of his department that have been authorized by the assembly. Each officer is held responsible for the acts of his subordinates and therefore must have the power of appointing them.

These officers need not necessarily be members of the assembly. In the U. S. House of Representatives the chairman, or speaker, is the only officer who is a member of the House, and in the U. S. Senate none of the officers are members of the Senate. In ordinary societies it is generally customary, though not obligatory, to elect all of the officers from the membership of the society. Sometimes, however, personal feeling has run so high in societies that no member could preserve order in a meeting, and it has been found advisable to invite a good presiding officer, who was in no way connected with the society, to preside at an adjourned or special meeting where an attempt was to be made to settle the difficulty in the organization. Where much money is handled, the treasurer and auditor are often not members of the organization, some banker or trust company being appointed treasurer, and the accounts being audited by a certified public accountant. Such organizations as engage a parliamentarian often find it advisable to go outside the organization to secure a suitable expert. There is no reason why any society, except a secret one, should not appoint any of its officers from outside its membership if it chooses to do so, provided it is not prohibited in its by-laws. But it must be borne in mind that holding office neither gives nor deprives one of the rights of membership. The right to make or to second motions, to engage in debate, to make inquiries or requests, to raise a question of order, to appeal from the decision of the chair, to vote—all these are the rights of membership, not of office. The office carries with it no rights except what are necessary for the performance of the duties of the office, and such as are given it by the by-laws. The society may by its by-laws make certain of its officers, or all of them, members of its board of managers, in which case they become members of the board by virtue of their being officers, not because they are members of the society. Their being members of the board does not give them any rights of membership in the society, but they have whatever rights are necessary for the performance of their duties as members of the board. The U. S. Senate gives to its president, who is not a member of the Senate, the right to vote when the vote is a tie.

Most clubs and other societies, whether incorporated or not, are organized for purposes that cannot be accomplished by the society in session as a deliberative assembly. While they do not usually need all of the officers required by legislative bodies, few permanent societies could well accomplish their work with no officers except a president and a secretary.

In most societies it is customary to provide for the absence of the president by having a vice-president, who presides in such cases. Some organizations have two or more vice-presidents, the first vice-president, if present, presiding in the absence of the president, the second vice-president presiding in the absence of the president and the first vice-president, and so on. Should one be appointed who is unfamiliar with the rules of the society and of parliamentary law, he should immediately remedy this defect. Sometimes a great many vice-presidents are elected simply as a matter of honor, with no idea of their being suitable presiding officers. In such cases there is no impropriety in one's accepting the honor without preparing himself to preside. When the presiding officer has another title than president, the word "vice" is prefixed to it, as Vice-Chairman, Vice-Commander, etc.

If there is much correspondence, it is usual to have a Corresponding Secretary to attend to it. In this case the other secretary is usually called the Recording Secretary, as he keeps the records and acts as the secretary of the society at its meetings. Since the work of different kinds of societies differs greatly, the division of duties between the secretaries must necessarily vary, and should therefore be clearly defined by each society for itself, as otherwise there is a great liability to trouble in regard to the division of duties between these officers.

If the society is small and they have no property and no receipts except the annual dues, the secretary can act also as treasurer. Usually it is necessary to have a treasurer to be responsible for the funds, disbursing them on the orders of the society or its authorized agent. When the secretary acts as treasurer he is sometimes called Secretary-Treasurer.

In some national organizations it has been found advisable to have an Executive Secretary, who is usually a paid officer giving his entire time to the work of the society. He has charge of the office of the society, and executes the orders of the society and of its board. Since he conducts the correspondence, there is no corresponding secretary when there is an Executive Secretary. He is also secretary of the board and of the executive committee.

In addition to the president, vice-presidents, recording secretary, corresponding secretary, and treasurer, all incorporated societies and nearly all unincorporated ones find it necessary to have some additional officers, called either managers, directors, or trustees. These managers, as they will be called hereafter, together with such of the other officers as the by-laws specify, constitute the Board of Managers, who control the business of the society between its meetings, subject to the by-laws and the orders of the society, as shown under Boards, page 247.

In some state and national organizations it has been found advisable to engage an expert parliamentarian as adviser to the president at the annual meetings, while in others it has been found more satisfactory to employ the parliamentarian for the year, so that he could advise the board and committees during the year. The president's preference should always be considered in this selection. In some cases the parliamentarian is made an officer of the organization. The advisability of this is doubtful, as he should not take part in debate or vote in meetings of the society or board, as explained on page 325.

Some organizations need still more officers, as a librarian, a curator, etc. Every society should provide in its by-laws for all the officers it requires, specifying those duties of each that are not stated in its parliamentary authority. The only persons called officers are those so called in the by-laws. Every society has a right to determine the division of duties among its officers, and it should not leave the duty of any officer in doubt. Much trouble arises from failure to do this.

The officers should always be selected by ballot, so that members who wish to do so may keep their votes secret. They should be elected at the annual meeting, and, except the managers, be elected for one or two or three years, or until their successors are chosen. In most organizations it has been found better to elect at each annual meeting half of the managers for two years, and thus prevent all of the managers being at one time new to the business. In some state and national societies half of the officers also are elected each year for two years. Which method is the better one depends upon the organization. This method is more conservative and renders sudden changes more difficult. On the other hand, it may prevent a new administration from making much-needed reforms. Where national organizations meet only biennially or triennially, all the officers should be elected at each convention.

The term of office begins as soon as the officer is elected, unless the society has specified the time. Some organizations meeting only annually elect their officers at the opening of the convention, the term of office beginning immediately upon the election. Others provide in their by-laws that the term of the officers shall begin at the close of the annual meeting. Still others provide that the term of office shall not begin for four or five months. This occurs in societies having the annual meeting in April or May, with no meetings until September or October, when the regular weekly, bi-weekly, or monthly meetings begin and continue for seven or eight months. It is doubtful whether this is as good a plan as the more usual one of having the term of office begin during or at the close of the annual meeting. Some organizations provide that the term of office shall not begin until the officer is formally in stalled with some ceremony established by rule or custom.

Vacancies in office in local societies sometimes are filled by the board of managers, and sometimes by the society. If the society has business meetings as often as monthly, it is usually better policy for the society itself to fill the vacancy. If the society has turned over its business entirely to the board, then the by-laws of the society should authorize the board to fill all vacancies in office. This should always be done with organizations meeting only once a year or once in two or three years. When the term of office exceeds a year, the board should be authorized to fill vacancies until the next annual meeting.

Reports of Officers. The officers do not make reports in an ordinary deliberative assembly. But in many societies the officers have duties outside their duties in the assembly, and are required by the by-laws to report at least annually to the society. These reports should be written in the third person, headed similarly to this: "Report of the Corresponding Secretary for the year ending June 30, 19—." The report need have no address. The signature should be followed by the official title of the officer. Ordinarily no motion should be made to accept the report of an officer. If recommendations are made, a motion should be made to refer them to a committee, or a resolution may be offered in conformity with the recommendation. In no case does the officer make a motion relating to his own report, whereas the chairman of a committee is the one who should make the motion to dispose of the committee's report.

The duties of the president, the vice-president, the different kinds of secretaries, the treasurer, the auditor, and the parliamentarian are shown in the following pages; the board of managers is treated on pages 247–249.

CHAPTER XXVIII

PRESIDENT AND VICE-PRESIDENT

PRESIDENT

The President as Presiding Officer, or Chairman. The presiding officer of a deliberative assembly is responsible for seeing that the business of the assembly is transacted in proper order and expedited as much as possible; that members observe the rules of debate; that order and decorum are always observed; and that the rules of the assembly are enforced with as little friction as possible. If the assembly is disorderly, in nine cases out of ten it is the fault of the presiding officer, just as it is the fault of the company commander if there is lack of discipline in a company of soldiers.

In order to perform the above-mentioned duties, the president of a society should first of all have the ability to command others. Without this he is unfitted to control an excited assembly. He should have good common sense, and be tactful and courteous, gentle but firm, and impartial in all his acts, so that all parties will feel confidence in his fairness.

Even with all these important qualifications, it is necessary for the presiding officer of an assembly to be familiar with the fundamental principles of parliamentary law and with the by-laws and rules of the society. If he is ignorant of these when he is elected, it is his duty to study them immediately so as to be prepared to preside, or else he should decline the office. No one has a right to accept an office while he is unwilling to do the work that is necessary to perform its duties properly. It is not a difficult matter, for any one who is otherwise fit to preside, to learn how to state and put questions, and to learn the order of precedence of the various motions, which motions are undebatable, those that cannot be amended, and those that require a two-thirds vote. All of these, except the stating and putting of questions, are shown in the three charts on pages 548–550. Where there is any possibility of trouble, he should have on his table the parliamentary authority and the by-laws of the society, so that he can quickly refer to them. He should always have with him a memorandum of all the business to come before the meeting, and a list of all the committees. He may at any time be called upon to appoint new committees, and as far as consistent with efficiency he should study to vary the membership of the committees. Societies would nearly always place upon the presiding officer the responsibility of appointing the committees if they were assured of his fairness and impartiality. This would generally be better than leaving the appointment of the committees to a large assembly where those first nominated are usually elected.

The president has not by virtue of his office the power to create or appoint committees, nor is he ex-officio a member of any committee. If it is desired to place upon the president these duties, it is necessary to provide for it in the by-laws or other rules, or in a special case by the adoption of a motion to that effect.

As a general rule, the presiding officer should avoid expressing his opinions on pending questions. Should he think it best to take either side on a question upon which there is some feeling, he should call some one else to the chair before making his speech, and he should not resume the chair until the pending question has been disposed of. After he has shown himself an advocate of one side, he cannot expect the other side to consider him an impartial judge in deciding any point of order that affects the pending question.

The presiding officer in an excited assembly should keep cool and calm, realizing the absolute necessity for this in order to control the assembly. He should bear in mind that he is placed in the chair to preserve order, and that the greater the disorder the greater the necessity for the exercise of his self-control and good sense.

The presiding officer of a deliberative assembly, unless some special title is assigned to him, is known as the Chairman. In the early times he was the only one provided with a chair, the rest of the assembly sitting on benches. The term "chairman" is now used for the presiding officer of a mass meeting, and for the presiding officer of an organized society, except in case of the president, or vice-president, etc., who are addressed as "Mr." or "Madam President," etc. The term "chairman" is also applied to the presiding officer of a committee, whether it be the committee of the whole or one of only two persons. The presiding officer of a board is sometimes called Chairman and sometimes President, there being no uniform practice.

The regular presiding officer of an organized society or club is usually called the President, and that term is generally used in this work. Different organizations have different titles, as Moderator, Commander, etc. In addressing the presiding officer the title should be preceded by "Mr." if a man, and by "Madam" if a woman. In no case should the title be preceded by "brother" or "sister," as such expressions imply that the speaker is also a presiding officer. Nor should a woman presiding be referred to or addressed as the "Chairwoman" or "Presidentess." A vice-president while presiding should be addressed as "Mr. President," on the same ground that a Vice-Admiral is addressed as Admiral and a Lieutenant-General as General. If any one except the president or vice-president is presiding, he is addressed as "Mr." or "Madam Chairman." This is the case regardless of the title of the regular presiding officer.

The term "chairman," or "the chair," covers the presiding officer regardless of his special title. He should never refer to himself except in the third person. If the reference is to his acts or opinions as presiding officer, he should not say, "I decide," or "I think," but he should say, "The chair decides," or, "The chair is of the opinion that the amendment is not germane, and therefore must rule it out of order"; or, "The chair is in doubt and will ask the club to decide." When a member appeals, he "appeals from the decision of the chair," not from the decision of Mr. ——, or the president. The individuality of the chairman should be lost in the office. A member should never address or refer to the presiding officer by his name, but should always address him by his official title, and should refer to him by his title, or as "the chair."

These formalities are necessary in order to emphasize the fact that the chairman represents and acts for the assembly. His decision is the decision of the assembly, unless the assembly exercises its right to reverse it. When he calls a member to order

he acts for the assembly. Any discourtesy to him is a discourtesy
to the assembly that he represents, and he should never treat such
an act as personal.

The president should always be in the hall a few minutes before
the hour set for the meeting, and when the hour arrives, if a
quorum is present, he should step to the platform and, while standing, strike on the table with the gavel, if there is one, and say,
"The meeting [or convention, or assembly, or society, or club]
will come to order." One stroke is usually sufficient, and the
blow should not be any stronger than is required to attract the
attention of everybody in the hall. It is a great mistake for the
president to pound on the table as if trying to drown the noise in
the hall by making more noise himself. It is the duty of every
one in the hall to be seated immediately and to cease conversation.
After calling the meeting to order, the president should remain
standing with his eyes on the assembly until it is quiet. If persons
continue talking or standing, he can generally bring them to order
by merely keeping his eyes on the disorderly members and thus
drawing the attention of the assembly to them. If this does not
suffice, he should say, "The chair is waiting for the members to
come to order." He should avoid speaking any louder than necessary to be heard, since the more quiet the chairman is the greater
the probability of the assembly's being quiet.

In case there is no gavel, the president should rap on the table
with his hand, or in a small hall a tap with a pencil will suffice.
The object is simply to attract the attention of all present, so
they will listen to what the president is about to say.

As soon as the assembly has come to order, the president should
say, "The secretary will read the minutes," and then he should
take his seat. If, when the president states a question, members
rise and address him, he recognizes the one that rose first, except
that the member who offered the pending motion has the preference to the floor even if others rose before him. But there are
many things affecting the right to the floor of rival claimants, as
explained in "Rules of Order Revised," pages 27–33, with which
every presiding officer should be familiar. The president recognizes a member by announcing his name so that the entire assembly may hear it, though in small meetings, where the members are
all acquainted, he may recognize a member by merely bowing to
him. In large conventions, where the president and the secretary

do not know all the members, it is necessary for a member, when he addresses the president, to give his own name distinctly, so that the president may announce it correctly.

During debate the president should keep his seat and pay attention to the discussion. He should see that the speaker observes the rules of debate, is not interrupted unnecessarily, and that order is preserved in the hall. If a motion that is not in order is made and seconded, he should rule it out of order as courteously as possible so as not to hurt the feelings of the mover. Instead of bluntly saying, "The motion is out of order," it is better to say, "The motion is not in order just now, but will be in order as soon as the pending question is disposed of," or something of a similar nature adapted to the circumstances. If a member expresses a motion incorrectly, the chair should state it correctly. If the president is not sure as to what motion is intended, he should ask the mover's intention. If it is moved "to postpone the question" without stating any time, the chairman should state it as the motion to lay on the table; if the motion is made to lay the question on the table until the next meeting, it should be stated as the motion to postpone the question until the next meeting. If a member makes a motion without waiting for recognition, the president is under no obligation to recognize it; and if, before the chair has stated the question, another member rises and claims the floor, the latter is entitled to it and the former motion should be ignored. Such motions as to lay on the table and to adjourn are frequently made while members are sitting, or while rising, and before the chair has recognized the mover as having the floor. Motions made in such a manner are out of order and can be recognized only by general consent. If members call "Question" when no one has the floor or has risen and addressed the chair, it is merely an expression of the wish of the assembly for the debate to cease and the question to be put, and should not be treated as disorderly. But to call for the question while a member is claiming the floor, or has it, is disorderly conduct and should be reproved by the president. The proper way to stop the debate and have the question put is to limit the debate or order the previous question. [See page 67.]

The president should always be careful to make it perfectly clear what is the question to be voted on. If necessary, before taking the vote on an amendment, besides reading it, he should read the resolution as it will be if the amendment is adopted. After the vote has been taken he should clearly state the result, and should then announce the question before the assembly, or the next business in order. Every time a motion is made, the president should clearly state it, if it is in order, so that every one may know what is before the assembly. A great deal of time is often wasted and confusion caused by the neglect of the president to state the question before the assembly every time a motion that is in order is made, or a vote is taken. Either of these acts changes the question before the assembly, and it is the duty of the president to state the new question. Often members do not hear the motion when made, and if the president fails to state the question, members cannot always be sure that a motion that has been made is in order and has been recognized by the chair. One cannot always be sure as to which way a vote has gone unless the chairman announces it. In fact, a vote is not complete until it is announced and an opportunity given to challenge its correctness by calling for a division. [See page 168.]

The chair should never put the negative of a complimentary motion, such as thanking a committee or an officer, unless it is called for by a member. This any member has a right to do. It is possible that such a motion of courtesy to which even a majority is opposed may be introduced, in which case some one should immediately demand that the negative be put.

If a frivolous motion is made, the president should not recognize it. [See page 179.] If a parliamentary inquiry is made, he should answer the question if it relates to pending business, or to a motion which the inquirer wishes to make. If the president is in doubt, he may ask for the opinion of one or more persons whom he designates, as no one has a right to express an opinion on the question unless it is called for by the president.

The president should not permit members to be interrupted unnecessarily by parliamentary inquiries, requests for information, etc. Such inquiries and requests should never be made while a member is speaking, unless the urgency is so great that the object of the inquiry or request would be defeated by delaying until the speaker has yielded the floor. If a member violates this rule the chair should refuse to answer the inquiry, and if the offense is repeated the offending member should be reproved for the violation of the rules. The chair should not allow members to rise to a question of privilege for the purpose of making an explanation. As stated under that head, on page 127, a question of privilege can scarcely ever arise in an ordinary society. It is the duty of the chair to protect the assembly from this improper use of parliamentary forms.

In the case of a large convention where there is a probability of troublesome parliamentary questions arising which the president is incompetent to handle, it is well to engage an expert in parliamentary law as an adviser. This adviser is usually authorized and the compensation fixed by the board of managers, but the appointment should be left to the president, subject to confirmation by the board or the assembly. The parliamentarian, as this adviser is called, should be consulted by the president during the recesses, so as to avoid as much as possible the necessity for consultation during the meetings. [See Parliamentarian, page 325.] The president cannot avoid the responsibility of every decision, whether the advice of the parliamentarian is followed or no, except, in rare cases, by leaving the question to the assembly to decide, as shown on page 147.

In enforcing the rules there is need for the exercise of tact and good sense. In small assemblies, and especially when the members are unfamiliar with parliamentary procedure, a strict enforcement of the rules is unwise. It is usually a mistake to insist upon technical points, as long as no one is being defrauded of his rights and the will of the majority is being carried out. The rules and customs are designed to help and not to hinder business. Brief consultations should be allowed on undebatable motions, provided they help the business.

The president, by being placed in the chair, does not lose his rights as a member of the assembly when the exercise of these rights would affect the action of the assembly. When they will not affect the result, however, he has no right to their exercise when he thereby lessens the confidence of the assembly in his impartiality. Thus he should never vote unless the vote is by ballot or his vote will affect the result. In the case of a ballot he must vote before the tellers commence counting the ballots. In the case of voting by yeas and nays (roll-call) his name is called last. If there is a tie vote he can abstain from voting, in which case the motion is lost, or he can say, "There are 25 ayes and 25 noes. The chair votes with the ayes [or affirmative], so that the ayes have it and the motion is adopted." Or, suppose there are 25 ayes and 24 noes; he may say, "The chair votes No, making 25 ayes and 25 noes, so the motion is lost." Or, suppose the motion requires a two-thirds vote, and the vote is taken by rising: if there are 25 in the affirmative and 12 in the negative, the president may say, "The chair votes in the negative, making 25 in the affirmative and 13 in the negative. There being less than two thirds in the affirmative, the motion is lost." If the presiding officer is not a member of the assembly, he cannot vote except in cases authorized by the by-laws.

On the principle mentioned above, the president should not, as a rule, take part in debate or express his opinion on pending questions. If he does speak on a question, he must call some one else to the chair and speak from the floor, and if there is much feeling on the question, as heretofore stated, he should not resume the chair until the question is disposed of.

If a motion is made that is personal, relating to the president, it should be stated and put to vote by a vice-president, or by the secretary, or by the maker of the motion. In a large convention the president should ask a vice-president, if one is present, to put the question. The vice-president should do this standing where he happens to be. In small assemblies without a vice-president, the secretary usually puts the question without being called upon by the president. If the secretary neglects to put it, the maker of the motion should stand and put the question. In no case should he go to the platform to do so. If the motion includes others with the president, as in case of appointing delegates, the president should usually state and put the question himself. If a motion censuring the president with others is made, he should call to the chair some one not included in the motion. It is very indelicate and improper for an officer to preside, for instance, while a motion is pending requesting his resignation. If he has not the delicacy to vacate the chair and leave the hall, some one should make a motion requesting him to do so. If the secretary does not state the question immediately, the maker of the motion should state and put it.

The president should never try to avoid debate by hurriedly stating and putting the question. Members cannot be deprived of their rights by such action. Even after a vote has been announced, it must be ignored and a member must be recognized, if it is shown that he rose and addressed the chair with reasonable promptness after the chair had asked, "Are you ready for the question?" If the chair puts a debatable question without making this inquiry, any member who rises and addresses the chair promptly must be recognized and be allowed to resume the debate or to make any proper motion. But it is the duty of members to be prompt in claiming the floor, and to speak sufficiently loud to be heard by the president. The president must not allow time to be wasted in waiting for members to claim the floor.

In most assemblies business can be greatly expedited by a tactful president's making use of General Consent, when he is confident that no one objects to a motion. Instead of taking a formal vote, he may ask, "Is there any objection?" and if there is no response he adds, "There being none, the motion is adopted." [See General Consent, page 190.]

The President's Duties in Addition to Those as Presiding Officer. In most clubs and other societies the president has other duties to perform besides presiding at the business meetings. In many organizations these other duties are so important that in comparison with them the duty of presiding sinks into insignificance. In such cases the president, of course, is selected on account of his fitness for his most important duties, regardless of his ability to preside at a meeting of the organization. Thus no one would think that the president of a business corporation or of a college, or the pastor of a church, should be chosen on account of his knowledge of parliamentary law, or excellence as a presiding officer. Still, as presiding is one of the duties of even such officers, they should prepare for it by familiarizing themselves with the fundamental principles of parliamentary law, and with their own by-laws and parliamentary authority, so that they can readily refer to any rule in the latter when needed. They would be well repaid for their labor by the increased efficiency of their work resulting from the elimination of much friction in the business meetings of the organizations.

The duties of the president vary so greatly in different organizations that they cannot be defined here. They should always be prescribed in the by-laws. If the by-laws are silent on the subject, his duties are limited to presiding at the meetings, as heretofore described. If, as presiding officer, he is to have special privileges or duties, as being authorized to appoint all committees, or being ex-officio a member of all committees, or ex-officio a member of the board of managers, these should be assigned him in the by-laws.

VICE-PRESIDENT

The prefix Vice in compound words means, "one who acts in the place, or as deputy, of another." A vice-president is the alternate of the president, or one who acts in his place whenever, from any cause, the president is unable to act at a time when there is a necessity for such action. In case of the resignation or death of the president, the vice-president automatically becomes president, unless the by-laws provide otherwise for filling the vacancy. If it is desired that the duties or privileges of the vice-president shall be different from those just mentioned, then it must be so stated in the by-laws.

In the meetings of a society the vice-president, if present, should preside in the absence of the president, and should be called to the chair whenever the president vacates it. If the president is absent from the locality and there is need for immediate action, the vice-president can assume the authority of president for the emergency. An example of this is the case when an emergency demands that a special meeting of the society or the board be called during the temporary absence of the president. Except in such an emergency, the temporary absence of the president does not entitle the vice-president to exercise any of the functions of the president other than that of presiding at meetings.

In the case of a prolonged absence extending over months, the vice-president exercises all the functions of the president, except that he cannot modify any rules or regulations made by the president. It is a general rule that no temporary officer can countermand or in any way change the rules or customs established by the permanent officer. If it were otherwise, great confusion might result from frequent changes made by temporary officers. Where the by-laws provide that certain vacancies shall be filled by the president, and such a vacancy occurs during the temporary absence of the president, it cannot be filled by the vice-president during the president's absence.

As to the occasions when the vice-president may act as president, there is need for the exercise of a great deal of common sense. The society evidently intends the president to perform all the duties of that office as far as possible. To prevent the society's work being injured because of inability of the president at times to perform his duty, a vice-president is elected to fill the gap. He cannot interfere with the plans of the president while taking his place during short intervals. To illustrate: Suppose a local society is entitled to representation in the state organization by its president and delegates. The society may elect alternates to the delegates, who are really vice-delegates, but it cannot elect an alternate to the president, nor can he appoint one, as the by-laws provide for his alternate, the vice-president, who has already been elected. The words "vice" and "alternate" when applied to officers are practically identical. In the case mentioned, if the vice-president had been elected a delegate, and the president is absent from the convention, the vice-president takes the place of the president and his own place is filled by an alternate.

If the president has prepared his annual report, or the report to the state convention, and he cannot attend the meeting, the vice-president is entitled to present it. The vice-president, while acting in the president's place, cannot write the report unless the president has neglected to perform that duty. He is only the temporary alternate of the president and cannot take advantage of the temporary absence of the president to modify in any way a report that the president has prepared.

In case of the death or resignation of the president, the vice-president automatically becomes president, and the vice-presidency becomes vacant, unless the by-laws provide to the contrary. If he is unable, or unwilling, to perform the duties of the president, his only recourse is to resign. In the case of several vice-presidents, each one is promoted, the second becoming first, and so on.

Some national organizations have a number of vice-presidents whose duties, if any, are entirely different from those of the vice-presidents of an ordinary society. The by-laws should specify these duties where they differ from those laid down in their adopted rules of order. In many cases of this kind it is inadvisable for the vice-presidents to change their duties whenever a vacancy occurs in their number. Some societies do not wish their vice-presidents to become presidents in case of the death or resignation of the latter. In such cases a by-law like this should be adopted: "All vacancies in office, including the presidency, shall be filled for the unexpired part of the term [or, filled until the next annual meeting]," etc., stating the method of filling the vacancy.

CHAPTER XXIX

SECRETARIES

SECRETARY

THE title of Secretary, or its equivalent, is applied to the officer who records the doings of a society or a deliberative assembly. In this work he is referred to as secretary. In legislative assemblies, and usually in city councils, he is called Clerk; in mass meetings, ordinary societies, and boards he is usually called Secretary; in secret societies he usually has some other title than secretary or clerk.

In most state and national organizations and in many large local societies the work of the secretary is divided between two officers known, respectively, as the Recording Secretary and the Corresponding Secretary, the duties of each being indicated by his title. Whenever the simple term "secretary" is used, it means the recording secretary in a society having two secretaries, unless the duty referred to is assigned by the rules to the corresponding secretary. The duties of the secretary will be treated under the heads of Recording Secretary and Corresponding Secretary, it being understood that the duties of both devolve upon the secretary in societies having no corresponding secretary.

Recording Secretary. This officer keeps a record of the transactions of the society, called the Minutes or Records; keeps a roll of the membership and "calls" the same alphabetically when directed to do so by the presiding officer; calls the meeting to order at the designated time in the absence of the president and vice-presidents, and presides until the election of a temporary chairman; has at every business meeting of the society the minutes

313

of its previous meeting, and all others that have not been approved, its by-laws and other rules, a list of all committees, and the order of business or list of all business to come before the meeting, arranged in its proper order; provides the stationery required for ballot voting at meetings where tellers have not been appointed previous to the meeting; is custodian of the records of the society; and in general performs all the duties of the secretary that are not assigned by the rules or well established custom to the corresponding secretary. The society has the right to modify these duties to any extent, the changes being placed in the by-laws.

The recording secretary is never addressed as such, but as the secretary, as he is secretary of the meeting, or secretary of the society when gathered together as a deliberative assembly. Thus the chair says, ''The secretary [not qualifying it by the word 'recording'] will read the minutes.''

The recording secretary is responsible for keeping alphabetically the membership roll, corrected to date so that it will show who are entitled to vote. In societies that disfranchise members delinquent in paying their dues, he should obtain from the treasurer before every business meeting a list of the disfranchised members, and he should check on the roll with a pencil the names of such members. These names should be omitted in calling the roll, as the object of calling the roll is to ascertain the voting members present, or else to obtain the vote of the voting members on the pending question.

As custodian of the records of the society, it is the secretary's duty to turn over to the various committees such documents as they require for the performance of their duties. Thus a committee may require the book of minutes, or a report of a committee, etc. If the secretary thinks the book should not go out of his possession, he can take the book to the committee and remain while it is being consulted. If he thinks the book is not required by the committee in connection with the duty assigned it, he should submit the question to the president, whose decision is final, unless the committee brings the matter before the society or board. Any member has a right to examine the minutes, but this privilege must not be abused to the annoyance of the secretary.

Whenever a committee is appointed, the recording secretary should hand to its chairman, or in his absence to a responsible member of the committee, a list of its members and all the documents referred to it. The secretary should see that all of these papers are returned to him with the committee's report.

When it is said that the recording secretary is custodian of the records of the society, it is not meant that he is custodian of the treasurer's books, or of the records of the board or standing committees, etc. The records referred to are the minutes, and all reports, resolutions, etc., that have been presented to the society. The treasurer's books are in charge of the treasurer, and the records of the board and standing committees are in charge of their respective secretaries. Since resolutions are entered in the minutes, they are not kept on file. Neither are reports of committees that have been entered in the minutes. Those that are not copied in the minutes are in some societies filed, and in others they are destroyed unless the society orders them ''to be placed on file.'' Their disposal depends upon the wishes of the society. Where the society has an office, it is usual to file reports of the boards and committees, but where there is no office it is not customary or practicable to keep for years files of all such documents. In the latter case very important papers, when acted upon, should be ordered ''placed on file.''

Minutes. The minutes of a meeting should be entered in a substantially bound blank book. They should contain a record of what is done by the society at each meeting, and not usually what is said. The object is to have a permanent record of what has actually been done. Therefore it is unnecessary to enter all secondary motions and the names of speakers in debate, etc. All main motions (except such as are withdrawn), whether adopted or rejected, should be entered, and usually the names of the makers of very important main motions, but not the seconders; points of order and appeals, whether sustained or lost; and all other motions that were not lost or withdrawn. For detailed information concerning minutes, see ''Rules of Order Revised,'' pages 247–250; ''Parliamentary Practice,'' pages 115–117 and 128; and in this book Forms, page 565, and Questions and Answers, pages 499–502.

Corresponding Secretary. In local societies there is rarely enough general correspondence to justify the appointment of a corresponding secretary, but in state and national organizations his duties are usually very important. He has charge of all the general correspondence of the society. that is. of the correspondence that does not relate to the work assigned to some other officer or to a committee. Each officer writes the letters relating to his own work, and the chairman of each committee attends to the correspondence of that committee. Thus the librarian would write a letter notifying a member who has retained a book too long; the treasurer would write a letter enclosing a check in payment of a bill; and the chairman of the lecture committee would conduct the correspondence with a lecturer whom the committee wishes to engage. In other words, there should be as little red tape as possible, and each officer should attend to the business, including the correspondence, connected with his own office.

All communications relating to the general work of the society received by any other of the officers should be referred to the corresponding secretary for reply. Letters received by the corresponding secretary relating specially to work under charge of another officer may be referred to that officer for reply, or the corresponding secretary may obtain the desired information and answer the letter himself. In the general correspondence in his charge is included sending out notices of meetings and communications that have been ordered by the society to be sent.

The difference between the duties of the recording and the corresponding secretaries may be illustrated by the case of a society's adopting resolutions expressive of its appreciation of a deceased member and of sympathy for his family, and directing that a copy of the resolutions be sent to the family. The resolutions would be prepared by a committee and submitted to the society, which would adopt them. The recording secretary would make a copy of the resolutions, heading it, ''Copy of Resolutions Adopted by the Alpha Club February 15, 19—.'' The resolutions should be followed by the words, ''A true copy,'' and signed ''A——— B———, Recording Secretary.''

The names of the committee should never be copied, since they are not a part of the resolutions adopted by the society. The copy of the resolutions should be handed to the corresponding secretary, who sends it to the family with a suitable letter.

It is sometimes desirable that the corresponding secretary should have duties additional to those mentioned. Such duties should be specified in the by-laws. In some state and national organizations, he is the paid executive officer having the duties assigned to the executive secretary in the next article.

EXECUTIVE SECRETARY

Some societies have many employees, sometimes scattered even in distant countries, so that it is necessary to maintain a regular office under the supervision of an officer, usually called the Executive Secretary. Sometimes he is called Corresponding Secretary, but that title does not fit the office. Where there is much work to be done in foreign countries, the work is sometimes divided between two secretaries, called the Home Secretary and the Foreign Secretary. In such a case the division of the work should be clearly defined.

The executive secretary is in charge of the headquarters or office of the society. He is a salaried officer elected by the society, unless it authorizes the board to elect him. He is the executive officer of the society, acting under the immediate direction of the executive committee. He is often the secretary of the board and always of the executive committee, and, together with the executive committee, is subject to the orders of the board. He prepares the annual report of the board, which, after being adopted b˳ʳ the executive committee, is submitted to the board for its adoption. It is usually presented at the society's annual meeting by the executive secretary.

When a society has an executive secretary, it is not usual for the president to have any more to do with the details of the work than any other member of the board, unless he is a member of the executive committee. His duty is that of presiding officer in the meetings of the society, and also of the board if so provided in the by-laws, which is usually the case. The board meets only quarterly or semiannually, hears the report of the work done by the executive committee, and takes such action in the case as it deems best. It may, if it desires, give any instructions to the executive committee, and the executive committee may instruct the executive secretary. The president cannot give orders to the executive secretary.

A society has a right in its by-laws to assign to its officers any duties it pleases, and in some societies joint action in many things has been required of the president and executive secretary. The result of such a policy is disastrous where the two officers differ. If it is desired that the president should be the head of the administrative work, there should be no executive secretary.

FINANCIAL SECRETARY

Some societies have dues or subscriptions payable weekly or monthly, necessitating so much clerical work that it has been found advisable to intrust it to an officer called the Financial Secretary. This is specially necessary when the payments are made weekly.

The financial secretary should never retain funds on hand longer than is necessary to enable him to post his accounts, as the treasurer is the only custodian of the society's funds. Usually, where payments are made weekly, each member is furnished with fifty-two envelopes, dated for each week, with the member's number printed on them. If the amount of the weekly dues is the same for all the members, there is no use for its being stated on the envelope. If the amount is a voluntary subscription for the year, it should be written on the envelope.

The contributions are put in the envelopes, and the envelopes are collected at the weekly meeting and turned over to the financial secretary. He opens each envelope and sees that the amount enclosed is correct. He then turns over the total amount to the treasurer, taking a memorandum receipt therefor, which he retains until after the auditing committee's report has been adopted.

The account with the different members is usually kept in a blank book ruled in vertical columns and filled as follows: the lines in the first column are numbered consecutively 1, 2, 3, etc.; the second column contains the names of the contributors, one on each line; the third column contains the amount to be contributed weekly; then follow 52 columns, in each of which is entered a check mark or x opposite the member's name when that week's contribution is paid. In actual practice many members will be behind in their payments, while in rare cases payments are made in advance. By this plan, each week the financial secretary checks off the additional week or weeks that are paid for, as shown by the envelopes collected that week. The envelopes for the week are tied together with the treasurer's receipt, and kept during the year, or at least until audited, so that they may be referred to in case any question arises as to the correctness of the treasurer's accounts.

At the close of each quarter a statement of his account should be sent to every delinquent member, as members are often unaware that they are delinquent. If the society has any penalty for such delinquency, the financial secretary must furnish a list of delinquents to the recording secretary at such times as the rules require or the secretary requests. Unless the rules or a resolution of the society require it, he makes no report of individual delinquencies.

SECRETARY-TREASURER

In some societies the work of the secretary and of the treasurer is so slight that the two offices are combined, and the officer is called Secretary-Treasurer, or simply Secretary. His duties comprise those explained under Secretary, Recording Secretary, Corresponding Secretary, and Treasurer.

In other organizations the title secretary-treasurer is given to the chief executive officer, a salaried officer whose duties combine those of the executive secretary and treasurer. In all cases where this title is used the duties of the officer should be fully defined in the by-laws.

CHAPTER XXX

TREASURER; AUDITORS; PARLIAMENTARIAN

TREASURER

THE Treasurer of a society is always the custodian of its funds, and usually receives its funds and disburses them on the order of the society or its board or its executive committee. In some societies the treasurer pays bills on their approval by a finance committee or by the president. In every case he must have some authority for the disbursement.

When the treasurer handles large sums of money, it is prudent and customary to have him bonded for a sum sufficient to protect the society from loss. The bonds should be furnished by a corporation, not by individuals, and the expense should be borne by the society in all cases where the treasurer is not a salaried officer.

In many societies that handle very little money the treasurer is likely at any meeting to receive funds, and may also wish to make payments. On this account he should have with him at every meeting a pocket memorandum book in which he enters at the time every receipt and every disbursement. He should always keep the society funds separate from his own, and from time to time compare the society funds on hand with his books. If the funds are sufficient to open a bank account, they should be deposited in a bank in his name with the word "Treasurer" added. This will prevent mixing the society and personal accounts. If he thus has a treasurer's bank account, no payment should be made on the society's account except by check. If a bank account cannot be started, the funds should be kept in a separate package in a safe, or surplus funds could be deposited in a savings bank.

The Report of the treasurer is usually made for a definite period, as a quarter or a year. The period should terminate a few days before the time the report is to be made, so as to allow time for writing the report and having it audited. Since the funds handled annually by treasurers of societies vary from a few dollars to hundreds of thousands of dollars, and since the objects for which they are disbursed vary from half a dozen to hundreds, the reports will necessarily vary from simple to very complicated ones. The essential things in the report are (1) Receipts; (2) Disbursements; (3) Assets, or amounts due to the society; and (4) Liabilities, or amounts due by the society. The report should always show the balance on hand at the beginning and at the close of the period for which the report is made. These are all necessary to enable one to understand the financial condition of the society.

(1) *Receipts.* The statement of receipts should be so made as to show the total amount of receipts of each class for the quarter or year, as "Initiation Fees," "Dues," "Fines," etc.

(2) *Disbursements.* This statement should show the disbursements in a similar way, giving the total expenses of each kind, as "Janitor," "Rent," "Fuel," "Lights," etc.

(3) *Amounts Due to the Society.* This statement should include only such amounts due to the society at the close of the quarter or year as the board considers are collectible. Amounts due that cannot be collected should be ordered by the board, or the society, to be struck from the treasurer's books. It is a mistake to retain on the treasurer's books as assets notes or dues that are practically worthless. Societies have been found to be in debt thousands of dollars, while the treasurer's reports showed larger assets than liabilities.

(4) *Amounts Due by the Society.* This should include every liability of the society, even though no bill has been rendered for it. Thus, if the year's supply of coal has been ordered but has not yet been delivered, the amount of the bill should be reported as due by the society. If a report is dated the last day of a month and the rent is due the first of the ensuing month, it should be reported as a liability. Without such facts the society may be in debt while the treasurer's report shows a balance on hand.

It will be observed that the treasurer's report as above described does not report details. It informs the society as to its financial condition, and not as to the dates of the receipts of each dollar and of the payment of each bill. In submitting his audited report, the treasurer may make an oral supplementary report showing the condition of the treasury at that time. If loans have been made and renewed, the report may be misleading to any members who notice mainly the aggregate receipts and disbursements, which may largely exceed, even double, the net amounts. In such a case the treasurer should always add to the report a statement of the actual total receipts and total expenses of the society, independent of bank transactions. In societies handling large sums of money, the treasurer's report should be accompanied by a number of exhibits, which are usually lettered, as "Exhibit A," "Exhibit B," etc. Each exhibit gives a special financial report of some branch of the work.

Auditors or Auditing Committee

The treasurer's accounts should always be audited at least annually, for his own protection as well as that of the society. A vote of the society adopting the treasurer's unaudited report is of no value and should never be taken. It does not relieve the treasurer of responsibility, because the society has nothing on which to base its judgment except the word of the interested party, the treasurer. The treasurer should insist, if necessary, upon his accounts being properly audited, as the adoption of the auditor's report that his accounts are correct relieves him of responsibility for the period covered by the report, except in case of fraud.

When the amounts involved are very large and the reports complicated, it is usual and necessary that they be audited by registered public accountants. But in ordinary societies it is practicable to have the treasurer's reports properly audited without expense by an auditing committee of two or more members of the society. Some societies prefer to elect one or more auditors, who may or may not be members of the society. In nearly all cases it is better to appoint the auditors, as the auditing committee will be called, in advance, so that the treasurer's report may be audited before it is submitted to the society.

The duty of the auditors is to examine the report of the treasurer, and his books and vouchers, and see that all the money received is properly accounted for. The treasurer must show a receipt for every disbursement, and must show that it was authorized. The balance in the treasury must be deposited in a bank to the credit of the treasurer in his official capacity, unless the amount is too small for such a deposit. When the auditors are satisfied that the report is correct, they certify to the fact at the bottom of the report. This certificate may be as brief as this: "Examined and found correct." It should be signed by the auditors officially, their title being written underneath or on the side.

Action on Report. It is preferable for the treasurer to have his report audited before he submits it. If this has been done, as soon as the auditors' report is read the chair says, "The question is on the adoption of the auditors' report." This being adopted, the society has endorsed the report of the auditors, which certifies that the treasurer's report is correct. The chair need not wait for such a routine motion as one to adopt the auditors' report. When the report is made, the question is necessarily on its adoption, and it is a waste of time to wait for a motion to that effect.

If the report has not been audited, and there is an auditing committee, the chair as soon as it is read says, "The report is referred to the auditing committee." If there is no auditor or auditing committee, the chair says: "The treasurer's report should be audited. A motion to appoint such a committee is in order"; or something to that effect. Instead of suggesting a motion he may ask, "How shall the auditing committee be appointed?" If the response is, "By the chair," and no other suggestion or motion is made, he immediately appoints the committee, usually consisting of two. This is the usual method. If more than one way of appointing the committee is suggested, the chair proceeds as described on page 48. As soon as the committee is appointed he says, "The treasurer's report is referred to the auditing committee."

Some societies wish to know at each meeting how their finances stand. Such a report should be made orally from a memorandum, and no action should be taken on it. It should not be confounded with the formal written report of the treasurer, usually made quarterly or annually, which should always be audited and action should then be taken upon the auditors' report.

PARLIAMENTARIAN

The rapid growth of clubs has necessitated in some cases the election of presiding officers who are not familiar with parliamentary law. This has led, especially in large conventions, to the employment of an expert parliamentarian to assist the president in ruling on points of order and answering parliamentary inquiries. In legislative bodies it is customary to have one clerk who is an expert in parliamentary law, and is especially familiar with the decisions made in that particular assembly, and can quickly refer to them. He is known as the "Clerk at the Speaker's Table," and the presiding officer can consult him at any moment, but the decision or opinion must be given by the presiding officer. In parliamentary bodies the presiding officer alone can rule on a parliamentary question, but he has the right to consult others before rendering his decision. At times in Congress the speaker has left the chair and conferred with an ex-speaker before rendering his decision. He has the right to call publicly upon any member for his opinion, but no member has a right to express an opinion until there has been an appeal, unless asked to do so by the presiding officer. After the chair has ruled on the question, any member may appeal, as explained on page 151, and the appeal is debatable except in certain cases.

The parliamentarian, as the parliamentary expert is called in ordinary conventions, should be appointed by the president, subject to the approval of the board, in advance of the meeting at which he is to serve. To enable this to be done, it would be well in large conventions, the only ones where a parliamentarian would usually be needed, to have a by-law authorizing the president, with the approval of the board, to appoint a parliamentarian to serve during the president's term of office at the conventions and the board meetings held in connection therewith, at a compensation to be fixed by the board of managers. A committee on revision of the by-laws should always consult a parliamentary expert. Still better, the parliamentarian for the ensuing annual meeting should be appointed before the revision committee commences its work, with the understanding that he act as parliamentary adviser to the committee. This should insure a better revision. In many large conventions, in which all resolutions should be referred to the committee on resolutions, it would often be well for the committee to have the advice of the parliamentarian.

The parliamentarian should be assigned a seat near the president, so as to be convenient for consultation. The chair has a right to ask the parliamentarian to explain any point to the convention, but the dignity of, and respect for, the presiding officer would be much better preserved if this right were never exercised.

If the chair, after a brief consultation with the parliamentarian, is not able to decide and explain questions of order, he is hardly fitted to preside at all.

If the parliamentarian is asked by the chair for an opinion on a point to be given publicly to the convention, this opinion cannot be appealed from, any more than if it had been given by a member at the request of the chair. Until the chair has ruled, no appeal can be made. Parliamentary law gives to the chair alone the power to rule on all questions of order, and he or she cannot be relieved of this responsibility except by submitting the question to the assembly for its decision, in which case the question is debatable, the same as an appeal. Therefore, after the parliamentarian has expressed an opinion on the point at the request of the chair, the chair must make the ruling, the same as if the parliamentarian had been consulted privately.

If the parliamentarian notices something being done out of order, he should call the attention of the chair to it unobtrusively, so that the assembly will not notice it. This can be done by writing a word or two on a slip of paper and handing it to the chair. But the main work of the parliamentarian should be done outside the meetings. The president, knowing the business to be attended to and the questions likely to arise, should confer with him about them before the meetings open and during the recesses, so as to avoid as far as possible the necessity for conference during the meetings. During the meetings the work of the parliamentarian should be limited to assisting the chairman with his advice, and to finding and handing to the presiding officer the section in the by-laws or rules which covers the case that has arisen. On this account he should be familiar with all the rules governing the organization, so as to be able instantly to turn to the one applicable to the matter in hand. Usually it is the rule that is desired rather than an opinion.

The parliamentarian should never be a member of the board, or serve on a committee or in any other capacity that makes it necessary for him to take sides in matters upon which his opinion as parliamentarian may be desired afterward. Hence, if the by-laws make the officers members of boards, the parliamentarian should be excepted if he is an officer. In fact, it is better if the parliamentarian of a convention is not a delegate, as the two positions are not compatible. A delegate has a right to make motions, to take part in the debate, to raise questions of order, to appeal from the decisions of the chair, and to vote. The parliamentarian, even though one of its officers, unless a member of the convention, has none of these rights, not even the right to speak in the assembly unless asked to do so by the chair. He is simply an adviser to the chair, who must decide whether to follow the advice or not. On this account the parliamentarian should always be appointed by the president, subject to confirmation by the board or the convention. There will be greater confidence in the impartiality of the opinion given, if the parliamentarian takes no part in the proceedings except when requested to express an opinion on a point of parliamentary law.

In some large national organizations there are many difficult questions involving interpretation of the by-laws and rules arising during the year in connection with the work of their own officers and of the subordinate societies. As a result some such organizations have found it expedient to .employ during the entire year a parliamentarian whom the officers may consult on different matters. This service calls for a fair judicial mind òn the part of the parliamentarian more than for a knowledge of parliamentary law, though both are valuable. As has been stated pre· viously, the president is not obliged to follow the advice of the parliamentarian. But no self-respecting parliamentary expert would continue to hold the position of parliamentarian in an organization where the advice given is not followed, just as no physician would continue to attend a patient who refused to take the prescribed remedies. It is better to have no guide than to have one in whom the responsible head has not confidence and whose advice will not be followed. Hence the importance of having the parliamentarian appointed by the president rather than elected by the society.

CHAPTER XXXI

MEMBERS; HONORARY OFFICERS AND MEMBERS; RESIGNATIONS

MEMBERS

MEMBERSHIP in a society carries with it obligations as well as privileges, and where these are peculiar to the society they should be defined in the by-laws, but it is not necessary or advisable to encumber the by-laws with a statement of duties that are common to members of all societies, such as those herein mentioned.

Duties. It is the duty of every member to obey the rules of the society, whether he approves of them or not; to try to further the objects of the society; to attend its meetings with reasonable regularity; to pay respect to its officers in their official capacity as its representatives; to abstain from acts or remarks outside of the meetings that will in any way interfere with the work being done by the officers or committees of the society and by its authority; to pay attention to the speaker during debate and to the business of the assembly at all times; to observe the rules of decorum in debate; to attend faithfully to any duty assigned him, and, when that is impracticable, to ask to be excused.

It is not to be expected that with a number of persons working together there should always be unanimity of opinion. Very little would be accomplished if nothing could be done to which a single member objects. While the question is under consideration members are free to express their opinions, always observing the rules of debate. After the question has been decided it is the duty of the defeated party to acquiesce in the decision and to refrain from further criticism. They have no right to talk outside in a way to interfere with the carrying out of the policy adopted, and such a course makes them liable to having charges preferred against them for their improper conduct. A case of this kind is that of a society which decides to have a course of lectures, and of members opposed to it talking against the course so as to interfere with the sale of tickets. The members opposed to the action of the society have a perfect right, however, to try to have the society rescind its action, as explained on page 110.

During a meeting no one has a right to do anything that prevents others from seeing or hearing the presiding officer or the speaker. No one has a right to converse, or to move about, or to stand except to address the presiding officer. Especially is a member prohibited from passing between the chairman and a member who is speaking. When several members rise together to claim the floor, all, except the one to whom the floor is assigned, should immediately be seated. Members should bear in mind that one who is standing when the speaker yields the floor is not entitled to the floor if any one afterward rises and claims it. He is out of order when he rises before the speaker finishes his speech, and can receive no benefit from his breach of the rules.

A member of a special committee is under obligations to attend every meeting of the committee and to be punctual. Since the report of the committee ought to be agreed to by a majority of the entire committee, it is important that all the members be present to discuss the question. A member who is ten minutes late has virtually stolen that much time from each of the members who were on time. If a member knows that he cannot attend a meeting he should, if possible, notify the chairman, either directly or through some other member of the committee. If it is probable that he cannot, or will not, regularly attend the meetings of the committee, it is his duty to decline the appointment.

Since a standing committee lasts usually about a year, it is to be expected that some members will be absent from each meeting. Still, the obligation to attend the meetings is much stronger than in the case of the meetings of the society. The quorum of any society, except a delegated one, is usually small, rarely as large as ten per cent., while the quorum of a committee is a majority, thus rendering attendance on the latter much more obligatory.

Privileges. All members have an equal right to attend all the meetings of the society; to propose and to debate any question that relates to the objects of the society, provided that debate is not prevented by a two-thirds vote; to vote on all questions before the society; to hold office; and to present their views to a committee on a question referred to it, provided they request a hearing of the committee.

If a member resigns, or is dropped, and afterward wishes to become a member again, he is subject to all the rules governing the reception of members the same as if he had never been a member of the society. If the by-laws at the time of his second application make him ineligible, he cannot be admitted. The fact of his previous membership does not remove his ineligibility. Thus, if the by-laws at the date of the second application do not admit members who have reached the age of fifty or who are not residents of the state, such provisions would prevent the reception of one who had been a member previously, but who is now over fifty or who is not a resident of the state. The fact that there are members who are over fifty, or who are not residents of the state, does not affect the case.

Honorary Officers and Members

Sometimes a society wishes to show its appreciation of the services or character of a person by conferring some honor upon him. This it does by electing him an honorary member, or an honorary officer, of the society. If the person is not a member of the society, the more usual course is to elect him an honorary member. If the person is retiring from an office he has long filled with credit, and it is desired to specially honor him, he may be elected an honorary member; but it is more usual to elect him to the honorary office that he has so well filled. Thus, a retiring president would be elected an Honorary President, a retiring secretary would be elected an Honorary Secretary, and so on.

An honorary office or membership carries with it no obligations whatever, such as dues, etc., and it confers the privilege only of attending the meetings and speaking upon pending questions. The honorary president should be given a seat on the platform. If the vice-presidents occupy the platform, then as far as practicable the honorary vice-presidents are seated there also. An honorary officer or member, unless he is also a member of the organization, cannot make motions or vote, or raise questions of order, etc. He is not an officer or member of the society by virtue of his honorary office or membership, but like any one else he may become a member, or continue his membership, in which case he is obliged to pay the dues and is eligible to office the same as any other member. He does not vacate his honorary office by being elected to or accepting an office in the society. Honorary office or membership continues for life, unless the appointment is rescinded, just as in the case of an honorary degree of a university.

No honorary officer or member should be elected until it is provided for in the by-laws. It is doubtful whether any one would like to accept an honorary office or membership conferred by an assembly whose right to do so might well be questioned, if the act were not authorized by the by-laws. The by-laws should require at least a three-fourths vote to confer an honorary office or membership, since the value of such an honor depends upon the difficulty of getting it. There would be but little honor attached to an honorary presidency that could be conferred by a bare majority vote.

RESIGNATIONS

No one can be made a member or officer of a society, or a member of a committee, without his consent, either expressed or implied, unless such service is made obligatory by the by-laws. After he has accepted membership or office, he has a right to resign; but before accepting a resignation the society has a right to a reasonable time to select a successor in case of an officer, and to ascertain whether his dues have been paid in case of a member. A resignation sent in to escape charges need not be accepted. The charges may be preferred and the trial should proceed the same as if the resignation had not been sent in.

A member in good standing with his dues paid cannot be compelled to continue his membership so that additional obligations are incurred. His resignation should be accepted immediately, and if it is not he incurs no obligation after his resignation has been sent in, provided he does not avail himself of the privilege of membership. It is different with members who have not paid their dues up to the date of sending in their resignations. Until they have settled their dues the society is under no obligation to accept their resignations, and thus additional amounts may become due. If their dues are not paid within a reasonable time, instead of accepting their resignations the society may expel them.

An officer or a member of a board or of a committee is under obligation, after handing in his resignation, not to embarrass the society by suddenly abandoning duties intrusted to him. He should always turn over to his successor all papers relating to his office, and give such help as his successor may need in order to take up his work.

On the other hand, a society has no right to compel one, to continue in office against his will any longer than is absolutely necessary for the election of a successor. In cases where the interests of the society will not suffer from the immediate acceptance of the resignation, this should be done. Thus, the president cannot be compelled to hold office longer than the first opportunity to accept his resignation, while the treasurer's resignation should not take effect until his successor has been appointed and has furnished satisfactory bonds where bonds are required. A resignation should always be addressed to the body that fills the vacancy, since that body has the power to accept the resignation. If presented in a meeting, it may be made either orally or in writing. It is a question of privilege, as is also the filling of a vacancy. These questions relate to "the organization of the assembly," or else to "the individual as a member of the assembly." If the resignation is made orally the member proceeds as described under Questions of Privilege, page 127. If made in writing the resignation of membership should be addressed to the secretary. Resignations of office or of membership should be addressed to the secretary. Resignations of office or of membership of boards or committees, when not made in person in a meeting, should be addressed to the president or the secretary of the society or of the board, according to whether the society or the board fills the vacancy. At the same time the chairman of the board or the committee, as the case may be, should be notified. Societies differ so greatly that there is no need for uniform practice in addressing resignations to the secretary, although he is the officer to whom communications should be addressed. The party authorized to fill the vacancy must know, so that it may be filled promptly; and the chairman of the board or committee must know that one of its members has resigned, as the resignation may affect the quorum and other matters in so small a body.

The resignation of the president of a society should be addressed to the society, and, if not made orally or read by him, should be sent to the secretary.

CHAPTER XXXI

DISCIPLINE

SLIGHT BREACHES OF ORDER

IN case of a slight breach of order, like the speaker's alluding to a member by name when he could be described otherwise, the chairman should not call the speaker to order and direct him to be seated, as in a more serious case, but he should merely rap and say: "The gentleman will please avoid the use of names. No name can be used where the member can be described otherwise." With this warning, if he stops speaking when the chair raps, the member should be allowed to resume speaking. If the offense is more serious, and yet not so serious as to demand punishment beyond being deprived of the right to continue speaking, the chair should, or any member may, call the speaker to order, and he should immediately take his seat. The chair should then put to the assembly the question, "Shall the member [or Mr. A] be allowed to continue speaking?" This question is undebatable, but the chair should state clearly what was the breach of order, since it is to be assumed that it is not known by all the members. In case of more serious offenses it is necessary to adopt more severe measures in order to protect a society from being imposed upon.

Right of an Assembly to Control Its Hall

A society has the control of its hall during its meetings, and has the right to determine who may be present, provided it does not discriminate against any of its members. All members have equal rights to attend the meetings of the society, and, except as a penalty for some offense, the society has no right to prevent any member from attending one of its meetings. But the society may exclude any non-member or class of non-members, and admit others, at its own discretion.

Disorderly Non-Members. Every person in the hall, whether a member of the society or not, is under obligation to obey the orders of the presiding officer. If a member thinks the order unjust, even though the order does not apply to him personally, he has a right to appeal to the assembly. If the decision or order of the chair is not reversed, it must be obeyed. If the order is not obeyed and the offender is not a member, the presiding officer should order him to leave the hall. If he does not obey this order the chairman should appoint a committee of two to remove him from the hall. The chairman of this committee acts as the sergeant-at-arms and the other member as his assistant. They have all the rights and power of a policeman as far as relate to removing the offender from the hall. They have a right to use all the force necessary for that purpose, but if they go beyond the necessities of the case and maltreat the offender unnecessarily they are individually liable for damages for assault and battery. Neither the presiding officer nor the society is responsible in the case, as they did not exceed their rights.

Disorderly Conduct of Members in a Meeting

If the offender is a member of the society, and he refuses, or fails, to obey the order of the presiding officer, the latter cannot detail a committee to remove him from the hall, as when the offender is a non-member. The presiding officer has no authority to punish members, however disorderly they may be. If a member will not come to order when directed to do so by the chair, the chair should "name" him; that is, he should address the member by his name and repeat the order. This should be entered in the minutes, since "naming" a member is virtually the same as the chairman's preferring charges against him for disorderly conduct.

The chairman should not proceed to this extremity until the member has shown obstinacy or insubordination in failing to obey the repeated order of the presiding officer. If, when named, the member immediately obeys the order and takes his seat, no further notice need be taken of the incident if the offense was slight. But if the member was guilty of conduct for which he should apologize or be otherwise punished, any member can make an appropriate motion, or the chair may ask, "What punishment will the assembly impose upon the member for his disorderly conduct?" An apology may be required; or a vote of censure may be adopted; or he may be required to leave the hall during the meeting or until he is ready to apologize; or he may be suspended from the rights of membership for a specified time; etc. The extreme punishment is expulsion from the society. During the deliberation and voting on the punishment, the member may be required to leave the hall or not, as the assembly by a majority vote may decide. But before withdrawing he has the right to be heard in his own defense. A two-thirds vote is required for expulsion, and the vote must be by ballot unless general consent is given for its being taken otherwise. When censuring, suspending, or expelling members, it often occurs that many timid members are unwilling to vote openly in accordance with their own judgment, and therefore, if a single member objects, such votes should never be taken openly.

As soon as the case of discipline is disposed of, the chair states the question that was pending when the interruption occurred, and assigns the floor to the member who was entitled to it.

To illustrate the procedure in case of a slight offense committed in a meeting, suppose several persons claim the floor at the same time, and the chair recognizes one of them, Mr. A, and the others remain standing in order to obtain the floor as soon as Mr. A finishes his remarks. Since this is disorderly, the chair should say, "The gentlemen standing are out of order and will be seated." If they do not immediately sit down, the chair should continue: "Business cannot proceed until the members are seated." If now all take their seats except Mr. B, the chair should say, "The gentleman is out of order and will be seated." If he still remains standing, the chair should "name" him thus: "Mr. B is out of order and will be seated." If he takes his seat immediately, the chair indicates by bowing to Mr. A, who has remained standing, that he may proceed with his remarks. If Mr. B does not sit down when named, the chair inquires, "What punishment shall be inflicted on Mr. B for his disorderly conduct in failing to obey the repeated orders of the chair to be seated?" Mr. A now takes his seat, and some one offers a motion appropriate to the case, as, for instance, that Mr. B be reprimanded by the chair, or that he be deprived of the right to the floor during the present meeting. The chair then puts the question in the ordinary way unless some one objects or asks that the vote be by ballot. If it is voted that Mr. B be reprimanded by the chair, Mr. B is directed to stand on the floor just in front of the chairman, while the chair proceeds to tell him of his offense and the necessity for observing the rules and obeying the orders of the chairman. Mr. B then resumes his seat, and the chair says: "The pending question is on adopting the resolution, 'Resolved, That ——.' Mr. A has the floor."

As still another illustration, suppose during debate a member, alluding to the expenditures made under a certain committee, says that he cannot see how the work could cost so much unless there were dishonesty and graft. As soon as he hears the word "dishonesty," the chair should rap on the table and, rising, say, "The gentleman is out of order." If the objectionable words are not immediately withdrawn, the chair directs the secretary to write them down as he repeats them, and tells the gentleman to be seated. If he refuses to obey the order, and even keeps on talking and insults the chair (all of which has happened in meetings), the chair must take no notice of it except again to tell him that he is out of order and to be seated, and then to direct the secretary to write down the unparliamentary language used, the chair repeating the words to be written down. The chair should explain to the assembly that the secretary will read the unparliamentary language, and that the gentleman will be called upon to state whether he used these words. If he denies using them the assembly will be called upon to decide whether or not he used them. This question is debatable. If he acknowledges using the words, or if it is decided that he used them, and they are not immediately withdrawn, the assembly will be called upon to decide what punishment is to be inflicted upon the member for his unparliamentary language. This explanation may have to be made while the member is speaking. In no case should the chair try to drown the member's voice by continuous pounding with the gavel, or by talking loudly himself. The better way to avoid a disturbance is for the presiding officer to be calm and quiet and not even to resent insulting language addressed to him. If this course is pursued, in most cases the offending member will be calmed, and will withdraw the objectionable words when they are read by the secretary. If he does so, the chair should, in case the member has defied the chair or used insulting words to him, call his attention to the insult, and to the fact that, while the chair might be indifferent in the matter, yet as the insult was to the presiding officer of the assembly while acting officially, it was an insult to the assembly, and therefore the chair is obliged to insist upon an apology as public as the offense. If the member apologizes, the chair should call the attention of the assembly to the importance of a member's stopping his speech, even in the middle of a word, the moment he hears the chair rap. After this the chair states the pending question, and the business is resumed where it was interrupted, except that if the member guilty of the breach of order had the floor, he has now lost his right to it.

If the offending member refuses to withdraw his unparliamentary language, or to apologize when called upon to do so, a motion like this should be made: "I move that Mr. B be required to leave the hall, and that he be deprived of the privilege of the floor until he is prepared publicly to withdraw the unparliamentary language used in debate to-day, and to apologize for the insulting language addressed to the presiding officer." The "privilege of the floor" means the privilege of being present in the hall of the assembly. The adoption of the foregoing debatable motion by a majority vote would require Mr. B to leave the hall at once and not to attend any meeting of the society until he is prepared to withdraw his offensive language and to apologize publicly. If Mr. B does not leave the room immediately, the presiding officer should appoint a committee of two to escort him to the door and prevent his return, as explained in case of removing a non-member guilty of disobeying an order of the chair.

In the cases just mentioned the offenses occurred in a meeting of the society, and therefore the members of the assembly were present and knew what occurred. There is no need, in such a case, of a formal trial with witnesses, because the witnesses are all present and form the assembly that is to determine the punishment.

If the punishment extends so as to include the next meeting, and injustice has been done, the unexpired part of the sentence can be remitted by the same vote as is necessary to rescind a motion (page 110). If, however, the offense involves matters that cannot be determined properly without an investigation, then a committee should be appointed as described below.

PROCEDURE IN CASES OF OFFENSES COMMITTED OUTSIDE OF A MEETING

In all cases of offenses other than those committed in a meeting of a society, it is necessary that charges specifying the offense or offenses be preferred against the members by the society, and that the society or a committee appointed by it, be furnished with evidence that the accused is guilty of the charges. When the offense is some special act it should be specified, but it is not necessary to go into details as if drawing up an indictment. With many organizations it is generally understood that a respectable reputation as well as moral character is essential to membership. This is true of religious societies and of most benevolent, literary, and social clubs—in fact, of most societies not organized for pecuniary profit. Consequently it is not necessary to prove some special act in order to justify the expulsion of the accused. Even when charged with a definite act, legal proof cannot be obtained, because the witnesses are not sworn and they cannot be compelled to testify. Not only do those who are not members of the society generally refuse to give testimony before the society or a trial committee, but the members themselves will not testify thus publicly in cases of scandal. Although the society has a right to require members to testify under pain of expulsion for refusal, yet it is loath to take so extreme a measure. Again, in cases of scandal, much that is known has been learned in confidence that ought not to be betrayed. The persons who know the facts may be willing to state them to a single member, or even to a committee of two or three under the pledge that the details will not be revealed, nor will the informants be in any way connected with the affair.

Legal Evidence Not Necessarily Required. Since a society has no power to procure legal testimony, it is obliged to act without it, using its best judgment upon the information it can procure. Hearsay evidence and common talk may constitute the only evidence upon which the society must form its opinion. Each member must make up his own mind as to the probability of guilt, not the certainty. If most of the members of a society believe a certain member is a thief, they should not retain him as a member. He should be excluded on the ground of his general reputation, though no offense can be proved. It injures a society to retain in its membership persons of bad reputation.

The following case illustrates this difficulty of obtaining evidence, and shows how a society may be obliged to base its action upon the opinions of others in whom it has confidence. A society had what was termed an Advisory Committee, consisting of all its officers and a few other members. Among its duties was one to endeavor to reform members who failed to live up to the obligations assumed upon becoming members of the society. If the committee failed, it was its duty to prefer charges against the delinquent members. A member of this committee, Mr. A, learned from a reliable friend, not a member of the society, that a very popular member of the society, X, had been guilty of certain disgraceful conduct. He gave the facts as far as he knew them to Mr. A upon condition that his name should not be connected with the affair. Mr. A then had an interview with the accused member, who denied the charge. It was then brought before the committee and discussed without going into details. The case was an extremely delicate one, but the committee was unwilling to act in it unless it knew all the facts. Mr. A contended that this was impossible, as those who knew the facts were not members of the society, and were unwilling to give any information in regard to the scandal except to a few personal friends of the delinquent member, whom they could trust to keep the details secret. Consequently he declined to serve on the sub-committee appointed to investigate the case. The sub-committee was unable to learn anything about the matter except the denial of the accused, which it reported. Mr. A then proposed that the case be referred to a committee consisting of four of the most intimate friends of the accused, including Mr. A and two very near relatives of the accused, all anxious to dispose of the case with the least possible publicity and injury to the accused, as well as to the society. This committee was to be instructed to investigate the case and to report, without giving the facts, whether, in their judgment, X should be expelled from the society for conduct unbecoming a member. Mr. A said the committee would be willing to serve, provided the Advisory Committee would accept their judgment without demanding the evidence upon which it was based, but that otherwise they would not serve, as they could not get to the bottom of the affair without pledging themselves not to reveal the details or the names of their informants. The Advisory Committee, finding it impossible to get at the facts, and feeling that the proposed committee was so friendly to the accused and was composed of such judicious persons that, if it found the accused guilty and recommended expulsion, the society would endorse its action, finally agreed to the proposition. The investigating committee was then appointed. With the assurance of secrecy on their part, the members of the investigating committee found no difficulty in getting at the facts, and were prepared to recommend unanimously the exclusion of the accused, as unworthy of membership in the society. Before submitting its report, however, Mr. A had another interview with the accused, stated what had been learned, and obtained a request that the name of the accused be dropped from the roll of membership. The investigating committee thereupon limited its report to this fact, the name was dropped from the roll at the request of the member, and the incident was closed quietly without publicity, the mass of the members never knowing that there was any scandal connected with it.

A little common sense and tact would prevent many of the troubles in societies resulting from cases of discipline injudiciously managed. In this case, if the accused had not asked to be dropped from the roll, the investigating committee would have reported its unanimous opinion that the accused should be expelled from the society for conduct unworthy of a member. The Advisory Committee would have made a similar report to the society, stating that the case had been investigated by a committee consisting of ——, ——, ——, and ——, who had interviewed various persons, not members of the society, who had stated the facts from their personal knowledge under a pledge of secrecy from the committee; they had afterwards interviewed the accused, who had denied the charges but made no attempt to disprove any of them; and that the committee was unanimously satisfied of the guilt of the accused, and recommended the exclusion of Mr. X for conduct unworthy of a member of the society. The report should close with this recommendation in the form of a resolution, the adoption of which should be moved by the reporting member. The adoption of this resolution would end the case, which was of such a serious nature that the mere reading of the charges against so popular a member would have created ill feeling on the part of many who could not believe they were true. This extreme case shows how it may be advisable to settle a case of discipline without even preferring charges. In this case, when the accused found that the committee had the evidence in its possession, and that by asking to be dropped from the roll the committee would be relieved from the necessity of recommending expulsion, the request was at once made.

Preliminary Steps to Be Taken in Case of a Trial. Indecorum in debate and other breaches of order involve only what the assembly has witnessed, and therefore there is no need of a trial. If the assembly is of the opinion that the offense merits punishment, it proceeds to determine what punishment shall be imposed for the offense, as already described. This punishment, however, does not prevent charges being preferred against the member guilty of the breach of order for anything else than that breach of order. For instance, suppose in a meeting A reports for the building committee the expenditures for the quarter, and B, having learned of certain graft or fraud, asks for an explanation of a certain item, the question showing his doubt of its accuracy. This question irritates Mr. A, who says, "Any man who insinuates that there is anything crooked in the work of the committee is a liar." His being punished for this breach of order does not interfere with charges being preferred against him or any other member for the dishonesty referred to. Or, suppose while A is reading an item or a statement in the report B says, "That is a lie!" B should be punished for his breach of order, but that does not prevent his preferring charges against Mr. A for dishonesty or for whatever was the offense.

In all cases of offenses requiring punishment, except breaches of order in a meeting, it is necessary that charges be preferred against the member, that he be given a reasonable opportunity to defend himself, that the accusers have an equal opportunity to prove the charges, and that the society vote directly, or indirectly through a committee, on the guilt of the accused and, if he is found guilty, on the punishment for the offense.

Committee to Investigate and Report Charges. It is generally advisable that charges against a member be prepared by a committee and adopted by the society. In this way the personal element is reduced to a minimum. In some organizations there is a standing committee on discipline whose duty it is to investigate cases that appear to require discipline, and, when they deem proper, to recommend charges to be preferred against the offending member. When there is such a committee, members knowing facts calling for its action should report them to the committee. When there is no standing committee, a member should offer a resolution to appoint a committee to investigate the case and to recommend suitable action. The matter to be investigated should usually be described in very general terms, the resolutions being in a form similar to the following:

Whereas, Rumors affecting the character of Mr. X, one of our members, are current which, if true, render him unworthy of membership in this society; therefore, [or, therefore, be it]

Resolved, That a committee of five be appointed by the chair to investigate said rumors sufficiently to enable it to decide whether or not charges should be preferred against Mr. X.

Resolved, That the committee be, and hereby is, instructed to report a resolution or resolutions covering its recommendation, and that these resolutions, in case charges are to be preferred, shall include the charges and specifications and shall provide for the trial of the case.

The resolutions should state the size of the committee, how it is to be appointed, and what is required of it. The committee should always report all the resolutions necessary to carry out its recommendations, even though it is not so stated in the instructions. The preamble should state the cause of the appointment of the committee. In case of a member's making a charge against another, it is best to postpone the resolution indefinitely, and to adopt resolutions similar to those above, except that the preamble should be worded similar to this: *"Whereas,* Mr. X has been accused of conduct unworthy of a member of this society [or, demanding the censure of the society], therefore" etc. Or the resolution may be referred to a committee with instructions similar to those given above. In stating the cause of the appointment of the committee, only very general terms should be used. No members should be allowed, under the cloak of such a resolution, to publish scandalous rumors, or to insult another member by false insinuations while making no false assertion.

If a member offers a resolution containing improper words or insinuations, the chair should call him to order and stop him at the first impropriety, and prevent his continuing the reading unless permission is given by a vote of the society. If the chair neglects this, some member should call the speaker to order. The resolution may be so worded as to justify the censuring or other punishment of the member offering it. As a general rule the motion is improper if it mentions the details of the offenses or rumors. Sometimes, however, it may be necessary to go somewhat into detail in order to enable members to vote intelligently. This would be the case where members refuse to vote for the resolutions unless they are more specific. But nothing that might injure the accused member should be done except what is necessary for the protection of the society or of other members. The society has a right to go that far, but no farther. Thus the above-mentioned resolutions would be improper if the preamble read thus:

Whereas, It has been reported that Mr. X has been found cheating at cards; and

Whereas, It has also been reported that he was seen after midnight on the fourth of last April in a disreputable part of the town dead drunk; therefore, etc.

Publishing rumors of such a kind by including them in a preamble or resolution should be prevented, and the attempt should be punished. Nothing should be in a resolution except what is necessary to enable the society to take proper steps to protect itself by removing unworthy members, which it has the right to do.

There should be a meeting of the committee at the close of the meeting at which it is appointed, when it should hear the statements of such members as know anything bearing on the case, or else a time should then be appointed for such a hearing. It should appoint one or more sub-committees of one or two members to investigate certain matters, or, if thought advisable, to interview the member whose conduct is being investigated. The committee should usually request the member to appear before it, so that it can get from him his side of the case. He should have an opportunity for full explanation, but in case of his guilt he may decline to appear before the committee. The committee should understand that it is not prosecuting the member, but simply trying to ascertain whether the welfare of the society requires any action in the case.

Report of the Committee. If the case is of a kind that it is possible to settle without a trial, the committee should make every effort to do so. If it succeeds, it should report that fact and recommend that no further action be taken in the matter. If the committee is satisfied that there is no ground for the accusation and that it was made with malice, it should report its opinion and a resolution censuring the one who made the charge. If the committee is of the opinion that the interests of the society demand the trial of the accused member, it should report its opinion, and should conclude with recommending the adoption of resolutions similar to the following:

Report of the Committee on the Case of Mr. X

The committee appointed to investigate certain accusations against Mr. X respectfully submits the following report:

The instructions of the committee are contained in the following resolutions, adopted by the society at its meeting June 4:

"*Whereas,*" etc. [Copy resolutions in full.]

The committee has interviewed a number of persons claiming to be acquainted with the facts in the case, including Mr. X, and has notified them that the committee would be glad to hear any persons desirous of presenting any additional facts. In talking over the matter with Mr. X the committee was not satisfied with his explanations, and is therefore of the opinion that the best interests of the society demand that charges be preferred against Mr. X for conduct unworthy of a member of this society.

Your committee therefore recommends the adoption of the following resolutions:

"*Resolved,* That when we adjourn we adjourn to meet at 8 P. M. on Saturday, June 26, 19—

"*Resolved,* That Mr. X be, and hereby is, cited to appear before the society at its meeting at 8 P. M., Saturday, June 26, 19—, to show cause why he should not be expelled from the society on the following charge and specifications:

"*Charge.* Conduct unworthy of a member of this society.

"*Specification* 1. In this that Mr. X has so conducted himself as to establish among a number of his associates a reputation for cheating at cards.

"*Specification* 2. In this that Mr. X on or about the 4th of April appeared after midnight in public on or near ——— and ——— streets in an apparently intoxicated condition.

"*Resolved,* That Messrs. B and D act for the society as its managers at the trial."

Committee.

The details of this report should vary according to circumstances, but the form given shows its main features. No names other than that of Mr. X should be mentioned. The opinion of the committee should always be given, and if it is favorable to the accused the report should close with a resolution exonerating him. If the opinion is unfavorable, it should be followed by a series of resolutions providing for the trial of the case, as shown above. The first resolution should provide for an adjourned meeting, as it is not usually good policy to have a trial at a regular meeting. The second resolution should cite the accused to appear at the adjourned meeting for trial on a charge or charges which should be stated. Generally each charge should be followed by specifications, unless they are of such a nature that both the committee and the accused prefer them to be suppressed. In such a case, of course, the committee and the accused know what they are, and there is nothing gained by placing them on the record unless one of the parties desires it. The main object of the specifications is to enable the accused to prepare his defense. In making specifications it is well to give dates only approximately. Sometimes only the month or the season is necessary. If the offense was committed, the time is of no importance except so far as is required by the accused in order to prepare his defense.

The last resolution should provide for appointing two or three "managers," whose duty it is to present at the trial the charges and the evidence to sustain them, and at the same time to see that justice is done the accused. Their aim should be to see that all the facts are presented that are necessary to enable the society to arrive at the truth, regardless of technicalities. Generally two managers are sufficient. They should usually be appointed from the committee that has conducted the investigation and preferred the charges, since they are familiar with the case. This resolution may name the managers, or it may authorize their appointment by the president or by the committee that investigated the case.

If the society has a standing committee whose duty it is to attend to cases of discipline, its report should begin in a manner similar to this:

"The [or Your] committee on discipline, having learned of rumors derogatory to the character of Mr. X, a member of this society, deemed them of such importance as to demand an investigation. Consequently they interviewed ——, etc." Of course a standing committee would never report a case unless it was sure that the accused was guilty.

It is not necessary, and in many cases it is not expedient, that a trial should be conducted before the entire society, any more than it is necessary that a criminal case should be tried by the entire community, or county, or state. If the case is one involving morals, or if the society is very large, the case should be tried by a committee sufficiently large and fair-minded to command the confidence of the society in its decisions. In such a case the following should replace the first two resolutions in the committee's report as given above:

"*Resolved*, That a trial committee consisting of Mr. L, chairman, and Messrs. ——, be, and hereby is, appointed to try the case of Mr. X.

"*Resolved*, That Mr. X be, and hereby is, cited to appear before the trial committee at the society hall at 8 P. M., Saturday, June 26, 19—, to show cause why he should not be expelled from the society on the following charge and specifications [or, for trial on the following charge and specifications]:" [Here follows the charge and specifications.]

When the report has been adopted by the committee, it should be signed by every member agreeing to it, as the vote of members of the society may be dependent upon who sign the report. If the charges are recommended by only a majority of one, and those the least judicious of the members, it is still the report of the committee, but would probably not carry much weight with it. In such a case the minority may submit their views and move to substitute the resolutions that they submit for those recommended by the committee.

When the president calls on the committee for its report, the reporting member rises and, addressing the presiding officer, reads the report and says, "By direction of the committee I move the adoption of the resolutions." The president then says: "It is moved and seconded to adopt the resolutions recommended by the committee. They are as follows: [reads the resolutions]. Are you ready for the question?" These resolutions are now open to debate and amendment or any other disposition the assembly may decide upon.

Form of Citation to Appear for Trial. If the resolutions are adopted, it is the duty of the secretary immediately to notify the accused that he is cited to appear for trial. This he should do by mailing to the accused a copy of the resolutions as adopted, except the first one providing for an additional meeting, or for the trial committee, as the case may be. Even if the accused is present when they are adopted, he must be furnished with a written copy of the citation, including the charges and specifications. The letter may be in this form, after the date and address:

Dear Sir:
The —— Society at its meeting June — adopted the following resolutions:
"*Resolved,* That Mr. X. be, and hereby is, cited to appear [copy remainder of resolutions]."
You will please be present at the society hall at the appointed time.
Respectfully yours,
L—— M——,
Secretary.

If the words "and hereby is" are omitted, then the adoption of the second resolution reported by the committee, page 345, does not cite Mr. X, but orders that he be cited, so the secretary should send him a citation in this form:

Dear Sir:
You are hereby cited to appear at the society hall on Saturday, June 26, 19—, for trial on the following charge and specifications [or, June 26, 19—, to show cause why you should not be expelled from the society on the following charge and specifications]: [Copy the charge and specifications.]
By order of the —— Society.
L—— M——,
Secretary.

THE TRIAL

At the appointed time for the trial of the case, the president calls the meeting to order, and the procedure is similar to the following:

PRESIDENT [*standing and rapping*]. The meeting will come to order. The secretary will read from the minutes the resolutions adopted by the society relating to this adjourned meeting and the trial. [*Takes his seat.*]

SECRETARY [*standing*]. The following resolutions were adopted at the meeting of the society held on the —— day of June. [*He reads all the resolutions as adopted.*]

PRES. [*standing*]. The special business of this meeting is the trial of Mr. X on the charges that have been read. [*Addressing the secretary.*] Was Mr. X furnished with a copy of the charges? [*The reply being in the affirmative, he continues.*] The case for the society will be managed by Messrs. B and D. [*Addressing Mr. X.*] Have you counsel? [*Mr. X replies that he has Mr. Y.*] [1] The secretary will read the charge and specifications, and Mr.

[1] Mr. Y must be a member of the society.

X will be called upon to plead guilty or not guilty. [*Secretary reads charge and specifications.*] Mr. X, how do you plead to the first specification, guilty or not guilty? [*Mr. X answers, "Not guilty.*] To the second specification, guilty or not guilty? [*Mr. X answers, "Not guilty."*] To the charge, guilty or not guilty? [*Mr. X answers, "Not guilty."*] Mr. X pleads not guilty to the charge and specifications, so the trial will proceed as follows: The managers will present the facts in the case as they have learned them without calling on any witnesses, and then the defense will state its side of the case. The managers will then bring forward whatever evidence they choose to substantiate such of their statements as are denied by the defense, and to prove the inaccuracy of any statements of the defense, after which the defense will have an equal opportunity to defend its statements, and to prove the incorrectness of the statements on the side of the managers. Any witnesses brought forward by one party may be cross-questioned by the other. After the evidence on both sides has been presented, each side will be allowed —— minutes to present its side of the case, the defense speaking first. The accused will then leave the hall, and the assembly will proceed to the consideration of the question, "Is Mr. X guilty of the charge and specifications preferred against him?" The question will then be before the assembly for debate and amendment. Up to this time no one is entitled to the floor except the managers and the accused and his counsel. Members may privately make suggestions to either party, which may be followed or not. The managers and the defense may consult with members quietly, and may even interrupt the other side to ask a question, but the request must be addressed to the presiding officer as in ordinary meetings of the society. Witnesses will be questioned directly and not through the chair. If the accused is found guilty of the charges, the society will then be called upon to decide upon the punishment. The chair calls the attention of the members to the fact that while engaged in this trial the society is in executive, or secret, session, and members should avoid talking to non-members about what occurs in the meeting. The managers will now present the case against Mr. X. [*The president takes his seat.*]

Mr. B [*standing*]. Mr. President, the committee of which Mr. D [*the other manager*] and I were members interviewed two of our members, Mr. L and Mr. M. and five others, not members of the society, who are unwilling that their names should be known. All of them had played cards with Mr. X and were convinced that he was in the habit of cheating, and they said they knew many others who had had the same experience and were of the same opinion. These men, the committee believed, were fair-minded and worthy of credence. The committee had talked with Mr. X on the subject, but was not at all satisfied with his explanation of this reputation which he had acquired. The committee also interviewed two non-members who assured it that while on the way from the railroad station to their homes late on the night of the —— day of ——, they passed Mr. X near the corner of —— and —— streets, apparently so intoxicated that he could not walk straight. The committee made inquiries as to the character of these two men, and found that they stood high in the esteem of their neighbors, and it believes that their statements are worthy of credence. Nothing that Mr. X said in any way shook the confidence of the committee in the veracity of these two men.

PRES. [*sitting*]. The defense will now be heard.

Mr. X now makes his statement standing. He may allow his counsel to make it for him, but it is generally bad policy to do so. If he is innocent, he can plead his case with more chances of success than any counsel, especially if he is frank and does not try to conceal anything. The remarks should be addressed to the presiding officer. While making them, his counsel may quietly make suggestions to him or he may consult his counsel. When he has finished his statement, the president, sitting or standing, asks, "Have the managers anything further to present?" Mr. B answers, "Mr. President, I should like to ask Mr. X some questions." He then proceeds to question Mr. X directly, not through the president. This he follows up, if he thinks it advisable, by calling on witnesses and questioning them. As he finishes with each one, the accused has the privilege of cross-questioning the witnesses. The parties conducting the trial are not supposed to be lawyers and the rules of courts are not in force. There is no objection to either party's questioning a witness again after the other has questioned him a second time. The president should prevent improper questions from being asked, but any of his decisions may be appealed from and thus the society be called upon to decide the question.

When the managers have brought forward all of their witnesses.

the president asks the accused if he wishes to produce any witnesses or evidence. When all witnesses and evidence have been presented, the president asks, "Has Mr. X anything further to say in his defense?" Mr. X, standing and addressing the chair, proceeds to state his defense. When he has finished the president says, "The managers will now close the case." One of the managers now presents the case, not from the standpoint of a prosecutor, but of one who wishes justice done. He should avoid all appearance of partizanship, but at the same time he should clearly present the case, and, where the evidence produces a moral conviction of guilt, he should say so.

When the managers have made their closing speech, the president should say "The case is closed, and Mr. X will retire to another room." The managers, the counsel for the accused, and all witnesses who are members of the society remain in the hall, being entitled to take part in the discussion and to vote, the same as the other members. All non-members, if any are present, and the accused must leave the hall. The hall being cleared, the president says, "The question before the assembly is, 'Is Mr. X guilty of the charge and specifications preferred against him?' Are you ready for the question?" The question is now open to debate and amendment. The specifications, or the charge, or all of them, may be modified by amendments. When the debate is exhausted the business proceeds thus: The president says: "Are you ready for the question? The secretary will read the first specification. As many as are of opinion that Mr. X is guilty of this specification, say 'Aye.' Those [or, As many as are] of a contrary opinion, say 'No.' The ayes have it, and Mr. X is found guilty of the first specification. The secretary will read the second specification." The question is put in a similar manner on the second specification, and then on the charge. If the accused is found guilty of the charge, the president says: "Mr. X having been found guilty of the charge of 'conduct unworthy of a member of this society,' the next business is to determine the punishment to be imposed upon him." A member, preferably one of the managers, should now make a suitable motion, which the chair states. This motion may be debated and amended and should finally be put to vote. If different punishments are suggested, they should be treated as in filling blanks rather than as amendments. The advantage of this is that the different suggestions are voted on in the order of their severity, the vote being taken first on the most severe one. The motion to expel a member requires a two-thirds vote for its adoption. If the motion is lost a lesser punishment may be adopted by a majority vote. As soon as the vote is taken and announced, the president directs a member (the doorkeeper, if there is one) to bring Mr. X back to the hall. The chair informs him of the finding and sentence in a manner similar to this: "Mr. X, you have been found guilty of the first specification, not guilty of the second specification, and guilty of the charge of conduct unworthy of a member of this society, and have consequently been expelled from its membership. There being no further business, a motion to adjourn is in order."

If a single member objects to voting as above described, it is necessary to vote by ballot on the charge and specifications, and also on the punishment. The secrecy of the ballot can be waived on these votes only by general consent. If the vote is taken by ballot, the president appoints two or more tellers, and directs them to distribute blank slips of paper, one to each member. The business then proceeds as follows:

Pres. The secretary will read the charge and specifications. [*The secretary reads these as modified, if they have been amended.*] The question is, "Is Mr. X guilty of the charge and specifications?" Each member will write on the left side of his blank ballot the words, "First specification," and to the right either "guilty" or "not guilty." Beneath this on the next line he will write, "Second specification, "guilty," or "not guilty"; and on the next line below he will write "Charge, guilty," or "not guilty." The members will prepare their ballots.

The ballots are collected and counted as described under Elections The vote on the charge is always announced last, the form being similar to this: "The number of votes cast, 100. Number necessary for conviction, 51. Vote on first specification: guilty, 78; not guilty, 22. A majority voting guilty, Mr. X is found guilty of the first specification. Vote on the second specification: guilty, 40; not guilty, 60. There not being a majority voting guilty, Mr. X is found not guilty of the second specification. Vote on charge: guilty, 77; not guilty, 23. A majority voting guilty, Mr. X is found guilty of the charge. The next business in order is to determine upon the punishment." If a motion is made to expel Mr. X, the vote being by ballot, the president puts the question thus: "The question is, 'Shall Mr. X be expelled from the membership of this society?' Those voting in the affirmative will write 'Yes' on their ballots, and those voting in the negative will write 'No.' It requires a two-thirds vote to adopt this motion. Prepare your ballots." After the tellers have reported, the president announces the vote thus: "Number of votes cast, 100: number voting 'Yes,' 70; number voting 'No,' 30. There being two thirds in the affirmative, the motion is adopted, and Mr. X is expelled from the membership of this society." Mr. X is then sent for and informed of the finding and the sentence as heretofore described.

If no punishments are proposed, the chair directs the members to write on their ballots the punishment voted for. If no punishment receives a majority vote, then a ballot vote should be taken on each punishment voted for, beginning with the severest, until one receives more votes for it than against it.

GENERAL REMARKS ON TRIALS

Before the specifications and charge are voted on, they should be amended so as to conform to the facts brought out by the trial. If, even after these changes, the accused is found guilty of a specification and yet is found not guilty of the charge, a lighter charge should be voted on, and so on, until he is found guilty of a charge commensurate with the offense described in the specification. No technicalities should be allowed to interfere with the object of the trial, namely, to do justice to the accused and to the society. The method of trial described is designed as a guide. Some modification of it can be found to fit each case.

Additional charges may be preferred against the accused at the time of the trial by members of the committee or by any other member. If members of the committee wish to prefer additional charges, and if it is a special committee, they cannot do it as a committee, because the committee was automatically discharged when its report was made to the society. Their proper course is to put the additional charge and specification in writing, and to have as many as practicable of the committee sign it. Then one of their number should obtain the floor, and state that the members of the committee since making their report had felt it their duty to prefer the following additional charge against Mr. X, and that he therefore moves that the following charge and specification be added to those adopted by the society. He then reads them with the names signed to them, and hands them to the presiding officer, who states the question upon them and puts it to vote.

If a member wishes an additional charge or specification to be preferred, he should present it to the chairman of the committee, even if the committee has been discharged, and should ask him to attend to it. In no case can a member be tried without his consent on the same day that charges are preferred, unless it is for something occurring at the meeting, so that the witnesses are present.

Preceding a statement by "if" does not necessarily relieve it from its insulting or accusing character, as illustrated by the following incident:

A member of a society wrote a letter to the president which was similar to this: "I have heard that at the last meeting of our society you made a speech condemning certain actions without mentioning names, which speech was certainly aimed at me. If you have made false statements about me I freely forgive you. Go and sin no more." The letter was handed to the standing committee on discipline, which appointed a sub-committee of two to interview the writer. He refused to apologize or withdraw any words in the letter, claiming that he had not written anything improper, as he made no accusation against the president. The sub-committee reported to the committee, which promptly recommended that the charges that they submitted be preferred against the member. This was done, and the member was cited to appear for trial on these charges at an adjourned meeting, at which time, as he refused to withdraw his statement or to apologize, he was expelled from the society.

A society should pay no attention to technicalities. Its aim should be to get at the truth, and the accused simply injures his case by a lack of frankness. Declining to answer a question necessarily produces the impression that the facts are damaging, unless a satisfactory explanation is made. The safest course, if one is innocent, is to conceal nothing, but to make a clean breast of the whole affair. This should be done with the committee, so that the case will never come to trial. A member's confession of the truth, even if he is guilty, and his promise to reform, will usually be as effective with the committee as with the society. If the offense is of such a nature that the committee would be obliged to recommend that he be expelled, he should ask that he be dropped from the roll of members, and thus the matter would usually be ended without a trial.

A member cannot necessarily escape expulsion by resigning or asking to be dropped from the roll of membership. If the offense is of such a nature that, for the protection of similar societies, he should be expelled and not merely dropped, the case should be pressed to the end, and no notice taken of his resignation or request to be dropped. If the member does not come in contact with other similar societies with which he might affiliate or unite, there is usually nothing gained by expulsion.

A member cannot prevent the trial of his case by failing to attend the meeting or by neglecting to procure the attendance of his witnesses. If he is not present, or if, when present, he refuses to plead or answer questions, the trial goes on just the same. This conduct only aggravates the case and justifies additional charges to be acted upon immediately.

The meetings at which charges are preferred or tried should always exclude all but members and witnesses. A secret session of this kind is commonly known as an executive session. The minutes of an executive session where business of this kind is transacted must be read and approved in executive session.

The society should not make public the charges and specifications upon which a member was tried if such publicity can in any way damage the accused. Members should be careful about circulating scandalous charges against a member. The society has a right to make public the fact that the accused is no longer a member of the society, but it has no right to publish this in the newspapers unless the publicity is necessary for the protection of the society or affiliated societies. The secretary of a certain society was obliged to pay damages for publishing, by order of the society, the charges upon which a member was expelled. The court refused to hear the evidence of the guilt of the plaintiff, declaring that it had nothing to do with the case.

CHAPTER XXXIII

QUORUM; SESSIONS AND MEETINGS

QUORUM

SINCE it is impracticable to secure the attendance of all the members of a society at many of its meetings, it is necessary to allow a certain proportion of the membership to transact the business of the society. Long-continued usage has established this proportion, called the Quorum, as a majority of the membership. If, then, a majority of the membership are present in the hall, business can be transacted regardless of the number voting. Those who abstain from voting acquiesce in the action of those who vote, because if they do not agree with the majority they have the privilege of expressing their views by voting.

In conventions, boards, and committees, this rule that a quorum consists of a majority of the members is satisfactory, because the members are selected for the special purpose and have no right to accept unless they intend to be present at the meetings. But, in ordinary societies, members are not under moral obligation to attend all the meetings, and it is therefore necessary to adopt a by-law establishing a smaller quorum. What number is best depends upon the society, and each one must ascertain it by experience. In a small society where there is great interest in the meetings the quorum may with safety be as large as one fourth of the membership, whereas in a very large society, long established, it may prove inconvenient to have a quorum as large even as ten per cent. of the members. The quorum of the English House of Commons is about six per cent. and of the House of Lords less than one half of one per cent. Too large a quorum discourages members from attending meetings during bad weather for fear there will not be a quorum, while too small a quorum enables a few members to take advantage of stormy weather to adopt ob-

356

jectionable measures. This latter action, however, can generally be nullified by the proper use of the motion to Reconsider and Enter on the Minutes, as explained on page 101.

Usually the presiding officer does not take the chair until a quorum is present. When he is satisfied that there will be no quorum, he calls the meeting to order and says, "As there is no quorum, a motion to adjourn is in order." Some one moves to adjourn, and, the motion being adopted, the meeting is declared adjourned. If it is the annual meeting when certain specified business, as the election of officers, should be transacted, the time for holding an adjourned meeting should be fixed before adjourning. As an ordinary society cannot compel its members to attend its meetings, the above-mentioned business is all that can be done when no quorum is present.

If, while a meeting is in progress, members should leave, so as to reduce the number present to less than a quorum, the debate may continue, but no vote can be taken except to fix the time to which to adjourn and to adjourn or to take a recess. The debate cannot continue if the point of "no quorum" is raised by a member and sustained by the chair. The point of "no quorum" cannot be raised so as to interrupt a member while speaking, but may be raised at any other time.

Sometimes bad weather prevents the attendance of a quorum at a meeting when it is necessary to take certain action, as electing delegates, engaging a lecturer, or accepting an invitation. If certain of the approval of the society, those present, though less than a quorum, may act in the emergency, and report at the next meeting of the society their informal action and ask that it be ratified. [See Ratify, page 12.] They take the risk of their action's not being ratified, as the society is under no obligation to endorse their informal act.

If it is desired to have a smaller quorum than a majority of the members in a board or a committee, it must be authorized by the same body that determined the size of the board or committee. If the by-laws prescribe the size of the board or committee, the by-laws alone can make the quorum less than a majority of the members. In such a case a unanimous vote of the society making a different quorum would be null and void. But if the size of the committee was established by a vote of the society, a majority vote of the society can determine the quorum.

A board or committee has no power to determine its own quorum. [In "Rules of Order Revised" (under Quorum), pages 257-261, will be found additional information on this subject.]

SESSIONS AND MEETINGS

The terms "Session," "Sitting," and "Meeting" have been used so interchangeably in different parts of the country that it is necessary to define clearly these terms as used in this work. Some by-laws refer to the different sessions of a meeting, others to the different sittings of a meeting. This is because the term "meeting" is applied to any assemblage of the members, as the annual meeting. But the term "session" has been applied from time immemorial to the meetings of the English Parliament from the time it first meets until it is prorogued, though the various daily meetings constituting the session may cover several years. A somewhat similar practice is followed by our national Congress and our state legislatures, a session, however, never lasting longer than a year. Parliamentary law is based on this meaning of the word "session," and consequently the word is so used in this work. Each separate meeting of a society provided for by its by-laws is a session. A called special meeting is a special session. A session, however, may be prolonged over several days by adjourning from one day to another. When the assembly lasts only a few hours the meeting and session are synonymous. But if the assembly lasts all day, a recess being taken for meals, the session consists of the morning meeting, the afternoon meeting, and the evening meeting. A recess taken for a few minutes does not break the continuity of a meeting. At the close of the recess the assembly resumes its sitting. All the meetings of a convention, regardless of the number of days it lasts, constitute one session. If the convention were to adjourn to meet a month later, the adjourned meetings together with the previous meetings would constitute one session.

The importance of keeping in mind the distinction between a session and a meeting will be seen by examining the article on Renewal of Motions, page 113. As a general statement it may be said that those rules relating to renewing motions apply to motions made at the same or a previous meeting of a session, but they do not apply to a motion made at a previous session. One session cannot tie the hands of the majority at a future session, excepting as expressly provided in the by-laws or rules of order. Thus, a motion cannot be postponed beyond the next session, but it may be postponed beyond the next meeting, provided it is postponed to a meeting of the same session or of the next session. A meeting can adjourn to meet shortly before the time for the next session to begin, but when that time arrives the majority will continue the adjourned meeting only as long as it wishes; therefore there is no interference with the will of the majority at the next session. [Further information on this subject will be found in ''Rules of Order Revised,'' pages 253-257.]

Executive Session. As it is customary for the U. S. Senate to consider executive business in secret session, the expression ''Executive Session'' has come to be synonymous with ''secret session,'' and is used in contrast with ''open'' or ''public session.'' None but members of the society and such persons as the society invites are permitted to be present in the hall during an executive session, and members are in honor bound not to divulge what occurs, and they can be punished for violating this rule. The minutes of executive sessions should not be read in open session, except the minutes of meetings at which no business is transacted other than the reading and approval of the minutes of the preceding executive session. Matters relating to discipline should usually be attended to in executive session, and trials involving character should always be so conducted.

CHAPTER XXXIV

BY-LAWS AND OTHER RULES

A MASS MEETING

A MASS MEETING lasts for only a few hours, and therefore has no need of any by-laws. It is called for some specific purpose, and it is customary at the opening of the meeting to have the call read, thus notifying the assembly as to the objects of the meeting. Motions that have no relation whatever to these objects should be ruled out of order by the presiding officer. Although the assembly has not adopted this statement of the objects of the meeting, yet they are the ones set forth by the promoters of the meeting who have engaged the hall, and have the control of it, and have the right to specify the objects of the meeting which they have called. In the case of an ordinary society the hall is controlled, at least for the time of the meeting, by the society itself: therefore the society, unless it has adopted a different rule previously, has a right by a two-thirds vote to suspend the rule prohibiting the introduction of questions having no relation to the objects of the society. But in a mass meeting this cannot be done if objection is made by the promoters who have signed the call and engaged the hall. If such a privilege were permitted, the meeting could be diverted to objects to which those who called the meeting, and are responsible for the expenses, are indifferent or even opposed.

The call may specify the class of persons invited, and none other need be admitted. The promoters of the meeting may appoint door-keepers, who are instructed to refuse admission to those known to be opposed to the object of the meeting. Thus, the meeting may be called in the interest of a political party, and the door-keepers may be authorized to refuse admission to known opponents of that party. Or, the call may state that tickets of admission will be required, and that they can be obtained at certain specified places. Such precautions are sometimes necessary, especially when there is a liability that the seating capacity of the hall will be insufficient.

The call for a mass meeting, then, takes the place of the by-laws of an organized society. It determines the object of the meeting, and who may attend, and who may vote. No other rules are required in a community where there is no difference of opinion as to what is the common parliamentary law. Since, however, there is usually diversity of opinion on this subject, it is safer for the assembly at the opening of the meeting to adopt some standard rules of order for its government. This can be done by a majority vote. The method of organizing and conducting business in a mass meeting is described in "Rules of Order Revised," pages 275-284.

A Permanent or Organized Society

A Permanent or Organized Society must have some rules for its government. These rules may be divided into three classes in the case of unincorporated societies, namely, By-Laws (including a Constitution, if used); Rules of Order (including Special Rules of Order); and Standing Rules. If the society expects to own property, it should incorporate, in which case it has a fourth set of rules, called the Charter, which outranks all other rules. The scope of these various rules is as follows:

Charter or Act of Incorporation. An unincorporated society cannot hold property or make legally binding contracts or sue or be sued as a society in its name as such or have a legacy left it. Therefore, any unincorporated society which proposes to do business or enter into contracts which involve liability or to own property must incorporate. This is done in some states by obtaining an act of the legislature, and in others by filing with the Secretary of State, Articles of Association giving the name and object of the society, etc., the paper being signed by all the incorporators. These Articles of Association, or the Act of Incorporation, are usually called the Charter. The members of the society at the time of the incorporation are "Charter Members," though sometimes societies apply this term to all who unite with the society before a certain date.

When it is desired to incorporate a society, a small committee on incorporation should be appointed, who should prepare a memorandum giving the names of the incorporators, the name and object of the society, the location of its headquarters or principal office, or, if it has no office, the principal field of its operations, and the amount of personal and real estate it wishes to be authorized to hold. The committee should consult a lawyer as to the details of incorporating in that particular state. Since the laws on the subject vary in the different states and may be changed at any time, a local lawyer should always be consulted. As the charter is the fundamental law of the society, it should be adopted, or approved, by the society before the final steps required for the incorporation are taken.

The charter is the supreme law of the organization, outranking the constitution, by-laws, etc., which must not conflict with it. It cannot be suspended. Any amendment to it must first be adopted by the organization in the same way as the by-laws are amended, and then must be submitted for approval to the legislature or superior organization if the original charter was granted by either of them. If the charter was obtained under a general law, such steps must be taken as are prescribed by the law. On account of the difficulty of amending a charter, nothing should be placed in it except what is absolutely necessary in order to obtain it.

The term "charter" is applied also to the document given by a superior organization granting the right to form a subordinate society, chapter, or lodge, etc.

By-Laws. The by-laws of a society comprise all its rules, except those relating to the transaction of business, that are of such importance that they should not be changed except after suitable notice to the members, and then by a vote larger than a majority of those voting. These rules should prescribe the name and objects of the society; its organization, that is, its membership, officers, boards, committees, etc., and how they are elected or appointed; its meetings and quorum; its parliamentary authority; and the method of amending these by-laws. These by-laws cannot be suspended, like Rules of Order and Standing Rules, and therefore nothing should be put in them that is allowed to be suspended.

In organizing a club or society, the by-laws are adopted by a majority vote, but no business can be transacted until it is known who are the members. A recess is taken, and those who wish to unite with the society must sign the by-laws and pay the initiation fee and annual dues if such are required. It is not well, however, to insist on the payment of the dues at the first meeting, because many who wish to join the society may not be prepared for this requirement.

By-laws may be divided into a Constitution, containing the more important rules, and By-Laws, containing the others. The object of this division is to make the more important rules more difficult to amend than the others. But it is now the custom to make no distinction in the difficulty of amending these fundamental rules, and therefore there is nothing gained by dividing them into a constitution and by-laws. On the contrary, it is much simpler to call them all by-laws and to place under each head everything relating to that subject. They are treated that way in this work.

Rules of Order. Every society in its by-laws should adopt some standard rules of order for the government of its meetings. Without this there is a great liability to having unpleasant differences as to questions of parliamentary law, which will interfere with the society's work. Parliamentary law is designed to assist and not to hinder a society, and yet it becomes a positive hindrance in an active society that has no rules of order and recognizes no definite authority in parliamentary law. When an authority has been adopted it must be followed, and the only question is as to the interpretation of the adopted rules. What any other authority says on the subject has nothing to do with the case.

Special Rules of Order. In addition to some standard parliamentary authority, most societies need some special rules relating to the transaction of business in their meetings which modify the adopted standard rules of order. The Special Rules of Order, adopted after standard rules of order have been adopted, are in the nature of amendments to the adopted rules, and supersede them whenever the two are in conflict. They may be suspended by the same vote as the other rules of order. Most societies need a special order of business, and also a simple rule relating to the number and length of speeches. All rules relating to the transaction of business in the meetings that are required in addition to those in their adopted authority should be placed in these special rules of order, and should be printed with the by-laws. These special rules and any amendments to them should be submitted in writing, either at the previous meeting or in the call for the meeting at which they are to be acted upon, and should be adopted by a two-thirds vote, or a vote of a majority of the membership. It is generally better to have the special rules of order reported by a committee. The motion for their adoption may be made thus: "By direction of the Committee on Special [or Additional] Rules of Order, I move that the special [or additional] rules of order be adopted, and that all rules conflicting therewith be rescinded." Rules that are intended to be in force only during the session at which they are adopted, as in case of a convention, are Standing Rules, and are explained in the next paragraph.

Standing Rules. Many organizations need a few rules of a semi-permanent nature, which they can modify or rescind without the delay and trouble attending the amending of by-laws or rules of order. An example of this is a rule fixing the hour of meeting, which it is desired to be able to change at the will of the society. A convention usually adopts some rules to be in force during the convention, which are called Standing Rules, and may be adopted at any meeting by a majority vote, provided they in no way conflict with the rules of order or the by-laws. By a two-thirds vote a convention may adopt standing rules governing that session which modify for the session the rules of debate as to the number and length of speeches allowed. This is permitted because a standing rule may be suspended at any time by a majority vote, and therefore can never interfere with the majority. If notice is given at the previous meeting (not necessarily session) a standing rule may be amended or rescinded by a majority vote, or it may be done without notice by a two-thirds vote. [See page 398 for a model of Standing Rules to be adopted by a convention.]

CHAPTER XXXV

AMENDING CONSTITUTIONS, BY-LAWS, RULES OF ORDER, AND OTHER RULES

AMENDING CONSTITUTIONS, BY-LAWS, AND RULES OF ORDER

SINCE the same rules usually apply to all of these, the term "by-laws" will be used in this chapter as covering the other cases. By-laws before they are adopted are amended the same as any other proposition that consists of a number of paragraphs. This method is fully described in "Rules of Order Revised," pages 94 and 287. The motion to adopt the by-laws, etc., is a main motion, and the motion to amend the by-laws is a subsidiary motion requiring only a majority vote, so there is nothing peculiar about amending by-laws, etc., before their adoption.

After their adoption the case is different. The by-laws, having been previously adopted, are not pending, and the motion to amend the by-laws, therefore, is not a subsidiary motion but is a main motion, as explained on page 38 under Amend, and is subject to all the methods of amendment of main motions, provided such amendments are covered by adequate notice.

The motion to amend existing by-laws, being a main motion, is debatable, and what is to be inserted is subject to amendments of the first and second degrees. It may have any of the subsidiary motions applied to it. It cannot be made as freely as other main motions, but must comply strictly with the requirements of the by-laws for their amendment. If no provision is made in the by-laws for their amendment, they may be amended at any meeting by a vote of the majority of the entire membership without notice being given of the proposed amendment; or they may be amended at any regular meeting by a two-thirds vote, provided the amendment was submitted in writing at the previous regular meeting;

368

or they may be amended at a special meeting by a two-thirds vote, provided the call for the meeting contained a copy of the proposed amendment with notice that it was to be offered. In other words, the members must have fair notice of the proposed change in the by-laws.

On account of the requirement of notice of any proposed change of the by-laws, etc., there cannot be permitted the same freedom of amending the main motion "to amend the by-laws" as is allowed with other main motions. Primary and secondary amendments are allowed, but they must not increase the change that is proposed in the main motion to amend, since it is only the main motion of which notice has been given. Absentees have had no notice of these primary and secondary subsidiary amendments, and therefore while these amendments may diminish the proposed change they cannot increase it. If notice is given of an amendment and a member wishes a greater change than the proposed one, he should at once write out his amendment and give notice of it. When the other amendment is pending at the next meeting, since his amendment is germane to it, he can move his as an amendment to the other amendment, even though it makes a greater change, because notice of it has been given. Notice may be given even after it has been voted to adjourn, provided the assembly has not been declared adjourned.

Frequently it is convenient, in proposing an amendment to the by-laws, to rewrite a by-law and offer it as a substitute for the existing one. When there are several changes proposed, this is usually the simplest and the best way. But it must be borne in mind that this does not necessarily open to amendment all parts of the proposed substitute. If the substitute is only a change in the wording without affecting the essential requirements of the by-law, the notice of amendment is limited to the wording, and only that is open to further amendment when action is to be taken by the society. If the substitute changes only one of several requirements in the by-law, only that requirement is open to further amendment. Thus, if it is proposed to amend a by-law that specifies the salaries of several officers, by substituting a new by-law which differs from the old one only in increasing the salary of one officer, no amendment to the substitute is in order except one affecting the salary of that officer. Otherwise the object of requiring written notice of an amendment to the by-laws could be defeated by omitting, in giving notice of an amendment, the vital changes to be made, and thus concealing until the last moment the essential features at which the amendment was aimed. No amendment of an amendment of a by-law or a constitution is in order unless it is clearly covered by the notice given; and where the notice is given in the form of a substitute, such notice does not apply to those portions that are unchanged in the substitute. No amendment of a proposed amendment or substitute is in order which is of such a nature that, if notice of it had been given, some of the absentees would probably have attended the meeting at which action on it was to be taken. In the example just given, if a member wishes to have the salary of another officer also increased, he should immediately write out an amendment to cover the desired increase, sign his name to it and get the signature of another member, and hand it to the chairman or secretary, reading it first if he prefers. The chairman or secretary reads the proposed amendment, and the secretary retains it with his papers. If the amendment is to strike out a by-law, the friends of the existing by-law should give notice of such amendments as they think advisable, since they cannot perfect the existing by-law by amendments, except by those of which notice has been given.

The motion to strike out words or a paragraph in the by-laws may be amended in any way that any main motion may be amended, except that the only amendments to the proposed amendment that are in order are such as are covered by notices which have been given. [See "Rules of Order Revised," page 272.] For example, take Model By-Laws II, page 386: suppose that notice has been given to amend these by-laws by striking out section 1, Art. III, "The membership of this club shall be limited to six hundred active and fifty associate members." Since the effect of this amendment if adopted would be to make the membership of the club unlimited, sufficient notice has been given to cover amendments to the proposed amendments to any extent from that of the existing limits to that of an unlimited membership. It would, therefore, be in order to move the adoption of the following substitute for the pending amendment, "that the by-laws be amended by substituting for section 1, Art. III, the following: 'The membership of this club shall be limited to one thousand active and one hundred associate members.' " This amendment to the proposed amendment to the by-laws is an amendment of the first degree and is subject to amendments of the second degree provided they are covered by sufficient notice, and in putting to vote is treated as a substitute motion. It takes only a majority vote to adopt the subsidiary motion to substitute, but it requires a two-thirds vote to adopt the proposed amendment to the by-laws as amended. [See also Ques. 93, page 446.] When the amendments of which notice has been given are to be considered, those made to perfect the existing by-law must be disposed of before the chair can put the question on the motion to strike out the by-law. If a revision committee submits a substitute for the existing by-laws, and notice has also been given of specific amendments to the by-laws, the latter must be acted upon before the substitute by-laws are considered.

Committee on Revision of By-Laws. When a society appoints a committee on revision of the by-laws, that in itself is sufficient notice that the committee may submit an entirely new set of by-laws, and therefore members should be prepared for any kind of change. The proposed revision should be printed or typewritten, so that at least a few copies can be distributed among the interested members. In large societies they should be printed and distributed in advance. The restrictions imposed upon amending ordinary amendments proposed to by-laws do not apply to amending a revised set of by-laws submitted by a committee on revision. The proposed new by-laws before being adopted may be perfected by amendments with all the freedom allowed when by-laws are originally adopted. The old by-laws are not pending and therefore are not open to subsidiary amendments. When the chairman of the committee reads the proposed revised by-laws he should say, "By direction of the committee on revision of the by-laws, I move to substitute these for the existing by-laws." The president states the question on the substitute, and then directs the first by-law or paragraph of the substitute to be read, and asks if any amendments to it are proposed. When it has been suitably amended, which requires only a majority vote, the next paragraph or by-law is read and it is open to amendment, and so on to the end. When no further amendments are proposed, the president puts the question on adopting the substitute. If the motion is carried by a two-thirds vote, the substitute immediately becomes the by-laws of the society. No vote should be taken on adopting the separate paragraphs or by-laws.

If the report of a committee on revision is due at a certain meeting, that is sufficient notice of the amendment so that it can be adopted at that meeting, provided only notice of the amendment is required. But if the committee is not under obligation to report at a certain meeting, notice must be given, in accordance with the by-laws, before the report of the committee can be acted upon. Every requirement of the by-laws for their amendment must be strictly complied with, the same as if the amendment had been proposed by a member instead of by a committee. If the existing by-laws require the proposed amendment to be submitted at the time the notice is given, the amendment (substitute) cannot be acted upon when reported by the committee, but must lie over until the next meeting. Of course it may be informally considered without voting on it.

Notice of Proposed Amendment. Giving notice of a proposed amendment to the by-laws is incidental to the business of the assembly, and may to a certain extent interrupt business, if necessary, in order to insure its being given. The notice may be given even after the assembly has voted to adjourn, provided the chair has not declared the assembly adjourned. It should not interrupt one while speaking, but if the member is unable to obtain the floor he may say, "Mr. Chairman, I rise to give notice of an amendment to the by-laws," provided he does it before the one to whom the floor has been assigned has commenced speaking. The chairman then directs him to read it, which he does, and hands it to the chairman, who reads it again. Or the member may hand the written notice to the secretary, whose duty it is to read it, or to hand it to the chairman, who will at a suitable time read it. The notice may be in this form:

Amendment to the By-Laws proposed by A. J. Lawton, Jan. 14, 19—.
Substitute for Sec. 2, Art. XII, the following: "Sec. 2 ——."
(*Signed*)   A. J. Lawton,
                    B. C. Bostwick.

The proposed amendment should be signed by two members because it is virtually a motion that the amendment be adopted, and therefore requires a second. Some organizations require as many as a dozen signatures to a proposed amendment to the constitution or by-laws. The title may be endorsed on the back of the paper and only the amendment and signatures be placed on the face of the sheet.

In an ordinary society, at the next meeting, when unfinished business is reached, the chairman says: "The next business in order is the consideration of the amendment of the by-laws proposed by Mr. Lawton at the last meeting. The amendment is as follows: "Substitute for Sec. 2, Art. XII, the following: [The chairman reads the new section.] The question is now on the adoption of the substitute." If no other notice of amendment to the section to be struck out has been made, the chair continues, "Are you ready for the question?" The proposed amendment is now open to debate, and the section to be inserted is open to limited amendment as heretofore described, after which the chair puts the question. If the amendment is adopted, it becomes a part of the by-laws and goes into effect immediately. If notice was given of other amendments to the section to be struck out, the chair states the questions on them first in the order in which they were proposed, and after they have been disposed of he states the question on the substitute.

When no further amendments are proposed, the chair reads first the present by-law and then the substitute as amended, and puts the question thus: "The question is on substituting the proposed section for the present one. As many as are in favor of the substitute will rise," etc.

It will be noticed that this main motion to substitute or amend in case of by-laws requires a two-thirds vote, while the subsidiary motion to substitute or amend never requires more than a majority vote. Furthermore, only a single vote is taken in this case, in which the substitute is a main motion, because the effect of that vote is to place the new section in the place in the adopted by-laws previously occupied by the section that has been struck out. The vote on amending the by-laws should always be counted, and the number on each side recorded in the minutes. Should the sum of the affirmative and the negative votes not equal the quorum, the minutes should state that a quorum was present. More than usual care should be taken, when the by-laws are amended, to have the record show that the amendment has been legally adopted, every required step having been taken.

The requirements for amending by-laws (including constitutions and rules of order) cannot be evaded by using some other word than "amend." Any motion that has the effect of inserting or adding a word, or of striking out a word, in the by-laws, is a motion to amend the by-laws, and is subject to every rule affecting amendments to the by-laws, regardless of whether the result is accomplished by adopting the motion to rescind, to repeal, to annul, to substitute, to adopt a revision, or any other motion.

AMENDING STANDING RULES

Standing Rules may be amended by a majority vote if notice of the proposed amendment was given at the previous meeting, or they may be amended without notice by a two-thirds vote, or by a vote of a majority of the membership of the society or convention.

CHAPTER XXXVI

SUGGESTIONS TO COMMITTEES ON BY-LAWS

A COMMITTEE to prepare a set of by-laws usually should be large, and should include, in addition to the most judicious persons interested, all those who are likely to consume much time in discussing the by-laws. By this means the thorough discussions that should and will require many hours, and probably days, will be confined to the committee. After this large committee has had one or two conferences on the subject, it should appoint a subcommittee of two or three to make a draft of the by-laws. This sub-committee will usually find it best to appoint one of its members to draw up a set of by-laws, which it discusses and amends, and then reports to the full committee. The committee, after discussion and amendment, reports the by-laws to the society or the mass meeting that appointed it. In "Rules of Order Revised," pages 287, 288, is given the method of making the report of the committee, and the method of its amendment and adoption by the assembly. The entire procedure in the organization of a society is given in "Rules of Order Revised," pages 284-291.

All members of the committee should read this chapter and the next carefully, noticing in this chapter especially the General Plan of By-Laws and the Principles of Interpretation. In the next chapter are given three models that will be of great assistance to the committee. The first one is very simple; the second is a more complicated case of a local club, and is completely filled out for a hypothetical case to show how the blanks left in the other models should be filled; the third model is for a state or national federation of local clubs. The Additional Suggestions following each of the three models should be read carefully. In addition to these helps, the committee should procure copies of the by-laws of similar societies and copy such good features as they find. It is better to take a great deal of time in preparation of the by-laws, and to have them thoroughly discussed before their adoption, in order to avoid the necessity of frequently amending them.

The chairman of the committee reporting by-laws should carefully explain every section, and call special attention to any change in the custom or previous by-laws affected by the proposed by-laws or amendments. No society should adopt by-laws, or amendments to by-laws, that the members cannot interpret.

When a rough draft of the by-laws has been prepared, it should be carefully criticized to see that there is no ambiguity in the statements. Such an expression as "holding office" applies to managers or directors as well as to officers, and regardless of whether they are called officers or not. Even if the by-laws are so worded as not to call the directors "officers," the expression, "No member shall hold office longer than four years consecutively," applies to the office of director, so that service as director is counted also. If it is not intended to include service as director, the word "member" should be replaced by "officer," and then it is clear that the directors are not included, because in the supposed case they are not called officers. The better plan, however, is to class the directors as officers, as is done in the Models for By-Laws given hereafter; and if it is desired not to include the directors in a certain rule, the expression, "the officers, exclusive of the directors," should be used. The use of the expression "active officers" is objectionable unless it is always used whenever these officers are referred to. If that term is used, the word "officer" when used alone must include "honorary officers," who are really not officers, but must be included as officers if the real officers are called the active officers, since the only other possible kind of officer is an honorary officer. Thus, when the by-laws in the article on Officers provide for active and honorary officers, and state that no officer shall serve longer than four years consecutively, the honorary officers hold their office for only four years instead of for life. [See Honorary Members and Officers, page 331.] So with members: if active and associate members are the only ones referred to in the article on Members, the word "members" applies only to them, even though elsewhere honorary members are provided for. The latter are not members, just as honorary officers are not officers, of the society, and should never be referred to as such. The title is purely complimentary. If it is desired to provide for honorary members and officers, the wording should show clearly that the compliment carries with it only a title.

A committee appointed to revise existing by-laws should follow a plan similar to the one heretofore described. It should be careful to see that everything relating to a subject is placed in the same or adjacent articles. Thus, everything relating to the requirements for membership should be placed in Article III in a set of by-laws based on the models in the next chapter. By this means the chances for conflict between different by-laws will be diminished. There should be nothing in the by-laws the effect of which the committee does not understand. When reporting the revision, the committee chairman should fully explain every section, and also explain the changes that will result from the changes proposed. The society should know not only the words of the amendments proposed, but also what changes from their former customs will result if the amendments, or revision, are adopted.

In drawing up or revising by-laws the following General Plan will be found helpful.

GENERAL PLAN OF BY-LAWS

NAME. The first article should state the name of the organization.

OBJECT. The second article should state its object. In preparing this article it should be borne in mind that, as it requires a two-thirds vote to prevent the introduction of a resolution relating to the objects of the society, so it requires a two-thirds vote to permit the introduction of a resolution having no relation to the objects.

MEMBERS. In the next article the different classes of members should be specified and the distinction between them explained. The method of uniting with the organization should be clearly described.—It should be stated that the initiation fee must be paid before the privileges of membership can be exercised. The time for payment of the annual dues should always be stated, and the treasurer or the corresponding secretary should be required to notify delinquents, who should be given a reasonable specified time for payment of the dues. If the arrears are not paid within the specified time after notice has been given, the member should be dropped from the roll without any action of the club.—If it is desired to provide for honorary members, this should be done in a separate section of this article, and it should be clearly shown that the title does not confer membership. The title of Honorary

Member should never be conferred except at the annual meeting, and by a vote at least as large as three-fourths of the voting members present.

OFFICERS. In the next article should be given a list of the officers, and the method of their election should be prescribed. If the time of beginning is not specified, the term of office begins the instant the chair declares the officer elected. If the term is stated simply as "two years," at the end of two years the term expires, whether or not a successor has been elected. By using the expression, "or [or and] until his successor is elected," the officer holds over until his successor is elected, in case of a failure to elect a successor at the annual meeting. Whether the expression "or until his successor is elected" should be used or "and until," etc., depends upon what the society wishes. If "or" is used, the society has a right to declare an office vacant by the same vote that is required to rescind any action taken. [See page 110.] If "and" is used, the society cannot vacate an office except by a trial on charges preferred, or else by amending the by-laws so as to legislate the incumbent out of office. It is scarcely to be conceived that a society would declare an office vacant unless the officer has grossly neglected his duty or abused his trust, and in such case the society should not be put to the trouble of a trial.— In some organizations it is found best to elect one half of the officers in the odd years and the other half in the even years. This has the advantage of conservatism, only half of the officers, and therefore of the Executive Board, being changed each year. On the other hand, it prevents a new administration's making such thorough reforms as are possible when all the officers are elected at the same time.—If it is desired to elect by a plurality vote, it must be so stated in this article, as a majority vote is always understood when there is no rule to the contrary. It is doubtful whether a plurality vote should ever be allowed to elect in a local society. Adjourned meetings can easily be held and the balloting be continued until all the officers are elected. If it is desired to avoid balloting when there is but one candidate for an office, it must be provided for in this article, since otherwise the society cannot, even by unanimous consent, do away with the formal ballot. [See page 157.] To accomplish this, insert after the word "ballot," Section 3, Article IV, page 387, the words "except when there is but one candidate for an office," or whatever provision is desired. Or, the following sentence may be added to the article: "If there is only one candidate, by unanimous consent the secretary may be instructed to cast the ballot." There is no need to state in the by-laws the duties of officers, except such as are peculiar to the society. They are fully stated in the parliamentary authority adopted by the society, to which reference should be made as in Article IV, Section 2, page 384.

MEETINGS. In specifying the time for the meetings, the days of the week should be used, never those of the month. Provision should usually be made for changing the day of the meeting in an emergency, such as when it falls on a holiday; for calling a special meeting; and for the quorum, the proper size of which is discussed in the article on Quorum, page 356.

BOARD. Most societies need a Board, the duties and powers of which are fully explained under Boards, page 247, and in Article VI, pages 387, 393.

EXECUTIVE COMMITTEE. If it is desired that there should be an Executive Committee, it should be provided for, because unless authorized by the society the Board has no power to appoint one. Delegated power cannot be delegated unless so authorized by the principal.

COMMITTEES. This article should provide for all the standing committees that will certainly be required. It should also provide for the appointment of such additional standing committees as experience has shown are needed. If it is desired to place in the hands of the president the appointment of such committees as are authorized by the society or the board, it should be so stated in this article.

DEPARTMENTS. If the organization desires to have different departments, they should be provided for in a separate article, as in Article VIII, page 388.

PARLIAMENTARY AUTHORITY. Every society should adopt some parliamentary authority, so as to avoid as much as possible doubt as to the rules under which it is working. "Robert's Rules of Order Revised" has been inserted in the models, because the name has been so frequently inaccurately printed in by-laws, and because the author wishes to call attention to the fact that it is the only one of his works that should be adopted by a society as a parliamentary authority. While all his three books are in harmony, "Rules of Order Revised" is the only one specially prepared for this purpose.

AMENDING THE BY-LAWS. By-laws should be carefully drawn up and seldom amended. Never use any other term for changing the by-laws except "amend" or "revise," as they include all changes. Of course, a revision is an amendment. A two-thirds vote should be required for amendment, and it is well to require the amendment to be submitted in writing at the previous meeting. When the amendment has been taken up for consideration, it may be postponed to another meeting, or it may have any other subsidiary motion applied to it. Amending by-laws is fully treated in Chapter XXXV.

SOME PRINCIPLES OF INTERPRETATION OF BY-LAWS AND OTHER RULES

The following principles of interpretation should be kept in mind while preparing by-laws and other rules, as well as when interpreting them.

(1) *Each society must decide for itself the meaning of its by-laws.* They should be carefully worded. When the meaning is clear, the society, even by a unanimous vote, cannot change that meaning. Where a by-law is ambiguous it must be interpreted, if possible, in harmony with the other by-laws. If this is not possible, it should be interpreted in accordance with the intention of the society at the time the by-law was adopted, as far as this can be ascertained. A majority vote is all that is necessary to decide the question. The ambiguous or doubtful expression should be amended as soon as practicable.

(2) *When a by-law or a clause is susceptible of two meanings, one of which conflicts with or renders absurd another by-law or clause, and the other meaning does not, the latter must be taken as the true meaning.*

(3) *A general statement or rule is always of less authority than, and yields to, a specific statement or rule.*

It is impracticable, every time a rule or principle is referred to, to state it in detail with all its limitations. Sometimes it is stated or referred to in general terms, and these general statements are seldom strictly correct. To ascertain the exact details it is necessary to examine the specific statement of the rule or principle that professedly gives the details.   For instance: when the statement is made, on page 153, that an appeal that does not adhere to the pending question may have any subsidiary motion, except to amend, applied to it, it is not necessary to except also the motion to postpone indefinitely, because in the article on Postpone Indefinitely it is expressly stated that it can be applied to nothing but a main motion.   Therefore, whenever it is stated in regard to any motion, except a main one, that any or all of the subsidiary motions may be applied to it, the subsidiary motion to postpone indefinitely is excepted.   No one has a right to quote a general statement as of any authority against a specific statement.

(4) *Whenever the by-laws authorize specifically certain things, other things of the same class are, by implication, prohibited.*

It is to be assumed that nothing is placed in the by-laws without some reason for it, and there can be no possible reason for authorizing certain things to be done that can be done unquestionably without the authorization of the by-laws, unless the object is to specify the things of this class that may be done, none others being permitted.   Thus, when the by-laws state that a certain number of honorary presidents and vice-presidents may be elected, it virtually prohibits the election of any other honorary officers.

(5) *A permission granting certain privileges carries with it a right to a part of the privilege, and a prohibition of greater privilege.*

If a man has permission to take a bushel of apples from an orchard, he has permission to take only a single apple if he prefers it, but he is prohibited from taking two bushels.   If in debate a member is permitted to speak ten minutes, he is permitted to speak two minutes, but is prohibited from speaking twelve minutes.

(6) *A prohibition or limitation prohibits everything greater than what is prohibited, or that goes beyond the limitation: it permits what is less than the limitation, and things of the same class that are not mentioned in the prohibition or limitation, and that are evidently not improper.*

If the by-laws prohibit a member from walking in the hall during debate, this prohibition carries with it the prohibition of his running under the same circumstances.   If the rules prohibit a member's speaking three times on the same question, it prohibits his speaking four times and allows his speaking twice. If the by-laws prohibit their amendment except in a specified way, they prohibit their being rescinded or replaced by a substitute, except in a way specified for its amendment. If the change of a single word is prohibited unless certain steps have been taken, certainly the change of a paragraph, or of the entire by-laws, requires these same steps to be taken. If it requires certain notice and a two-thirds vote to strike out a word, it requires the same notice and vote to strike out the entire by-laws, that is, to repeal or rescind them, or to substitute a new set for the old ones, which is really a motion to strike out the old by-laws and insert the new ones. If the rules prohibit a child from entering an art gallery, children are also prohibited, and adults are permitted to enter. If, in a park, signs are put up prohibiting persons from walking on certain grounds, it is equivalent to granting permission to walk elsewhere in the park.

(7) *The imposition by the by-laws of a definite penalty for a certain offense in effect prohibits the increase or diminution of the penalty.*

If the by-laws state that a member who has been dropped for non-payment of dues can be restored to membership upon the payment of all arrears of dues, he cannot be restored on any milder terms, nor can severer penalties be imposed. If a definite fine is imposed for failure to perform a certain duty, the society can neither increase nor diminish the fine. If it is desired to allow the society to diminish the penalty, the by-law must not make it definite.

(8) *When the by-laws use a general term and also two or more specific terms that are included under the general one, any rule in which the general term only is used applies to all the specific terms.*

If the by-laws state that members may be active, associate, or honorary, then whenever the term "member" is used it applies to all three classes of members. If, under the head of Members, it is stated that they may be either active or associate members, the term "member" applies only to those two classes of members, even though elsewhere honorary members are provided for. When the by-laws call its real officers "active officers," and provide for electing also "honorary officers," and also provide that "all officers" shall hold office for one year, this provision applies to honorary as well as to active officers. If, however, the word "active" is not used to describe the real officers, the word "officer" applies only to them, and not to the honorary officers. Honorary membership or office is not real office or membership, and is not included in those terms unless the by-laws are so worded as to force it. The word "members" or "officers" should be used to describe only real members or real officers.

CHAPTER XXXVII

MODELS OF BY-LAWS AND STANDING RULES

MODEL I

BY-LAWS OF THE —— SOCIETY

ARTICLE I.

Name.
The name of this organization shall be the ——.

ARTICLE II.

Object.
The object of this organization shall be ——.

ARTICLE III.

Members.
Section I.   Any person who is interested in the object of this organization shall be eligible to membership.   The name of an applicant for membership must be presented to the organization by a member, and if the applicant receives a majority vote in the affirmative, he shall be declared elected.
Section 2.   The dues of this organization shall be ——, payable in advance on or before — of each year.

ARTICLE IV.

Officers.
Section 1.   The officers of this organization shall be a President, a Vice-President, a Secretary, and a Treasurer.   These officers shall be elected at each annual meeting, and shall hold office for one year or until their successors are elected.
Section 2.   The officers of the organization shall perform the duties prescribed for them in the parliamentary authority adopted by this organization.

ARTICLE V.

Meetings.
Section 1.   Regular meetings shall be held on the — of each month, unless otherwise ordered by the organization.
Section 2.   The regular meeting in — shall be known as the annual meet-

ing, and shall be for the purpose of electing officers and for any other business that may arise.

Section 3. Special meetings may be called by the President, and shall be called upon the request of — members.

Section 4. — members shall constitute a quorum at any meeting of the organization.

ARTICLE VI.

Parliamentary Authority.

The rules contained in "Robert's Rules of Order Revised" shall govern this organization in all cases to which they are applicable, and in which they are not inconsistent with these by-laws.

ARTICLE VII.

Amendment to the By-Laws.

These by-laws may be amended at any regular meeting of the organization by a two-thirds vote, provided notice was given at the previous meeting.

Additional Suggestions Applying to First Model

These by-laws are for the simplest form of a local society.

Article III prescribes the simplest method of receiving members in which a vote of the society is required. If it is desired to receive members without a vote's being taken on their reception, the last sentence of Section 1 should be omitted, and the first should be continued thus, "and may become a member by presenting his name to the secretary and paying the dues." Every society has some expenses, and should require some dues, however small. The time before which the annual dues are to be paid should always be stated in the by-laws. If an initiation fee is to be required, it should be so stated, as in the second model, Article III, Section 3, page 386.

Article IV provides for four officers, which may be reduced to three by having the secretary perform the duties of treasurer where there is but little money to handle. In this case, instead of "a Secretary and a Treasurer," the by-law should read "and a Secretary who shall also perform the duties of a Treasurer," or "and a Secretary-Treasurer."

Article V. The blank in Section 1 should be filled thus, "second Monday," or "second and fourth Mondays." The date of the month should never be used, because the meetings should be held on the same day of the week. If the meetings are to be held weekly, strike out "on the — of each month" and insert "every Monday." If the meetings are to be held only in certain months of the year, insert before "unless" the words, "from October 1 to June 15," using the proper dates. The blank in Section 3 should be filled with a number not much less than the quorum, which is stated in the next section.

MODEL II

BY-LAWS
OF
THE WOMAN'S CLUB OF ELYRIA

ARTICLE I.

Name.

The name of this organization shall be the Woman's Club of Elyria.

ARTICLE II.

Object.

The object of this club shall be the mutual improvement of its members in literature, art, and science; civic work; and the discussion of the vital interests of the day.

ARTICLE III.

Members.

Section 1. The membership of this club shall be limited to six hundred active and fifty associate members.

Section 2. Any woman residing in Elyria shall be eligible to membership in the club. An applicant for membership, either active or associate, must present her application in writing, signed by two members of the club, to the recording secretary, who shall notify the club at its next regular meeting that such application has been made. The executive board shall then vote upon the application at its next regular meeting. If the applicant receives an affirmative vote of a majority of the executive board, she shall be declared elected a member of the club upon the payment of the initiation fee.

Section 3. The initiation fee for all members shall be five dollars. The annual dues shall be three dollars for active members, and five dollars for associate members. Dues are payable in advance on or before November 1. The treasurer shall notify members two months in arrears, and those whose dues are not paid within sixty days thereafter shall be dropped automatically from the roll of membership of the club.

Section 4. Associate members shall have all the privileges of the club excepting those of voting and holding office, and shall not be required to take part in the program.

Section 5. Any member desiring to resign from the club shall present her resignation in writing to the corresponding secretary, who shall present it to the executive board for action. No member's resignation shall be accepted until her dues are paid.

Section 6. The title of honorary member may be conferred for life upon a woman by a two-thirds vote by ballot of the voting members present at any annual meeting. The title of honorary member shall carry with it none of the obligations of the club, but shall entitle the holder to all of the privileges except those of making motions, of voting, and of holding office.

ARTICLE IV.

Officers.

Section 1. The officers of the club shall be a President, a First Vice-President, a Second Vice-President, a Recording Secretary, a Corresponding

Secretary, a Treasurer, and four Directors. These officers shall perform the duties prescribed by these by-laws and by the parliamentary authority adopted by the club.

Section 2. At the regular meeting held the third Monday of May a Nominating Committee of five members shall be elected by the club. It shall be the duty of this committee to nominate candidates for the offices to be filled at the annual meeting.

Section 3. The President, the Second Vice-President, the Recording Secretary, and two of the Directors shall be elected at the annual meeting held in the even years, and the First Vice-President, the Corresponding Secretary, the Treasurer, and two Directors shall be elected at the annual meeting held the odd years. All officers shall be elected by ballot to serve for two years or until their successors are elected, and their term of office shall begin at the close of the annual meeting at which they are elected.

Section 4. No member shall hold more than one office at any one time, and no officer shall be eligible to two consecutive terms in the same office.

ARTICLE V.

Meetings.

Section 1. The regular meetings of the club shall be held on the first and the third Mondays of the month, from October to June inclusive, unless otherwise ordered by the club or the executive board.

Section 2. The meetings held the third Monday of the month shall be known as business meetings. At the regular meetings, held the first Monday of the month, no business other than is provided for in the program shall be transacted, unless consent is given by a two-thirds vote.

Section 3. The regular meeting the third Monday in June shall be known as the annual meeting, and shall be for the purpose of electing officers, receiving reports of officers and committees, and for any other business that may arise.

Section 4. Special meetings may be called by the executive board, and shall be called upon the written request of twenty members of the club.

Section 5. Twenty-five members of the club shall constitute a quorum.

ARTICLE VI.

The Executive Board.

Section 1. The officers of the club and the chairmen of departments shall constitute the Executive Board.

Section 2. The Executive Board shall have general supervision of the affairs of the club between its business meetings, fix the hour and place of meetings, and perform such other duties as are specified in these by-laws. It is subject to the orders of the club, and none of its acts shall conflict with action taken by the club.

Section 3. Regular meetings of the Executive Board shall be held once a month from September to June inclusive. Special meetings may be called by the president, and shall be called upon the request of three members of the board.

ARTICLE VII.

Committees.

Section 1. A Program Committee of five members shall be appointed by the president as soon as convenient after each annual meeting, whose duty shall be to arrange a program for the club and to submit the same to the executive board at their regular meeting in September for approval.

Section 2. An Auditing Committee of two shall be appointed by the president at the last business meeting prior to each annual meeting, to audit the treasurer's accounts and to report at the annual meeting.

Section 3. Such other committees shall be appointed by the president as the club or the executive board shall from time to time deem necessary to carry on the work of the club.

ARTICLE VIII.
Departments.

Section 1. There shall be the following departments: Civic, Literature and Arts, Dramatic, and Musical. Such other departments may be created by the club as it may deem necessary.

Section 2. A department is authorized to adopt rules for the transaction of its business, provided they do not conflict with the by-laws of the club. A department may, in its rules, provide for dues for its own use.

Section 3. Each department shall hold an annual meeting, prior to the close of the club year. At this meeting the department shall elect a chairman and such other officers as are provided for in its rules.

Section 4. Each department shall submit a plan of work for the current year for the approval of the executive board at or before the regular meeting of the board in October.

Section 5. Any department entering into a project for the purpose of raising money for its own use shall pay into the club treasury not less than ten per cent. and not more than twenty-five per cent. of net proceeds of that project. The amount shall be determined by the executive board. This percentage does not apply to money raised from dues.

ARTICLE IX.
Parliamentary Authority.

The rules contained in ''Robert's Rules of Order Revised'' shall govern the club in all cases to which they are applicable and in which they are not inconsistent with these by-laws.

ARTICLE X.
Amendment to By-Laws.

These by-laws may be amended at any regular business meeting of the club by a two-thirds vote, provided the amendment has been submitted in writing at the previous regular business meeting.

Additional Suggestions Applying to Second Model

The second model takes a representative case of a local society with active and associate members and a limited membership; with provisions for protecting the club from undesirable applications for membership; and with an executive board empowered to transact most of the business of the club, thus relieving the society from the necessity of attending to this business. In these by-laws names and dates are filled in.

Article III. Members. This article provides for both active and associate members, limits the number of each, and gives in detail the steps necessary to be taken in order to become a member. Like the other articles in this model, it is filled in for a hypothetical case. This article should be adapted to each society using it as a guide. Section 2 provides that an application for membership shall be endorsed by two members and handed to the recording secretary. The secretary notifies the society of the application at the next regular meeting and then hands the application to the executive board, who must act on the case at its next regular meeting. Members thus learn of the application, so that they may have ample time to present to the executive board any objections they have to the reception of the applicant. An affirmative vote of a majority of the entire board is required to receive a member. This vote in some societies should be larger. Where a board elects the members, the by-laws should require the vote to be a certain part of the entire board. Section 4 states the limitation in the privileges, and the duties of, associate members, which would vary in different societies. Section 5 provides for the resignation of a member. If a member has paid his dues and there are no charges against him, or about to be preferred against him, his resignation must be accepted unless he withdraws it. [See Resignations, page 332.]

Article IV. Officers. Section 1 specifies the officers, among whom are four directors. The directors, or managers, as they are variously called, hold very important offices, as is shown by the power given them in Article VI, and it is better to classify them as officers. The only additional duties beyond what are specified in the parliamentary authority adopted by the club mentioned in this model are those assigned to them in Article VI as members of the executive board. Section 2 provides for the election one month before the annual meeting of a nominating committee. According to this model, this committee is elected by the club, since this is the fairest way where it is practicable, which it usually is in local societies. The wording of the section leaves it to the discretion of the committee whether to nominate more than one candidate for an office. If it is desired to limit the committee to a single candidate for each office, it is necessary to strike out the words "candidates for the offices" and insert "a candidate for each office." The expression "nominate candidates for the offices to be filled," etc., applies to directors or managers, whether they are called "officers" or not. Section 4 provides that no member shall hold more than one office at the same time. If the by-laws do not provide a limit, a member may hold all the offices to which he is elected. With this limitation, a member who is elected to more than one office, if present, chooses which office he will accept; if he is absent from the election, the society by a majority vote decides which office he shall fill, voting first on the highest office. It is provided that no officer shall be elected to fill two consecutive terms in the same office. This is a good rule in some societies and a bad one in others. If an officer has served more than half a term, he is considered as having served that term and would be ineligible for the next term. No provision is made in these by-laws for filling vacancies in office, because the society has monthly business meetings at which vacancies should be filled.

Article V. Meetings. Section 1 provides for the regular meetings to be held on a certain day of the week, and provision is made for changing the day of the meeting in an emergency by a vote of the society or the executive board. Without such a provision there is no way to make such a change. Section 2 provides that one of the meetings each month shall be known as the business meeting, at which business may be transacted; and at the other meeting no business that is not on the program shall be transacted, unless consent is given by a two-thirds vote. In such a society with an executive board there is no necessity for, or advantage in, allowing business to be attended to more than once a month. Section 3 provides for the annual meeting to be held at the close of the club year, which allows time for the new administration to get into working order before the club year begins in October. Section 4 provides that special meetings may be called by the executive committee, and shall be called at the request of a certain number of members, which number should always be about the same as the quorum in a society. Section 5 provides a quorum which is only four per cent. of the possible membership. [See Quorum, page 356, for the proper size of a quorum.]

Article VI. Executive Board. Section 1 makes the officers, which include the directors, and the chairmen of the different departments, constitute the executive board. This makes a board of at least fourteen, of which a quorum is eight. Section 2 gives the board ample power to attend to all the business that the club does not take care of itself at its monthly business meetings. By this means the club is not obliged to attend to any business except in regard to its program and the annual meeting, while it may take up any business in regard to its work that it desires to act upon itself. Since the board has "general supervision of the affairs of the club" and is "subject to the orders of the club," it follows that where no orders are given the board may, and should, attend to all business of the club requiring immediate attention. This covers the expenditure of funds, but it does not authorize the board to incur a debt. Nor is the board authorized to forestall action by the society in a matter that can wait until the next business meeting of the society. Where a club wishes to turn over all of its business to the board, all the words in this section after the expression "affairs of the club" should be struck out.

Article VII. Committees. All committees that it is known will be needed should be specified in this article. Section 1 provides for a program committee and designates the time that it shall present to the executive board a program for its approval. When approved, the program should be printed, usually under the direction of the program committee. Another method that would be preferred by many clubs is to have the program committee appointed in the winter, with instructions to report at the next business meeting the outlines of two programs on different subjects for the club to choose between. When the club has decided upon the subject, the committee completes the program under any instructions the club may choose to give, and submits the complete program for the approval of the club at its annual meeting, or at the meeting preceding. When approved, it is printed and distributed before the opening of the session in October. Section 2 provides for an auditing committee to be appointed a month before the annual meeting to audit the treasurer's report for the year and report at the annual meeting. The treasurer's report should always be audited before the annual meeting. Section 3 empowers the president to appoint all committees that have been authorized by a vote of the club or the board. He cannot appoint any others.

Article VIII. Departments. Section 1 provides for four departments, and allows the club to form others as they are deemed necessary. As the section is worded, only a majority vote is required to form a new department.

MODEL III

BY-LAWS OF THE
FEDERATION OF CIVIC CLUBS OF THE
STATE OF ——.

ARTICLE I.

Name.
The name of this organization shall be The Federation of Civic Clubs of the State of ——.

ARTICLE II.

Object.
The object of the federation shall be to unite the influence and endeavors of the civic clubs of the state of ——; to promote legislative, civic, educational, moral, and social measures that are conducive to the welfare of the state; and to compare methods of study and work.

ARTICLE III.

Members.
Section 1. Any civic club in the state of —— shall be eligible for membership in the federation. Application for membership must be made to the membership committee, who may act upon the application by mail. A unanimous vote of the entire committee shall elect or reject an applicant for membership in the federation. If the committee fails to agree, the application shall be referred to the board of directors for final action. It shall require a majority vote of the entire board to admit the applicant to membership. The corresponding secretary shall notify each newly elected club of its admission to the federation, enclosing a statement of the amount of the dues, which shall be payable within sixty days.

Section 2. The amount of annual dues payable to the federation shall vary according to the number of members composing the various clubs that are members of the federation. Clubs having less than fifty members shall pay annual dues of five dollars ($5); those having fifty or more members, but less than one hundred members, seven dollars and fifty cents ($7.50); those having one hundred or more members, but less than two hundred members, ten dollars ($10); those having two hundred or more members, but less than three hundred members, twelve dollars and fifty cents ($12.50); those having three hundred or more members, but less than four hundred members, fifteen dollars ($15); those having four hundred or more members, seventeen dollars and fifty cents ($17.50).

Section 3. Bills for dues shall be sent by the treasurer during March of each year to all clubs that are members of the federation, and are payable on or before the next October first. Clubs in arrears for dues shall not be entitled to be represented at meetings of the federation, and if their dues are not paid by the following March first they shall be dropped from the federation.

ARTICLE IV.

Officers.
Section 1. The officers of the federation shall be a President, a Vice-President, a Recording Secretary, a Corresponding Secretary, a Treasurer, and ten Directors. These officers, with the exception of the directors, shall be elected at the annual meeting held in the odd years, and shall hold office for two years or until their successors are elected. Five of the directors shall be elected at the annual meeting in each odd year, and shall hold office

for four years or until their successors are elected. All of the officers shall be elected by ballot.

Section 2. A nominating committee consisting of — members shall be elected at each annual meeting, whose duty it shall be to nominate a candidate for each office to be filled at the next annual meeting. The committee shall send a report of these nominations to the corresponding secretary, who shall send a copy to each club in the federation at least thirty days before the election. Additional nominations may be made from the floor, and voting shall not be limited to the nominees.

Section 3. The duties of the various officers shall be such as are specified in these by-laws and in the parliamentary authority adopted by the federation.

Section 4. A vacancy occurring in an office shall be filled until the next annual meeting by the board of directors. The election shall be by ballot. If proper notice of the election has been given a majority vote shall elect; otherwise an affirmative vote of a majority of the entire board shall be necessary for an election.

Section 5. The title Honorary President may be conferred for life upon a person at any annual meeting by a three-fourths vote, which shall be taken by ballot unless by unanimous consent the ballot is dispensed with. The title of honorary president shall carry with it none of the obligations of the federation, but shall entitle the holder to all of the privileges except those of making motions, of voting, and of holding office.

ARTICLE V.

Meetings.

Section 1. A regular meeting of the federation shall be held annually in October, the date and place to be fixed by the board of directors. A notice of this meeting shall be sent by the corresponding secretary to all clubs that are members of the federation at least thirty days before the meeting.

Section 2. The federated clubs shall be entitled to be represented at the meetings of the federation by delegates elected by the individual clubs in proportion to the number of members as follows: Clubs of less than fifty members, one delegate; of fifty or more members, but less than one hundred, two delegates; of one hundred or more, but less than two hundred, three delegates; of two hundred or more, but less than three hundred, four delegates; of three hundred or more, but less than four hundred, five delegates; of four hundred or more, six delegates. No club shall be represented by more than six delegates, and no delegate shall represent more than one club.

Section 3. The meetings of the federation shall be open to all members of the federated clubs. The privilege of making motions, debating, and voting shall be limited to the officers of the federation, the delegates from the federated clubs, and the chairmen of the standing and special committees that have been authorized by these by-laws, or the federation, or the board of directors, and have been instructed to report at the meeting. A voting member shall have but one vote, although entitled to vote in either of several capacities.

Section 4. One hundred voting members present at any meeting of the federation shall constitute a quorum.

ARTICLE VI.

Board of Directors.

Section 1. The officers of the federation shall constitute the board of directors.

Section 2. The board of directors shall have all power and authority over the affairs of the federation during the interim between the meetings of the federation, excepting that of modifying any action taken by the federation.

Section 3. The officers of the federation shall ex-officio be the officers of the board of directors.

Section 4. Regular meetings of the board of directors shall be held immediately before and after the annual meeting, and in February and June, the place and date to be fixed by the president.

Section 5. Special meetings of the board of directors may be called by the president, and shall be called upon the request of five members of the board.

Section 6. The board of directors is authorized to adopt rules for the transaction of its business, provided they do not conflict with these by-laws.

Section 7. The board of directors shall make an annual report to the federation.

ARTICLE VII.

Executive Committee.

Section 1. The board of directors, at its first meeting following the annual meeting of the federation, is authorized to elect from its own body three members, who, together with the president and the recording secretary, shall constitute an Executive Committee.

Section 2. The board of directors may authorize the Executive Committee to perform between the meetings of the board such duties as the board may from time to time deem expedient.

Section 3. The Executive Committee shall meet at the call of the president, or upon the request of three of its members. It shall make a complete report at each meeting of the board.

ARTICLE VIII.

Committees.

Section 1. A Membership Committee of five, of whom the corresponding secretary shall be one, shall be appointed annually by the president. It shall be the duty of this committee to act upon all applications for membership as provided in these by-laws.

Section 2. The president shall appoint annually five members who, with the president, shall constitute a Program Committee. It shall be the duty of this committee to arrange a program for the annual meeting, and to submit it at the opening of the annual meeting for approval. If approved, it shall become the order of business for the session.

Section 3. Such other committees, standing or special, shall be appointed by the president as shall be authorized by the federation or the board of directors.

ARTICLE IX.

Parliamentary Authority.

The rules contained in ''Robert's Rules of Order Revised'' shall govern the federation in all cases to which they are applicable and in which they are not inconsistent with these by-laws.

ARTICLE X.

Amendment to the By-Laws.

These by-laws may be amended by a two-thirds vote at any annual meeting, provided the amendment has been proposed by the board of directors, or by a committee authorized by the federation, or by a federated club, and has been sent in writing to the corresponding secretary, and a copy of the proposed amendment has been sent by him to each club in the federation at least thirty days before the annual meeting.

Additional Suggestions Applying to Third Model

These by-laws are adapted to a state or national organization composed of local clubs. This model, like the others, is merely designed as a guide, each organization varying from it to suit its own needs. The General Plan of By-Laws and Suggestions Applying to Second Model should also be read, as they are not usually repeated even though applicable here.

Articles I and II should conform exactly to the wording of the charter, such organizations being usually incorporated. The object of this federation is so extensive that it would be difficult to find a subject that is not included. But in many state and national organizations it would be well to add to Article II the following: "No subject can be considered or acted upon in the meetings, except those included in the object of the society, unless permission is granted by a vote of two thirds [or three fourths] of the registered delegates." Delegates are usually put to much expense in attending the meetings, and it is unfair to them to occupy the time with subjects outside the declared object of the convention.

Article III. Members. Section 2. If it is desired to require an initiation fee, insert after "Section 2" the words, "The initiation fee shall be — dollars," or, "The initiation fee shall be the same as the annual dues." The annual dues vary according to the size of the club, just as does the number of delegates to which the club is entitled, according to Article V. In order to prevent the large clubs from having too many votes, the dues and delegates are not increased after the club has reached the limit of four hundred members. Section 3. In order to ascertain what clubs are entitled to representation at the meeting of the federation in October, the recording secretary should ascertain from the treasurer the names of the clubs that have paid their dues on October 1, as only such clubs are entitled to representation at the meetings. Such delinquent clubs as have not paid their dues by the following March 1 are automatically dropped from membership.

Article IV. Officers. Section I provides for a term of two years for all the officers except the ten directors whose term of office is four years. Half of the directors are elected in the even years, and the rest of the officers in the odd years. It may be preferred to elect half of the officers each year, in which case the term of the directors might be the same as that of the other officers, the object being to avoid having all the directors go out of office at the same time. See Section 3, Article IV, of the second model. Elections are by ballot, as they should always be in organizations where there is competition for office. This by-law provides for election by a plurality vote on account of the difficulty of holding the delegates long enough to repeat the balloting when the first ballot fails to give a majority vote for some of the offices. Where it is practicable to continue the balloting at the same or at an adjourned meeting, as in local societies, it is more satisfactory to require a majority vote for an election, which is the case unless the by-laws allow a plurality to elect.

Section 2 provides for the election at each annual meeting of a nominating committee, whose duty it is to prepare a ticket for the election at the next annual meeting. This ticket should be printed in a form suitable to be used at the election, and therefore should provide ample space for writing the name of a different candidate beneath each printed one. The last sentence of this by-law, while unnecessary, since it enumerates a simple principle of parliamentary law, is inserted because so many persons appear to be ignorant of it.

Section 3 makes the duties of the officers such as are specified in the by-laws and in the parliamentary authority adopted by the club. This is generally better than to attempt to specify in the by-laws the duties of the officers. Section 4 provides that the board shall fill all vacancies in office until the next annual meeting, the election to be by ballot. To provide against sharp practice in withholding a resignation until a board meeting when certain parties are absent, and immediately filling the vacancy, an affirmative vote of a majority of the board is required to elect unless suitable notice of the election has been given. Section 5 provides for conferring the title of honorary president. If it is desired to limit this title to those who have served as president, the words "a person" should be replaced by "an ex-president" or by "one who has served as president."

Article V. Meetings. Section 1 provides for holding the annual meeting in October, the exact day to be determined by the board. This leeway is needed by many state organizations in order to avoid having the meetings conflict with the annual meetings of national organizations which delegates may wish to attend. Thirty days' notice of the meeting must be given the federated clubs. No provision is made for holding special meetings, since the necessity for an extra meeting of such an organization could hardly occur.

Section 2 provides for the clubs' being represented at the meetings by a number of delegates in proportion to their membership, up to four hundred. This is similar to the scale of the annual dues. Section 3 permits the attendance of members who are not delegates. This is a good plan in state federations. This section limits the privileges of such persons to attendance at the meetings.

Article VI. Board of Directors. Section 1. The board is called here board of directors. It might be called board of managers, in which case the word "directors" should be changed everywhere in these by-laws to "managers." Section 2 does not give the board authority to incur any debt beyond the funds at its disposal. To do that it must get the special authority of the federation. Section 5. One third of the board should have the power to call a board meeting if the president is absent or declines to call a meeting.

Article VII. Executive Committee. Section 1 authorizes, but does not require, the board, at its first meeting just after the annual meeting, to elect three of its members who, with the president and the recording secretary, shall constitute an executive committee. Section 3 provides no regular meetings of the executive committee, but states how a meeting may be called. The board, under the authority given it by Section 6, Article VI, may appoint regular meetings of the executive committee.

Article VIII. Committees. Section 1 provides for a membership committee of which the corresponding secretary is made a member because this officer attends to the correspondence in connection with the reception of new members.

Article X. Amendments to the By-Laws. Amendments to the by-laws of a state or national organization should never be allowed to be proposed by one or two delegates. This article designates those who can propose an amendment, and requires that a copy be sent to each of the federated clubs at least thirty days before the annual meeting. This gives the clubs an opportunity to discuss the proposed amendment and, if they so wish, to instruct their delegates.

MODEL FOR STANDING RULES

The following is an example of Standing Rules that some conventions may adopt in a modified form to their advantage: [Read also page 367.]

STANDING RULES FOR THE —— STATE CONVENTION OF ——
SOCIETIES —— [DATE].

Rule 1. The credentials committee, immediately after the president's address of welcome, shall report the number of members registered as present with the proper credentials, and it shall make a supplementary report each day that additional delegates register.

Rule 2. All recommendations made in the report of officers, or boards, or committees of the convention, that are not in the form of resolutions, and all resolutions offered by individual members, shall be referred without debate to the committee on resolutions. Each member who offers a resolution shall be given an opportunity to explain it to the committee on resolutions. This committee shall prepare suitable resolutions to carry into effect the recommendations referred to it, and shall recommend suitable action to be taken by the convention on each of these resolutions. This committee shall also recommend suitable action to be taken by the convention on all resolutions referred to it, except such as the committee by a vote of three fourths of its members may refuse to report. The convention by a majority vote may suspend this rule and immediately consider any question, or may order the committee to report a question at any specified time, even if the committee has voted not to report it.

Rule 3. All resolutions, except those contained in the reports of officers, boards, or committees, shall be in writing and shall be signed by the mover and the seconder.

Rule 4. No member shall speak in debate more than once on the same question, or longer than three minutes, without the permission of the convention.

Rule 5. Delegates will be furnished badges by the credentials committee when they register, and will be required to wear them in order to obtain admission to the main floor of the convention hall.

[Abbreviations, etc.: "R. O. R." is used for "Robert's Rules of Order Revised," and "Par. Prac." for "Robert's Parliamentary Practice." References enclosed in brackets thus, [See p. 137], refer to pages in this book.]

These questions and answers have been selected from the author's parliamentary law correspondence as covering difficulties actually occurring to-day in clubs and other societies. The questions were asked usually by officers of societies or teachers of parliamentary law. Many of them have been greatly abridged so as to eliminate all unnecessary matter, and also to avoid repeating what is covered by other questions. In doing this the language of the writers has been retained as far as possible. When questions involving the same principle have been asked by several persons, the author has sometimes prepared a question that will best illustrate the principle involved. The references to "Robert's Rules of Order Revised" ("R. O. R.") have been retained, even though the matter is equally explained in this book, since that is the parliamentary authority of the clubs involved. To find what this book says on the subject, consult the cross references and the General Index at the end of the book.

Attention is called to the fact that the answers given to the following questions are in accordance with parliamentary law. Parliamentary law is subordinate to state law, which is not the same in all the states, and is constantly liable to change. By allowing proxy voting, and giving to the Board of Managers nearly all the power of the organization in incorporated societies, some states have nearly destroyed the deliberative character of their incorporated societies. As in the case of state laws, so by-laws outrank rules of order and answers to these questions.

401

CHAPTER XXXVIII

QUESTIONS ANSWERED

AMENDMENTS: RECONSIDER AND RESCIND

AMENDMENTS

[See page 368 for Amendments to By-Laws.]

1. QUESTION. What is meant by "an amendment to something already adopted?"

ANSWER. An amendment to by-laws, standing rules, resolutions, etc., that have been previously adopted. This kind of an amendment is a main motion and is treated differently from an ordinary amendment. See R. O. R., p. 55. [See Ques. 13, 14, 15, 34.]

2. QUES. Can any one offer two amendments at the same time to different parts of the by-laws, if no one objects?

ANS. Yes, since it is done by general consent. The chair, however, before stating the question, should ask if there is any objection.

3. QUES. If a club is discussing having an entertainment, and the resolution is offered, "*Resolved,* That we take a boat ride on the Severn River, (*a*) Is it not germane to strike out Severn River and insert Placid Lake? (*b*) It would not, however, be germane to strike out "boat ride on the Severn River" and insert "dinner at the Oriental," for that would be changing the subject, would it?

ANS. (*a*) Yes, the amendment is germane. (*b*) The latter amendment is also germane if having the boat ride would interfere with having the dinner at the Oriental. If having one of them does not affect the question of having the other, then the amendment is not germane. [See Ques. 4, 5.]

4. QUES. While a motion "that we build a brownstone club house," etc., is pending, it is moved "to amend by adding the words, 'the cost not to exceed $30,000.'" Then it is moved "to amend the amendment by striking out '30,000' and inserting

'35,000.' "   Is this amendment to the amendment in order, or should the first amendment have been voted down and then the second one offered? There is a difference of opinion on this question in our parliamentary law club.

ANS. The amendment to the amendment is in order. It could have been ruled out of order only on the ground that it was not germane. The adoption of the first amendment would have prevented the offering of the second amendment, and therefore the second was germane to the first amendment, and in order. Read R. O. R., pp. 143–146, and you will see that this is not included in Improper Amendments. [See pages 19–24 and Ques. 3, 5.]

5. QUES. While a motion "to place on the ponds in the public parks swan boats" was pending, and also an amendment "to add the words 'equipped with roller-skates,' " it was moved "to amend the amendment by striking out 'roller' and inserting 'ice.' " This last motion was ruled out of order. It was stated that, according to your ruling, it was necessary to incorporate the first amendment in the main motion before the second could be offered. Is that correct?

ANS. No. If the first amendment were adopted, the second amendment would be out of order until the vote on the first amendment was reconsidered. A word that has been inserted or added cannot be struck out except after a reconsideration, unless the motion to strike out includes much more than the word, as explained in R. O. R., p. 138. The error probably arose from the fact that if the secondary amendment is not germane to the first primary amendment, the secondary must wait until the primary is voted on, and then it is moved as a primary amendment. Thus, suppose in the above-mentioned case the secondary amendment had been "to add the words 'and a reasonable charge shall be made for their use.' " This second amendment, if the charge is for the use of the boats, is germane to the main motion, but not to the first amendment. The question of making a reasonable charge for the use of the boats usually has nothing to do with the question of how they shall be equipped, and therefore should be moved as an independent amendment of the main motion. Suppose, however, it was desired to make a special charge for the boats when used with skates, then a secondary amendment to that effect would be germane to the primary amendment, because the special price might affect the expediency of incurring the expense of the special equipment. No amendment should be ruled out of order unless it evidently has no bearing on the immediately pending question. [See Ques. 3, 4.]

6. QUES. When an amendment to a motion has been voted upon and lost, is the original motion then open for further discussion, and does the same rule apply to an amendment to a motion after an amendment to the amendment has been voted upon and lost?

ANS. Yes; see R. O. R., p. 280.

7. QUES. (a) Must the discussion on an amended motion be confined to the amendment? Or (b) is the original motion, together with the amendment or amendments, open to discussion up to the time the question is put?

ANS. (a) No. Read R. O. R., pp. 39, 40. (b) When the amendment is voted on, it is finally disposed of, whether adopted or lost. The question is then on the main motion as it then stands, whether amended or not. The pending question may be debated again and further amended. The same principle applies to amending an amendment. When the amendment of the amendment is disposed of, the amendment as it now stands is open to discussion and further amendment.

8. QUES. Before the question is put, the mover consents, without objection from his second, to change his motion, and does so, partly conforming to the suggestion of another member, and the question as restated is put and lost: (a) Is it proper for the president at the next regular meeting to say he made a mistake in not putting the "original" motion when the "amendment" was lost, and then and there to proceed to put said question to a different attendance, the mover being absent and others present who were not at the former meeting? (b) If it were an amendment offered after the question was put in the usual way, and the chair failed to put the original question after the amendment was lost, would it be proper to put the question at the next meeting on his own initiative?

ANS. (a) No. The chair did not put the question on the amendment. A member suggested an amendment which the mover accepted in part, and with general consent (no one objecting) the mover modified his motion accordingly. The modified main motion was put and lost. That ended the matter. (b) After the main question has been "put" no subsidiary amendment can be offered, because there is nothing pending before the assembly to amend. If, when an amendment is lost, the chair fails to put the main question, but proceeds to other business, some member should at once raise a question of order. If this is neglected and the assembly adjourns without acting on the main question, that question drops, and can be acted upon at the next or a future meeting only by being renewed. It is not unfinished business that can be called up by the chair. It is new business, requiring a new motion. If, however, the assembly adjourns while the main motion is pending, at the next meeting it comes up as unfinished business.

9. QUES. A makes a motion which is seconded, and then B offers an amendment to the motion, which A will not accept. The presiding officer, however, incorporates the amendment with the original motion, despite A's objection. Now, is the presiding officer compelled to ask the mover for his acceptance, or can he of his own accord accept the amendment? I cannot find in R. O. R. an answer to this question.

ANS. The presiding officer has no authority to incorporate the amendment in A's motion without A's consent. If A wishes to modify his own motion, or if he is willing to accept B's suggested amendment, it can be done as explained in R. O. R., pp. 100, 101, under "Leave to Withdraw or Modify a Motion." If he is unwilling to accept the amendment, the only way to get the motion amended is for the assembly to adopt the amendment by a vote. Section 10 of R. O. R., pp. 43–50, shows what motions to use to accomplish certain objects. On p. 44 of R. O. R. you will find how the assembly may modify a motion. On pp. 236-244 of R. O. R. are stated the duties of the presiding officer, and you will not find that he has any such power as exercised in your case.

10. QUES. While an original motion, A, is pending, a substitute motion, B, is offered and passed by a large majority. Should the chairman then put the original motion, A, or consider that as the substitute motion, B, has been passed, the motion in its original form, A, is not open to further consideration?

ANS. The chairman should not put the original motion, A, because it has been replaced by a new motion, B, and has thus in its original form been finally disposed of. The new motion, B, that has replaced it is the pending question, and must be put to vote or otherwise disposed of. There appears to be much misunderstanding of this form of amendment. To substitute is simply to strike out all of a resolution or paragraph and insert in its place another resolution or paragraph on the same general subject. When one resolution is substituted for another, the substituted resolution becomes the pending question, just as the original resolution was, and must be adopted or rejected, or otherwise disposed of. It has simply taken the place of the original resolution, and members may have voted for the substitute with the intention of voting against the amended (substituted) resolution. They may think it easier to kill the new, or substituted, resolution than the original one. When the motion to substitute has been adopted, the chair immediately states the question on the resolution as amended, that is, the resolution as amended by striking out one resolution and inserting another. While it may appear like voting on the substitute twice, it is not so, as the first vote was merely on substituting the new for the original resolution. Since the original resolution had not been adopted, replacing it by the new resolution does not adopt the new one, but leaves it as the pending question. The method of amending a substitute is explained in R. O. R., pp. 141-143. [See also Par. Prac., Second Drill, p. 40.]

11. Ques. While a primary amendment in the nature of a substitute is pending, is a secondary amendment in the nature of a substitute in order?

Ans. Yes, after opportunity has been given for amending the paragraph or resolution to be struck out, and the chair has asked whether there are any amendments to the paragraph or resolution to be substituted. [See Ques. 12.]

12. Ques. A certain motion was amended by substitution. Can that substitute be amended in the same way, that is, by substitution?

Ans. It depends upon what you mean. If you mean exactly what you say, the answer is, No, except by adding, unless the vote making the substitution is reconsidered. If you mean to ask whether, while the motion to substitute is pending, it is in order to move to substitute a new paragraph or resolution for the pending one to be substituted, the answer is, Yes. It is stated in R. O. R., p. 142, that "A paragraph that has been substituted for another cannot be amended afterward except by adding to it." What is stated of a paragraph is true of any paragraph, whether the paragraph comprises the entire resolution, or motion, or is simply one of several paragraphs. [See Ques. 11.]

13. QUES. A club at a regular monthly meeting voted to engage Mrs. X to deliver a course of three lectures. At the next regular meeting it was moved to amend this motion by striking out "three" and inserting "five." This was ruled out of order. What was the correct procedure in order to make the change?

ANS. If the lecturer had been engaged before the amendment was moved, the amendment was out of order and the proper course was to move that Mrs. X be engaged for two additional lectures. If the lecturer had not been engaged when the amendment was moved, the amendment was in order, but required a two-thirds vote for its adoption, unless previous notice had been given. An adopted resolution that still requires action to be taken is of the nature of a standing rule and can be amended in the same way. [See Ques. 1, 14, 15, 34.]

14. QUES. Is it in order to amend something already adopted, before the time for moving to reconsider has expired?

ANS. Yes; but, unless notice of the amendment was given at the previous meeting, it requires a two-thirds vote or a vote of the majority of the membership to adopt the amendment. [See Ques. 1, 13, 15, 34.]

15. QUES. A society adopted a budget for the year. One item of this budget authorized the payment of a certain sum for enforcement of the prohibition law. Some of the payments authorized by the budget have been made, but none for prohibition. The society now wishes to decrease the amount for that cause. It is too late to reconsider. How should they proceed?

ANS. Move to amend the budget by striking out the amount authorized for the enforcement of the prohibition law and inserting the desired amount. This is a main motion, and, unless previous notice has been given, it requires for its adoption a two-thirds vote or a vote of a majority of the membership. If the motion is voted down, give notice that you will offer the amendment at the next meeting. [See Ques. 1, 13, 14, 34.]

RECONSIDER AND RESCIND.

16. QUES. Can the motion to reconsider be made or seconded by one who is entitled to debate and make motions but not to vote?

Ans. No; the motion to reconsider can be made only by one who voted with the prevailing side. In a committee it may be moved by any one who did not vote with the losing side.

17. Ques. In R. O. R., p. 156, it is said in reference to the motion to reconsider that "It can be made only on the day the vote to be reconsidered was taken, or on the next succeeding day." My interpretation of this is that the next succeeding day means the next meeting in organizations meeting weekly or twice a month. Others claim that in a society working under "Robert's Rules" and having meetings twice a month the motion to reconsider would have to be made at the meeting at which the vote was taken, or else a special meeting would have to be called for the next succeeding day for the purpose of reconsidering. Which is correct?

Ans. The latter. The motion to reconsider may be made on the day the vote that it is desired to reconsider was taken, or on the next succeeding calendar day. It does not matter whether the meeting on the second day is a regular, an adjourned, or a special meeting. A recess or a legal holiday is not counted as a day. At the next meeting, regardless of the time elapsed, the previous action may be rescinded; but this requires a two-thirds vote, no notice of the motion to rescind having been given. This partially protects the society from the danger of having a small quorum. Every good rule at times is inconvenient. [See Ques. 18, 25, 26.]

18. Ques. Can a question that has been carried at a regular meeting of an organization be reconsidered at the next meeting, either regular or special? My interpretation according to "Robert's Rules," p. 164 of the 1915 edition, and pp. 76, 79, 185, and 186 of the 1904 edition, is that it may be reconsidered at the next meeting. Is my interpretation correct?

Ans. Yes, provided the motion to reconsider was made "on the day the vote to be reconsidered was taken, or on the next succeeding day," as stated in R. O. R., p. 156. All the references you give relate to the time during which the motion to reconsider may be "called up" and acted upon. It cannot be "called up" unless it has been previously moved, and the time for that expires with the calendar day after the motion to be reconsidered was made. [See Ques. 17, 25, 26.]

19. Ques. Can a motion decided by secret ballot be called up for reconsideration?

Ans. If you mean, "Is it in order to reconsider a vote taken by secret ballot?" the answer is, Yes. The member making the motion to reconsider must state that he voted with the prevailing side, and the vote on the reconsideration must be taken by ballot. The principle is the same as laid down in R. O. R., p. 202, in the case of voting to make a ballot unanimous. The secrecy would be of little benefit if members could be forced to show their colors by taking a viva voce vote on the reconsideration.

20. Ques. Instead of reconsidering the ballot vote in an election, can the club order that another ballot be taken?

Ans. No. When an election has been decided, the assembly cannot order the vote to be taken again, unless members misunderstood the question when put, or fraud has been discovered. In an election by ballot, the balloting is continued until all the offices are filled.

21. Ques. Can a vote taken by secret ballot be rescinded?

Ans. Yes, the same as any other vote, but the vote on rescinding must be taken by ballot to prevent exposing the votes of members. The votes or actions that cannot be rescinded are stated in R. O. R., p. 169.

22. Ques. Our by-laws provide "That the same name cannot be proposed [for membership] more than once during the club year." They also provide that two negative votes will defeat the application, the vote being taken by ballot. The rejection of an application for membership is not among the votes mentioned in R. O. R., p. 169, that cannot be rescinded. Can a defeated application be brought up again by a motion to rescind the vote rejecting the application for membership?

Ans. No. The vote could be rescinded were it not for your by-law prohibiting the proposing of the same name more than once in a club year. The motion to rescind the vote rejecting an application brings the matter again before the club just as effectually as renewing the application. [See Ques. 31.]

23. Ques. The vote adopting an ordinance was reconsidered. The ordinance was then amended. Should a vote now be taken on adopting the ordinance?

Ans. Yes. If the ordinance is not adopted after it has been reconsidered, it is not adopted at all. It is not proper, however, to make a motion to adopt after the reconsideration. As soon as the chair announces the result of the vote on the reconsideration, he should state the question before the assembly thus: "The question is on the adoption of ordinance No. —." After a resolution has been amended you cannot move to adopt the resolution, because the amendment was not in order unless there was already pending a motion to adopt the resolution.

24. QUES. An ordinance was legally passed in a city council by a vote of eight ayes to seven noes. One week later a motion to reconsider the vote adopting the ordinance was moved by a member who voted for the ordinance, and the motion to reconsider has never been called up. In what condition is the ordinance now?

ANS. The motion to reconsider was not in order unless the city council has a special rule allowing the motion to reconsider to be made at the next regular meeting. But, assuming that the motion to reconsider was in order when made, since it was never called up, its effect terminated at the close of the next regular meeting, and the ordinance at once went into effect on the adjournment of that meeting.

25. QUES. If an organization holds its regular meetings or sessions once in two or three months, and has directors' meetings called specially in the intervals, must reconsideration be brought up at the next directors' meeting, or can it hold over until another regular session?

ANS. The question is not clear whether the action to be reconsidered was taken by the organization or by the board of directors. In either case, the reconsideration could be moved only on the day the action was taken or on the next succeeding day, and in a meeting of the body that took the action it is proposed to reconsider. The motion to reconsider, if made at the proper time, can be called up at any time before the close of the next regular session of the same body. If the motion to reconsider was made at a meeting of the organization, it cannot be called up in a meeting of the board of directors. If it was made in a meeting of the board of directors, it cannot be brought up in a meeting of the organization. [See Ques. 17, 18, 26.]

26. QUES. Our constitution has the following provision for its amendment: "No amendment shall be made to the constitution unless it shall have been proposed by a state society, communicated to all other societies by the national recorder, returned

to her on or before the first Thursday in March in order to append the two-thirds vote of the state societies to the call for the annual meeting, said two-thirds vote of all societies to constitute the adoption of the amendment.'' An amendment was sent out to the state societies and did not receive the necessary two-thirds vote. A member proposes at the annual meeting to move to reconsider the vote by which the amendment was rejected. Is this motion in order? Our national society is governed by R. O. R.

ANS. No. If you refer to the Table of Rules on p. 6 of your parliamentary authority you will see that a negative vote on the motion to amend a constitution may be reconsidered. But a reconsideration must be moved by one who voted with the prevailing side, in this case the negative, and ''on the day the vote to be reconsidered was taken, or on the next succeeding day.'' [R. O. R., p. 156.] The voting units appear to be state societies, and therefore the reconsideration would have to be proposed by a state society that voted against the amendment. It is impossible, however, for the motion to be made now, as more than a day has passed since the vote was taken. Your constitution is so worded that it cannot be amended at the annual meeting, nor can a vote on amending it be reconsidered. [See Ques. 17, 18, 25, 27, 101.]

27. QUES. In a convention composed of delegates from various counties, which delegations were instructed to vote as units upon a resolution, a member of one of the units voting in favor of said resolution moved to reconsider the vote by which the motion was carried, the unit of which he was a member having previously ordered the vote of the delegation recorded solid for the resolution. It is wished to know whether or not the said delegate had the right to make the motion to reconsider, and whether or not the chair's ruling, that said delegate was out of order, was right.

ANS. The individual members were not entitled to vote in the convention on the resolution, and therefore could not make the motion to reconsider. The delegates from a county voted as units; consequently the motion to reconsider could be made only by a unit that voted for the resolution. Any member who did not vote against instructing the county delegation to vote in favor of the resolution had the right in a meeting of the county delegation to move to reconsider the vote ordering the county vote on the resolution to be cast in the affirmative. If the reconsideration is carried and the vote is reversed, any member can move to instruct the delegate's chairman, or some other member, to move the reconsideration of the vote adopting the resolution, and to cast the county's vote against the resolution. [See Ques. 26.]

28. Ques. Is a motion to rescind in order after a motion to reconsider has been defeated?

Ans. No, not in the same meeting, because by refusing to reconsider the vote the club has shown that it will not at that meeting change the action taken. Rescind is in order, however, at a future meeting.

29. Ques. A bill is rejected and then reconsidered and again rejected by one house of a legislature. Can that house afterward, at the same session, adopt a similar or identical bill that comes to it from the other house, which has adopted it?

Ans. Yes. That is not a case of renewing a motion or reconsidering a vote, but is treated as a new question coming from a coordinate branch of the government, which simple courtesy requires to be considered regardless of action previously taken. Technically a reconsideration applies only to acts of the same assembly. It is not a reconsideration to consider again an amendment that was rejected before the bill was sent to the other house, provided the other house had adopted that amendment before returning the bill. So the rules of reconsideration do not apply to the consideration of a vetoed bill that is returned by the executive. [See Ques. 25.]

30. Ques. A motion is made to reconsider a vote, and the request is made that the reconsideration be entered on the minutes. Can the chair refuse this request on the ground that the meeting is representative and that such delay would defeat the purpose of the motion?

Ans. If delaying action until the next day will defeat the motion, the chair should rule it out of order. For instance, a vote inviting a person to address the society before the next day is not subject to the motion to reconsider and have entered on the minutes. But if delaying action until the next day will not defeat the object of the motion, the motion to reconsider and have entered on the minutes is in order. If improper use of this motion is made, as was apparently done in your case, the remedy is to appoint an adjourned meeting for the next day, as explained in R. O. R., p. 167.

31. QUES. Can you rescind a vote and leave the motion in the form it was before the vote was taken?

ANS. No. Reconsider has that effect, but not rescind. To rescind a resolution is to strike it out, to repeal it. To rescind a by-law is to amend the by-laws by striking out that by-law. See R. O. R., middle of page 169. [See Ques. 22.]

32. QUES. When a member gives notice of intention at the next meeting to rescind a vote, is it brought before the meeting by the president as unfinished business, or by the member who gave notice, or can any member call for the motion?

ANS. Any one of these methods may be pursued. The same principle applies to all motions where previous notice is given. The giver of the notice is usually allowed the preference as to the time of making or calling up the motion, as long as he makes no improper use of the privilege. But the convenience of the assembly is more to be considered than that of any member, and no member should be allowed to prevent the assembly's taking up at a reasonable time a question of which notice has been given. If this were not so, a member could prevent the motion's being acted upon by giving the notice and then failing to make it or to call it up. This applies to all motions requiring notice.

33. QUES. We wish to rescind a resolution adopted at a convention last year. It is a delegated body. How can it be done?

ANS. Any member at any succeeding convention may make a motion to rescind the resolution. The vote required for the adoption of this motion is explained in R. O. R., p. 169. Since the convention has several meetings each day, the easiest way is to give notice of the motion to rescind at one meeting, and then it may be adopted by a majority vote at the next meeting, even if the two meetings are on the same day.

34. QUES. Our club voted "to send a delegate to Washington and to pay all her railroad and hotel expenses." It was afterward found that we could not pay more than $50 of the expenses. It was too late to reconsider the vote. If we rescind the resolution, how can we get it again before the club in the desired modified form?

ANS. The desired object can be attained in two ways. First, rescind the resolution and then adopt a new resolution in the exact form desired. This, of course, is a main motion. Or, the resolution previously adopted may be amended by striking out all after the word "pay" and inserting "$50 toward her expenses." This motion to amend, like the motion to rescind, is a main motion requiring a two-thirds vote for its adoption unless previous notice has been given, in which case it requires only a majority vote. See R. O. R., pp. 147, 169, 268. [See Ques. 1, 13, 14, 15.]

35. QUES. Can the vote rejecting an application for membership be reconsidered or rescinded in a society whose by-laws require the vote to be taken by ballot, either with black and white balls or with slips of paper?

ANS. Such a vote can be reconsidered. It is not in the list of votes that cannot be reconsidered, as given in R. O. R., p. 158. If the by-laws of the society do not prohibit the renewal of the application, the action of the society in rejecting the application may be rescinded. This is not among the votes that cannot be rescinded, which are stated on p. 169, R. O. R. If the by-laws prohibit the application's being considered again for a certain period, then during that period the vote cannot be rescinded; but it can be reconsidered if the motion is made the day the vote was taken, or the next calendar day, by one who voted for rejecting the application.

36. QUES. A society at a regular meeting expelled two members, all the provisions of the by-laws and parliamentary law for the expulsion of members being complied with. Three days thereafter a meeting was called for the next day for the specified purpose of rescinding the vote expelling said members. Had the members at this called meeting the legal or parliamentary right to rescind the vote expelling the two members?

ANS. No. See R. O. R., p. 170.

37. QUES. A member resigned, and was present when the resignation was accepted. He now wishes the resignation to be reconsidered. Can this be done?

ANS. No. See Par. Prac., p. 173.

38. QUES. A motion was made and carried to discharge the credentials committee, and count all present as members except certain ones challenged. At the next meeting a motion as follows was made: "To rescind the previous action in regard to the credentials committee, and to consider everybody present members."

This motion was ruled out of order by the chairman on the ground that the motion to rescind should be a single motion without the rider attached to it. Was the chair correct?

ANS. No, because the motion to be rescinded is in conflict with the motion to be adopted, and the repeal is a necessary part of the motion to adopt. It is like placing in a resolution a provision repealing everything in conflict with the resolution.

39. QUES. It is customary in our club to have the board minutes read once a month, and then to vote to accept the report, that is, the minutes. This is understood as approving what has been done and authorizing what is recommended. The club accepted the minutes of a meeting of the board that contained the record of the adoption of a resolution instructing the treasurer to leave signed blank checks with the financial secretary for her to fill out whenever she (the treasurer) left the city. A member who was going to oppose the acceptance of this part of the report did not arrive until after the report was accepted, and therefore could not move a reconsideration. After the meeting it was found that many members had not heard the report distinctly and were unaware of their having approved such action. Now they want to rescind it; but the report that they accepted approved bills which have since been paid, hence the vote cannot be rescinded. Can we rescind our action in accepting that part of the report of the board? How can we reverse our action?

ANS. Although you cannot rescind the vote accepting the report, because bills have already been paid as the result of the vote, yet you can rescind the approval of the instructions given the treasurer as far as the future is concerned. A law may be repealed, but the repeal does not affect the legality of actions taken after the passage of the law and before its repeal. Resolutions similar to the following should be adopted:

Whereas, On the — of —— the club accepted the report of its board, thereby approving of the board's action in instructing the treasurer to leave signed blank checks with the financial secretary whenever the treasurer left the city; and

Whereas, The club wishes to rescind that action and to express its disapproval of said instructions; therefore, be it

Resolved, That the action of the club on the — day of —— in accepting the report of the board is hereby rescinded as far as relates to the instructions given to the treasurer in regard to leaving signed blank checks with the financial secretary when the treasurer leaves the city.

Resolved, That it is the sense of the club that no officer of the club is justified in allowing a blank check with his signature to go out of his possession.

The board should rescind its action at the first meeting after the adoption of these resolutions by the club. Consult also R. O. R., pp. 169, 268. [See Ques. 354, 379.]

40. QUES. (a) Is the motion to rescind in order before the time has expired for making the motion to reconsider? (b) If the motion to rescind a resolution is made while there is yet time to move to reconsider, should the chair ask whether there is any one both able and willing to move to reconsider before stating the motion to rescind? (c) If there is some one both able and willing, should the chair rule the motion to rescind out of order?

ANS. (a) Yes; but to rescind requires a two-thirds vote or a vote of a majority of the membership, while to reconsider requires only a majority vote. (b) Not necessarily. (c) No.

41. QUES. Can you rescind the unexecuted part of a motion? ANS. Yes. [See Ques. 42.]

42. QUES. Just previous to the annual meeting of a society, a resolution was adopted, almost unanimously, prescribing certain qualities for officers. At the annual meeting a motion to rescind this resolution was made out of the regular order, and was ruled out of order. Failing to complete the elections, the society adjourned for a week. At the adjourned meeting another attempt to rescind the resolution was made, but the motion was ruled out of order and the balloting was proceeded with. Again the meeting was adjourned for a week. The board, which is empowered to call special meetings, now called a special meeting for the day before the day to which the society had adjourned. The meeting was called ostensibly for another purpose which was not urgent. Its real object was to rescind the resolution mentioned above. As soon as the special meeting was called to order, a point of order was made that "the meeting was improperly called and was therefore out of order." The chair ruled that the point of order was not well taken. From this decision an appeal was made and the decision of the chair was reversed and the meeting adjourned. (a) Was the society right in reversing the decision of the chair at the special meeting? (b) Was the motion to rescind the resolution in order at the time of the election of officers?

ANS. (a) I think so. It is possible that there may be an emergency of such urgency that a delay of one day, until the adjourned meeting, would prove injurious. But the urgency should be evident, and under such circumstances no business except that for which the meeting was called should be transacted. (*b*) Since the resolution related to the qualifications of the officers to be elected, the motion to rescind that resolution was incidental to the election, and was in order when the election was the order of business. Even after some of the officers had been elected it would have been in order to rescind the unexecuted portion of the resolution. As no previous notice had been given of the motion to rescind, a two-thirds vote would be required for its adoption. But a bare majority vote could have suspended the resolution for that meeting, as stated under Standing Rules, p. 268, R. O. R. The majority at one session cannot bind the majority at another session, as explained at bottom of p. 255, R. O. R. [See Ques. 41.]

CHAPTER XXXIX

QUESTIONS ANSWERED

BY-LAWS AND CONSTITUTIONS: AMENDMENT OF BY-LAWS AND CONSTITUTIONS

By-Laws and Constitutions

43. Ques. Is it desirable for a society to have both a constitution and by-laws, or may it have only by-laws?

Ans. It is entirely optional with the society. The society is the supreme authority. It is simpler, however, to have only by-laws. Formerly the more important fundamental rules of a society were made more difficult to amend than the others, and were called the constitution, the less important being called the by-laws, just as the rules or laws made by the state were called laws, and those made by a *by*, a town, were called the by-laws. But, in case all the fundamental rules require the same notice and the same vote for their amendment, there is nothing gained by separating them into a constitution and by-laws. On the contrary, the rules can be classified better if not separated. If incorporated, the charter corresponds to the constitution, because the charter cannot be amended as easily as the by-laws, which include the rest of its fundamental rules. If it is not incorporated, the club is under no obligation to divide its fundamental rules, but may require the same notice and the same vote for their amendment, and may call them the constitution or the by-laws, as it pleases. "By-laws" is the more usual term. [See Ques. 46.]

44. Ques. The rules of a society consist of a constitution and by-laws. One article in the constitution conflicts with one of the by-laws. Which is in force?

Ans. The article in the constitution. A by-law that conflicts with the constitution is null and void. For instance, if the constitution limits the services of officers to two years, all of the by-laws must be interpreted so as to be in harmony with that rule.

423

There is less liability of conflict in the rules if there is no separate constitution. [See answer to preceding question.]

45. QUES. Is it possible to divide a set of by-laws into articles?

ANS. Yes. The word "article" has many meanings. The Century Dictionary gives eight distinct meanings besides obsolete ones. The fourth one is, "A separate member or portion of anything." This has under it six particular meanings, the second of which is: "A distinct proposition in a connected series." This covers the case of by-laws, regardless of its meaning in law, or botany, or commerce, etc. It is usual to divide by-laws into articles and sections.

46. QUES. Is it true that "the law has decided that corporations should have simply by-laws"?

ANS. I know of no such law. Corporations are the creation of the state, and each state has its own laws. The legal term "by-laws" includes the fundamental rules of a society that may be called the constitution, or by-laws, or standing rules; or a part may be called by one name and another part by another of these names. Frequently in incorporated societies the charter takes the place of the constitution, the other fundamental rules being called by-laws. It is probably better to call all the fundamental rules of a society by-laws, except those relating to the transaction of business in the meetings and the duties of the officers and committees, which are called rules of order. [See Ques. 43.]

47. QUES. (a) When a resolution conflicts with an existing law or rule, is it necessary to repeal the law or rule before the resolution can be acted upon? (b) Is it necessary that the words "this resolution hereby repeals all conflicting laws or rules" follow the resolution? (c) Or does the resolution automatically repeal such laws without further action?

ANS. (a) Yes. If you consult the Index of R. O. R., you will find under the word "Resolution" the words: "Not in order if conflicting with Constitutions, By-laws, Rules of Order, or Standing Rules, 201, 269." On p. 201, under "Votes that are Null and Void even if Unanimous," the first sentence is: "No motion is in order that conflicts with the laws of the nation, or state, or with the assembly's constitution or by-laws, and if such a motion is adopted, even by a unanimous vote, it is null and void." On p. 269 at the end of the section on constitutions and other rules you will find this sentence: "No standing rule, or resolution, or motion is in order that conflicts with the constitution, or by-laws, or rules of order, or standing rules." (b) No. Rules after being adopted cannot be repealed or otherwise amended by a resolution adopted by a majority vote and without notice. (c) No. The rule or by-law must first be amended so that the resolution will not conflict with it. Read R. O. R., pp. 268, 269. [See Ques. 353.]

48. Ques. Is it necessary to designate the fiscal year in the by-laws or the constitution in any other way except by setting the time of payment of dues and the annual meeting?

Ans. No, unless it is desired to have the fiscal year close at some other time than at the close of the annual meeting.

49. Ques. How long do officers serve who are elected at the time of permanent organization?

Ans. Until the first annual meeting, unless the by-laws specify a longer term. [See Ques. 68, 207.]

50. Ques. Should the auditor be a member of the executive board and of the finance committee?

Ans. No. It is better for the auditor to be in no way connected with authorizing the expenditures which he is to audit. Where large expenditures are involved it is better to have the accounts audited by a certified public accountant who is not a member of the organization.

51. Ques. Our state constitution contains the following: "This organization shall be composed of associations —— the minimum dues to be at the rate of 20 cents for each member— 5 cents going to the national congress, 10 cents to the state, and 5 cents to the district—dues to be forwarded with application for membership. Dues shall be paid by April 1, and become delinquent two weeks prior to the annual convention." (Our convention is the last week of May annually.) Now, the two questions I am asked are these: (a) Does this paragraph give to the districts of the state the power to make their dues as much as they wish? (b) Is a new association forming in April, and sending dues with application for membership in state organization, paying dues for the current year, or can these dues apply as dues for the ensuing year beginning in July?

Ans. (a) No. The minimum dues prescribed are divided between the national, the state, and the district organizations, leaving nothing for the associations. Apparently each association is permitted to increase the dues of its members and thus provide for its own expenses. Your by-laws should make this clear. (b) The dues paid during the fiscal year are for that year. If anything different is desired it should be clearly stated in the by-laws. Some organizations provide that dues paid after the annual meeting shall apply to the next fiscal year.

52. QUES. The executive board consists of one president, three vice-presidents, one treasurer, two secretaries, and four directors. The only standing committee is one on membership. 'Other committees are book and art, philanthropic, hospitality, and printing. It is proposed to amend the constitution to make these chairmen members of the board. (a) Would this be proper? (b) If so, would they have to be elected by the club, or would the president still appoint them? According to the by-laws, the president now appoints committees subject to ratification by the board.

ANS. (a) Yes. (b) The president would still appoint the committees unless the by-laws are amended. If all your five committees are appointed for the year, as I assume they are, they are all standing committees. See R. O. R., p. 211. [See Ques. 53.]

53. QUES. The by-laws of a society provide that the executive board shall consist of the officers, chairmen of departments, and chairmen of standing committees. Elsewhere is a clause empowering the president to appoint the chairmen of standing committees. A member has contended that this is illegal, and that an appointed chairman cannot properly be present at any board meeting excepting to present his special work, after which he shall retire. Is the contention correct?

ANS. No. The constitution or by-laws is the organic law of the society, and as long as it does not conflict with national or state laws, or the vested rights of members, or plain principles of justice, you may place in it any provision you choose. Nothing in your by-laws can be illegal as long as it complies with the above, any more than an article of the constitution of the United States can be illegal. If your constitution or by-laws conflict with your rules of order, it is the latter that must yield. In the special case referred to, the method of choosing the chairman of a committee in no way affects the question of his rights and duties. Furthermore, if the society wishes to do so, it could make all the members of committees members of the executive board, or merely give them the privilege of attending the meetings. [See Ques. 52.]

54. QUES. Is it "unconstitutional" for a constitution to require payment of dues in advance?

ANS. No. Nothing in a constitution can be unconstitutional. Unconstitutional means "in violation of the constitution." A society has a perfect right to make such a provision in its constitution.

55. QUES. One of our by-laws reads as follows: "Section 3. The executive committee shall manage all affairs of the association, subject to the approval of the members in regular meetings, authorize all expenditure of funds, approve all applications for membership passed by the membership committee, act as judges in case of complaints filed by members, and direct all officers and committees in their work." Does this authorize the executive committee to dispose of all bills and debts contracted for without submitting them to a meeting of the association?

ANS. The by-law makes it the duty of the executive committee "to manage all the affairs of the association subject to the approval of the members in regular meetings." If the by-law made no exception to this general rule it would undoubtedly be the duty of the executive committee at every meeting of the association to report all its acts since the last meeting of the association for its approval. This report might be made by reading the minutes of the executive committee, which should always be kept and from which nothing should be omitted that was actually done by the committee. Four things are excepted, however, from this rule and do not require the approval of the association. These exceptions must be so construed as not to make the general rule just stated absurd. If they are interpreted in their broadest sense the general rule is made null and void. What would be the use of the rule making the management of "all the affairs of the association subject to the approval of the members in regular meetings" if the executive committee could expend the funds in any way it pleased, regardless of the approval of the association, and could direct its officers and committees in opposition to the views of the association? Construed together it would seem that the intent of the by-law is to require the executive committee to report to the association its doings sufficiently fully to enable the association to understand the management of its affairs, so that it may express its approval or disapproval. If the association disapproves of anything, it has the power to give the executive committee orders in the case, as otherwise "subject to the approval of the members in regular meetings" would be meaningless. But it is not necessary to submit all the bills or the directions that have been given to the officers and committees for approval. It is assumed that these bills are incurred and the directions are given by the executive committee in accordance with the plan of management that has been approved by the association. But the association is the supreme authority, and if it feels that additional information is needed in a special case in order to determine whether something has been done of which it would disapprove, it has a perfect right to order the information to be furnished. The action of the executive committee on applications for membership that have been approved by the membership committee, and its action as judges in case of complaints of members, are final and do not have to be submitted to the association for its approval.

56. QUES. An amendment to the constitution is proposed empowering the board of managers "by a two-thirds vote of its entire membership (which vote may be taken by mail)" to reduce the annual dues. (a) Is it proper to give the board so much power? (b) Is a mail vote legal or advisable?

ANS. (a) Yes, it is proper. A society may give the board any power it pleases. Whether your organization desires to give this power to its board must be determined by the organization itself. In some societies the board is very large and representative and is given great power, while in others very little power is given it. Usually, however, it has great power. I know of no reason for having the above-mentioned provision in your constitution, and yet I see no reason why two thirds of the entire membership of the board should not be empowered to lower the dues when they think best. (b) Yes, it is legal and is often advisable, and is used largely. Some organizations adopt that method of voting on all important matters, such as election of officers and amendments of the constitution. Where members are scattered over a large area it is the only fair way. [See Voting by Mail, p. 191.]

57. QUES. Because of illness the president of a state congress resigned, and the board of managers filled the vacancy by electing a president, on the ground that all the officers are members of

the board, and the by-laws state that "The board of managers shall have power to fill all vacancies occurring in its body." It is claimed by some that it is illegal to have the board fill a vacancy if the officer was elected for a term of two years. Is the claim correct?

ANS. No. Nothing in the by-laws of a society can be illegal unless it conflicts with the national or the state constitutions or laws, or the city ordinances, or the constitution or by-laws of an organization to which it is subordinate, or its own constitution. Your organization has chosen to authorize its board to fill all vacancies occurring in its body, and it had a perfect right to do so. It has the right, in its by-laws, to authorize its board to appoint and depose at will any or all of the officers of the society, or it could have given this power to one man, provided, in an incorporated body, that no state law is violated thereby. [See Ques. 58, 61, 65, 216, 217, 382.]

58. QUES. There was no limit to the length of time a member could hold office until last year, when the by-laws were amended by adopting the following section: "No member shall hold more than one office at the same time. No member shall hold the same office more than two successive years, except the registrar. No member shall hold any office more than four successive years, except that the office of regent may be filled without regard to previous service in other offices." Another section of our by-laws reads as follows: "The officers of the chapter shall be ——; these officers, together with ten members, —— shall constitute the board of management." (a) As the by-laws do not include the ten managers among the officers of the chapter, does the expression "holding office" apply to them? (b) Does the expression "No member shall hold any office more than four successive years" apply only to the registrar, or does it mean that after holding office four successive years a member is ineligible for any office whatever? (c) When an amendment to the by-laws is adopted, is it retroactive? That is, in our case is service in office previous to the adoption of the amendment counted?

ANS. (a) Yes. The managers "hold office" as well as the officers. If the by-laws were designed to apply only to officers, the word "officer" should have been used throughout instead of "member." A manager holds a very important office, a much more important one than is held by some who are called officers.

The better form for the by-laws would be, "The officers shall con-sist of —— and ten members —— who shall constitute the board of management." Service on the board, however, is counted as holding office, whether the managers are called officers or not.

(b) The latter construction is the correct one, as shown by the office of regent being excepted from its limitation, which would be absurd if the clause applied only to the registrar. The by-law allows a member to hold office for four consecutive years, provided he does not hold the same office longer than two years consecutively. After this he is for one year ineligible to any office except that of regent, which may also be held for two con-secutive years. Thus, a member may continue in office six years.

(c) The amendment is not retroactive. It cannot make illegal the acts of an officer who was legally elected to the office as the by-laws then stood. It cannot, by limiting the length of time for holding the same office to two consecutive years, in any way affect the legality of acts of officers who had held the same office for ten consecutive years at a time when there was no limitation on the length of service. The amendment takes effect the instant it is adopted, and if an officer at that time has held the office more than two consecutive years, he is legislated out of office. Previous service in office is counted, but takes effect only when the amend-ment is adopted. Thus, if any of the officers or managers had for the last four years held office, they would be ineligible for any office except that of regent. If the regent had held that office for two consecutive years and any offices the two preceding years, he would be ineligible to office as an officer or manager.

To make this still plainer, take the case of the act of Congress retiring officers of the army automatically when they have reached the age of sixty-four. It would be incorrect to say that the law does not take into account the time an officer has lived before the law was passed. When the law took effect, all officers over sixty-four years of age were automatically retired. At noon on an officer's sixty-fourth birthday he is automatically retired, no order being necessary. But the law was not retroactive, as it did not go back and make the retirement take effect on the sixty-fourth birthday of officers who were more than sixty-four years old at the time the law was passed. [See Ques. 108.]

59. Ques. If a society amends its by-laws shortening the

terms of its officers, does it affect the officers previously elected for a longer term?

ANS. Yes. A society may amend its by-laws regardless of unexpired terms of any of its officers. The new by-laws go into effect as soon as adopted, unless some provision to the contrary is adopted by the society previous to, or simultaneously with, the adoption of the new by-laws. If, for instance, the new by-laws omitted directors, the moment the new by-laws were adopted the present directors would be legislated out of office. [See Ques. 103, 106, 108, 109, 383.]

60. QUES. Our state federation has the following by-law: "All members of —— clubs within the state shall have the right to participate in the deliberations, but only the delegates shall have the right to vote." Do members of the clubs who are not delegates have the right to make motions?

ANS. If it were not for the last clause the answer would be No. Neither making motions nor voting is included in the strict meaning of "deliberations," and if the by-law had stopped with that word the by-law would naturally be construed as giving non-delegates the privilege of debating but not of making motions or voting. But the last clause excludes the privilege of voting, thus indicating that the word "deliberations" is used in the broad sense of including making motions, debating, and voting, and consequently non-delegates may make motions as well as debate them. If this is not the wish of the federation, the by-law should be amended.

61. QUES. Our state federation at its annual meeting elected a state president and a state vice-president whose term of office should begin at the close of the next annual meeting of the national federation after their election had been confirmed by the national federation, as provided for in the constitution. The state president died before her election was confirmed. How shall the vacancy be filled?

ANS. If the by-laws of your state federation do not provide for the filling of a vacancy in the office of state president, the state vice-president becomes the state president. The fact that his election has not been confirmed does not enter into the case. If the President of the United States, elected in November, should die before taking his oath of office March 4, the vice-president elected in November would take the oath in his place and become President. [See Ques. 57, 65, 216, 217, 382.]

62. QUES. Our constitution provides that "The corresponding secretary shall conduct and have charge of the general correspondence of the federation. She shall sign and send all notices and invitations," etc. Can the president and the executive board employ some one else to act as secretary at headquarters to receive and answer federation mail?

ANS. No, unless the person is employed as an assistant to the corresponding secretary and is under her orders. A unanimous vote of the federation itself cannot deprive the corresponding secretary of the charge of the general correspondence of the federation except by amending the constitution.

63. QUES. When the words "duly elected and installed" are used in the constitution, (a) does that mean that it is necessary then to have installation exercises? (b) or can the officers assume their duties without any special installing?

ANS. (a) No, unless there is a rule or custom prescribing a form of installation. (b) Yes, if a form of installation is not prescribed.

64. QUES. The by-laws of our national organization provide that "All state branches shall work under a constitution in harmony with the national constitution." What is the status of a state branch that changes its constitution so as not to be in harmony with the national constitution?

ANS. The state branch is a subordinate body, not a constituent one. Its constitution is subordinate to and cannot conflict with the national constitution. Any amendment in conflict with the national constitution, if adopted, is null and void in accordance with the principles laid down in the section on "Votes that are Null and Void even if Unanimous," R. O. R., p. 201. If the majority of the state branch refuses to recognize the national congress as its superior, the minority may resolve itself into the branch, and it should be recognized as such by the parent society. In case the branch is incorporated and property is involved, I think the courts would award it to the minority, in accordance with the principles laid down by the U. S. Supreme Court as quoted on pp. 300, 301, R. O. R. [See Ques. 104.]

65. QUES. The by-laws of a society provide that vacancies in all offices shall be filled by the executive board. An election was

held and a member who was not present was elected president. The other officers elected were present and did not decline. The member who was elected president, when notified of her election, refused to serve, and the recording secretary was elected in her place. Who fills the vacancy in the office of recording secretary?

ANS. The executive board. The fact that the member who was elected recording secretary was present and did not decline when elected shows that she accepted the office and therefore was the recording secretary until elected president. She should then resign the office of recording secretary, and the executive board should fill the vacancy. [See Ques. 57, 61, 216, 217, 382.]

66. QUES. The by-law prescribing the annual dues has been amended, increasing the dues. Are the members who paid their dues for the current year before the by-laws were amended to pay the additional amount this year?

ANS. Those who had paid their annual dues before the adoption of the amendment would not have to pay the additional amount. Those who had not paid their dues for the year would come under the amended by-laws, and would have to pay the newly prescribed fee, because the new by-law took effect immediately. The society, however, should have settled all this before or while adopting the amendment. It is careless to adopt an amendment of the by-laws without knowing what its effect is to be. Many might have voted differently had they understood the exact effect. The society had a perfect right, before the amendment was adopted, to decide by a majority vote at what time in the future it would go into effect if adopted.

67. QUES. The by-laws provide that officers shall serve one year or until their successors are elected. The president and secretary elected at the annual meeting did not decline, but they resigned before entering upon the duties of their offices. Do the president and secretary who were in office up to the annual meeting continue in office until their successors are elected?

ANS. If their successors had not been elected they would continue in office; but their successors were elected and did not decline, consequently they go out of office at the time of the election of their successors.

68. QUES. There is a rule in the constitution of a society that no officer can serve longer than two consecutive terms in the same office. Now, suppose, without amending the constitution, the club

wished to have one of its officers serve longer than two years. Would it be permissible to elect some one else at the annual meeting, and then for her to resign after she had served a month or so in the next club year, and then for the executive board to fill the vacancy with this other officer whom they wanted? The constitution prescribes that vacancies in the offices of the club shall be filled by the board. If this can be done, would this officer then be eligible at the next annual meeting for two other terms?

ANS. Both of these questions must be answered in the negative. The meaning of the constitution is clear, and these acts suggested are evident violations of it. If it is not desired to conform to the constitution, it should be amended. Constitutions of clubs very commonly provide that no officer shall serve longer than two consecutive terms in the same office, and there are constantly arising questions as to the proper application of this rule. An officer may resign near the beginning, near the middle, or near the end of the term, and the question arises as to whether he has served that term. The question also arises in each case as to whether his successor has served the term. Before answering these questions it is well to consider a similar provision in many constitutions, namely, that no officer is eligible to succeed himself. This is evidently intended to prevent an officer's holding the same office for two consecutive terms. If an officer resigns so that his successor is elected at the last meeting before the annual meeting, which officer has served that term and is ineligible for the same office during the next term? If it is held that it is the second officer, then the constitutional provision is a farce, because one person may hold the same office continually except for a few days before the expiration of each term. Again, suppose, for illness or necessary absence, the president resigns at the end of the month. Should he be ineligible for the presidency the next term because a year before he had held the office a month, while his successor is eligible and may hold the same office for nearly two years? Fairness requires that the term should be charged to the one that served the majority of the time, regardless of whether the service was in the early or the latter part of the term, and regardless of how the person acquires the office. It is all the same whether a vice-president becomes president by virtue of the resignation or death of the president, or by being appointed by the board to fill a vacancy. If one is ineligible to a certain office at the annual meeting, he is not qualified to hold that office during any part of the year or term beginning with that annual meeting. If any one has served less than half the term, that term is not charged against him. These principles apply, whether the holding of an office is limited to one term or to two or more terms. [See Ques. 49, 207.]

AMENDMENT OF BY-LAWS AND CONSTITUTIONS

69. QUES. What is meant by the term "previous notice" in regard to an amendment to the by-laws?

ANS. "Previous notice" means nothing more in parliamentary law than reading the notice, or giving it orally, at a previous meeting, or including it in the call for the meeting. The notice must give the purport of the amendment. When the amendment is offered at the next meeting it need not be in the exact words used in giving the notice. But no important change can be made in the effect of the amendment. The notice must be such as to enable members to know what change is proposed, but it does not necessarily give the wording of the motion to accomplish this change. See R. O. R., p. 271. [See Ques. 70, 74, 75, 76, 79, 83, 96.]

70. QUES. What do you consider "ample notice" of an amendment?

ANS. What is "ample notice" of a proposed amendment to the constitution of a society must be determined by each society for itself. In a case like a commandery of the Military Order of the Loyal Legion of the United States, where the members are scattered over a large territory and where the members vote by mail on amendments of the constitution and in elections, to give ample notice requires every member to be notified by mail. In a religious organization with a congregational form of government, ample notice is given when it is announced from the pulpit at the public services on Sunday. In a board of education ample notice is given by announcing it at the preceding regular meeting of the board. It all depends upon the organization. In many societies the secretary does not keep a record of the addresses of the members and could not mail them the notices. In others the labor would be too great, unless the secretary was authorized to pay for having the work done. The society to which you refer has two thousand members, all living in the same city. It would be very troublesome to notify every member by mail, and in fact is impracticable. On the other hand, notice should not be given at an unimportant weekly meeting, provided more important meetings are held, say, monthly or quarterly. [See Ques. 69, 74, 75, 76, 79, 83, 96.]

71. Ques. A point of order was raised at the last meeting of our society against an attempt to amend the by-laws without notice. It is now proposed to consider the attempt to amend as a "previous notice" of the proposed amendments. Is this proper?

Ans. No notice was given that the amendments were to be proposed at the next meeting, and therefore they cannot be acted upon at that meeting, unless it was understood by every one that what had been done was equivalent to previous notice that the amendments would come up at the next meeting.

72. Ques. At a regular meeting some four years ago, after discussing the subject of changing its name, our association unanimously referred the question to the executive committee with power to act. Under this vote of power the executive committee changed the name of the association. No one has raised a question of the legality of this procedure, but some of us now are in doubt and would like to know whether the amendment was legally adopted.

Ans. The amendment was not adopted by the method prescribed in the constitution. The method pursued was adopted, however, by a unanimous vote, and no one appeared to doubt its propriety. No one has raised a question as to its legality in the four years that have passed since the name was changed, and no one is injured by the action taken. Therefore I think the amendment should be considered as adopted. The error in the procedure was the result of a misunderstanding of what is meant by "with power to act." The committee seems to have understood the expression to mean that the committee was given the power to adopt the amendment to the constitution. An assembly cannot give to a committee a power that it does not possess. The power given by that vote was the power to decide precisely what change ought to be made in the name of the association, and to see that the proper steps were taken to secure the adoption of the change, including giving notice of the proposed amendment. The association could not, even by a unanimous vote, dispense with the previous notice.

73. Ques. Our by-laws require amendments to them to be presented at the previous regular business meeting. At the annual meeting, being desirous of taking action that conflicted with the by-laws, the article on amendments was suspended, and then the

by-laws were immediately amended and the desired action taken. Was this legal?

ANS. No. The article of the by-laws providing for their amendment cannot be suspended, R. O. R., p. 267, and hence the amendment was never legally adopted. The votes suspending an article of the by-laws, amending the by-laws, and adopting the motion in conflict with the by-laws, are all null and void.

74. QUES. The by-laws of our state convention contain the following article:

These by-laws may be amended at the annual convention by a two-thirds vote of those present and entitled to vote, notice of the proposed amendment having been given at a previous meeting, or appended to the call of this meeting.

Notice of an amendment to the by-laws was given, a recess of five minutes was taken, and then the amendment to the by-laws was adopted. It was claimed that the meeting after the recess was a different meeting from the one before the recess at which the notice was given. Is this correct?

ANS. R. O. R., p. 254, says: "In this manual the term Meeting is used to denote an assembling of the members of a deliberative assembly for any length of time, during which there is no separation of the members except for a recess of a few minutes, as the morning meetings, the afternoon meetings, and the evening meetings, of a convention whose session lasts for days. . . . An adjournment to meet again at some other time, even the same day, unless it was for only a few minutes, terminates the meeting." Therefore the notice was not given at a previous meeting, and the amendment, having been adopted in violation of the by-laws, is null and void. [See R. O. R., p. 201.]

Your by-laws cannot be amended unless notice has been given "at a previous meeting or in the call for this meeting." The word "meeting" undoubtedly is used in the same sense as when we refer to the "annual meeting," because a "call" is never issued for the separate meetings of a session. If the different meetings of each day of the session of the convention are referred to, there would be no sense in the provision for inserting the notice in the call for the meeting of the convention. Notice could be given at any meeting, and the amendment could be adopted at any succeeding meeting, even on the same day. But it is a very reasonable provision if the intention of the by-law was to give notice to the constituent societies by having the notice given at a previous session of the convention, or else in the call for the session at which it is to be acted upon. If the convention meets only once a year, notice of the amendment must be given at the previous annual meeting, or else in the call for the meeting at which it is to be acted upon. [See Ques. 69, 70, 75, 76, 79, 83, 96.]

75. QUES. The by-laws read, "An amendment to the constitution or by-laws must be conspicuously posted for one month preceding action." An amendment was posted three weeks, after which the club season closed. What is the proper method of handling this amendment? Does it drop to the floor and have to be revived, or should it be considered one week after the club season opens?

ANS. The amendment should again be posted in accordance with the by-laws, ignoring the previous posting. [See Ques. 69, 70, 74, 76, 79, 83, 96.]

76. QUES. Our by-laws require that proposed amendments shall be read at the meeting previous to the one at which they are acted upon. Is it complying with this by-law for the proposed amendments to be printed and furnished to every member a few days before the meeting, provided this is done by order of the society?

ANS. Yes. While not literally complying with the by-law, it carries out its spirit more thoroughly than a literal compliance would. When the amendments are numerous, as in case of a revision, it is much more satisfactory to have them printed and furnished to the members, so that they can be carefully examined in advance. In some cases it is advisable to print the existing by-laws and the proposed substitute in parallel columns. [See Ques. 69, 70, 74, 75, 79, 83, 96.]

77. QUES. The by-laws of a society state that they may be amended at any regular meeting. May they be amended at a special meeting called for the purpose?

ANS. No. As the by-laws state that they may be amended at any regular meeting, it follows that they cannot be amended at any other time. The regular meeting may, however, adjourn to another day for the purpose of considering the amendments, and thus the desired object be obtained.

78. QUES. At the regular meeting of a society a committee on revision of the by-laws submitted a new set of by-laws as a substi-

tute for the old set. At the previous meeting, and in the notice of this meeting, it was stated that "the new by-laws would be voted on." Outside of the meeting a member has urged the necessity of having copies of the new by-laws sent to the members, or else of having them read at the meeting previous to the one at which they were to be voted on. It was claimed that this was unnecessary, as "these are not amendments but entirely new by-laws." At the meeting the by-laws were taken up for action, and were read through and adopted as a whole, though a member objected to the reading because the new by-laws had never been seen by the members. The same member also claimed that the new by-laws should be read and considered article by article, but it was not done. The objecting member did not vote, claiming that the proceeding was irregular. The question is now raised, Which are the by-laws of the society, the old ones or the new ones?

Ans. The statement of the case seems to show a lack of appreciation of the importance of by-laws, and almost indifference as to their contents. If a society is willing to adopt by-laws without knowing what they contain, there is no help for it. No one can know anything of by-laws that they have read only once. Your parliamentary authority, R. O. R., gives nearly five pages to Amendment of By-Laws, pp. 269-273, in addition to pages 92-94 showing the procedure when anything like by-laws are being considered. These instructions appear to have been ignored. However, the society appears to have been virtually unanimous in not caring to be informed as to the contents of the substitute by-laws reported by the committee, and they had a right, if they preferred, to adopt the substitute without hearing it at all. Notice was fully given that a revised set of by-laws was to be submitted at the specified meeting, so those interested were doubtless on hand. In my opinion, the new by-laws were legally, but very carelessly, adopted. Assuming that the society has its by-laws printed, the committee should have had the substitute by-laws printed and distributed to all the members either before or at the meeting. At the meeting the entire by-laws should have been read, and then each article should have been taken up separately and read and explained by the reporting member of the committee, and amended if desired, but not adopted, as explained in R. O. R., pp. 93, 94. Attention is called to the statement you quote that a revision is not an amendment. Any change in the by-laws is an amendment, whether it is called a revision or a substitute, or whether the change is made by rescinding or repealing a part or all of the by-laws. If the intention of the member who moved to appoint the committee on revision was to have the entire by-laws revised, he should have moved, "That a committee on revision of the by-laws be appointed by the chair, with instructions to report at the next annual meeting a revised set of by-laws." The revision, or substitute, which would be open to unlimited amendment, should be treated as explained in the answer to Ques. 90. [See Ques. 79, 85, 86, 87, 88, 89, 90.]

79. QUES. There being dissatisfaction with two provisions of our by-laws, the executive committee took the matter up and recommended their modification, and asked for an appropriation to enable it to employ a parliamentarian to prepare suitable amendments. This was done and the amendments were prepared. The notice of the regular society meeting in April stated that the proposed amendments would be presented at the next regular meeting in May. At the April meeting the president gave the same notice. At the May meeting the amendments were submitted and adopted unanimously. Has the new president, six months later, the right to declare the action adopting the amendments null and void on the ground that "written notice" of the proposed amendments was not given at a previous meeting, as required by the by-laws?

ANS. No, though it was a mistake on the part of those in charge of the revision not to have submitted the amendments in writing, especially as they were all prepared. But as a people we have not learned to obey laws strictly, and it is not well to attempt suddenly without warning to enforce them to the letter. More harm than good is done by such a course. In this case the spirit of the by-laws was carried out, and every one appeared to approve of what was done. If, at either the April or the May meeting, the point of order had been raised that the notice given of the proposed amendments was not in writing, and the society had adopted the amendments without written notice, the action would have been null and void. But no such point was raised. Ample notice had been given, though not exactly as the by-laws required, and the amendments were adopted unanimously, and they are now a part of the by-laws. If the president declares any past action of the society illegal, and thus null and void, an appeal should be made, as the society, not the president, has the power to decide the question. [See Ques. 69, 70, 74, 75, 76, 83, 96.]

80. QUES. The by-laws provide that they "may be amended at any regular meeting, notice in writing having been given at the previous meeting." The notice was given, but the amendments were not taken up at the next regular meeting. The question is now raised whether the amendment to the by-laws cannot be adopted at a special meeting called therefor, the object being stated in the call, and then have this action ratified at the next regular meeting.

ANS. No. An assembly cannot ratify an action that it could not itself have legally taken.

81. QUES. Some time ago the state law regarding the revision of incorporated organizations not organized for profit was changed. Previous to that time it was possible to revise the by-laws only at an annual meeting. Now revision is legal at any regular business meeting or adjourned session thereof. Some parliamentarians hold that any one can, according to the law, present an amendment at any regular meeting and have it acted upon without giving any notice, although the rules of the organization stipulate that a five or ten days' notice must be sent or given. Are they correct?

ANS. No; the notice required by the by-laws must be given. The change in the state law affected only the kind of meeting at which the by-laws can be amended.

82. QUES. Our constitution provides that it may be amended at any regular meeting of the union by a two-thirds vote of the members present and voting, notice thereof having been given at a previous meeting. At the last annual convention an amendment to the constitution was adopted, and at the succeeding semi-annual convention the vote adopting the amendment was rescinded. (a) Was the motion to rescind legal? (b) Is the amendment still a part of the constitution? (c) A motion to lay on the table the motion to rescind was ruled out of order; was the ruling correct?

ANS. (a) No. (b) Yes. (c) No. This whole case is fully covered in R. O. R., p. 169: "To rescind is identical with the motion to amend something previously adopted, by striking out the entire by-law, . . . and is subject to all the limitations as to notice and vote that may be placed by the rules on similar amendments. It is a main motion without any privilege . . . and all the subsidiary motions may be applied to it." As soon as the amendment was adopted at the annual convention, it became a part of the constitution, and could not be struck out except by the prescribed method of amending the constitution. Since the prescribed notice was not given, the vote rescinding the vote on adopting the amendment is null and void, and the constitution remains as it was before the motion to rescind was made. As the motion to rescind is a main motion, it may be laid on the table the same as any other main motion. [See Ques. 94, 102, 111.]

83. QUES. The constitution of our congress provides for its amendment at any annual convention, "due notice of such proposed amendment having been given at the preceding annual convention." Last year a member gave notice of amending the entire constitution without giving any details as to what amendments were to be proposed. Is it parliamentary or constitutional to present a notice that the entire constitution will be amended, not naming a single item that is to be considered?

ANS. No. Your parliamentary authority, R. O. R., in referring to notices of proposed amendments to constitutions where the amendments themselves are not required to be submitted, says at the top of page 271: "Only the purport of the amendment is necessary, unless the rule requires that the amendment itself be submitted." It is no legal notice unless the purport of each amendment is given so members may know what changes are proposed, though the exact wording of each amendment is not required. Since the proposed amendment must be endorsed by five members, it would appear that it should be in writing. There is no reason why the five members, or even one person if the by-laws did not prohibit, could not give notice of amendments to every article of the constitution, or notice of a substitute for the present constitution, provided the gist of every change is given. When the substitute is presented, unless confidence is felt in the good judgment of those submitting it, the congress should refer it to a committee, which may be ordered to report during the session, or to the next congress. No revision of the constitution should be adopted by an organization until after thorough examination by a carefully selected committee. The exact effect of every change should be understood before the amendment or revision is reported to the organization. If the intention of the member was to have the entire constitution revised, he should have moved that a committee be appointed to revise the constitution, with instructions to report at the next annual convention. This revision would then be open to amendment to an unlimited extent. [See Ques. 69, 70, 74, 75, 76, 79, 96.]

84. QUES. Article IV, Section 2, of our by-laws made our past presidents an advisory committee to the executive board, with the privilege of attending the board meetings, making motions, debating, and voting. This by-law was amended last spring on the recommendation of the committee on revision. The chairman of the committee, instead of moving the amendment in a proper form, said: "Article IV, Section 2, to be changed in the phrasing to read, 'The past presidents shall form an advisory committee to the executive board.'" This was adopted. There is difference of opinion as to the effect of adopting this amendment. Some think that the past presidents have lost their privilege of attending and taking part in the meetings of the board, and others think they have not. Which is right? Is it a legal amendment when worded in this way, "It shall be changed in the phrasing"?

ANS. If nothing more was said by the committee chairman or by the presiding officer to explain the scope of the amendment to Article IV, Section 2, the vote of the society merely changed the wording of the part of the section relating to there being an advisory committee to the board, without changing the sense. This was what the committee recommended, according to the chairman, and was what the society adopted. The privileges of the members of the advisory committee were not alluded to, and therefore were not affected by the vote. If the committee intended to substitute the words quoted for the entire section, its chairman should have so stated, and the old section should have been read and then the new one, and the difference between them explained, so that every one might understand exactly what was being voted for. The legality of the amendment is not affected by the fact that the motion was not made in the usual parliamentary form. The amendment might have been offered in perfect form, and yet, if the committee chairman had misrepresented the effect of the amendment and the voting members had no copies of the amendment and by-laws to examine for themselves—in such a case the amendment would have been adopted by means of fraud, and the vote should be declared null and void. Fraud vitiates any act.

The amendment as offered, though not in parliamentary form, could be understood by every one as an amendment to change the "phrasing," that is, the method of expressing the matter of the section without changing the sense. These questions would never have arisen if the effect of the adoption of the by-law had been thoroughly explained, as it should have been, when the questions were open for debate. Consult R. O. R., p. 94, and Par. Prac., p. 145.

85. QUES. Can a motion be made to substitute the by-laws recommended by a committee for the original by-laws?

ANS. Yes; that is the proper motion when a committee submits a revised set of by-lawsfl [See Ques. 78, 79, 86, 87, 88, 89, 90.]

86. QUES. Should the by-laws be amended, if desired, section by section, before a motion is made to substitute the recommendation of the committee for the original by-laws?

ANS. No. Until the motion to substitute is made and is stated by the chair, there is no question before the assembly for it to amend. When the chairman of the revision committee reports, he should, as soon as the revised by-laws are read, say: "By direction of the revision committee, I move to substitute the by-laws just read for the present by-laws." This is a main motion. When the chair states the question on adopting the substitute, it, the substitute, is open to amendment, section by section, by a majority vote, after which the vote is taken on adopting the substitute. No motion to amend the existing by-laws is in order, because those by-laws have been previously adopted and are not pending. After the substitute has been adopted it becomes the new set of by-laws, and cannot be amended excepting by giving notice and by a two-thirds vote, and by complying with every other of its requirements for its amendment. [The difference between the procedure in adopting a substitute for by-laws that have been previously adopted and adopting a substitute for by-laws that have not been adopted but are pending, is explained on page 34. [See also Ques. 78, 79, 85, 87, 88, 89, 90.]

87. QUES. When the revision committee brings in an entire new constitution and by-laws and wishes them substituted for the old ones, what motion should be made?

ANS. "To substitute the constitution reported by the committee for the present one." The motion to substitute is a main motion, not a subsidiary one, because the existing constitution and by-laws are not pending.

88. Ques. In offering a substitute for the constitution or by-laws, should the old constitution be read first?

Ans. No. The method is described in R. O. R., p. 94. The chairman of the revision committee should, in explaining each section, show wherein it differs from the existing constitution. [See Ques. 78, 79, 85, 86, 87, 89, 90.]

89. Ques. Do the rules governing the amending of the constitution control the revision of the constitution?

Ans. Yes; because it is impossible to revise the constitution except by amending it, that is, by adding words to it or taking words from it. It is correct English to speak of revising the constitution, but when the revision committee reports a new constitution the parliamentary motion is to substitute it for the existing one. When the constitution prohibits its amendment (*i. e.,* its alteration), except by a prescribed method, the prohibition cannot be evaded by using another word than "amend," such as "rescind" or "revise," to accomplish the same object. If the by-laws prohibit the executive board of a club from expending, without the club's authority, more than $200 between any two consecutive meetings, the board cannot legally evade this and purchase a club-house for $10,000, claiming that they had not expended any money, but had only purchased property, which was not prohibited by the by-laws. The purchase necessarily involves an expenditure. Does any one think for a moment that the U. S. Supreme Court would hold valid a revision of the U. S. Constitution that was adopted without conforming to the rules governing the amending of the constitution? It must be borne in mind that the constitution cannot be changed in the slightest degree without amending it. Shylock had the right to cut out a pound of Antonio's flesh, provided he did not draw a drop of blood; so the constitution may be rescinded or revised without observing all the rules governing its amendment, provided not one word is added to nor one word struck out of the constitution. [See Ques. 78, 79, 85, 86, 87, 88, 90.]

90. Ques. Cannot a society amend a proposed revision of its constitution to any extent it pleases?

Ans. It depends upon the nature of the revision. If the revision is a new constitution submitted as a substitute for the old one, the answer is, Yes. In that case the members have notice that a new constitution is to be adopted, and consequently all of those interested should be present, since there is the same freedom of amendment as if the society were adopting a constitution for the first time. But the case is different when a revision committee reports amendments to certain articles of the constitution. In this case members attend who are interested in the particular changes made, and the amendments to these proposed amendments are very limited, as explained in R. O. R., p. 272.

91. QUES. Does the rule given in R. O. R., p. 272, for amending the dues apply to amending the number of members of a society?

ANS. Yes.

92. QUES. In our advanced class we had an example of a proposed amendment to the by-laws, to strike out "25" and insert "50" before the word "members." When the amendment came up for action at the next meeting, it was moved to strike out "50" and insert "100." Was the motion in order?

ANS. The motion was not in order, as it "increases the modification of the rule to be amended" without any previous notice of the greater change being given, which is prohibited by the rule as laid down in R. O. R., p. 272. It is clearly explained there why such amendments are out of order. If they were allowed, the object of requiring notice could be defeated. When notice of the proposed amendment was given, notice should also have been given of the amendment of the amendment to strike out "50" and insert "100." [See Ques. 90, 91, 94, 100.]

93. QUES. The by-laws of a society read: "The membership of the club shall consist of 70 active, 50 associate, and 40 non-resident members." A member has given notice to amend the by-laws by striking out "70," her idea being to make the active membership unlimited. A number of members are opposed to this, but wish to increase the active membership to 150. How can this be done?

ANS. The notice of the motion to strike out "70" and thus have an unlimited active membership covers an increase to 150 members. The motion to strike out "70" is a main motion, and it therefore is in order to move to substitute for it the motion to strike out "70" and insert "150." A subsidiary motion to strike out cannot be amended in that way. However, the better way to accomplish the desired result would have been for some one, when notice of the proposed amendment was given, to have given notice of the desired amendment. [See page 369.]

94. QUES. A revision committee, a month before the annual meeting, sent out printed notices of proposed amendments to the by-laws, showing how the amended articles would read if the amendments were adopted. One of these changes the initiation fee from $5 to $10, but leaves the dues as they were. An amendment to this amendment was adopted at the annual meeting, increasing also the annual dues from $5 to $10: no motion to reconsider was made or entered on the minutes. Would it therefore be in order to rescind this amendment at the next meeting, which is an adjourned annual meeting? If so, would it then be in order to pass it again for the same amount of dues?

ANS. These questions are based on the supposition that the secondary amendment (increasing the annual dues from $5 to $10) was adopted legally. But it was not. The notice of the proposed amendment did not specify the changes to be made, but gave the section as it would read if the amendment was adopted. In this case the notice does not apply to any provision in the section that has not been changed in the proposed new section. The annual dues were not changed in the proposed new section, and therefore no notice had been given of their amendment, and any change made in the annual dues is null and void.

If it were allowed to amend a proposed substitute by-law to an unlimited extent, the whole object of requiring previous notice would be defeated. Notice of the proposed amendments could be evaded by simply giving a substitute with some trifling change from the existing by-law. The real amendments could be held back until the last moment, increasing also the annual dues from $5 to $10. To take an extreme case, suppose the notice had reprinted the entire article, merely improving its style without making any change in the initiation fee or annual dues; would any one contend that at the annual meeting, without any notice, it would be in order to amend the amendment by increasing the initiation fee and annual dues from $5 to $50 each? If the notice of the amendment had proposed to change the "$5" to "$6," an amendment of the amendment striking out "$6" and inserting "$10," while in order with an amendment of an ordinary motion, would be out of order with existing by-laws, because notice of a proposed increase of annual dues from $5 to $6 is not sufficient notice to justify increasing the dues to more than $6. If such methods of amending by-laws were permitted, advantage would be taken of it, and the notice of proposed amendments would be so worded as to avoid attracting attention to the vital changes really aimed at. A club cannot be too careful in amending its by-laws. The amendment changing your annual dues was adopted without the notice required by the by-laws, and is therefore null and void. See R. O. R., p. 272. If the committee had been authorized to submit a revised set of by-laws as a substitute for the existing ones, the revision would be open to amendment as fully as if the society were adopting a set of by-laws for the first time. [See Ques 90.] Your questions call for a reminder that an amendment to a by-law, when adopted, immediately becomes a part of the by-laws, and cannot be changed except in accordance with the rule for amending by-laws. Therefore the vote adopting an amendment to an existing by-law cannot be reconsidered. It cannot be rescinded without taking all the steps required for amending the by-law. [See Ques. 82, 91, 92, 100, 102, 111.]

95. QUES. As a proposed revision of the by-laws is an amendment, is it not improper to lay the revision on the table? Is it not out of order to apply any subsidiary motion to it except to amend or motions to close or limit debate?

ANS. No. The revised by-laws are proposed as a substitute for the existing ones; but as the existing ones are not pending, the substitute (amendment) is not a subsidiary but is a main motion, as stated in R. O. R., pp. 55, 273, and the various subsidiary motions may be applied to it, as to any other main motion. [See page 38 and Ques. 96, 97.]

96. QUES. When an amendment to the constitution is laid on the table in a society having regular sessions as frequently as quarterly, can it be taken from the table at the same or the next session and acted upon without further notice?

ANS. Yes.

97. QUES. A revised constitution is submitted by a committee on revision, and one article after much discussion is laid on the table. Was that a correct procedure?

ANS. No. The pending question was on substituting the revised constitution for the existing one, and that question might have been laid on the table, but not a part of it. The different sections are considered separately only for amendment.

98. QUES. The constitution requires for its amendment "a two-thirds vote of those present and entitled to vote." The vote on an amendment was 99 in favor and 7 opposed; 48 other members were present but did not vote. It did not appear fair to the parliamentarian to count the 48 silent ones in the negative, and so she ruled that the amendment was adopted. Was the ruling correct?

ANS. The parliamentarian gave her opinion. The chairman is the one that can give a ruling. While the parliamentarian's opinion of the unfairness of counting in the negative the 48 who neglected to vote is perfectly sound, yet the constitution required for its amendment a two-thirds vote of those present and entitled to vote. There were 154 of these present, two thirds of which is 103, not 99. Her duty was to obey the constitution, however unjust or even absurd it may be, provided the meaning is clear. In this case there can be no doubt as to the meaning of the constitution. [See Ques. 99, 342, 343.]

99. QUES. Our by-laws provide that they may be amended by a two-thirds vote of the members present. Twenty members were present; 12 votes were cast in the affirmative, 6 in the negative, and 2 were blanks. The club accepted the ruling of the chair that two thirds of the votes cast ignoring blanks was a two-thirds vote of the members present. Was the amendment adopted or lost?

ANS. The fact that the club accepted the ruling that two thirds of the votes cast ignoring blanks is the same as "a two-thirds vote of the members present" does not make it so. The amendment was lost, and the announcement that it was adopted is null and void. See R. O. R., p. 204. [See Ques. 98.]

100. QUES. Article III of our constitution contains the following: "The annual dues for each club shall be $3 for 30 members or less, and 10 cents per capita for each additional member." Appended to the call for the last meeting was a proposed amendment to the constitution "to strike out of Article III '$3' and insert '$6.'" The amendment was adopted, and then, in order to make the larger clubs bear their proper share of the burden, the article was further amended by striking out "10" and insert-

ing "25." (a) Was the latter amendment permissible not hav-ing been stated in the call? (b) If not permissible, does it mean that a proposed amendment that involves expenditure of money cannot be further amended from the floor?

ANS. (a) No. (b) No. A proposed amendment to consti-tutions or by-laws already adopted may be amended when it is pending, provided the secondary amendment does not increase the proposed change and is therefore fully covered by the notice. Thus, in the case stated, it would have been in order to move to amend the proposed amendment by striking out "$6" and inserting "$4." This is thoroughly explained in R. O. R., p. 272. [See Ques. 91, 92, 94.]

101. QUES. On the first day of a convention, one of the pro-posed amendments to the by-laws was defeated. Outside of the convention, a number of parliamentarians discussed the question of reconsidering the vote rejecting the amendment on the follow-ing day when the other amendments to the by-laws were to be considered. One thought the vote could be reconsidered by a two-thirds vote; another thought it would require a unanimous vote; but the majority were of the opinion that a vote on an amend-ment to the by-laws cannot be reconsidered. (a) May a defeated amendment to the by-laws be reconsidered? (b) If it can be re-considered, what vote is required?

ANS. (a) Yes. (b) Only a majority vote. In the Table of Rules, p. 6, R. O. R., opposite Amend Constitutions, By-Laws, Rules of Order, in the column headed Can Be Reconsidered, will be found the figure 2. Note 2 says, "An affirmative vote on this motion cannot be reconsidered," which means that a negative vote can be reconsidered, because the rules at the heads of the columns apply to every case not marked by a star or excepted in a note. On page 158 of R.O.R., Amend the By-Laws is in the list of motions affirmative votes on which cannot be reconsidered. [See Ques. 26.]

102. QUES. After an amendment to the by-laws or constitu-tion has been adopted, may the vote be reconsidered or rescinded at this same convention, if two thirds of the members present at the convention desire to do so?

ANS. No, not if the desire was unanimous. By-laws should not be amended so carelessly that it could be possible within a few days that even a majority would be in favor of a reconsideration. [See Ques. 82, 111, 383.]

103. QUES. Has the president or chairman any authority or power to state when the amendment to the constitution or by-laws is to go into effect without the consent of the society?

ANS. None at all. Before its adoption a motion or resolution may be adopted specifying a time for the amendment to go into effect. Or, the motion to adopt the amendment may prescribe the time for it to go into effect. But, if neither of these things has been done, the amendment goes into effect immediately upon its adoption, and it is too late for even the society, much less the president, to change that time. [See Ques. 59, 108, 109.]

104. QUES. A national organization amended its by-laws so that certain requirements were made mandatory upon its subordinates. The by-laws of one of its subordinates require a three-fourths vote of the entire membership for their amendment. So large an attendance at any meeting cannot be obtained. What can be done?

ANS. The order of the superior body is superior to the by-laws of subordinates and must be obeyed. If the state enacts a law that conflicts with the by-laws of a society, the state law must be obeyed. In both cases the conflicting by-law or clause is null and void and is repealed. [See Ques. 64.]

105. QUES. Is it legal for a club to require a vote of three fourths of the membership to amend the by-laws?

ANS. A by-law cannot be illegal unless it conflicts with the constitution of the club or some state or national law. Your club has a perfect right to adopt a by-law requiring a vote of three fourths of the membership to amend its by-laws, but it would be unwise. When clubs are old and very large it is impossible to secure an attendance of a majority of the membership. [See Ques. 107.]

106. QUES. A president of a society was elected for a term of two years at the annual meeting held in April of an even year. Six months later an amendment to the by-laws was proposed changing the time of the election of the president from the even to the odd years. This amendment will be voted on at the next meeting. When will this amendment, if adopted, go into effect? As the next annual meeting is in an odd year, will it be necessary for the society to elect a president at that meeting?

ANS. If this amendment is adopted at your next annual meeting it will go into effect immediately, and since that meeting is in an odd year, it will be necessary to elect a president at that time. If it is desired not to legislate the present president out of office, it can be done as follows: You can amend the motion to adopt the proposed amendment by adding a proviso similar to this: "Provided that the term of office of the present president shall not expire until the close of the annual meeting two years hence." If the motion to amend the by-laws is thus amended, its adoption reëlects the president for two years. The amendment should be acted upon before electing the officers. In the notice do not place the proviso as a part of the proposed by-law. See R. O. R., p. 271. [See Ques. 59, 103, 108.]

107. QUES. The by-laws of a society provide that they may be amended by a three-fourths vote of the entire membership, notice having been given at the previous regular meeting. These by-laws were adopted when the society was very small. Since that time it has grown to more than 600 members. It is a necessity that the by-laws be amended to meet the requirements of such a large organization. Repeated attempts have been made for two years to amend them, but it is impossible to get an attendance of three fourths of the entire membership. What can be done about it?

ANS. Since the society has adopted a provision for amendment in its by-laws that is impracticable to carry out, the only thing that can be done is to change that provision to a reasonable one, complying, in making the change, with the spirit of the existing by-laws as nearly as possible. The makers of the by-laws did not foresee that the time would come when it would be impracticable to secure the attendance of three fourths of the membership at a meeting. If notice of the amendment of this by-law is given as required by the by-laws, and it is adopted by a three-fourths vote of the members present, and then a mail vote is taken on the adoption of the amendment as described in R. O. R., pp. 199, 200, and three fourths of the votes cast are in favor of the amendment, the amendment is adopted by a method as nearly in the spirit of the by-laws as is practicable. While voting by mail is not allowed by R. O. R. unless it is provided for in the by-laws, yet this rule must be broken in order to comply with the spirit of an unwise by-law. In R. O. R., p. 270, the committee on by-laws is warned against similar provisions in by-laws. [See Ques. 105.]

108. QUES. (a) When an amendment to a by-law is adopted a month after an officer was elected at the annual meeting to serve

two years under the by-laws then in force, is it retroactive? (b) That is, can a by-law that provides that no member can hold office for more than four successive years legislate out of office one who was legally elected under the old by-law, which had no limit as to the length of time a member could hold office?

ANS. (a) No. (b) Yes. The by-law does not affect anything done in the past and is not retroactive. It does not affect the officers of the society until it is actually adopted, and then it immediately goes into effect, as stated in R. O. R., p. 271, last paragraph. A society may so amend its by-laws as to do away with certain offices, and thus legislate out of office those filling them. Such an amendment is not retroactive, as it did not affect anything prior to its adoption. Suppose a society has by-laws that allowed it to elect officers for life, and they had so elected them: this does not prevent the amending of the by-law so as to limit the term of office to such an extent as to legislate every officer out of office.

In the case of your society, if you do not wish the amendment to affect the term of the present officers, a motion to that effect should have been adopted before voting on the amendment, as explained at the bottom of p. 271, R. O. R. [See Ques. 58, 59, 109.]

109. QUES. What is the effect upon incumbent officers of the adoption of an amendment of the constitution or by-laws affecting their offices, when no motion is adopted protecting them at the time the amendment is adopted?

ANS. They are affected by the amendment even if it legislates them out of office, as the amendment takes effect immediately upon its adoption. If it is desired that the amendment should not affect those in office, it is necessary to adopt such a motion before the amendment is adopted, or to incorporate it in the motion to adopt the amendment. [See Ques. 59, 108.]

110. QUES. May an organization composed of its officers and of delegates from auxiliary societies amend its constitution so as to restrict the amending of the instrument to conventions held in alternate years? Or, in other words, is it in the power of one convention to prevent the next succeeding convention from amending the constitution?

ANS. Yes, provided the constitution is amended in strict compliance with the provisions for its amendment. The constitution, or by-laws, adopted at one convention is binding on succeeding conventions, just as the by-laws of a society adopted at one session are binding on future sessions. R. O. R., p. 256.

111. QUES. At the last annual meeting of a state federation of clubs, an amendment to the constitution was adopted, and a motion made that it should not go into effect until the next annual meeting. There is now a wish that it should not go into effect at all. Can the action of last year be rescinded, thus leaving the article as it was before it was amended?

ANS. No. Your statement omits essential things. You state that the motion specifying the time the amendment was to take effect was made, not that it was adopted, and even if it is assumed that it was adopted, it is not stated whether it was adopted before, at the same time, or after the adoption of the amendment. From the way the statement is worded, it would appear that the motion was adopted after the adoption of the amendment. If so, it was null and void, as the amendment had become a part of the constitution and was already in effect. See R. O. R., p. 271. If the motion specifying the time for the amendment to take effect was adopted before or at the same time the amendment was adopted, it could be rescinded at another meeting, as explained under Rescind, R. O. R., p. 169. But the effect of rescinding the motion is not to rescind the amendment to the constitution, as the question implies, but rather to cause the amendment to take effect immediately. There is no way to rescind the amendment except by taking the steps provided in the constitution for its amendment. [See Ques. 82, 94, 102.]

112. QUES. An organization has a by-law to the effect that "notice of an amendment to a by-law must be given in writing to members one month previous to action." At a regular meeting a member proposed an amendment to a by-law, which was thereupon referred to a committee. Said amendment was printed in the notice of the meeting for the following month. At this second meeting the committee reported, its report consisting of a substitute amendment for the one proposed the month before. The chairman had the assembly consider the amendment according to R. O. R., p. 271, on the ground that, as due notice had been given of the amendment, the report of the committee could be acted upon as a report regularly presented. (a) Was the ruling correct? (b) The criticism has been made that the substitute amend-

ment itself should have been referred to a committee and consideration of it deferred for another month. Is this criticism correct?

ANS. (a) A committee to which is referred a proposed amendment to the by-laws is not a "committee appointed to revise the by-laws," which is referred to on p. 271, R. O. R. The substitute reported by the committee should have been treated in accordance with the principles stated on p. 272 R. O. R. for amending proposed amendments of by-laws. (b) The substitute reported by the committee should not have been referred to a committee. It had already been in the hands of a committee. If the substitute varied enough from the ·original amendment to require it to be sent to the members, then it was out of order, as shown on p. 272, above referred to.

As the case is stated, it does not appear that "notice of the proposed amendment was given in writing to members one month previous to action," as required by the by-laws. The notice appears to have been given in connection with the notice of the meeting at which action was taken, and therefore not a month in advance. If so, the amendment was not legally adopted.

CHAPTER XL

QUESTIONS ANSWERED

COMMITTEES AND THEIR REPORTS

113. QUES. A committee is composed of four members. One is absent. (a) Can the chairman vote? (b) If so, when?

ANS. (a) Yes. (b) He may vote at any time, but it is his duty to vote whenever it will affect the result.

114. QUES. In a society in which the president appoints, and is ex-officio a member of, all committees, (a) Has he the power to call a meeting of a committee, or does that power rest with the chairman? (b) Has the president any more authority in the committee than any other member?

ANS. (a) The chairman of the committee is the only person who can call a committee meeting. If he neglects to do it, a meeting may be called by any two members. See R. O. R., p. 212. (b) No. See R. O. R., p. 210. [See Ques. 233, 234, 235.]

115. QUES. According to parliamentary practice, ought the president to name the chairman of committees, or is it customary for the executive board to appoint them?

ANS. It depends entirely upon circumstances. There is no uniform practice in the case. In some clubs the committees are elected by the club, in some they are appointed by the president, and in some by the executive board. Whoever appoints the committee has the power to appoint its chairman, provided the appointment is made at the time the committee is appointed. If no chairman is appointed, the first member appointed is chairman, unless the committee elects its own chairman. In many clubs the chairman of each standing committee is appointed by the president or by the club, and he is authorized to appoint the other members of the committee. This plan has many advantages.

116. QUES. The by-laws provide that certain committees shall be appointed by the president as soon as convenient after his elec

tion. The president appointed the committees and then resigned. Does the resignation of the president affect the committees?

ANS. No. When the president has appointed a committee and they do not decline, the appointment is complete, and it is not affected by the resignation or death of the president who appointed them.

117. QUES. When the chairman of a committee resigns, who appoints a new chairman?

ANS. Whoever appointed the chairman originally. If no one attends to it within a reasonable time, the committee should elect its own chairman. [See Ques. 118, 119, 120, 121, 171.]

118. QUES. Mrs. A. was appointed chairman of a committee by her club, with power to appoint her committee. Mrs. A now wishes to resign. What should be done about the committee?

ANS. If the committee has not been appointed, the club should elect another chairman and authorize her to appoint her associates. If the committee has been appointed, there are three courses open to the club: (1) It may discharge the committee and appoint another chairman, authorizing her to appoint the rest of the committee; (2) it may appoint another chairman; or (3) it may take no action, in which case the committee elects its own chairman from its membership. Which is the best course to pursue depends upon the circumstances of the case. [See Ques. 117, 119, 120, 121, 171.]

119. QUES. A committee of three was appointed by the executive committee to do a special piece of work. The chairman resigned. (a) Should the remaining two members have completed the work? (b) The president appointed a new chairman. Was this proper?

ANS. (a) Yes, if no additional member is appointed. (b) It was proper if the president originally appointed the committee, not otherwise. The appointing power alone has the right to fill vacancies unless the by-laws provide differently. [See Ques. 117, 118, 120, 121, 171.]

120. QUES. The society appointed a permanent club-house committee with full power. It is now desired to change the chairman. Can this be done, and, if so, by the society or by the executive board?

ANS. The society. The body that appointed a committee can remove or replace any of its members, or can appoint another committee in its place, or can replace any member, unless the by-laws prescribe a term of office. Its being called a permanent committee does not affect the case. [See Ques. 121.]

121. QUES. In case a member of a committee remained away from several meetings without an excuse, could he be removed from the committee by the chairman?

ANS. No. The chairman of a committee has no power to remove a member of the committee for any reason unless he appointed the other members of the committee. He may request the body that appointed the committee to remove the delinquent member. [See Ques. 120 and page 266.]

122. QUES. Our society elected as chairman of a committee one who is not a member of the society. Was such action legal or in good form?

ANS. Yes, the action was legal. Whether it was in "good form," by which I understand you mean expedient, can be decided only by each society for itself. Officers and committees are chosen by a society for certain purposes, and it has the right to select such persons as it thinks will accomplish those purposes most efficiently. While the society can elect any one as a member or chairman of a committee, neither the president nor the board can place on a committee any one who is not a member of the society, unless specially authorized by the society. The society cannot elect as a delegate to the parent society any one who is not a member of the society. [See Ques. 123.]

123. QUES. When an officer is authorized to appoint a committee of a local society, can he appoint a person who is not a member of that particular local society, provided the person appointed is a member of the state or national organization of which the local society is a subordinate?

ANS. No, an individual cannot. A society may appoint on a committee one who is not a member of the society, but authorizing its president to appoint a committee does not empower him to place on the committee any but members, unless permission to do so is expressly given. [See Ques. 122.]

124. QUES. In a convention composed of delegates from local organizations, should the committee on resolutions, credentials, and the like be appointed from the members of the convention, or may they be appointed from members of local organizations, re-

gardless of the fact that they may not become delegates to the convention?

ANS. It is optional with the convention. In some very large conventions the members of these committees are kept so busy that they have no opportunity to attend the meetings and engage in the debates and voting. Societies whose delegates are appointed on these committees are virtually deprived of representation in such conventions.

125. QUES. What are the duties of the credentials committee?

ANS. The committee should receive and examine the credentials of all delegates and alternates, and furnish all who have proper credentials with suitable badges. They should report to the convention from time to time the number of accredited delegates and alternates, and furnish a list of the names promptly to the tellers, or assist the tellers in identifying those entitled to vote. In cases of doubt they should report the facts to the convention and ask for instructions. [See page 281.]

126. QUES. Please explain the exact duties of a resolution committee at a convention. (a) Is it not to receive any resolutions referred to it and report amendments, etc., back to the convention, and move their adoption, and also to frame resolutions of thanks, etc.? (b) They have no power to take any action themselves, have they?

ANS. (a) Yes. (b) I understand this question to mean, "Has the resolutions committee the right to report any resolution, except of thanks, unless the resolution has been previously referred to it by the society?" The answer to this question is: The committee may originate resolutions, unless the society prohibits it. Generally it is allowed. A committee is under the orders of the society, and the duties of the resolutions committee are whatever the society prescribes by rule or custom. [See Ques. 136 and Model for Standing Rules, page 398.]

127. QUES. A committee was appointed to furnish the clubhouse and to build an addition. The next year, at a special meeting called for the purpose, it was voted almost unanimously to continue the committee, "with full power," to serve until the completion of the building. At the annual meeting the next year, the report of a committee appointed by the executive board, con-

taining three recommendations, was accepted by the club. One of these recommended the discharge of the committee. Afterward at the same meeting a vote of confidence in the chairman of the building committee was adopted. In my opinion, all the members present and voting (more than one hundred) understood that the vote meant the retention of the building committee. That was the intent of the motion. For nearly two years afterward the quarterly and annual reports of the committee were called for by the president, were made by the committee, and were accepted and filed by the club, no one objecting. At the last annual meeting a new president was elected, and he has ruled that the building committee was discharged two years before by the club's accepting the report of a committee recommending the building committee's discharge. The ground was that accepting the report adopted its recommendations. Is that ruling correct?

ANS. The statement involves several errors that need explanation. (a) The committee that reported the recommendation that the building committee be discharged should have reported a resolution to carry out its recommendation, as stated at the bottom of p. 214, R. O. R. On p. 215, after giving two examples to show the importance of the committee's submitting resolutions to carry out its recommendations, the statement closes with: "The committee should never leave to others the responsibility of preparing resolutions to carry out their recommendations. They should consider this as one of their most important duties."

(b) The new president is correct in saying that the acceptance of the committee's report adopted the committee's recommendation that the building committee be discharged. The effect of that vote was to make the recommendation the recommendation of the club. The club should then have voted to discharge the committee, which requires a two-thirds vote, as notice of the motion had not been given. If a two-thirds vote could not be obtained, notice should have been given that the motion to discharge the committee would be made at the next meeting, at which time only a majority vote would be required for its adoption.

(c) The vote of confidence in the committee's chairman did not reverse the vote recommending the discharge of the committee, though this seems to have been the understanding of the voters at the time. If it had that effect, the motion was out of order until after the vote accepting the committee's report had been reconsidered, and the recommendation to discharge the committee had been struck out. It is absurd to endorse a recommendation that a committee be discharged, and then immediately to vote to continue the committee.

(*d*) The fact that, notwithstanding the endorsement of the recommendation to discharge the building committee, its quarterly and annual reports were called for by the president, and were made by the committee and were accepted by the club for nearly two years without any protest, shows that the club understood that the committee had not been discharged. It is too late now to raise the question as to the effect of that vote. The club acquiesced in the action of its president in calling for the building committee's reports, thereby approving the ruling that the committee was not discharged.

(*e*) The vote of the club endorsing or adopting a recommendation that the building committee be discharged did not discharge the committee, according to R. O. R., the parliamentary authority of the club, and the club by its action afterward showed that its members did not at the time understand that the committee was discharged. The committee is still in existence, and can be discharged only as prescribed on p. 133, R. O. R.

128. QUES. When a committee's report contains recommendations or resolutions, (*a*) is not action on the recommendations or resolutions the only action necessary? (*b*) Is it necessary first to adopt the report in order to act upon the resolutions separately? (*c*) Is it necessary to adopt the "report as a whole" after action has been taken on the recommendations or resolutions?

ANS. (*a*) Yes. (*b*) No. The adoption of the report carries with it the adoption of the recommendations or resolutions. (*c*) No. See R. O. R., pp. 223, 224.

129. QUES. (*a*) When a report contains a recommendation, and some one moves that the report be accepted, does not that adopt the work and also the recommendation of the committee? (*b*) It is useless to move to accept the work done and then move to adopt the resolution, is it not? (*c*) Often in meetings a long report is read that does not include recommendations, and it does not seem necessary really to take any action, but some one will move to adopt the report. Is it not proper to move to accept in such cases?

ANS. (*a*) Yes, if the motion is adopted. (*b*) Yes. (*c*) Yes but no action is necessary. See R. O. R., pages 223, 224. [See Ques. 128, 130, 131.]

130. QUES. A motion that a club give $10 to the Civic Association is referred to a committee, and the committee recommends that the club make no contribution this year. The motion to adopt the report of the committee is lost. What is the next step?

ANS. No motion to adopt the report should have been made. The chair should have said, "The question is on the adoption of the motion that the club give $10 to the Civic Association, the recommendation of the committee to the contrary notwithstanding." If this motion is lost, the matter is ended and other business is taken up. In the case you mention the next step should have been for the chair to state the question as given above. [See Par. Prac., pp. 65, 66, for an illustration, and also Ques. 128, 129, 131.]

131. QUES. If the society adopts an officer's report with recommendations in it, do the recommendations then become the recommendations of the society?

ANS. Yes, recommendations, but they do not become resolutions. [See Ques. 128, 129, 130.]

132. QUES. At an annual meeting held for election of officers, is it proper for an outgoing president to appoint committees for the incoming administration?

ANS. No.

133. QUES. What is the most approved and satisfactory method of appointing a nominating committee?

ANS. Every method has its objectionable features. No one method is best for all organizations. In some societies it is difficult to find competent persons who are willing to accept office. In other organizations there are many candidates scrambling for office. In a state organization that meets only once a year, the best plan generally is to have the nominating committee appointed by the executive board at least a month before the committee reports, .or at the time of election.

134. QUES. Do all standing committees go out of existence at the expiration of the term?

ANS. No. If not provided otherwise in the by-laws, the terms of members expire when their successors are elected or appointed. [See Ques. 135.]

135. QUES. Do special committees die with an outgoing ad-

ministration, whether such committees have completed work assigned them or not? Do they die when they fail to report at the time specified?

ANS. No, to both questions. A special committee appointed by the society to do a piece of work continues in existence until its duties are performed, unless discharged sooner. Take, for instance, a committee appointed to recommend a site for a club building. Such a committee is not affected by the occurrence of the annual meeting or by the change of the administration. The society to which it reports is the same.

But in a body like a convention of delegates, or a city council, or a board of directors, which ceases to exist at a definite time, a special committee expires with the body that appointed it, unless it is appointed expressly to report to the next convention, as in case of a committee to revise the by-laws. If it does not report, its life does not continue after the close of the convention to which it was to report. If it is desired to continue the committee, it can be done by adopting a motion to that effect. [See Ques. 134.]

136. QUES. When a resolutions committee brings in resolutions of various kinds, including those of courtesy, does it report those of courtesy first or last, in giving its report?

ANS. In any order that suits the committee, though usually the courtesy resolutions are brought in last. [See Ques. 126.]

137. QUES. If a motion has been made to substitute the minority report for the report of the committee, (a) is the question put on the substituting, or (b) is the committee's report open for amendments first, and then the minority report open for amendments, and then the question put on substituting and then on adopting? In other words, (c) is a report treated as a resolution would be?

ANS. (a) Yes. (b) Yes; this is the method of treating the motion to substitute. (c) Yes. [See Par. Prac., p. 26.]

138. QUES. Has a society the right to demand that the minutes of its executive board be read to the society?

ANS. While the minutes of an executive board cannot be demanded by a member of the society, yet the society may by a two-thirds vote, or by a vote of a majority of the membership, require them to be produced and read. If previous notice is given, only a majority vote is necessary. [See Ques. 260.]

139. QUES. May an organization resolve itself into a com-

mittee of the whole for the purpose of discussing the report of a committee?

Ans. Yes. [See Ques. 140.]

140. Ques. When we come out of committee of the whole can any one make a motion, or only the chairmen of the different committees? How do we get back into the regular order of business?

Ans. The instant the chairman of the committee of the whole declares the adoption of the motion for the committee to rise and report, the committee of the whole ceases to exist and the assembly is in session. The president resumes the chair, which has been vacated by the chairman of the committee of the whole. The latter, instead of resuming his seat, stands and addresses the president, stating that the committee of the whole has had under consideration such and such a matter [describing it], and has directed him to report the following resolution, or amendment, or whatever the committee has agreed to. The business is then in exactly the same condition as if the report had been made by a special committee. The chairmen of the different committees have no more right to the floor than other members. Any member has a right to debate or make such a motion as he could make when considering the report of a special committee. This whole procedure is more fully described on pp. 229–233, R. O. R. [See Ques. 139.]

There is seldom, if ever, an occasion in an ordinary society when the committee of the whole is of any advantage. If it is used, the society should limit each speech in committee to two or three minutes in length. But, without going into committee of the whole, the society may extend the number of speeches to any desired limit, at the same time cutting down their length, which should generally be done whenever the number allowed is increased. Or the subject may be considered informally as described in R. O. R., p. 234.

CHAPTER XLI

QUESTIONS ANSWERED

NOMINATIONS; ELECTIONS

NOMINATIONS

141. QUES. What is the difference between a nominating committee and a committee on nominations?

ANS. None. Either title is applied to a committee appointed to submit nominations.

142. QUES. An organization has an annual convention which is a delegated body. Can a member of the organization who is not a member of the convention nominate a member for an office?

ANS. No. A nomination can be made only by one who has the right to make a motion.

143. QUES. A county superintendent of schools is to be elected by the county school directors. In nominating persons for the position, can the nominator talk against the other candidates? In other words, are the rules of decorum in debate applicable to a case of this kind?

ANS. The nomination is debatable, and since the nominees are not members of the board of school directors, the rules of decorum in debate as far as avoiding personalities do not apply. The relative merits of candidates for employment may be freely discussed.

144. QUES. How can the statement in the table, R. O. R., p. 7, "Nominations, to Make," be reconciled with that on p. 96, next to the last line, which says, "It is undebatable?"

ANS. The "it," p. 96, refers to the *method* of making nominations, that is, from the floor by ballot, etc., and not to making the nominations. The method of making nominations is undebatable, but a nomination itself may be debated.

145. QUES. Our constitution requires that the general officers shall be nominated by ballot. Can the whole number of general officers be nominated on one ballot?

Ans. Yes.

146. Ques. Is it necessary for a candidate to be nominated in order to be elected an officer of a society?

Ans. No. The person receiving the requisite number of votes at an election is elected if qualified in other respects, regardless of whether he was nominated or not. [See Ques. 159, 172, 173, 212, 213.]

147. Ques. Has a member of a society the right to nominate herself for an office?

Ans. Yes, she has the right, but it is scarcely conceivable that one would commit such an indelicate act. It implies that she has not one friend who is willing to nominate her, and lessens her chances of election.

148. Ques. (a) Does the fact that a member has accepted a nomination from the nominating committee preclude his being nominated from the floor for another office? (b) May a candidate be voted for on the same ticket for two offices?

Ans. (a) No. (b) Yes.

149. Ques. At a recent election one man arose and nominated every man in the organization as a director. A new board of directors was to be elected and there was some trouble among the members in regard to the election. How many can one nominate for one office?

Ans. Only one, except by general consent, until every other member has had an opportunity to nominate a candidate. In no case can one nominate more candidates than there are places to fill.

150. Ques. The nominating committee has had the custom of inviting suggestions for nominations for office. Is the committee at liberty to ignore these suggestions?

Ans. Yes.

151. Ques. Has a nominating committee a right to nominate themselves for offices?

Ans. Yes, they have the right. If a rule were adopted preventing it, the presiding officer, or whoever was authorized to appoint the nominating committee, could keep off the ticket the names of prominent candidates for office by placing them on the nominating committee. The committee is perfectly free as to its nominations, except as limited by the by-laws. When a nominating committee takes advantage of its power and nominates an unreasonable number of its own members, the remedy is to nominate from the floor other persons for the same offices, or to move to appoint another nominating committee composed of the opposition, to report another ticket.

152. QUES. Is it necessary for the nominating committee to consult every person they wish to nominate, before nominating them, to ascertain if they will take the office if elected?

ANS. It is not necessary unless required by the by-laws, but it is desirable when there is any doubt as to the acceptance of the office by the nominee if elected. This is especially necessary in conventions and other bodies meeting only annually. [See Ques. 213.]

153. QUES. The by-laws specify that it shall be the duty of the nominating committee to prepare two tickets to be voted at the annual meeting. Under this by-law may the committee present two tickets with the same name for president on both?

ANS. Yes. Frequently all parties are united on one officer, particularly the secretary or treasurer. If it were desired to prevent any name's being on both tickets, the by-laws should have so specified.

154. QUES. A motion was made that nominations be made by ballot, and before it was put to vote a substitute motion was made that the nominations be made by acclamation. The chair ruled it out of order, on the principle that it merely made the affirmative of the amended question equivalent to the negative of the original motion. Was that correct?

ANS. No. The affirmative of the motion that nominations be by acclamation is not the equivalent of the negative of the motion that nominations be by ballot. Deciding that nominations would not be by ballot left the assembly the choice between nominations from the floor, nominations by the chair, and nominations by a committee.

I am not sure that I understand what you mean by a motion "to make nominations by acclamation." Acclamation in deliberative assemblies is defined in the Century Dictionary to be "the spontaneous approval or adoption of a resolution or measure by unanimous viva voce vote, in distinction from a formal division or ballot." The only way a nomination can be made by acclamation is for every one to call out the same name spontaneously.

155. QUES. The by-laws of our organization provide that nominations of officers of the lodges shall be conducted by a

nominating committee consisting of the president and all the ex-presidents of the lodges. This committee is required to "consider and vote upon all recommendations sent in by members upon blanks supplied to them for that purpose. It shall select the candidates by a majority vote, and report the result thereof to the lodge at its next meeting. The nominating committee shall secure the consent of each candidate before it presents its report." Under these by-laws, with R. O. R. as parliamentary authority, (a) Are nominations from the floor permissible after the committee reports? (b) May the nominating committee present two names, or must they decide on one? (c) If the vote of the nominating committee is by written ballot and the result is a tie, the chairman having voted, what decision is made?

Ans. (a) No. Your by-laws outrank the rules of order and prescribe a definite method of nominations for your society. All the members have an opportunity to submit nominations to the committee, but of these names only the ones that receive a majority vote of the committee will be presented to the society as nominees. (b) Yes, they may present two or more. They are required to vote on every nominee suggested by the members, and every nominee that receives a majority vote should be reported by the committee to the society as a nominee. There is no limit to the number of nominees for each office, according to your by-laws. (c) The ballot vote being a tie, the candidate has failed to be nominated by the committee. [See Ques. 156, 157.]

156. Ques. A society having voted that nominations shall be by ballot, are nominations from the floor also in order?

Ans. No, unless the society authorizes it. The main object of making nominations by ballot is to get at the real wishes of the members, uninfluenced by the importance of the person making the nomination, and this object is defeated by allowing nominations from the floor. If the object of the ballot were not secrecy, it would be simpler to allow nominations from the floor, and for the chair to ask those in favor of each nomination to rise and be counted. In this way in a fraction of the time the number in favor of each nomination could be found. But the object of the ballot is secrecy, and therefore, the society having ordered the nominations to be made by ballot, it is not in order to make open nominations. [See Ques. 155, 157.]

157. QUES. Some of our clubs have one of the following by-laws. Does either of them preclude nominations from the floor?

(1) Nominations for office shall be by ballot, and the two candidates having the highest number of votes shall be the nominees for election.

(2) During the first two days of the convention each delegate may deposit in the ballot-box her choice of officers. The nominating committee shall present the names of the two receiving the highest number of votes for each office.

ANS. Yes. Each of these rules provides for nominations by ballot. Every member has had an opportunity to nominate, and therefore nominations from the floor are not allowed. An instance of this will be seen in Par. Prac., p. 150. These by-laws are of very doubtful utility. They are a source of trouble, because many understand them to limit the voting to the two nominees, which is not the case. A society, on account of this misunderstanding, felt bound to elect the minority candidate, who had only 5 votes on the nominating ballot, because the other candidate, who had 95 votes, declined election. The legal effect of such by-laws is simply to limit the names of candidates printed on the ticket to two for each office. Members may vote for any one they please. [See Ques. 155, 156.]

158. QUES. Is it legal for a nominating committee to present two names for the same office to the voting body?

ANS. Yes. If the assembly in such case wishes the committee to submit only one name, it can refer the report back to the committee, with instructions to that effect. Sometimes the committee is required to submit two names for each office.

159. QUES. What would be the procedure in the event of a nominating committee's failing to nominate a president, provided nominations from the floor are not allowed under the by-laws?

ANS. Ballot for officers, without nominations; or, if preferred, a nominating ballot could be taken first. [See Ques. 146, 172, 173, 212, 213.]

160. QUES. If A nominates B and the motion to close nominations is carried, may A then withdraw the nomination of B?

ANS. No, not until nominations are reopened, unless with the consent of B.

161. QUES. A name is presented for membership, in accordance with the by-laws, to the board of directors, and is laid on the

table. Can the name be brought before a new board, the same as if it had never been proposed before?

Ans. Yes. Even if your by-laws prohibited a rejected name's being proposed again for a year, it would make no difference. The name has not been finally acted upon. When it was laid on the table it was presumably for the purpose of investigation and could have been taken up at the next meeting.

162. Ques. Is it necessary to have a motion that nominations close?

Ans. No. When the election is by ballot, the chairman should announce that ''nominations are closed'' after he has asked whether there are any further nominations, and no more are proposed.

163. Ques. Has a nominee for an office the right to move that nominations close when she is the only nominee?

Ans. No, unless a reasonable time has been given for other nominations, in which case she may do so. See R. O. R., p. 97.

164. Ques. Since it requires a two-thirds vote to close nominations, is it reasonable that a majority vote can immediately reopen them without any change in conditions?

Ans. When nominations were closed, those in favor of keeping them open must have been not more than one third of those voting. Is it conceivable that this minority of one third or less should become a majority ''immediately without any change in conditions?'' Is it not reasonable that, when a majority wish to reopen nominations, they should have the power to do so, as long as a much smaller number could have prevented their being closed? It might be argued with some show of reason that, since a two-thirds vote is required to close nominations, it should require a similar vote to keep them closed. But experience has shown that it is better to allow a majority to prevent the reopening of nominations. A two-thirds vote is required for closing nominations, the polls, or debate, because in each of these cases members are deprived of some inherent right to membership in a deliberative assembly. No one is deprived of a right when the polls are reopened.

165. Ques. Three negative votes defeat a candidate for membership in our club. Is the candidate defeated for all time, or may he be nominated again and again at future meetings, the same as if he had not been previously defeated?

Ans. In the article on Renewal of Motions, p. 171, R. O. R., the rule on this question is fully stated. The nomination may be renewed at any future session, the same as if it had never been made. If this right to renew motions again and again is abused, the remedy is to adopt a rule or order or by-law prohibiting the renewal of certain motions for, say, three or six months after their rejection. [See Note on Session, R. O. R., p. 257.]

166. QUES. A nominating committee was to be elected. Rival factions each nominated a member for chairman. Both were elected but neither received as many votes as another member. Who is chairman, the member who received the most votes, or the nominee for chairman having the most votes?

ANS. If the chairman was voted for directly, it is impossible that two candidates should both receive a majority of the votes cast for chairman. The one receiving the majority of votes for that office was elected. If the committee was voted for without specifying who was chairman, the member receiving the most votes should call the committee together, and it should elect its own chairman. The fact that any one was nominated for chairman has nothing to do with the case. Even if members put the word "chairman" in connection with the name of a nominee, it does not affect the case unless the voters are instructed to indicate which one they wish for chairman, in which case the one elected chairman is the one who receives a majority of the votes so indicated. The presiding officer may direct voters simply to head the list with the name of their choice for chairman, or to indicate their choice in some other way. [See Ques. 115.]

167. QUES. A society uses a nominating ballot to avoid giving offense by making open nominations when they wish to change officers. They then declare the nominating ballot to be the electing ballot. Is this the best procedure?

ANS. No. The simplest way to obtain the result desired would be to vote to proceed to the election of the officers by ballot without nominations. The method you describe is to nominate by ballot, and then to elect viva voce. It is a viva voce election when by a viva voce vote you declare a nominating ballot to be the electing ballot, after you know what the nominating ballot is. You simply vote to elect the candidates who have received a majority of the votes on the nominating ballot. This is illegal if the by-laws require a ballot election. [See Ques. 168.]

168. QUES. Is it proper to declare the nominating ballot the formal or electing ballot?

Ans. Declaring the nominating ballot the electing ballot does away with the secrecy of the ballot just as much as the cases referred to in R. O. R., p. 194, and therefore is out of order if the by-laws require the election to be by ballot. If the by-laws do not require a ballot, but the society has ordered the vote to be by ballot, this order may be reconsidered on the same or the succeeding day, if it has not been partially executed. If it cannot be reconsidered, the unexecuted part may be rescinded at the same meeting or any time thereafter. [See Drill in Par. Prac., p. 151, and Ques. 167.]

169. Ques. A nominating committee makes its report and is appointed election committee. The candidate for president withdraws, and no action is taken on the withdrawal. The election is to be held at the next meeting three weeks later, the polls being open one half-hour before the meeting begins. The Australian ballot is used. (a) Because the committee has reported, has it finished its work? (b) May the committee try to find another candidate? (c) If not, will there be a blank after the president's space on the ticket, or will the candidate refusing to serve be obliged to have her name there?

Ans. (a) Yes, usually; but in this case the nominating committee has not fully performed the duty assigned it. The nominees should have been consulted and their consent assured before the report was made, unless the committee was reasonably sure of their consent. If a nominee withdraws, the work of the nominating committee has not been fully performed, and the committee should at once complete its nominations. In this case, since the ballots must be printed and the polls be open before the club meets again, the committee should fill the vacancy in the ticket, and report the fact at the opening of the next meeting. (b) Yes. (c) No name of a candidate who declines to serve should be printed on the ticket.

170. Ques. The nominating committee submitted its report, naming two candidates for each office. Immediately, before the president had called for nominations from the floor, the second nominee for president resigned and nominated a member in her place. Should not the resignation have been given to the nominating committee whose duty it was to accept the same and to select another candidate? Was the nomination made in this way legal?

Ans. A nomination or a candidacy cannot be resigned, like an office or membership. It is assumed that you mean that the second nominee for president declined the nomination. If the nominee knew of the intended nomination before the committee reported, and was not willing to be a candidate, the committee should have been notified, so that it could have filled the vacancy. While it was in order for the nominee to decline the nomination as soon as the report was read, it was not proper to make a nomination to fill the vacancy. The committee's nominations cannot be amended. Other nominations may be made as soon as the president calls for nominations from the floor, but they are not the committee's nominations. In the case mentioned the president should have stated that the nominee declined and "that nominations from the floor are now in order. A is nominated for president. Are there any further nominations for president?" The president should recognize the nomination made by the declining nominee as a nomination from the floor. The nominations from the floor for the different offices should be taken up in the same order as in the report of the nominating committee. [Read preceding answer.]

171. QUES. We have a nominating committee that prepares a ticket containing two names, if possible, for each office to be filled. This ticket is presented at the meeting preceding the annual meeting. (a) Now, are nominations from the floor in order at this time, or two weeks later on election day? (b) If there are not two names brought in for each office, has the club the right to nominate persons to fill these places at the time the ticket is presented, or must all nominations be made on election day? (c) The nominating committee consists of nine members, three appointed by the president and six elected by the club. After this committee has been named and announced, if any member resigns, has the club or the president the right to fill the vacant place? I understand that a vacant place would be filled by the appointing or electing power; but would the president, for instance, have the right to fill one of the three places made vacant, when the club would not have the opportunity to fill any place made vacant in the six, because they report at the next meeting?

ANS. (a) Nominations from the floor are in order both times. [See Ques. 175.] (b) The nominations made by the committee cannot be amended by the society, but members can make additional nominations from the floor when the nominating committee reports. (c) The appointing power can fill the vacancies. If the society feels this may give the president too much power, the remedy is to modify the by-law by reducing the number of members appointed by the president, even to the extent of having all the nominating committee elected by the society. [See Ques. 117, 119.]

172. QUES. Is it democratic to have no nominations?

ANS. Yes. [See Ques. 146, 159, 173, 212, 213.]

173. QUES. (a) In R. O. R., p. 263, line 12, you state: "This nomination is not necessary when the election is by ballot or by roll-call." Do you mean by printed ballot? (b) Many organizations are using a form of electing on the first ballot when no nomination has been made. They quote this passage in your book as their authority. Is it right?

ANS. (a) By printed or written ballot. (b) Yes. An illustration of the procedure in elections is given in Par. Prac., Seventh Drill, pp. 147–158. This drill is devoted to elections. [See Ques. 146, 159, 172, 212, 213.]

174. QUES. (a) Is it necessary or wise to have the names on an informal ballot, with the number of votes each received, placed upon the blackboard? (b) Is it better to omit the number of votes cast?

ANS. (a) Yes, in order to guide the voters in the formal ballot. They know that ballots cast for candidates who received only three or four votes are valueless. (b) No.

175. QUES. Before postponing the election of officers for seven months, nominations were closed with one nominee for each office. Before proceeding to the election, should the chair call for nominations?

ANS. Yes. The case is somewhat like that of closing debate. The reasons for closing debate or nominations at one meeting do not usually exist at the next meeting. The members present at the two meetings may be different, and those at the second meeting should not be limited, in their right to debate and to make nominations, by those present at the first meeting. [See Ques. 171, 176.]

176. QUES. A club was having its annual election of officers. Ballots were cast for all the officers on one ticket. The club adjourned before the tellers finished counting the ballots. When the balloting was finished, it was found that 224 votes had been cast for first vice-president; Mrs. D received 112, Mrs. S 111, and Mrs. L 1. Since no one received a majority, there was no election for this office. (a) Will the election of a first vice-president come up at the next meeting as new business or as unfinished business?

(*b*) Will nominations from the floor be in order, or must nominations be reopened in order to have additional nominations to those made at the last meeting?

ANS. (*a*) Unfinished business. (*b*) Nominations from the floor are in order. [See Ques. 175.]

ELECTIONS

177. QUES. May a person who is not a member of the society be elected an officer of that society?

ANS. It is not necessary that the officers of a deliberative assembly be members of the assembly, unless it is required by the by-laws. None of the officers of the national House of Representatives are members of Congress, except the presiding officer. In the United States Senate not even the presiding officer is a member of the Senate. In many societies the treasurer and the auditor are not members of the society. And even where the regular officers are required to be members, on special occasions an assembly sometimes chooses a presiding officer who is not a member of the assembly. This is done in serious cases in which the presiding officer and other prominent members are involved, and it is important to have an impartial outsider as presiding officer. [See page 296.]

178. QUES. May a member of a society hold more than one office at a time?

ANS. Yes, unless limited by the by-laws. In most societies it is generally understood that no member is to hold two offices, such as president and treasurer. Hence, if a member is elected to two offices and he is present, he should choose the one he accepts. If he is absent, the society should determine by vote which office is assigned to him, and then proceed to fill the other office. This is done because it is assumed that it was not intended that one member should fill two offices unless previous to the election the society had voted to adopt that policy. In small societies where it is desired that the work of two offices should be attended to by the same person, it is better to provide for it in the by-laws. [See Secretary-Treasurer, page 319, and Ques. 211.]

179. QUES. The first vice-president is nominated for president. Is she obliged to resign as vice-president at once, or may she retain that office until elected president?

ANS. She may retain her position as vice-president until she is elected president.

180. QUES. In an election of officers, the tellers had collected part of the ballots when a member arose and asked a parliamentary question relating to the election. Upon being answered by the chair, the member said she had voted under a misunderstanding, as had many others, and moved that the ballots collected be destroyed and the balloting be begun again. This motion was adopted and a new ballot taken. Was the procedure correct?

ANS. Yes, if done before members had left after voting; or it could be done by a two-thirds vote after members had left. The object of the voting is to ascertain the choice of the assembly, and if a vote is taken under a misunderstanding that might affect the result it should be ignored. If no member who has voted has left the hall, the chair or a majority may order a new ballot immediately. If members have voted and left the hall, it requires a two-thirds vote to order a new ballot at the same meeting. If a new ballot at the same meeting is not taken, another ballot should be taken at the next meeting, which may be an adjourned meeting.

181. QUES. There being no election on the first ballot, another ballot for officers was cast, and before the polls were closed three members arrived who had not been there when the first ballot was cast. Can these three members now vote?

ANS. Yes. [See Ques. 199.]

182. QUES. Have the tellers a right to vote?

ANS. Yes.

183. QUES. Can a candidate for an office serve as teller at the election?

ANS. Yes, as otherwise persons might be appointed tellers to prevent their being candidates. But no known candidate for a prominent office should be appointed a teller. If a teller is nominated for such an office, he should either decline the nomination or ask to be excused from serving as a teller. A teller should not ask to be excused from serving, simply because votes are cast for him.

184. QUES. In a meeting where there is only one ticket and no way provided in the constitution as to how officers are to be elected, (a) Cannot the secretary be instructed to cast the ballot? (b) Cannot a member move to make the vote unanimous?

ANS. (a) Yes. (b) Yes; but the motion should be made by the leading opponent, or by one who voted for that opponent. One negative vote, however, defeats the motion. [See Ques. 185, 186, 187, 188, 189.]

185. Ques. When a vote on nominating ballot is unanimous except one vote, is it necessary to have the motion for the secretary to cast the ballot of the convention for A?

Ans. Yes; or elect him in some other way. Nominations never elect.

186. Ques. What is the correct procedure when the secretary is asked to "cast the ballot"?

Ans. The secretary is not asked, but is directed, or ordered, to cast the ballot for a certain person for a specified office. In such a case, he writes the name of the candidate on a blank piece of paper, and standing says: "Mr. Chairman, by order of the club, I cast its ballot [or, unanimous ballot] for Mr. A for treasurer." He then hands the ballot to the chairman and resumes his seat. The chairman, standing, says: "The ballot [or, unanimous ballot] of the club has been cast for Mr. A for treasurer, and he is therefore elected treasurer." This is not a vote by ballot, but is a viva voce vote, and cannot be done legally if the by-laws require the election to be by ballot. R. O. R., pp. 194, 202. [See Ques. 184, 185, 187, 188 189.]

187. Ques. In an organization where the constitution requires an election of officers to be by ballot, and there is but one name for each office, and every opportunity is given for other names to be presented from the floor, and none is given, could the secretary be instructed to cast the ballot?

Ans. No; the election must be by ballot, as the constitution requires. See R. O. R., p. 202. [See Ques. 184, 185, 186, 188, 189.]

188. Ques. In most women's organizations where there is but one candidate, if there is a unanimous vote, the secretary is instructed to cast the ballot. (a) Is not this according to pp. 265 and 266 of your book (R. O. R.)? (b) Or, do you mean that this provision must be in the constitution?

Ans. (a) No. (b) Yes. It is a waste of time to ballot when there is only one candidate, but it must be done if required by the by-laws. [See Ques. 184, 185, 186, 187, 189.]

189. Ques. Our national organization has this provision in its constitution: "In case there is but one nominee, or one person receiving a large majority of votes cast on the nominating ballot,

by a unanimous vote the secretary or some member may be instructed to cast the ballot of the convention." Is this all right?

ANS. Yes, it is a very good provision. It might be improved by changing the "large majority vote" to a definite amount, as a two-thirds or three-fourths vote. [See Ques. 184, 185, 186, 187, 188.]

190. QUES. When several members are nominated for the same office, as for secretary, and the election is to be by voice, if the first one nominated is not elected and the second name is to be voted on, may any members who voted for the first one (the defeated one) vote for the second one?

ANS. The same question arises in filling blanks. Each question is distinct, and every member has a right to vote on each nominee until one is elected, just as he may vote on each proposition for filling a blank until one is decided on.

Laws are usually made to restrain the individual, or to give him some privilege of which existing laws deprive him. Therefore, in the absence of a by-law or rule of order prohibiting a nominating committee from nominating its own members, or prohibiting a member from voting on each nominee for office until one is elected, you know that those practices are not prohibited, unless they are so clearly wrong as not to require any rules, which is not the case in the above instances. Thus it is not necessary to have a rule prohibiting a member from throwing a brick at the presiding officer, but it is necessary to have a rule prohibiting a member from speaking discourteously to him, or from charging improper motives to a member in debate. The first is out of order without any rule, but there may be doubt as to the other two. By keeping in mind this general principle, most questions of the nature of the one mentioned can be answered.

191. QUES. In an organization chartered for the purpose of dispensing charity to worthy poor, and having no clause in its by-laws from which to infer that it is a secret organization, although its meetings are held behind closed doors, does the presence of a non-member invalidate the results of an election of officers?

ANS. No. Any society can adopt a by-law prohibiting the presence of non-members at an election, but in the absence of such a by-law their presence has no effect on the validity of an election or of any other business.

192. QUES. An election was held and a certain person declared

elected. After the meeting it was found that five persons had voted who had not paid their dues. The number of votes cast for each nominee was nearly the same, so that the five votes might have affected the result. What should be done?

ANS. If the organization does not have a by-law providing that members who have not paid their dues shall not vote, the five persons in arrears cannot be disfranchised, excepting by suspending them from membership. If the organization has a by-law providing that such members shall not vote, but it has not been customary to enforce the by-law, and the question was not raised at the meeting, it is too late to raise it after the meeting. A single objection during the meeting would have enforced the by-law, and if the election had proceeded and the five members who were in arrears had been allowed to vote, the election would be invalid. As the right of these persons to vote was not raised at the meeting, the members present virtually gave unanimous consent for them to vote. Therefore the election stands, unless a by-law that has been habitually enforced covers the case. [See Ques. 200, 286.]

193. QUES. Since any action taken by a body when there is no quorum is invalid, although no person raises the question of no quorum, is not an election invalid when members vote who are not entitled to vote, even though no one raises the question?

ANS. If the votes cast by persons not entitled to vote affect the election so that a new election is necessary in order to ascertain the choice of those entitled to vote, then the election is invalid and a new election must be held. The election is not invalid if the number of improper votes is not sufficient to affect the election; or if the assembly is willing to accept the word of the illegal voters, and also accept the ballot as thus corrected. The object is to ascertain the choice of those who are entitled to vote. But if long-established custom has waived certain requirements of the by-laws, such by-laws cannot be invoked to invalidate an election after the adjournment of the session at which the election was held. Custom long established has the force of a rule until the society sees fit to vary from it, or attention is called at the time to its being in conflict with the by-laws or other rules. If the society had for a long period ignored the rule as to the quorum and it had been customary to transact business with less than a quorum, business transacted at such meetings held before attention is called to the by-law is not invalid. If for a long time elections have been viva voce, or by directing the secretary to cast the ballot for the assembly (which is the same thing), they are not invalid, even though the by-laws require ballot elections, unless attention is called to the violation of the by-laws before the adjournment of the session at which the election was held. [See Ques. 200, 203, 204, 205.]

194. QUES. When it is found that the ballot is being stuffed, what is the proper thing to do?

ANS. If sufficient precaution is taken, this cannot occur if you have honest tellers. See R. O. R., page 195. [See pages 215–217.] If it is ever detected during balloting, the balloting must be stopped and all done over again, and those guilty of the fraud should be expelled from the society. If the fraud evidently does not affect the result of the ballot, it is not necessary to take a new ballot. [See Ques. 180.]

195. QUES. Have the tellers the right to omit to report to the assembly the fact that one candidate received only one vote?

ANS. No. The full report of the tellers should be given in all cases, accounting for every vote, unless the assembly decides otherwise. [See Ques. 206.]

196. QUES. A formal ballot for the election of an officer resulted as follows: total number of ballots cast 20, of which A received 10; B 9; and 1 was blank. Was A elected or were 11 votes necessary to elect?

ANS. A was elected. There were only 19 ballots and A received a majority. Blanks are not ballots. [See Ques. 197, 346.]

197. QUES. If a member is nominated for an office and her name is withdrawn, are the ballots cast for her thrown out, the same as blanks?

ANS. No; the ballots for her are counted, the same as any other ballots. If she gets a majority she is elected, and may accept, even though she declined the nomination. All ballots are counted. Blank pieces of paper are not counted as ballots. [See Ques. 196, 346.]

198. QUES. If a member moves that the ticket be accepted and it is adopted, would that not constitute an election?

ANS. Yes, provided no rule or order adopted by the society requires the election to be by ballot. If the society has ordered the election to be by ballot, the motion to accept the ticket is out of order.

199. Ques. What is the difference between reopening the polls and a second ballot?

Ans. The polls are reopened before the ballots are counted, for the purpose of permitting members who have not voted previously to vote at that time. A second ballot is taken after the first ballots have been counted and it is found that some of the offices have not been filled. A second ballot should then be taken for the offices still vacant. All members present can vote at the second ballot, the same as at the first. If the second ballot fails to fill all the vacancies, the balloting should be continued until they are filled. Each balloting is independent of the others, and the polls for each may be reopened for the benefit of those arriving after the polls have been closed. [See Ques. 181.]

200. Ques. The constitution reads: "The election of the proposed member may take place at any regular meeting after the name has been placed in nomination at the previous regular meeting. The election must be by personal ballot, three adverse votes defeating the candidate. New members shall be declared members if within two weeks they signify their acceptance and pay dues."

At an election a member received three adverse votes. However, the following irregularities occurred at that election: The tellers did not count the votes or the number of members present, and one new member present, not knowing of the rule concerning payment of dues, voted without having paid her dues. This rule, however, has never been enforced. Can the election be declared illegal on the above-mentioned grounds?

Ans. I think not. It was not necessary to count the votes or the members present. The three adverse votes are sufficient to defeat the candidate. The clause regarding the payment of dues never having been enforced, it is too late now to raise the question of order. Had this matter been brought up at the time of voting, the illegal ballot should have been rejected. It is assumed that a quorum was present. [See Ques. 192, 193, 203, 204, 205.]

201. Ques. Formerly the officers of a society were elected annually. At the last annual meeting, in an even year, the by-laws were amended so that the term of office is two years, certain officers to be elected in the even years and the others in the odd years. After the amendment was adopted, all the officers were elected

without anything being said as to their term of office. Does the term of office of those to be elected in the odd years expire at the next annual meeting, which is in an odd year?

ANS. Yes. The by-laws require certain offices to be filled in the odd years, so that every odd year there must be an election of these officers. At the last annual meeting these offices were vacant, and they were filled by an election, even though it was an even year. That could not, however, interfere with the by-law requiring them to be filled in the odd years. The by-laws did not allow the two-year term of these officers to be filled in an even year: it was only the unexpired part of the two-year term that was filled.

202. QUES. The secretary resigned, and the society proceeded to elect his successor by ballot, as is the custom, though there is no by-law requiring it. The ballot showed a tie vote for the two candidates, A and B. One of the candidates, Mr. B, moved to elect the other candidate, Mr. A, by acclamation. The chair ruled this out of order, as there were two candidates, unless Mr. B should withdraw his own nomination. From this decision an appeal was taken, and the decision of the chair was reversed, and Mr. A was elected by acclamation. Was this ruling correct?

ANS. Mr. B, in moving that Mr. A be elected by acclamation, in effect withdrew his candidacy. When a candidate makes such a motion, it is not necessary for him to say also that he is no longer a candidate. His motion shows that. As the by-laws did not require the election to be by ballot, it was in order to vote to elect in any way the society pleased. If the by-laws had required the election to be by ballot, an election conducted in any other way, though it had been unanimously so ordered, would have been null and void.

203. QUES. Only 15 members of a club of 63 attended the annual meeting for the election of officers. Before the meeting they prepared a "slate" and had it adopted without opposition by a vote directing the secretary to cast the ballot of the club for the prepared ticket. It has always been the custom of the club to direct the secretary to cast the ballot, though the by-laws require the election to be by ballot. Was such an election legal?

ANS. If only 15 of the 63 members chose to attend the annual meeting, and they were a quorum according to your by-laws, they had a right to elect the officers. And they had a perfect right to talk over the matter beforehand and agree upon a ticket. If they failed to conform strictly to the by-laws, but followed the established custom of the society, the officers elected are just as legally elected as those of previous years. That those present did not consider the election illegal is evident, because they had the power to elect their candidates legally, and would not have adopted a method the legality of which they doubted. If they had thought the officers were not elected legally, they certainly would have taken a legal ballot and elected the same ticket. As no one has been deprived of any rights, and as the result would have been precisely the same if the by-laws had been conformed to, my opinion is that the election should stand. If at the time a point of order had been raised that the ballot was required by the by-laws, and the society had persisted in following the custom, the election would have been null and void, even though in accordance with the established custom.

Suppose, however, that the by-laws assigned certain duties to an officer or a committee, and the society were to adopt a resolution assigning these duties to another officer or committee, and it was afterward discovered that this was in violation of the by-laws. As soon as the point is raised that the action taken is in violation of the by-laws, the chair should rule that said action is null and void.

In the first case, the election was necessary and in accordance with custom, and the election would have resulted the same if a proper ballot had been taken. In the other case there was no necessity for the adoption of the resolution, and the result would have been entirely different if the by-law had been conformed to. In the first case the action should stand, and in the second it is null and void. [See Ques. 193, 200, 204.]

204. QUES. The by-laws of our society require the officers to be elected by ballot at the annual meeting. Most of our officers were elected as usual by the formula, "The secretary is directed to cast the ballot," etc. As the election was illegal, how can we make it legal? Do the officers of the preceding year hold over until there is a new election?

ANS. The election was held at the prescribed time, the annual meeting, and was conducted according to the method established by custom, which was not in conformity to the by-laws. If a point of order had been raised and the club had persisted in violating the by-laws, the election would be null and void and the old officers would continue in office until their successors were properly elected.

As a general rule, a law that has been ignored for years, so that its existence is not known by most persons, should not be suddenly enforced against those who have violated it in ignorance of its existence. If, at the time, attention had been called to the violation of the by-laws, and the error had not been corrected, the election would have been illegal and the old officers should continue in office until new officers could be elected, which should be done as quickly as possible, notice thereof being given. But the violation of the by-laws was not intentional, and the best interests of the society are subserved by allowing the election to stand. [See Ques. 193, 200, 203, 205.]

205. QUES. The constitution of our city federation of clubs says that all officers shall be elected at the annual meeting, that the annual meeting shall be held in April, and that no officer shall hold office longer than three terms. At our last annual meeting new officers were nominated, the old officers having been in office three terms. Before the election, by request of the nominees, the annual meeting adjourned until November 21, the officers to be then elected. The request was made because our city is to entertain the state federation convention next November, and it was thought this could be done better if the old experienced officers of the city federation were still in office. One or two members only thought our action unconstitutional. Were we wrong?

ANS. Yes; you violated your constitution. If you could adjourn your annual meeting for seven months, why not for twelve months, and thus continue the old officers in office for another year? It was the duty of the city federation to proceed to the election of officers at the annual meeting. If the election could not be completed on that day, it should have adjourned to another day. It would be reasonable to adjourn for a week, but not longer. The spirit of the constitution should be carried out as far as practicable. Since no one is injured by the error and it is impracticable to correct it now until a few days previous to the November meeting, it is better to let the action stand. [See Ques. 175, 193, 200, 203, 204.]

206. QUES. When a society votes for all its officers on one blanket ballot or on a voting-machine, and provides in its con-

stitution that the "majority of votes cast shall elect," how is the majority computed? That is, must a successful candidate for an office on the ballot have a majority of the total number of votes or ballots cast by the voting-machine, or only a majority of the votes cast for the office for which he is running, which may be a much smaller number? That is to say, the number of votes cast for each office may vary, while the total number of votes cast is an exact count of all the ballots. Which number determines the majority for an office?

ANS. When several officers are voted for at the same time on the same ballot or on a voting-machine, each office is treated separately, the same as if it were the only office to be filled. The "number of votes cast" is the number cast for that office. Those ballots that have no name of a candidate for that office are treated as blanks as far as that office is concerned. The tellers' report must give a full report for each office. [See Par. Prac., page 177, and page 561 in this book, and Ques. 195.]

207. QUES. The by-laws read: "Club officers shall be elected every two years by ballot. Said officers shall not be eligible for reëlection until two years after their term of office expires." If a club secretary resigns after serving three months, and a successor is appointed by the board (without ballots being cast), is this second secretary eligible for election at the next election? Was she a "said officer"?

ANS. A person who has filled an office more than half the time should be considered as having filled that term, regardless of how she was appointed or elected. In the case stated the first secretary is eligible, and the second, who has served longer than a year, is ineligible for office at the next election. [See Ques. 49, 68.]

208. QUES. The by-laws read: "The election shall be by ballot biennially. In case of tie the tellers shall obey the instructions of the club." What ought to be the instructions of the club? Is it a square deal to have the candidates draw papers, the member drawing the longer slip being placed in office? Should not a second election be held, with ballots cast?

ANS. Where there is time, it is always best to repeat the ballot until the officers are elected by a majority vote. When this is impracticable, the method of drawing lots described above seems equally fair to both candidates.

209. Ques. When printed ballots are used, and new names are written in the blank spaces, and the voter neglects to comply with the requirements to erase the other name or place a cross opposite the new name, should the vote be thrown out as illegal?

Ans. No. The essential thing is for the ballot to show without any doubt for whom it is cast. When a name is written in a blank space in a ballot, there can be no doubt for whom that vote was cast. Requiring a cross to be placed in front of the written name is absurd. The erasing of the printed names is unnecessary. One of these methods is essential if the vote is intended for one of several candidates whose names are printed on the ballot, but is not essential if there is only one name for the office, or if one name is in writing. [See page 225, and Ques. 211.]

210. Ques. At an election of officers the tellers reported 129 votes cast, of which 65 were for A and 64 for B. A was declared elected. But the tellers failed to report two votes that they had rejected as illegal because one voter put her ballot in the box before it was marked by the inspector, but immediately noticed her mistake and called the inspector's attention to it. The other wrote her own name in two ways on the ballot, besides the name of the candidate for whom she wished to vote. Should these two ballots have been included in the whole number of votes cast?

Ans. Yes. The tellers should have reported 131 votes cast. Every ballot should be counted, whether legal or not. The number necessary to elect is a majority of all the votes cast, legal or illegal. In the case mentioned the tellers should have reported 131 votes cast, 66 necessary for election, 65 for A, 64 for B, and 2 illegal, even though they were unanimous in declaring the votes illegal. If they had not been unanimous, before reporting they should have stated the facts to the assembly and have asked for instructions. If the assembly had declared those ballots legal and one had been for A, A would have had 66 votes and been elected. If the assembly had declared the votes illegal, the chair would have announced that there was no election. The assembly is the supreme authority, not the tellers. In asking for instructions as to these ballots, the tellers should give no clue as to the candidates for whom the ballots were intended.

The difference between a political election and an election in a society is often overlooked. In the former the voters are not in session. They cannot decide questions and continue balloting until candidates are elected by a majority, as in an assembly. In this country, in political elections, it has been found best to allow a plurality to elect and to give to judges of election the power to decide questions which in ordinary assemblies would be decided by the assembly itself.

In the case mentioned, it would have been better for the assembly to have allowed the two rejected ballots to have been accepted as regular. There was no doubt as to their being cast by members entitled to vote, and there was no doubt for whom each ballot was cast. It is a mistake to be so technical when there is no attempt at fraud.

211. QUES. The Australian Ballot system was used at an election of officers. The nominating committee reported a printed ticket, with Mrs. A as candidate for president and Mrs. B as candidate for director, both having accepted the nomination. Mrs. B was nominated from the floor for president also. The number present and voting was 100. The tellers reported for president, 46 votes for Mrs. A, and 45 votes for Mrs. B, and 67 votes for Mrs. B as director. 3 ballots for Mrs. A and 6 for Mrs. B as president were thrown out by the tellers because they did not have the required cross before the names. Who is president, Mrs. A or Mrs. B?

ANS. The object of an election is to ascertain whom the voters wish to fill certain offices. When it is apparent from a ballot itself for whom the voter intended to vote, it should be so credited. In the case mentioned it appears that 49 ballots were cast with no name for president except Mrs. A's, which was printed on the ballot. Can there be any possible doubt as to whom these ballots were voted for? Did the fact that 46 had a cross before the name make these votes any more certain for Mrs. A than the other three where the cross was omitted? It is absurd to require a cross to indicate which candidate is voted for, when there is only one name printed on the ballot for the office. So it is equally absurd to require a cross to show which candidate is voted for when the voter writes the name of his candidate. The 49 ballots that contained the name of no candidate for president except Mrs. A should be credited to her, and the 51 ballots that had the name of Mrs. B written for president should be credited to Mrs. B. The fact that the president stated that the cross was necessary does not make it so. The vote actually stood Mrs. A 49, and Mrs. B 51, so that Mrs. B was elected. Since Mrs. B was also elected director,. it was for her to decide which office she preferred, provided she was present. If she was absent from the meeting, it would be assumed that she would prefer the higher office, and the election of a director would immediately take place. If the two offices were of equal importance and she was not present, the society by a majority vote should decide which of the two should be assigned to her, and then proceed to fill the other.

The Australian Ballot was designed for political elections where the names of a number of candidates for each office, and the necessary instructions, are printed on the ballot. It is not at all adapted to a case where only one ticket is printed, with no directions on it. [See page 225, and Ques. 178, 209.]

212. QUES. Our by-laws contain the following: "The officers of this club shall be elected by ballot. The person receiving the highest number of votes for any office shall be declared elected. The tellers shall report to the chair only the names of the persons receiving the highest number of votes." I find nothing in "Robert's Rules of Order," which our society has adopted, that recognizes this method of making the nominating ballot the formal ballot. What is your opinion of this method, and of reporting only the names of the successful candidates? By this method an officer might be elected by a small minority of votes, which seems to me unfair.

ANS. The method you describe does not make the nominating ballot the formal ballot. It simply does away with a nominating ballot and allows a plurality to elect. On p. 24, R. O. R., you will see that "a plurality never elects except by virtue of a rule to that effect." Your society has adopted such a rule, which it has a perfect right to do. I think a plurality vote should never elect in a local society where the balloting can be repeated until some one receives a majority vote. It is unfair to the officer to expect him to serve when he has the support of perhaps only a small minority. As for a nominating ballot, you are under no obligations to have one. Your society has a right to adopt a rule allowing the tellers to report nothing but the names of the successful candidates, though I have never before heard of any society's taking such a step. It puts the society absolutely in the power of the tellers as far as the election is concerned, and if the tellers are unprincipled and in collusion, the election would be a farce. As the object of your by-law is to prevent any one from knowing what candidates were voted for, and how many votes were cast for each, there is no possible way to detect fraud or to correct errors. [See Ques. 146, 159, 172, 173, 213.]

213. QUES. Our by-laws provide for electing a nominating committee, and also for nominations from the floor. All nominations must be placed on the bulletin-board one month before the election, and the names of all nominees must be sent with the notice of the proposed election to each club member, and must be printed on the ballots. The consent of each nominee must be obtained. (a) If a member writes on her ballot a name of one who was not nominated, is that vote counted? (b) If a group on the day of election agree among themselves to write another name on the ballot for, say, president, and their candidate receives a majority vote, is their candidate elected over the one whose name is printed on the ballot?

ANS. (a) Yes. (b) Yes. It is better to cross out the printed name or names not voted for, though the fact that a name is written shows that the vote is intended for that person. The rule that the consent of nominees shall be obtained does not apply to those that are not nominated, and the voting is not limited to nominees. [See Ques. 146, 152, 159, 172, 173, 212, 213.]

214. QUES. If a ballot for officers and directors is all correct except that too many directors are voted for, must the ballot be thrown out, or may the votes for officers be counted?

ANS. The votes for officers should be counted. The vote for directors is thrown out, because it is impossible from the ballot to decide to which ones the vote should be credited.

215. QUES. In voting for directors or delegates, where there are several to be elected, often the voters vote for only one in order to insure a favorite's receiving the highest number of votes. This is unfair to the other candidates. Is there any way to offset this pernicious practice?

ANS. None, unless all the members adopt the same practice and each member votes for only one candidate, or the assembly ballots for only one director at a time. The second plan takes a great deal of time. The first plan takes just as much time, unless a rule is adopted that the required number receiving the largest number of votes are elected.

216. QUES. We understand that our newly elected president

intends to resign at the next meeting, which is the last one until next fall. Our constitution states that vacancies shall be filled at any regular meeting in the same manner as at an annual meeting. Of course, our annual meeting is the day of election, when we vote by ballot, the nominating committee reporting the ticket two weeks before. What is the manner of electing a president to fill the vacancy in a case like this? Can a president be nominated from the floor and elected the same day?

ANS. Under no circumstances, except at the annual meeting, should a vacancy in the presidency be filled at the same meeting at which the resignation is presented. The society should know in advance when so important an election is to take place, so that those interested may attend. Your constitution providing that vacancies may be filled at any regular meeting in the same manner as at the annual meeting evidently intended that the elections should be equally public and guarded in both cases. If it is customary to have a nominating committee for the annual meeting, the same method should be followed in filling a vacancy. As the resignation will probably be presented at the last meeting of the season, I would suggest the following procedure: Accept the president's resignation, the vice-president taking the chair, and then adopt a resolution similar to this:

Resolved, That when we adjourn we adjourn to meet at 3 P. M. on Saturday, May 15, the special order of business being the election of a president.
Resolved, That we now proceed to the election by ballot of a nominating committee of five, to nominate a president at the adjourned meeting, the five members receiving the largest number of votes to be declared elected, lots to be drawn in case of a tie.

These resolutions provide for an adjourned regular meeting and for a nominating committee. Of course, when the nominating committee reports, nominations from the floor are in order. [See Ques. 57, 61, 65, 217, 382.]

217. QUES. When the by-laws make no provision for a special election, and no provision for the filling of vacancies by a board, is there any legal time when an election may be held, except at the annual meeting?

ANS. Yes. In an ordinary society the election may be held at any regular business meeting, notice of the election having been given at a previous meeting. In a delegated body, such as a state organization, an election to fill a vacancy not provided for by its rules may be held at any meeting of the board, provided notice has been given at the previous meeting, or in the notice for this meeting. However, in these circumstances the board cannot fill a vacancy beyond the next meeting of the organization. [See Ques. 57, 61, 65, 216, 382.]

CHAPTER XLII

QUESTIONS ANSWERED

OFFICERS; HONORARY OFFICERS AND MEMBERS

PRESIDENT

218. QUES. Can the president of a local society call a special meeting of the society to be held at a considerable distance from the usual meeting place, as in another part of the state?

ANS. No. The place must be the usual place of meeting, unless it is impossible to meet there. In that case the place must be one that is as convenient as possible for the entire membership.

219. QUES. Should the president stand during the transaction of business?

ANS. He should stand while putting a question, while giving his reasons for a decision on a point of order, and while speaking on an appeal. While members are speaking in debate, the chairman should be seated and should pay strict attention to the debate, since the remarks are addressed to the chairman. At all other times it is optional with him whether he sits or stands. In a very large assembly it may be advisable for the chairman to stand whenever speaking, in order to make himself heard through the entire hall.

220. QUES. Has the president of a society control over the seats of members?

ANS. No, unless it is given him by some special rule of the society.

221. QUES. When the president of a society is absent, would it be proper to nominate and elect the recording secretary to fill the chair, and then nominate and elect a recording secretary pro tem.?

ANS. Yes, if no vice-president is present; but it is seldom

desirable. In the absence of the president and vice-presidents, the recording secretary calls the meeting to order and then calls for nominations of a chairman pro tem. [See Ques. 222.]

222. QUES. If the president desires to address the assembly on a question when one or more of the vice-presidents are present, is it not unparliamentary for him to ask the secretary to take the chair?

ANS. Yes. [See Ques. 221.]

223. QUES. Should the chairman ever read a paper without calling some one else to the chair?

ANS. Yes. He need not call any one else to the chair unless he wishes to take part in the debate; or unless he is so involved in the matter under consideration that the assembly may not have confidence in the impartiality of his decisions; or when, in a large body, he is to make a report that will require action by the assembly.

224. QUES. When a president is making a report with recommendations, the vice-president having the chair, is it correct for the president to move the adoption of his recommendations?

ANS. No. [See page 301.]

225. QUES. Has the chair the right to appoint a secretary pro tem.?

ANS. The duties of the secretary are such that usually no one wishes to take the office temporarily. Consequently in small societies the chair frequently asks some one to serve as secretary pro tem. But the chair can do this only with general consent. A single objection would necessitate an election of a secretary, as described in R. O. R., bottom of p. 276.

226. QUES. Has the president of a board of aldermen a right to vote with the minority to make a tie, and then cast the deciding vote? Has the presiding officer under any circumstances the right to vote twice, once as a member and once as chairman?

ANS. No, to both questions. The right to vote comes from membership, not from office. These questions are answered in R. O. R., p. 192. [See Ques. 273, 375.]

227. QUES. When the vote is by ballot and the result has been announced, may a president vote who has not voted before?

ANS. Not unless the consent of the society has been obtained.

228. QUES. Should the president cast the deciding vote in case of a tie, when the vote is taken by ballot?

Ans. No, the president is entitled to vote before the tellers begin to count the ballots, but not afterward. See R. O. R., p. 238. [See Ques. 226, 227.]

229. Ques. Does the president of an organization have any more authority in the chair than any other presiding officer?

Ans. No; he can no more reverse the action of a temporary presiding officer than the latter can reverse his action. In eithei case, the society may reverse the ruling of the presiding officer, and if this is not done it is assumed that the society acquiesces in that ruling. [See Ques. 239.]

230. Ques. Should the president leave the chair during an annual election of officers, in case he is a candidate?

Ans. No, not unless he chooses to do so.

231. Ques. At the annual meeting, all of the officers were elected except the president. Who should preside at the next meeting?

Ans. The vice-president who was elected at the annual meeting should preside until a president is elected, unless your by-laws provide that the officers shall hold office until their successors are elected, in which case the old president continues in office until his successor is elected.

232. Ques. (a) Is it the business of the chair to take questions from the table? (b) Should the chair announce a special or a general order?

Ans. (a) No; but he may suggest it. He should give the preference to one rising for the purpose of moving to take a question from the table, over one who rises to make a new motion. [R. O. R., p. 155.] (b) Yes, it is the duty of the chair to announce the order, or to state that the time has arrived to take up a special order. [R. O. R., top of p. 70.]

233. Ques. The president is made ex-officio a member of all committees. If he is absent for a couple of weeks, would the vice-president attend committee meetings occurring during his absence?

Ans. No. Where the president is made ex-officio a member of all committees, it is to enable him to attend and to take part in their meetings whenever he wishes to, so that he may be familiar with their work and may influence their actions. This applies only to the president. He is under no obligation to attend the meetings, and is not regarded as a member in counting a quorum. See R. O. R., p. 210. [See Ques. 114, 235.]

234. QUES. The by-laws state that the president is a member ex-officio of all committees. Had the nominating committee a right to ignore him by failing to notify him of their meetings?

ANS. Of course not. They should ignore him no more than they would ignore their chairman or any other member. Delicacy would usually prevent his attending the meetings of the nominating committee if he is a candidate for office. But the president should never be made a member of the nominating committee. [See Ques. 114, 233, 235.]

235. QUES. What is the position or authority of a chairman ex-officio?

ANS. The same precisely as if he had been appointed chairman by a vote of the society. [See Ques. 114, 233, 234.]

236. QUES. A member of a society was elected president in June. A few weeks later he resigned before having presided at a meeting of the society. Can he now be said to be a past-president?

ANS. Yes. The member was elected in June and immediately became president. His resignation some weeks afterward, before he had presided at a meeting, does not destroy the fact that he was the president for a time, and therefore is now a past-president.

237. QUES. Should a president, who has been working delegate at a convention, in making her report from the platform, refer to herself as "your president" or "the chair," or can she be human and speak of herself as "I"?

ANS. She does not report as the presiding officer, but as the working delegate. It would be decidedly improper to refer to herself as "the chair." That term applies exclusively to the presiding officer of the assembly as such, whether it is the president or a member who has been temporarily called to the chair. If it is the custom to appoint the president working delegate, then she might refer to herself as "your president." But she should usually refer to herself as "your working delegate." That is the best form. The third person should be used as much as possible. There is not, however, the same objection to the use of "I" in the report of an officer or delegate, or committee of one, as there is in the report of a committee of two or more, or in any remarks by the presiding officer, who, above all things, must be regarded as judicial and whose personality must be kept in the background.

238. QUES. When the presiding officer leaves the chair, is it

not a fact that all power as president of the association leaves him, and he becomes as any other member, save and except such power as may be vested in him between meetings, such as being served with a summons of court, or the calling of a meeting without the request of members?

ANS. The duties of the president of a society may include other things besides presiding at the meetings. His authority as presiding officer, for instance, to decide questions of order, exists only while the society is in session and he is in the chair. If he desired to participate in the debate and called another member to take the chair, the acting chairman could rule him out of order, as the power to decide questions of order rests with the chairman, and the president, not being in the chair, has none of the power of the chairman.

If the president, while not in the chair, is asked his opinion upon a question of order, he has a perfect right to express it. But that is not ruling on the question of order, as that can be done by the chair only while the society is in session. The member has the right of immediate appeal.

239. QUES. Has the president of a society the authority, as president, to decide questions relating to administration of the policy of the society between its meetings and those of the board of directors?

ANS. There may be questions of the kind arising that require decision before there is a meeting of the society or of the board. In such case the president may be obliged to decide it. He should report the matter at the first meeting of the board for its approval. The authority does not rest with the president, and his decision may be reversed. [See Ques. 229.]

240. QUES. When a chairman tenders in writing his resignation, to take effect at once, does such resignation take effect immediately upon its receipt by the secretary of the organization, or not until formally acted upon by the authority that has the power to fill the vacancy?

ANS. A reasonable time must be given for the acceptance of the resignation. This question is answered in R. O. R., p. 103.

241. QUES. In organizing a permanent society a president was elected who had not signed the constitution. Was this correct?

ANS. In organizing a permanent society it is entirely proper to elect a president who has not signed the constitution and thereby become a member. If he accepts the presidency he should at once become a member, though he may preside without being a member.

242. Ques. As a general rule, has the chair the right to refuse to recognize a member to make a nominating speech?

Ans. A nomination for an office is a debatable motion that the office be filled by the nominee. If the member making the nomination wishes to make a nominating speech, he should obtain the floor and make his nomination and his speech without waiting for the chair to state the nomination. In a similar way, it may be seconded with a speech, or sometimes it is seconded by two or three members in succession, each making a speech. This is all the debate that is customary. The opponents, instead of attacking this nominee, should in the same way advocate the election of a rival candidate. It would be difficult to speak against a nomination without bringing in personalities that would be out of order. If the nominee is not a member of the organization, but an employee, the case is different, and the merits of the different candidates can be debated. While the chair has not the power to stop debate on a debatable question, he has the power, and it is his duty, to stop any speaker who is speaking off the question, or in a foolish or frivolous way. The chair cannot prevent two or three nominating speeches for each candidate if they are evidently made in good faith, but if he finds that a group is taking advantage of this privilege to waste the time of the assembly by making long or numerous nominating speeches, it is his duty to protect the assembly by stopping it. It must be borne in mind that the assembly has rights, as well as individual members. Of course the assembly may by a vote adopt a motion limiting the nominating speeches to any desired extent.

243. Ques. (a) What can an assembly do with a chairman who cannot, or will not, at all events does not, put motions? (b) Is there any way by which an assembly can rid itself of an incompetent or malicious chairman? (c) Could a member gain the floor, state the situation, receive a motion asking the chairman to surrender the chair, and put such motion to vote? (d) Has any one except the duly elected chairman a right to present a motion to be voted upon?

Ans. If the chairman is the president of an organized society, he should be censured by a vote of the society. In this case the member making the motion of censure should state and put the question, and declare the vote. He should stand on the floor of the hall, not on the platform. If after this the president persists in neglecting his duty as chairman, charges should be preferred against him for continued neglect of duty as presiding officer, and he should be deposed from office by a two-thirds vote, if found guilty. The vacancy should be filled as in other cases.

In all cases except that of the president of an organized society, the questions asked are answered as follows: (*a*) Raise points of order every time the chairman fails to put a proper motion. If the chair rules against you, appeal. (*b*) Yes; if he is not the president of an organized society, move "to declare the chair vacant and proceed to elect a new chairman." This is a question of privilege, since it relates to the organization of the assembly. (*c*) Under certain circumstances, yes. [R. O. R., p. 238, last sentence.] (*d*) Yes.

While the above-mentioned procedure is correct, assuming the facts to be as stated, yet one should be very sure that he has a large majority of the assembly with him before adopting such an extreme course. The probability is that a man who would be elected chairman has the support of a majority of the assembly, and therefore that your effort would result in your embarrassing defeat.

244. Ques. You say that the chairman cannot put the question on a debatable motion so long as any one desires to speak. What if there is a set time for adjournment adopted in the order of business? Should the chairman let the debate run over the hour unless rules are suspended?

Ans. No. The chairman must obey both rules. He cannot stop the debate so long as members who are entitled to speak wish to do so; and yet, when the hour appointed for adjournment arrives, unless the rules are suspended, he must declare the meeting adjourned. In this case the question goes over to the next meeting as unfinished business. [See Ques. 284.]

245. Ques. After the business meeting, should the chairman call for a formal motion to adjourn, before the social hour that follows the business meeting?

Ans. No, not necessarily. The chairman should usually ask whether there is any further business, and if there is none he should say something like this: "There being none, the business meeting is adjourned."

246. QUES. If a chairman is authorized to appoint a committee after the meeting adjourns, does he give the names of those appointed to the secretary to insert in the minutes?

ANS. At the next meeting he should announce the names of the committee, which would consequently be entered in the minutes.

SECRETARY AND MINUTES

247. QUES. (a) Should the secretary append "Respectfully submitted" to the minutes, or the name only? (b) Can the secretary make motions and vote?

ANS. (a) Only the name, followed by the title "Secretary." (b) Yes, the same as any other member.

248. QUES. When the minutes are being approved, is a motion in order to strike out a portion that may be thought best not to have entered in the minutes?

ANS. Yes; but striking from. the minutes does not in any way modify the action previously taken. A resolution or order is just as much in force whether recorded or not. Anything that the rules require to be in the minutes cannot be struck out, except by a two-thirds vote. [R. O. R., p. 247.]

249. QUES. If a member requests that his vote be recorded in the minutes, is it proper for the chair to state the request and ask if there is any objection?

ANS. Yes. If there is no objection the chair directs the secretary to make the entry. If objection is made, the chair puts the question to vote.

250. QUES. Are the names of the makers of main motions always entered in the minutes?

ANS. It is well to enter in the minutes the name of the person offering a main motion, or the motions to reconsider, to rescind, or to take from the table, and the person raising a question of order or making an appeal from the decision of the chair. The name of the seconder should not be entered. But every society has the right to decide what names shall be entered in its minutes. [See Par. Prac., p. 128, for a copy of the minutes of the meeting described in the Drill, pp. 104–112.] [See Ques. 251, 253, 261.]

251. QUES. (a) Am I correct in understanding that a lost motion and one withdrawn are not entered in the minutes? (b) Is a record kept only of motions favorably voted on? (c) When

a motion is reconsidered and lost after the reconsideration, is not that fact entered in the minutes?

ANS. (a) Main motions, points of order, and appeals should be entered in the minutes, even when lost. They are not necessarily entered when withdrawn. Other motions that are lost are usually not recorded. See R. O. R., p. 247, for the seven essentials that should be entered in the minutes. (b) No; main motions that are lost are entered in the minutes. (c) Yes. [See Ques. 261, 250, 252, 253.]

252. QUES. On p. 249 of R. O. R. it is stated that when a count is ordered or a vote is taken by ballot the votes on each side should be entered in the minutes. Does this rule apply to elections?

ANS. Yes, it applies to such votes on all questions. The assembly may, however, at any time by a two-thirds vote suspend the rule for that meeting. Or, any society may adopt a rule prohibiting, in the case of elections, the recording in the minutes of the number of votes cast for candidates.

253. QUES. What is the preferable form of record for all main motions?

ANS. If the motion was not in the form of a resolution the record should read: "On motion of Mr. Jones, it was resolved that we have a banquet." If the motion was in the form of a resolution the entry would be thus: "The following resolution offered by Mr. Jones was adopted: 'Resolved, That we have a banquet.'" If the resolution was amended before adoption the minutes should read thus: "A resolution offered by Mr. Jones, after amendment, was adopted as follows: 'Resolved, That,' etc." [See Ques. 250, 251, 252, 261.]

254. QUES. How should the report of the tellers be recorded? Is it sufficient simply to state who was elected?

ANS. No. The full report of the tellers should be recorded, unless the assembly orders it not to be done, which the assembly has the power to do. [See Form of Tellers' Report, page 561.]

255. QUES. In a society having regular meetings, held monthly from October to April, the annual meeting being in April, (a) What minutes are read at the annual meeting? (b) What minutes are read at the first meeting in October?

ANS. (a) The minutes of the meeting held the previous month. (b) The minutes of the preceding meeting, which is the annual meeting held in April. The interval between April and October is so great, however, that it is better, in case there is a possibility of difference of opinion as to what occurred at the meeting, to appoint a committee on the minutes, consisting of two or three of the old officers and an equal number of the new ones, including the old and the new secretaries, with instructions to report at the meeting in October. In this way the record prepared by the secretary is examined before the facts are forgotten, and there is a much greater possibility of the truth being ascertained. If the committee cannot agree, the society will have to decide the disputed points. [See Ques. 257.]

256. QUES. Has the presiding officer of a meeting or convention authority to insert in the minutes of the convention anything that was not said or read during the convention?

ANS. No. Neither the president nor any one else has a right to insert in the minutes a false statement, and it certainly is a false statement to say that certain things were said or done that were not said or done. But this does not necessarily prevent the committee in charge of compiling and publishing the proceedings of a convention from including matter that did not come before the convention. In doing so, however, they run the risk of a vote of censure at the next meeting of the convention if anything is inserted that is disapproved by the convention.

257. QUES. At the annual meeting of a federation composed of delegates appointed to the meeting, when the secretary reads the minutes of the last annual meeting, are they approved by the meeting assembled?

ANS. A convention of delegates should not have read, nor should it take action upon, the minutes of the previous convention. Each convention must attend to its own minutes. It is well to have the executive committee or the board empowered to approve the minutes, as far as they have not been acted upon before adjournment of the convention. Or, a special committee may be appointed for the purpose. [R. O. R., p. 249.]

258. QUES. May a society authorize its board of managers to approve the minutes of a meeting of the society?

ANS. Yes.

259. QUES. Can any one vote to amend the minutes, whether present or not at the time the action was taken?

ANS. Yes.

260. QUES. (a) Are the minutes of the board meetings open

for inspection of a club member not on the board? or (b) Can such inspection be demanded of a board?

ANS. (a) No, unless by permission of the board. (b) No, not by a member. Only the society has that power. [See Ques. 138.]

261. QUES. The minutes of one of our meetings contain the following record of the proceedings:

"Moved by Mr. A that $500 be donated to the Orphans' Home. Moved by Mr. B that, with the consent of the mover, an amendment to the motion be made that the amount appropriated be $400 and with a different disposition. The original mover reduced the amount to $450, and the motion was stated as follows: Moved that the sum of $450 be appropriated from the treasury and donations be made as follows: $300 to the Orphans' Home, $100 to the Foundling Asylum, and $50 to the Children's Hospital. The motion was put, and failed to carry." Is the record made correctly?

ANS. One does not move an amendment with the consent of the mover of the main motion. This is a suggestion, not a motion, that the mover modify his motion. The question having been stated, the mover cannot modify his motion without the consent of the assembly, and the minutes should show that he had this consent. Since no one objected, he had general consent. The minutes would have been better if written thus:

"Moved by Mr. A that $500 be appropriated to the Orphans' Home. Mr. B suggested that Mr. A modify his motion in a certain way, whereupon Mr. A, partially accepting the suggestion, with general consent, modified his motion to read as follows: That $300 be appropriated to the Orphans' Home, $100 to the Foundling Asylum, and $50 to the Children's Hospital. The motion as modified was put, and lost." [See Ques. 250, 251, 252, 253, 261.]

HONORARY OFFICERS AND MEMBERS

262. QUES. (a) Can a member be elected to the office of honorary president who has never served as president? (b) If possible, is it customary?

ANS. (a) Yes. (b) No.

263. QUES. If an amendment to the by-laws creating the office of honorary president is proposed, can it be amended so as to limit the office to one who has formerly served as president?

ANS. Yes. The society may adopt any limitations it pleases,

and may require the vote to be unanimous. But an honorary presidency should never be made an office. It is only a title.

264. QUES. When a retiring president is made honorary president, is there any rule that prevents the club's renominating him at a later period for the presidency again, or any reason why he may not serve as chairman of any committee to which they may choose to elect him?

ANS. No. [See page 332 and Ques. 270, 272.]

265. QUES. Can an honorary president hold office on an executive board, be a member of a committee, or be elected to serve as a duly elected delegate or alternate to state or national conventions?

ANS. Yes, if he is a member of the society. The honorary office neither gives nor takes away any of his rights, except that it entitles him to be present and to speak at the meetings. If he is not a member of the society the answer is, No.

266. QUES. Do honorary presidents have any right to attend board meetings and other committee meetings and take active part in them by virtue of their office?

ANS. No.

267. QUES. Do honorary officers or members have the right to make motions or to vote?

ANS. No, honorary officers or members do not have the right to make motions or to vote by virtue of their honorary offices, but they have the right to debate. Holding an honorary position does not deprive one of any rights he would have if he did not hold the honorary position. Thus, an honorary president, if a member of the organization, may be elected to any office without vacating his honorary office.

268. QUES. Is it permissible for a chapter to give an honorary regent the power to vote on the board of management?

ANS. No, it is not permissible unless your by-laws provide for it. As an honorary office is not a real parliamentary office, the privilege of voting in either the chapter or the board of management does not go with it. A chapter has just as much right to place upon the board of management an honorary member or an honorary secretary or one who is not a member of the society as an honorary regent. For honorary officers see R. O. R., p. 267. [See Ques. 269.]

269. QUES. If no provision is made by the constitution or

by-laws to give a vote to honorary presidents, can such vote be given by vote of convention, and if so, can it be cast on constitutional amendments and in elections?

ANS. The convention has no more authority to give the privilege of voting to an honorary president than it has to give it to any one else who is not a member of the convention. The right of voting belongs only to members of an organization, unless the by-laws provide otherwise. [See Ques. 268.]

270. QUES. (*a*) When an honorary president is elected active president, is she both active and honorary president? (*b*) When an honorary member of a club becomes again an active member, is she then both an active and an honorary member?

ANS. Yes, to both questions. But each society has a perfect right to settle these questions for itself in its by-laws. [See Ques. 264, 271, 272.]

271. QUES. (*a*) If an honorary member becomes an active member, does that do away with the honorary membership? and (*b*) Do their names not have to be put up and voted on before they can become active members again?

ANS. (*a*) No. (*b*) Honorary membership is simply an honor conferred on some one, and in no way affects real membership unless the by-laws make it otherwise. If an honorary member wishes to become a member of a club, the same steps must be taken as with any one else. If he afterward terminates his membership, his honorary membership continues, since that is for life unless the society terminates it sooner. If an active member is elected an honorary member or honorary officer, it in no way affects his active membership. [See Ques. 270.]

272. QUES. After an honorary title has been conferred on a retiring officer, such as honorary president, regent, etc., (*a*) May this person be later reëlected to active service in this same office? If so, (*b*) is the honorary title dropped?

ANS. (*a*) Yes. (*b*) No. [See Ques. 264, 270.]

273. QUES. (*a*) Has an honorary president who holds another office always the right to vote by virtue of the second office? (*b*) Has an honorary president, holding another office, the right to leave the platform and come to the floor and make motions and vote?

ANS. (*a*) No. Holding office gives no right to vote. (*b*) Yes, if a member of the society. No, if not a member. It is membership, not office, that gives the right to vote. [See Ques. 226, 375.]

274. QUES. If a regent resigns in the middle of her term, can the chapter elect her an honorary regent, when we already have an honorary regent?

ANS. Yes, unless you have a by-law preventing it. In fact, you can elect every member of the chapter, and any one else, an honorary regent if you wish. An honorary office is not a real office. It is simply a compliment, and, unless there is something in the by-laws on the subject, there is no reason why you should not pay the compliment to any one the chapter may wish to honor. Of course, the value of the compliment diminishes as the number upon whom it is conferred is increased, and its value increases with the difficulty of obtaining it. Therefore it should require at least a three-fourths if not a unanimous vote to elect a member to an honorary office. It does not give any privilege whatever, except to attend the meetings of the chapter and to speak. If there is no by-law on the subject, it may be conferred by a majority vote. The vote conferring it may be rescinded, like any other resolution. The compliment is of little value unless provided for in the by-laws and made difficult to obtain.

275. QUES. If a member of a society is made an honorary officer for life, how may that honor be taken from him?

ANS. The society should rescind the resolution conferring the honor. The motion may be made, "To rescind the resolution making Mr. A an honorary vice-president of this society." This is not a privileged motion, but must be made like any other main motion. If notice is given, it may be adopted by a majority vote at the next meeting, even on the same day. Without notice, a majority of the registered members or a two-thirds vote may adopt it.

CHAPTER XLIII

QUESTIONS ANSWERED

MISCELLANEOUS

276. QUES. Is a roll-call necessary to make a meeting legal?
ANS. No. A roll-call is unnecessary in most organizations, and is an inexcusable waste of time. Not only does calling the roll occupy time, but time must be consumed at the next meeting in reading the list of members who were present, because this list must be recorded in the minutes whenever there is a roll-call. The roll should be called in meetings of societies that impose a fine for absence, provided the attendance is too large for the secretary to check the names of those present. In small bodies like city councils, boards of education, etc., where the names of the attendants and the absentees are recorded and published, the roll may be called, or the secretary may make the record without a roll-call. [See Ques. 360.]

277. QUES. Are there any "U. S. Laws," "U. S. Statutes," or "Laws of Congress" that govern parliamentary law in general?
ANS. There are no laws or U. S. statutes relating to parliamentary law. A law or a U. S. statute requires the joint action of both houses of Congress and of the President of the United States. But all of them combined have not the power to regulate the proceedings in either house after the members have taken the oath of office, because Section 5 of the U. S. Constitution provides that "Each house may determine the rules of its proceedings." A law was passed, however, in 1789, requiring the election of a clerk before proceeding to business; yet the house has held that it may adopt rules before electing a clerk, the law to the contrary notwithstanding. Each house has its own rules, and they do not agree with each other.

278. QUES. Does the fact that the meeting was not called to order until fifteen minutes after the hour designated in the by-laws, though a quorum was present at that hour, affect the legality of the action taken?

ANS. No. The hour for the meeting should be provided for in a standing rule, never in a by-law.

279. QUES. If a district meeting is called for two o'clock and the chairman is not there at two-thirty, and the members then elect another chairman and transact the business that the meeting was called for, has the regular chairman any right to contend that the procedure was illegal because they did not wait for her? She appeared after it was all over with, being nearly an hour late.

ANS. The meeting was legal and the chairman had no cause of complaint. There was no necessity for waiting thirty minutes. Ten minutes was sufficient delay.

280. QUES. If the chair puts a question to vote without its being seconded, and no objection is made at the time, does his failure to call for a second affect the legality of the action taken?

ANS. No.

281. QUES. A motion was made, but, not being immediately seconded, another motion was made and seconded, after which the first motion was seconded, and each mover claimed that his motion was the pending one. Which was correct?

ANS. The one who made the first motion. When a motion is made, the chair has no right to recognize any one to make a motion until the first motion has been stated by the chair, or until he has taken the proper steps to ascertain whether any one wishes to second it, and has announced that the motion is not seconded. See R. O. R., pp. 36, 37. Before a motion is seconded a point of order may be raised or suitable requests may be made, as that the motion be modified. But the motion, after being made, has the right of way in preference to other motions until the chair states the question on it, or rules that it is not before the assembly because of its not being seconded, or because of its being out of order.

282. QUES. Can this question be divided? Moved "That we give a whist, the proceeds to go to the French Orphans."

ANS. No, because the second proposition is absurd if the first is lost. The proper course to be pursued by those who wish separate votes taken on the two propositions is to move "to strike out all the words after 'whist.'" The vote on this motion will show whether the society wishes these words retained, just as effectually as if the original motion were divided. See R. O. R., p. 91.

283. QUES. Are there any motions that cannot be withdrawn? If so, please state them.

ANS. No, provided the withdrawal is made before it is too late for the motion to be renewed. Thus, the motion to reconsider cannot be withdrawn after it is too late for any one else to make the motion. Notice of a motion to be made at the next meeting may be withdrawn at any time during the meeting at which the notice was given, but not afterward.

284. QUES. If a club has adopted a certain hour for the adjournment of the weekly meetings and the club wishes to adjourn before that time, could it be done without suspending the rules?

ANS. No. The rule having been adopted, members who come late have a right to expect the club to be in session. If it is only a standing rule it may be suspended by a majority vote. [See Ques. 244.]

285. QUES. Can a member be compelled to pay his dues if the by-laws do not prescribe a penalty for not doing so? If so, how?

ANS. No; but after reasonable delay and efforts to secure the payment, he should be suspended from membership. If he fails to do so, he should be expelled.

286. QUES. Can a member be deprived of his right to vote if he is in arrears for his dues, if there is no provision for it in the by-laws?

ANS. No, not unless he is suspended from membership. See preceding question. [See Ques. 192.]

287. QUES. A society in its by-laws provides that members who are in arrears for dues cannot vote. Can these members be counted for a quorum?

ANS. No.

288. QUES. A case of discipline was being tried. A member refused to testify. The society expelled the member. Did it have the right to do so when there was nothing in the by-laws about it?

ANS. Yes.

289. QUES. Is it better form to say "opposed" or "contrary" when taking a vote on a motion?

ANS. "Opposed" is the word used in Congress and in R. O. R., and is preferable, except when the question is put in the following form when "contrary" is used: "As many as are of the opinion that the amendment is germane to the pending resolution [or question] say 'Aye.' Those of a contrary opinion say 'No.' ''

290. QUES. What is the difference between a recommendation and a resolution?

ANS. Sometimes they amount to the same thing, but not usually. If a recommendation is adopted that no further action be taken in the case, the effect is the same as if a similar resolution had been adopted. But if a club adopts a recommendation of a committee that charges be preferred against a member for a certain offense, that does not prefer the charges. As a general rule, a committee should close its report with resolutions to put into effect all of its recommendations, and the reporting member should move their adoption.

291. QUES. What is the difference between a motion and a resolution?

ANS. A motion is defined in R. O. R., p. 33, as "a proposal that the assembly take certain action, or that it express itself as holding certain views." Those motions that are made to bring before the assembly for its consideration a particular subject that is not at the time in the possession of the assembly are called main motions. A resolution is the common form of an original main motion, and rules relating to the former apply equally to the latter. The term "resolution" is generally used instead of "original main motion," even though the proposition is not in the form of a resolution.

292. QUES. The following resolution was adopted by our club: "*Resolved,* That the club do not accept the offer of a site for a club-house for $75,000." Is such a negative resolution in order?

ANS. Yes. It is much more emphatic than voting down a resolution to accept the offer. A member has as much right to offer a resolution in the negative form as in the positive form. The only objection to a negative resolution is that it often confuses some members in regard to the effect of a negative vote.

The objections to a negative amendment do not apply to a negative resolution. In the case of an amendment, it is out of order when the effect of its adoption is to make the adoption of the amended resolution have the same effect as the rejection of the original resolution. In such a case the negative amendment only wastes time and becomes a dilatory motion, and is out of order.

293. QUES. Is it proper to ask an opponent for permission to ask a question while he is speaking?

ANS. Yes, but the request must be made through the chairman. The opponent may consent or decline to be interrupted. If he consents, the interruption is charged to his time. If this were not so, a speaker could keep the floor indefinitely by having his friends ask him questions that he wishes to discuss.

294. QUES. Is it fair, in a parliamentary contest, to prevent a member's reading an extract as a part of his speech?

ANS. It depends upon what it was proposed to read. A speaker does not ask for permission to read, but continues until objection is made. He then stops, and the chair immediately puts the question to the assembly as to whether the article may be read. Permission is never refused, except in case an attempt is made to impose upon the assembly by reading irrelevant matter, or for filibustering purposes. The rule against reading was adopted originally when there was no limit to the length of speeches, and is still the rule in the U. S. Senate and in the British Parliament. It is still necessary to protect the assembly from advantage being taken of the rule allowing each member two speeches of ten minutes each on each question. If members could not be prevented from reading, a minority opposition larger than one third could occupy twenty minutes each in reading papers bearing on the question, or one member could write out a lengthy article on the question to be read by different members, so as to occupy hours. In this way, members who could speak only a few minutes, if confined to their own resources, could consume their full time. The rule is not intended to prevent a member from quoting printed or written articles bearing on the question at issue when used in good faith to strengthen his argument. R. O. R., p. 102, lines 5-7, reads as follows: "It is customary, however, to allow members to read printed extracts as parts of their speeches, as long as they do not abuse the privilege."

In the case you mention, it does not appear that any vote was taken on granting the permission to read, but the chair seems to have assumed that a single objection prevented the reading. This was an error.

295. QUES. When may a man rise to a point of order? I cannot find this in R. O. R.

ANS. The last paragraph of R. O. R., p. 79, under Questions of Order says: "It is also the right of every member who notices the breach of a rule to insist on its enforcement. In such a case he rises from his seat and says, 'Mr. Chairman, I rise to a point of order,' etc." He may rise to a point of order whenever the rules are violated.

296. QUES. When a very important question was being acted upon at our last general conference, the vote by show of hands was declared to be a tie and the action lost. The count was doubted, a rising vote was taken, and the same result declared. This count was also doubted, and it was decided to take the yeas and nays. On this count the action was declared carried by a majority of one, but it was known that one member on the affirmative side had meanwhile come into the assembly and voted, and it was his vote that carried the action. Now, the questions are these: (a) During a recount, can any member vote who did not vote when the original vote was taken? Or, (b) Is the recount simply a recount of the first vote? Or, (c) Does it afford an opportunity for a member to vote who was present when the first vote was taken, but did not then vote? (d) Can a member who voted on the first vote change his vote on the recount? (e) Can either side bring in other members to vote who were not present when the first vote was taken?

ANS. (a) Yes. (b) No. (c) Yes. (d) Yes. (e) Yes. The old common parliamentary law, following the English practice, prohibited the voting of any member who was not present when the chairman put the question. But our Congress has no rule on the subject, and has followed the more reasonable practice of permitting members to vote, regardless of whether they were present or not when the question was put. The object of taking the vote is to ascertain the views or the will of the members, and this object is better attained by the practice of Congress than by that of Parliament. In my opinion, your conference acted properly in admitting the vote of the member who entered the hall after the question was put.

The term "recount" is scarcely a correct expression for the subsequent voting, which was actually a division and a vote by "yeas and nays," which you will find described in R. O. R., p. 95. You did not have a recount of the vote originally taken. You had two new votes taken, at which members could vote as they thought best, regardless of how they voted before, or whether they voted at all.

297. Ques. When the chair was in the act of putting the question to vote, a member moved to lay the question on the table. The chairman ignored the motion. Was he right?

Ans. It depends upon circumstances, as explained in R. O. R., pp. 182, 183. As stated there, debate, and therefore the right to make motions, "is not closed by the chairman's rising and putting the question, as, until both the affirmative and the negative are put, a member can rise and claim the floor and reopen the debate or make a motion, provided he rises with reasonable promptness after the chair asks, 'Are you ready for the question?'" The chair cannot cut off members from making motions or debating by hurriedly putting the question. It is not for the chair to decide when the question shall be put. When the chair has given ample opportunity for members to claim the floor for debate, or for making motions, and they do not take advantage of it, they lose their right to claim the floor for these purposes after the chair has started to put the question.

298. Ques. Ten days before our convention of city clubs the resolutions committee met to determine which of the resolutions would be brought to our women for business. One week before the convention the delegates and presidents met to fully determine on those to be brought before the convention. When one of the resolutions was reached, a member moved to lay it on the table. Was not the motion out of order? Do not these resolutions comprise the orders of the day, a "class of motions" that cannot be laid on the table, according to R. O. R., p. 106? I understand that the resolution could have been sent back to the committee.

Ans. It is not clear what was the pending question when the motion to lay on the table was made. If the question stated by the chair was on the adoption of an order of business consisting of the resolutions submitted, the motion to lay on the table one of the resolutions was out of order. Nothing can be laid on the table but the pending question and what adheres to it. The only subsidiary motions that could be applied to one of the resolutions is to amend. If members object to it, they should move to strike it out, not to lay it on the table. The pending question is not on the resolution, but on the motion to adopt an order of business, and it is only this latter motion that may be laid on the table. The orders of the day, or order of business, cannot as a whole be postponed or laid on the table, because they are not pending as a whole. But a single order, when pending, may be laid on the table, etc. The orders were not pending in your case, but a motion to adopt a certain order of business, and this could be laid on the table.

299. Ques. A convention adopted a program that included a set of resolutions. One of these resolutions was contentious, and a motion was made to lay it on the table. This was ruled out of order on the ground that the resolution was the order of the day and therefore could not be tabled, according to R. O. R., p. 106. Was this ruling correct? Is not each resolution a pending question as it is taken up?

Ans. R. O. R., p. 71, says: "After the order has been announced and the question is actually pending, it is debatable and may be amended or have any other subsidiary motion applied to it, the same as any other main motion. The orders of the day in a mass cannot be laid on the table or postponed, but when an order has actually been taken up it may, by a majority vote, be laid on the table, or postponed, or committed." The statement on p. 106 of R. O. R. is that "it is not in order to lay on the table a class of questions, as the orders of the day, or unfinished business, or reports of committees, because they are not pending questions, as only one main motion can be pending at a time." The two extracts are in complete harmony; the first statement answers your question.

300. Ques. A resignation of a member is laid on the table and is not taken up. What becomes of it?

Ans. If the member is in good standing, the resignation, unless withdrawn, takes effect when the time for taking it from the table has expired. [See next question and Resignations, page 332.]

301. Ques. When can you take from the table; i. e., how long after the question has been laid on the table?

Ans. Until the close of the next regular meeting, provided that meeting is held within three months. If there is no regular meeting within three months, it cannot be taken from the table after the close of the session at which it was laid on the table. See R. O. R., p. 154.

302. Ques. Can lay on the table and the previous question be moved at the same time on a main or secondary motion?

Ans. No. The combination is useless, even if it were allowed.

303. Ques. (*a*) Does tabling the main motion while objection to consideration is pending kill the objection to consideration? or (*b*) Is it voted upon when the main question is taken from the table?

Ans. (*a*) No. (*b*) Yes. R. O. R., p. 155, states: "When taken up the [main] question with everything adhering to it is before the assembly exactly as when laid on the table."

304. Ques. If the motion to limit debate to one minute for each person has been carried, is it then in order to move the previous question, with or without qualifications?

Ans. Yes. The last sentence beginning on p. 119, R. O. R., answers your question. [See Ques. 305.]

305. Ques. If the previous question is ordered after the motion to limit debate to one minute for each person has carried, would it cut off the one-minute speeches?

Ans. Yes. The order closing debate now supersedes the order limiting debate. [See Ques. 304.]

306. Ques. If a special order is interrupted by one made before it was, is it necessary to make a motion to lay it on the table?

Ans. No. The special order is announced, thus interrupting the pending business, which is resumed as soon as the interrupting question is disposed of.

307. Ques. When may the orders of the day be called for?

Ans. Only when the order of business is being deviated from without the assembly's having authorized it by a two-thirds vote. See R. O. R., pp. 68, 69.

308. Ques. When the main motion and the motion to postpone indefinitely are pending, a motion is made to amend the main motion, and the amendment is carried; is it in order now to put the motion to postpone indefinitely to vote?

Ans. Yes. As soon as the amendment is voted on, the motion to postpone indefinitely becomes the immediately pending question.

309. Ques. It is stated in R. O. R., p. 50, that a resolution or other main motion that has been rejected at one session may be introduced anew at any future session. Does this mean that the one who offered the resolution, and voted for it and was defeated, can make the same main motion at any future session?

Ans. Yes; any member may make it.

310. Ques. A motion that 40 typewriters be purchased was rejected by a vote of 13 yes and 14 no. One who voted yes, knowing that he cannot move to reconsider, plans to open the question again by moving to buy 30 typewriters. (*a*) Can he do this at a meeting that is the adjournment of the meeting at which the first motion was made? (*b*) Could he move to rescind action and then make his motion?

Ans. (*a*) No. The new motion is so similar to the one rejected by the assembly at the same session that it would be out of order. (*b*) Yes, provided the motion to rescind is adopted by a two-thirds vote. This vote is required because no previous notice was given.

311. Ques. At a regular business meeting of a society, the officers were elected though a quorum was not present, on the ground that a quorum was present at the luncheon accompanied by speaking and music preceding the business meeting. It was contended that those who remained until the business meeting was called to order had a right to proceed to the election, even though there was no quorum. Was this legal?

Ans. No. This question is fully answered in R. O. R. under Quorum, pp. 258, 259. The members remaining could proceed to an election, and then submit their action to the society at an adjourned meeting, and have it ratified. [See Ques. 364.]

312. Ques. Our state conference appointed a committee to investigate a certain matter and report at the next conference. When the committee was prepared to report, a special meeting of the conference was called in strict conformity to the by-laws, and the resolutions recommended by the committee were adopted. The chairman of the committee, who was opposed to the committee's report, then resigned from the committee. (*a*) Was there any committee, after its report had been made, from which to resign? (*b*) It is now claimed by some members that the action of the conference at its special meeting was illegal, and they propose to rescind it at the next regular meeting of the conference. Was it illegal? (*c*) Can it be rescinded, and if so, what vote is required and who may make the motion?

Ans. (*a*) The committee ceased to exist the instant its report was made. [R. O. R., p. 133.] (*b*) The committee was ordered to report at the next conference. The by-laws provided a method for calling a special meeting of the conference, which very properly required a notice of the business to be transacted. All the constituent societies had notice that the committee's report was to be acted upon. At the meeting no one appeared to doubt the right of the committee to report, and I think it too late now to raise that question, which is as to the difference between the "next conference" and the "next meeting of the conference." That is a question for the conference itself to decide, and by acquiescence at the special meeting it decided there was no difference in the meaning, so far as concerned the report of that committee. (c) Yes, the action taken at the special meeting may be rescinded at the regular meeting by a two-thirds vote, provided nothing has been done under the original action that cannot be undone. If notice is given of the proposed motion to rescind in the call for the meeting, the motion to rescind may be adopted by a 'majority vote. [See R. O. R., p. 169.] Any member may make the motion to rescind.

313. QUES. The vice-president of a society moved away a month ago, and left no address with the treasurer or secretary, nor did she resign as vice-president. The board of directors propose to meet and appoint her successor. Have they the authority to do this?

ANS. Yes, if the by-laws authorize the board to fill vacancies. Officers and members of committees and boards of a local society are understood to be residents of the locality. The removal of their residence to a distance that would render the performance of their duties impracticable is virtually the abandonment of their office, and should be treated as the equivalent of a resignation. An officer, in the circumstances described above, should resign.

314. QUES. Should officers who resign during their term of office make a report at the annual meeting?

ANS. No. Officers who resign, if they ever make a report should make it at the time they resign. When the resignation goes into effect they are no longer officers, and-are not entitled to make a report unless it accompanies the resignation. For example, the president at the time the convention meets is the one to make the president's report, even though he has held the office but a short time. The previous president should furnish him with data, or send him a report that he could include in his.

315. QUES. The by-laws of a society provide that the board

shall fill all vacancies in office. An officer resigned. Should the resignation be sent to the society or to the board? The society and board meetings are held one month apart.

ANS. To the board, because it fills the vacancy.

316. QUES. A member of a society wishes to resign. He presents his resignation. (*a*) May he now move that the resignation be accepted? (*b*) May he vote on the question of accepting his resignation?

ANS. (*a*) Yes. (*b*) Yes. In the case mentioned he is a member of the society until his resignation is accepted, and is entitled to make any proper motion and to vote. While the general rule is that "no one can vote on a question in which he has a direct personal or pecuniary interest," R. O. R., p. 192, you will notice that this rule does not prevent one's voting for himself for office. The same principle would allow his voting to accept his own resignation of office or membership.

317. QUES. Does appoint ever mean the same as elect?

ANS. Appoint includes elect. Thus, one who is elected may be said to be appointed to an office. But one who is appointed to an office by the president cannot be said to have been elected to the office.

318. QUES. If one wishes to leave a meeting before adjournment, is it necessary to go through the motion of personal privilege?

ANS. No; such a course is decidedly improper.

319. QUES. Do occasions often occur in ordinary societies that justify raising a question of personal privilege?

ANS. No. So seldom do they occur that I cannot recall a case in my own experience. Ninety per cent. of the instances of persons rising to a question of personal privilege that I have seen recorded in the proceedings of societies were not questions of privilege. The member rose to make an explanation or to make a request, which are not questions of privilege.

320. QUES. Are charter members of an unincorporated club the ones who first sign the constitution, or are they merely original members?

ANS. "Charter members" originally meant the persons whose names are mentioned in the charter, that is, those who originally formed the corporation. When used to-day in ordinary societies it is synonymous with "original members," and therefore can be used in an unincorporated society.

321. Ques. Does a resolution previously adopted, permanent or otherwise, become null and void by a revision of the constitution?

Ans. No, unless it conflicts with the revised constitution.

322. Ques. In the absence of a special rule, has an organization a right to assess its members?

Ans. No. It would require a by-law to authorize an assessment.

323. Ques. (a) Can a member move "that a two-thirds vote shall be necessary for the adoption of this motion"? (b) Could a majority vote on this incidental motion bind the meeting?

Ans. (a) Yes. (b) No. A two-thirds vote is required for the adoption of the motion, which practically suspends the rules relating to voting.

324. Ques. Does the statement, "One negative vote defeats a motion to make a vote unanimous," in R. O. R., p. 203, mean that it requires a unanimous vote to adopt a resolution requiring a unanimous vote for a certain election?

Ans. No. The rule quoted is nothing more than saying that the assembly cannot declare a vote unanimous if there is one negative vote. Adopting a resolution or order that there will be no election unless the candidate receives a unanimous vote is a very different thing, and requires only a two-thirds vote. It requires a two-thirds vote because it suspends the rule that a majority elects. A two-thirds vote would have been necessary to require a two-thirds or three-fourths vote for the election. If you read a few sentences preceding the quotation, I think you will see that the sentence quoted does not apply to your case.

325. Ques. Does not an organization suffer a loss if the chairman is a member and is allowed to vote only when his vote will affect the result?

Ans. No. How can there be a loss when the result is not affected? [See Ques. 377.]

326. Ques. Is a motion to declare an office vacant a question of privilege?

Ans. Yes. The office may be declared vacant by a two-thirds vote, or by a vote of a majority of the entire membership, if there is no rule specifying the term of office, or if the by-laws specify the term as "one year *or* until the successor is elected." If reasonable previous notice has been given of the proposed action, it requires only a majority vote to declare such an office vacant. If, however, the by-laws make the term of office one year, or "one year *and* until the successor is elected," the office cannot be declared vacant. The only way to get rid of the officer is to prefer charges against him, and after trial to dismiss him from office. [See chapter on Discipline, page 334, and Ques. 331.]

327. QUES. What is meant by the "privilege of the floor"?

ANS. The expression "privilege of the floor" means nothing but the privilege of admission to the hall of the assembly during its session. In legislative assemblies, and in many others, no one has the right to enter the hall during a session of the assembly, except members and employees and such other persons as are entitled to the "privileges of the floor" by virtue of a rule or vote of the assembly. It carries with it no right to debate or to make or to second motions, or even to address the chair by way of inquiry, much less to vote. For instance, while a commissioner of the District of Columbia, the writer had the privilege of the floor of the U. S. Senate so that he could go into the Senate chamber when it was in session. But, while he might speak to a senator, he could not, of course, address the presiding officer.

The "privilege of the floor" is a meaningless expression in assemblies whose meetings are so public that any one is entitled to admission to the hall. Where the general public is excluded it gives the possessor of the privilege the right to admission.

328. QUES. (*a*) What is a majority vote? (*b*) Why are illegal votes counted in determining the number necessary for an election by ballot, as stated in R. O. R., p. 196?

ANS. (*a*) A majority vote is more than half of the votes cast, or, in other words, more than are cast for all other candidates combined. It may be found by dividing the entire vote by two and taking the next whole number above it. Or you may state it as half of the even number next larger than the vote. The majority of any even number is the same as that of the odd number just above it. Thus 3 is a majority of either 4 or 5, as it is half of 6, the next larger even number. *Majority* is from *major,* the comparative of *magnus,* great, and means the greater part. If there are only two candidates voted for, and there is not a tie, one must have a majority vote. The term "plurality" is never used except when there are more than two candidates and neither one has a majority. In that case the one that has the largest vote is said to have a plurality, that is, more votes than any other candidate. A majority vote must not be confused with a vote of a majority of the members. (*b*) The object of the vote is to ascertain the choice of the majority of the members who choose to vote. The illegal votes are not cast by illegal voters. They are due generally to ignorance, or to carelessness, or to foolish rules. The choice of the majority of the voters cannot be ascertained in the example given in R. O. R., p. 196, unless the illegal votes are counted. Mr. A, who received a majority of the legal votes, was the choice of but little more than one third of the legal voters, the majority of the ballots being cast for an ineligible candidate. The only way, in such a case, to ascertain the choice of a majority of the legal voters is to take another ballot. [See Ques. 384.]

329. QUES. What is the difference between an adjourned meeting and one held after a recess?

ANS. Congress has varied as to using the term "recess." Previous to 1883 there was in the House Rules no such motion as to take a recess. In the revision of the rules that year, it was made a privileged motion, ranking next after to adjourn. It was dropped in 1890, and since then has not been restored.

The term "recess" is used for an interval of a few minutes during which the assembly is permitted to separate; or it may be for several days, as the holiday recess; or for several months, as the recess between the first and second sessions of Congress. In ordinary societies the sessions rarely extend beyond a day, and then for only three or four days, and the term "recess" should be limited to interruptions of the meetings during the session. Thus, there may be recesses for dinner and for supper, and a recess while the ballots are being counted. Or, in a convention lasting for several days, there may be a recess for an entire day for the purpose of sight-seeing, etc. The expression "adjourned meeting" should, in the case of a society whose ordinary sessions do not last beyond a day, be limited to a meeting adjourned to another day.

330. QUES. What is the difference between the terms "executive session" and "secret session"?

ANS. None. The use of the term "executive session" as equivalent to secret session has become very common. Strictly speaking, an ordinary society cannot have an executive session, as there is no executive business for it to transact. So there is no such thing as an executive session in the lower house of Congress. But the U. S.

Senate has two kinds of sessions, legislative and executive. All confidential business in connection with the chief executive is attended to in executive session. The Senate Rules use the term "session with closed doors" for a secret session, and, as executive sessions are usually held with closed doors, the expression "executive session" has gradually come to be used as synonymous with "secret session."

331. QUES. The president resigned, and then motions were adopted by a majority vote "to vacate all offices and committees." The president was reëlected, the other offices were filled by election, and new committees were appointed. Where is the authority obtained for such procedure?

ANS. It is based upon the principle of the majority ruling. In an assembly like the one referred to, the officers and committees are elected at the will of the assembly, like the speaker in Congress, or in the English Parliament. A motion to declare the ·chair vacant and to proceed to elect a new speaker is a privileged motion in Congress. As such action rescinds what ·the assembly has done previously, it requires the same vote as to rescind, or to discharge a committee. In the case mentioned it is assumed that the majority vote was a majority of the entire organization, because a majority of a quorum cannot adopt such motions unless previous notice of the motion has been given. [See page 378 and Ques. 326.]

332. QUES. A member of a society sent in his resignation as a member, stating it was to take effect at once. A short time after he sent in his resignation, and before a meeting was held at which it could be acted upon, he withdrew ·it. (a) Did he have the right to withdraw the resignation? (b) Is he still a member of the society?

ANS. (a) Yes. (b) Yes. A member or officer may withdraw his resignation at any time before the chair has stated the question on its adoption. [See Ques. 240.]

333. QUES. Has a member of an organization the right to cite another member to appear before a body and answer to charges without being authorized to do so by the body?

ANS. No. A member may notify another one that he intends to prefer charges against him at a certain meeting, but the "citation" is made by the secretary (or clerk), by order of the assembly. The first is an unofficial act that may be ignored, but an official citation must be obeyed on peril of the severest punishment the body can inflict for the offense. In other words, the failure to obey the citation exposes one to the same punishment as a plea of "guilty." [See page 347 for further information on Citations.]

334. QUES. If a member of a society is expelled, may he be restored to membership?

ANS. Yes. If a society expels a member, it can at any future time take up the question and restore the member. This can be done even if there does not remain a single member of the body that expelled the member. The same notice and the same vote are required for restoring a member as are required to elect a member. A body may take up again a case where an officer or an employee has been dismissed, and restore the person to his position for the unexpired term, provided the vacancy has not been filled. The same procedure and vote are necessary as are required for an election. See R. O. R., p. 170.

335. QUES. Can a member hold an office in the national federation and also in the home club?

ANS. Yes.

336. QUES. (a) In a convention that has adopted R. O. R., would a motion to limit or extend the limits of debate during the entire session be allowed? (b) If a single speaker wishes time extended, can the chair grant the permission, or must a vote be taken?

ANS. (a) Yes. (b) Either course may be pursued, but when the chair grants the permission he should preface it by saying, "If there is no objection." If there is a single objection, the chair should put the question to vote on granting the request. See R. O. R., page 104 (f). [See Ques. 337.]

337. QUES. When a rules and regulations committee is appointed for a meeting, and the constitution reads that R. O. R. shall·be used, can a rule be adopted that speeches are to be five minutes in length and that each member is to speak only once to a subject? Is that in conflict with the Robert's rule that allows ten-minute speeches? If the above-mentioned motion can be made, should it be to "suspend the rules" and require a two-thirds vote? And if this rule is made, that would not debar a motion to extend the time from five minutes to longer, would it?

ANS. The rules committee can report a rule regulating the length and number of speeches allowed in debate, but, like all motions to limit debate, it requires a two-thirds vote for its adoption.

It is not in conflict with R. O. R., because these rules provide for limiting debate by a two-thirds vote. The motion is not made in the form of suspending the rules, but is described on p. 120, R. O. R. Adopting the limit of five minutes for speeches does not prevent changing this limit at any time by a two-thirds vote. This is all explained in the article above referred to on Limiting Debate. [See Ques. 336.]

338. QUES. If a program has been adopted, and it has been found impossible to carry out some part of it, could the program committee make the necessary changes without taking another vote of the assembly, the president, without taking a formal vote, announcing that if there is no objection the following changes will be made? I know that Robert's Rules say a change cannot be made without taking a two-thirds vote and suspending the rules.

ANS. The statement to which you refer is, "No change can be made in it [the program] after its adoption by the assembly, except by a two-thirds vote." Anything that can be done by a two-thirds vote can be done by general consent, which is equivalent to a unanimous vote. The proceeding you describe is the proper one under the circumstances.

339. QUES. (a) When a special meeting is called, must the business to be transacted be specified in the call? (b) If a very urgent matter came up just before the special meeting, could it be considered at the special meeting, though not mentioned in the call? (c) If a majority of the entire membership were present, would that affect taking up something urgent that was not in the call? (d) Or may a special meeting be called with a statement that "other business of importance may be considered"?

ANS. (a) It depends upon the by-laws. If the by-laws do not require the business to be specified, it is not absolutely necessary, but it is customary and is advisable. All important questions to come up should be stated in the call, and a clause like this should be added: "and such other business as may properly come before the meeting." This should cover minor matters, but would not comply with the by-laws, so far as an important question is concerned. (b) If the by-laws require notice of the business to come up, no question of which notice was not given can be considered, except informally, if it is so important that the attendance, if notice had been given, might have been affected sufficiently to change the action of the society. If, after the notice is sent out, the secretary receives an invitation for the society to go on an excursion, or to a banquet, before the next meeting, the society could act upon such a matter. If it is found desirable to take important action of which notice was not given, the action being informal the same as if no quorum was present, it must be ratified by the society at a regular or a special meeting in order to legalize it. (*c*) It would insure the ratification of whatever action was taken. (*d*) Not if the by-laws require notice of the business to be transacted.

340. QUES. An annual meeting adjourned sine die. After adjournment a number of the members of the society found that a sine die adjournment defeated the purpose they had in view, and they rallied enough members together to form a quorum in accordance with the by-laws, and adopted certain measures that would have been taken by the executive board. Was their action legal?

ANS. No. The sine die adjournment of the annual meeting ended the meeting, and the reconvening of the meeting afterward was illegal, and all action taken at the illegal meeting is null and void. If such proceedings were allowed, the friends of a measure that could not be adopted in the regular meeting could agree to linger after adjournment and then reconvene the meeting, in which they would have a majority, and adopt their resolution.

341. QUES. Should any action be taken on a president's annual address which contains no recommendations?

ANS. No.

342. QUES. When a club has a parliamentarian as one of its officers, (*a*) Should her duties be defined in the by-laws under duties of officers? (*b*) If so, how would you word it?

ANS. (*a*) Yes. (*b*) It could be worded thus: "It shall be the duty of the parliamentarian to advise the presiding officer on points of parliamentary law, and also to give similar advice to the society and the board of managers, when they request it." [See Ques. 98, 343.]

343. QUES. Must an organization abide by the decision of its parliamentarian?

ANS. No. The parliamentarian has no authority to decide questions for an organization. It is an incorrect use of parliamentary terms to speak of the "decision" or the "ruling" of the parliamentarian. The presiding officer is the only person authorized to decide questions of order or to make rulings. She has the right to call on persons of experience for their opinions on a point of order before making her decision, but no one has a right to express her opinion until requested to do so by the presiding officer. See R. O. R., page 78. [See Parliamentarian, page 323.] [See Ques. 98, 342.]

344. QUES. Would it be wise for a society to adopt a rule prohibiting the chair's counting on either side the members who do not vote, or requiring members who will not vote to leave the room?

ANS. There is no authority for counting as voting those abstaining from voting, or for requiring members who will not vote to leave the room. It would be as absurd to adopt a rule prohibiting the counting of a member as voting, when he does not vote, as it would be to prohibit the counting of absentees as present. There is as much reason for the one as for the other.

The rules of Congress require that all the members, unless excused or unavoidably prevented, shall attend all the meetings, and that all shall vote unless personally interested or excused. Congress does compel the attendance of absentees frequently, but, in the more than one hundred years' existence of that rule, it has never been able to compel members to vote. Members ought to vote if they have an opinion on the question, but there is no way yet devised to compel them to do their duty. However, the principle is that those neglecting to vote acquiesce in the result following from their non-action, the same as if they voted. If there is present a quorum of an organization of 1000 members, and one member votes in favor of and none against the resolution, that resolution is legally adopted, as all the silent members acquiesced in the action. They cannot be counted as voting with the majority, but the effect is the same.

Again, suppose you have a by-law requiring a vote of two thirds of the members present to amend the by-laws, and there are 100 present, and 60 vote in favor of the amendment and 10 against it. The amendment is lost, the same as if the thirty silent members had voted in the negative. But that is a different thing from counting them as voting with the minority. They did not vote at all. Nor could they be required to leave the room so that the amendment could be adopted, as that would defeat the very object of the by-law requiring a two-thirds vote of those present instead of only a two-thirds vote. [See page 576, Two-Thirds Vote]

345. QUES. The following motion is recorded as adopted by our

society: "*Resolved,* That in the future, when a death occurs in the club, the place shall be left vacant for the rest of the calendar year." It is now desired to fill at once a vacancy caused by a death. How must we treat the former motion to do it correctly?

ANS. Adopt a motion "to suspend the rule relating to filling vacancies caused by death, and to proceed to fill the vacancy in our membership caused by the death of ——." See Standing Rules, R. O. R., p. 268. This motion requires only a majority vote for its adoption, and when adopted the chair announces the election to fill the vacancy as the next business in order.

346. QUES. There were fifteen members of an executive board present at a meeting. One member moved that the salary of a certain officer be increased a certain amount. The question was put to vote. The "ayes" had a strong response; nobody voted "no," but three members did not vote "yes." Can this be called a "unanimous" vote?

ANS. Yes. All blank ballots are ignored, and the same principle applies to all other forms of voting. Those not voting are not counted in deciding whether it is a majority, two-thirds, or unanimous vote. [See Ques. 196, 197.]

347. QUES. Is approving a budget the same as approving the bills for the expenditures?

ANS. No. Approving a budget is very different from approving the bills for expenditures. The U. S. government may authorize the expenditure of $50,000,000 for improvement of rivers and harbors, under the direction of the Secretary of War; the Secretary of War may authorize certain expenditures; but still the disbursing officer is not relieved of his responsibility for the money turned over to him until his detailed vouchers or bills have been approved by the U. S. Auditors and the U. S. Comptroller. The budget is approved in advance, and the bills are approved after the expenditures.

348. QUES. In a society meeting monthly, the treasurer is asked at each meeting to read the condition of the treasury—really for information. Should such a report be accepted by a motion and vote?

ANS. No. A society should never vote to accept a treasurer's report. If the report is of such a nature as to require the approval of the society it should go to an auditing committee, and it is their report that is accepted. If it is merely a "report of facts for information" it requires no action of the society. In the article on

Treasurer, R. O. R., pp. 251-253, you will notice that the only reports of the treasurer referred to are those that are to be audited, like the annual report. See also what is said in third paragraph, p. 223, R. O. R., concerning reports of facts for information only. [See page 323.]

349. QUES. If a club has an auditor who makes a yearly report, is the treasurer's report accepted at the monthly business meeting, or referred to the auditor?

ANS. Neither. [See answer to preceding question.]

350. QUES. A motion was made that the treasurer be censured for the careless manner in which he had kept the accounts, and the motion was referred to a committee. The committee recommended that the treasurer be censured. Does the motion to adopt the report of the committee, if carried, censure the treasurer.

ANS. It depends upon the form of the report. In such a case the report should always end with a resolution which the committee recommends be adopted, and as soon as the report is read the chairman of the committee should move the adoption of the resolution. The report would end in a form similar to this: "In conclusion your committee recommends the adoption of the following resolution: 'Resolved, That the treasurer be, and he is hereby, censured for the careless manner in which he has kept his accounts.' " If this motion is adopted no further action is necessary. Or the resolution may be worded thus: "Resolved, That the treasurer be publicly censured by the president for the careless manner," etc. In this case the president calls the treasurer to stand in front of the platform, and then censures him publicly.

351. QUES. An executive board authorized to transact the business of an organization in the interim between the meetings of the organization takes certain action during a recess of the convention, and the convention immediately takes opposite action. Which action holds?

ANS. The convention's action is supreme. The action of the executive board is in force as long as the superior body does not interfere with it. While the superior body is in session, even during a recess, the executive board is not authorized to transact the business of the organization. The words "between meetings" in the by-law are used in the sense of "between sessions." [See Ques. 354, 379.]

352. QUES. Has a club the right to refuse to hear the minutes

of its executive board, which would have explained an action the board had taken?

ANS. Yes, the legal right. The law does not oblige any one to be courteous.

353. QUES. Do motions adopted by the executive board of a club, and ratified by the club, hold over from one year to another, or are they void at the end of the club year?

ANS. Any resolution of a society continues in force until it is rescinded or amended. If a board adopts a resolution and it is ratified by the club, it remains in force until it has been amended or rescinded by the club. [See Ques. 47.]

354. QUES. If the society is not satisfied with action taken by its executive board, can it change that action?

ANS. Yes, unless the by-laws place the matter at issue under the charge of the board. For instance, when the by-laws authorize the executive board to fill vacancies in office, the society cannot instruct the board in the matter, or reverse its action. [See Ques. 351, 379.]

355. QUES. (a) Has a board of a society the right to adopt a resolution censuring the conduct of one of its members? (b) What vote is required to censure a member?

ANS. (a) No. The board's recourse is to direct its chairman, or some other member, to report the facts to the society, which alone has the power of censuring or otherwise disciplining a member of the board. Boards, in this respect, are the same as committees. See R. O. R., p. 218. (b) A majority vote.

356. QUES. Has the board of a society the authority to create an office in the society?

ANS. No. [See Ques. 357.]

357. QUES. Has the board of a society the authority to restore an office that has been dropped and is no longer provided for in the by-laws of the society?

ANS. No. [See Ques. 356.]

358. QUES. When the by-laws of a national organization contain one section specifying certain classes of names that its subordinate local societies are prohibited from taking, can the board by a resolution add to that list ?

ANS. No. The national society itself cannot add to the list of prohibited names, except by amending their by-laws. The presumption is that the society, having specified a prohibited list, included all that it intended to prohibit. If the list is incomplete, the proper course is to amend the by-law. Of course it is not necessary to specify frivolous or absurd names, such as the "Benedict Arnold Society," as a name for a patriotic society.

359. QUES. When the executive board numbers 11, is 3 a sufficiently large quorum? When the club numbers 250, is 5 a sufficiently large quorum?

ANS. No, to both questions. The quorum of a board is a majority of its members unless the club has authorized a smaller number. It is seldom that a quorum smaller than one third should be authorized for a board. It is best to have the quorum an even number, because the majority of an even number is the same as that of the next larger number, which is always an odd number. Thus, if the quorum of a board of 11 is 4, it is about as safe as if it were 5, because in either case it would require 3 votes to adopt any measure, while with a quorum of 4 there is a greater possibility of having a quorum at every meeting. A club of 250 members should have a quorum of not less than 12, and in most cases not less than 20. A board of 11 should have a quorum of not less than 4. The proper size for a quorum depends upon the importance of its duties. Where the board has great responsibilities and power, its quorum should be large. The proper size for the quorum depends upon the number that usually attend the meetings when the weather is unfavorable.

360. QUES. Should not the roll of delegates be called at each meeting in order to see if a quorum is present, or how else could you ascertain if there is a quorum?

ANS. No. It would probably take at least half an hour to call the roll of a convention of 400 or 500 delegates. If there is doubt as to a quorum's being present, the president should appoint tellers to make a count. By dividing the hall into sections and appointing a teller for each section, a convention of 1,000 delegates can be counted in five minutes when there is reason to doubt the presence of a quorum. If there were more than 600 present to count, it would be evident that a quorum was present and there would be no use in making a count. If the president does not order a count, a member may raise a point of "no quorum." If the president decides the point not well taken, and the member is still confident that no quorum is present, he may appeal from the decision, or he may simply move that a count be made. In either case, if the majority agrees with him, tellers are appointed and those present are counted. [See Ques. 276.]

361. QUES. An organization has no provision for a quorum. Their annual convention meets and its credentials committee reports 100 members entitled to vote registered as present. On the second day the credentials committee reports 150 voting members registered. On the third day 75 of the members have left for home. What is the quorum (a) On the first day? (b) On the second day? (c) On the third day?

ANS. The quorum is (a) 51 on first day; (b) 76 on second day; and (c) 76 on third day. The quorum at any time is a majority of the members registered up to that time as attending the convention, even though many may have left.

362. QUES. An exact quorum was present, but one member refused to vote on the question of adopting a certain resolution. Was the resolution legally adopted?

ANS. Yes.

363. QUES. Is a majority of the membership necessary for a quorum at a special meeting?

ANS. No. The quorum is the same as at a regular meeting.

364. QUES. No quorum was present, but the question of "no quorum" was not raised. Business was transacted. Was the action taken legal?

ANS. The business transacted when there was no quorum was illegal. If the club approves it, however, they may afterward ratify the informal action. A majority vote may ratify anything that a majority may adopt. See Ratify R. O. R., p. 173. If the club is not willing to ratify what was done, the minutes should be amended by striking out all the proceedings when there was no quorum, except what relates to adjournment. [See Ques. 311.]

365. QUES. A town board, consisting of supervisor and town clerk and four justices of the peace, has power by law to fill vacancies in its membership, to hold office until the next biennial town meeting. Some time ago one member of the board died, and it was not thought necessary to fill the vacancy immediately. Before the vacancy was filled, a second member died. If a third member had died before it was possible to call a meeting to fill the vacancies, could the three remaining members have made the appointments, there being no provision in the state law for this contingency?

ANS. No. A quorum of the board consists of four elected members. The board cannot reduce its quorum by neglecting its duty to fill vacancies immediately. To allow it would be to offer inducement to the board never to fill vacancies.

366. QUES. A board of trustees consisting of 8 members, authorized by law to buy and sell property for the organization they represent, hold a regularly called meeting for the transaction of business. Only 5 members are present, the president, the secretary, and another being absent. Temporary president and secretary are elected. Upon a vote of 3 to 2 it is voted to sell a piece of property, and the permanent president and secretary are instructed to sign the deed for the organization. The three absent members are unalterably opposed to the proposition, making 5 in all who are opposed to it and 3 who are in favor of it. Can the president and secretary be forced to sign the deed?

ANS. Yes, unless the order is rescinded, which can be done by a majority vote after notice, as described under Rescind, R. O. R., p. 169.

367. QUES. While debate on certain resolutions is in progress, a member who has to leave before the vote is taken hands to another member a written memorandum to the effect that he is in favor of the pending resolutions, and requests that the club's attention be called to it when his name is called, the vote being by yeas and nays. While the paper was not a formal proxy, could not the club suspend the rules and accept this paper as a proxy?

ANS. If the charter or by-laws allow proxy voting, the answer is, Yes. In that case the club can suspend the rules as to the exact form of the proxy and waive formalities. But if neither the charter nor the by-laws provide for proxy voting, the club has not the power to permit it. Your parliamentary authority, R. O. R., explains proxy voting, but it expressly states in the second sentence that "It is unknown to a strictly deliberative assembly, and is in conflict with the idea of the equality of members, which is a fundamental principle of deliberative assemblies." The whole article shows that it is intended for stock voting, or for voting where all absentees know they have the privilege.

368. QUES. Can a board delegate its power? In other words, can a board appoint an executive committee?

ANS. Not unless it has been authorized to do so by the by-laws of the club. No delegated power can be delegated to others, unless authorized by the principal. This is explained in R. O. R., p. 207.

Of course a board can appoint a committee to investigate and report to it, or to carry out something that the board has decided on. [See Ques. 369.]

369. QUES. Is it true as a general principle that delegated authority cannot be delegated?

ANS. This question may be answered generally in the affirmative, but there are numerous exceptions. A picnic committee may divide itself into sub-committees, one on transportation, another on securing the grounds, a third on refreshments, a fourth on finances, and so on, without authority being given them by the society. The nature of the committee requires the subdivision. [See Ques. 368.]

370. QUES. May a delegated body take action on matters of policy that have not been presented to the constituent organizations?

ANS. This depends upon the constitution of the delegated assembly. In a case like that of a state convention of churches with independent congregational government, the answer is, Yes. As a rule the questions acted upon by the convention have not been presented to the constituent organizations. Again, a convention of delegates may be empowered to attend to only such matters as have been previously submitted to the constituent organizations.

371. QUES. Our by-laws require the registrar's books to be closed "fifteen days before date for assembling of convention," and that "credentials received after this time shall not be recorded until after convention." Our convention meets May 5. Should credentials received April 20 be recorded?

ANS. The strictest interpretation of the words of the by-laws would require the books to be closed fifteen full days prior to the beginning of May 5, that is, at midnight of April 19. But similar language is used very commonly where it is meant that the books are to be closed on the fifteenth day before the convention, and this interpretation of the language would require the recording of the credentials received April 20. Where a law is capable of two interpretations, the more liberal one should be adopted, if the interests of the society are not injured thereby. As, in this case, no one is injured by the more liberal interpretation of the by-law, I should answer your question in the affirmative.

372. QUES. In a meeting of delegates in convention, can others than delegates take part in debate by permission of the chair, if there is no rule to the contrary?

Ans. Yes, if no one objects. If a single objection is made, the chairman must submit the question to the assembly.

373. Ques. Can others than delegates at a convention offer resolutions?

Ans. None but members of the convention are entitled to offer resolutions. The by-laws should prescribe the membership, which should include, besides the delegates, the officers of the convention and the chairmen of all committees that are required to report to the convention. In many if not most cases, it is desirable to include the presidents of the constituent societies. The officers of the society, whose duties require them to be present, certainly should be members of the convention, and yet they may not be elected delegates. The same is true of chairmen of committees that are required to report to the convention.

374. Ques. Has a delegate who is also secretary of a convention a right to two votes?

Ans. No. No member is entitled to more than one vote, except where proxy voting is allowed. [See Ques. 375.]

375. Ques. If no one is entitled to two votes at a convention, even though holding two offices, either one of which would give him a vote, is it necessary to put this in the by-laws?

Ans. No. An office does not make one a member of the convention or entitle him to a vote, unless it so specified in the by-laws. It is membership, not office, that entitles one to vote. [See page 298.] [See Ques. 226, 273, 374.]

376. Ques. May a club delegate an ex-officio member to represent it at a convention?

Ans. Yes. An ex-officio member has all the privileges of membership, the same as any other member. See R. O. R., p. 210. ⌐See Ques. 233, 234, 235.]

377. Ques. When a delegate is elected president of the body, does his alternate have the right to vote in place of the delegate?

Ans. No. A delegate does not, by being elected president, lose his right to vote whenever that vote will affect the result. Electing a member of Congress to the speakership does not create a vacancy or deprive him of his right to vote. [See Ques. 325.]

378. Ques. If the fourth delegate resigns, is the vacancy filled by the fourth alternate?

Ans. No, unless by virtue of some special rule of the society. In the absence of any rule on the subject, the first alternate automatically fills the first vacancy, the second alternate the second vacancy, and so on, so that the vacancy then exists in the alternates, not in the delegates. If the vacancy occurs before the convention meets, credentials of a delegate should be given to the one who fills the vacancy.

379. Ques. A society has a scattered membership and only an annual meeting. Between meetings there is a council which convenes quarterly and is in general charge. The council has control of the admission of members, and may promulgate rules on the subject. One of their rules established a membership committee, whose practice has been to O. K. applications before the council admitted members. An application for membership was received and transmitted to the membership committee, but the latter did not act on it in time to report to the recent annual meeting of the entire society. At this meeting, and included among the members in attendance, was a quorum of the council and a majority of the membership committee. It was highly desired to admit that applicant. The president ruled that the annual meeting was superior to the council, and entertained a motion that the society admit the member. The motion prevailed unanimously. Was the member legally admitted?

Ans. If the constitution, as you state, provides that the council "has control of the admission of members," the society cannot take away this control, except by amending the constitution. The society is superior to the council, but not to the constitution, and the constitution cannot be suspended by general consent. The member was not legally admitted. [See Ques. 351, 354.]

380. Ques. Can the president and the majority form an agreement by telephone, and disburse a sum of money from the club funds for a certain thing when the other members are opposed to the movement?

Ans. No. There can be no action of a deliberative body except when it is in session, whether it is a society, or a board, or a committee. Members, of course, may consult together, but even if the agreement is unanimous the action must be ratified in a formal meeting. For the case of a committee see R. O. R., p. 217. In the case mentioned, if the funds were disbursed, it was done without legal authority and at the risk of the one who paid the bill. The club is under no obligation to approve it. The auditor could not pass the account unless approved at a formal meeting. Sometimes officers, in the best interests of the society, are obliged to go beyond their legitimate authority, and depend upon their action's being ratified by the club or board. But only a great emergency ever justifies such action. See Ratify, p. 173, and Quorum, pp. 257–259, R. O. R.

381. Ques. A society authorized its editor, who is an officer of the society, to employ a managing editor. This was done and afterward the editor resigned and a new editor was appointed. (a) Does the resignation of the first editor cancel the contract with the managing editor? (b) If not, has the new editor the authority to dismiss her and to employ another?

Ans. (a) No. The resignation or death of the appointer does not affect the appointee. (b) If the first editor did not exceed her power in making the contract, her successor and the society are bound by it. The second editor has all the power of her predecessor and no more. If the first editor could not legally dismiss the managing editor, the second one cannot, assuming that the contract was not made conditional upon the editor's remaining in office.

382. Ques. The constitution of a society provides that "the consent of a candidate shall be obtained before her name is presented." This provision has been virtually a dead letter. The constitution also says that "the executive board shall fill all vacancies." Three officers were elected—a president, a vice-president, and a secretary. The member who was elected president was absent when elected, and resigned when she was notified, explaining that if she had been asked she would not have accepted. At the next meeting a motion was made to accept her resignation, and that the vice-president fill the vacancy. A point of order was raised against this motion, on the ground that the election was illegal, as the consent of none of the candidates had been asked. The chair ruled that the point was not well taken. (a) Was the election legal? (b) If the election was legal, does the board fill the vacancy? Or, shall a special election be held?

Ans. (a) Yes. The nominations were not made in accordance with the constitution, and the chair should have ruled them out of order. But members are not limited to voting for nominees, and their improper nomination does not affect the legality of the election. They were elected as unnominated candidates. (b) A special election should be held. But, since the member who was elected president was absent, and declined the office when notified of her election, she never was president. The office is not filled until some one is elected who has consented in advance, or who does not decline when she learns of her election. The condition, then, is the same as if the meeting had adjourned without electing a president. If nothing had been said in the constitution about filling vacancies, a special election should be held, because the election had never gone into effect. If the president had not declined, but after accepting the office had resigned, and nothing had been said in the constitution about vacancies, the vice-president would become president. The constitution of the society provides that a vacancy in an office shall be filled by the executive board, but failure to hold or to complete an election does not create a vacancy. There was no complete election of president, the one elected not having accepted the office, and therefore if the constitution provides that officers shall hold office until their successors are elected, the former president continues in office until her successor is elected, and it is in order to provide for holding a special election, proper notice thereof to be given. If the former president went out of office at the close of the annual meeting, the new vice-president acts as president until a new one is elected.

Whether the member who was elected said or wrote that she "resigned" instead of "declined" the office is a matter of no moment. The material facts are that, when notified of her election, instead of accepting the office, she said that if her consent had been asked she would not have accepted, and before performing any of the duties of the office she notified the proper authorities that she resigned it, which under the circumstances was not a resignation but a declination. [See Ques. 57, 61, 65, 216, 217.]

383. QUES. A club at a meeting June 2 adopted legally some amendments to its by-laws, and then adjourned to meet June 9, not having completed the scheduled business. At the meeting on June 9 only 16 were present, the quorum being 40. The meeting was called to order by the president, and proceeded to the transaction of business A member stated that she thought they had made a mistake in adopting a certain by-law at the meeting of June 2. She was interrupted by a point of order that there was no quorum. Then it was claimed that the executive board could act in the case for the club under the following by-law: "At any regular or special meeting, when the attendance is less than a quorum, the executive board may transact any regularly scheduled or unfinished busi-

QUESTIONS ANSWERED: MISCELLANEOUS   537

ness.'' The chair sustained the claim, and the vote of the club adopting the amendment to the by-laws was reconsidered by the executive board on the motion of one of its members, 3 voting for it and none against it. The motion to reconsider was then laid on the table by the board, 2 voting for it and none against it. The executive board consists of 11 members, with a quorum of 6. Is that amendment a part of the by-laws or not?

Ans. (1) The fact that no quorum voted in the executive board does not affect the case. Assuming that a quorum was present, the vote was legal if only one person voted, provided it was legal in other respects. Those who abstained from voting acquiesced in the action taken by others. (2) The amendments were acted on at a club meeting on June 2, and immediately became part of the by-laws and beyond the control of the assembly, except as prescribed by the by-laws, which outrank the rules of order. No change can be made in the by-laws, except as prescribed for its amendment, and therefore, after an amendment to the by-laws has been adopted, the vote adopting it cannot be reconsidered even by the club itself, at any time whatever, and consequently the action taken is null and void. See bottom of p. 158, R. O. R. (3) As this was an adjournment of a regular meeting, and there was no quorum present, the by-laws empowered the executive board to "transact any regularly scheduled or unfinished business." The terms used are evidently intended to limit the board to acting only on such questions as the club knows are to come before the club or board at that meeting. If the amendment, though scheduled for June 2, had not been finally acted upon, the club would know that it would come up for action at the adjourned meeting, and those interested in it would try to attend. While an adjourned meeting is a continuation of the original meeting, only such scheduled business as has not been finally disposed of can be properly said to be scheduled for the adjourned meeting, and the reconsideration was not scheduled. The board cannot reconsider or rescind a vote of the club, except where there is no quorum of the club present, and notice of such a motion has been given at the previous meeting of the club. Hence, supposing the club had the right to reconsider the vote on the amendment, the executive board had no such right, and its action taken at the adjourned meeting of the club, June 9, is null and void. (4) Supposing that the executive board had the power to reconsider a vote of the club without notice, their rules of order expressly state that the motion to reconsider can be made only "during the day on which a motion has been acted upon, or on the next succeeding day." The club adopted the amendment June 2, so that after June 3 the motion to reconsider was illegal, even if made in the club itself with a quorum present. Therefore the vote of the executive board, June 9, reconsidering a vote of the club taken June 2 is illegal, and is null and void. [See Ques. 102.]

384. QUES. The constitution of our club provides that "There shall be such additional assessments as may be voted by the club for special purposes, but no special assessment shall be binding on the members unless voted for by a majority of the members in good standing."

A series of four resolutions, one of which levied an assessment of $25 on each member for club quarters, was voted on, the affirmative vote being a majority of those present and voting, but lacking 6 of being a majority of the members in good standing. The chairman ruled that the resolutions were lost. Was the ruling correct?

ANS. I think the resolutions were adopted. If the intention of the constitution was to require a vote of a majority of the membership to adopt a resolution levying an assessment, it should have said so. It would have been expressed in some such manner as this: "No additional assessments shall be made except for special purposes and by a vote of a majority of the members in good standing." Instead of that, a much longer form is used, which permits special assessments, but states that they are not "binding on the members unless voted for by a majority of the members in good standing." While the resolution has been adopted, the fact that the assessment is not binding on the members makes its effect equivalent to a request for voluntary contributions of $25 from each member. [See Ques. 328.]

385. QUES. How are mistakes corrected? If an amendment or motion was carried, but should have been ruled out of order when moved, is such an action null and void?

ANS. If the action violates the by-laws, or is to the detriment of any one, or is of such a nature that it could not be authorized by a unanimous vote, as described in R. O. R., p. 201, it is null and void, and should be so declared by the chairman as soon as attention is called to the fact. If, however, the mistake does not violate the by-laws, nor is any one injured by it, there is no need to correct the error. By general consent the improper proceðure was allowed. If objection to the improper procedure was made at the time, and the assembly still persisted in taking the improper action, such action is null and void, and should be so declared as soon as the fact of its illegality is recognized.

386. QUES. A temporary board of officers, before the adoption of constitution and by-laws and election of officers, voted to make the then temporary president an honorary president and a permanent member of the board. The by-laws afterward adopted do not provide for an honorary president. How can this mistake be rectified? (a) Can the business of the old temporary board, which was not regularly completed, be called "unfinished business" which died when it went out of office? Or (b) must we rescind that motion—move to amend the article on "officers" to include an honorary president—and legally elect at our next annual meeting?

ANS. (a) No. The society came into existence when its by-laws (or constitution if it had one) were adopted. Any action taken before that is temporary in its nature, and should be limited to what is described in R. O. R., pp. 284–291, where will be found the correct procedure for organization. The action of the temporary board in electing an honorary officer of a society not in existence is null and void. (b) No. The society has nothing to do with the actions of the mass meeting that organized it, or of any of its officers or boards.

387. QUES. If voting is allowed by proxy, and each county organization is allowed ten votes, even if only one delegate is present, must that delegate cast ten separate ballots, or will one ballot answer—that is, can he write it, "10 votes"?

ANS. Each assembly decides for itself the method of voting, subject, of course, to its own rules. Where proxy voting is allowed, some method must be adopted to see that no one casts more votes than he is entitled to. If each district is entitled to ten votes, the tellers must see that the rule is enforced. If ballots are distributed, only ten must be given to the chairman of each district delegation. If members write their own ballots, it must be seen that each delegation casts only ten ballots for each office, whether these are separate or all on one ballot.

388. QUES. Our year book provides that one of our practice hours shall be devoted to a prepared debate. Two members are assigned to the affirmative and two to the negative, and the question is to be open to general debate. When is the general

debate in order, and who should close the debate? In other words, what would you suggest as the order of the proceedings?

ANS. Every society is at liberty to adopt such an order as it chooses. Experience has led to the established custom of allowing the affirmative to open and to close the debate. I would therefore suggest the following plan where the meeting lasts an hour.

At a previous meeting a resolution similar to this should be adopted:

Resolved, That the debate to be held January 17 next shall be conducted under the following rules:

(1) The question to be discussed shall be as follows: "*Resolved,* That," etc.

(2) Thirty minutes shall be allowed the designated speakers, fifteen minutes to each side. The time allotted to each side is to be divided between the two speakers, as they may decide.

(3) The debate shall be opened with a speech on each side of the question, made by the designated speakers, the affirmative speech being first. After these two speeches there shall be twenty minutes of general debate, equally divided between the two sides, in which each speaker shall be limited to one speech of three minutes' length. In recognizing members the chair shall give the preference, as far as practicable, to one opposed to the last speaker.

(4) When the general debate is closed, the chair shall assign the floor to the second designated speaker in the negative, who will close the debate for his side. The floor will then be assigned to the second speaker designated for the affirmative, who will close the debate. In this closing speech no new matter can be introduced, except what is necessary to refute statements of the negative. The chair shall enforce this rule strictly, in order to protect the negative side, which has no opportunity to reply to this closing speech.

(5) The question shall be put on the resolution as soon as the debate is closed.

When the debate is to begin, the chair states the question thus: "The question is on the adoption of the resolution, '*Resolved,* That,' etc. [reading the resolution]." He then assigns the floor to the first speaker in the affirmative by announcing his name. The chair should be informed of the division of time between the designated speakers, and should stop each speaker when his time has expired. If requested, he should give a warning signal a minute, or a half-minute, before that time.

389. QUES. A society wishes to disband. How should it be done?

ANS. Appoint a committee "to consider and report the steps to be taken in order that the society may disband." If the society is incorporated and owns property, the committee should consult a lawyer, just as is done when a society incorporates. The committee's report should consist mainly, if not entirely, of resolutions for the society to adopt. If there is any property, it may be disposed of before the society disbands, or it may be put into the hands of trustees to be sold, the proceeds to be disposed of in a specified way. The disposition of the records should be provided for. In no case should a society disband before it has attended to all such matters. Since disbanding is virtually annulling the constitution and by-laws, the motion to disband is the same as the motion to amend by striking out the entire constitution and by-laws, and therefore requires previous notice and a two-thirds vote. One resolution submitted by the committee should be like this: ."*Resolved*, That notice is hereby given that at the next regular meeting a motion will be made to disband this society." If it is desired to have quicker action, notice of the motion to disband could be given at the time of the appointment of the committee, so that it could be voted on as soon as the committee reports.

390. QUES. Two societies wish to unite to form a new society, neither one being willing to disband and unite with the other. How is it to be done? Please state procedure from beginning to end.

ANS. Each society should appoint a large representative committee, to coöperate with a similar committee, to be appointed by the other society, in preparing by-laws for the new organization and in recommending the proper action to be taken by each society. The following is a suitable form for such a motion:

Whereas, The objects of the Alpha and the Beta societies are nearly identical; and

Whereas, Combining their membership would greatly increase the interest in the meetings; therefore be it

Resolved, That a committee of seven be appointed by the president to coöperate with a similar committee of the —— Society in preparing by-laws for a new society to comprise the entire membership of both organizations, and in recommending suitable steps to be taken by each in order to effect their combination into one society.

Resolved, That the committee be, and hereby is, instructed to report at each meeting of the society the progress made.

The two committees should meet as a joint committee, electing a chairman and a secretary, and then go over the constitution and by-laws of each society, section by section, selecting the best out of each. After the conference a sub-committee of one or two should be appointed to draft a set of by-laws (or a constitution and by-laws if preferred) based on those preferred by the committee. These by-laws are submitted at the next meeting of the committee, and discussed and amended section by section. It may be necessary for the committee to report several times to their societies, so as to be sure that their joint action will be endorsed by a two-thirds vote of each society.

After the joint committee has agreed upon the new by-laws, it should agree upon identical reports for each committee. A draft of this report should be prepared by a sub-committee previously appointed. Each committee reports, orally if preferred, to its own society that the two committees have agreed upon by-laws for the combined society, and that notice is given of certain motions to be made at the next meeting. This notice should be in writing, signed by the chairman of the committee, and similar to this:

NOTICE

The committee on combining the Alpha and the Beta societies hereby gives notice that at the meeting to be held on the — of —— the following questions will be introduced for consideration and action:

Resolved, That the by-laws reported by the committee on revision be considered section by section for amendment, and if any amendments are adopted, that the by-laws be recommitted with instructions for the committee to report as soon as practicable.

Resolved, further, That as soon as the committee reports a set of by-laws which neither society insists on amending, a vote shall immediately be taken on the following resolution: *"Resolved,* by the Alpha and the Beta societies, That the by-laws of the Delta Society reported by the joint committee be, and are hereby, adopted as a substitute for their present by-laws; that the tenure of office of all officers be, and is hereby, terminated; that the Delta Society, consisting of all the members of the Alpha and the Beta societies, shall immediately meet in —— to elect a nominating committee consisting of — former members of each society, who shall report nominations for all the offices; and that, until the election of officers, the former president of the Alpha society shall act as chairman, and the secretary of the Beta society as secretary, of the meetings of the Delta Society."

As soon as the notice has been read, the reporting member should say: "By direction of the committee, I move that the resolutions of which notice has just been given, and the actions required by them, be made the special orders for the next meeting, and all adjournments thereof, until the Delta Society is fully organized." This motion requires a two-thirds vote for its adoption.

The by-laws should then be read section by section, the reporting member explaining all changes from the old by-laws. Every one should be free to ask questions bearing on the meaning or effect of each by-law, which the reporting member should answer. No vote should be taken on the matter, as it is read only for information.

When the meeting is held at which the new by-laws are to be

acted upon, immediately after the reading and approval of the minutes, the president announces: "The special order for this meeting is the consideration of, and action on, the resolutions of which notice was given at the last meeting by the committee on uniting with the —— Society." The resolutions are then read and voted on. If they are adopted by a majority vote, the president immediately directs the proposed revision to be read section by section, asking in regard to each section if there are any amendments proposed, as described in R. O. R., p. 93.

If no amendments are made, the chairman of the revision committee should confer with the chairman of the revision committee of the other society, to see if it has made amendments. If neither society has made amendments to the proposed revision, the president proceeds to state the question on the resolution contained in the second resolution previously adopted. As this resolution amends the by-laws by substituting a new set for the old ones, it requires a two-thirds vote for its adoption.

For convenience the two societies should meet in adjoining rooms to act on the proposed revision of their by-laws. Both societies, having adopted the joint resolution, should immediately adjourn, and then meet together with the temporary chairman and secretary prescribed by the joint resolution. The nominating committee, elected as prescribed in the second resolution, retires and agrees upon a ticket, which is at once reported. After nominations from the floor, the election by ballot proceeds until all the officers are elected. The new combined society is now fully organized and ready for its regular business. If the original societies were incorporated, a local lawyer should be consulted as to amending the charter and arranging for the transfer of the property from the old to the new trustees.

It is possible that the proposed revision of the by-laws reported by the committee may be amended by either or both of the societies. In this case the president announces that the revision is recommitted. The joint committee discusses the difference between the two societies, and tries to agree upon amendments that will be adopted by both societies. It may be necessary for each committee to consult its society more than once in order to modify the proposed revision so as to insure a favorable vote of two thirds. When this is accomplished the procedure is as described above.

PART VIII

MISCELLANEOUS

CHAPTER XLIV

CHARTS; VARIOUS LISTS OF MOTIONS

CHARTS [1]

Explanation of Signs Used in the Charts.

@ This sign indicates that the motion which it precedes can be amended. The other motions cannot be amended.

—— A single underscore shows that the motion is debatable. Motions not underscored are undebatable.

==== A double underscore shows that the motion is debatable, and that at the same time the pending main motion is open to debate.

– – – – A single broken underscore shows that the motion is sometimes debatable and sometimes undebatable. Thus, to Amend is debatable only when the motion to be amended is debatable, and an Appeal can be debated except when it relates to indecorum, or to the transgression of the rules of speaking, or to the priority of business, or if made while the immediately pending question is undebatable or during a division of the assembly.

= = = = A double broken underscore, which is used only for the motion to Reconsider, shows that the motion is debatable whenever the motion to be reconsidered is debatable; and, also, that when debatable the question to be reconsidered is at the same time open to debate.

⅔. A motion followed by ⅔ requires a two-thirds vote for its adoption, the other motions requiring only a majority vote. In the case of an objection to the consideration of a question, since the question is put on the consideration, and not on the objection to the consideration, a ⅔ vote in the negative is required to prevent the consideration.

⅔? This sign shows that the motion preceding it requires a ⅔ vote unless previous notice of the motion has been given, in which case it requires only a majority.

[1] These charts, by permission, are copied from "Robert's Parliamentary Law Charts," copyright, 1915, by Henry M. Robert. They are based, by permission, on the tables on pages 5, 44, 57, and 58 of "Rules of Order Revised," copyright, 1915, by Henry M. Robert, and published by Scott, Foresman & Co., Chicago and New York.

CHART I

ORDER OF PRECEDENCE OF MOTIONS

@ Fix the Time to which to Adjourn (when privileged).
Adjourn (when privileged).
@ Take a Recess (when privileged).
Raise a Question of Privilege.
Call for the Orders of the Day.

PRIVILEGED

Lay on the Table.
Previous Question (⅔).
@ Limit or Extend Limits of Debate (⅔).
@ Postpone to a Certain Time.
@ Commit or Refer.
@ Amend.
Postpone Indefinitely.

SUBSIDIARY

@ Main Motion.

The ordinary motions rank as shown above: the lowest in rank are at the bottom and the highest at the top of the list. When any one of them is immediately pending, the motions above it in the list are in order and those below it are out of order. The first three motions are not always privileged. When not privileged they are main motions and therefore of the lowest rank and are debatable and amendable. To Fix the Time to which to Adjourn is privileged only when made while another question is pending, and in an assembly that has made no provision for another meeting on the same or the next day. To Adjourn loses its privileged character if in any way qualified, or if its effect, when adopted, is to dissolve the assembly without any provision for its meeting again. To Take a Recess is privileged only when made while other business is pending.

CHART II

INCIDENTAL MOTIONS

Questions of Order and Appeal.
Suspension of the Rules. (⅔)
Objection to Consideration of a Question. (⅔)
@ Division of a Question, and @Consideration by Paragraph or
    Seriatim.
Division of the Assembly, & @Motions relating to Voting.
@ Motions Relating to Nominations. (⅔?)
Requests Growing out of Business Pending or That Has Just
    Been Pending; as,
    Parliamentary Inquiry,
    Request for Information,
    Leave to Withdraw a Motion,
    Reading Papers,
    To Be Excused from a Duty,
    Request for Any Other Privilege.

CERTAIN OTHER MOTIONS

Take from the Table.
Reconsider.
@ Rescind. (⅔?)
@ Ratify.

Incidental motions cannot be arranged according to rank like privileged and subsidiary ones. They take precedence of the pending motion or business out of which they arise. On account of their privilege to interrupt business they are undebatable, excepting an appeal in certain cases as shown in the explanation of a broken underscore (— — — —).

Of the Certain Other Motions mentioned, Reconsider is the only one that can be moved when another question is pending. Its privileges are very great as will be seen by consulting page 89. The motion to Take from the Table has the right of way over any main motion that has not yet been stated by the chair.

CHART III

WHAT MOTIONS TO USE

To MODIFY OR AMEND.

@ Amend.
@ Commit or Refer.

To DEFER ACTION.

@ Postpone to a Certain Time.
@ Make a Special Order (⅔).
Lay on the Table.

To SUPPRESS OR TO LIMIT DEBATE.

Previous Question (⅔).
@ Limit Debate (⅔).

To SUPPRESS THE QUESTION.

Objection to its Consideration (⅔).
Prev. Ques. (⅔) and Reject Question.
Postpone Indefinitely.
Lay on the Table. (?)

To CONSIDER A QUESTION A SECOND TIME.

Take from the Table.
Reconsider.
@ Rescind. (⅔?)

To PREVENT FINAL ACTION ON A QUESTION IN AN
UNREPRESENTATIVE MEETING.

Reconsider and Enter on the Minutes.

[For explanation of the signs used in the charts, see page 547. For a brief explanation of the circumstances under which each of these motions should be used, see R. O. R., pp. 44-50.]

VARIOUS LISTS OF MOTIONS

(1) In Order When Another Has the Floor.
(2) Do Not Require a Second.
(3) Cannot Be Debated.
(4) Open Main Question to Debate.
(5) Cannot Be Amended.
(6)   "   "   Reconsidered.
(7)   "   "   Rescinded.
(8)   "   "   Renewed.
(9) Require a Two-Thirds Vote.

(1) In Order When Another Has the Floor.

Appeal.
Call to Order.
  " for the Orders of the Day.
  "   "   Division of the Assembly.
  "   "   "   "   " Question.
Objection to Consideration of the Question.
Parliamentary Inquiry.
Request of Any Kind.
Raise a Question of Order.
  "   "   "   " Privilege.
Reconsider.

[By comparing this list with the next one it will be noticed that none of these motions, except an Appeal and Reconsider, require to be seconded.]

(2) Do Not Require to Be Seconded.

Call to Order.
  " for the Orders of the Day.
  "   "   Division of the Assembly.
  "   "   "   "   " Question.
  " Up Motion to Reconsider.
Filling Blanks.
Leave to Withdraw or Modify a Motion.
Nominations.
Objection to Consideration of a Question.
Parliamentary, or Any Other, Inquiry.
Request of Any Kind.
Raise a Question of Order.
  "   "   "   " Privilege.

(3) Cannot Be Debated.

Adjourn, Fix the Time to Which to Adjourn, and Take a Recess
—whenever these motions are privileged. [See note, page 548.]

Appeal, if undebatable question is pending, or if it relates to indecorum, or to transgression of the rules of speaking, or to
priority of business.

Amend and Reconsider an Undebatable Motion.

Call to Order, and Questions of Order.
" for Orders of the Day.
" " Division of the Assembly.
" " " " " Question.
" Up Motion to Reconsider.

Close or Limit or Extend Limits of Debate.
" " Open Nominations.
" " " the Polls.

Dispense with Reading the Minutes.

Fix the Time to Which to Adjourn (when privileged, see note,
page 548.)

Incidental Motions (except Appeal as shown above).

Lay on the Table and Take from the Table.

Leave to Continue Speaking after Indecorum.
" " Read Papers.
" " Withdraw or Modify Motion.

Limit Debate.

Objection to Consideration of a Question.

Parliamentary, or Any Other, Inquiry.

Previous Question, and Close, or Limit, or Extend the Limits of
Debate.

Questions of Order.

Raise a Question of Order.
" " " " Privilege.

Reconsider an Undebatable Motion.

Request of Any Kind.

Take a Recess (when privileged, see note, page 548).
" up a Question Out of Its Proper Order.
" from the Table.

Voting, Motions Relating to Methods of.

(4) Open a Debatable Main Question to Debate While the Secondary Motion Is Immediately Pending.

Postpone Indefinitely.
Reconsider.
Rescind.
Ratify.

(5) Cannot Be Amended.

Adjourn (when privileged, see note, page 548).
Amend an Amendment.
Appeal and Questions of Order.
Blank, to fill a.
Call to Order.
" for the Orders of the Day.
Call for Division of the Assembly.
" Up Motion to Reconsider.
Lay on the Table and Take from the Table.
Leave to Continue Speaking after Indecorum.
"   " Read Papers.
"   " Withdraw or Modify a Motion.
Make a Nomination.
Objection to Consideration of a Question.
Parliamentary, or Any Other, Inquiry.
Postpone Indefinitely.
Previous Question.
Questions of Order.
Raise a Question of Order.
"   "   "   " Privilege.
Reconsider.
Requests of Any Kind.
Suspend the Rules.
Take from the Table.
" Up a Question Out of Its Proper Order.

(6) Cannot Be Reconsidered.

Adjourn.
Division of the Assembly.
"   "   " Question.
Lay on the Table.

Motion that Has Been Reconsidered, unless it has been materially amended since it was reconsidered.

Nominations, to Make or to Close.

Questions of Order.

Parliamentary, or Other, Inquiry.

Proceed to the Orders of the Day.

Raise Questions of Order.

"   "   " Privilege.

Reconsider.

Suspend the Rules.

Take a Recess.

Take from the Table.

" Up a Question Out of Its Proper Order.

Affirmative Votes which Cannot Be Reconsidered.

Adopt, or after adoption, to Amend, Repeal, or Rescind the Constitution, By-laws, or Rules of Order or any other rules that require previous notice of their amendment.

Elect to Membership or Office, if the member or officer is present and does not decline, or is absent and has learned of his election in the usual way and has not declined.

Accept Resignation, if member is present or has been notified.

Consideration of Question that Has Been Objected to.

Commit, after the committee has taken up the subject referred to it.

Previous Question, after vote has been taken under it.

Reopen Nominations.

Negative Vote which Cannot be Reconsidered.

Postpone Indefinitely.

(7) Cannot Be Rescinded.

A Vote cannot be rescinded after something that the assembly cannot undo has been done as a result of that vote, or if a vote is in the nature of a contract and the other party is informed of the vote; or when one has been elected to, or expelled from, membership or office, and was present or has been officially notified.

If a Question can be reached by calling up the motion to reconsider, which has been previously made, the vote cannot be rescinded.

With the above exceptions, all votes on Main Motions, and on Questions of Privilege and Orders of the Day that have been acted upon, and on Appeals, may be rescinded without previous notice by a two-thirds vote or by a vote of a majority of the entire membership; or by a majority vote if notice was given at the previous meeting or in the call for this meeting.

But, since "Rescind" is identical with "Amend something already adopted," the rules for amending by-laws, standing rules, etc., apply to the motion to rescind a by-law, a standing rule, etc.

(8) Cannot Be Renewed.

Adopt.

Amend.

Appeal.

Fix the Same Time to Which to Adjourn.

Objection to Consideration of a Question.

Question of Order.

Reconsider a Question, unless it was materially Amended when previously Reconsidered.

Suspend the Rules for the Same Purpose at the Same Meeting.

[None of the above motions, except the last one, can be renewed at the same session. As a general rule no motion can be renewed at the same session unless there has been such a change in conditions as to make the question a new one. Thus, to commit a motion after voting on a material amendment is a different question from the one of committing it before voting on the amendment.]

(9) Require a Two-Thirds Vote.

Amend, Annul, Repeal, or Rescind any part of the Constitution, By-laws, or Rules of Order previously adopted; previous notice is also required.

Amend or Rescind, etc., a Standing Rule, Program, or Order of Business, or a Resolution previously adopted, without notice being given at the previous meeting or in the call for this meeting.

Extend the Time Appointed for Adjournment or for Taking a Recess.

Previous Question.

Close, Limit, or Extend Limits of Debate.

Suspend the Rules.

Take up a Question Out of Its Proper Order.

Make a Special Order.

Refuse to Proceed to the Orders of the Day.

Discharge an Order of the Day Before it is Pending.

Sustain an Objection to the Consideration of a Question.

Close Nominations or the Polls.

Limit Names to Be Voted for at an Election.

Expel from Membership; requires also previous notice and trial unless for an offense committed in the assembly.

Depose from Office that is not held for a definite period, and previous notice has not been given.

Discharge a Committee, unless previous notice has been given.

Reconsider in Committee when one of the majority is absent and has not been notified of the proposed reconsideration.

CHAPTER XLV.

FORMS

The forms of making the various motions and of stating and putting the question on them are given in the text in connection with each motion, and are therefore omitted here. To find these forms, refer to the motion in the Index. To find a particular form in this chapter, consult the Index, under the word Forms.

FORMS OF REPORTS OF COMMITTEES.

(1) A Resolution Referred to a Committee.

The committee to which was referred the resolution, *"Resolved,* That we issue $50,000 worth of five per cent. bonds payable in 30 years for the purpose of improving the electric light plant,'' recommends that the resolution be adopted [or, be not adopted].

This report is given orally, and no motion is made because the pending question is on "the adoption of the resolution," if the report is favorable; and on "the adoption of the resolution, the recommendation of the committee to the contrary notwithstanding," if the report is unfavorable. See pages 269–271.

(2) Resolution with Pending Amendment Referred to a Committee.

The committee to which was referred the resolution, *"Resolved,* That Emerson Avenue be paved with brick,'' together with the pending amendment, ''to add the words, 'provided the cost is not more than $20,000,' '' recommends that the amendment be adopted, and that the resolution as thus amended be adopted [or, that the amendment be not adopted and that the resolution be adopted].

Report is given orally and no motion is made. The question is stated as given on page 270 (b).

(3) Resolution Referred to a Committee, the Committee Recommending an Amendment.

The committee to which was referred the resolution, *"Resolved,* That it is the sense of this meeting that the gymnasium of the high school be equipped with suitable apparatus, the cost not to exceed $1,000,'' recommends that it be amended by striking out ''$1,000'' and inserting ''$1,500,'' and that as thus amended the resolution be adopted.

This report is given orally, the reporting member moving the adoption of the amendment recommended by the committee.

(4) Resolution Referred to a Committee, the Committee Recommending a Substitute.

The committee to which was referred the resolution, ''*Resolved*, That a new county court-house be built to cost $100,000,'' recommends the adoption of the following substitute: ''*Resolved*, That the old court-house be repaired and an annex be built.''

ASA JONES,
Chairman.

This report may be oral or written. If in writing it should be signed by the chairman. If the report is oral, the substitute should be in writing on a separate sheet of paper from the resolution. In either case, the reporting member moves to substitute the committee's resolution for the original. See pages 271, 272.

(5) Resolution with Pending Amendment Referred to a Committee, the Committee Recommending Further Amendment.

The committee to which was referred the following resolution, ''*Resolved*, That it is our duty to take an interest in public affairs and show that interest by voting,'' and the pending amendment ''to strike out 'our duty' and insert 'the duty of every citizen,' '' having considered the same, recommends the following:

(1) That the pending amendment be amended by adding to the words to be inserted the words ''of a republic,'' and that as thus amended the amendment be adopted;

(2) That the resolution be amended by inserting the word ''to'' before the word ''show'';

(3) That the resolution as thus amended be adopted.

Chairman.

This report should be in writing. As each recommendation is read, the chairman should read enough of the resolution to show exactly the effect of adopting the recommendation. When he has finished reading the report, he moves ''the adoption of the amendments reported [or proposed, or recommended] by the committee,'' and hands the report to the presiding officer. It is well for the committee chairman to have a duplicate of the report for his own use during the debate that follows. The example given here illustrates this style of report. This method is useful when there are several amendments to a long resolution, or a series of resolutions, or a set of by-laws, and it is not desired to submit a substitute. If many changes are desired in a short resolution, the preferable plan is to report a substitute as shown in the preceding example.

(6) A Committee Appointed to Investigate a Matter.

The committee appointed to investigate the conditions of the City Hospital begs leave to submit the following report:
The committee visited the hospital, taking with it a State Examiner. It found that the hospital is badly in need of accommodations for its nurses. The committee, therefore, recommends the adoption of the following resolution: "*Resolved*, That $50,000 be, and is hereby, appropriated for a nurses' home in connection with the City Hospital."

CLEMENT CORBIN,
EMILY CUTTER,
DAVID STARR,
Committee.

This report should be in writing and the reporting member should move the adoption of the resolution recommended by the committee. See page 277.

(7) A Recommendation of a Standing Committee, Followed by a Resolution Covering the Recommendation.

The house committee reports that the kitchen is in need of a new stove, and, bearing in mind the shortage of gas this winter, recommends the adoption of the following resolution: "*Resolved*, That a combination coal and gas stove be purchased for the kitchen, at a cost not to exceed $125."

A——— B———
Chairman.

This report should be in writing, and be signed by the chairman or by all the members of the committee agreeing to it. The reporting member should move the adoption of the resolution.

(8) Report of Work Done by a Standing Committee.

Your committee on relief work for orphans begs leave to state that it has been very successful in securing both funds and clothing for more than one hundred orphans. The committee thus far has sent to the asylum 50 layettes, 100 outfits for boys and girls, and $500 in cash.

SARAH JORDON,
Chairman.

This report should be in writing and be signed by the chairman, since it reports only work done. If important recommendations are made, it is better to have the report signed by all the members agreeing to it. See page 285.

(9) Membership Committee.

The membership committee reports favorably upon the applications of Mr. A, Mr. B, and Mr. C, and recommends that they be received as members of the society. On behalf of the committee, I move that they be received into membership.

This report is made orally, but a written list of the names in full of those recommended for membership should be handed to the president when the report is made.

(10) Report of a Committee on Revision of the By-Laws, Reporting a Substitute, some Provisions of which Should Not Take Effect Immediately.

[*The chairman of the committee reports orally as follows, the resolutions being in writing:*]

The committee on revision of the by-laws submits a revised set of by-laws as a substitute for the present ones, and reports that all the preliminary requirements of the by-laws for their amendment have been complied with. By direction of the committee I move the adoption of the following resolutions:

"*Resolved*, That the by-laws submitted by the committee on revision of the by-laws be, and they are hereby, adopted as a substitute for the present by-laws; provided, however, that the terms of office of officers and directors heretofore elected shall not be affected thereby, and that at the first election of directors one third shall be elected for one year, one third for two years, and one third for three years; and provided further that members who have already paid their dues for the present year shall not be required to pay for this year the additional dues required by the new by-laws.

"*Resolved*, That 1,000 copies of the new by-laws be printed under the direction of the executive committee, and that each member hereafter shall be furnished one copy free and be entitled to purchase extra copies from the secretary at 5 cents each."

The by-laws take effect immediately upon adoption, unless exception is made previously or in the motion adopting them. The above form will show how to carry out the wishes of the society. After the resolutions have been read and handed to the president, the revised by-laws are read and amended (but not adopted) paragraph by paragraph, as shown on page 371, after which the resolutions are taken up for amendment and adoption. The adoption of the first resolution adopts the new by-laws. The substitute should be signed by every member of the committee agreeing to it. The word "chairman" should never be written after the name of the chairman except in case he signs the report alone by order of the committee. In large organizations the resolutions and substitute should be printed in advance and distributed. In small societies they should be typewritten in triplicate, the committee's chairman retaining one copy, the others being for the president and the secretary.

(11) Report of Committee on Discipline, See p. 345.

(12) Report of Treasurer and Auditing Committee.

Report of the Treasurer of the —— Society for the year ending Dec. 31, 19—.

Receipts.

Balance on hand Jan. 1, 19—..........		$ 178.53
Initiation Fees	$ 120.00	
Membership Dues	1,170.00	
Fines	15.50	1,305.50
Total		$1,484.03

Disbursements.

Rent	$ 48ს.00	
Janitor	360.00	
Fuel	110.00	
Light	105.00	
Stationery and Postage	76.00	
Printing	25.00	
Furniture	55.00	
Sundries	36.15	1,247.15
Balance on hand Dec. 31, 19—		236.88
Total		$1,484.03

Membership dues amounting to $75.00 have not yet been paid, and the rent ($40.00) for December is due Jan. 1. If these items were paid, our balance would be increased by $35.00.

A. B. LARKIN,
Treasurer.

Examined and found correct.
A. L. BANKS,
M. JENKS,
Auditing Committee.

FORMS RELATING TO TELLERS AND DELEGATES.

(13) Report of Tellers in an Election of Officers by Ballot.

President.

Number of votes cast	106
Necessary for election	54
C. S. Kerr received	62
W. W. Boyd ''	34
C. R. King ''	6

Illegal Votes.

A. C. Spofford (ineligible) received	3
B. M. Lewis received 2 votes folded together	1

Vice-President.

Number of votes cast	101
Necessary for election	51
etc., etc., etc.	

ALBERT BARNES,
JOHN WINTHROP,
HENRY JONES,
WILLIAM ASH,
Tellers.

The reports for the other officers are made the same as the one for the president. The number of votes cast must include the illegal votes. Blank ballots are ignored. The report and the duties of the tellers, including the tally sheets, are explained on pages 221–228. See also R. O. R., pages 195, 196 and Par. Prac., pages 149, 153, 158, and 176–178. If the same number of votes are cast for each of the offices, this form may be modified by placing the number of votes cast and the number necessary for election at the beginning of the report, and omitting this statement in connection with each office.

(14) Tally Sheet.

President.

Boyd, W. W.	𝍸 𝍸 𝍸 𝍸 𝍸 𝍸 𝍷𝍷𝍷𝍷	34
Kerr, Mrs. C. S. (Susan L.)	𝍸 𝍸 𝍸 𝍸 𝍸 𝍸 𝍸 𝍸 𝍸 𝍸 𝍸 𝍸 𝍷𝍷	62
King, C. R.	𝍸 𝍷	6
Lewis, B. M.	Two folded together	1
Spofford, A. C.	𝍷𝍷𝍷 Ineligible	3

If there is liability of a recount's being ordered, which is within the power of the society, the tally sheet entries should be in ink, and each sheet should be signed by the tellers, and all the sheets should be turned over to the secretary, who should retain them until it is certain that a recount will not be ordered. See page 223, and R. O. R., p. 196, and Par. Prac., p. 178.

(15) Form of Credentials of Delegates and Alternates.

(*a*) *Where the secretary of each club writes the credentials.*

Akron, Cal.,
April 9, 1922.

This is to certify that the Akron Improvement Club has appointed John Jones a delegate [or first, or second, etc., alternate of the delegates] to the State Convention of Improvement Clubs to be held in May, 1922.

ALEX. V. LARKIN,
Secretary.

JAMES LAWTON,
President.

(*b*) *Where the convention secretary furnishes the constituent, or subordinate, societies with printed blank credential cards.*

Vermont Federation of Medical Societies.

Credentials Card.

This is to certify, that ———————————— is a delegate to the annual meeting of the Vermont Federation of Medical Societies, from the Medical Society of ————————————————.

———————— ————————
President.

———————— ————————
Recording Secretary.

———————— 19—.

This card must be presented in person to the Credentials Committee.

The credentials for delegates and for alternates are more convenient if printed on different colored cardboard. In large conventions a list of delegates and alternates should be sent by the secretary of each constituent, or subordinate, society to the chairman of the credentials committee several days before the convention meets, so that the register of delegates and alternates, as described below, may be prepared in advance. This list may be similar to the first form of credentials above, only striking out, "John Jones a delegate [or, etc.]" and inserting, "the following delegates and alternates," and then writing the list of delegates and alternates in their proper order above the secretary's signature. A copy of this may be taken to the convention and presented to the credentials committee instead of giving each delegate and alternate separate credentials. In this case the holder of the certificate must identify each delegate and alternate. [See Credentials Committee, page 281, for further explanation.]

(16) Form of Register of Delegates and Alternates.		Delegates	Alternates
Lafayette Medical Society	(Present)		
Delegates			
Lakin, Arthur T................	*Arthur T. Lakin*	/	
Lewissohn, Abram N...........			
Morrison, John Louis...........	*John Louis Morrison*	/	
Alternates			
Loomis, George..................	*George Loomis*		/
Love, Joseph....................			
Martin, James P................	*James P. Martin*	/	×
Laporte Medical Society	(Present)		
Delegates			
Barton, Louis...................	*Louis Barton*	/	
Wiley, John P...................			
Alternates			
Harding, William S.............	*William S. Harding*	/	
Johnson, Milton H.............	*Milton H. Johnson*		/

The societies should be in alphabetical order, and the delegates and alternates of each society should be alphabetically arranged, except that the name of the president of the society, or in his absence the chairman of the delegates, should head the list. In very large conventions, where the president of each constituent society is ex-officio a delegate, it may be more convenient to have a separate register for all ex-officio delegates. For quick reference it is well to write the surname first. Each delegate registers by signing to the right of his typewritten name. When a delegate has signed, a pencil check mark should be made in the first column to the right of his signature. In the case of an alternate the mark should be in the second column. The total check marks in each column show the number present. When an alternate becomes a delegate he is checked in the delegate column. If he has been previously checked as an alternate, that mark should be crossed out.

FORMS FOR ANNUAL MEETING OF STOCKHOLDERS.

(17) Notice of Annual Meeting of Stockholders.

The annual meeting of stockholders of the Excelsior Manufacturing Company will be held at the general offices [or office, or chief office] of the company, 322 Arnold Ave., Lonsdale, Nevada, on Wednesday, April 12, 19—, at 2 o'clock P. M. for the election of directors and for such other business as may properly come before the meeting.

If unable to be present, please execute the enclosed proxy and return promptly in the enclosed stamped and addressed envelope.

The stock-transfer books will be closed on Tuesday, March 28, 1922, at 3 P. M., and will be reopened on Thursday, April 13, 19—, at 10 A. M.

Lonsdale, Nevada,   JULIUS KUHN,
                                                                           Secretary.

The purpose of this meeting is sometimes expressed in terms like these: "for the election of three directors to serve for a term of four years, for the ratification of all action of the board of directors of the company since the last annual meeting of stockholders, and for the transaction of such other business as may properly come before the meeting."

(18) Proxy.

Know all men by these presents,

That I do hereby constitute and appoint Alvah Thomas attorney and agent for me, and in my name, place, and stead, to vote as my proxy at the annual meeting of stockholders of the Excelsior Manufacturing Company to be held Wednesday, April 12, 19—, at the company's office, 322 Arnold Ave., Lonsdale, Nevada, or at any adjournment thereof, according to the number of votes I should be entitled to vote if then personally present; and also to appoint a substitute under him for like purpose.

In witness whereof, I have hereunto set my hand and seal, this — day of ——, 19—.

Witness: ———————————— L. S.

When a stockholder desires to authorize two or more persons to act as or appoint a proxy for him, the above form may be used striking out the words, "Alvah . . . stead" and inserting "A, B, C, D, and E, F, or any of them, attorneys and agents for me, irrevocable, with full power by the affirmative vote of a majority of said attorneys and agents to appoint a substitute or substitutes for and in the name and stead of me."

FORMS OF MINUTES OF A MEETING.

(19) Minutes of a Regular [or Stated] Meeting of a Society.

A regular [or stated] meeting of the Civic Club was held on Thursday evening, Jan. 19, 19—, the president and secretary being present. The minutes of the last meeting were read and approved. The reports of the committees on —— and —— were received and ordered to be placed on file. The committee on —— reported a resolution on child welfare, which after being amended was adopted as follows: [Copy the resolution.]

The house committee reported that at their request an excellent carpenter inspected the roof of the club-house and stated that it needed immediate repairs at an estimated cost of $50.00. On motion of the committee it was "*Resolved,* That the house committee be, and hereby is, authorized to have the roof of the club-house properly repaired."

The committee to which was referred the resolution relating to the club's contributing to the village library reported it back with certain amendments, and with the recommendation that as thus amended the resolution be adopted. The amendments were adopted, and the resolution as thus amended was then adopted as follows: [Copy the resolution as adopted.]

The resolution on entertainments which was laid on the table at the previous meeting was taken from the table on motion of Mr. Jones, and after amendment was adopted as follows: [Copy the resolution as adopted.]

On motion of Mr. Boden the vote adopting the resolution relating to contributing to the village library was reconsidered and the word "thirty" was struck out and "forty" was inserted in its place. As thus amended the resolution was adopted.

At 9.30 P. M. the club adjourned.

ABEL BROWN, JR.,
Secretary.

In many societies the minutes need not state that the president and secretary are present, that being assumed unless stated to the contrary. When one of them is absent, the first sentence in these minutes should end with the date. If the president is absent, say: "The secretary was present, and in the absence of the president, Mr. Abel was elected chairman"; or: "The president was present, and, the secretary being absent, Mr. Larkin was elected secretary pro tem." Such elections are usually viva voce. For other forms of minutes, see R. O. R., p. 248, and Par. Prac., p. 128.

(20) Minutes of a Special or Called Meeting.

A special meeting of the club was held on Thursday evening, Feb. 2, 19—, the president and the secretary being present. The call for the meeting was read by the secretary as follows:
' A special meeting of the Civic Club will be held in its hall at 8 P. M. Thursday, Feb. 2, 19—, for the purpose of electing a treasurer to fill the vacancy caused by the death of Mr. Dawson.

"ALECK SIMPSON,
"*President.*"

The secretary said that the by-laws had been complied with, the notice having been sent by mail to every member five days before the meeting.
The president expressed the appreciation of the loss that the club suffered in the death of Mr. Dawson, and suggested that a committee be appointed to prepare suitable resolutions in the case. Mr. L moved "that a committee of three be appointed by the chair to draft resolutions concerning the death of Mr. Dawson, with instructions to report it at the next meeting of the club." The motion was adopted, and Mr. Lane, Mr. Moore, and Mr. Lewis were appointed the committee.
The chair announced that the special business for which this meeting was called was the election of a treasurer. Upon motion of Mr. Thorne it was ordered that nominations be by ballot. Messrs. Seely, Jason, Link, and Hope were appointed tellers and the club proceeded to take a nominating ballot, resulting as follows: Mr. A, 75; Mr. B, 60; Mr. C, 25; Mr. D, 3. The club then proceeded to ballot for treasurer, with the following result:

```
Number of votes cast.............................. 163
Necessary for election............................  82
Mr. B received....................................  85
Mr. A    "    ....................................  77
```
Illegal (void) votes.

Mr. A received 2 ballots folded together.............. 1

The chair declared Mr. B elected treasurer. At 9 P. M. the club adjourned.

ABEL BROWN,
Secretary.

The minutes of the regular meetings should not be acted upon at a special meeting, nor should any business of importance be considered unless it was specified in the call. See page 315 for further explanation.

(21) Minutes of an Adjourned Regular Meeting.

At an adjourned regular meeting held April 27, 1922, the president and the secretary being present, the minutes of the last meeting were read and approved. The president announced that the first business in order was the continuation of the balloting for directors, as only two of the five required were elected at the last meeting. The club then proceeded to ballot for 3 directors to serve 3 years, the vote being as follows: etc., etc.
At 9 P. M. the club adjourned.

ABEL BROWN,
Secretary.

If the meeting was the adjournment of a special meeting, the minutes of the previous regular meeting would not be acted upon.

(22) Minutes of a Regular Meeting of a Village Board, or of a Board of Directors.

Wednesday evening, June 12, 1922.

Regular meeting of the board of village trustees, the following members being present: President ——————— and Trustees ———————,
———————, ———————, ———————, ———————,
———————.

The minutes of the last meeting were read and approved.

The following bills were audited and ordered paid [or, approved for payment]:

A——— B———————, street labor	$24.00
C——— D———————, ,, ,,	13.50
E——— F———————, team	20.00
Repairs for Fire Department	14.75
	$72.25

On motion of Mr. Dennis the board voted to pay one half the cost of motorizing the wagon of the Bronson chemical engine, the estimated cost being about $800.

· ·

At 9.30 P. M. the board adjourned.

LOUIS JONES,
Village Clerk.

This brief form is sufficient for boards of any kind. The members present should be named, and sometimes the absentees. The latter, however, is useless except in the case of municipal boards when the proceedings, or minutes, are published, and then it is well to inform the public as to who are absent. If the meeting is a special one, the minutes would begin thus: "Special meeting of the board of ——, held pursuant to the call of the president, there being present," etc. The call need not be read or recorded.

CHAPTER XLVI

DEFINITIONS

Accepting the report of a committee is the same as adopting it.

Amend, in a parliamentary sense, is to change the wording of a resolution, etc., by inserting or adding, or by striking out, or by striking out and inserting, one or more words, or one or more paragraphs. When one or more paragraphs are replaced by others, or the entire resolution is replaced by another, the amendment is called a Substitute. When the amendment has the effect of striking out an entire resolution that has been previously adopted, the motion is called to Rescind, or to Repeal. All of the restrictions on amendments apply equally to the motions to substitute and to rescind, since these motions are really amendments. An amendment of an amendment is called a Secondary Amendment, or an Amendment of the Second Degree.

Announcing the Vote is the declaration by the chair of the result of the vote. No vote is complete until announced. See page 307.

Apply. See Precedence.

Assembly is used to designate the members of a society actually assembled for the transaction of business. In the case of a mass meeting it includes all present. In making motions the word "assembly" should be replaced by the word "club," or "society," or "church," or "convention," or "board," etc.

Aye and No. These terms are used in the ordinary forms of voting, the aye (pronounced the same as "eye" or "I") meaning yes.

Board. A Board is a group of members of an organization which is authorized to act for the organization between its meetings, with specified limitations, as a Board of Managers; or which, as the agent of the organization, has the entire charge of a certain part of its work, subject, however, to the orders of the organization, as a Board of Trustees. [See R. O. R., pp. 207–210, and this book, Chap. XXIII.]

By-Laws are the fundamental rules or laws of a society, which include among other things its objects, its membership, its officers, how and when it meets for business, how many must be present in order that business may be transacted, and how they, the by-laws, may be modified. Sometimes they are divided into two parts, one being called the Constitution and the other the By-Laws, but both are included in the general term By-Laws.

Call Up. If, when other business is pending, a motion is made to reconsider a vote finally disposing of a main motion, the motion to reconsider cannot be taken up until the pending business is disposed of. Even then it is not taken up until some one "calls it up," that is, demands that it be taken up for consideration. If it is moved to reconsider a vote and have it entered on the minutes, the motion to reconsider cannot be called up on the day the reconsideration is moved. The motion to reconsider is dead if it is not called up before the close of the next session in an assembly having regular meetings as often as quarterly; and in other assemblies its effect terminates with the session at which it is made.

Carried. The same as Adopted.

Chair. The Chair is the term generally used to designate the presiding officer, regardless of his official title, when referring to him or his acts as presiding officer. One is said to be "in the chair" when he is presiding, regardless of whether he is sitting or standing.

Chairman means the person "in the chair"; that is, the one presiding. The presiding officer of a committee is always called the chairman. The chairman of a board is often called the president of the board.

Chairman pro tem. and **Temporary Chairman.** Where there is a regular presiding officer, any other person acting as chairman is called the chairman pro tem.; that is, chairman for the time being. The "pro tem." is not used, however, in addressing him. Where the assembly has no regular presiding officer a "temporary chairman" is appointed to preside until the regular presiding officer is elected. Thus, when a society is being organized, a "temporary chairman' is elected to serve until the adoption of the by-laws and the election of the president. If the "temporary chairman" is absent or vacates the chair for a time, his place is filled by a "chairman pro tem."

Commit To is to refer something to a committee.

Division. When a vote is taken viva voce or by show of hands, any member not satisfied that the vote is a true expression of the opinion of the assembly, or thinking that the chair has made a mistake in announcing the vote, may compel the vote to be taken again, this time by a rising vote, by simply calling out, "Division." [See Division of the Assembly, page 167.].

Ex-Officio means "from the office," or "by virtue of the office." Thus, if the by-laws make the president of the society president ex-officio of the board of managers, it means that the society's president, by virtue of that office, is also president of the board of managers. The moment he ceases to be president of the society he automatically ceases to be president of the board. A member or officer ex-officio is as much a member or officer as if elected to the position.

Floor, Obtaining the. A member is said to have "obtained the floor" when he has risen and addressed the chair by his proper title and has been "recognized" by the chair, that is, the chair has announced his name to the assembly. In small assemblies, instead of announcing the name of the speaker, the chair commonly recognizes the member by bowing to him.

General Consent. Instead of taking formal votes on questions to which it is apparent no one objects, much time can be saved by the chairman's saying, for instance, "Are there any corrections to the minutes? There being none, the minutes stand approved." It is useless to make a motion and take a vote in such a case. Sometimes a request is made for general consent to take up a question out of its proper order, or to do something that is not exactly according to the rules. The chair inquires whether there is any objection, and if none is made he says, "There being no objection," etc., and proceeds to entertain the proposed business, the same as if the rules had been suspended for that purpose by a formal action and vote. Clerical errors should usually be corrected by general consent.

General Order. See Orders, General.

Germane. An amendment is said to be germane to a resolution when it relates to the subject of the resolution so closely that the two can be considered and acted upon together as well as separately. If the adoption of the resolution would necessarily prevent the introduction of a new resolution containing the substance of the proposed amendment, the amendment is germane to the resolution.

An amendment is not in order unless it is germane to the resolution or motion to be amended. [See page 19.]

Honorary. The title of Honorary President, Honorary Member, etc., is similar to a degree conferred by a college. Honorary officers or members of a society are not real officers or members, and have none of the responsibilities of officers or members. They have the privilege of attending the meetings of the society and of speaking, but no other privileges of membership. [See page 331.]

Immediately Pending. See Pending.

Incidental Motions or Questions. [See Chart II, page 548.]

Main Motions are motions that bring a subject before the assembly for its consideration and action.

Majority, Plurality, Two Thirds. A majority is more than half. A candidate has a plurality vote when he receives more votes than any other candidate. A majority vote is more than half of the votes cast, which is usually a very different thing from a vote of a majority of the members present, or a majority of the members. Thus, if 12 members vote, and 21 are present at a meeting of a society having 80 members, a majority vote is 7; a vote of a majority of the members present is 11; and a vote of a majority of the members is 41. So a two-thirds vote is 8; a vote of two thirds of the members present is 14; and a vote of two thirds of the members, or a two-thirds vote of the members, is 54. The by-laws of an ordinary society should never require for any purpose a vote of a majority of the members, or of two thirds of the members, unless they also allow voting by mail.

Mass Meeting. A Mass Meeting is a public meeting called for some specific purpose, in which all of those who attend have the right to vote. It has no by-laws or permanent organization. [See page 363.]

Meeting and Session. A Meeting of a society is an assembly of its members for a time during which they do not separate longer than for a recess of a few minutes. A recess or adjournment for a meal terminates with the meeting, so that a convention lasting several days has usually three meetings each day. Each of the meetings of an ordinary society, whether regular or called, is usually a session. But if it adjourns to meet at another time the adjourned meeting is a part of the same session. A regular meeting, together with all its adjourned meetings, constitutes one session.

Minute and Minutes. A Minute is a record of some act, statement, or opinion of the assembly. The Minutes of a meeting are a record of the business transacted at the meeting. What the minutes should contain is shown on page 315.

Motions. A Motion is a proposal that something be done, or that a certain statement expresses the sense or opinion, or wish, or will of the assembly. For convenience motions are divided into Main, Subsidiary, Privileged, and Incidental. All the motions except main motions are sometimes referred to as Secondary motions. See Questions for the difference between Motions and Questions. For further information consult the Index under Motions.

Notice. See Previous Notice.

Order of Precedence. See Precedence.

Order, Point of, Question of. A member or a proceeding is "in order" when the rules are not being violated; he or it is "out of order" when the rules are being violated. One "makes a point of order" when he objects to a proceeding as being out of order. He "raises a question of order" when he asks the chair whether a certain proceeding is not out of order.

Orders of the Day means the program or the business of the meeting, arranged in its proper order as prescribed by the rules or by vote of the assembly. A "Call for the Orders of the Day" is a demand that the business prescribed for that particular time be taken up.

Orders, General and Special. A General Order is a motion or subject placed in the order of business without the privilege of interrupting another question, as when a motion is postponed to a certain time. A Special Order is a motion or subject that has been assigned to a certain time and made a special order by a two-thirds vote, so that when that hour arrives it interrupts and supersedes any pending business except the consideration of another special order which was made previous to it or at the same time.

Outrank equals "Take precedence of." See Precedence.

Pass. In legislative bodies a bill is said to have "passed" when it has been enacted. The term is also used in connection with the passage of a bill from one stage to another, as, "The bill has passed its second reading."

Pending and **Immediately Pending.** A motion is pending after it has been stated by the chair until it has been disposed of either permanently or temporarily. [See pages 80, 82.] There may be a number of motions pending at the same time. The pending motion that was last stated by the chair is called the Immediately Pending Motion.

Plurality Vote. See Majority.

Point of Order. See Order, Point of.

Polls. When a vote is taken by ballot the polls are said to be open all the time during which members may deposit their ballots. After the polls are closed (which requires a two-thirds vote) no more ballots can be received unless the polls are reopened. This may be done by a majority vote.

A **Preamble** is the introduction to a resolution or constitution. The preamble to a resolution, or to a set of resolutions, states some of the reasons for its adoption. It begins with the word "Whereas" and closes with "therefore" or "therefore be it." [See pages 35, 164.] The preamble to a constitution, when there is one, usually states by whom it was adopted or the causes of its adoption.

Precedence and **Apply.** The motion A is said to Apply to another motion B, when it is in order to move A while B is immediately pending, and when A is adopted its effect is limited to the immediately pending question B. Thus, "to amend" applies to the motion "to postpone" because, if adopted when to postpone is immediately pending, the amendment affects only the motion to postpone. The motion A is said to Take Precedence of, or to Outrank, another motion B, when it is in order to move A while B is immediately pending, and if A is adopted its effect is not necessarily limited to the immediately pending question B. Thus, "to postpone" takes precedence of, outranks, "to commit," because it can be moved while to commit is pending and, if the postponement is adopted, not only is the motion to commit postponed, but all other pending questions are also postponed. The motion to postpone does not apply to the motion to commit, because the latter motion cannot be postponed without carrying with it all pending questions.

Previous Notice unless otherwise specified in the by-laws, may be given at the previous meeting, or by mail to every member, or in the call for the meeting.

Previous Question is the name given to the motion to close debate and take a vote at once on the immediately pending question and such other of the successive pending questions as are specified in the motion. It requires a two-thirds vote for its adoption.

Privileged Motions. See list in Chart I, page 548.

Proxy Voting. See Voting.

Putting the Question is submitting to the assembly the question whether it will adopt [or agree to] the immediately pending motion. The assembly answers the question by voting, usually, "Aye" (yes) or "No." The different forms of putting the question are shown in various places referred to in the Index under "Question, Putting the."

Question. The Question is whether the assembly agrees to, or will adopt, the immediately pending motion. No other motion can be made, nor can any one be recognized to speak in debate until the chair has stated the question to the assembly.

A Quorum is the number of members required to be present at a meeting in order that the assembly may transact business. In an organized society, or a board, or a committee, the quorum is a majority of all the members unless the by-laws authorize a different quorum.

Raise a Question of Order. See Order, Question of.

Rank is the same as the order of precedence. See Precedence.

Receiving a Report. Receiving a Report or Communication is merely permitting it to be presented, that is, to be read, to the assembly, and therefore after a report has been read, the motion to receive it cannot be entertained since the report has been received already.

A Recess is a short intermission taken by the assembly. In an ordinary society, when the meeting lasts only a few hours, a recess would be for only a few minutes, as while counting the ballots. In case the session lasts all day there are usually recesses for the different meals. If the session lasts for several days a recess is sometimes taken over an entire day.

Recognize. A member is "recognized" by the chairman's announcing his name, or in case of a small assembly by merely bowing to him, after the member has risen and addressed the chairman by his proper title. No member can make a motion or speak in debate until he is "recognized" by the presiding officer.

The Reporting Member is the member of a committee that submits the committee's report to the assembly. Usually this is the chairman of the committee, but he may not be in sympathy with the report, or another member may be much better able to defend the committee's report if it is attacked. In either of these cases it is better for the committee to appoint another member, who is called the reporting member, to present the report.

Rescind. See Amend.

A Secondary Amendment is an amendment of an amendment. It is also called an amendment of the second degree.

A Secondary Motion is any motion except a main motion.

Second Degree. See Secondary Amendment.

A Seconder is one who seconds, or endorses, a motion. Most motions require to be seconded before they can be stated as before the assembly. In an ordinary society the seconder does not rise, but from his seat says, "I second the motion," or simply, "I second it." In large conventions of delegates he rises when he seconds a motion, and in some cases is required also to announce his name.

Session. See Meeting and Session.

Sine die means "without day." When an assembly adjourns sine die it is dissolved, and that assembly ceases to exist. An organized society has by-laws that provide for future meetings, and therefore such an assembly never adjourns sine die.

Speaker, as used in this manual, refers to the person who has the floor and is, or has just been, speaking. In Congress it refers to the regular presiding officer of the House of Representatives.

Standing Rules are rules and regulations for the guidance of an assembly which have been adopted, the same as ordinary resolutions, by a majority vote without previous notice. They do not interfere with any future session, because at any meeting a Standing Rule may be suspended by a majority vote. A Standing Rule may be amended or rescinded at any time by a two-thirds vote, or, if notice has been given, by a majority vote. Standing Rules are usually adopted from time to time, as they are needed, in the form of resolutions.

Stating the Question. As soon as a motion is made and seconded, if it is in order, the chair states the question on its adoption, so that the assembly may know exactly what is before it for action. He usually does this by saying, "It is moved and seconded that [or to]," etc., repeating the motion. For the different forms see Index under Question, Stating the.

Subsidiary Motion or Question. See page 6.

Substitute. See Amend.

Table. The same as to Lay on the Table. See pages 62–66.

Tellers are practically a committee appointed to count the votes and to report the same to the assembly. When a rising vote is taken in a large assembly, and always when the vote is by ballot, it is necessary to have tellers.

Tie. An equality of votes of the affirmative and the negative, or of the votes for rival candidates.

Two Thirds. See Majority.

A **Vote** is a formal expression of the will, or opinion, or preference of the members of an assembly in regard to a matter submitted to it. See page 188.

Yeas and Nays. A vote is said to be taken by Yeas and Nays, or by roll-call, when the question is put and the alphabetical roll of the members is called, each member as his name is called answering either "Yes" [or Yea] or "No" [or Nay]. Members not wishing to vote either way answer, "Present." This method of voting takes much time and is useless in ordinary societies. See R. O. R., p. 197, and this book, page 191.

Yields. A motion, A, is said to yield to another, B, if B is in order when A is pending. In this case B supersedes A for the time being and becomes the immediately pending question.

INDEX

577